DISCOVER AUSTRALIA

National Parks

The wait

After a 10 year wait, the all new 1998

Discover Australia

National Parks

Edited by Ron and Viv Moon

 RANDOM HOUSE

Published in Australia by
Random House Australia Pty Ltd
20 Alfred St, Milsons Point, NSW 2061 Australia
tel 61 2 9954 9966
fax 61 2 9954 9008
http://www.randomhouse.com.au

ISBN 0 09 183772 3

Sydney New York Toronto London Auckland Johannesburg
and agencies throughout the world

First published in 1997
Second edition published 1998

National Library of Australia
Cataloguing-in-Publication Data

Discover Australia: national parks.

3rd ed.
Includes index.
ISBN 0 09 183772 3.

1. National parks and reserves – Australia –
Guidebooks. I. Moon, Ron. II. Moon, Viv. III.
Title: Discover Australia: national parks.

333.7830994

Printed by Dah Hua, Hong Kong
Film separation Pica Colour Separation, Singapore

Publisher	Gordon Cheers
Chief consultants	Ron and Viv Moon
Managing editors	Heather Jackson
	Margaret Olds
Contributors	Ron and Viv Moon
	Heather Donovan
	Willie Kempen
	Colin Kerr
	John McCann
	Sharyn Vanderhorst
	Vic Widman
Cover design	Bob Mitchell
Designer	Robert Taylor
Cartographer	John Frith
Cartographic coordinator	Gordon Cheers
Cartographic consultants	Brian Stokes
	Bruce Whitehouse
Park maps	Robert Taylor
	Warren Penney
Map coordinator	Valerie Marlborough
Map editors	Marlene Meynert
	Janet Parker
	Jane Cozens
	Joan Sutter
	Denise Imwold
	Heather Martin
	Jenny Lake
Copy Editor/proofreader	Doreen Grézoux
Tables and research	Jane Cozens
Keyboarding	Deanne Lowe
Index	Dee Rogers
	Marie-Louise Taylor
Line drawings	Tony Pyrzakowski
Photo research	Gordon Cheers
Publishing manager	Linda Watchorn
Publishing coordinator	Sarah Sherlock

PHOTOGRAPHS
Half-title: Mungo National Park, NSW
Page iv: Mt Warning National Park, NSW
Page xi: Nigli Gap in Keep River National Park, NT

KEY TO ROAD MAPS

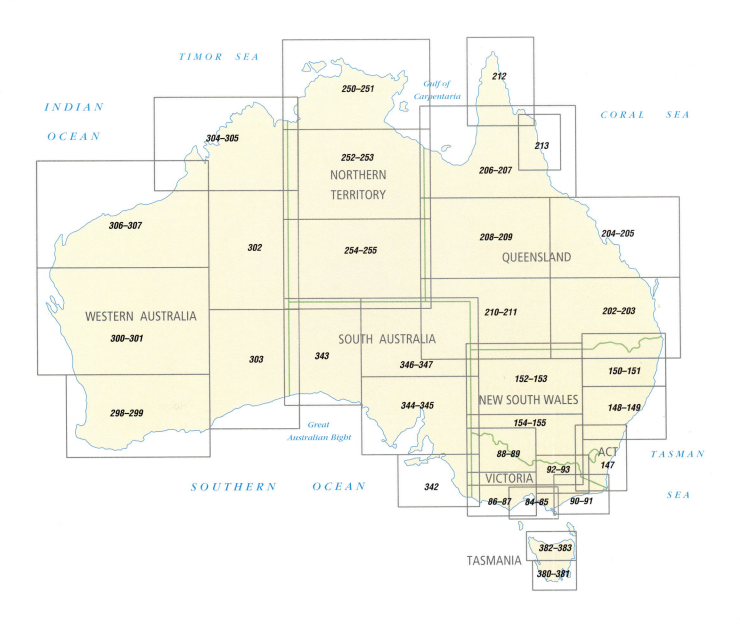

TIMOR SEA

INDIAN OCEAN

Gulf of Carpentaria

CORAL SEA

250–251

304–305

212

213

206–207

252–253
NORTHERN
TERRITORY

204–205

306–307

302

254–255

208–209

QUEENSLAND

WESTERN AUSTRALIA

300–301

210–211

202–203

303

343

SOUTH AUSTRALIA

346–347

150–151

152–153

148–149

298–299

344–345

NEW SOUTH WALES

154–155

ACT
147

TASMAN

88–89

92–93

Great Australian Bight

342

VICTORIA

90–91

SEA

SOUTHERN OCEAN

86–87

84–85

382–383

TASMANIA

380–381

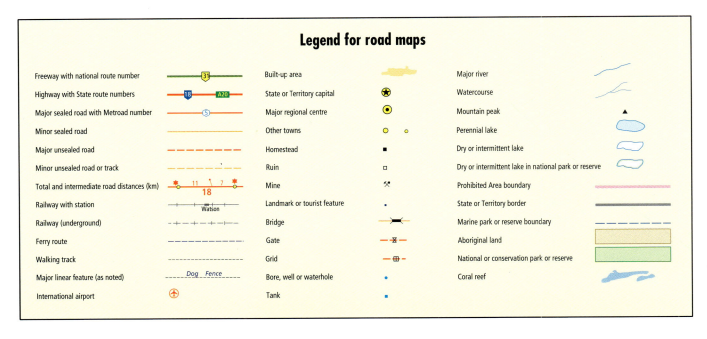

Legend for road maps

Freeway with national route number	Built-up area	Major river
Highway with State route numbers	State or Territory capital	Watercourse
Major sealed road with Metroad number	Major regional centre	Mountain peak
Minor sealed road	Other towns	Perennial lake
Major unsealed road	Homestead	Dry or intermittent lake
Minor unsealed road or track	Ruin	Dry or intermittent lake in national park or reserve
Total and intermediate road distances (km)	Mine	Prohibited Area boundary
Railway with station	Landmark or tourist feature	State or Territory border
Railway (underground)	Bridge	Marine park or reserve boundary
Ferry route	Gate	Aboriginal land
Walking track	Grid	National or conservation park or reserve
Major linear feature (as noted)	Bore, well or waterhole	Coral reef
International airport	Tank	

CONTENTS

THE PARKS

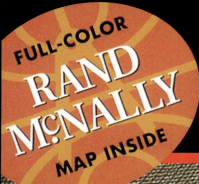

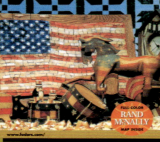
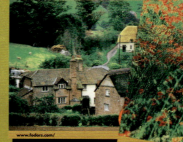
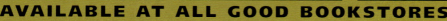

AUSTRALIA'S NATIONAL PARKS AND RESERVES

A rich tapestry of parks and reserves covers Australia from the southern tip of Tasmania to the northern tip of Cape York and from the Great Dividing Range in the east to the far western extremity of Western Australia.

Alpine meadows in the high country of New South Wales and Victoria; towering gums in the southwest of Western Australia; rich verdant rainforests in Queensland; impenetrable temperate forests and untouched rivers in Tasmania, the floodplains and escarpments of the Northern Territory and the untracked desert country and outback mountain ranges in South Australia, all offer a safe, vibrant habitat for our unique flora and fauna. They are also places where we, as part of nature, can seek solace, enjoyment and adventure.

Australia is fortunate in that it has the landmass and the lack of population pressure to incorporate much of its natural treasures in parks and reserves of significant size. In the last 20 years, with a growing awareness of our natural heritage, each state and territory has increased vastly the amount of land protected in national parks and reserves and many of those parks are in excess of one million hectares. A number are bigger than some European countries! Even so, there are some anomalies and no standard is followed by the states in what constitutes a national park, a conservation park, a state park, or whatever. It is a little confusing!

Bird's nest fern, typical rainforest flora

Queensland has the largest number of reserves in Australia with over 730 listed, about 340 of which are national parks. Many are just 249 hectares in size (one square mile) and were designated as national parks to 'protect' any area that wasn't used for mining or agriculture. It is hard to imagine how these parks can rate national park status beside such magnificent Queensland national parks as Lamington, Hinchinbrook, Great Sandy (Fraser Island and Cooloola), Carnarvon, Daintree and others. All told Queensland has around 4 per cent of its landmass protected in parks and reserves—the least amount of any state except the Northern Territory, which has just over 2 per cent—and over 50 per cent in Aboriginal land.

Other states have much tougher criteria for their reserves to be declared as national parks, with South Australia having fewer than 20 national parks but a wide range of conservation parks, nature reserves and regional reserves—the latter being a ground-breaking land management system where all groups involved, such as miners, pastoralists and national park departments, work together to protect the designated land. In South Australia much of the northern semi-arid desert lands, which still support gas and oil production as well as cattle grazing, are open to travellers and are managed by the state's Department of Environment and Natural Resources.

With such a classification system in place, South Australia has nearly 17 per cent of its area protected in parks and reserves, representing the biggest percentage of any mainland state. Only the island state of Tasmania has more, with 26 per cent protected. Western Australia takes the award for the largest amount of land in reserves, with slightly more than South Australia at just under 17 million hectares, but only 7 per cent of the state's area.

Victoria, with its large area of forest, has 13 per cent of its area

protected in parks and reserves, while the most populous state, New South Wales, has around 5 per cent of its landmass protected with over 70 national parks, coming second after Queensland in the total number of national parks.

Many guide books that look at our favoured natural areas concentrate on the national parks in each state but we preferred to take on all-encompassing approach. After all, much of our best country is protected in areas other than national parks. As well, while these protected areas are very important as biological reserves and places where animals can exist in their natural habitat, free from the encroachment of humans and their rabid development, the parks and reserves dotted across the landscape offer suburban Australians, surrounded by tar and cement, a real escape from everyday work and living pressures.

This guide, while acknowledging the wildlife and vegetation these parks protect, and their scenic beauty and the rich heritage they possess, is more about what people can see and do in these often wild places.

Some of the parks are extremely well developed, with resorts and sports facilities within their boundaries, though these are generally close to the major cities and are in the minority. Most of these parks are a hangover from times gone by and include parks such as Belair National Park in South Australia, where football fields and tennis courts are dotted within its borders. Kosciuszko National Park in New South Wales has huge ski and resort developments within its boundaries but it is such a vast park that much of its area retains its wilderness character, attracting thousands of cross-country skiers in winter and bushwalkers in summer.

Across the border in Victoria most of the developed ski resorts with their lodges and restaurants are not included within surrounding national parks and this has been the concept with most of the more recently declared parks in Australia. So we have, for example, an upmarket resort on Lizard Island off the northern Queensland coast which is in its own special enclave while the rest of the island is national park, or in Kakadu in the Northern Territory, where a whole town and mine are surrounded by the national park.

While in the latter cases the park can be said to be pristine or natural, in the case of parks such as Belair and Koscuiszko, the managing national parks organisation has at least some control on what happens within the developed area of the park. However, on Lizard, or within Jabiru surrounded by Kakadu, the controlling parks' body has no sway. Which management strategy is better is a vexed question, with supporters of each system considering their option to be the better one for conservation of the area.

Many national parks, forest scenic reserves, state parks and conservation parks and the like have facilities such as developed camping grounds, picnic areas and walking tracks with wheelchair access, while other parks have remote-area camping with few, if any, facilities. In fact, most of the parks and reserves within Australia fall within these two levels of development. Some, like Drysdale River National Park in the far north of the Kimberley in Western Australia, offer no more than a rough 4WD track, a couple of signs leading the way and an area on a river bank which is the designated camping area.

A bandicoot cleans the dishes

A rainforest skink, commonly found in Border Ranges National Park

The less remote parks and those more popular with visitors normally have good access to one or more features within the park. In many cases, that access is suitable for the family car while the better known parks have access for buses and the like. Bushwalking is permitted in most of the parks, with some great bushwalking experiences available while a number also have designated day walking trails, radiating from the access point. A few parks and reserves in Australia have no access and no facilities at all. Some of these are small and are reserved for scientific purposes, but others, such as the Staaten River National Park on Cape York in Queensland, or the Prince Regent Nature Reserve in Western Australia, are quite large but aren't really available to the public.

Don't expect to visit Australia's parks and reserves for nothing. In today's 'pay as you go' world, many parks have a fee for camping and, as time goes on, this practice is sure to increase. Fees vary from state to state and from park to park. Some states, like New South Wales, have a system of fees that relate directly to the camping facilities in the park, while some states seem to have no system at all, charging the same amount to camp in a park with good facilities as they do to camp in a park with no or poor amenities.

Other parks, though they are in the minority, even have an entry fee whether you are going to stay overnight or not. Uluru National Park, where that icon of outback Australia, Uluru (Ayers Rock), is found, is one such place: you pay a fee just to visit it.

Some states, like New South Wales, have a pass system where for an annual fee you can camp in most of the parks and reserves in that state for a considerable saving over the daily rate. Other states, such as South Australia, have an annual or monthly pass system for a certain area, such as the annual Desert Parks Pass which gives you access to the reserves in the north of the state for 12 months, or a Kangaroo Island Pass which allows you to camp in the parks on that delightful island for either a month or a year. It is worth contacting each state's national parks organisation—under whatever government department name they are currently known—for information on any parks pass system in operation.

Then there is the matter of rules and regulations. These vary from state to state and even from park to park. National parks generally don't allow hunting or pets within the park, but there are exceptions. Within Victoria's Alpine National Park there are a number of hunting areas, if you have the right permits at the right time of the year, while in the Northern Territory there are a couple of parks where you may take a dog, provided you keep it under control. In most states you are allowed to fish in a national park but in Queensland that is not the case. About the only exception to that rule in that state is Lakefield National Park, where you can fish for barramundi—under strict guidelines, of course.

The rules and regulations covering state parks, conservation parks and others vary even more widely and can be just as strict as for a national park. The best idea is to get in touch with each state parks organisation who will let you know what the situation is in that state and within a certain park.

So, where to go and what to see?

In New South Wales a visit to the Blue Mountains National Park is almost obligatory. It is right on Sydney's doorstep and offers bushwalking, climbing and canyoning. Kosciuszko is great for walking, skiing and fishing while Deua and Wadbilliga National Parks are enjoyable for 4WD tours and camping. Out west, try the Outback parks of Sturt and Kinchega for a different experience.

In Victoria there is the Prom—Wilsons Promontory for the uninitiated—with its great coastal scenery, pleasant walks and fine fishing and diving. The vast Alpine National Park is a delight for 4WDs but it also offers some of the best bushwalking, skiing and canoeing experiences available in the country. In the north of the state you could try any of the parks along the Murray River or head west and enjoy the myriad delights of walking, climbing, or camping in the Grampians National Park.

Down in Tasmania walkers can tramp through the Southwest National Park while rafters can paddle down the spectacular Franklin River in the Franklin–Gordon Wild Rivers National Park. For the less adventurous the more gentle coastline around Freycinet National Park or Russell Falls in Mt Field National Park would be more suitable.

Head up to Queensland for the walking trails of Lamington, as well as the beaches, fishing and freshwater lakes of Great Sandy National Park (Fraser Island in particular). Some of the island parks that dot the coast not only offer fishing and diving but also pleasant walking and camping, while the parks of the far north present the adventurous soul with some of the best bush experiences on the planet.

Over in the Northern Territory 2 parks stand out above all others: Uluru in the central deserts and Kakadu in the tropical wet north. These parks offer experiences vastly different to one another but shouldn't be missed by any Australian or overseas visitor.

South Australia has some of the best desert experiences you can imagine within the Witjira National Park and adjoining Simpson Desert Regional Reserve. Further south there are the parks through the Flinders Ranges while along the coast there are Coffin Bay, Innes and the Coorong National Parks to tempt you with their fine fishing, great scenery, surfing, diving and camping.

From the bottom of Western Australia to the top there is so much choice it's hard to pick a few outstanding ones. Leeuwin–Naturaliste National Park in the southwest corner cannot be beaten for delightful coastal scenery, good fishing, pleasant walking and great diving and surfing, while further north is the Cape Range National Park and the adjoining Ningaloo Marine Park, a world-class diving area. In the Kimberley and the desert country some of our most remote parks offer the desert traveller magnificent adventures and experiences.

Snorkelling off Lady Musgrave Island

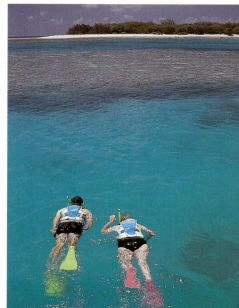

Within Australia's parks and reserves there are adventures and experiences to last—and to take—a lifetime. Now is the time to discover Australia's national parks.

ENJOYING OUR NATIONAL PARKS

Most of our parks offer a variety of things to do, from simply soaking up the scenery and atmosphere or having a picnic, to more adventurous pursuits such as bushwalking, climbing, diving and vehicle touring.

NATURE WATCHING

Many parks close to major populated areas are great spots to watch the delights of nature. You need nothing more than a good pair of eyes and some patience, but in some parks the latter isn't even required.

Animals

In a number of parks and reserves animals have become so used to seeing humans in close proximity that they either ignore them, pester them for food, or sneak food at the earliest opportunity. In rare instances the animals have become such a problem that the authorities have had to erect enclosures for the humans, so that they are not molested by over-friendly animals looking for a free feed.

Alpine daisies growing in Kosciuszko National Park

Even so, some of our most magical moments in parks have been when animals have visited us, or allowed us to approach them closely. Children will love this interaction with animals, to the point where you may have to subdue their enthusiasm, and noise, a little. By being quiet and moving slowly, the animals will allow you to get closer, for longer. Don't use food to tempt wildlife as animals soon realise that humans mean food and they will become a pest. They may also be harmed by eating foodstuffs that are not part of their natural diet.

Out in the more remote parks where kangaroos and eagles roam, you'll find that animals will tolerate people in a vehicle more easily than they will a person on foot, so getting close is easy—just stay in the car! Remember, though, that you must stay on the road or track—heading into the scrub off the track in a vehicle is definitely frowned on, and liable to a fine!

Remember, too, that no matter how friendly an animal appears, it is a wild creature and deserves respect, not only for what it is, but also for what it can do. A kangaroo, even if it is not large, can easily hurt a young person, while a large red kangaroo can disembowel an adult human with one swift kick. An emu can do likewise. Watch and enjoy!

Birdwatching

This can be an all-consuming pastime and, in fact, can be the main reason for travelling to different areas and parks of Australia.

A good pair of binoculars, such as an 8 x 40 or even a 10 x 40 roof prism, is ideal, but can be expensive. The generally cheaper porro prism binoculars are the most common but they are heavier and bulkier. Whichever type you choose, get the best you can afford, with Nikon, Tasco and Pentax, to name a few, being a good starting range.

There are a number of good bird books available for birdwatchers and no matter how keen or experienced you are, you definitely need a guide-book. Choose a general, all-Australian guide at a good bookshop.

Plants and Flowers

Viewing the flora is another enjoyable pastime, and some parks are a kaleidoscope of colour at certain times of the year. In the Alps, daisies and other plants burst into life in early summer while in the desert colour adorns each and every dune four to six weeks after rain. In Western Australia the southwest puts on one of the great displays of wildflowers in Australia with the flush of colour appearing to the north of Perth in early spring and then rolling down to the south coast later in the summer. Early spring is also good for wildflowers in the Flinders Ranges.

It's tempting, but remember, you are not allowed to pick plants in a park, and in most places in southwestern Western Australia you are not even allowed to pick wildflowers from the roadside. At times the flowers can be so profuse, it's hard not to walk on them, but please take care. Footprints in a bed of flowers are not a pretty sight.

Once again, there are some excellent field guides, but the best ones are those that describe plants from a particular region or group. Check out the bookshops in the area, or the park information centre, for the appropriate books, or browse through a good bookshop in any of the major cities.

PHOTOGRAPHY

Bringing back treasured memories from the bush is what photography is all about and it can be as simple, or as demanding (read expensive), as you want to make it.

Most people own a camera, and they have become so easy to use and so good in recent years that even the most basic camera can take reasonable shots of scenery and the like.

Once your interest extends to taking photos of delicate flowers or wildlife, or if you want more than just a sunlight scene, then you need to purchase something a little better.

An SLR camera with interchangeable lenses is what you need, preferably a good camera with a couple of zoom lenses. If you have a 30–70 mm zoom (most come with macro capability for ultra close-up work) and a 70–200 mm lens, you will have enough equipment to give you quite professional results.

Camping by a beach

However, even though you don't need to be an expert photographer, and even if you own the best photographic equipment, taking a good photo is more than just pointing and shooting. Composition, perspective, depth of field and exposure all contribute to making a photo and by reading a little (there are heaps of books available on photography from good bookshops around Australia) and practising in the field, you'll soon be turning out stunning photos of your latest visit to a park.

Once again, it's a hobby that can become the main reason for visiting a park or travelling around Australia and many hours of enjoyment can be had by just chasing that special shot.

WALKING

The simplest and possibly the most enjoyable pastime in our parks is walking. It demands the least equipment, no training, and gives each of us the opportunity to get back to basics.

There is, however, a certain amount of skill required in travelling on foot in the bush and those that have it seem to simply glide across the ground, using a minimum of effort and making the least amount of noise. On the other hand, some of us crash our way along a track, stumbling over a rock here, tripping over a tree root there and tiring ourselves out in the process. Yes, you do get better with practice, but it seems silly to practise walking. Just get out and do it—and enjoy it!

Day Walks

If you are heading off on a walk that is longer than a stroll to a favoured lookout or a top swimming hole, you really ought to do some planning and carry some extra gear.

Wear good walking shoes. A good pair of runners will do for most jaunts, but if you have them, your favourite walking boots would be more suitable. Carry a daypack with a few snacks, and maybe even lunch, if you are going further afield. When we're up in the mountains, or when the weather is changeable, we always carry a waterproof jacket because the weather can go from delightful to diabolical in just a few hours, or even less. As well, there is always a box of matches or a lighter, along with a compass, a pocket knife and a torch in the pack. A water bottle, containing nothing more than water, is essential, and if there is the slightest chance of heading off the track, or if we're in an unfamiliar area, then we also carry a map. Sunglasses, sunscreen and a hat are either worn or carried. If you have children with you make sure they are suitably attired and protected from the elements; they burn easily and get colder more quickly. They also run out of energy, so take enjoyable snacks as well as a few drinks.

Longer Bushwalks

From gentle day walks it is a natural progression to overnight hikes and longer forays into the bush. But that step needs more equipment and more skills and experience. Backpacks, sleeping bags, tents, lightweight cooking stoves, and other essentials will be required for most of us to enjoy an overnight bushwalk. There is a wide choice of equipment available and a number of books that can help you, not only in the choice of equipment but also where and when to go.

Stores such as Paddy Pallin, Mountain Design, Kathmandu and other speciality backpacking stores in every major city around Australia are a good starting point as most of the staff in these places are keen bushwalkers. Each capital city has a number of bushwalking clubs, as do the major regional centres, and the Federation of Bushwalking Clubs will also be pleased to help. You should find them under 'Bushwalking' in the *White Pages* of the telephone directory in each state's capital city.

SKIING

Downhill and cross-country skiing are such vastly different activities that the only thing they have in common is snow—even the skis are quite different, as is all the equipment.

A strangler fig in Eungella National Park

Downhill skiing is the glamour winter activity of the High Country. In Kosciuszko National Park the hills around Thredbo, Perisher Valley, Smiggin Holes and others are cut by the long line of poles and cables of the chairlifts that carry thousands each day to the top of the ski runs.

Cross-country skiers generally shun such places, heading as quickly as possible to the quieter back country for a day's skiing or for longer overnight excursions.

While most resorts hire out cross-country skis, anything more than an easy day run should be left to those who are well equipped and experienced. Even on an easy day trip it is imperative that a small daypack is carried with warm and protective clothing, including gloves, a warm cap, waterproof jacket and overpants, a down vest and a pile jacket. And don't forget such things as sunscreen and sunglasses. Something to sit on, such as a foam mat, will come in handy, as will lots of high-energy snacks along with lunch and a water bottle or a thermos.

There are a number of adventure tour operators who organise trips into the High Country during winter and joining an operator is one of the best ways to experience the back country with the right equipment and the right support. Once again, stores such as Paddy Pallin are great places to start learning about cross-country skiing. It is a fabulous experience and one easy to get hooked on.

CANOEING

Canoeing is such a diverse activity it encompasses everything from lazily paddling a canoe across a tranquil inlet, to paddling down a remote wilderness river, to shooting huge rapids. It brings to any region a completely different aspect and experience.

It doesn't matter where you go, a canoe will add to your appreciation of the region. Down along the delightfully peaceful rivers of the Victorian Croajingolong coast, or up on the Cooper Creek near Innamincka in northeastern South Australia, or paddling under the cliffs in Yardie Creek Gorge in northwestern Western Australia, a canoe will add pleasure and excitement to any trip.

There are a number of basic styles of canoe but most people will opt for an open Canadian canoe for their first experience as these are best for gentle paddles or trips down wide, open rivers that have few or no rapids.

A good quality buoyancy vest should be worn by all, while helmets and protective spray decks should be used if you're travelling through whitewater or rapids.

There's a great deal more to handling a canoe properly than first meets the eye and if you want to do more than a very lazy paddle it would be best to do some reading or attend a basic course on the main points of canoeing. Sweep strokes, J-strokes and bow strokes will help you become a more efficient paddler and you'll enjoy the experience much more.

CLIMBING

Climbers have some of the best rocks and mountains to climb within the parks dotted around Australia, while in winter the Alps offer snow and ice climbing.

Mt Buffalo in the northeast, the Grampians and Mt Arapiles in the west of Victoria are well-known spots, with Arapiles considered to have the finest rock climbing in Australia. Mere mortals like us gape in astonishment at what the experts can do on vertical slabs of granite and sandstone.

In New South Wales the vertical walls of the Blue Mountains make fine climbing venues, while in South Australia the southern walls of Wilpena Pound are considered the best in the state.

For ice-climbing buffs the area around Blue Lake in Kosciuszko National Park and Mt Feathertop in the Alpine National Park, across the border in Victoria, offer the only real chance for mountaineering experience on this continent.

There are a host of other spots and the best place to start is at the speciality outdoor shops or within the pages of magazines such as *Wild* and *Rock*. There are also a number of climbing schools located around Australia, generally close to the best climbing areas, or in the capital cities where you can learn the skills required. While you need to be fit to climb the top grades, most of us would be capable of tackling the minor climbs and getting a fantastic buzz out of it. Give it a try!

DIVING

Many of our parks and reserves fringe stretches of spectacular coastline that are perfect for divers and snorkellers. In some areas marine parks have been established while in others underwater trails have been marked where divers can follow a series of signs to wrecks or other points of interest.

While SCUBA diving is a skill that demands training and a range of expensive equipment, snorkelling can be enjoyed by most people—with a minimal outlay on equipment. Both open up a whole new world, with fish,

Pogona vitticeps, the bearded dragon, found in desert landscapes

colour and movement surrounding you wherever you choose to go. Of course, snorkelling on a coral reef is everyone's dream, but southern Australia also offers plenty of fabulous opportunities to delight in the underwater world.

For snorkelling, you'll need fins that fit firmly but comfortably, a mask that seals around the face and is comfortable, and a snorkel. While you could spend well over $200 on these three items alone, for $70 or so you should be able to buy some reasonable gear. And, because it is expensive, wash your equipment in fresh water after you have used it.

Of course, there are a few skills to learn, but the most common mistake for first-timers is that, as they lie on the surface looking down, they splash too much with their fins, using up energy and scaring away any fish. Keep your fins down and under water and use slow, steady strokes to propel yourself along.

Most of the dive shops around the country can arrange to teach you

SCUBA diving, but if snorkelling is all you want to do you can learn most of the basics from a book and with practice you'll soon be snorkelling with the best of them.

Once again, diving can become an all-encompassing passion and the prime reason for travelling and visiting our wild, magnificent places.

FISHING

Fishing is the biggest recreational pastime in Australia and it is no wonder that thousands of people each year pack their vehicles and head off fishing. Some save up for that one big trip north to the barra capitals of the Territory or the Cape; others with less time head up to a local stream for a weekend's trout fishing or along the coast after a snapper or mulloway. It is an activity that is worth millions to the economy, and one that in recent years has become more and more controlled. It's not that governing bodies want people to stop fishing, but they want to manage the resource so that the fishing will be just as good in years to come.

Fishing Regulations

Fishing regulations vary from state to state. However, recreational fishing in a marine environment is normally free of any licensing requirements unless you want to use nets, pots or take selected species like crayfish; in these cases state requirements vary.

Fishing in freshwater habitats generally requires a licence of some sort. Once again the regulations vary by state.

Most states have minimum sizes for all fish and other marine life. Some species also have maximum sizes, while other species are protected altogether. Bag limits also apply and once again the requirements vary from state to state.

Most states have areas of coastline that are marine habitat reserves, or marine national parks. These can include areas where no fishing, collecting or the removal of any item from the water is allowed, as well as others where there are bag and size limits. Check with each state body, individual parks, reserves etc. as to their regulations.

MOUNTAIN BIKING

Designed for riding on rough and rocky trails, the mountain bike is an ideal way to see and experience many of our wild places. Day trips and longer overnight forays are possible on a mountain bike, but in our parks these bikes often suffer the same restrictions as motor vehicles. In other words, you are often confined to public roads and tracks, with walking trails and even Management Vehicles Only (MVO) tracks being out of bounds. There doesn't seem to be a standard ruling on mountain biking, even within parks in the same state, so it pays to check before setting out on two wheels.

In some places, such as Thredbo, you can hire mountain bikes (though riding to the crest of Mt Kosciuszko is not allowed). Otherwise you could spend a lot of dollars buying a mountain bike, with prices topping out at an incredible $8000!

Clothing for bike touring needs to be light and snug fitting, and you need good windproof and waterproof gear as well. Much the same gear as for bushwalking needs to be carried for either day jaunts or extended overnight trips.

Mountain biking is a much faster way to travel through the back country than on two feet and there is ample opportunity for excitement on exhilarating descents and narrow trails.

VEHICLE TOURING

In many of our larger parks, vehicle-based touring is a pleasant and easy way to enjoy what the parks have to offer. It doesn't matter whether you have a 4WD or the family car, most of the

Pipis cooking on the hot plate

parks close to the more settled areas of Australia have access routes and through routes which are suitable to explore, and the chances of finding a delightful place to camp are good.

In the more remote country a 4WD is a better choice, but even so, parks such as Sturt National Park in far northwestern New South Wales, the Innamincka Recreation Reserve in South Australia, Litchfield National Park in the Northern Territory, Carnarvon National Park in Queensland and the Big Desert National Park in Victoria, to name just a few, can all be visited and enjoyed in the family car, driven with care.

Contact the ranger headquarters of the particular parks you wish to visit and they will let you know which roads and tracks are suitable for you and your vehicle, and if there are any seasonal closures or roads temporarily closed due to recent rains or floods.

Travel in remote areas demands some special precautions such as carrying some water, maybe an extra spare tyre, as well as tools, camping gear, food and drink See the relevant sections for some helpful information in the following pages.

OTHER ACTIVITIES

Canyoning, caving, paragliding and a host of other activities can all be enjoyed in our parks and wilderness areas. Whatever your particular interest, it can be found in our parks and wild places. Go forth and enjoy!

Cape Peron and its beautiful waters, part of François Peron National Park

A day visit to a nearby national park can be a most enjoyable way to spend a few hours. At the opposite end of the scale is a visit to a park on the other side of the state—or even country. Clearly this would involve much more detailed planning, particularly if travelling off road through the Outback is part of your trip. Touring this great country of ours can be exciting, enjoyable, an adventure and a challenge. It pays you to check out the gear you have and what you need to take before setting out on any trip, whatever its length or duration.

The main ideas are to have an itinerary—a flexible one—and to enjoy yourself. Enjoying yourself is a lot easier if you haven't got a cast-iron set of times and places to stick to.

PLANNING THE ITINERARY

Once you have decided on where you are going and for how long, you need to do a little planning. Distances to be travelled, how long you'll be away, and where to stay will all be important when working out costs. At that point you'll need a budget, and while food costs may be a little higher on the road than they are at home, the big cost for most travellers is fuel.

Plan ahead and thoroughly check all the equipment you take away with you, from your vehicle, to the tent and the zips on the sleeping bags.

Before you go, let somebody know your travel plans, and if you are going away for any length of time and you say you are going to contact them every week, make sure you do! If you are heading into very remote country, of course, this becomes even more important.

Should you need more information than is given here, there are a host of places to go, including state government tourist offices, state national park bodies, the state motoring organisations, dedicated map shops that sell a wide range of maps and guides, as well as the local tourist information centres.

TRAVELLING LONG DISTANCES

Setting off on any trip is not to be undertaken too lightly and you should set yourself modest goals in terms of distance covered and time taken.

Long-distance truckies might be able to sit behind the wheel for six to eight hours on end, but most people cannot. A lot of accidents happen on holidays because people try to drive too far too quickly. So take it easy, plan plenty of breaks and don't try to drive for more than, say, 10 hours a day.

If the road is rougher than you expected, the weather rainy and windy, or you are towing a trailer or caravan, allow for a lower speed and more time, and stop earlier as you will find that driving in these conditions will be more tiring.

If you are planning to travel at night make sure your lights are in first-class condition.

Travelling with Kids

Ah, the joys of travelling with kids! Be they tiny tots or teenagers, they bring a new dimension to touring and camping.

Taking the kids camping and touring can be an enjoyable and rewarding experience—it just takes a little effort, planning and compromise. These days, when work and family commitments make it difficult to spend much time as a family unit, camping and touring provide a great

Sunset in Kinchega National Park

opportunity to enjoy each other's company amid the delights of the bush.

Keep in mind that, for both parents and children, being confined to the vehicle for long periods with nowhere to go to get away from each other can lead to tempers flaring and disagreements and arguments. Kids need regular breaks every couple of hours as do most adults.

If you start taking the children camping when they are young, you sort of 'advance' with their needs as they grow.

Life on the road can also be a lot easier if you travel in the company of friends who also have children.

Around Camp

We've found that kids usually disappear once you get to your camp site. While this may be a relief after a full day's travel, you should set clear guidelines on how far they can go when exploring around the camping area. It is very easy for them to get lost in the bush.

It is also very important to have strict rules around the camp fire and near water. A fire for cooking your meals and to sit around at night is one of the great experiences of camping in the bush, but keep a watchful eye on young children especially.

It is worth mentioning that most snakes are nocturnal and are active at night, so don't let the kids go wandering off in the bush unsupervised. If they need to go to the toilet, make sure they carry a torch with them. In fact, children should each have their own torch, which they can also take to bed with them.

LEGAL ISSUES

We are relatively lucky in this country that the road rules are similar right across the board. A few years ago there were some anomalies, but these have been rectified.

Driving licences, car registration and the like are all valid wherever you are in Australia. Likewise, you will be liable for a speeding fine or an unroadworthy vehicle sticker no matter what state you are in or where you come from.

Speed Limits

All speed limits are well signposted; on the open highway it is between 100 and 110 kph, except in the Northern Territory where at present there is an open speed limit.

TRAVELLING IN PASTORAL AREAS

- Don't impose on property owners along the way for help unless you are in *real* trouble. Property owners are not geared up to receive or resupply tourists. Before planning to enter their property write to them for permission. At the very least, if you enter a property, proceed directly to the homestead and speak to the manager or owner.
- Leave all gates as you find them unless otherwise requested by the occupier. A gate may have been left open to allow stock to get to water.
- Refrain from lighting fires unless approved by the occupier. If you do have a fire, cover it completely with earth and ensure it is out before going to sleep or leaving camp. One small spark can start a devastating bushfire.
- Littering is an offence by law, the same as anywhere else, and plastics and tin cans can be fatal if chewed or swallowed by livestock. Remove all litter and rubbish.
- Chasing or upsetting livestock can cause broken fences, injuries and even death, especially around calving time.
- Livestock need water too, so please do not bathe, swim or wash clothes in water tanks or troughs, and do not camp near a watering place as stock will not come in to drink.
- Fences must not be cut, removed or driven over.
- Travelling on wet, unsealed roads can cause expensive damage and take months to repair. You could be made to pay, so always check with the local Shire office, Department of Transport or the occupier before driving on unsealed roads after rain.

Careless acts by insensitive, non-thinking people have spoilt it for others, as well as themselves if they ever want to come back. Please take care and consider the rights of others.

WILDLIFE

One of the attractions of travelling our great continent is the wildlife that inhabits it. Ever since the first seafarers landed on our shores our unique animals have amazed and delighted people. Modern travellers are no different. For those who want a good idea of what there is to see, and also help in identifying what they see, then a good field guide to wildlife is essential.

Birds

There are over 700 species of birds which call Australia home either all the time or for at least part of the year. Found in every region, from arid desert country to the most dense rainforest, they range in size from tiny bush birds the size of a matchbox to the emu which is taller than a man. Any time in the bush can be enhanced by watching birds and a long trip will be appreciated more if you take the time to watch and learn about birds and their habits.

Mammals

The mammals of this country vary from the seals that inhabit many of our southern offshore islands to the majestic kangaroo, to the introduced species that have caused so much damage to the land and the native and unique marsupials.

For most people the larger kangaroos are the most common native mammal seen, while luckier or more observant people will spy koalas, possums, wallabies and small marsupials. Most of our native fauna will go unnoticed by the majority of travellers, which is rather sad.

Reptiles and Frogs

Snakes and lizards may send a shiver up most people's spines, but Australia has a vast array of reptiles and outdoor people are sure to meet up with some. One species of crocodile and several snakes are dangerous, so unless you know what you are looking at, leave well alone!

The lizards are a variable lot, ranging from tiny geckoes to large monitor lizards over a metre in length. While not dangerous, the larger animals can bite and scratch if cornered, so once again leave them alone.

The frog fauna of Australia takes in the whole of the continent, with some specially adapted frogs making their home in ephemeral pools in the central deserts of Australia. They are incredible.

A pelican in the surf off Stradbroke Island

Looking Out for Wildlife

When travelling you need to take a little care as far as our wildlife is concerned. Wombats wander quiet country roads in the mountains of the southeast and kangaroos or other marsupials can be found on most country roads at one time or another, as can many of our birds.

Without getting too melodramatic about it, the toll of wildlife on our roads is shocking. It is near impossible to travel the Outback and not add to the carnage, but you can lessen the toll by driving more slowly, watching out for animals on the side of the road and keeping travelling at night, in the early morning, or the evening, to a minimum.

If you do hit an animal on an outback road, do the right thing: stop and make sure it is dead. It's not nice, but it's better than leaving the animal to die a painful and lingering death.

Approaching Wildlife

Remember the animals you see in a national park or in the bush, are wild! Most animals will tolerate you approaching to within a certain distance and then they will want to flee. If you are in their way they could very well attack you. Feeding wild animals is a definite no-no!

Dangerous Wildlife

Barring the animal that will attack you because it feels threatened or trapped, we have very few animals that could really be called dangerous.

Snakes

There are a few species of snake that will attack with little provocation and others that may not be so willing to attack but are still poisonous. Generally the best rule by far is to leave them well and truly alone and they will do the same. I have yet to hear of the snake that has gone out of its way to spring an unprovoked, surprise attack on a human! Wear above-ankle boots or similar, and take particular care when walking through thick undergrowth or gathering wood for a camp fire.

Prevention is much better than any cure, but we have included information about snakebite in the First Aid section of this book, just in case.

Sharks

There are a few shark attacks on humans each year in Australia, most of them around the well-populated areas of our coastline.

There is only one sure way of not getting attacked and that is not to go swimming in the ocean or in a river that has unrestricted access to the sea. However, the chances of being attacked are pretty slim and most of us take the risk each summer.

When travelling in more remote areas the same risks apply, but you may be a little further from help than if an attack happened on a major suburban beach.

Our section on First Aid has details on how to stop bleeding, in the unlikely event that an attack occurs.

Crocodiles

When travelling north for the first (or even the 20th) time this is the animal that strikes fear into most people's hearts.

Australia has two species, the freshwater crocodile and the estuarine (or saltwater) crocodile.

The freshie only inhabits freshwater streams, waterholes and billabongs; it grows to around 3 metres and is a shy, retiring creature. Basically, it won't hurt you, but again, it will bite if you corner it. In a word, do the right thing and they are not a problem.

Salties are an entirely different matter. They grow to well over 6 metres, live in fresh and salt water, and have been recorded 300 km offshore as well as hundreds of kilometres upstream. They are aggressive, cunning and eat large mammals. If you are in their territory you are potential prey!

HOW TO BE CROCODILE WISE

In areas where estuarine crocodiles may be present you should follow this code:

- Be aware of crocodiles—keep your eyes open
- Do not feed or otherwise interfere with crocodiles
- Avoid areas where large crocodiles or their nests have been seen
- Camp at least 50 metres from the water's edge
- Stand at least a few metres back from the water's edge when fishing and don't stand on logs overhanging deep pools
- If you're going for a swim pick a shallow spot, e.g. over a rapid; don't swim in deep, dark waters; swim in a group rather than alone
- Dispose of fish offal and any other animal refuse well away from camp sites; carcasses of dead animals attract crocodiles
- Don't set a regular routine in these areas, such as cleaning fish on the side of a river at the same spot each day. Salties are cunning hunters and have been known to observe such behaviour and wait for an opportune time before launching an attack
- Take note of any warning signs around

A misty morning in a rainforest

ABORIGINAL COMMUNITIES AND LAND

Much of inland Australia is Aboriginal land. These areas can be cattle stations that are now owned and run by Aboriginal communities, or vast areas of old reserve land that have been deeded to an Aboriginal community as freehold land or areas of Crown land that have been handed back to a particular group of Aboriginal people. In the Northern Territory over 50 per cent of the land is now owned by Aboriginal groups, while other states have lesser amounts.

Permits and Access

You need an access permit to enter or to cross most Aboriginal land. While some are easy to obtain, like the permits required to use the Gunbarrel Highway west of Uluru (Ayers Rock), other areas are almost impossible to enter.

For further information and requirements concerning access permits, write to or contact the Aboriginal authorities concerned, and remember to allow plenty of time before your planned trip as it can take months to get a permit.

FUEL

Getting fuel in the Outback isn't as easy as it first seems. In big towns and on the major highways it is not a problem, but once you start heading into remote country fuel is just a little harder to organise.

Autogas may be common on the east coast, but away from the main highways elsewhere it can be hard to get. For example, north of Cooktown on Cape York you cannot get autogas, and there are plenty of other places the same. For the autogas vehicle owner there are a couple of annually updated guides that give you a listing of outlets. These are essential for planning. If you can't buy one at a good newsagent or bookstore, the RAA of SA has an LPG Outlets Directory, or alternatively, contact the Energy Information Centre in Adelaide.

MONEY MATTERS

Don't expect to find your bank while travelling around the country. Once you are away from major town centres, most small communities have only one or two banks represented, and they mightn't be yours. As well, you can't count on the banks having full banking facilities, and if the computers go down, it can create a few problems.

When touring in more remote areas, it pays to have a Commonwealth Bank passbook account—not just a keycard account—as every post office in Australia is a Commonwealth Bank agency, and even though they may not be able to offer ETPOB (Electronic Transfer Point of Banking) facilities for you to use your keycard and the like, they can certainly let you withdraw money from a passbook account.

Certainly these days electronic banking is becoming more readily available even in isolated communities, but it should not be relied upon. It is also possible to do a lot of transactions, such as shopping and buying fuel, through EFTPOS (Electronic Funds Transfer Point of Sale) terminals.

While credit cards, especially Mastercard, Bankcard and Visa, are widely accepted as payment, they cannot be depended upon, and trying to get a cheque accepted as payment for goods and services is near impossible unless prior arrangement has been made with the shop owner. Australian dollar travellers' cheques can also be used and cashed in many places, but once again they aren't universal and we wouldn't suggest that they be your main source of cash, especially when travelling in outback areas.

In many cases you will find that cash is the only form of money wanted, so try to gauge how much you will need for fuel and food, along with incidentals, between banking points, especially if you don't have a Commonwealth Bank passbook account.

INSURANCE AND THE LIKE

Travelling off the beaten track in this vast country does open one up to a new range of experiences, including exposure to having equipment lost, stolen or damaged in ways not covered by your normal insurance policies.

Automobile Association Membership

We are great believers in joining your state motoring organisation, especially if you are about to set off on a long trip around Australia. It might also pay to upgrade your membership to include any extra benefits the association might offer in your home state.

Not only does membership give you access to a vast range of cheap, often free, touring and accommodation information, there are also the roadside assist schemes that are a great help when touring. The 'Plus' schemes give even more coverage, including such things as return fares home, hire cars, accommodation, and more. It *can* pay to belong!

The southern rim of Wilpena Pound, Flinders Ranges National Park

How much planning and preparation you will need to do for a visit to a national park or other protected area will depend on where you are going and how long you'll be away. For a day's jaunt you may only need to take a portable cooler with a few cool drinks and lunch.

For an overnight trip you may need to plan where you will stay and what you would like to see. Obviously if you intend to camp you'll also need a swag or a tent plus sleeping gear and food.

On long trips you will need to do a lot more planning and take a heap more gear. Questions about fuel requirements, and a dozen other things, need to be answered before you set off. This section aims to give you some idea of what you require, but you will need to think about the trip you have planned, the style of accommodation or camping you enjoy, and your gear. There are places where you shouldn't go if you haven't the right equipment. While Cape York is fine without a High Frequency (HF) radio, a more remote and difficult trip to the Simpson Desert or any outback national park really demands at least one HF radio in your group.

PLANNING THE TRIP

• Make a plan of your proposed trip—where, what season, time allowed, distance, fuel.
• Check on fuel availability, where you can resupply, places to see, history, attractions and things to do.
• Make a rough, and flexible, itinerary.
• Apply for any permits that may be necessary, such as for certain national parks and Aboriginal land. Advance bookings are necessary for camp sites in some national parks, and during holiday periods they often operate on a ballot system. It is also very important to apply well ahead for any permits for access to Aboriginal land as these can take some time to obtain.
• It may be advisable to book accommodation at some of the more popular destinations.
• If you are going bush, then let someone know your itinerary, and if you change it significantly, contact them so they don't panic. Keep in regular touch.
• For some areas it will be necessary to check the conditions of the roads, whether they are open to vehicular traffic, whether conventional or 4WD only.

PREPARING THE VEHICLE

Your vehicle is your lifeline. Break down on a remote mountain track in Victoria's Alpine National Park and you could be in for a long, hard walk. If you have the same sort of breakdown in the Kimberley or the Gulf Country your bones, bleached by the sun, may be all they find.

It pays to have a well set up vehicle, and remember that a vehicle that can handle a 300 km day trip to the mountains may not be at all suitable for a visit to the Simpson Desert Regional Reserve.

Checking the Mechanicals

Many people can service and maintain their own vehicle and that will certainly be of help if you are heading for the bush. It doesn't take a lot of skill and knowledge to do a basic service on your vehicle so maybe it would be a good idea to learn before you head off onto the wild.

If you are not mechanically minded, before setting off get your vehicle checked by a reputable mechanic.

PACKING A VEHICLE

Packing a vehicle is a skill; it gets easier—and better—with practice. Once you have done a few long trips you will know the things you require to be kept handy and those you can afford to bury.

Keep in mind the equipment and stores you'll be using all the time. Cameras, a lolly jar and a pillow, plus a few cassette tapes you may want always at hand, while everyday food items, water and the basic cooking gear need to be pretty close. On the other hand the stores required to cook bread over the camp fire can be buried a little deeper because you won't be doing that every day.

The clothes bag will need to be fairly handy, as will a basic first aid kit. Depending on where you're going, the shovel and toilet paper need to be very handy as you will need it whenever anyone wants a nature walk.

A basic toolroll should always be part of your equipment, along with a can of WD40.

An emu visitor to a camp site near Yerranderie

If you have just bought a 4WD it may come as a shock to you that this is not the perfect tourer you thought. Of the host of gear you can fit to your machine some is a near necessity while some is only as good as it looks. Equipment you may wish to consider fitting to your vehicle includes:

Bullbar: for added protection from wayward kangaroos and stock

Driving lights: a necessity if driving in the bush at night

Towbar: make sure it can carry the load you wish it to

Roofrack: just to carry light bulky gear

Long-range fuel tanks: worthwhile if you intend doing long trips

Suspension kit: most 4WDs need some help in this department to carry the loads required for a trip. You can opt for just a pair of Polyair springs or a complete replacement suspension

Snorkel: to raise the level of the air intake; a real life saver, especially if you have a diesel engine and are going anywhere near water

Dual battery system: excellent if you plan to use an electric fridge, winches and the like

Cargo barrier: a very good safety feature in the back of a wagon

Storage system: helps you use the available space effectively

There is lots more you can fit to a 4WD such as turbos, diff locks, seats, etc. but that is beyond the scope of this guide. Use the *Yellow Pages* or your favourite 4WD magazine to find your closest dealers.

BASIC EQUIPMENT, SPARES AND TOOLS

While some of the following may not be required for a day trip to Stradbroke Island or the like, they make sense for longer trips.

Basic Equipment Always to Be Carried

> Basic recovery equipment
> Basic first aid kit (see First Aid)
> Fire extinguisher
> CB radio
> Tool kit and spare parts (see below)
> 10 litres of water (in semi-remote and remote desert country you'll need much more)
> Map of area and surrounds
> Matches, compass, torch, knife
> Space blanket

Basic Tools to Carry

> Set of ring and open end spanners (to suit your vehicle)
> Adjustable spanner, Plug spanner
> Wheelbrace, jack and jacking plate (30 cm square x 2.5 cm thick board)
> Screwdrivers/Phillips head screwdriver
> Hammer, chisel
> Hacksaw and spare blades
> Files, including a points file
> Pliers and wire cutters
> Feeler gauges
> Tyre levers
> Pump and pressure gauge for tyres
> Tube/tyre repair kit
> Battery jumper leads
> Repair manual
> WD40, or similar

Basic Spares to Carry

> Radiator hoses, heater hoses
> Fan belts (an emergency Uni-Belt is handy and easier to fit)
> Fuses, globes, electric wire
> Spark plugs, plug leads, points

One of the entrances to Main Range National Park

> Coil, condenser
> Tyre tube

On longer trips you could include a more comprehensive range of tools and spares.

Carrying Extra Fuel

There is no better way to carry extra fuel than in dedicated long-range fuel tanks. If you are going to do more than one trip where a long-range tank is required, it is worth having one fitted.

Many people still opt to carry their extra fuel in jerry cans. While metal jerry cans were once the only type, today there are a number of excellent plastic drums that offer a better, safer and cleaner option.

Carrying fuel in or on a vehicle is fraught with problems. Fuel, especially petrol, is a real hassle inside a vehicle. While I'd carry diesel inside a car, I wouldn't carry petrol.

Carrying fuel on the roof rack is not much better because its weight raises the vehicle's centre of gravity and makes it easier to tip the vehicle over. However, that is where most four wheelers who carry fuel in jerry cans are forced to carry their extra fuel, the only other option would be carrying it in a trailer.

If you need to carry fuel on a roofrack make sure the rack is strong enough, and keep the amount of fuel to a minimum. As fuel is used up in your tank, transfer fuel from the drums into the tank, aiming to get rid of the weight on the roof as quickly as possible.

OFF ROAD DRIVING TECHNIQUES

Knowing what you can—and can't—do with your 4WD is a skill that needs to be learned; it comes only with a lot of time spent behind the wheel in all sorts of terrains and conditions. It is also important to understand a vehicle's capabilities, and these vary considerably.

Most of the older vehicles (pre-1984) do not have power steering, or great brakes. Their suspension is truck-like, giving a rather harsh ride, a touch or more of understeer, and on rough roads a fair amount of bump steer. Later model 4WDs are a lot more car-like in their design and performance, with the latest models being well set up, very capable vehicles, and also very expensive.

THE FUNDAMENTALS OF 4WD

First off you need to understand the operation of such things as free wheeling hubs and the transfer box gear selection. On bitumen or hard dirt surfaces the vehicle should be driven in 2WD, high ratio, or if it's a

Camping in the High Country in Victoria

General

• It is always wise to check out the ground ahead if you are unsure of a situation, and especially if there is mud or water involved.

• It's crucial not to change gear in the middle of a difficult section, so if you don't know which gear to select, always choose the lower gear.

• Remember to keep your thumbs outside the steering wheel, otherwise you are likely to end up with broken bones caused by the sudden, unexpected spin of the wheel—this is especially true for vehicles without power steering.

• Tyre pressures play a very important part in four wheel driving. Too hard and the vehicle's ride will be uncomfortable and you will get bogged more often. Too soft and you will destroy tyres. The load you are carrying will dictate what pressure you use, but for general touring we normally run pressures between 210 and 280 kPa (30–40 psi). If you are in the mountains and want more traction decrease tyre pressures to 175–210 kPa (25–30 psi). In soft beach sand you can drop tyre pressure to 140 kPa (20 psi) or lower, even down to 70 kPa (10 psi), while on the Canning Stock Route and heavily loaded with fuel, somewhere around 210 kPa (30 psi) would be more suitable.

• Cross small ridges square-on, while ditches should be crossed at a slight angle.

Corrugations

Corrugations can make for very unpleasant driving conditions. They can be so bad they will seem to be vibrating the vehicle to pieces. Going too fast on these stretches can be dangerous as well as detrimental to you and your car, while going too slow might not be as dangerous but it will certainly be tiring on you and wearing on your vehicle.

In most cases a speed of around 80 kph is the optimum, as at that speed the vehicle will tend to 'float' across the hollows, giving a smoother ride. Mind you, what sort of ride you get will depend on how good your suspension is—if you have poor shock absorbers you are going to feel every bump!

On Steep Hills

• Low second or third gear is generally best for going uphill, while low first is best for steep downhills.

• Use the footbrake sparingly and with caution and keep your feet well away from the clutch.

• Don't turn a vehicle sideways on a hill and if you stall going uphill, don't touch the clutch or accelerator. See our Stall Start advice below.

• Try to stay out of the ruts. However, if you are on a steep downhill gradient and it is slippery, the ruts may be the safest place.

• A more aggressive tread pattern on your tyres makes a difference here.

Snow

Chains are an essential part of the snow driving experience. It pays to practise fitting these at home, in comfort. This makes the first time you have to do it in the cold and dark so much easier. It is compulsory to carry chains to most of the snowfields. With a 4WD chains can be fitted to either front or back tyres, but front are generally favoured.

Drive slowly, keeping gear changes to a minimum and any braking slow and steady. Use gears to slow down instead of the brakes if possible.

Don't use the handbrake when you park the vehicle—it is preferable to chock the wheels instead.

Watch for patches of 'black ice' on shaded or cold sections of the road or track.

Vehicles going downhill should give way to those going uphill as it is more difficult to get going again when facing uphill.

In an emergency it's better to head into a snow bank or the hill side of the road than to drop off the edge of the mountain.

constant 4WD vehicle such as a Range Rover, leave it in normal, without the centre diff locked.

Once the road or track gets sandy, muddy or just slippery you can engage 4WD high ratio, or lock the centre diff of a constant 4WD vehicle.

When the going slows and it is rough and sandy or boggy and muddy you can engage 4WD low ratio, or low ratio with the centre diff locked in a constant 4WD machine. This will give you the maximum traction and power.

Don't get confused about 'diff locks' and 'centre diff locks'. Centre diff locks are found on constant 4WD vehicles and are operated as detailed earlier. Diff locks can be found on part-time 4WD vehicles and constant 4WD vehicles. They are located in either or both axles and actually lock the axle so one wheel cannot spin.

Diff locks give the ultimate capability as well as making those hard-to-traverse areas a lot easier on the vehicle. They shouldn't be regarded solely as an addition for extremely hard country.

It should be made clear that a 4WD won't guarantee that you won't get bogged, but it will help you get bogged less often.

The downside of a 4WD is that when you do get bogged you are normally deeper and further into the quagmire than a normal car is when it gets bogged!

OFF ROAD CONDITIONS

If you follow these points you should be able to approach most situations with some confidence—well, at least, you'll know what you are *supposed* to be doing!

Sand Driving

• Speed and flotation are the keys to success and high ratio is best, if possible.

• Tyre pressures are important. Generally 140 kPa (20 psi) is a good starting point but if you are heavily loaded this may be too low and 175 kPa (25 psi) could be more appropriate. If you are lightly loaded 105 kPa (15 psi) may be the way to go.

• Stick to existing wheel tracks, avoid sudden changes in direction and tackle dunes head on.

• When descending a dune avoid braking at all costs. Keep the nose pointing downhill, and don't travel too fast, but don't go so slow that the wheels stop turning.

• If you do get stuck, rock the vehicle backwards and forwards, building up a small stretch of hard-packed sand that you can move off from. Don't spin the wheels.

Melaleucas lining a lake on Stradbroke Island

Water Crossings

• Always check the crossing before you plunge in. A 4WD should be able to tackle a crossing of around 60 cm deep without any problems or preparation, but a soft sandy bottom or a strong current flow can change all that.

• Spray electrical components with WD40 or similar, loosen the fanbelt unless the fan has an auto clutch, and in deep water fit a canvas blind to the front of the vehicle.

• Enter the water at a slow pace—low second gear is generally the best— and keep the engine running even if you stop.

• Don't forget to dry your brakes out once through the water crossing, and if you were stuck, check all your oils for contamination.

Mud

Speed and power are essential. In deep mud, low second or third are probably best. Keep a steady pace and if possible keep out of ruts.

STALL START OR KEY START

When you stop on a steep uphill, don't panic, stay calm. *Do not* touch the clutch.

• Engage both the handbrake and the footbrake.

• Switch the engine off if it hasn't already stalled.

• Ease the clutch in and select low range reverse gear; ease the clutch out.

• Ensure that the track is clear and the wheels are pointing straight ahead.

• Take the handbrake off and the footbrake, but keep your foot close to the brake just in case.

A rainbow lorikeet enjoying a feast

• Keeping your feet away from both clutch or accelerator, start the engine and slowly back the vehicle down the hill. Slight feathering of the brake is possible, but take care.

ONCOMING TRAFFIC

When another vehicle approaches in dust, move over to the left and slow down and if need be, stop. Probably the most dangerous thing to do is travel in somebody's dust—oncoming traffic will never see you.

• Don't forget, a *road train* will never get out of your way—appreciate that he has a huge load on behind him and keep out of his way.

• When approaching bridges, watch for oncoming traffic and obey any giveway signs.

• When you see an oncoming *bike rider*, slow down to a walking pace. Whilst it may seem easier for the rider to pull off to the side, wheel ruts and deep sand often make this impossible.

4WD DRIVER TRAINING COURSES

Not everybody who owns a 4WD is a proficient off road driver, and although the greatest teacher of all is experience, it certainly helps to have some good instruction. The best way to obtain that is through a driving course which specialises in 4WD techniques. This will give you both the experience (under the watchful eye of an instructor) and the ability to find the limitations of your vehicle, as well as an opportunity to explore your own skills.

4WD INSURANCE

There are a number of vehicle insurance schemes and for the general motorists these are fine. When it comes to 4WDs that may be fitted with thousands of dollars worth of accessories, including wide tyres, turbo diesel motors, HF radios and the like, it may be a different ball game. When those vehicles head up into the mountains, along the beaches, crossing rocky streams or ploughing over the tall sandridges and vast distances of the Outback there just might be some small print in your insurance policy which can see you out of pocket if your vehicle is damaged while off the main roads.

It pays to check and to cover yourself, and your vehicle, in writing.

CAMPING

One of the real delights of a trip away from home is setting up a tent and being close to nature. Today there is absolutely no reason why you can't be comfortable when you are in the bush; good tents to keep the bugs and elements at bay, refrigerators to keep the food and beer cold, showers to keep you clean and sleeping gear that is comfortable and warm all provide the ingredients for a happy and successful camping trip.

What camping equipment you buy will really depend on how much money you have to spend, how much time you are going to be in the scrub and where you plan to go. Whatever you do, buy the very best you can afford. Not only will it keep you drier and warmer, it will last longer and if you want to sell it later you will get more for it.

CAMPING AND PERSONAL REQUIREMENTS CHECKLIST

Portable light	Boots/shoes
Torch	Hat
Tent or swag	Wet weather gear
Sleeping gear	Sunglasses
Clothes—to suit where you are going	
Portable refrigerator/ice chest	First aid kit (see First Aid)
Jerrycan(s) of water	Paper and pencils
Folding chairs	String
Fire extinguisher	Plastic sheet
Toilet paper	Tarpaulin
Toiletries bag	Poles, ropes and pegs
Camera, film and spare batteries	Bucket
Compass and maps	Shovel, Axe
Insect repellent	Food
Sunblock cream	Cooking equipment

CAMPING GEAR

What you take with you will depend on where you go and for how long. A swag may be good for the Outback, but a tent is better for the Alps in spring or autumn when it can rain at any time. If you're on the road for a long time a camper may be the best answer as it does give a lot more luxury. Decide on your style of camping and buy the appropriate gear.

Swags

A swag is an excellent option for sleeping when touring the Outback. It is quick: while everyone else is struggling with a tent, a swag is a throw-down winner. Although they are basically just a protected sleeping cocoon, the models of swags now available keep you comfortable and secure from all the elements. They are especially suitable for trips in central Australia, or up north in the warmer areas, and there is no greater feeling than sleeping under a clear, star-studded sky.

A basic swag consists of a large piece of good quality canvas in which you put all your sleeping gear—mattress, blankets or sleeping bag, pillow and mossie net. Today, however, you can get swags that are more like a small tent and these are definitely better in the rain. This type also prevents the bugs and creepy crawlies from getting into your sleeping gear, while still having all the advantages of the normal traditional swag.

As with buying a tent, make sure you are getting a high standard of workmanship, that good quality material is used in the canvas, flywire and zips, and that the mattress is made of high density foam.

Tents

Tents are the long term favourite of Australians going bush and how you camp will depend on which is the best for you. Think about your requirements, then buy the very best tent you can afford.

Are you a tourer or a stay-in-one-place camper, an overnight bushwalker or a vehicle-based camper? Clearly weight and packed size are of prime importance to bushwalkers, mountain climbers and the like. A 'minute camper' that is easy to erect is great for overnight stops, while a more palatial tent may suit longer stays but is a pain to erect each and every night. The smaller tents, at around 3 metres square, are acceptable overnighters.

It's hard to beat an Australian or New Zealand made tent. Look for quality when you're choosing a tent: quality of canvas, floor material, zips (go for the YKK brand and check to make sure that they are protected from the weather), even and close sewing, reinforced seams, corner peg points, and even the poles, pegs and ropes, are all important. Flyscreens on the windows should be double-stitched and fibreglass screens will generally outlast nylon. Don't select by floor size alone, as lower wall heights and sloping walls will greatly reduce the amount of usable space. The bigger the tent, the longer it takes to erect and the harder it gets.

When you get your new tent home, hose it down and saturate the tent thoroughly so that the new canvas stretches and fills up any sewing holes—you don't want it leaking on your first outing simply because you couldn't be bothered to give it a thorough soaking at home.

Never put your tent away wet. If you have to pack it wet, erect it again as soon as possible to dry out the canvas, or the canvas will deteriorate!

If purchasing a tent made from a synthetic like nylon, stick to the better brands such as Fairydown, Tatonka or Eureka. Tents made from these materials can vary in size from a one-person bivvy, through small bushwalking dome and tunnel tents to larger family-style dome and A-frame tents.

Be aware that nylon is usually not UV stabilised and can lose its colour and become weak in areas constantly exposed to heat and sunlight. Make sure you get a double skin tent, or one with a fly. Also ensure that stress areas like peg loops and seams are reinforced and, as with canvas tents, that zippers are a good quality (such as YKK).

It is worth noting that alloy poles are more durable than fibreglass poles.

The better outdoor shops such as Paddy Pallin, found around Australia, are the best places for these types of tents, but the top of the line ones are expensive.

A magpie lark and its young

Caravans

The choice of vans available for the tourer is immense and your choice will be determined by where you want to go. There are only a few that come anywhere near real off-road capability. The final choice will depend on your wallet and the layout of the van.

No matter what style and size, a van will limit your travels. In places such as Cape York and the Simpson Desert, to name just two, you will be forced to leave the van behind and take a tent or a swag.

Sleeping Gear

You spend nearly a third of your life in bed asleep and it's not much different when you're in the bush, so it pays to be comfortable and pleasantly warm.

Mattresses

You can use a layer of foam, a camp stretcher, a normal air mattress or one of the newer, self-inflating air mattresses.

While the latter may be the most expensive, they have the advantage of taking up a minimum amount of room when packed, they're well padded for sleeping on and being insulated they keep the cold from the ground away from you. There are a number of different sorts of self-inflators around.

A layer of foam is the simplest form of mattress and is very comfortable; its main drawback is its size when packed away.

Camp stretchers are comfortable, yet they tend to break at the most inopportune times. The original canvas stretcher is still around, but today there is a wider selection of makes and models.

Normal air matresses are fine once you've learnt what's the right amount of air in it for you, and they pack down to a small size for travelling.

Camping in the Bunya Mountains National Park

Sleeping Bags

Sleeping bags come in all shapes and sizes, but it's what is on the inside that makes the difference—and that makes the choice confusing. Be guided by the price—the more expensive the bag is, the better it will be. It certainly pays to select a bag from a specialised camping store where the staff are well qualified to guide you.

Sleeping bags are priced according to their filling and lining. At the lower end of the market acrylic and polyester filled bags are only suitable for home use or strictly in warmer climates. Hollofill is a good all-round filling and Quallofill, which is lighter in weight than Hollofill, has good heat retention, even if wet.

The warmest, and the fill that packs down to the smallest size, is down and the best you'll find is 90 per cent down/10 per cent feathers. Some of the cheaper down bags will be less than 50 per cent down—so they're bulkier and colder!

You need to keep your bag clean as the things that destroy a bag's insulating qualities are dust, dirt and body oils. While most bags are washable, it pays to keep washing to a minimum. To do that and to preserve your bag the best idea is to make up an inner bag out of an old sheet that will fit nicely into your new sleeping bag. That will not only keep the bag clean, it is great for warm nights when you can use it on its own, and on cold nights it adds a little more insulation.

Another point well worth remembering when sleeping out is that it's no use just throwing blankets on top of you if you're cold—the cold will come in from underneath you as well. So either wrap yourself and bag in a blanket or put one blanket on the bottom and one on the top!

Upon returning home, don't leave the bag in its stuffsack. Store it loosely and that way the filling won't break down so quickly.

Whatever you do, think about your needs and shop around at specialty camping stores. Remember the old adage: You get what you pay for!

THE TRAVELLING COOK

Cooking in the bush, whether it be from a van or tent, using a camp oven or a gas stove, need not be a daunting task. Plan ahead the meals you hope to cook—it only has to be a very rough plan, but this will give you an idea of the staples you will need to carry. If you go through your favourite recipes you can list the necessary ingredients and include them in your shopping list. A great help in this regard is to start your own camping cookbook, a ready reckoner for camping meals.

As well, make a list of the items you think you might need for each meal, for example, Breakfast—cereal, toast, bacon and eggs for the first few mornings, tea/coffee, sugar, milk, etc. Do the same thing for lunch and dinner, then estimate how many days you might be away from civilisation and a corner shop. From this you can gauge your food requirements.

Space and Time Savers

With weight and space at a premium in most vehicles or backpacks on any trip, dehydrated and long-life products make catering for wilderness camping much easier. However, no matter how hard you try you can't get away from taking some canned food.

CAMP HYGIENE

Let us say something about camp hygiene. We detest people who use any form of soap in a river, stream, waterhole or lake. It is not necessary, does nothing for the water quality (even if you feel the amount is inconsequential), does nothing for the people downriver except give them belly aches, and does nothing for the aquatic life (plant and animal) except kill them!

If you want to swim and wash in a river or lake, it's not a problem: wet yourself and then, with a bucket of water, walk a whole 15 metres or so from the water's edge, soap yourself up and then rinse it off, making sure the waste water doesn't run down the bank back into the river or dam. Then you can go back and enjoy the swim.

Toilets should be erected well away from a water source, a short distance from camp. We all like our privacy but if you need a cut lunch and a water bottle to get to the loo it is a bit far!

For a toilet pit, dig a deep hole about a metre long and 40 cm wide. A folding toilet seat makes it more comfortable. Always cover any waste with soil and leave a shovel or trenching tool at the toilet for this purpose. When you are moving on, make sure the trench is covered with a deep layer of soil before you pack the shovel.

For the quick loo stop you'll need a shovel—a small garden one or a trenching tool is ideal. Scrape a hole at least 20 cm deep and once you have finished bury all the waste with soil. Better still, before burying the waste, burn the paper and then bury what remains. Obviously, you need to be careful not start a fire or let young kids out into the scrub with matches lighting paper at the drop of a hat!

When setting up a toilet, remember not to erect it where wastes can run back into the water system.

INSECT PROBLEMS

Bush flies can be a real hassle and at times can spoil a great holiday. And insect repellent isn't too effective either. In warm weather in central Australia or places further north, a fly veil or a hat with a set of corks is a must. At mealtimes an insect-free enclosure, either inside the vehicle or in a specially erected insect-screened gazebo, may be the answer.

Young kids can be driven to despair by flies, so make sure they have a fly veil during the day when the flies are bad and a net that keeps the insects away when they are having a nap.

Freshwater yabbies, a tasty meal

Mosquitoes too can be a problem in the Outback. Claypans and water-holes topped up with occasional seasonal rains provide ideal breeding places, and in the evening and at night they can be a real pain. Insect repellents work better on these little pests, with Rid or tropical strength Aeroguard being the best. Even so, a long-sleeved shirt or an insect-free enclosure, either a tent or a fly-screen gazebo, is more effective.

In northern Australia, anywhere near the coast or an estuary, sandflies can drive you insane. Once bitten, the damage is done—the bites will itch and itch. If you are in sandfly country cover up, especially just before sunset, and use plenty of Rid on exposed flesh.

We make up our own north Queensland proven anti-sandfly mix of baby oil and Dettol in an 8:1 ratio. You can add 1 part methylated spirits, along with some citronella for that little extra something that may help.

Camp fire cooking

SETTING UP CAMP

This is one aspect of camping that you learn as you go along. We'll give some pointers here, but there is nothing like experience to teach you what you have done wrong. It is easy to say, 'Don't set your camp up on low ground'. But sometimes it's only when it rains that you know where the low ground is!

Camp Sites

Many people are happy in camping grounds and caravan parks. We tend to look for uncrowded camp sites, where we and a few travelling companions can enjoy some peace and the delights of the bush.

Getting away from it all doesn't mean the back of beyond. It just takes a little forethought. Nearly every summer, over the school break, we take a beachside holiday. We stay away from the east coast though, saving our favourite camping spots in the Myall Lakes National Park or Great Sandy (Fraser Island) National Park for when school is back. No, over the Christmas break we head for the west coast of South Australia where, believe it or not, you can still camp and have a beach to yourself.

If you want an east coast holiday it's surprising how quickly the crowds drop away just a few kilometres inland from the coast. We have often camped beside a delightful stream within easy distance of the Gippsland 'Riviera' coast and not seen another soul from one day to the next.

Overnight Bushcamps

Travelling down the main highway it isn't easy to find a good camp site, though you can be lucky. The more remote the area, the better your chances of finding a good site near the road. Even so, you'll have a better camp, quieter and more private, if you head off the road a short distance. Use your maps and head along a side road; ones that follow a creek or cross a river or stream often give access to small areas ideal for a camp. Unless you are in a hurry it's best to set up camp while there is some day-light left, especially if you have kids or are unfamiliar with your equip-ment. Setting up camp at night after a long day's drive is bound to bring tempers to the boil.

If you want to get away in the morning and have dry canvas when you do, make sure your tent or camper is sited to catch the early morning sun.

If you aren't in a hurry and you're working on that flexible timetable we recommend earlier, don't drive past a great looking camp site, even if it is only mid-afternoon. Chances are it will be the last decent one you see.

Choosing a Camp Site

Pick a site protected from the wind. A line of trees or scrub can break the wind while a small hollow tucked into the side of a hill can be a very sheltered spot. If you're in a vehicle, it can, at a pinch, act as a windbreak;

CAMPING AND TOURING ETIQUETTE

It's one of the greatest disappointments of a trip to travel through pristine wilderness and come across a delightful camping site marred—no, vandalised—by rubbish! For everybody's sake

• Leave the camp site clean and take ALL your rubbish out with you. Don't even bury it, as wild animals, other people and flooding rivers can uncover the junk and spread it over the countryside.

• Use a shovel to dig a deep hole for your toilet requirements; keep it away from running water and other campers.

• Set up camp well away from any stock or water point.

• Don't use soap, shampoo or detergent in streams, waterholes, dams or water troughs. Use a bucket or a bush shower well away from the water to wash and rinse yourself. Also use a bucket to wash clothes and dishes, away from where animals and other humans may drink. Nobody likes to drink water tainted by soap!

• Take care with fire—clear an area around the fireplace before lighting it. Before you leave, make sure the fire is well and truly out.

• Use old fireplaces—don't erect new ones.

• Observe all fire restrictions.

• Observe all rules and regulations pertaining to the use of public land.

• Keep to constructed vehicle tracks, never 'bush bash'.

• Avoid areas which are easily damaged, such as swamps, alpine snow plains and vegetated sand dunes.

• Respect our wildlife.

• Respect private land. Always ask permission before crossing pastoral land.

• Leave gates as you find them.

• Observe all park regulations: when in doubt consult the ranger.

more than once on a flat featureless plain, with a howling wind, we have used the vehicles for shelter. The prevailing winds can often be picked, especially near the coast, by the trees and scrubs all leaning in one direction. In the mountains, stay away from ridges and saddles between two hilltops; when on the coast, avoid those bare unprotected headlands.

Don't select the lowest ground. Water can gather there, while in a valley or larger depression cold air can be trapped, keeping your camp cool, while just a little higher both you and the camp could be warmer.

Check out where the shade is going to be. You'll need to know where north is to do this, so use a compass, or a watch, and work out the sun's path. If it is blistering hot during the day you'll want to try and be in the shade during those hot hours. If it's a winter camp you'll be happier if your tent or camper trailer catches some sun. Select the site accordingly.

Don't camp underneath old gum trees. This rule is probably broken by everyone sooner or later. Those shady red gums along the river attract the eye, and the shade they cast can be a delight on a hot summer's day. However, red gums, yellow box gums and the like are notorious for dropping branches, and it doesn't have to be windy before they decide to shed a bough or two. Visible dead branches are a sign that should be heeded. We've seen cars crushed by a fallen branch, so it doesn't take much imagination to figure out what a large bough would do to a tent and its occupants.

Don't camp in a dry river or creek bed. West of the Great Divide and away from the well-watered regions of this country you will come across many dry river beds. Flat, soft and sandy, with few of the weeds and burrs

that mar the surrounding areas, they seem to offer an ideal camp site. They can be a trap! A distant rainstorm can send down a torrent of water to catch you unprepared, and even steady rain can produce enough water to bog your vehicle.

A river flat or a sandy tropical beach front may look a nice spot to camp, but the insects, mosquitoes especially, can drive you nuts. It might be better to camp away from the stream and the floodplain, or the beach, by just 100 metres or so—the difference in annoying insect life is amazing.

Two other things make for an ideal camp. Being close to a good, reliable water supply makes life a lot easier. Remember, though, in the Outback not to crowd a water point. It may be the only waterhole for kilometres, which all the wildlife and stock in the area depend on. Your actions could cause them to go thirsty and die a horrible death.

Wood for a fire makes for an easy camp. You'll be surprised how quickly the easily collected wood is used up and you'll then have to walk 100 metres or more to get some. Use wood conservatively and don't cut or chop down live trees and scrub to feed a fire. It won't burn well and you will destroy the area. Bring out the gas stove if there is no firewood. Some parks provide firewood, whereas others prohibit wood fires. Check on the regulations before entering the park.

There is one other point to consider before setting up your canvas home. Is there anybody else there? Most people who are camping in the bush prefer not to have somebody camp right on their doorstep. If there is another site not far away, or even a kilometre or so, think before you crowd up close to someone else. Ask if they mind; they might be pulling out next morning and then you will have the site to yourself.

Setting Up the Camp

Once you have found an area that looks good, pick a flat-looking site, making sure there is enough room for your tent, swag or camper. Once the tent is up, the camper erected or the swag laid out (the latter is the easiest and quickest of the three), the pegs hammered in and everything shipshape, it's time to think about what the weather will do.

If it is about to rain or you think a storm is likely, it will pay to dig a gutter or two to keep any flooding water away from your canvas home. You don't need to dig a gutter all the way around your tent. One across the slope on the high side of your tent will be fine.

A most important rule to observe when leaving a camp site

You may think you will never need to be proficient at first aid but everybody should have some training in this essential skill. Prompt action, correctly carried out, can go a long way to save lives.

There are quite a few good handbooks on first aid, such as those produced by the St John Ambulance Association and the Red Cross, and one is essential in any glovebox.

PRACTICAL FIRST AID

In the bush the main aspect of first aid is clear, logical thinking, prompt action and the ability to improvise. We've included the treatment for some of the more dangerous situations and the more common situations travellers will come across. Much of the information has been taken from the free book *Aids to Survival* produced by the WA Police Force.

IN AN EMERGENCY

The acknowledged order of urgency when assessing a situation is
D R A B C:
Danger—move the cause from the patient or the patient from the cause
Response—shake and shout
Airway—maintain an open and clear airway
Breathing—look, listen and feel
Circulation—check the carotid pulse

Further action

• Stop bleeding
• Minimise pain
• Reassure the patient
• Seek further aid if necessary
Always attend to the most urgent needs first!

Making a Diagnosis

Before you can commence rational treatment, a diagnosis must be made. You need to find out quickly:
History—how the injury occurred
Symptoms—what the patient feels
Signs—what you can observe by examining the patient

UNCONSCIOUSNESS

A patient may be unconscious for many reasons including heart attack, drowning, electrocution, a head injury, fainting, and smoke inhalation.

Diagnosing an unconscious patient is a little more difficult than a conscious one. Apply principles of DRABC, then check the level of consciousness by seeing if the patient responds to speech or reacts to a more painful stimulus.

Check head, neck, spine and upper and lower limbs for any sign of injury. Treat as required and place the patient in the coma position.

See our chart for the resuscitation of an unconscious patient.

SHOCK

Shock is brought on by a fall in blood pressure; if unchecked it can result in death or irreversible damage. The onset of clinical shock is often delayed, that is, when a person first starts bleeding, they may not be shocked, but if they go on bleeding (externally or internally) they will eventually go into shock.

Early detection, or better still, anticipation of shock and commencement of treatment or prevention is extremely important, because the patient's condition can deteriorate very quickly.

Signs and Symptoms of Shock

• Patient is cold, clammy and pale, has a rapid, feeble pulse and may have fast, shallow breathing
• Thirst
• Weakness, anxiety, restlessness, incoherence
• Nausea

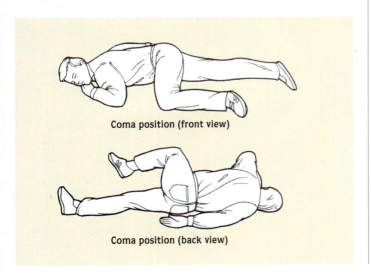

Coma position (front view)

Coma position (back view)

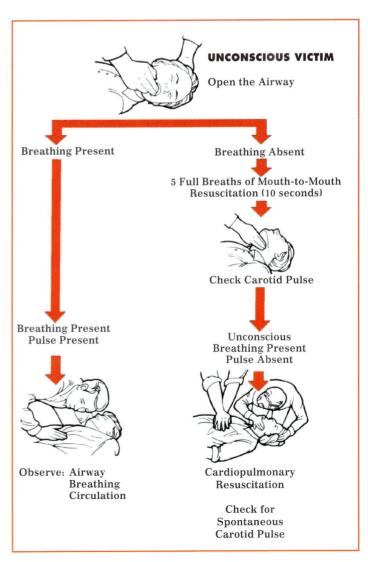

UNCONSCIOUS VICTIM
Open the Airway

Breathing Present

Breathing Absent

5 Full Breaths of Mouth-to-Mouth Resuscitation (10 seconds)

Check Carotid Pulse

Breathing Present
Pulse Present

Unconscious
Breathing Present
Pulse Absent

Observe: Airway
Breathing
Circulation

Cardiopulmonary
Resuscitation

Check for
Spontaneous
Carotid Pulse

Treatment of Shock

Cover patient and keep warm, raise the legs, protect from the elements, minimise fluid loss (e.g. from bleeding), reassure, moisten lips and DO NOT give alcohol.

FRACTURES

The key to the treatment of fractures is immobilisation. A mobile fracture is painful, may cause internal bleeding, may become compound (break through the skin) and is a major cause of shock.

Treatment of Fractures

Check and assess—can you immobilise the limb?

Reduction (repositioning) can be dangerous. Only reduce a fracture if you must, say, to move the person to safety. In this case, if the patient faints with pain, don't stop! Reduce and splint the fracture while the patient is unconscious.

Methods of Immobilisation

Finger—strap the broken one to the adjacent finger
Leg—strap legs together or splint
Pelvis—strap legs together
Upper arm—collar and cuff sling, then bandage upper arm to chest
Ribs—leave alone

Fractures of the Spine

Fractures of the spine may be complicated by damage to the spinal cord. Therefore, to avoid permanent damage, careful protective handling aimed at minimising spinal cord damage is essential. The signs and symptoms may range from severe pain to loss of sensation and lack of control over limbs.

Treatment

• The aim is to prevent further damage by immobilising the spine.
• If patient is unconscious, normal resuscitation procedures MUST take precedence.
• The patient should then be immobilised by strapping the legs together, maintaining body position with improvised padding and keeping the head straight and in extension to ensure an open airway.

SPRAIN

Sprains result from abnormal stretching or partial tearing of the supporting ligaments of any joint. Ankles are the most common. There is pain, swelling, tenderness and bruising, but the patient can still use the joint or limb.

Treatment

• In a bushwalking situation it may be better NOT to remove the boot if the boot comes above the ankle.
• Otherwise, remove shoe, elevate and support the foot and apply a cold compress for 15 minutes, then support joint with a firm elastic bandage.

HEAD INJURY

If a patient is unconscious and has not obviously been electrocuted or drowned, etc., think of head injury. There may be no obvious signs. Bleeding from the nose, mouth or ears may indicate a fracture of the skull.

If a patient who has been unconscious recovers and then loses consciousness again, you may assume head injury.

Treatment

• Put patient into recovery position.
• Transport to hospital.

BURNS AND SCALDS

These can happen anywhere around a camp and they can be extremely painful.

Treatment

• Apply cold water to any burn.
• Do not attempt to remove clothing from burned area.
• Do not use butter.
• Leave blisters intact.
• For minor burns and all peripheral burns apply antibiotic cream or Betadine and cover.
   (Antibiotic cream or Betadine is useful to prevent infection.)

BLEEDING

Blood flows through a system of arteries and veins. If there is a break or a hole in them, bleeding occurs.

Primary treatment

Plug the hole. Don't worry about whether it is arterial or venous bleeding. If there is a lot of bleeding the patient will develop shock quickly.
• First wipe away any blood (or remove clothing) so you can see where the bleeding is coming from.
• Apply direct pressure with a pad or bandage (or your hand) to the source of the bleeding.
• Elevate the bleeding site, if practicable, to reduce blood flow.

Tourniquets

A big NO-NO—only to be used if you cannot stop the bleeding in any other way. Tourniquets can cause damage and the patient may lose the limb altogether.

However, use common sense. If the limb is severed, use a tourniquet first up—you can't do any further damage to a limb which is not there.

SNAKE BITE

Ninety per cent of snake bites in Australia are at the ankle or below; 8 per cent occur on the hand and 2 per cent elsewhere. Hence the best guard against snake bite is protection. If you wear above-ankle boots, and/or thick socks and/or long trousers, you are less likely to be bitten.

Treatment

• Apply a pressure bandage straight over the bite, then wind the bandage up the limb towards the body.
• Do not cut or bleed the site of the bite. A cut will only allow poison into the body.
• Do not wipe or wash the site of the bite because the residual venom on the skin may be identifiable in the laboratory when the patient arrives at the hospital. Venom is harmless on skin contact.
• Patient should avoid excessive activity; carry the patient or walk him slowly.
• Reassure the patient.
• Endeavour to get medical aid within 8 hours.

BITES AND STINGS

The only fatal bites from an insect come from ticks. Funnel web spider bites can cause death: redback spiders and scorpions cause pain but almost never death.

Bees, Wasps, Ants

The major problem with stings of bees, wasps and ants is an allergy to the bite. If you know you are allergic to insect bites, or whatever, be careful, and carry the appropriate medicine/first aid treatment. A liquid antihistamine is often of some help while an antihistamine tablet has a slower effect.

Ammonia and methylated spirits may be useful as counter irritants.

In the case of bee stings, the poison sac is attached to the sting, and the sting being barbed will often remain in the skin. It should be removed 31with the edge of a knife, or the edge of a piece of paper, not between the fingers as the squeezing action of the fingers will squash the venom sac and inject more venom.

Ticks and Leeches

In areas where ticks and leeches are prevalent you can reduce your chances of attracting them by covering up (long trousers, socks and boots, long-sleeved shirt, a hat) and applying Rid or similar to your boots, socks, neck and wrists.

Leeches are mainly a nuisance; they feed, injecting an anticoagulant into your bloodstream, which makes the tiny wound bleed profusely, then they drop off. Wash the wound to remove the anticoagulant, then apply a dressing until the bleeding stops.

Ticks, on the other hand, can cause paralysis, breathing failure, even death, if not removed. At the end of the day, check your body carefully for ticks, particularly soft skins areas (armpits, groin, navel, behind ears, etc.). Check children similarly.

If a tick is attached to/embedded in the skin, DO NOT attempt to pull it off; this could leave the toxin-containing mouthparts there. Do not try to prick or burn the tick; this will make it release more toxin; do not apply petrol or kerosene.

To remove the tick, use fine-point tweezers to grasp the tick's mouthparts, and then pull gently, with steady pressure; do not jerk or twist the tick. When it is removed, wash the area carefully with soap and water, pat dry and apply Betadine. If you are unable to remove the tick, seek medical attention urgently.

Eucalyptus woodwardii, **the lemon-flowered gum**

Spiders and Scorpions

Treat as for snake bite, with a pressure bandage (see Snake Bite). Seek medical aid and ,if possible, take the spider or scorpion for identification.

CUTS AND ABRASIONS

These are common on any bush trip and treatment is simple:
• Clean with water.
• Apply antiseptic cream or solution as this may prevent infection later.
• Cover with a Bandaid, dressing, or bandage.

BLISTERS

Everybody will get them if they are doing a fair amount of walking.
• Leave them intact.
• Pad away from the area causing pressure (use 4 Bandaids, 2 felt strips, or a felt pad with a hole cut in it). Do not put the dressing on the blister as this increases pressure.

HYPOTHERMIA

Hypothermia is the abnormal lowering of body temperature and can cause death!

Mild Hypothermia
• Skin feels cold
• Skin looks blue or livid (mottled)
• Patient shivers
• Patient complains of feeling cold

Severe Hypothermia
• Skin cold and mottled
• No shivering—shivering response has failed
• Irrational behaviour and speech, may be uncooperative
• May be unconscious; if so, the patient is near death!

Note: A victim of cold can be resuscitated after a much longer period of 'technical death' (when no pulse or breathing can be detected) than a patient at normal temperature.

Treatment
• Shelter in warm, dry environment.
• Replace wet clothing with dry clothing.
• Leave arms and legs cold, but insulate body with blankets to minimise further heat loss.
• Rewarm critical areas—chest, neck and head—by body-to-body contact with two or more persons, or by placing heated objects (such as hot rocks wrapped in towels to prevent burning the skin) about these areas; particularly the sides of the chest.
• Breathe warm air in the vicinity of the patient's mouth (several people if possible) to warm the air breathed into the lungs.
• If conscious, rehydrate with warm drinks (non-alcoholic).
• If unconscious, transport to hospital; leave the patient cold while transport, just insulate with blankets to prevent further heat loss.

HYPERTHERMIA

Hyperthermia is heat stroke. This can occur quite easily in the Outback.

Factors Influencing Development
• High air temperature, reduces radiation
• High humidity, reduces sweat evaporation
• Clothing, reduces sweat evaporation
• Level of exercise—sustained exercise causes internal heat generation
• Body build—big, well-muscled or fat people are more susceptible

- Level of fitness—an unfit person has poor blood flow to muscles and skin
- Dehydration—reduces blood volume
- Age—babies and the elderly are at higher risk
- Acclimatisation to hot conditions reduces risk

Recognition (in Hot Conditions)
- Skin feels hot
- Face flushed
- Rapid pulse at rest
- Dizziness
- Excessive fatigue
- Lethargy, no will to go on
- Irrational behaviour
- Cessation of sweating

Treatment
- Transfer to a cool, shaded location
- Immerse in cold water or apply ice packs, water or alcohol to the skin
- Concentrate on cooling head, neck and chest
- Rehydrate by giving cool fluids orally
- Keep at rest

FIRST AID KIT CHECKLIST

A basic first aid kit including a manual from the Australian Red Cross should always be carried in the vehicle and updated as items are used so the kit is always intact. Bushwalkers should carry as many of the following items as possible. Include items such as

- Antiseptic fluid (Betadine, Dettol, or similar)
- Antiseptic cream
- Eye bath and eyestream drops
- Assorted Bandaids, strips, spots
- Steristrip wound closures
- Elastic and crepe bandages for sprains and snake bite
- Sterile gauze bandages (50 and 75 mm)
- Triangular bandages to support limbs and hold dressings in place
- Adhesive tape, cotton wool, tissues
- Scissors, safety pins
- Thermometer
- Calamine lotion, Stingose or similar for insect bite
- Fine-point tweezers

PLANNING FOR THE UNEXPECTED

Becoming stranded or lost, the first rule of survival is: Don't Panic!

Once you realise that you are stranded or lost there are certain questions you must sit down and ask yourself: How much water do I have? How much food do I have? How much food or water is in the surrounding area? What protection from the elements do I have?

If you have a radio, use it.

If you have notified someone of your intended route and dates, then it might just be a matter of sitting tight, opening a good book and waiting patiently for a search party to arrive. Meantime, concentrate on the four main requirements of water, food, shelter and warmth, until help arrives.

If you have a vehicle, stay with it as it is a source of shelter and contains all your supplies. Only leave your vehicle if you know, absolutely, that there is help within walking distance in the direction you have come.

Water

The average person can expect to survive without water for three to four days, depending on the climate and what you try to do. It is possible to perish after only hours if you do anything too strenuous. Water is needed to replace fluid loss, so by conserving body fluid you need less water.

Your body loses fluid in six ways: Perspiring, breathing, urinating, vomiting, crying and talking.
- Perspiring and urinating are normal bodily processes that cannot be ceased, but if you stay still in the shade your body will perspire less.
- Move around in the evening only; your body will retain more fluid. A person standing still in the heat requires about three times more fluid than someone standing still in the shade.
- Crying and talking should be avoided, and vomiting can be avoided by leaving harmful food alone to avoid sickness.
- Cover as much of the body as possible to avoid sunburn as blistering causes water loss. By keeping your clothes on, you slow down the rate at which perspiration evaporates; this maximises the cooling effect.
- Light coloured clothing is recommended as it reflects the sun; loosen clothing at the neck waist, wrists and ankles for better ventilation.
- Take advantage of cool breezes and try not to rest on the ground; the temperature may be up to 16°C cooler 30 cm above the ground than it is on the ground.
- If near the sea, keep your clothes wet during the day to cool your body.

What Water Can I Drink?
- Do not drink salt water.
- Infection and sickness must be avoided; dirty water can only be drunk after it has been boiled and strained through a piece of cloth.
- Urine shouldn't be drunk, but it can be used on the surface to cool the skin.
- Do not suck on stones as it encourages salivation.
- A good idea is to carry a filter-style drinking straw, available from bush-walking stores and the like. These can be used to filter water but are no use for filtering salt water.

Shelter

When you erect your tent to wait for rescue the following points should be onsidered:
- Select your camp site carefully.
- Look for shelter that is near fuel (wood).
- Don't place a tent on a windswept ridge, in a draughty gully, or on a river bed at the base of a steep slope or cliff.
- Don't face the tent into the wind.

If you haven't a tent, construct a shelter of some sort to protect you from wind, cold and sun. Shelter, as survival experts will tell you, is the most important thing to have and must be organised before anything else.

Conserving Food and Energy

It's important that you plan for an extended stay, and ration the water and food accordingly.
- Estimate the number of days you expect to be stranded and divide food into thirds; allow two-thirds for the first half, one-third for the second half.
- If members of your party go back for help, divide food and give them twice as much as is allocated for those at camp.
- Eating increases thirst. If you have minimal water, avoid dry, starchy food, highly flavoured foods and meats.
- The best foods to eat are those that are high in carbohydrates: sugar, cereals and fruit.
- Do as little work as possible.
- If you have plenty of water, drink more than normal.
- Eat regularly and cook all food, if possible, to avoid sickness.

VICTORIA

With nearly a tenth of its area devoted to national or state parks, reserves and protected historical sites, the small state of Victoria is truly a wonderland for the outdoor enthusiast. An incredible diversity of terrain and climate enables Victoria to boast a plethora of activities from snow skiing on the peaks of the High Country to SCUBA diving off its majestic coastline, or even camel riding in the remote desert areas of the Mallee in the far northwest of the state—there is something on offer for everyone.

The state can easily be divided into eight different regions, each unique in its terrain, flora and fauna, with many locations only a short drive from the capital city of Melbourne.

Around Melbourne itself there are numerous picnic grounds and short walks, perfect for taking a close look at wildlife such as koalas, kangaroos and possums, as well as birdwatching. Popular haunts include the cool, fern-filled gullies of the Dandenong Ranges National Park less than an hour from the city, where families gather for picnics, and the energetic use the cooler climate of the mountains for bushwalking or birdwatching.

Further afield, Murrindindi Scenic Reserve, Eildon State Park and Fraser National Park to the north of town, all offer scenic forest drives, excellent walking tracks, (many of which lead to waterfalls), along with challenging 4WD tracks.

Of a more historical nature are the Bunyip State Park and Kurth Kiln to the east of Melbourne, and the Lal Lal Blast Furnace to the capital's west. Both of these locations provide information about the enormous industries, such as gold or iron mining, that were operating in these country towns last century. Those interested in historical towns would also enjoy a visit to the restored townships of Beechworth in the state's northeast and Walhalla in West Gippsland. The discovery of gold saw both of these towns flourish last century, while today they are quiet reminders of our yesteryear.

The central region of Victoria over the Dividing Range includes large tracts of farming land but also boasts many interesting parks such as the Whipstick, Kamarooka and Terrick Terrick State Parks, dry parks that are home to the blue and green mallee—stunted eucalypts that have diversified to suit arid conditions. These plants have been used to harvest eucalyptus oil for over one hundred years, and the old distilleries still function today.

In the far north of the state the Murray River flows west marking the

Mist surrounds a snow gum on Mt Baw Baw

A typical forest scene in Dandenong Ranges National Park

border between Victoria and New South Wales. On its southern bank lies the Barmah State Park and the Barmah Forest. These areas, once inhabited by the Yorta Yorta Aboriginal tribe, consist of open plains and wetlands which are full of bird life, along with the largest stand of the majestic river red gums in Victoria. This region of northern Victoria is popular with birdwatchers, campers and drivers of 4WD vehicles while the river itself is perfect for water sports.

The northeast region of the state follows the mountainous High Country region of the Great Dividing Range. This is the home of the Alpine National Park, Victoria's biggest and most popular park. The high reaching peaks offer snow-based activities and once the winter snow has melted and the water has reached the deep gorges and rivers, it provides exciting white-water rafting and canoeing action.

This alpine country is popular with campers, bushwalkers and cyclists, and with many of the roads in the parks being gravel, or minor tracks, it also attracts a large number of 4WD tourists.

This is the home of the mountain pioneers, the cattlemen of the High Country, and the many huts found in the park are evidence of their days spent watching over grazing cattle on the higher peaks during summer. Craigs Hut is

a relic from the film set of the popular Australian film, *The Man From Snowy River*. It is northeast of Mansfield and is an ideal weekend destination for walkers or those with 4WD.

The attractions of the High Country for 4WD drivers, walkers or horse riders also include the historic Wonnangatta Station where lonely ruins sit in the lush green valley surrounded by the Alpine National Park and the old goldmining areas of Grant and Talbotville.

The Alpine Walking Track cuts across this region, trekking along the Dividing Range from Walhalla in Gippsland, through to the north of the state, crossing the border and finally finishing in the ACT.

Gippsland can be divided into western and eastern regions with both boasting large tracts of rugged forests inland and coastlines offering white sandy beaches and remote stretches of seashore.

The Errinundra National Park is an outstanding area of cool temperate rainforest which is best viewed by a scenic drive along the Baldwin Spencer Trail. Bushwalks and an excellent interpretation centre are also popular for learning about the area.

Cavers, both experienced and novice, may like to visit the Buchan Caves, a series of large limestone caverns that are open to the public. There is a large picnic area and camping reserve surrounding the region.

To the east, the Snowy River National Park encompasses two large tracts of wilderness and is popular with canoeists. The Snowy River cuts its way through a series of gorges providing exciting white-water thrills before finally reaching the ocean near Orbost.

The gem of the Gippsland's coastline is the large lake system at Lakes Entrance which is home to a variety of bird life including terns. These nest on islands created at the mouth of the lake system near Lake Tyers. Nearby Rotamah Island, a bird observatory accessible by boat or small causeway only, offers courses on birdwatching and natural history.

For a more remote coastal experience, Croajingolong National Park is another of Victoria's large parks offering unspoilt beaches, rocky inlets and extensive coastal foreshores—an ideal destination for walking, birdwatching or just relaxing. With tall coastal dunes, and a large array of plants and wildlife, this area is extremely delicate and numbers are restricted for overnight use.

The rugged coastline on Victoria's western side is dominated by the Great Ocean Road, a magical road which follows the coastline as it winds through fern-filled gullies, from the seaside resort of Anglesea, an hour's drive from Melbourne, through to the regional seaside township of Warrnambool. The road itself is very

A kookaburra, symbol of the open woodlands

popular and many, including motorcycle riders, enjoy the winding roads of the coastline.

The eastern section of the road drives around the edge of the Otway Ranges, where a moist climate supports a huge forest which was harvested for timber up until the formation of protective parks in recent years. Heading west the lush verdant trees and ferns change to the white surf beaches which play host to summer surfers and beach lovers.

Beyond the beachside resorts are the shipwrecks and historical sites such as Loch Ard Gorge where two survivors spent their days after their ship hit the reef off the coast, and the Twelve Apostles, large limestone stacks sitting off the coastline, continually pounded and thus

4WD in the snow is for experienced drivers only

altered by the treacherous ocean waves.

On the state's western border lies Lower Glenelg National Park where the Glenelg River has created large gorges, a perfect location for canoeing. The river banks are ideal for camping.

Northward, away from the ocean and moist climate, stand the Grampians, the rugged tail-end of the Great Dividing Range. This series of spectacular blue mountain peaks cuts across the horizon and forms a playground for rock climbers and bushwalkers. The large rock structures are covered during spring in wild-flowers, such as orchids, grevilleas and flame heath, while the flora supports a large species of bird life including colourful lorikeets and corellas. Hidden among the rocks lie Aboriginal artwork, much of which is accessible to visitors.

Just out of Horsham is another rock structure, Mt Arapiles, which rises up from the horizontal plains as a beacon for mountain climbers, walkers and sightseers.

Tucked away in the far northwest of the state you will find the open plains, and low scrub of the Mallee, a dry, arid region of the state that is home to a number of parks, including Hattah-Kulkyne, Murray–Sunset and the Big Desert Wilderness.

Much of this region is devoid of water and the most popular way to travel is via 4WD on the sandy tracks, and conventional vehicles on the firmer, clay-based roads. Only 5 to 7 hours' drive from Melbourne, this remote corner of the state offers visitors an insight into the desert regions of Australia.

Victoria is fortunate indeed to have this diversity and large number of multi-use parks, where walkers play alongside climbers, horse riders and four wheel drivers—all joined by their common interest in the outdoors, and its conservation through the network of excellent parks and reserves.

VICTORIA NATIONAL PARKS AND RESERVES

#	Park	Ranger/Park Tel.	Ranger/Information	Camping	Caravan	4WD Access	BBQ/Fireplace	Picnic Area	Marked Walking Tracks	Bushwalking	Kiosk/Restaurant	Fishing	Swimming
1	Alpine National Park	(03) 5754 4693	*	*		*	*	*	*	*			
2	Angahook–Lorne State Park	(03) 5263 3144	*	*	*	*	*	*	*	*			
3	Annuello Flora & Fauna Reserve	(03) 5035 1261				*				*			
4	Ararat Hills Regional Park	(03) 5349 2404						*					
5	Arthurs Seat State Park	(03) 5987 3093					*	*	*	*			
6	Avon–Mt Henrick Scenic Reserve	(03) 5148 2355								*		*	*
7	Avon Wilderness Park	(03) 5148 2355								*			
8	Barmah Forest Park & State Park	(03) 5866 2702	*	*		*		*		*		*	*
9	Baw Baw National Park	(03) 5165 3204	*	*			*	*	*	*	*		*
10	Beechworth Historic Park	(03) 6055 6111	*	*			*	*		*			
11	Bemm River Scenic Reserve	(03) 5161 1375					*	*				*	
12	Bendigo Bushland Trail	(03) 5444 6666	*				*	*		*			
13	Big Desert Wilderness Park	(03) 5022 3000				*				*			
14	Big River State Forest	(03) 5772 0200	*					*		*		*	
15	Birdcage Flora & Fauna Reserve	(03) 5083 3411	*							*			
16	Brisbane Ranges National Park	(03) 5284 1230	*	*		*	*	*	*	*			
17	Buchan Caves Reserve	(03) 5155 9264	*	*			*	*			*		*
18	Bunurong Marine Park	(03) 5672 1066						*			*	*	*
19	Bunyip State Park & Gembrook Park	(03) 5968 1280	*			*	*			*			
20	Burrowa–Pine Mountain National Park	(03) 6076 1655	*			*	*	*		*			
21	Buxton Silver Gum Reserve	(03) 5963 3306					*	*		*			
22	Cape Conran Coastal Park	(03) 5161 1375	*	*		*	*	*		*		*	*
23	Cape Nelson State Park	(03) 5523 3232					*	*	*				
24	Carlisle State Park	(03) 5235 8301					*	*					
25	Cassilis Historical Area	(03) 5159 4344								*			
26	Castlemaine–Chewton Historic Reserve	(03) 5472 1110					*	*	*				
27	Cathedral Range State Park	(03) 5963 3396	*			*	*			*			
28	Chiltern Regional Park	(03) 5726 1234	*					*		*			
29	Churchill National Park	(03) 9796 8763					*	*	*	*			
30	Colquhoun Regional Park	(03) 5152 0400					*			*			
31	Coopracambra National Park	(03) 5158 6351				*	*			*			
32	Corner Inlet & Shallow Inlet Coastal Parks and Nooramunga Marine Park	(03) 5682 2133	*				*					*	*
33	Croajingolong National Park	(03) 5158 6351	*	*		*	*	*		*		*	*
34	Dandenong Ranges National Park	(03) 9758 1342	*				*	*	*	*	*		
35	Delatite Arm Reserve	(03) 5775 2788	*							*			
36	Dergholm State Park	(03) 5581 1311					*	*		*			
37	Discovery Bay Coastal Park	(08) 8738 4051	*	*		*	*	*		*		*	
38	Eildon State Park	(03) 5772 0200	*	*			*	*		*		*	*
39	Enfield State Park	(03) 5333 6782						*		*			
40	Errinundra National Park	(03) 6458 1456	*			*		*		*			
41	Fraser National Park	(03) 5772 1293	*	*			*	*		*		*	*
42	French Island State Park	(03) 5980 1294	*				*	*		*			
43	Gippsland Lakes Coastal Park	(03) 5152 0400	*	*				*		*		*	*
44	Grampians National Park	(03) 5356 4381	*	*		*	*	*	*	*	*	*	*
45	Grant Historic Area	(03) 5140 1243		*				*		*		*	
46	Green Lake Regional Reserve	(03) 5070 1018		*	*			*				*	*
47	Gunbower Island State Forest	(03) 5456 2266		*		*		*		*		*	*
48	Hanging Rock Reserve	(03) 5427 0295						*			*		
49	Hattah–Kulkyne National Park	(03) 5029 3253	*	*		*	*	*		*			
50	Holey Plains State Park	(03) 5144 3048						*		*			
51	Howqua Hills Historic Area	(03) 5775 2788		*		*		*		*		*	
52	Kamarooka State Park	(03) 5444 6666								*			
53	Kara Kara State Park	(03) 5405 1115						*		*			
54	Kinglake National Park	(03) 5786 5351	*	*			*	*	*	*			
55	Kings Billabong Wildlife Reserve	(03) 5024 1904						*				*	
56	Kooyoora State Park	(03) 5438 3066		*			*	*		*			
57	Lake Albacutya Regional Park	(03) 5395 7246	*	*		*	*	*		*		*	*
58	Lake Lascelles & Lake Coorong Reserves	(03) 5083 3411		*				*				*	*
59	Lake Tyers Forest Park	(03) 5152 0400						*	*	*		*	
60	Lal Lal Blast Furnace	(03) 5444 6782						*					
61	Langi Ghiran State Park	(03) 5349 2404		*				*		*			
62	Lerderderg State Park	(03) 5367 2922		*						*		*	*
63	Lind National Park	(03) 5158 6351						*		*			
64	Little Desert National Park	(03) 5389 1204	*	*		*	*	*		*			
65	Lower Glenelg National Park	(08) 8738 4051	*	*	*	*	*	*		*		*	
66	Lysterfield Lake Park	(03) 9796 8763	*					*		*			*
67	Macedon Regional Park	(03) 5426 1866	*					*		*			
68	Macleods Morass Wildlife Reserve	(03) 5152 0400						*				*	
69	Maldon Historic Reserve	(03) 5444 6666		*				*					
70	McKenzie Flora Reserve	(03) 5772 0200								*			
71	Melba Gully State Park	(03) 5237 3243						*	*	*			
72	Mitchell River National Park	(03) 5152 0400		*		*		*		*		*	
73	Moondarra State Park	(03) 5136 3204		*				*		*		*	
74	Mornington Peninsula National Park	(03) 5984 4276	*				*	*	*	*		*	*
75	Morwell National Park	(03) 5122 1478	*					*		*			
76	Mt Alexander Regional Park	(03) 5472 1110		*			*	*		*			
77	Mt Arapiles–Tooan State Park	(03) 5387 1260		*		*		*		*			
78	Mt Buangor and Mount Cole State Forests	(03) 5349 2404	*	*		*		*		*			
79	Mt Buffalo National Park	(03) 5755 1466	*	*			*	*	*	*	*	*	*
80	Mt Eccles National Park	(03) 5576 1338	*	*	*		*	*		*			*
81	Mt Granya State Park	(03) 6071 2604								*			
82	Mt Lawson State Park	(03) 6071 2604				*				*			
83	Mt Napier State Park	(03) 5576 1338								*			
84	Mt Richmond National Park	(03) 5523 3232					*	*		*			
85	Mt Samaria State Park	(03) 5761 1611		*		*		*		*			
86	Mt Worth State Park	(03) 5628 9507						*		*			
87	Murray–Kulkyne Park	(03) 5029 3253	*	*		*		*		*		*	*
88	Murray–Sunset (Yanga–Nyawi) National Park	(03) 5094 6267	*	*		*		*		*			
89	Nyerimilang Park	(03) 5156 3253	*					*				*	
90	Organ Pipes National Park	(03) 9390 1082	*					*		*			
91	Otway National Park	(03) 5237 6889	*	*	*	*	*	*		*		*	*

	Ranger/Park Tel.	Ranger/Information	Camping	Caravan	4WD Access	BBQ/Fireplace	Picnic Area	Marked Walking Tracks	Bushwalking	Kiosk/Restaurant	Fishing	Swimming
92 Paddys Ranges State Park &												
Maryborough Regional Reserve	(03) 5461 1066	*				*	*	*				
93 Points Reserve Arboretum	(03) 5575 2134					*						
94 Port Campbell National Park	(03) 5598 6382	*	*	*		*	*					*
95 Red Cliffs Scenic Reserve	(03) 5024 1904	*				*			*			
96 Reef Hills Park	(03) 5761 1611					*	*	*	*			
97 Rocklands–Black Range Area	(03) 5574 2308	*			*	*	*	*	*			*
98 Snowy River National Park	(03) 6458 0290	*	*	*	*	*	*		*			
99 Tarra-Bulga National Park	(03) 5196 6166					*	*	*	*			
100 Terrick Terrick State Park	(03) 5456 2266	*				*	*					
101 The Lakes National Park	(03) 5146 0278	*				*	*				*	*
102 Tower Hill												
State Game Reserve	(03) 5565 9202	*				*	*			*		
103 Tyers Park	(03) 5165 3204					*	*		*		*	*
104 Upper Goulburn Historic												
Recreation Area	(03) 5775 2788		*	*							*	

	Ranger/Park Tel.	Ranger/Information	Camping	Caravan	4WD Access	BBQ/Fireplace	Picnic Area	Marked Walking Tracks	Bushwalking	Kiosk/Restaurant	Fishing	Swimming
105 Victoria Falls												
Historical Area	(03) 5159 1231					*	*	*	*			
106 Walhalla Historic Area	(03) 5165 3204	*				*	*	*	*			
107 Wallpolla Island	(03) 5028 1218	*									*	
108 Warby Range State Park &												
Killawarra State Forest	(03) 5721 5022	*				*	*	*	*			
109 Wathe Flora &												
Fauna Reserve	(03) 5083 3411				*							
110 Werribee Gorge												
State Park	(03) 5367 2922					*	*		*			
111 Whipstick State Park	(03) 5444 6666	*				*	*		*			
112 Whroo Historic Reserve	(03) 5856 1434	*	*			*	*		*			
113 Wilsons Promontory												
National Park	(03) 5680 9555	*	*	*		*	*	*	*	*	*	*
114 Wyperfeld National Park	(03) 5395 7221	*	*			*	*	*	*			
115 You Yangs Regional Park	(03) 5282 3356	*				*	*	*	*			

ALPINE NATIONAL PARK

IN BRIEF

MAP REFERENCE: PAGE 93 J 7

Location Extends across the Great Dividing Range from Mansfield, through to the northeastern border of NSW, with access between 230 and 500 km from Melbourne
Best Time Year round
Main Attractions Natural beauty of the mountains, skiing in winter, swimming, walking, 4WD tours, cycling, horse riding, canoeing, nature study, photography, historical interest
Ranger Phone Parks Victoria: (03) 5755 1577 (Bright); (03) 5729 8266 (Whitfield); (03) 5775 2788 (Mansfield); (03) 5148 2355 (Heyfield)

Alpine Resorts Commission, phone (03) 5759 3531
Alpine Trail Horse Riders Association, RMB 1705, Broadford, Vic 3653

Last light on Mt Feathertop, Alpine National Park

The Alpine National Park is Victoria's biggest and one of Australia's finest parks, offering rugged mountains, powerful rivers, remote snowfields, open plains where cattle once grazed and deep gorges which open out to reveal green valleys. Reaching far across the Dividing Range this park forms an important natural corridor for its unique flora and fauna.

HISTORY

Aborigines resided in this mountain region for thousands of years, but it was in 1824 that Hume and Hovell explored and named the Australian Alps. Many years later, during the 1850s, Baron Ferdinand von Mueller extensively explored the botany of the alpine region and thus expanded our knowledge of the diverse alpine flora.

Many people were to venture across and inhabit the peaks, including miners during the mining booms, loggers, graziers and workers on hydro-electric schemes.

During the 1950s controls were imposed on graziers to limit stock numbers and prohibit grazing of sheep and horses in the High Country. These controls were later extended even further when concern arose over the impact the cattle were having on the fragile environment and many grazing licences were withdrawn. Today, very few permits are still valid allowing cattle to graze in the spectacular High Country.

The push for a national park first came from the newly formed Victorian National Parks Association during the 1960s, but it was not until several public enquiries had been held and there was a change in attitude in many of the users that the Alpine National Park was proclaimed in December 1989.

A CORRIDOR THROUGH THE MOUNTAINS

The alpine region is ever-changing, snow covers the upper reaches for most of winter, while summer brings heat to the lower reaches and the mountains. The weather can change from extreme heat to freezing temperatures very quickly, and snow is not uncommon during the warmer months.

With most of the continent being relatively flat, the Great Dividing Range, and this park in particular, protects a myriad wildlife, many species of which are endangered. It also provides a playground for Melburnians.

Perhaps the most enduring image of the High Country is that of tall timbers, and the park is dominated by eucalypts such as the mountain gum and stringybark, on the higher peaks the alpine ash, and above the snow line, the colourful, gnarled, stunted snow gum. During spring, as the winter snow melts, a carpet of alpine daisies, alpine marsh marigold and the alpine hovea greet walkers who utilise the ski tracks for their forages on foot.

The changing weather and the different types of vegetation lead to a diversity in the wildlife and the most common form of wildlife you will encounter on a visit to the park is the bird life. Species include the noisy gang-gang cockatoo, colourful crimson rosellas and the distinctive long-beaked wattlebird.

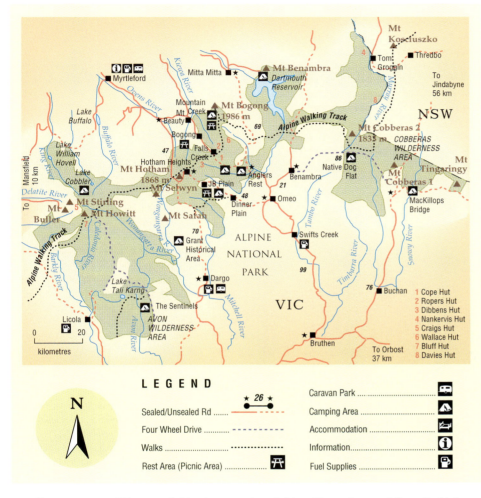

LEGEND

N

Sealed/Unsealed Rd .... ★—26—★	Caravan Park ....
Four Wheel Drive .... - - - - - - -	Camping Area ....
Walks .... ··········	Accommodation ....
Rest Area (Picnic Area)	Information.......................................
	Fuel Supplies ....

(Map labels)

1 Cope Hut
2 Ropers Hut
3 Dibbens Hut
4 Nankervis Hut
5 Craigs Hut
6 Wallace Hut
7 Bluff Hut
8 Davies Hut

---

surrounding area boasts a remote mountain range for the ski tourer. Many cross-country skiers base themselves at nearby Dinner Plain while the adventurous head cross-country along the Razorback trail to Mt Feathertop. This is an 18 km trek that can be completed in a day with snow camping possible near Federation Hut down from the summit of Feathertop.

Walking tracks abound after the snow melts, and the Alpine Walking Track cuts through this region towards Falls Creek.

For up-to-date information, contact the Alpine Resorts Commission.

Wombargo–The Cobberas

With only one access road suitable for conventional vehicles, this section in the north of the state abuts the NSW Kosciuszko National Park to the north of the park, and the Buchan Headwaters Wilderness Area to the south. Although there are still some 4WD tracks in the area, visitors with conventional vehicles should use Black Mountain Road to access the popular camping areas of Native Dog Flat, Willis on the Snowy River and the Cobberas Wilderness Area.

The peaks of Mt Cobberas One and Two are popular bases for walks, as is Cowombat Flat with its wreckage of a DC-3 aircraft which crashed in 1954, killing one crew member.

Tingaringy

As the highest peak east of the Snowy River, Mt Tingaringy offers commanding views of the NSW Kosciuszko Range and the peaks down south towards the Snowy River. Most of this region is classified as a wilderness area and at the border of NSW adjoins the Kosciuszko National Park and Byadbo Wilderness Area. Because vehicles,

---

Patient visitors will be rewarded by chance meetings with kangaroos, bats, echidnas or the hearty wombat, which can be found foraging at night. There are also some reclusive emus living in the park, but they are rarely spotted.

Many species of animals are endemic to the region, including the brush-tailed rock wallaby and the mountain pygmy possum, the latter once thought to be extinct.

VICTORIA'S LARGEST PARK

The Alpine National Park, Victoria's largest park, covers a vast area of 635 580 hectares. It is, therefore, best treated as 6 sectors: Mt Hotham–Feathertop; Wombargo–The Cobberas; Tingaringy; Bogong High Plains; Wonnangatta–Moroka; and Mt Buller–Stirling.

Mt Hotham–Feathertop

Mt Feathertop, standing at 1922 metres, and Mt Hotham, a mere 1862 metres, are amongst Victora's highest peaks and provide a perfect playground for skiers and snowboarders in winter and walkers and cyclists during summer.

Situated in the heart of the Apline National Park, this sector is best known for its winter

activities with regular snowfalls on the higher reaches during winter. The Hotham Heights village caters for the downhill skier, while the

The view from Mt Victoria

and all other mechanical means of transport, are not permitted, it is mainly bushwalkers who use this remote and inhospitable region. Water can be scarce here in summer, so bushwalkers need to be well prepared and self-sufficient.

Bogong High Plains

Originally, the Bogong High Plains heralded the birth of skiing in Victoria in the early 1900s, but long before that the pioneers grazed their cattle on the lush, grassy plains during summer. Today the area is popular with visitors in both summer and winter as it offers snow skiing, bushwalking, bike and horse riding and trout fishing in the Rocky Valley Dam and Pretty Valley Pondage.

Popular walks include the 5 km moderate trek from Rocky Valley Dam up to Ropers Lookout which takes 1½ hours return, or the difficult day journey along the Mt Bogong Staircase which is 16 km return and for the seriously fit only.

South of Rocky Valley Dam you will find Wallaces Hut, built by the Wallace Brothers in 1889, the oldest of the huts still standing in the park. The woollybutt roof shingles were replaced by galvanised iron in the 1930s and it is now classi-fied by the National Trust. This building is not far from the Bogong High Plains Road, near Falls Creek.

Wonnangatta–Moroka

This section of the park, only 335 km from Melbourne, is one of the more popular, offering a wide range of walking and 4WD tracks, ski trails in winter for cross-country skiers, and excellent camping areas, many of which have access for conventional vehicles. For many, the main attraction is the Wonnangatta Valley with its majestic green valley floor where many pioneers settled last century.

Hidden deep in the mountains at the head of the Wellington River is the jewel of the High Country, Lake Tali Karng, which is accessible on foot, and can only be viewed from the Sentinel and Echo Point on Rigalls Spur. Many walkers enjoy the 28 km return descent to the lake which should be undertaken only by the fit and healthy. The trek takes 2 days and is best enjoyed by spending more than one night camped by the sapphire blue lake.

Another popular walk is along the Moroka Gorge where sections of the Moroka River carve their way through the rock and include 3 water-falls and excellent swimming holes in summer when the water level is low. A walking track leading to the gorge can be found at the popular camping area of Horseyard Flats.

Further east, the Moroka Road heads to the Pinnacles Lookout where a fire tower watches over the surrounding country and makes the most of the superb views. You can drive to within 1 km of the peak, then take the moderate walking track to the lookout for breathtaking views you will long remember.

The Buffalo Plateau in the distance

Mt Buller–Stirling and Lake Cobbler

Only 2½ hours' drive from Melbourne, Mt Buller and Mt Stirling stand atop the Delatite Valley where the cool streams of the Delatite and King rivers flow. These 2 mountains are Melbourne's playgrounds, with Stirling offering excellent cross-country skiing and popular walking trails while Buller caters for Melbourne's downhill ski set. With many trails surrounding the 2 mountains and leading up to Lake Cobbler, 4WD touring and cycling are popular pastimes.

HAZARDS

Weather in the alpine region is changeable and it is not uncommon for fierce storms to deluge the area during the warmer summer months, sometimes provoking a snowfall. Generally, in the Alps, for every 100 metres you increase in altitude, the temperature will drop roughly 1°C. Be prepared for any weather and always carry warm clothing and adequate food and water.

Seasonal road closures apply in winter due to snow and heavy rainfalls. Check the local Parks Victoria office for details of track closures before planning your trip.

HUTS OF THE HIGH COUNTRY

Scattered throughout the Alpine National Park are a number of huts which represent part of the rich cultural heritage of the alpine region. Many of these huts once belonged to the pioneers that grazed their cattle on the high plains during summer. Today, the huts are visited for their historical significance and are used as temporary or emergency shelters.

The popular huts to visit include Wallaces Hut on the Bogong High Plains, and Bluff Hut and Bindaree Hut, which, along with Craigs Hut, are in the region near Mansfield. Off the Howitt Road, north of Licola, you will find Guys Hut and the ruins of the Old Wonnangatta Station, while in the north of the state is Davies Plain Hut.

4WD TOURING

In recent years, the 4WD vehicle has become a very popular way to enjoy the park where access is impossible by conventional vehicles.

One of the most popular areas to visit, Wonnangatta Valley, can be found in the centre of the park, north of Licola. Zeka Spur Track, the road into Wonnangatta from the Howitt High Plains Road, was once a very challenging track, but with the increase in visitors the track has been upgraded and shouldn't pose a problem for novice drivers of 4WD vehicles.

An ideal weekend jaunt would be to camp on the Wellington River outside Licola on Friday night, then travel the 82 km north to the Zeka Spur Track which winds down for 30 km to the valley floor. This is now of a moderate standard and should take you 3 or 4 hours from Licola. There is camping aplenty in the valley and attractions include the site of a burnt-out station on the banks of Conglomerate Creek and a cemetery which is perched on the hillside under towering pine trees.

Other interesting tours in the alpine park include Dargo and the Crooked River–Talbotville area, Jacksons Crossing on the Snowy River, and the Deddick Trail. The more adventurous and experienced might like to tackle Butcher Country Track or the mountain country around Davies Plain in the north.

WALKING FOR FUN

This park is extremely popular with walkers. Popular short walks include the return trek from the Bogong High Plains to Wallaces Hut,

one of the most picturesque. This easy walk is only 2 km long and will take less than an hour.

Another easy walk is to Bryces Gorge which starts at Howitt Road, 70 km north of Licola. This moderate walk covers 8 km return and takes in Bryces Plain and Gorge, Guys Hut and the Pieman Falls. Allow 3 hours for the journey.

While there are many short walks, by far the most impressive is the Alpine Walking Track which extends a lengthy 650 km from the old goldmining town of Walhalla in Gippsland, across the rugged mountain range, into New South Wales, finally finishing in the ACT at the Namadgi Visitor Centre. The Alpine Walking Track was devised in 1968, before the area was declared a national park, and passes through areas rich in history and natural wonders.

The entire trail takes more than 10 weeks to complete, but most walkers tackle it in sections.

OTHER ACTIVITIES

The Alps of Victoria represent premium mountain-bike riding country, with tracks running alongside deep river gorges, imposing clifftops, large plateaus and verdant valleys.

Cyclists must remember that temperatures in the Alps are generally lower than the rest of the state, with the peaks rarely recording temperatures above 20°C, even in summer.

Details of treks in the region can be found in the book *Cycling in the Bush* by Sven Klinge.

There are restrictions imposed on cyclists in parks and wilderness areas so it is best to ring and check before assuming you may use vehicular or Management Vehicle tracks.

Other recreations that can be enjoyed in the park include canoeing, which is popular on the Wellington, Macalister and Snowy Rivers, and horse riding along the mountaintops. For information on horse riding contact the Australian Trail Horse Riders Association in Broadford.

ACCESS AND CAMPING

Many bitumen and good quality roads lead to the major regions of the Alpine National Park.

The Mt Buller–Stirling area can be reached via Mansfield, north of Melbourne, along good quality gravel roads.

The Wonnangatta–Moroka area is accessed via Licola, on a well-maintained gravel road, or from Dargo on 4WD tracks.

Mt Hotham is serviced by a good bitumen road from Harrietville to the north and Dargo from the south. The Snowy River Road provides access for the Tingaringy unit, while Benambra and the Black Mountain Road lead to the Cobberas region in the northeast of the state.

Remote camping is the best way to experience the magnificent alpine park in areas where there are no facilities provided. There are, however, a number of popular camping sites where toilets and fireplaces can be found. For conventional vehicle access, MacKillops Bridge on the Snowy River in the northeast is a great camping area, as is Sheepyard Flat and Lake Cobbler near Mt Buller, Wellington River north of Licola, Anglers Rest north of Omeo and the numerous camping sites at the top end of the Snowy River Road.

Drivers of 4WDs might like to try areas such as Wonnangatta Valley, Grant Historical Area, Rams Head at the Cobberas, or Davies Plain.

Walkers have the best camping opportunities and can take in the delights of the wilderness areas within the national park at the Avon and Buchan Headwaters Wilderness Zones.

For details of camping locations, contact the regional Parks Victoria office.

Winter views from the Bluff in the Alpine National Park

BAW BAW NATIONAL PARK

MAP REFERENCE: PAGE 85 N 3

IN BRIEF

Location 95 km north of Moe. Southern access is the Thomson Valley Road via Moe and Erica, or to the Baw Baw Alpine Village via Drouin or Powelltown
Best Time Winter for snow, spring for wildflowers
Main Attractions Cross-country and downhill skiing in winter, bushwalking, camping, canoeing, fishing, scenic drives
Ranger Phone (03) 5165 3204

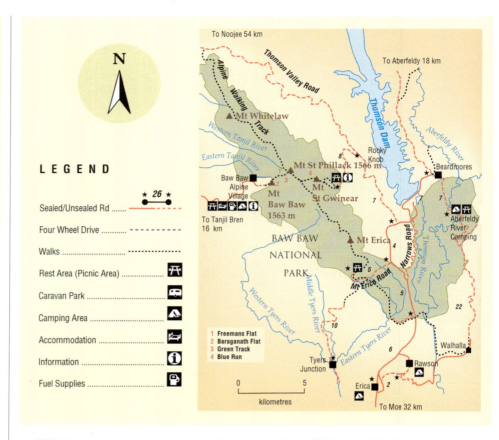

LEGEND

Sealed/Unsealed Rd	★ 26 ★
Four Wheel Drive	
Walks	
Rest Area (Picnic Area)	🌲
Caravan Park	🚐
Camping Area	⛺
Accommodation	🛏
Information	ℹ
Fuel Supplies	⛽

1 Freemans Flat
2 Baraganath Flat
3 Green Track
4 Blue Run

Rich ochres and mossy greens form brilliant bands down the length of the twisted and gnarled snow gums. These subalpine trees provide a palette of colour against the pristine snow-covered mountaintop of Mt Baw Baw.

William Dawson, an early surveyor of the area, believed that this mountain was a forbidden site for the Braiakaulung tribe, and stone artefacts have been found well up the mountainside. Today, ties to the area's original inhabitants remain, with the name Baw Baw being a derivative of the Aboriginal word Bo Bo, meaning 'echo'. The area was first explored by Baron von Mueller in 1860, and being close to Melbourne it has become a base for walkers and cross-country skiers with the Mt Baw Baw Alpine Village providing lodging and supplies for visitors. Buildings on the mountain, however, were obliterated in the horrific 1939 fires and with the village well established, it was not until 1979 that the area was actually declared a national park.

SUBALPINE PARKLAND

Apart from the Alpine National Park, the Baw Baw National Park is the only other Victorian park with large areas of subalpine vegetation, such as the colourful twisted snow gum and the wildflowers that carpet the area once the snow melts into the Thomson Dam.

The diversity of mountaintops and river flats encourages an equally varied plant life, with huge alpine ash trees leading down to messmate and stringybark, while the Baw Baw berry is endemic to the Baw Baw Plateau.

Within the 13 300 hectare park visitors will find the amphibian Baw Baw frog along with the rare Leadbeater's possum and other wildlife such as wombats, cockatoos, and many lyrebirds which often race across the walking track or road in front of visitors.

WINTER WONDERLAND OR SUMMER ESCAPE

The busiest time for this alpine park is during winter, when many skiers head downhill in the village area, or cross-country on the many and varied tracks, including the 1.5 km Green Track which runs from Barawanath Flat to Freemans Flat, or the 2 km Blue Run which continues on

The forest floor in Baw Baw National Park

from Mt St Phillack to Mt St Gwinear.

In the milder months bushwalkers can be seen on the tracks scattered over the mountaintops or traversing the Alpine Walking Track which passes over Mt St Phillack and heads north towards the ACT.

On the edge of the park is the Thomson Dam, which supplies water to the Melbourne and Gippsland irrigation system. Fantastic views can be had of the reservoir from the Silvertop Picnic Ground where you will find fireplaces, tables and toilets.

ACCESS AND CAMPING

Access to the park is via 4 different routes: the main access is from Drouin through Nerrim South and Tanjil Bren where a narrow, winding road leads to the village, or from the Thomson Valley Road to the Mt Erica car park or, by taking another turn-off on the Thomson Valley Road, to Mt St Gwinear. Access to the Aberfeldy River in the far eastern side of the park is via Walhalla. Note that snow-chains are to be carried in your vehicle during the snow season.

Dispersed bush camping is allowed on the Baw Baw Plateau while there are official camping and caravan parks at Erica and Rawson, where toilets and showers are provided. There are also motels and lodges at Mt Baw Baw Alpine Village.

BEECHWORTH HISTORIC PARK

IN BRIEF

MAP REFERENCE: PAGE 92 G4

Location Northeastern Victoria, 40 km from Wangaratta

Best Time Year-round, although autumn is best for leaf colour

Main Attractions Historic buildings, bridges, museum, cemetery, gardens, mine sites, trout farm nearby, antiques and craft shops

Ranger Phone (03) 5728 1501

Chinese headstones in Beechworth Cemetery

Sitting amid the natural beauty of the northern Victorian Alps is the old goldmining town of Beechworth, so well preserved it allows visitors to assimilate the lifestyles of the earlier diggers.

While nearby forests of brittle gum and peppermints are a natural drawcard, it is history that brings visitors to this 1130 hectare historical park, with 30 of the buildings in town classified by the National Trust.

By the time the town was first declared in 1853, the infamous Spring and Reedy Creeks housed over 8000 gold diggers on their banks. Now it is the best preserved gold town in Victoria. You can also see a restored powder magazine, built to house mining explosives.

A visit to the historical town will show that Beechworth is not famous just for the gold production during the 1800s. In the Loch Street Museum you will find a display on Robert Burke, of Burke and Wills fame, who was a police chief in the district's early years. The museum is open most days, phone (03) 5728 1420. It's also possible to visit a jail cell where Ned Kelly spent time both as a youth and just before the trial which led to his execution.

A STEP BACK IN TIME

A drive or stroll through the park will reveal amongst the eucalypts and native cypress many historical features of the goldmining era. At Woolshed Falls a self-guided one hour walk goes through the Reids Creek Goldfield. The region illustrates different methods of gold extraction including water channelling, stream diversion and the most destructive, water hosing of banks.

Eldorado Dredge sits abandoned on Reedy Creek and has huge buckets which were once capable of removing 153 000 square metres of soil in one month.

Established as a historical park visitors will be rewarded with an abundance of historic and heritage buildings, bridges, museums, gardens and mining sites—although for many the main interest is browsing in the antique shops, or marvelling at the many craft displays in town. Surrounded by stone cottages, and with the large canopies of majestic deciduous trees overhead, a stroll along the historic Ford Street really does take you back in time.

FOSSICKERS' DELIGHT

If you want to try your hand at mining, fossicking is allowed within the park area with a Miner's Right, but only within the Two and Three Mile Creeks. Outside the park, Reedy Creek is a very popular fossicking area.

Browsing, walking, fishing, horse riding and swimming are all on offer in this area of northern Victoria. Brochures outlining the different walks and drives can be obtained from the Information Centre. These brochures should be studied before heading off on your own as there are many shafts still open in this area.

For something different, a short drive to the south-east of the park, past the Fletcher

Chinese Burning Towers in Beechworth Cemetery

Dam, will take you to a magnificent stand of Californian redwood trees which were planted in 1936, along with samples of the Douglas fir, also from the west coast of North America.

ACCESS AND CAMPING

The park can be accessed via the Hume Freeway to Wangaratta, then follow the Ovens Highway for around 28 km to Beechworth.

There is no camping in the park other than bush camping at Woolshed Falls. There are 2 caravan parks—Lake Sambell and Silver Creek—and numerous hotels and motels in the town, along with guesthouses, bed and breakfasts, farms and resorts.

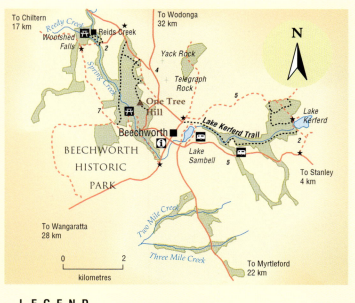

LEGEND

Sealed/Unsealed Rd	★ 26 ★
Four Wheel Drive	- - - - - - -
Walks	·············
Rest Area (Picnic Area)	🛆
Caravan Park	🚐
Camping Area	⛺
Accommodation	🛏
Information	ℹ
Fuel Supplies	⛽

CROAJINGOLONG NATIONAL PARK

IN BRIEF

MAP REFERENCE: PAGE 91 M 5

Location 500 km from Melbourne, via the Princes Highway, in far eastern Gippsland
Best Time Summer for water sports, wildflowers in spring
Main Attractions Walking, camping, coastal scenery, fishing, boating, swimming, nature study, birdwatching
Ranger Phone
(03) 5158 6351 or
(03) 5158 0219

The wide expanses of the Thurra River glistening in the sun

Nestled on the eastern coast of Victoria, the Croajingolong National Park is a remote wilderness area where cool freshwater streams trickle down the mountains within pockets of temperate rainforest, before filtering through the sand dunes and merging with the sea.

HISTORY

Aboriginal people are thought to have lived in the Croajingolong area for over 40 000 years and it's not hard to understand their attraction for the place. With prolific plant life and an abundance of birds, fish and marsupials around the ocean and the freshwater systems, this area provided a perfect food source for the local tribes.

The name Croajingolong is a derivative of the name of the local tribe that roamed this region, the Krauatungalung, meaning 'people of the east', and often refers to the whole of East Gippsland. The name of Ben Boyd's station at Bendoc, Kirkenong, is also believed to have been derived from this Aboriginal word.

The park was established in 1979 with the formation of the Mallacoota, Wingan and Captain James Cook National Parks along the coastline of far eastern Victoria.

Captain Cook was, in 1770, the first European to discover this coast, and after seals were spotted a few years later, the area was under siege by hundreds of sealers who had all but wiped out the seal population by the 1820s. While pastoralists have occupied much of the land, this magnificent coastal wilderness has always appealed to holiday-makers, and the combination of temperate rainforests, coastal heathlands and freshwater lakes makes this region important for its conservation value.

COASTAL ISOLATION

The natural, unspoilt beauty of this 87 500 hectare park attracts hundreds of visitors each year, many of whom are drawn to the freshwater estuaries of the Thurra, Mueller and Wingan Rivers that wind their way down from the rain-

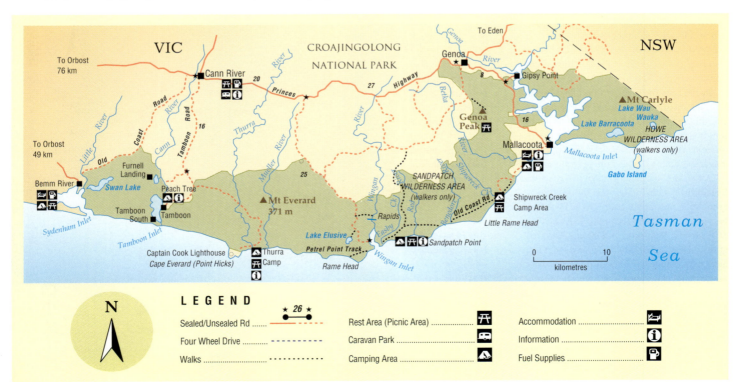

LEGEND

Sealed/Unsealed Rd ......
Four Wheel Drive ....
Walks ....

Rest Area (Picnic Area) ....
Caravan Park ....
Camping Area ....

Accommodation ....
Information ....
Fuel Supplies ....

forests, through the tablelands of the park, to finally emerge at the rugged southeast coastline of Victoria. These rivers, which were once an important source of fresh water for the local

inhabit the warmer climates of southern New South Wales, such as the silvertop and red bloodwood, with Victoria's cooler-climate species such as the stringybark.

Genoa Falls in Croajingolong National Park

spring and, finally, stunted banksias and tea-trees which sit upon the windswept cliffs.

Nature study and birdwatching are popular pastimes among park visitors, and over 300 species of birds can be found, including water-birds such as pelicans. The elusive lyrebird can be seen darting out from the rainforest and colourful parrots and vocal cockatoos can be found in the heathlands and forests.

Although the seal population was almost wiped out during the early 1800s, the Australian fur seal can still be seen, protected now in the shallow waters of this important coastal park.

BUSHWALKERS' VIEW OF THE COASTLINE

Popular walks within the park include the Dunes, a 2 hour walk of moderate difficulty, which takes you over the high sand dunes and offers a superb view over Point Hicks and out to the ocean. In the same area is the Lighthouse Trek, which is easier and takes 3 hours to explore Point Hicks.

From Wingan River camp site you can take the Petrel Point Track which is signposted and is moderate to difficult, and will take 5–6 hours return to explore the eastern coastline. The trail through the forest to Lake Elusive is easier and will take only one hour return, while the Wingan Rapids can be accessed via an easy walk along the Wingan River taking between 3 and 5 hours return. For a full day's walk, take the Easby Track from Wingan Point which joins up with the Sandpatch Track and the Old Coast Road to Shipwreck Creek camp site and eventually joins up with the main road into Mallacoota. This trek, however, is for the experienced walker.

With the freshwater estuaries meeting the ocean, anglers will be rewarded with a large variety of species, and nearby Mallacoota is the centre of the Gippsland fishing industry.

ACCESS AND CAMPING

The road from Mallacoota is sealed but unsealed roads leading into the park from the Princes Highway may deteriorate after rain, forcing a closure until the roads dry out. Check with the ranger on conditions before leaving.

Camping is allowed at Peach Tree Camping Area on Tamboon Inlet, Shipwreck Creek, Wingan River, Mueller River and Thurra River. Camping is allowed outside the park at Cape Conran, Bemm River, Marlo and Mallacoota. Most of the camp sites have pit toilets, fire-places and picnic tables but you must bring in your own water for many of the sites, and check on fire restrictions before entering the park.

During the peak holiday periods, a ballot system is used for allocation of camping sites within Croajingolong due to its popularity. Contact the ranger for camping information.

Aborigines, now not only provide water for campers, but also offer an opportunity to explore the area by canoe.

One of the fascinations of the park is the merging of 2 climates, resulting in the interesting combination of plants which normally

Inland, the park features woodlands which lead down into gullies where temperate rain-forest plants such as tree ferns, mosses, orchids and vines can be found. As you venture closer towards the coastline, the large trees give way to headlands which offer a riot of colour in

DANDENONG RANGES NATIONAL PARK

IN BRIEF

MAP REFERENCE: PAGE 85 J 3

Location 40 km east of Melbourne, via the Burwood Highway
Best Time Year-round
Main Attractions Picnics, bushwalking
Ranger Phone (03) 9758 1342

Skyhigh Restaurant: phone (03) 9751 2266

Reaching upward from Ferntree Gully on the outskirts of Melbourne, over Mt Dandenong, lies the verdant sanctuary of the Dandenong Ranges National Park, a popular picnic ground for Victorians for more than 70 years.

HISTORY

In 1882 the local residents pursauded the Minister for Agriculture to set aside a 168 hectare area as a recreational park. The area was enlarged in 1927 and Victoria's second national park was proclaimed. This suburban park now spreads across 3 different sections of Mt Dandenong: the Ferntree Gully, Sherbrooke and Doongalla areas. The Doongalla area was first settled in 1885 and in 1908 a mansion was built which was later renamed Doongalla. The horrific fires of 1939 took the house but left the servants' quarters and stables untouched. Today the homestead site, along with the restored servants' quarters, is open to the public and sits in the central section of Doongalla accessed by the Doongalla Road.

A PARK IN SECTIONS

The first and most accessible section of the park is the Ferntree Gully block, which is just off the Burwood Highway in Upper Ferntree Gully and offers a variety of interesting walks and 3 picnic areas within its 450 hectares. Further along the Mt Dandenong Tourist Road, and flanking the Monbulk Road, is the Sherbrooke section which boasts 810 hectares of natural bushland and the tumbling Sherbrooke Falls. At the peak of the mountain and surrounding the observatory and Skyhigh Restaurant is the smaller 279 hectare area named Doongalla which means 'place of peace'. It is aptly named, with spectacular views and rugged bush trails leading down the western side of the mountain.

A BRILLIANT GREEN HAVEN

Mt Dandenong is a popular tourist retreat and is the home of many Melburnians who make the transit from their cool mountain haven each day and travel the hour-long journey to the city. You will see many houses perched on the side of the

William Ricketts Sanctuary on Mt Dandenong

LEGEND

Sealed/Unsealed Rd	★ 26 ★
Four Wheel Drive	
Walks	
Rest Area (Picnic Area)	
Caravan Park	
Camping Area	
Accommodation	
Information	ⓘ
Fuel Supplies	

Major National Parks

AUSTRALIA HAS MORE THAN TWO THOUSAND national parks, nature reserves and wildlife sanctuaries. They include tropical rainforests, deserts, snow capped mountains, tropical islands, coral reefs, estuaries and glacial lakes. Here is a sample – space has precluded many important and near city parks.

National Parks	Location	Description	Telephone No.	Information Centre	Camping Areas	Accommodation	Trails	Fishing	Swimming	Best time	Nearest Major Town
NEW SOUTH WALES											
Ku-ring-gai Chase	18m N Sydney	Sandstone plateau with enclosed waterways.	(02)4579322	●	●		●		●	Year round	Sydney
Barrington Tops	199m NW Sydney	Mountain knoll, rainforest, antarctic beech, snow gums.	(049)873108		●		●	●		Year round	Gloucester/Taree
Warrumbungle	310m NW Sydney	Volcanic ranges. Woodlands, heath.	(068)421311	●	●		●			Jun-Mar	Coonabarabran
Blue Mountains	44m W Sydney	Large eroded valleys surrounded by rolling plateaux & ridges.	(047)878877	●	●	●	●		●	Year round	Katoomba
Mootwingee	71m NE Broken Hill	Remote Aboriginal relic sites.	(080)880253	●			●			Apr-Sep	Broken Hill
Kosciusko	302m SW Sydney	Highest mountain in Australia, alpine snowfields.	(0648)62102	●	●	●	●	●		Year round	Thredbo/Cooma
Myall Lakes	151m N Sydney	Long sandy beaches, spectacular headlands.	(049)873108		●			●	●	Jun-Sep	Newcastle
QUEENSLAND											
The Scenic Rim	62m SW Brisbane	Several parks on rim surrounding Brisbane. Eucalypt & rainforests.	(07)2020200		●		●		●	Year round	Binna Burra
Carnarvon	446m NW Brisbane	Inland oasis, gorges, cliffs, eucalypt, grasslands.	(079)844505	●			●		●	Jun-Aug	Rolleston
Atherton Tableland	41m SW Cairns	Extensive tableland with several rainforest parks.	(070)953768		●		●		●	Year round	Atherton
Cape York Wilderness	N of Cairns	Several parks in wilderness areas are of world interest.	(070)519811		●		●			May-Nov	Cairns
Fraser Island	186m N Brisbane	Lakes, sand-dunes, forests.	(071)222455		●		●	●	●	Apr-Nov	Maryborough
Lamington	34m W Gold Coast	Magnificent rainforest, wet upland heath.	(075)333584 (075)451734	●	●	●	●		●	Dec-Feb	Southport
Bunya Mountains	250m NW Brisbane	Rainforest, eucalypt, open forest & grassland.	(074)683127	●	●	●	●			Year round	Kingaroy
Great Barrier Reef Islands	Various	Many of the resort islands have areas set aside as national parks.								Year round (Best times May-Nov)	See main map
SOUTH AUSTRALIA											
Flinders Chase (Kangaroo Island)	124m S Adelaide	Eucalypt woodland, mallee, heaths, superb island location.	(0848)37235	●	●	●		●	●	Sep-May	Kingscote
Flinders Ranges	211m N Adelaide	Ranges, natural amphitheatre, eucalypt, wildflowers.	(086)480017	●	●	●				Jun-Nov	Hawker
Coorong	115m S Adelaide	Sand-dunes, large bird rookeries.	(085)757014	●		●	●	●	●	Sep-May	Meningie
Lincoln	434m W Adelaide	Granite hills, rugged bluffs, mallee woodland.	(086)823936	●	●		●	●	●	Nov-Jan	Port Lincoln
VICTORIA											
Wilson's Promontory	142m SE Melbourne	Timbered coastal ranges, swamps, heaths, beaches.	(056)808538	●	●	●	●		●	Year round	Foster
Otway	116m SW Melbourne	Spectacular coastline, Otway forest woodland, coastal vegetation.	(052)376889		●		●			Year round	Apollo Bay/Colac
Wyperfeld	288m NW Melbourne	Wilderness of sandhills, mallee & native pine.	(053)957221	●	●		●			Jun-Nov	Rainbow
Hattah Lakes	314m NW Melbourne	Semi arid, grasslands, floodplains & forest.	(050)293253		●		●		●	Jun-Nov	Mildura
Port Campbell	182m SW Melbourne	Coastal strip, pounding seas.	(055)986382	●	●		●		●	Sep-Feb	Warrnambool
Bogong	217m NE Melbourne	Mountain peaks, spectacular scenery.	(C57)215022		●		●			Mar-Nov	Falls Creek/Omeo
Snowy River	280m E Melbourne	Unspoilt river scenery, cliffs, gorges & rapids.	(0648)80290		●		●	●	●	Dec-May	Buchan
NORTHERN TERRITORY											
Finke Gorge	82m W Alice Springs	Rough terrain. Livistona mariae.	(089)508211		●		●		●	Apr-Oct	Alice Springs
Uluru (Ayers Rock-Mt Olga)	28dm SW Alice Springs	Ayers Rock & Mt Olga, huge monoliths, sacred Aboriginal sites.	(089)508211	●	●		●			Jun-Nov	Alice Springs
Simpson's Gap	10m W Alice Springs	Rugged, arid ranges, gorges & chasms.	(039)508211	●			●			Mar-Sep	Alice Springs
Kakadu	155m E Darwin	Coastal plains, mangroves, eucalypts, wildlife.	(089)792101	●	●		●	●		May-Oct	Darwin
Katherine Gorge	20m NE Katherine	Sandstone plateau. Spectacular gorges & waterfalls.	(089)721886	●	●	●	●	●	●	May-Oct	Katherine
WESTERN AUSTRALIA											
...chep	31m N Perth	Limestone caves, heath, low scrub, wildflowers.	(095)611004	●			●		●	Wildflowers – Sep-Nov	Perth
...bung	151m N Perth	Sand-dunes, fascinating limestone formations.	(095)457043				●		●	Year round	Cervantes
...arri	400m N Perth	River gorges, wildflowers, coastal cliffs & dunes.	(099)371140	●	●		●		●	May-Oct	Geraldton
...ng Range	217m S Perth	Rugged peaks, heathlands, woodlands, wildflowers.	(098)279230	●	●		●			Sep-Mar	Albany
...ple/Nornalup	69m W Albany	Sheltered coastal inlets, extensive karri forests.	(098)401026	●	●		●	●	●	Sep-Mar	Albany
...Range	833m NW Perth	Rugged limestone ridges, scrub & heathlands.	(099)491428	●	●		●	●	●	Apr-Sep	Exmouth
...rsley Range	833m N Perth	River gorges, rugged ranges, spectacular white trees.	(091)898157	●	●		●			Apr-Sep	Wittenoom
TASMANIA											
...n & Gordon Rivers	128m W Hobart	Undisturbed wild river, quartz peaks, dense forest.	(004)717122		●	●		●	●	Dec-Feb	Strahan
...Mt-Lake St Clair	99m W Launceston	Rugged mountain peaks, moorland, lakes.	(003)635187	●	●	●	●		●	Oct-Mar	Mole Creek
...	44m NW Hobart	Dense rainforest, alpine vegetation, mountain ranges.	(002)881149	●	●		●			Dec-May	New Norfolk

New South Wales

The harbour is breathtaking, whether you're on it, in it or over it. Just hop on a ferry — any ferry — and go where it takes you. You'll get the Pacific's most spectacular panorama for pennies.

OUR FIRST BRITISH VISITORS didn't have much choice. They travelled steerage. And when they arrived in Sydney Harbour, Sydney wasn't even there. They had to build the place.

You can still see where the convicts carved the first town in Australia.

It's in the restored Rocks district, right under Sydney Harbour Bridge. The early colonial architecture now sits in the middle of our largest city — 3.5 million people living around a spectacular harbour and city skyline.

It's a leisure-loving city. Just go to Bondi Beach or any of the other 100 beaches and you'll see what we mean. Keep an eye out for the life savers crashing into the surf or marching by in their surf caps and '20s-style swim suits.

You can take a harbour cruise and dine on board (don't miss the famous Sydney rock oysters). Or you can go up Sydney Tower with its revolving restaurant and watch the scenery unfold into the horizon.

You'll see the harbour dominated by the 'coathanger' which is what the locals call the Harbour Bridge, and the wonderful billowing sails of the Sydney Opera House.

From Sydney branch out to the rest of New South Wales — the wine country of the Hunter Valley, the opal mines of Lightning Ridge, to sleepy coastal towns and the spectacular Blue Mountains. They really do look blue. It's the vapour from the eucalypt trees that creates the effect. Beyond the mountains is the sweeping sheep and wheat country and, at Dubbo, one of the world's largest open-range zoos.

Public transport: Buses, trains and ferries operate in city and suburban areas. Underground train circles the city, with connecting stations to suburban lines (daily, 5 am to midnight). Buses (daily 5 am to 11.30 pm), from Circular Quay, York Street, Wynyard Park and Railway Sq. Bus 777 (free) circles the downtown area Mon.-Fri. Ferry boats (daily 6 am to 11.30 pm) from Circular Quay to harbourside suburbs. Metered, radio taxis at all hours. Telephone timetable: Train 20918, Bus 20543, Ferries 219 4735.

Climate: Warm temperate; Sydney enjoys sunshine most days. Summer average max 25°C/78°F; Winter average max 17°C/65°F. Rain is fairly even throughout year but, January, February and March are warm/hot with occasional heavy rain.

Airport Transfers → Sydney Airport SYD (International & Domestic terminals are 1.6km/1 mile apart) transfers from both terminals to city centre by airporter bus or taxi; Distance 10km (6 miles) SW of city; Time 30 min; Rental cars available.

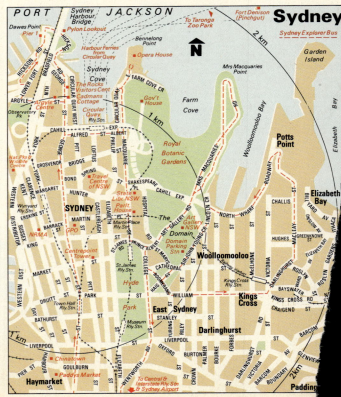

Facts & Figures as of June 1, 1986, subject to change

The straight trunks of eucalypts tower above ferns in Dandenong Ranges National Park

mountain and surrounded by large tree ferns and a variety of eucalypts; it's not hard to understand why so many people love this area.

Visitors will be rewarded with the sounds of many birds, with bellbirds and kookaburras very common, while once heard, the spectacular song of the lyrebird is not easily forgotten.

A WALKER'S DELIGHT

Apart from lazing underneath the forest canopy on a hot summer's day, the most popular recreation in the park is bushwalking and a number of excellent trails are on offer. Within the Ferntree Gully section the easiest and most popular is the self-guided nature trail which covers 3 km and takes roughly 1½ hours to complete. A leaflet can be obtained at the Lower Picnic Ground area at the park section headquarters. A series of markers correspond with

numbers on the trail providing information on the diverse number of plants found in this park. If you've got more energy to expend, then try the Ferntree Gully Track which also starts from the Lower Picnic Ground and extends for 5 km, finishing at the One Tree Hill Picnic Ground. This track is more difficult and takes in One Thousand Steps. The journey along the steep, narrow path should take 2 hours return.

Sherbrooke Forest features nature trails near Grants Picnic Ground; the Hardy Gully Trail is only 700 metres and should take visitors only half an hour to complete. Nearby is the Margaret Lester Forest Walk, which has a hard surface, suitable for wheelchairs. This walk will also take around half an hour to complete. Further north of the forest is the Sherbrooke Falls where access is via the main entrance at Sherbrooke Road.

ACCESS

Burwood Highway from the city is the best access for the park. The lower Picnic Ground of the Ferntree Gully section is on the Mt Dandenong Tourist Road in Ferntree Gully, just after the Burwood Highway turn-off. The Sherbrooke Forest section can be reached by following the Tourist Road and then onto the Sherbrooke Road. The Doongalla block can be reached from the top of the hill at Ridge Road, off Mt Dandenong Tourist Road, or from the Doongalla Road at the foothills of the mountain, a short drive from Mountain Highway.

Camping is not permitted within this metropolitan parkland, but there are a number of places where you can stop and enjoy a picnic, as well as an abundance of bed and breakfast cottages in the hills of the Dandenongs.

EILDON STATE PARK AND FRASER NATIONAL PARK

IN BRIEF

MAP REFERENCE: PAGE 92 E 8

Location 180 km northeast of Melbourne, via the Maroondah Highway
Best Time Summer for water sports; anglers, 4WD owners and trail bike riders year round
Main Attractions Camping, water sports, walking, trail-bike riding, 4WD, forest drives, horse riding, fishing
Ranger Eildon State Park, phone (03) 5775 2788 or (03) 5772 0200 Fraser National Park, phone (03) 5772 1293 or (03) 5774 2208

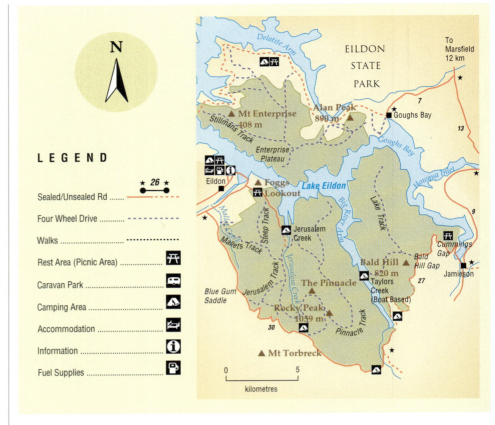

LEGEND

Sealed/Unsealed Rd	★ 26 ★
Four Wheel Drive	
Walks	
Rest Area (Picnic Area)	
Caravan Park	
Camping Area	
Accommodation	
Information	
Fuel Supplies	

With steep, rugged mountains and fresh rivers leading into the vast reservoir of Lake Eildon, these 2 parks, which have now combined to form Lake Eildon National Park, offer a natural playground, only hours from Melbourne.

HISTORY

White settlers first visited this mountainous area in the early 1800s in search of grazing land, and not long after gold miners followed with hopes of striking it rich. Today, careful exploration will reveal evidence of the goldmining era with shafts and old buildings scattered throughout the area. It was also at this time that much of the heavily timbered hills were cleared by graziers to produce open, grassy land for their cattle, while miners used the timber for buildings and mines.

More significant, however, was the damming of the Goulburn River, which began in the 1920s with a small dam for irrigation water in the dry Goulburn Valley region. The dammed area was well received by the local pastoralists who became dependent on the life-giving source. The size of the dam was significantly increased in 1955 when a large area of government land was flooded to form Lake Eildon. The droughts of the 1980s have seen the re-emergence of the buildings that were submerged in the flood, many of which are still intact.

It was not until 1957 that the Fraser National Park was proclaimed while 1980 saw the establishment of the Eildon State Park.

Eildon State Park encompasses 24 000 hectares which is set out in 3 blocks. The largest is just southeast of Eildon and is bordered by Lake Eildon, the Big River Arm and the Eildon–Jamieson road. The other 2 sections are of similar size and are to the north across the lake, and further east between the Big River Arm and Jamieson. The smaller Fraser National Park has a total landmass of only 3750 hectares, but is extremely popular in the warmer months with water-skiers.

WILDLIFE PARK

Visitors to both parks will be rewarded by the sights and sounds of the native wildlife which are used to the human intruders of their domain. During the day colourful rosellas, blue wrens and noisy miners keep a watchful eye on the camp sites, while gang-gang cockatoos are often heard squawking high up in the trees. On

Lake Eildon at dawn

the water's edge, cormorants, pelicans and ducks seek refuge among the trees and feed in the water, while wedge-tail eagles can often be spotted flying overhead.

At dusk and dawn, eastern grey kangaroos may be seen grazing on the grassy slopes or coming down to the water to drink, while koalas can be heard grunting in the trees surrounding the camp site.

OTHER ATTRACTIONS

Fishing is popular at Lake Eildon with the most common species being redfin, carp and trout. In the nearby rivers such as the Rubicon fishing is popular in May and June when the trout swim upriver to spawn. Bag limits apply and need to be checked with the local ranger.

Drivers of 4WD vehicles can tour the heavily forested areas of the Eildon State Park using tracks which extend from the Eildon–Jamieson road to the lake, such as the Pinnacle Track which starts near Blue Gum Saddle and extends over the Pinnacle, or the Steep Track which leads to Foggs Lookout. Further along the Eildon–Jamieson road is the turn-off to Mt Torbreck, and to the west is Rubicon where Australia's first hyrdo-electric scheme was established in the early 1900s, and still exists.

Fraser National Park offers adventure for the bushwalker, with many walks throughout the park. The energetic may like to try the Keg

Bushwalking in Fraser National Park

Spur Trek which heads high up into the mountains before leading back down to Aird Inlet on the lake foreshore and then across to Cooks Point, following the edge of the lake back around to Wallaby Bay. This is a moderate to hard trek of about 13.5 km and will take a total of 5 hours.

Easier walks include the Candlebark Gully Nature Walk Loop which is 2 km and takes around one hour.

Eildon State Park has a superb nature walk which is only 2 km long and takes roughly an hour. Starting near the kiosk, the Sheoak Nature Walk gives visitors a good introduction to what the forest has to offer.

Canoeists can also paddle their way around Coller Bay at Fraser National Park where the boating zone is restricted to 8 kph, while in the Eildon Park the Big River Arm of the lake is perfect for canoeists and kayakers with many day and camping areas along the river's edge, the Chaffe's Creek location being very popular.

ACCESS AND CAMPING

The Eildon Park can be accessed via the Eildon–Jamieson road from Eildon, or from Jamieson for the Big River block, and from Goughs Bay via Jamieson or Mansfield for the Delatite Arm.

At the Delatite Arm you will find more than 400 camp sites with fireplaces and toilets, while Jerusalem Creek has 73 sites. During the Christmas and Easter holidays, the camp sites must be pre-booked. There is also a camp site at Kendells Camping Area (no amenities are provided), and there are boat-based camp sites at Coopers Point and Taylors Creek.

Normal fire restrictions apply, so check fire ban information before you leave home.

Access to Fraser National Park, which is 145 km from Melbourne, is through Alexandra using the Maroondah Highway or through Seymour, Yea and Alexandra. Within the park are the Lakeside, Devil Cove and Candlebark camping areas where you will find toilets, showers, picnic facilities and 2 boat ramps.

LEGEND

Sealed/Unsealed Rd .... ★ 26 ★

Four Wheel Drive .... - - - - - - -

Walks .... ••••••••••••

Rest Area (Picnic Area) .... ⛶

Caravan Park .... 🚐

Camping Area .... ⛺

Accommodation .... 🛏

Information .... ⓘ

Fuel Supplies .... ⛽

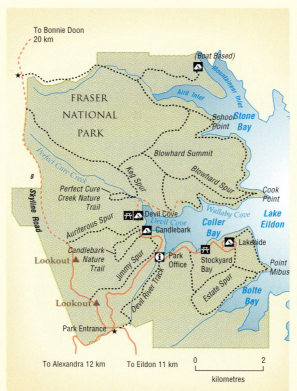

To Bonnie Doon
20 km

FRASER
NATIONAL
PARK

(Boat Based)

Mountaineer Inlet

Aird Inlet

School Point

Stone Bay

Blowhard Summit

Blowhard Spur

Cook Point

Wallaby Cove

Lake Eildon

Perfect Cure Creek

Keg Spur

Perfect Cure Creek Nature Trail

Devil Cove

Candlebark

Coller Bay

Skyline Road

Auriferous Spur

Lakeside

Candlebark Nature Trail

Jimmy Spur

Park Office

Stockyard Bay

Point Mibus

Lookout

Devil River Track

Estate Spur

Bolte Bay

Lookout

Park Entrance

To Alexandra 12 km   To Eildon 11 km

0   2

kilometres

GRAMPIANS NATIONAL PARK

MAP REFERENCE: PAGE 86 F 4

IN BRIEF

Location Central western Victoria, 260 km from Melbourne and 25 km south-west of Stawell
Best Time Spring for wildflowers and autumn for mild weather
Main Attractions Hiking, camping, sightseeing, cycling, scenic driving, rock climbing, nature study and wildflower exhibition (first week in October)
Ranger Phone: (03) 5356 4381

Brambuk Living Cultural Centre, PO Box 43, Halls Gap, phone (03) 5356 4452
Base Camp and Beyond, PO Box 37, Halls Gap, phone (03) 5356 4300
Grampian National Park Visitor Centre, phone (03) 5356 4381. Open daily 9 am to 4.45 pm
Stawell Tourist Information Centre, phone (03) 5358 2314
Victorian Climbing Centre, phone (03) 9782 4222

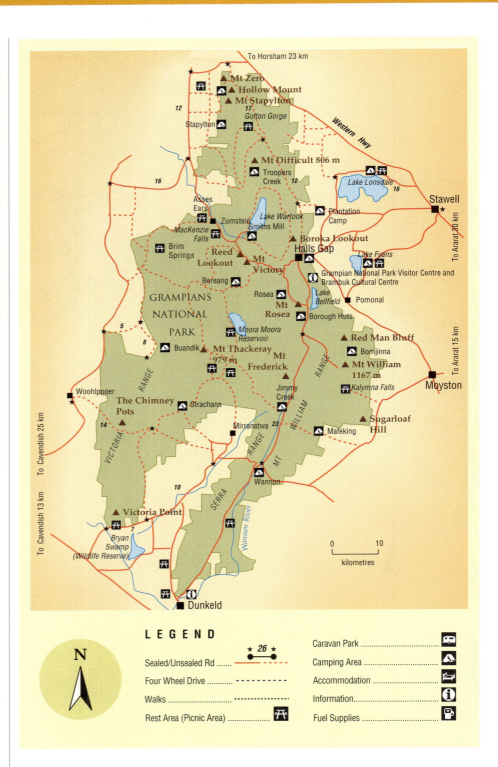

LEGEND

Sealed/Unsealed Rd ★ 26 ★
Four Wheel Drive
Walks
Rest Area (Picnic Area) 🎪

Caravan Park 🚐
Camping Area 🏕
Accommodation 🛏
Information ℹ
Fuel Supplies ⛽

Perched on the extreme western edge of the Great Dividing Range, a series of blue peaks known as Gariwerd form a striking outline on the horizon. A closer inspection reveals the ruggedness and grandeur of massive sandstone sculptures interspersed with a mosaic of colourful wildflowers.

Extending more than 80 km in length and 50 km at their widest point, the Grampians are a series of ranges which signal the end of the Dividing Range which starts near Cooktown in far north Queensland. These rugged mountain ranges offer the outdoors enthusiast the base for most activities, including walking, rock climbing, cycling and abseiling.

The sculptured structures started to emerge more than 400 million years ago when the land rose to form large islands of mountains. These rock formations have since been weathered by wind and rain and are now the main attraction of the Grampians National Park.

One of the more noticeable features of the range is that the western slopes are modest while the eastern slopes are very steep. Excellent examples of this can be found on the Wonderland Range near Halls Gap in the park's centre. This region has not always been protected under national park status, but it has long been recognised for its rugged beauty.

HISTORY

Thomas Mitchell was the first European to explore this region in 1836 and it was not long after that graziers occupied the foothills of the mountains. Other settlers included gold miners and loggers, who harvested the timber during its time as a state forest until the national park was formed in 1984. Since then, visitor numbers have markedly increased and now strict controls are in place to protect the region from feral animals, weeds and soil erosion.

Early evidence of settlement by Aboriginal people can be seen in the park's many art sites. It is also believed that the early settlers utilised the rock formations and caves for ceremonies. Many of the line drawings depict animal tracks, human figures and handprints, such as those at Wab Manja and Billimina art sites.

GRANDIOSE SANDSTONE FORMATIONS

The 167 000 hectare national park consists of 4 main systems of ranges: Victoria and Mt William in the park's lower sections, Mt Difficult in the north, and Serra, which cuts through the centre of the park from Dunkeld to Halls Gap. A smaller range to the southwest of Halls Gap is the Wonderland Range, which is popular with visitors to the area. Unusual rock formations and towering cliffs can be appreciated in a variety of walks which begin around Halls Gap.

The rugged sandstone peaks and valleys house an extremely diverse plant life, with many rare species of wildflowers found in this western Victorian park. Spring heralds the wildflower season and from August to November the colourful blooms carpet the rocky slopes and valleys and include species such as the brilliant red flame heath which is widespread on the hillsides, and the rare spectral duck orchid.

High up, the plateaus are covered in thick heathlands while the hillsides and most of the park are covered in woodland forests and eucalypts such as messmate and brown stringybarks. In contrast, the moist valley floors and folds within the rocks provide the nutrients needed for the swamp gums, succulent ferns and silver banksias to flourish.

The diversity of plant life provides a home to a large number of birds, with more than 200 different species recorded in the Grampians. Flowering gums attract lorikeets, while yellow-tailed black cockatoos soar above the stringybarks. Walkers will see crimson rosellas and honeyeaters in the heathlands, and campers will often be rewarded with the antics of kookaburras. These cheeky birds often forage around camp sites in the early morning, in search of food, retreating to the safety of the tree branches before letting out their famous call. To the south of the park is the Bryan Swamp Wildlife Reserve where an abundance of bird life roosts, including cormorants, ibises, blacks swans and whiskered terns.

The most common marsupial spotted within the park is the swamp wallaby, but other species such as the grey kangaroo and a number of possums inhabit the park. Zumstein picnic area in the centre of the park is popular for viewing kangaroos, but visitors are asked not to feed these friendly natives. Platypus also reside in many of the creeks, but it takes a keen eye and a great deal of patience to spot one of these reclusive monotremes.

A WALK ON THE WILD SIDE

With more than 200 km of maintained walking tracks throughout the park, it is no wonder that walkers head to this region for a wide variety of walks. These trails range from short strolls

A picnic on the Balconies, also known as the Jaws of Death, in the Grampians

The view from the Grampian Ranges Lookout

The magnificent MacKenzie Falls

through to overnight treks over rough terrain for the ambitious and fit. One of the most popular walks for tourists is the Wonderland Long Walk which starts at the Halls Gap camp ground and then climbs along the Pinnacle Track through eucalypt forests to the Pinnacle Lookout which rewards the energetic with spectacular views. Continuing along the Wonderland Track on the return walk to Halls Gap you will take in the Grand Canyon, Silent Street and the famous Elephant's Hide, a huge weatherbeaten face. This 10 km walk is moderate and should take a day to complete.

Another walk is Briggs Bluff, which is best undertaken by those without a fear of heights as it follows the cliff edge. Beginning at the car park near Rose Gap it follows the Beehive Falls track and then climbs steeply up onto the plateau for spectacular views of the Wimmera Plains. This 10 km round trip should not be undertaken on days of poor visibility and will take around 5 hours to complete.

The Balconies, also known as the Jaws of Death, can be reached via a track from the Reed Lookout car park and offers scenic views of the Victoria Valley. The walk is less than 2 km and is of an easy grade, taking 30 minutes to complete.

Information on all the walks within the park is available from the Grampians National Park Visitor Centre at Halls Gap. Informative handbooks and maps are available from the centre, and the helpful staff will answer any questions.

ROCK CLIMBERS' PLAYGROUND
Featuring a multitude of large, majestic sandstone formations, the Grampians National Park has a number of popular climbs.

Hollow Mountain, in the north of the park, is very popular with climbs that range from the beginner level to the very difficult.

Mt Rosea, in the heart of the park near Halls Gap, offers one of the best collections of sandstone climbing. The climbing area stretches for about 2 km and the average height of the cliffs is 100 metres along clean, sound rock. Obvious lines mark the popular climbs and the area can be reached from the Mt Rosea camping area.

For something different, nearby Bundaleer has a range of climbs. For details on climbing in the Grampians, or nearby Mt Arapiles, contact Parks Victoria and the Victorian Climbing Centre. Guided climbing tours can be organised through Base Camp and Beyond at Halls Gap.

OTHER ACTIVITIES
Heavy rain during winter causes much erosion in the Grampians National Park, so most of the vehicular tracks which were used during the logging era have now been closed, leaving cycling as the next best form of transport.

A popular one-day ride is the Wonderland which leaves from Zumstein picnic area and heads to Wonderland car park before returning to Zumstein. The length of this trek is 53 km and will take a day to complete. The difficulty of the ride is between 5 and 6 and the track rating is 4–5, so it should be undertaken using a well-equipped mountain bike, with good tyres and a fit rider. The trail takes in MacKenzie Falls and the Pinnacle Lookout.

For the more adventurous, there is a 3 day ride, leaving also from Zumstein, which heads to the Victoria Range in the south of the park, taking in the Glenelg River, Wallaby Rocks, and various Aboriginal sites. The distance is 100 km return and the ride and track grades are more difficult at 8 and 7.

The 2 lakes in the park—Wartook and Bellfield—offer the visitor canoeing, swimming and fishing. Brown trout, redfin, blackfish and the occasional rainbow trout can be taken, while nearby Rocklands Reservoir, Lake Fyans and Lake Toolondo are also popular. Yabbying is also a favourite pastime of the locals in many of the dams and waterholes in and around the park area. Victorian fishing licences must be obtained from the Parks Victoria for all waters.

Wartook offers restricted powerboat use, while Rocklands and Lake Fyans are the main bodies of water for powered water craft and water-skiers.

Gariwerd offers a cultural experience through a number of ancient Aboriginal rock art sites within the park, some of which are accessible to visitors.

Brambuk Living Cultural Centre near Halls Gap will give visitors an insight into the Aboriginal culture through displays, bush tucker and performances given by the local Aboriginal people.

The Grampians National Park Visitor Centre should be your first stop at the beginning of your exploration of the park. The centre houses extensive displays and provides pamphlets and publications, and ranger staff are on hand to answer any questions you may have on the available activities. The centre is open from 9 am to 4.45 pm daily.

ACCESS

The park is 260 km from Melbourne and can be reached via Ararat or Stawell to Halls Gap. Access to the park's southern boundary is via Dunkeld on the Glenelg Highway, and through Wartook to the west.

CAMPING

There are bush camping areas throughout the park and a number of excellent camps where fees apply. Most are operated on a self-serve system, where campers fill out forms and deposit them at the camp site.

Camp grounds in the central part of the park include Borough Huts, Mt Rosea and Boreang. To the southeast, covering the Serra and Mt William Ranges, you will find Bomjinna, Jimmy Creek, Mafeking and Wannon Crossing. Victoria Range to the southwest offers camping at Buandik, Chimney Pots and Strachan Hut. Camping in the northern sector can be found at Troopers Creek, Smith Mill, Hollow Mountain and Mt Stapylton. The more popular camping areas are those at Halls Gap.

The view from Reed Lookout

HATTAH–KULKYNE NATIONAL PARK/MURRAY–KULKYNE PARK

IN BRIEF

MAP REFERENCE: PAGE 88 F 3

Location Off the Sunraysia Highway, 580 km north of Melbourne via Ouyen, and 70 km south of Mildura
Best Time Spring and autumn
Main Attractions Camping, bushwalking, canoeing, fishing, driving, cycling, photography
Ranger Phone (03) 5029 3253

In this arid region of northwest Victoria, floodwaters from the Murray River form the Hattah Lakes, providing a life source for the birds, other animals and vegetation that thrive in the Hattah–Kulkyne National Park and Murray–Kulkyne Park.

Both of these parks lie west of the mighty Murray River in a typical mallee environment of native cypress pine woodland and vast mallee scrubland covering the fragile sandy soil.

As with much of the mallee, this area was grazed in the 19th century, but early in 1915 the lakes area was recognised as being significant and declared a sanctuary. Then in 1960 the Hattah Lakes National Park was formed before being added to the Kulkyne State Forest to form the park as we know it today.

As with much of the mallee region, rabbit infestation has taken its toll. However, a very intense revegetation program is now in place, and with the co-operation of visitors it is hoped that the area will successfully regenerate over the ensuing years.

ACTIVITIES IN THE PARK

A series of creeks serve as a passageway for water from the Murray River along the Chalka Creek, which in turn provides an oasis for the wildlife in the 48 000 hectare park.

Birds, kangaroos and other animals are abundant in the park, especially around the lakes, which are best explored by canoe. With the exception of very dry seasons, the lakes are connected by a series of small creeks which can easily be traversed by boat (non-powered craft only).

Covering a small area of only 1690 hectares the Murray–Kulkyne Park fringes the Murray River providing the visitor with inviting sandy shores and big river red gums along the shore-line. Camping is tranquil and during the hot summer months the Murray offers cool respite.

If dry ground is more your style, walking and cycling are both excellent ways to explore the park, taking in the many archaeological sites

including shield trees and middens. The many drives and walks available are detailed in the information brochure available from the park's information centre.

BIRDWATCHERS' MECCA

While other parks in the northwest of Victoria may be lacking in bird life, the Hattah–Kulkyne National Park and the Murray-Kulkyne Park contain an abundance of birds. Having both dry and lake environments, they provide a habitat for more than 200 species of birds. Many campers will awake to the raucous squawks of the Major Mitchell cockatoos, while leisurely walks will reward the keen eye with species such as the apostlebird, mallee ring-neck and the colourful Australian icon, the rosella.

ACCESS AND CAMPING

Access to the Hattah—Kulkyne National Park is via the Sunraysia Highway turning east at Hattah. From here the Hattah Lake camping area is only a short drive on a good road.

The Murray–Kulkyne Park can be accessed via the gravel River Track from Ouyen or Mildura. During periods of heavy rain, obtain advice on road conditions from the park ranger.

Mallee vegetation on the shores of Lake Hattah

Delightful camping areas can be found on the shores of Lake Hattah and Lake Mournpall which offer pit toilets, fireplaces and picnic tables. There is limited water available from the information centre and Lake Mournpall, and visitors are encouraged to carry in their own water. Camping is also permitted in the Murray–Kulkyne Park to the north.

Firewood is in short supply and fires must be lit in the fireplaces provided. As Murray–Kulkyne is not a national park, dogs are allowed in on a leash.

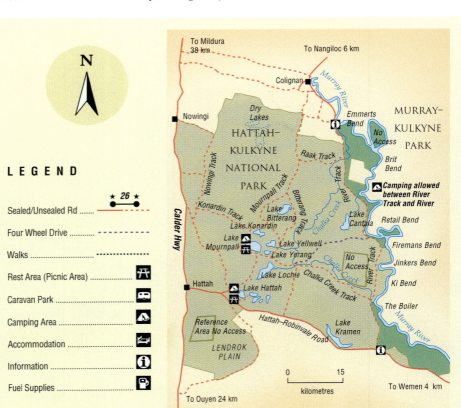

LEGEND

★ 26 ★

Sealed/Unsealed Rd ....
Four Wheel Drive ....
Walks ....
Rest Area (Picnic Area) .... 🛆
Caravan Park .... 🚐
Camping Area .... 🛆
Accommodation .... 🛏
Information .... ℹ
Fuel Supplies .... ⛽

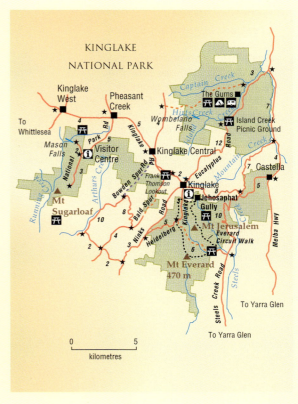

IN BRIEF

MAP REFERENCE: PAGE 92 B 10

Location One hour north of Melbourne, on the north-western slopes of the Great Dividing Range
Best Time Year round: autumn and spring are delightful, summer has warm, balmy days, winter can be cold with snow
Main Attractions Walking, horse riding, picnics, nature study, scenic drives, 4WD, birdwatching
Ranger Phone (03) 5786 5328

With magnificent views of the city, densely forested mountaintops, and fern-filled gullies, the Kinglake National Park offers Melburnians a cool respite from the summer heat.

The land was initially used extensively for logging to supply timber to Melbourne during the housing boom in the early part of the 20th century. Gold prospectors had also gathered in the area during the mid-1850s, but this was short-lived and they eventually made way for the loggers and pastoralists who made an enormous impact on this mountain landscape by clearing much of the land.

Fortunately, being only 65 km from Melbourne, the beauty of this region was recognised and in 1928 the national park was declared. It was used extensively by Melburnians who would retreat to the cool fern-covered mountains in summer.

The steep mountains in the northern section of the park are covered with eucalypts, stringybarks, peppermint gums and orchids while the wetter southern section has gullies filled with delicate ferns, mosses and tree ferns.

The park was eventually extended to its

Bushland in Kinglake National Park

LEGEND

Sealed/Unsealed Rd	★ 26 ★
Four Wheel Drive	
Walks	
Rest Area (Picnic Area)	
Caravan Park	
Camping Area	
Accommodation	
Information	
Fuel Supplies	

present size of 11 430, but in accommodating the private land on the top of the mountain, the park is divided into 3 sections which surround Kinglake township itself.

ACTIVITIES IN THE PARK

The area surrounding the park is scattered with farmland where horses can be seen grazing on the grassy slopes. These animals provide the perfect transport through the mountain ranges of the park, and there are designated areas where horses can be ridden. Due to seasonal closures it is best to check with the ranger first.

For walkers, the Wombelano Falls on Hirts Creek can be accessed via an easy short walk through the cool, fern-filled gullies, while ferns and messmate forests can be seen on the short walk to Mason Falls in the west of the park.

The more spectacular journey by foot is the 20 km moderate to hard trail from the Jehosaphat Gully picnic area south of Kinglake. Called the Everard Circuit Walk, the day-long trail takes you around Mt Jerusalem to the Jehosaphat Creek, and then heads west to Mt Everard which stands at 470 metres and offers superb views of the city as the mountains drop away towards Melbourne. The trail then heads north crossing the Heidelberg–Kinglake road and ending back at Jehosaphat Gully.

If you would like the view, but without the energetic walk, Frank Thomson Lookout can be

found just out of town, heading along the Whittlesea–Kinglake road. This small picnic ground has toilets and picnic tables, and offers a magical view of the city, especially at night.

If you have a 4WD vehicle you can venture down the Bowden Spur Road, just a few hundred metres past this lookout, and head down under the transmission lines. The drive along the steep, narrow, winding road offers views of the cityscape and Sugarloaf Reservoir, interrupted only by the buzzing powerlines overhead. If you continue down this road and then deviate left down Rankine Road which winds along the valley floor amongst farmland, you can then head northeast on Bald Spur Road which follows the spur back up the mountain, through the park, finally finishing back near the lookout. This route, which takes about an hour, is an easy drive, and since it is a fire trail, it is well maintained, but is suitable for 4WD vehicles only.

ACCESS AND CAMPING

Kinglake National Park can be accessed via the Melba Highway from Yarra Glen, from Whittlesea using the Whittlesea–Kinglake road, or the Heidelberg–Kinglake Road from Eltham.

The region caters more for day-trippers than campers, but there is a camp area at the Gums which has toilets, fresh water and sites for caravans. The area is small, and sites need to be booked ahead through the ranger.

THE LAKES NATIONAL PARK AND GIPPSLAND LAKES COASTAL PARK

IN BRIEF

MAP REFERENCE: PAGE 90 E 7

Location 35 km from Sale to Lakes Entrance
Best Time The warmer months, particularly summer
Main Attractions Extensive coastal lake system, Ninety Mile Beach, swimming, fishing, boating, forest and coastal bushland
Ranger Phone (03) 5152 0400 or (03) 5146 0278

Boat Hire: Lake Tyers Beach Boat Hire, phone (03) 5156 5666; Lakes Entrance Paddle Boats, phone (03) 5155 2753

In the coastal parks near Lakes Entrance in Gippsland you can sit quietly beside the tranquil lakes and rivers taking in the orchestra of birds, mingled with the laughter of children.

Encompassing the coastal region from Seaspray to Lakes Entrance, the Gippsland Lakes Coastal Park covers 17 200 hectares and boasts such natural features as the Ninety Mile Beach and the inland coastal lakes system.

LEGEND

Sealed/Unsealed Rd	★ 26 ★
Four Wheel Drive	- - - - - -
Walks	· · · · · · ·
Rest Area (Picnic Area)	⊞
Caravan Park	
Camping Area	
Accommodation	
Information	ⓘ
Fuel Supplies	

Lakes Entrance in the Lakes National Park

The fishing fleet at Lakes Entrance

HISTORY

The lakes were formed more than a million years ago, when the sea forced sand on the shore, creating a series of barriers along the coast. Eventually the lakes system was separated from the coast, occasionally penetrated during sea storms. It was not until 1889 that a permanent entrance to the lakes was made, and this is now used as entry to the lakes system and the fishing township of Lakes Entrance.

A HAVEN FOR WILDLIFE

The Lakes National Park, covering only 2390 hectares, is rich in wildlife and is a retreat from the bustling seaside villages that dot the coast in this part of Gippsland. Visitors can take one of the many walks along the beach, or stroll through banskia woodlands around the Point Wilson Picnic Area. Birdwatchers can use the bird hides in the park, while a trip to Murphy's Hill will reward the energetic with fantastic views of Bass Strait. Kangaroos can be seen feeding on the plains along Barton's Hill Track near Point Wilson while seabirds such as herons, pelicans and plovers are always nearby.

If your interest is in wildlife, take in one of the many wildlife reserves such as Lake Coleman State Game Reserve, Macleod Morass Wildlife Reserve, or Sale Common Wildlife Reserve. The Macleod Reserve is a 520 hectare marsh where a 300 metre boardwalk leads to a hide which produces the best results just before dusk. The Sale Reserve boasts many waterbirds including the Cape Barren goose.

Wildflowers flourish in this coastal environment and visitors in October will be rewarded with a fine display including a rare flower, *Thryptomene micrantha*, which, outside Tasmania, is found only in this area.

SEASIDE FROLICS

The seaside conjures up images of long walks along the sand, swimming, and family fun on the beach. An ideal family holiday location, this region has all of this to offer plus the spectacular lakes and forest areas.

Boat ramps can be found at Loch Sport, Goon Nure, Paynesville, Metung and Nungurner.

Nearby Lake Tyers Forest Park boasts ocean foreshores, and canoeists will enjoy the Nowa Arm of the lake which extends all the way to the township of Nowa Nowa, or the western arm which leads to Cherry Tree Creek. Near Cherry Tree Creek a rainforest walk of 40 minutes starts at the Silvertop Picnic Area.

Near the entrance to the lakes is Barrier Landing, accessible only by boat, which offers a lake and surf beach and is ideal for fishing or swimming. Dolphins and seals are regularly spotted searching the area for food and the location is also ideal for watching the boats negotiate the entrance.

ACCESS AND CAMPING

There is boat access from Paynesville in the north of Lakes National Park. The eastern end of the park is accessed from Bairnsdale. Rotomah Island is accessed by boat only.

Camping is available at Rotamah Island Observatory and Emu Bight in the Lakes National Park and also at Seaspray, Golden Beach, Paradise Beach, Eel Farm, Red Bluff, Bunga Arm, near the Moss Ball Swamp, and Seacombe in the Gippsland Lakes Coastal Park.

Campers will also find retreats along the thin stretch of land between Lake Reeve and the coast from the Honeysuckles and Golden Beach. There are also many camping areas along the edge of Lake Tyers. The only camping facilities are toilets.

LERDERDERG STATE PARK

The Lerderderg River, flanked with huge stands of eucalypt trees, cuts its way through this significant conservation parkland, only an hour from Melbourne's inner city.

During the last century the area was recognised by the gold diggers for its potential to produce alluvial gold. Evidence of the mining can be found along Byers Back Track, and Tunnel Point, where miners diverted the Lerderderg River, making a tunnel through the solid rock gorge of the river.

The park was originally a small forest reserve in 1963 and it has since been extended 3 times to its present size of 13 400 hectares. For its protection, it was declared a state park.

VALUABLE CONSERVATION REGION

The region is a very important conservation area, boasting the largest single area of eucalypt forest in north-central Victoria. It is also home to a colony of koalas, who nest in the large ribbony manna gums, the preferred tree for this species. The prolific bird life includes cockatoos, such as the sulphur-crested and gang-gang, and the mighty wedge-tail eagle.

Flora is abundant in this isolated bushland with the most popular eucalypts being the tall, fibrous messmate stringybark which is found in the mountain foothills, and the red ironbark, easily identified by the goblet-shaped fruit and dark, thick bark.

Closer inspection along the ground will reveal wildflowers, bush peas and orchids, the most impressive being the large duck orchid.

Lerderderg Gorge in Lerderderg State Park

A TRUE BUSH ENCOUNTER

The isolation of this park makes it ideal for bushwalking. Blackwood Mineral Springs walk will take you past Shaws Lake and onto Sweets Lookout, high above the river. This walk is 3.5 km long and takes around 2 hours return. To take in the tunnel, start at O'Briens Crossing and head along Byers Back Track which follows an old water-race around the valley and offers excellent views of the river and surrounds. This 2 hours, 3 km return trek takes you to the site where the tunnel has been carved into the rock to divert the Lerderderg River.

Touring in a 4WD vehicle is also very popular and can be combined with many of the walks to make for an enjoyable weekend or a day's outing. One such trip could include a drive along the Lerderderg Track, then setting off on foot to complete the journey along Spanish Onion Track down to the cliffs, which are perched above the Lerderderg River, and the East Walk, which heads northwest to O'Briens Crossing. Remember to check on seasonal track closures during winter and spring.

ACCESS AND CAMPING

The park can be entered using O'Briens Road from the Greenvale–Trentham road, or further north from Blackwood along the Golden Point road. From the south access is via the Lerderderg Gorge road off the Bacchus Marsh–Gisborne road.

There are numerous camp sites along the Lerderderg River within the park, but most have no toilet facilities. The picnic ground at O'Briens Crossing has fireplaces and toilets.

N

LEGEND

Sealed/Unsealed Rd	★ 26 ★
Four Wheel Drive	
Walks	
Rest Area (Picnic Area)	⊞
Caravan Park	
Camping Area	
Accommodation	
Information	ⓘ
Fuel Supplies	

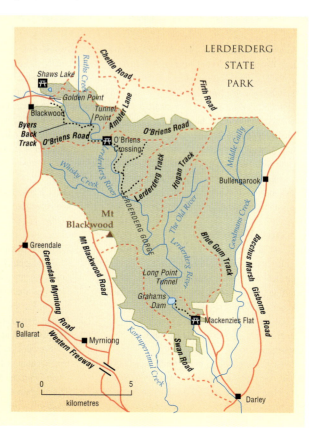

LERDERDERG STATE PARK

Shaws Lake
Ruths Creek
Chettle Road
Firth Road
Golden Point
Tunnel Point
Blackwood
Amber Lane
O'Briens Road
Byers Back Track
O'Briens Road
O'Briens Crossing
Whisky Creek
Lerderderg River
Lerderderg Track
Hogan Track
Middle Gully
Bullengarook
Mt Blackwood
LERDERDERG GORGE
The Old River
Lerderderg River
Blue Gum Track
Gwinhams Creek
Bacchus Marsh Gisborne Road
Greendale
Mt Blackwood Road
Greendale Myrniong Road
To Ballarat
Long Point Tunnel
Grahams Dam
Mackenzies Flat
Myrniong
Western Freeway
Korkuperrimul Creek
Swan Road
Darley

0   5
kilometres

IN BRIEF

MAP REFERENCE: PAGE 86 C 1

Location On the Vic–SA border, 375 km northwest from Melbourne
Best Time Autumn and spring, especially when the wildflowers bloom
Main Attractions Walking, 4WD, nature study, camping, fishing
Ranger Phone (03) 5389 1204 or (03) 5391 1275

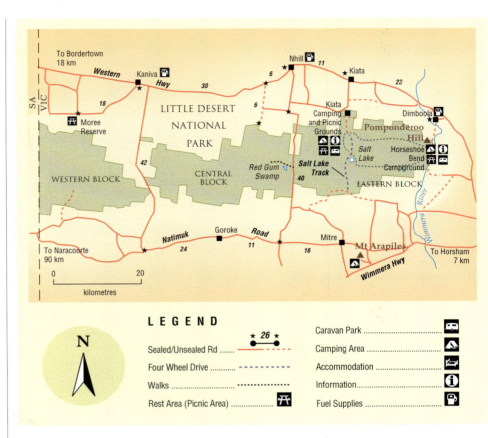

LEGEND

Sealed/Unsealed Rd .... ★ 26 ★	Caravan Park ....
Four Wheel Drive .... - - - - - - -	Camping Area ....
Walks .... ••••••••••	Accommodation ....
Rest Area (Picnic Area)	Information.................................
	Fuel Supplies ....

N

With a diversity of vegetation, this park conserves an important region of the Mallee in far western Victoria.

In 1988, Crown Land west of Dimboola was finally recognised for its conservation qualities and incorporated into the Little Desert National Park. This park is divided into 3 major blocks: the eastern which is closest to Dimboola, the central block which lies between the Nhill–Harrow road and Kaniva–Edenhope road, and the western block which occupies most of the land from the Kaniva–Edenhope road to the Victoria–South Australia border.

Many of the tracks in the area, especially in the central and western blocks, are neatly divided, and many date back to the time when the area was to be subdivided, cleared and used for pastoralists. Fortunately, this never occurred, but as you trek through the parkland there is evidence of the early settlement.

SANDY HEATHLANDS

The sandy soils support typical mallee vegetation such as the stunted mallee bush, grey mulga, colourful wattle, and the casuarina. Throughout the 132 000 hectares of the heathland park there is a diverse range of plants which, in spring, produce a spectacular exhibition of wildflowers. Smaller plants and shrubs, such as the holly grevillea, flame heath and the colourful broom bush, carpet the area and provide a haven for birds. Commonly found around the wildflowers are a number of parrots, honeyeaters and currawongs, and, making their mark with their huge mound nests, the malleefowl.

The keen-eyed may spot a brush-tail possum or a bearded dragon basking in the sun, but many visitors should be rewarded with glimpses of kangaroos and a number of different lizards.

4WD ON THE SANDY TRACKS

As most of the tracks in the sandy region are unsuitable for conventional vehicles, this remote area is perfect for 4WDs. Within the eastern block, the Salt Lake Track which leaves from the Kiata camp ground and extends to the very south of the park is an easy walk, as are most of the tracks in the area. This journey is a good introduction to the heathlands in this region of the park. Moving west on the Red Gum Track brings you through the central block and into a different region, extensively vegetated by

Wimmera River in Little Desert National Park

stringybark. Heading out on Crater Track, then north on Whimpeys Track, will bring you back to the Kiata camp ground. To explore the western block, with its magnificent woodlands of yellow and red gums and stands of cypress pines, enter this block from the Kaniva–Edenhope road. Tracks are often closed due to the wet weather which can cause damage to the clay-based tracks. The park ranger will have information on track conditions and seasonal closures.

Many walks in the area accommodate the day or overnight hiker, while short walks can be made from the camping areas.

ACCESS AND CAMPING

Access to the park from the east is along well formed gravel roads from Dimboola, or from the Western Highway on gravel roads from Horsham. Heading north, access is via Edenhope, Gymbowen, Goroke or Mitre.

Remote bush camping is allowed in the central and western blocks of the park, while camping sites have been set up in the eastern block nearer to the town. At the Horseshoe Bend camping ground, the closest to Dimboola on the Wimmera River, you will find sites for caravans and tents, information is provided and there are toilets, fireplaces, picnic tables and fresh water. Similar facilities can be found at the Kiata camp ground north of the eastern block near the Kiata South Road.

LOWER GLENELG NATIONAL PARK

IN BRIEF

MAP REFERENCE: PAGE 86 B 7

Location 73 km northwest of Portland, extending to the Vic–SA border
Best Time Summer
Main Attractions Cave tours, walking, picnics, camping, nature study, canoeing, boating, water-skiing, fishing
Ranger Phone (03) 8738 4051

Canoe hire, Nelson: phone (03) 8738 4048
Princess Margaret Rose Caves Guided Tours, phone (03) 8738 4171
Portland Tourist Information Centre, phone (03) 5523 2671

A magnificent limestone column in Princess Margaret Rose Caves

Before it finally meets the Southern Ocean, the Glenelg River carves a magnificent gorge from the tall limestone cliffs to form the most popular feature of the park.

HISTORY

Major Thomas Mitchell, the Surveyor-General of New South Wales, was the first European to explore this region and it was he who named the Glenelg River in 1836. Exactly 100 years later, Keith McEachern discovered the Princess Margaret Rose Caves and developed them into a tourist attraction. It was not, however, until the 1940s that settlers took up the surrounding land for pine plantation and in 1968 the park was first declared. However, it was not developed until 1975. The caves were included in the park system in 1980 to form the present park of 27 300 hectares.

CLIFFS AND CAVES

The best way to view the cliffs is by canoe, and with no rapids or fast currents, and plenty of overnight camps, the Glenelg River offers newcomers

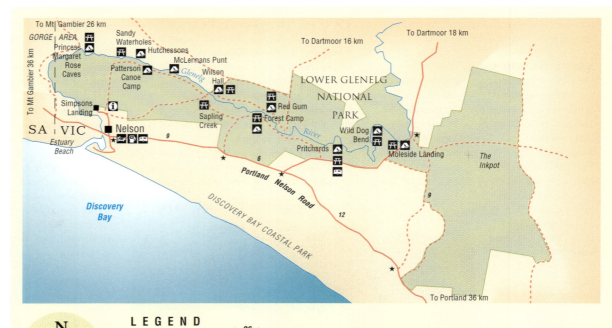

LEGEND

★—26—★

Sealed/Unsealed Rd .... (red line)
Four Wheel Drive .... (blue dashed)
Walks .... (dotted)

Rest Area (Picnic Area) ....
Caravan Park ....
Camping Area ....

Accommodation ....
Information ....
Fuel Supplies ....

the perfect overnight canoeing adventure.

While the Glenelg River Gorge and the river itself are popular for canoeing, fishing and boating, the limestone caves are a further attraction to the area. Keith McEachern cut steps into the limestone and installed electricity enabling the caves to be accessed by tourists. The caves have excellent examples of stalactites and stalagmites, shawls and columns. The Princess Margaret Rose Caves are open for guided tours on most days; phone for details.

The fishing is good, and the river is well-known for its catches of bass, southern black bream and Australian salmon.

Canoes can be hired in Nelson, and with the numerous camp grounds along its banks, the Glenelg River allows canoeists to make extended trips. Powered boats for water-skiing can be used in the lower section of the park. Check with the ranger for restrictions.

OTHER ATTRACTIONS

Many walking tracks crisscross the park and bushwalkers are blessed with wildflowers in spring and a large number of plants and animals. The park has the westernmost stands of tree ferns in Australia, and also plays host to many West Australian plants.

The park is along the route of the Great Southwest Walk, a 250 km trek which takes in the scenery of the southwest of Victoria. It's for the very fit only, taking 10 days to complete. The best times to tackle the walk are from October to very early December before the weather becomes too hot, and then late March to June before the winter chill sets in. Starting and finishing in Portland at the Tourist Information Centre, the trail takes in the Cobboboonee State Forest and the Lower Glenelg National Park as well as Discovery Bay Coastal Park before returning via the coast to Portland.

ACCESS

Dartmoor, on the Princes Highway, offers access to the northern edge of the park, while travelling from Portland to Nelson will give easy access to the southern and western ends of the park.

CAMPING

Camp grounds are scattered all along the Glenelg River and also at Dartmoor. Many include picnic tables and fireplaces—some, such as those at Pritchards, Wilson Hall and Simpsons Landing, also offer boat ramps. At Pattersons Canoe Camp there is canoe-based camping only. Camping is by permit only which is obtainable from the Park Office near Nelson on the edge of the park.

The Princess Margaret Rose Caves can be accessed via Bonds Road and you will find picnic tables and camping areas at this site.

The tranquil Glenelg River

MORNINGTON PENINSULA NATIONAL PARK

MAP REFERENCE: PAGE 87 N 8

IN BRIEF

Location 95 km south of Melbourne on the eastern side of the entrance to Port Phillip Bay
Best Time Summer, spring and autumn
Main Attractions Military fort, beaches, swimming (not at Point Nepean due to currents), surfing, bush and beach walks, historical significance
Ranger Western section and fort, phone (03) 5984 1586; eastern section and Cape Schanck, phone (03) 5988 6321

Bookings to visit Point Nepean, phone (03) 5984 4276

Port Nepean and the old military fort were out of bounds to the public for more than 100 years and thus gathered an air of mystery. They are now incorporated in the Mornington Peninsula National Park, accessible to all.

The newly named Mornington Peninsula National Park covers the 2686 hectare region formerly known as the Point Nepean National Park which amalgamated with the smaller Cape Schanck Coastal Park nearly 10 years ago to cover a large coastal region featuring craggy headlands, spectacular sandy beaches and an abundance of marine life.

This area also includes Port Nepean which covers an area of only 315 hectares and incorporates a section of Commonwealth land including the old Port Nepean Quarantine Station.

While many associate the area with sun, surf and fun, the Point Nepean region has for years been closed to the public, sheltering a historic fort, cemetery and quarantine station which was opened to the public only 20 years ago.

The quarantine station was set up in 1852 after an immigrant ship arrived with hundreds of passengers suffering from typhoid. One hundred passengers died during the voyage and another 68 died at the station and were buried in the Point Nepean Cemetery.

The fort was erected in 1882 in response to a fear of attack from countries such as Russia, but only 2 shots were ever fired in the fort's 63 year history of active duty.

A great deal of the fort is still intact and there are many tunnels and bunkers to be explored, while the large guns sit proudly on the top of this coastal fortress as a reminder of its origins.

LEGEND

Sealed/Unsealed Rd	⋆ 26 ⋆
Four Wheel Drive	- - - -
Walks	•••••
Rest Area (Picnic Area)	⛩
Caravan Park	🚐
Camping Area	⛺
Accommodation	🛏
Information	ℹ
Fuel Supplies	⛽

N

THINGS TO DO

Exploring Point Nepean is possible by boarding a tractor-pulled train, and once a month the fort area is opened for a bicycle day when cyclists can ride around the park taking in all the sights.

An excellent display at the Orientation Centre at the entrance to the park outlines the park and fortress through pictures, diagrams and models, and there is literature detailing the short history of the area.

The park is popular and visitor numbers are limited so it is advisable to book ahead.

The surf rolling in at Cheviot Beach on Point Nepean

Cheviot Beach is on the southern side of Point Nepean and was named after a ship that was wrecked there in 1887. Many years later, in 1967, it became famous as the place where the then Australian Prime Minister, Harold Holt, vanished while swimming off the coast. His body has never been found and many rumours surround his disappearance.

The back beaches of Sorrento, Portsea and Gunnamatta are well known among surfers. During low tide, the higher reaches of the Sorrento beach are exposed, revealing rocky platforms forming rockpools teeming with sea life such as sea-urchins, starfish and crabs. These pools are perfect for relaxing after an exhausting surf, or for use as wading pools.

Popular walks include the Farnsworth Track which covers the area between Portsea and the rocky structure named London Bridge. This easy walk is around 2.5 km return and takes in sand dunes and coastal heathlands and offers superb views along the clifftop. The return walk takes in a stroll along the beach, and the satisfaction of an invigorating ocean swim.

ACCESS

The Point Nepean section of Mornington Peninsula National Park is accessed from the Point Nepean road from Portsea.

Sorrento Back Beach is reached from Ocean Beach Road from Sorrento, while Browns Road provides access further down the beach.

Cape Schanck can be reached by travelling along the Cape Schanck Road.

The Mornington Peninsula National Park is for day-use only; toilets and picnic facilities can be found throughout the park.

MT BUFFALO NATIONAL PARK

Imposing granite boulders rise abruptly from the Ovens Valley—it's a sight long to be remembered. Encircled by the Ovens, Buffalo and Buckland Rivers this year-round park offers snow-covered mountaintops in winter and clear, warm days in summer. It was reserved as a national park in 1898.

For hundreds of years the Aboriginal people of the alpine area would gather at Mt Buffalo and celebrate the coming of the Bogong moth by catching and eating swarms of the large insect. It was not, however, until the early 1800s that Hume and Hovell passed through the Ovens Valley and named the mountain because of its likeness to the buffalo.

ADVENTURERS' WONDERLAND

It is the rugged nature of this 31 600 hectare park that beckons a wide variety of outdoor enthusiasts.

With crystal-clear waterfalls tumbling through the mammoth granite boulders, and alpine daisies carpeting the way, there is nothing more exhilarating than bushwalking through the Mt Buffalo National Park soon after the snow melts. There are more than 90 km of marked bushwalks in the park and a good starting point might be to the Eurobin Falls. The walk starts at the entrance to the park and leads to the falls. The distance is approximately 1.5 km and being an easy grade

Skiing in Mt Buffalo National Park

will take 45 minutes return. The more experienced might like to try the Mt Dunn Walk which takes in spectacular views of Mt Dunn and the Underground River. The distance of this walk is 15.5 km and with a moderate to difficult grade will take around 5½ hours to complete.

For the more adventurous, rock climbing over the towering boulders offers spectacular views of the surrounding river valley. The climbs including the Back Wall, Chalwell Galleries, Eurobin Falls, the Hump, the Gorge, the Leviathan and the Monolith, a balancing rock close to the Chalet.

During the winter months cross-country skiers are well catered for and information can be obtained from the Cresta Resort Office at Mt Buffalo, phone (03) 5755 1585, while downhill skiers have many trails to choose from.

Anglers will find brown trout in Lake Catani, while mountain-bike riders have use of the vehicular and management vehicle roads through the park for their exploration. The Reservoir Road is a great introduction to the Mt Buffalo area for cyclists. Put aside a day for this ride which is of an easy standard.

ACCESS AND CAMPING

Access to the park from Melbourne is via the Hume Highway on a sealed road through Porepunkah.

Camping is restricted to the camp grounds at Lake Catani on the Mt Buffalo Road from November to May. Facilities include toilets, fireplaces and picnic tables.

Motel or lodge style accommodation can be sought on the mountain. Try either the Chalet, phone (03) 5755 1500, or the Tatra Inn, phone (03) 5755 1988.

LEGEND

Sealed/Unsealed Rd	★ 26 ★
Four Wheel Drive	- - - - - -
Walks	·······
Rest Area (Picnic Area)	⛼
Caravan Park	🚐
Camping Area	⛺
Accommodation	🛏
Information	ℹ
Fuel Supplies	⛽

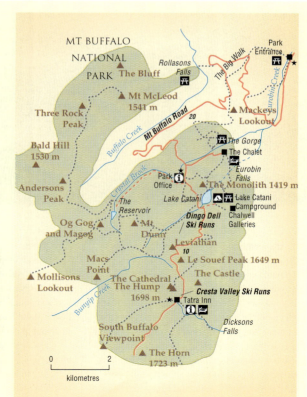

MT BUFFALO NATIONAL PARK

The Bluff
Rollasons Falls
The Big Walk
Park Entrance
Mt McLeod 1541 m
Three Rock Peak
Mackeys Lookout
Buffalo Creek
Mt Buffalo Road
20
The Gorge
Bald Hill 1530 m
The Chalet
Andersons Peak
Crystal Brook
Park Office
Eurobin Falls
The Monolith 1419 m
Lake Catani
Lake Catani Campground
The Reservoir
Dingo Dell Ski Runs
Chalwell Galleries
Og Gog and Magog
Mt Dunn
Leviathan
10
Le Souef Peak 1649 m
Macs Point
The Castle
Mollisons Lookout
Bunyip Creek
The Cathedral
The Hump 1698 m
Tatra Inn
Cresta Valley Ski Runs
South Buffalo Viewpoint
Dicksons Falls
0   2
kilometres
The Horn 1723 m

IN BRIEF

MAP REFERENCE: PAGE 88 C 4

Location On the Vic–SA border, 585 km from Melbourne, via Ouyen
Best Time Spring
Main Attractions 4WD, walking, nature study, photography, camping, cycling, remote desert
Ranger Phone (03) 5094 6267 or (03) 5092 1322

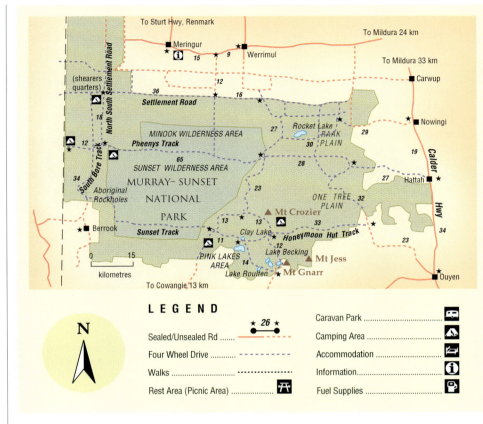

LEGEND

Sealed/Unsealed Rd	★ 26 ★
Four Wheel Drive	Caravan Park
Walks	Camping Area
Rest Area (Picnic Area)	Accommodation
	Information
	Fuel Supplies

Situated in the far northwest of Victoria, the Murray–Sunset National Park is the closest most Victorians will come to experiencing the arid Australian desert country. With the rolling pastures of wheat on either side of the highway, salt flats and sand dunes to the north and thick mallee scrub to the south, this corner of Victoria offers a series of contrasting vistas.

The second largest park in Victoria, the 633 000 hectare Murray–Sunset National Park was proclaimed in 1991 and houses 4 important wilderness zones within its boundaries. Originally the area was used for grazing, which was introduced in the mid-1800s, but this lasted only until the late 19th century when the land was mined for salt and gypsum. The mining continued until the original park was declared in the 1970s.

DESERT ON THE DOORSTEP

Located only 6 hours from Melbourne, this vast park offers visitors an insight into the arid desert regions of our country without the remoteness associated with larger areas interstate such as the Simpson Desert.

The park previously held the name of Sunset Country and is renowned for the magnificent Pink Lakes located in the southern end of the park. These closely grouped salt lakes take on a pink hue which contrasts well with the surrounding desert sands and dense mallee scrub. The Pink Lakes is the ideal base for a series of day trips by 4WD, bicycle or on foot.

It is, however, the remoteness of the region that has a lasting impact on visitors. With a 4WD vehicle you can drive through the vast areas of the park taking in such highlights as Mt Crozier, which offers superb views of the mallee heathland.

Walkers can take advantage of the wilderness areas and trek through the mallee-covered dunes and saltbush flats, possibly catching a glimpse of the malleefowl.

While wildlife is not abundant in this park, a large number of kangaroos can be seen, especially the red kangaroo which is prolific along the northern section of the park.

The word mallee comes from the Aboriginal word 'mallee' which describes the unusual growth form of the eucalypts in the area—in fact 20 different species of mallee eucalypts can be found in the region, many of which live to an age of 500 years.

It is most inadvisable to visit this region during the hot, dry summer months when

Lake Kenyon, one of the Pink Lakes

temperatures often reach the high thirties and low forties. This time of year also brings the threat of wildfires.

While you are travelling in the region, make an appointment to call into the Local History Resource Centre based in Ouyen (phone (03) 5092 1763) for information on the region.

ACCESS AND CAMPING

Two main highways border the south and east of the park. The Mallee Highway runs from Ouyen west to Adelaide, while the Sunraysia Highway reaches north towards Mildura.

The most popular access to the park is the drive to the Pink Lakes area via Linga. Fuel and supplies, however, are best sought in Ouyen.

Camping is very pleasant at Pink Lakes where you will find toilets, fireplaces, picnic tables, gas BBQs and a limited supply of water. If you have a 4WD vehicle you can venture deeper into the parkland, to the camping areas of Mopoke, Pheneeys Track, Mt Crozier and Rocket Lake—which can also be accessed via Settlement Track. These remote camping areas offer toilets, fireplaces and picnic tables.

Water is not available through most of the park, so it has to be carried in. During the wetter months it is advisable to check with the ranger on road conditions as heavy rain can make the tracks inaccessible for conventional vehicles.

OTWAY NATIONAL PARK AND ANGAHOOK–LORNE STATE PARK

IN BRIEF

MAP REFERENCE: PAGE 87 J 9

Location Otway Ranges, about 200 km southwest of Melbourne, via the Princes Highway or the Great Ocean Road
Best Time Late summer through to autumn
Main Attractions Bushwalking, scenic driving, camping, swimming, surfing, fishing, horse riding, canoeing
Ranger Phone (03) 5237 6889 or (03) 5237 3243 or for Angahook–Lorne State Park, phone (03) 5263 3144 or (03) 5289 1732

Triplet Falls in Otway National Park

A hinterland where the towering ash provide a protective canopy over the fern-filled gullies, the Otway National Park offers a cool respite from the surf beaches and rugged coastline.

HISTORY

Due to the rugged nature of the coastline, the park, named after its main feature, Cape Otway, was for many years seen only by passing ships. The lighthouse was built in the late 1840s and soon after loggers pillaged the area for the magnificent mountain ash trees that towered in the forests around Lorne and Apollo Bay. These huge trees were carted to the goldfields during the 1920s. The nearby Angahook–Lorne State Park and the Otway State Forest were also used extensively for logging and it has been reported that, at one time, 29 sawmills worked within 20 km of the dense forest. Unfortunately, farmers also cleared the land for grazing cattle and it was many years before the national park was formed to protect what remained of these magnificent forests.

RAINFOREST

The 12 900 hectare Otway National Park stretches from just west of Apollo Bay 60 km along the coastline to Princetown where it merges with the Port Campbell National Park. The Angahook–Lorne State Park is much larger and its 21 340 hectares extends from Cape Patton along the coastline to Aireys Inlet. These coastal parks are significantly different from the Port Campbell park, the main differences being the impressive mountain ash trees, waterfalls and lush, fern-filled ravines that can be found near the rugged southern coastline.

A high annual rainfall of around 1000 mm is common in these parks due to the towering Otway Ranges and the damp southwest winds from the Southern Ocean. Winter and early spring are the worst times for heavy rain and thick mist, which also make the unsealed roads hazardous. Road closures apply during these times, so check with the ranger before you set out. In late summer and autumn, however, temperatures in the forest are much lower than elsewhere.

The mountain and alpine ash, along with a variety of gums, form a dense canopy, creating a dark, cool environment which, combined with heavy rainfall, provides the perfect rainforest.

Avid birdwatchers will find the satin bowerbird and king parrot, along with the albatross, among the species of bird life in the park, while

LEGEND

Sealed/Unsealed Rd	Caravan Park
Four Wheel Drive	Camping Area
Walks	Accommodation
Rest Area (Picnic Area)	Information
	Fuel Supplies

ANGAHOOK-LORNE STATE PARK

❶ Teddy Lookout
❷ Sheoak Creek Picnic Area ℹ
❸ Sheoak Falls
❹ Blanket Leaf Picnic Area ℹ
❺ Grey River Picnic Area
❻ Mt Defiance Lookout

LEGEND

Sealed/Unsealed Rd .... ●★ 26 ★●
Four Wheel Drive .... ----------
Walks .... ·················
Rest Area (Picnic Area) .... 🏕

Caravan Park .... 🚐
Camping Area .... ⛺
Accommodation .... 🛏
Information.. ℹ
Fuel Supplies .... ⛽

---

there are also many bats in the dense, dark forest. Scurrying across the leaf-littered floor are the echidna and possum, while both the red-necked and swamp wallaby favour this area.

ACTIVITIES IN THE PARKS

In Otway National Park Johanna Beach is very popular, especially in summer when intrepid surfers gather to ride the waves and anglers line

up for the excellent surf fishing. Strong currents make the sea unsuitable for swimming—the nearby lakes and rivers are better suited for this.

An easy, but fairly long, walk for beachcombers is the trek from the Aire River camping area which follows the river then turns south along the coastline, past Point Flinders to the lighthouse at Cape Otway. You can then use the

inland route to return and it should take around 8 hours in total.

A more adventurous and more difficult walk is along the track which starts at Shelley Beach picnic area and heads down towards the mouth of the Elliott River. This 2 hour trek along the short loop explores the rugged coastline.

Off the Great Ocean Road, in the extreme west of the park, is Wreck Beach where a steep flight of steps leads down to the beach. Offshore lie the wrecks of the *Fiji* and *Marie Gabrielle*. The anchors of these 2 ships can also be seen here, while to the west, a walk along the beach from Moonlight Beach, along Pebble Point to Princetown, will give glimpses of the Twelve Apostles located further west along the coast.

Away from the beach and the surf, deep in the forest is the Maits Rest picnic area and a 40–50 minute self-guided rainforest walk.

Rivers such as the Aire and Ford, along with the lakes around the centre of the Otway park area, offer tranquil waters for canoeing and these peaceful waters are also home to the platypus and a large number of birds.

There are numerous hikes in the Angahook–Lorne Park including the moderate 3 hour return journey to Sheoak Falls which extends for a total of 8.6 km, starts at the picnic area and takes in the 15 metre drop of the Sheoak Falls and Castle Rock Lookout before returning. A shorter, easier, trail is to Teddy Lookout where a 40 minute walk takes you across 3 km of the banks of the St George River. Starting at the Allenvale car park this trek offers superb views of the ocean and the surrounding coastline.

ACCESS AND CAMPING

The Lorne park can be accessed from the Princes Highway, then south through Apollo Bay or Lavers Hill. Alternatively, you can take the Great Ocean Road, which cuts through the main section of the park.

Campers are catered for at the beachside Blanket Bay camping area at Point Lewis on the eastern side of the park, where there are picnic tables and toilets. Further west is Johanna camping area near Johanna Beach, an excellent fishing spot, where there are camping sites, picnic tables and toilets.

Aire River south of Lake Craven has camping sites, toilets and picnic tables and is popular with canoeists.

Angahook–Lorne has 7 camping locations along the beach—many of which are suitable for caravans—as well as numerous picnic areas. Access is from the Great Ocean Road or from Deans Marsh via Benwerrin.

Camp sites for both parks can be very popular during the summer holidays and sites should be booked in advance with the ranger.

The Big Tree in Otway National Park

PORT CAMPBELL NATIONAL PARK

IN BRIEF

MAP REFERENCE: PAGE 87 H 9

Location 280 km southwest from Melbourne along the Great Ocean Road

Best Time Winter can be chilly, but the warmer months of the year are ideal

Main Attractions Natural formations such as the Twelve Apostles, Loch Ard Gorge, the Blowhole, Gibson's Steps, London Bridge, Bay of Islands and Mutton Bird Island

Ranger Phone (03) 5598 6369

For camp site bookings at Port Campbell, Peterborough and Curdies Inlet, phone (03) 5598 6364
Glenample Homestead, phone (03) 5598 8209

With large stacks and caves carved into the sandstone cliffs by the unforgiving Southern Ocean, the weatherbeaten coastline of the Port Campbell National Park stands as a headstone for the numerous shipwrecks that lie on the nearby ocean floor.

HISTORY

On the lengthy voyage to and from England, the ruthless southern coastline of Australia was considered one of the worst stretches of the journey, with strong gales and dense fog making navigating through this passage extremely difficult. It was here, along the coastline of the Port Campbell National Park, that many ships ended their voyage and now lie in the shallows, providing a fascination for tourists and divers to the area. The most famous is the *Loch Ard* which was wrecked in 1878 taking the lives of 52 people. Amazingly, 2 survivors were found, along with a superb porcelain peacock which is now on display at the Flagstaff Museum in the coastal town of Warrnambool.

TWELVE APOSTLES—A SIGNIFICANT LANDMARK

Apart from a history of shipwrecks, the 1750 hectare coastal park forms the southernmost coast of Victoria. Over thousands of years the crashing ocean, gales and driving rain have carved stacks, caves and gorges into the imposing limestone cliffs. In contrast, at the western end of the coast, near Peterborough, the tall cliffs disappear and sandy dunes offer the perfect summer retreat, with safe waters for swimming.

Stacks are formed of hardened limestone and resist the battering of the ocean—this is how the Twelve Apostles were shaped. They were once a series of caves on the edge of the coastline, then the softer limestone wore away, leaving just the singular stacks. This was demonstrated in 1990 when the famous London Bridge formation collapsed in one section leaving the bridge standing as an island. Because of the fragile structure of the cliffs, visitors must take care when venturing near lookouts and stay within park boundaries.

The Great Ocean Road represents the border for most of the park, and the road itself was built by returned soldiers during the Depression from 1919 to 1932.

UNDERWATER GRAVEYARD

The best way to take in the delights of the rugged southern coast and to investigate the many shipwrecks is to take the historical shipwreck trail drive from Port Fairy all the way to Lavers Hill. Along this route, following the Great Ocean Road, trail signs will indicate the wreck sites, unfolding many mysteries involving these disasters. Sites visited on this day-long drive include the famous Loch Ard Gorge, as well as Mutton Bird Island and the Twelve Apostles.

The Loch Ard Gorge is one of the most popular attractions and to really appreciate it you should allow at least 3 hours to explore the area.

There are many interesting walks in the

The famous landmark, the Twelve Apostles in Port Campbell National Park

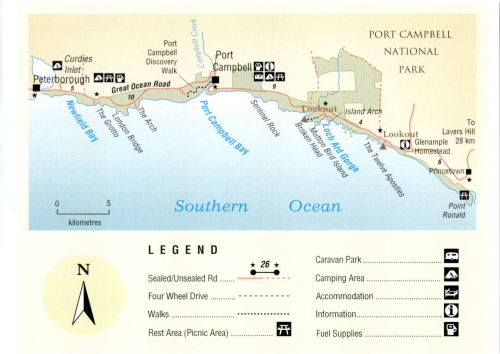

An aerial view of the Twelve Apostles

area, one of these is the Discovery Walk which gives an insight into life on the rugged land edged by the Southern Ocean. The walk is 2.5 km long, of a moderate grade, and will take about 1½ hours. Call into the Parks Centre at Port Campbell where you will find information on other walks.

The famous Glenample Homestead is now open to visitors. This is where the survivors of the *Loch Ard* shipwreck were taken after their rescue.

ACCESS AND CAMPING

Port Campbell National Park lies along the Great Ocean Road, between Princetown and Peterborough, 280 km from Melbourne via the Great Ocean Road, or 240 km via the Princes Highway.

Camping is available at the towns of Port Campbell, Peterborough and Curdies Inlet with all facilities.

Bookings are essential over the main holiday periods.

LEGEND

Sealed/Unsealed Rd ......
Four Wheel Drive ....
Walks ....
Rest Area (Picnic Area) ....
Caravan Park ....
Camping Area ....
Accommodation ....
Information....................
Fuel Supplies ....

SNOWY RIVER NATIONAL PARK

IN BRIEF

MAP REFERENCE: PAGE 91 H 3

Location Far East Gippsland, 390 km from Melbourne, via the Princes Highway
Best Time Year round, though the Snowy River is best in the warmer months
Main Attractions Snowy River, MacKillops Bridge, canoeing, camping, bushwalking, scenic drives, mountain-bike riding, 4WD, fishing, rafting
Ranger Phone (03) 6458 0290 or (03) 6458 1456

Victorian Canoe Association, phone (03) 9459 4277

Flanked by remote wilderness areas, the powerful Snowy River forces its way through deep, rocky gorges forming turbulent white water, cutting through the rugged Victorian High Country before it finally settles into a large, wide, tranquil waterway and trickles quietly south out to the ocean.

A stockyard near Jacksons Crossing

The mighty Snowy River

HISTORY

The Snowy River is known by many Australians because of its contribution to the infamous Snowy Mountains Hydro-Electricity Scheme which redirects about half of the river's water through the turbines to supply power to New South Wales and Victoria. But while the wide banks, covered in small shrubs, tell the tale of a river system that has been robbed of its life-giving source, the Snowy is still ferocious enough to flood towns to the south, such as Orbost.

Perched 256 metres above the river is MacKillops Bridge, the second such construction to span the river at this point. The first bridge was washed downstream only one day before its official opening in 1934, but the new bridge has withstood every fierce flood since.

NATURAL WILDERNESS

Covering 98 700 hectares, this remote alpine area is uncompromising with towering cliffs and harsh grey rock faces looking down on the small river. The narrow, one-lane gravel road winding down from Seldom Seen to MacKillops Bridge is not for the faint-hearted and is akin to a test for visitors to this wild region.

The park is considered to be extremely significant environmentally and its remoteness has allowed 2 wilderness areas to be incorporated within the boundaries. The Snowy River Wilderness lies east of the river while the Bowen Wilderness is on the far northeast of the park.

ACTIVITIES IN THE PARK

While the surrounding countryside is majestic, it is the mighty Snowy River that attracts thousands of visitors to this remote bushland high in the mountains of the Victorian High Country. Canoeing is the best way to appreciate the ruggedness of the river.

Although the Snowy Mountains Hydro-Electricity Scheme takes much of the water

from the river, there are still rugged gorges and rapids to thrill the most experienced canoeist.

The Snowy River can be canoed from the border, north of the park, all the way to Orbost from where it flows out to sea. The first section is from Willis to MacKillops Bridge and this is generally easy with low gradient rapids. The minimum level for paddling is 0.8 metre while the maximum for most would be 2 metres when the river starts to boil. This section, at the minimum height, which is in the peak summer holiday season, should take around 6–7 hours. The next section is from MacKillops Bridge to Buchan and flows through the Snowy River National Park and the adjacent wilderness areas. There are excellent camping areas and 3 gorges which are the highlight of the trip. The minimum water level is 0.7 metre and the maximum 1.1 metres, anything over that should be tackled only by experienced paddlers in closed boats. This section is of an easy to medium standard and should take 3 or 4 days to complete. For more information contact the Victorian Canoe Association.

Canoeists should register at Buchan or MacKillops Bridge before leaving on their journey. Be careful, however, as floodwaters during spring and winter can raise the level of the river by up to 8 metres overnight.

The best walk in the Snowy park is the Silver Mine Walking Track which is a very hard walk, 18 km long and takes 9–10 hours, though it would be better to do it in 2 days and camp alongside the river. A more moderate walk can take in an 8 km section of the Silver Mine Walking Track which takes 4 hours return. Leaflets on the Silver Mine Track can be obtained from the local Parks Victoria office.

A most satisfying and easier walk is the Snowy River Nature Trail which is a 1.5 km trip from MacKillops Bridge, while another is the 400 metre walk to the Little River Falls at the entry to the park on the Buchan–Gelantipy road. Also along this road, before MacKillops Bridge, is the Little River Gorge Lookout, which is only 200 metres off the road and takes only 10 minutes return. Raymond Falls can be accessed from the falls camp site in the south of the park, and the easy 30 minute return walk gives a fantastic view of the waterfall which plunges 20 metres into a deep, clear pool.

Walks in the area should be undertaken in the cooler part of the day, and walkers should ensure they have an adequate supply of drinking water as summer temperatures can soar.

Drivers with 4WD vehicles can take in the drier woodland at the peaks of the ridges of the northern section of the park, along with the temperate rainforests hidden in the folds of the mountains, by taking the Deddick Trail. This 4WD track starts at the Yalmy Road east of Buchan and cuts through the centre of the park for 43 km finishing near MacKillops Bridge. This trek is best completed over a couple of days.

ACCESS AND CAMPING

Park access is either from the Buchan–Gelantipy road to the turn-off past Seldom Seen and onto the road to MacKillops Bridge, or via the 4WD Deddick Trail, which is seasonally closed and runs from the south of the park to MacKillops Bridge. There is also access from the northeast via Bonang and the Bonang–Gelantipy road. The road in, however, is not for nervous drivers as it has very steep drop-offs .

The camping grounds at MacKillops Bridge, Waratah Flat and Balley Hooley have basic facilities; Raymond Falls and Hicks camp sites have none. Camping permits are required.

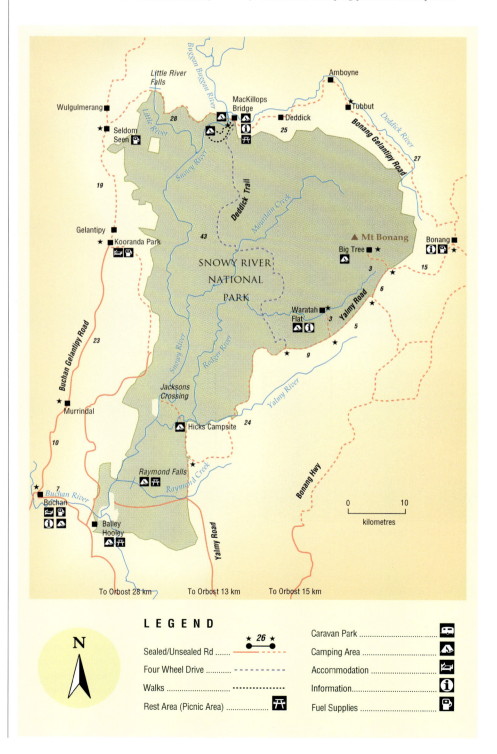

WILSONS PROMONTORY NATIONAL PARK

IN BRIEF

MAP REFERENCE: PAGE 85 N 9

Location South Gippsland on the southern tip of the Victorian coast, 200 km south-east from Melbourne
Best Time Year round
Main Attractions Camping, walking, photography, SCUBA diving, snorkelling, swimming, overnight bushwalking (permit required)
Ranger Phone (03) 5680 9555, or for flat and lodge bookings, phone (03) 5680 9500

Lighthouse tours, phone (03) 5680 8529

The promontory is a huge mass of granite which juts out to form the southernmost tip of the Victorian coastline. The huge granite rocks and pristine unspoilt beaches combine with the extensive mountain range to make this a very attractive and popular national park.

HISTORY

George Bass first sighted this part of the Australian coastline in 1798, but the park, commonly referred to as 'the Prom', once played host to the Brataualong Tribe, who utilised the park's diverse animal and plant life for their own survival.

Emus crossing a road in the Prom

It was the plant life that drew botanist Ferdinand von Mueller to the park on two occasions—1853 and 1876. But the flora and fauna has not always been respected in the history of the Prom.

On the southeast coast, Refuge Cove housed a whaling station in the early 1840s, while further north, Sealers Cove was named by George Bass who, when he sheltered there in 1798, had his men shoot seals for supplies. More than 50 years later, in 1854, a timber mill was established at this cove which employed up to 61 people, supplying timber to the booming

LEGEND

Sealed/Unsealed Rd .... ★ 26 ★
Four Wheel Drive .... - - - - - -
Walks .... · · · · · · ·
Rest Area (Picnic Area) .... ⛱

Caravan Park .... 🚐
Camping Area .... ⛺
Accommodation .... 🛏
Information............................ ℹ
Fuel Supplies .... 🅿

colony of Melbourne.

Since 1898 the park has been preserved, although it has expanded considerably in that time in an effort to escape the commercialism that has enveloped much of Victoria's coastline.

The park was closed to the public, however, during World War II when the large expanse of parkland was used for commando training, with Tidal River used as the base station.

TRANQUIL COASTAL WILDERNESS

The 49 000 hectare park, which encompasses 130 km of coastline, has an immense diversity of landscapes. Huge granite headlands protect secluded white beaches, while marshland and sand dunes gives sanctuary to a multitude of birds. Further inland, the land reaches up to form rugged forested mountain ranges which play host to fern-filled gullies and temperate

The coastline of Wilsons Promontory National Park

pockets of rainforest. Exploring this coastal wilderness will give visitors an appreciation of the beauty of these contrasting elements, including the ocean which laps the edges of this coastal park.

There are over 700 native plants in the park, illustrating the diversity of the flora. Tall euca-lypt forests are perched high in the mountains, with tree ferns and delicate mosses lining the protected gullies. Closer to the ocean, and away from the cooler mountains, the open heathland which blooms in spring extends down to the coastal vegetation which covers the dunes and stabilises them. There are even plants native to Tasmania which have remained in the park from the era when the mainland was joined at this juncture with Australia's most southern state.

WALKS AND WATER ACTIVITIES

Apart from photography, which is a popular pastime in the park, bushwalking is the favoured activity, and the only form of transport, as bicycles are not permitted past vehicle boundaries. There are walks of every degree available, from short 10 minute strolls to the rugged overnight hikes which require overnight permits.

Popular walks include Squeaky Beach to Picnic Bay, which provides excellent views of the coastline and a close-up look at some of the coastal vegetation that thrives in these harsh windswept conditions. With an easy grading, this 3.6 km walk takes only one hour to complete. A more difficult walk is to the Lighthouse which was built by stonemasons in 1859. This 10–12 hour trek takes you from the Mt Oberon car park up to Halfway Hut and through to the Roaring Meg camping area and covers 37.4 km. Much of the journey is over relatively easy heathland. Tours of the lighthouse are available with permission from the keeper.

On the east coast, an energetic walk covers Sealers Cove, Refuge Cove and Waterloo Bay starting at the car park at Mt Oberon. With a distance of 36.6 km it takes 2–3 days to traverse and crosses the width of the Prom.

Close to Tidal River is the Lilly Pilly Gully Nature Walk which starts at the car park and provides a great introduction to the park's plant life. The distance of this walk is 5 km and, with an easy grade, should take only between 2–3 hours to complete.

Many water activities can be enjoyed in the ocean and freshwater streams, including swim-ming, snorkelling and SCUBA diving. Check with the ranger at Tidal River for information.

ACCESS AND CAMPING

The park can be accessed from the South Gippsland Highway via Foster or Meeniyan and Fish Creek.

The Tidal River Village offers the only vehicle access to the park and has camping and caravan sites, along with flats and lodges. Demand for the sites and accommodation is extremely heavy, especially during peak holiday times when a ballot is drawn for allocation of the sites. (Phone the ranger for details.)

Facilities for campers include unpowered sites, fireplaces, kiosk, toilets, showers and picnic tables.

Other more remote camping areas in the park, which are accessed by walking tracks and have toilets, include Oberon Bay which is close to the Tidal River site; Roaring Meg at the south of the park; and Waterloo Bay. Refuge Cove and Sealers Cove are on the lower eastern section, while in the north of the park is Tin Mine Cove.

There is a further handful of sites which have no toilet facilities. These include Johnny Souey Cove, Five Mile Beach, Lower Barry Creek and Barry Creek.

You should be aware that the northern camp sites are often closed in summer due to the lack of fresh water.

WYPERFELD NATIONAL PARK AND LAKE ALBACUTYA REGIONAL PARK

IN BRIEF

MAP REFERENCE: PAGE 88 D 7

Location 450 km northwest of Melbourne, 47 km from Hopetoun
Best Time Autumn and spring, particularly for wildflowers
Main Attractions Walking, cycling, scenic drives, 4WD, birdwatching, wildflower study
Ranger Phone (03) 5395 7221

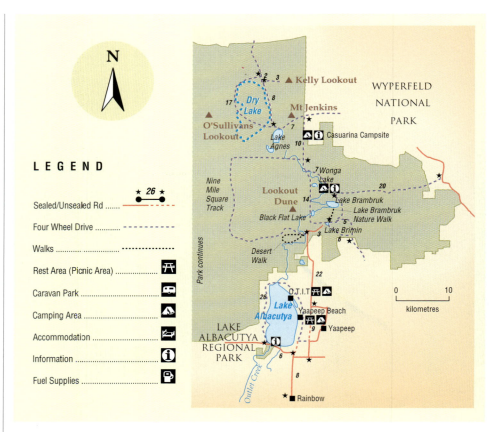

LEGEND

★ 26 ★

Sealed/Unsealed Rd .... ●——●

Four Wheel Drive .... - - - - -

Walks ....

Rest Area (Picnic Area) .... 🎋

Caravan Park .... 🚐

Camping Area .... ⛺

Accommodation .... 🛏

Information .... ℹ

Fuel Supplies .... ⛽

Perched in the arid mallee country of western Victoria lies a sporadic lake system that is host to a myriad birds, such as the sulphur-crested cockatoo and the tumultuous galah.

HISTORY

Before European settlement, Aboriginal people roamed this area as nomads, settling when animal and plant life was flourishing after rains and retreating to the north and the waters of the Murray River during the dry months, where they would trade with other tribes. In the mid-1800s pastoralists started using the area for grazing and wheat growing, but earlier in this century the government established the Wyperfeld National Park. This has now grown extensively from its original size of 3900 hectares, to become Victoria's third largest park covering an immense 356 800 hectares. Lake Albacutya Regional Park covers the small area around the lake and boasts a size of only 8300 hectares.

With much of the northwest of Victoria

Tree roots in the sand

cleared for grazing and wheat farming, this park protects one of the last large expanses of mallee country left in Victoria, but it has been undermined over the years by fire and rabbits. The low-lying growth which covers the sand dunes soon returns, but constant damage from the rabbits has left a scar on the countryside. Extensive regeneration programs, however, should help.

CYCLIC LAKE SYSTEM

The basis of this park is the large number of lakes which are connected by the Outlet Creek which runs north–south through the park. Many years ago the lakes filled on a 20 year cycle, taking 10 years to drain, and then remaining dry for another 10 years until floods came down and gave life to the dry mallee country. But the arid nature of the country that initially drove pastoralists away, motivated them to build irrigation systems further north which helped with the farming, but prevented the lakes and creek system of the Wyperfeld National Park from flourishing. The last flood was the big one of 1975, but even then the lakes drained within 2 years, with only Lake Albacutya holding water for around 9 years.

When rains do fall in the area, large pools of water accumulate in the sand, beckoning kangaroos and emus who graze on the nearby grassy plains. The emergence of water also attracts waterbirds, while the malleefowl makes its nest amongst mounds of rotting leaf litter and sand to incubate its eggs.

Also common to the area are raucous sulphur-crested cockatoos, galahs and many species of parrots, who make their homes amongst the red gum and heathlands that can be found in the park. The most prominent vegetation is, however, the scrubby mallee, which are forms of eucalypts that have adapted to the dry, inhospitable conditions, their stems forming from an underground lignotuber. This root stores food and sends shoots upwards when those above ground finally die off from the effects of the harsh elements. Different mallee species include the red and dumosa mallees, Christmas mallee, and the yellow mallee.

WALKS AND OTHER ACTIVITIES

There are 2 self-guided walks within the Wyperfeld Park, both of which are of an easy standard and 6 km in length, which give visitors a closer look at the flora and fauna of the park region. One trail is located at Lake Brambruk, the other at Black Flat Lake and they take from 2½ to 3 hours return.

Another 6 km circuit is the Desert Walk which is a relatively easy walk along a sandy track near Nine Mile Square. This takes around

3 hours to complete and offers excellent views of the Big Desert and Outlet Creek.

For more remote walks, use Casuarina camp ground as your base and seek local information from the ranger.

Bicycles can be used on the firmer tracks such as the Outlet Creek Track, Lowan Track and Dattuck Track, but other tracks will be too sandy.

Drivers of 4WD vehicles may enjoy this sandy desert country and the park ranger should be contacted for information on available tracks and seasonal closures.

Lake Albacutya is not a national park, so duck shooting is allowed within the seasonal boundaries, which is usually March to May, but check with the ranger. Dogs are allowed on a leash in the camping areas around the lake only.

ACCESS AND CAMPING

The best access is from the Henty Highway, then west from Hopetoun.

There are 3 designated camping sites within the park: Wonga Hut, Broken Bucket and, to the north of the park, Casuarina. Wonga Hut has a picnic shelter, limited water, a washing block, pit toilets and fireplaces. It is suitable for caravans, although there is no power. Broken Bucket has toilets and water, while Casuarina has pit toilets only. Vehicle-based camping is allowed at Wonga Hut and Casuarina. There are also 3 camping grounds on the shores of Lake Albacutya and these have toilets and picnic tables only. All water needed for your stay should be brought in, as water supplies are limited.

Wonga Hut Camping Site in Wyperfeld National Park

AVON MT HENRICK STATE RESERVE
5700 HECTARES

The powerful Avon River provides welcome relief from the harsh summer sun which reflects off rock walls, gorged by this river over thousands of years.

This Gippsland park, only a ½ hour drive from Maffra, is an ideal weekend hideaway, but the area around the Avon River was originally used as a holding ground for cattle in the colder months when the nearby alpine area was under snow. Cattle would be walked from the mountains and through this region before ending up at Bairnsdale where they would be transported by sea.

Perched above Lake Glenmaggie, Pearson Point offers superb views of the sunset over the lake and surrounding farmland. Walking and 4WD tracks lead to this popular rocky outcrop.

The park can be reached from the Newry–Glenmaggie road. Access to Huggetts Crossing is via Green Hills Road.

Bush camping is available along a walking track or an easy 4WD track to Huggetts Crossing, a natural bush camp alongside the Avon River. Pit toilets are nearby and a choice of walks can be made from this area.

Nearby Lake Glenmaggie offers commercial camp grounds.

Gorging its way through the sandstone, the Avon River is the main attraction of the area, with Huggetts Crossing an ideal base for exploration.

Bushwalking, 4WD touring, horse riding and trail-bike riding are among the more popular recreations in this region while the river lends itself to fishing and swimming. The river is subject to sudden flooding, however, and conditions need to be checked beforehand.

Popular walks of moderate standard include the Avon–Henrick 4 hour walk along the Avon River and half-day walks to Mt Henrick, while Golden Point Hut would make an ideal day-drive for 4WD vehicles, or for horseback or motorbike rides.

For further information, contact the ranger, ph: (03) 5148 2355.

AVON WILDERNESS
4000 HECTARES

One of Victoria's first declared wilderness regions, with no vehicle tracks or facilities, this rugged area of Gippsland is a true untamed park for those wanting to get away from modern city life.

Declared a wilderness in the 1980s, this dense forest of shining gum and mountain ash reaches over the subalpine region below the Alpine National Park, south of Lake Tali Karng.

The park is mostly dense bushland, offering walkers an opportunity for remote back-country walking. Because of the lack of tracks, only the very well prepared and experienced should tackle this remote wilderness. Conditions can vary from extremely hot and dry in the summer months, to alpine conditions in the winter with snow falling on the higher peaks. Spring and autumn offer the best conditions.

Access to the park is via the Heyfield–Jamieson road, turning off at Licola. There is no vehicle access into the park.

Remote area bush camping is all that is available with no facilities at all in the park.

Bushwalking, rock climbing and nature study are the recreations catered for within the park. Deer can also be found in the park and stalking is popular in winter.

For further information, contact the ranger, ph: (03) 5148 2355.

BARMAH STATE FOREST
79 000 HECTARES
BARMAH STATE PARK
21 000 HECTARES

The Barmah State Park, in northern Victoria, flanks the Barmah State Forest and, combined with the Moira State Park situated across the Murray River in New South Wales, forms the largest red gum forest in the world. These huge trees are one of the major attractions of the park.

The floodwaters of the Murray River form the wetlands of the Barmah State Park which acts as a breeding ground for a wide variety of bird life and fish which originally attracted the large Aboriginal population to the region.

Barmah can be accessed via the Murray Valley Highway from Echuca to the west or Nathalia to the east. During summer and autumn the whole region is available for recreationalists, but during winter and spring the area floods and even 4WD vehicles cannot access some areas of the park, so check road conditions before making your travel plans.

Camping is allowed at numerous sites throughout the forest, mainly near the Murray River. Because of the fragile wetlands, satisfactory toilet arrangements should be made.

The history of the region and of the Aboriginal people's ancestors can be learned by a visit to the Dharnya Centre just outside the township of Barmah. The Centre is run by the local Aboriginal people with the help of the Department of Conservation and also offers accommodation, phone (03) 5869 3302.

Kingfisher Cruises operate 2 hour cruises on Barmah Lake on Mondays, Wednesdays and Sundays from 12.30 pm. Bookings can be made by phoning (03) 5482 6788.

For further information, contact the ranger, ph: (03) 5866 2702.

BRISBANE RANGES NATIONAL PARK
7517 HECTARES

Situated 80 km southwest of Melbourne, and less than an hour's drive away, this park of rugged gorges and gullies is famous for its spectacular wildflowers during spring.

The Aboriginal Watheuang Tribe once occupied the Brisbane Ranges area and important archaeological sites have been recovered near the Moorabool River along with artefacts which support this claim. In the 1850s gold prospectors inundated the region hoping to strike it rich, but this was short-lived.

With the township of Geelong growing rapidly, 2 dams, the Upper and Lower Stoney Creek dams, were built late in the 1870s to ensure a supply of fresh water .

Nearly a quarter of the state's native flora can be found in this area of Victoria and it is during spring that the mass of colour forms a carpet, softening the rugged ranges.

Access to the park is via the Geelong–Ballan road or Meredith–Steiglitz road. Facilities in the

Red gums in Barmah State Forest

Ruins from the pioneering days in the Brisbane Ranges

park include fireplaces, toilets, water, picnic tables and camping at Boar Gully in the north of the park. Further south, at Stoney Creek and Anakie Gorge picnic areas, you can also find camping facilities including toilets, picnic tables and fresh water.

Bookings should be made in advance during the peak holiday periods and fuel stoves should be taken in rather than lighting fires as firewood is scarce.

During spring, various walks around the camping areas are ideal for viewing the wild-flowers. The most popular walk in the park for day visitors is the Anakie Gorge Trail which extends 3 km through the gorge, taking walkers from the Anakie Gorge picnic area to the Stoney Creek area. This walk is of moderate difficulty and walkers are required to negotiate a number of creek crossings but the return walk can be done in about 1½ hours.

Further on from the Stoney Creek area is the Outlook which can be reached via the moderately graded Outlook Track which climbs for 2 km over the saddle, offering magnificent views of the park.

Panoramic views can also be had from Nelsons Lookout which is accessed via Nelsons Track off the Anakie Gorge walking track. This track climbs upward for breath-taking views of the Anakie Gorge and Lower Reservoir, and

like the Outlook Track, takes around 1½–2 hours return.

For further information, contact the ranger, ph: (03) 5284 1230.

BUCHAN CAVES RESERVE

The small town of Buchan, nestling in hilly farm-land, is very charming, but the main feature that has drawn thousands of tourists for over a century is the large limestone cave system.

The cave system in East Gippsland, north of Lakes Entrance, was first recognised by the government and reserved in 1897, although it was not until 1907 that the Fairy Caves were

Spring in Anakie Gorge in the Brisbane Ranges

discovered by Frank Moon and later that year opened to the public. The Royal Cave was discovered in 1910, but it was 3 years before the public were allowed in for viewing.

Formed by underground rivers cutting their way through the limestone, it is the limestone formations, produced by droplets of the dissolved limestone that form stalactites, stalagmites, and eventually columns, that draw visitors to this magnificent place. For guided tour information, phone (03) 5155 9292.

Access to the reserve is off the Buchan road from Bairnsdale via Bruthen. The reserve has powered and unpowered sites available along with amenities for the disabled. Bookings are required for popular holiday periods.

There are 2 caves in the system that are open to the public for guided tours: Fairy Cave and Royal Cave. Further north of the township visitors may also tour the Shades of Death cave which is off the Gelantipy road.

For further information, contact the ranger, ph: (03) 5155 9264.

BUNYIP STATE PARK AND GEMBROOK STATE PARK
16 550 HECTARES

On Melbourne's doorstep, these parks offer forests, historical sites and wildlife.

While mining and gold fossicking lured the first European settlers to this area, which is east of Gembrook, northeast of Melbourne, the main industry has always been timber harvesting, and a scenic drive through the area will illustrate this. Mortimer Mill once stood proudly at Mortimer Picnic Ground within the Gembrook Park, while at Kurth Kiln Picnic Area an old charcoal kiln still remains. The kiln was built during World War II to produce charcoal from the stringybark forests abundant in the area.

Both forests can be accessed via the Warburton Highway to the north, Gembrook along the Belgrave–Gembrook road, or from the south through Tynong or Bunyip on the Princes Highway.

Numerous picnic grounds are scattered throughout both parks, but the official camping ground is at Kurth Kiln only 6 km from Gembrook, where you will find toilets, picnic tables and fireplaces.

With much evidence of early settlement still in the area, these parks provide the perfect location for fossickers and history studies. The nearby Puffing Billy Railway was originally built to take the timber from the Gembrook area and remnants of the railway can be found at places such as Dyers Picnic Area. The kiln site is also interesting, and offers a number of short walks in the surrounding country.

For further information, contact the ranger, ph: (03) 5968 1280.

CAPE CONRAN FORESHORE RESERVE
500 HECTARES

Offering fishing, surfing, swimming and SCUBA diving, this coastal foreshore reserve is popular with both day users and summer holiday-makers.

With sand, surf, rivers, heathlands, banksia woodlands and the ocean, visitors have the option to sit back and view the magnificent scenery, or participate in one of the many activities available. The energetic may like to stroll through the bush looking for wombats or wallabies, while the warmer weather is ideal for snorkelling or SCUBA diving off the coast. Tides and currents can be strong, especially in the Snowy River and the boat ramp, but Banksia Bluff and Yeerung Beach are ideal for ocean swimming and the Yeerung River can also be traversed by canoe.

The park, situated in far east coastal Gippsland, can be accessed from Orbost or Marlo using the Princes Highway and Cape Conran Road, or Conran–Cabbage Tree Road.

Camping is allowed at the Banksia Bluff camping area where you will find fireplaces, toilets and areas for swimming and fishing. A boat ramp is located at West Cape on the West Cape Road. Also along this road is Salmon Rocks which is ideal for snorkelling and diving. East Cape Beach Picnic Area has facilities for the disabled.

Drivers with 4WD vehicles may like to head along the Yeerung Gorge Road to the gorge while there are many short walks through the heathlands for bushwalkers, including the 5 km track to the gorge.

For further information, contact the ranger, ph: (03) 5154 8438.

CASTLEMAINE HISTORICAL RESERVE
3939 HECTARES

Central Victoria monopolised the state's mineral wealth, and the old goldmining area of Castlemaine is situated right at its very heart.

Throughout the reserve and in the surrounding forest, evidence of the goldmining era is present in the large mullock heaps, scarred hillsides and the open mine shafts that litter the area. During the 1800s the government

Historic Castlemaine

ensured that the Crown retained the land surrounding the township—land that was rich in mineral wealth. Light, scrubby forests of wattle and eucalypts surround the town and form this reserve.

The park is reached via the Pyrenees Highway or the Calder Highway and is about 135 km from Melbourne.

There is no camping in this reserve, but the nearby Vaughan Springs Reserve offers camping and caravan sites, phone (03) 5473 4282.

The main feature of the park is the relics that remain of the mining era, and various walks around the site lead to cyanide tanks, mines and batteries. At the centre of the park sits the Garfield Wheel, south of the Garfield Mine. The remains of this wheel and its enormous axle supports give visitors an idea of the size of the wheel and its potential to drive the large quartz crushing plant.

Other features of the park include 2 water-races and a number of old mullock heaps.

For further information, contact the ranger, ph: (03) 5472 1110 or the Vaughan Springs Reserve ranger, ph: (03) 5473 4282.

CATHEDRAL RANGE STATE PARK
3570 HECTARES

Towering sandstone escarpments overlooking the tranquil Acheron Valley dominate the Cathedral Range State Park only 100 km north-west of Melbourne.

Cathedral Mountain itself is 845 metres high and, combined with the escarpment, is the main feature of the park which was formed in 1979.

The park encompasses the lush growth in the valleys, which contrasts with the drier region in the northwest above the escarpment. This wooded area contains more peppermint trees and receives less rainfall than the lush valley below.

Access is via the Maroondah Highway, over the Black Spur from Healesville.

Camping is popular in the Cathedral Range State Park and there are numerous sites including Neds Gully and Blackwood Flat in the north of the park, which have toilets and fireplaces; Cooks Mill in the centre of the park also has these facilities and access for caravans. Sugarloaf Saddle in the south has toilets only, while the Farmyard has no facilities. Jawbone car park is in the centre of the park near the Cooks Mill camp site.

There are many tracks for walkers in the park, but there is sometimes a fine line between bushwalking and rock climbing. Walking along the track leading to the Sugarloaf Peak involves scrambling up rock faces and can be difficult for the inexperienced walker or climber. There are also many overnight hikes and information can be obtained from the ranger at Alexandra.

Take care on the rocky slopes of the Cathedral Range and seek local information before heading off on any of the longer, more difficult walks.

For further information, contact the ranger, ph: (03) 5772 1633.

COOPRACAMBRA NATIONAL PARK
38 800 HECTARES

Lying on the northern border, in the far east of the state, 500 km from Melbourne and with very few tracks and trails, Cooppracambra is one of the most remote parks in Victoria.

The sandstone gorge formed by the Genoa River is the main feature of this park which, apart from a couple of tracks on the southern and eastern sides of the park, is accessible only by bushwalkers.

The park incorporates the Genoa Wilderness Zone and this section does not allow entry to vehicles, horses, bike riders or canoeists. There are some areas outside the Wilderness Zone where 4WD vehicles and canoeing are allowed.

Access is via the Cann Valley Highway to the west from Cann River, or from the far southeast from the Princes Highway although this access is more suitable for 4WD vehicles. There are no designated camp sites, but bush camping is permitted.

It is the ruggedness of this region that attracts the more adventurous and experienced bushwalkers. The grading of the trails within the park is difficult and those who attempt them should have all the required maps, a compass

and detailed information on the area.

The best walk in the park is one that takes in the delights of the gorge and ventures into the Genoa Wilderness Zone. The return walk can vary, depending on the route selected, between a 2 to 4 day hike, the latter taking in the Yambulla Peak Track. The unpredictable Genoa River must be forded and local information from the Conservation Department should be sought before attempting this walk.

For the less experienced, a 300 metre return walk leads to the Beehive Falls off the Cann Valley Highway on the western side of the park.

For further information, contact the ranger, ph: (03) 5158 0263 or (03) 5158 6251.

ERRINUNDRA NATIONAL PARK
25 600 HECTARES

High on the Errinundra Plateau in northeastern Victoria, 463 km from Melbourne, you will find the largest stand of cool temperate rainforest in the state. Scenic drives and boardwalks help visitors appreciate this priceless beauty.

Sitting right in the middle of timber logging country, this extraordinary park protects a unique forest that has not seen fire for over 150 years. With such beauty, it is surprising that the park was not declared until 1988 when conservationists managed to stop efforts to log the ageing forest.

Most of the park is above 1000 metres and is inaccessible in winter when an abundance of rainfall and snow make the unsealed tracks impassable. With 2 catchment areas skirting the plateau, springtime also sees heavy rain in the park which helps maintain this spectacular rainforest area.

Access is restricted due to wet conditions, when closures will apply. The main entry is via the Errinundra Road from Club Terrace to the south, or the Bonang Highway from the east, taking the Errinundra Road. The main roads into the park are unsealed, winding, and should be driven with caution. They are unsuitable for caravans.

Camping sites can be found at the Gap Scenic Reserve in the north, on the Bonang River near the intersection of the Bonang Highway and the Gap Road. Goongerah Camping Area is to the west off the Bonang Highway and features toilets.

An interpretation display gives a good insight into the park before heading off on the self-guided nature walk. The William Baldwin Spencer Trail cuts through the forest and a guide for this trail and many others is available from the park office in Orbost or the information centre at Cann River.

Be prepared for wet weather, even in the warmer months and bring along a raincoat and a good pair of shoes.

For further information, contact the ranger, ph: (03) 5161 1375 or (03) 5161 1222.

GRANT HISTORIC AREA

The old goldmining towns of Grant and Talbotville offer the perfect base for exploring the surrounding mountain area, on foot or by 4WD vehicle.

More than 100 years ago, the thriving township of Grant was the main regional centre of the goldfields in this remote part of Gippsland, boasting a population of more than 3000. All the buildings have since been bulldozed and buried on this mountaintop, but cemeteries in Grant and nearby Talbotville, along with old chimney stacks and ruins, tell the tale of the hard lives led by the pioneers.

The Grant Historic Area, in the high country in central Gippsland, is 310 km from Melbourne. It is an excellent base from which to explore the sites of the many old goldmining towns which lined the Crooked, Wongungarra and Wonnangatta rivers last century. Old town sites such as Bulltown, Hogtown, Howitville and Winchester and the Old Pioneer Racecourse can all be accessed from Talbotville, although barely any trace of their existence remains today.

The park can be accessed from the Princes Highway at Bairnsdale, then from Dargo.

This reserve and the area surrounding it offer ideal camping locations, especially the old Talbotville township downhill from the Grant site, where you can find a large area of flat, grassy land for camping, an information board, pit toilets and the magnificent Wongungarra River. There is no water at all at Grant itself and while the road is unsealed, access by conventional vehicle is possible to the Grant township site.

Apart from the historical significance of the area, this region offers drivers of 4WD vehicles the chance to ascend steep hills and cross rivers and streams. The Crooked River trail from Talbotville is for experienced drivers and crosses the Crooked River many times before joining up with Bulltown Spur and heading up a very steep hill back onto the McMillan Track which heads back to Talbotville or up to Grant and Dargo. There are good camping sites along this trail near the river. Some tracks are closed during winter, and snow can fall on the peaks.

For further information, contact the ranger, ph: (03) 5140 1243 or (03) 5148 2355.

GUNBOWER ISLAND STATE PARK
2000 HECTARES

Magnificent stands of red gum cover much of this island park which is surrounded by the Gunbower Creek and the Murray River in far northern Victoria, 250 km from Melbourne.

This small park lies in a floodplain of the Murray River where river red gums have established themselves over the centuries, originally used by the loggers as timber for fencing and houses and for fuel for the ships that steamed down the Murray earlier this century.

Access is via the Murray Valley Highway from Echuca or Swan Hill and the Loddon Valley Highway from Bendigo.

There are numerous camping sites along the Murray River, which are accessed via a dirt road which is suitable for conventional vehicles in dry weather, but in wet weather requires a 4WD.

Errinundra Plateau, Errinundra National Park

With so much water, fishing is very popular in this park but Victorian licences must be held for the Victorian waters, while no licence is necessary for the Murray River.

Canoeists can paddle their way right through the forest along the Gunbower Creek and should be rewarded by the sighting of many species of waterbirds.

For further information, contact the ranger, ph: (03) 5452 1237 or (03) 5444 6666.

HOWQUA HILLS AND UPPER GOULBURN HISTORIC AREAS
1300 HECTARES

The Howqua Hills Historical Park in the Central Highlands near Mansfield, along with the Upper Goulburn Recreation Reserve further west at Jamieson, should fulfil those with an insatiable interest in relics from the gold mining era of the last century.

The larger Upper Goulburn Recreation Reserve extends along the Goulburn River and Gaffneys Creek from Jamieson to Walhalla in Gippsland.

Downstream from the Sheepyard Flat camp site at Howqua is an old water-race and brick chimney which was used for the Great Rand Mine, while other mining relics in the area include Mountain Chief and Tunnel Bend where miners dug a 100 metre tunnel through rock in the 1880s to link the Howqua River with their water-race. A short walk off the main road provides access to this tunnel.

Another water-race can be found at Tunnel Bend Reserve off the Jamieson–Woods Point road, along with cemeteries at Aberfeldy and mining relics at historic Woods Point.

Numerous camp sites are located in the Howqua area, the most popular being Sheepyard Flat on the Howqua Track which is an excellent base for exploration.

Camping areas abound in the Upper Goulburn Recreation Reserve, especially along the Jamieson River. These are popular in summer when the river is perfect for swimming.

This area is the base for the famous Annual Mountain Cattlemen's Horse Race and really is an ideal area for horseback rides. Drivers with 4WD vehicles will also enjoy exploring this region with many tracks open year-round, although higher tracks in the mountain country are closed during winter.

For further information, contact the ranger, ph: (03) 5775 2788

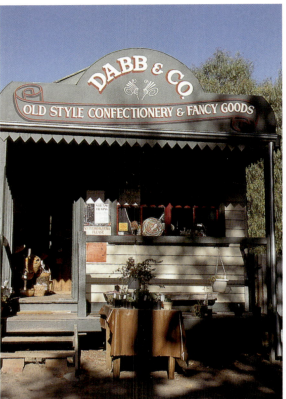
Dabb's General Store in Maldon

LAL LAL BLAST FURNACE
30 HECTARES

Standing defiantly on a hillside southeast of Ballarat is the ruins of the Lal Lal blast furnace, the last of its kind in Australia.

Located within the small park, the furnace is evidence of iron mining in this area last century. The Lal Lal Iron Mining Company was set up in 1873 after the initial discovery of the precious mineral. After experimental blasts, 100 tonnes of pig iron was extracted from the site. The furnace was built in 1881 but it took only a couple of years for the company to realise that the project was not commercially viable and the mine closed down in 1884.

Standing 12 metres high and surrounded by bushland, the furnace is by far the most impressive relic at the site. An information board explains how the furnace was used in the production of iron ore on this industrial site. The furnace is classified by the National Trust and is only one of 4 built in Australia.

To access the Lal Lal Blast Furnace, take the Navigators Road southeast from Ballarat to Lal Lal, then the Iron Mine Road to Blast-furnace Ruins.

There are no camping facilities provided here although there is a picnic ground with toilets, water, a wood fireplace and an information board.

For further information, contact the ranger, ph: (03) 5333 6782.

MALDON HISTORIC RESERVE

Seemingly unchanged since its early days as a goldmining town, historic Maldon township, 136 km from Melbourne, and the surrounding reserve, both educates and charms its many thousands of visitors.

Alluvial gold was first discovered in the area by a German prospector named John Mechosk. This was the start of a gold boom and with subsequent discoveries 40 years later, the prosperity of the miners shows in the township where magnificent old homes sit proudly with their delicate lace trimmings and cool, welcoming verandahs.

The town can be accessed via the Calder Highway out of Melbourne, turning off to Castlemaine, then Maldon.

Butts Reserve on the outskirts of town offers camping with fireplaces and toilets.

The pastime of most visitors is exploring the many mining relics which can be found in the reserve. One of the most interesting is the Beehive Chimney which stands 30 metres high and is situated on the edge of the town. South of Maldon is Carmen's Tunnel which was excavated through the quartz. On completion it boasted an incredible length of 570 metres. Some of the mine sites, such as the North British Mine and South German Mine, are now used as picnic grounds.

For further information, contact the ranger, ph: (03) 5444 6666 or (03) 5472 1110.

MITCHELL RIVER NATIONAL PARK
11 900 HECTARES

Whether on foot, by canoe or 4WD, the Mitchell River National Park offers a remote mountain wilderness just north of the Princes Highway in East Gippsland, 300 km from Melbourne.

Initially this region was owned by the Australian Paper Manufacturers who donated land to the government in 1963 to conserve the area. In 1986 additions were made and the Mitchell River National Park was formed, bringing the park to its present size.

Apart from the river, the best-known feature of this park is the Den of Nargun where a steep walking track, about 1 km long, leads from the car park at the south of the park to a limestone cave featuring stalactites. This car park is the most accessible and most favoured entry into the park.

Access is from the Princes Highway before Bairnsdale, taking the Dargo Road.

Numerous bush camping sites can be found throughout the park, especially along the Mitchell River.

Many visitors come to this Gippsland park to canoe and raft down the Mitchell River; the best time for this is in spring.

Drivers of 4WD vehicles can use tracks in the park including Billy Goat Bend Road which leads to a picnic site and lookout at the Mitchell River, or Adam Track on the east side of the park.

An excellent walking track takes in the Den of Nargun, the Bluff Lookout and the Mitchell River. There are steep sections making this trek moderate to hard. This 3 km trek will take around one hour.

For further information, contact the ranger, ph: (03) 5152 0400 or (03) 5152 6444.

MOONDARRA STATE PARK
6292 HECTARES

This popular picnic area north of Moe in Gippsland is 160 km from Melbourne. It features the remains of an old tramway amongst the densely timbered forest.

The extensive woodland forest in this park is most unusual in that it has a very dense undergrowth of plants such as the wattle, banskia and hakea which provide colourful blooms in springtime.

The southern section of the park is where you will find remains of the old tramway which was once used to haul timber down from the mountains so it could be sent to Melbourne to fulfil the demand for timber during the housing boom in the 1920s.

The park can be accessed by using the Moe–Erica road from Moe.

Remote bush camping sites can be found all through the Moondarra State Park, including the Seninis Visitor Centre at the eastern edge of the park.

When the Moondarra Reservoir was formed it destroyed the township of Gould, but the local hotel was dismantled and re-erected in the picnic ground of the reservoir where it is used as a shelter. Inside you can find old photographs which show the hotel and town in its original setting.

Many 4WD tracks can also be found throughout the park and walking is popular in the nearby Tyers Regional Park.

For further information, contact the ranger, ph: (03) 5165 3204.

A sulphur-crested cockatoo in Mt Arapiles

MT ARAPILES–TOOAN STATE PARK
5061 HECTARES

This isolated mass of rock rises from the surrounding Wimmera flats, enticing adventurous rock climbers and hikers to the quartzose sandstone.

Major Mitchell in 1836 was also drawn to this large rocky outcrop and named the mountain after 2 peaks he remembered from the Spanish battle of Salamanca. A cairn bearing his name can be found on the far western side of the park.

While grazing is carried out in the surrounding countryside, rock climbing has long been the major activity in this park.

Within this State Park, 320 km west of Melbourne, stands Mt Arapiles, known worldwide as one of the best crags available for rock climbers. There are in fact more than 2000 different routes available over, around and atop this large rock formation.

Apart from the rock itself, the weather in this part of Victoria is generally very predictable and fine for most of the year, although the summer months do tend to become very hot, especially against the rock face.

Access is very easy via the Wimmera Highway, with bitumen roads leading to the base of the park and the peak of Mt Arapiles. Centenary Park off Centenary Road offers parking, toilets, picnic area, water and camping sites while other picnic areas include the scenic view and summit areas of the mountain.

Varying climbs are on offer for the beginner through to the most experienced climber. The quartzose sandstone is very stable, and the crevices help provide protection for climbers.

There are numerous climbs including Atriade, Organ Pipes, Voodoo Buttress, Kitten Wall and the Pinnacle Face.

The many walking tracks, varying in their degree of difficulty, also attract visitors to the area. Some of these walks offer an excellent view of climbers hanging from rock faces, and also the caves and chasms that have formed in the rock over millions of years.

Information brochures on climbs and walks can be obtained from the local Department of Conservation.

For further information, contact the ranger, ph: (03) 5381 1255.

MT LAWSON STATE PARK
13 500 HECTARES

On the shores of the Hume Weir, where the mighty Murray flows into this huge reservoir, sits Mt Lawson State Park, just 16 km from the regional centres of Albury–Wodonga and 290 km from Melbourne.

Though fairly large, this park has very few vehicle or walking tracks but it is popular with bushwalkers and rock climbers who trek along the sandy and granite-based soils.

Access for conventional vehicles is via the Murray Valley Highway and the Burrowye and Tallangatta–Mt Lawson roads, or south via the Mt Lawson–Hempenstall road.

There are no designated camp sites in the park, but bush camping is allowed.

The park lends itself to 4WD touring, with a small number of tracks scattered throughout. These include Boulder Track which veers off the main road at the Mt Lawson Lookout and leads back down to the Hume Weir and Murray River Road via Thologolong Track, then either Stockyard Creek Track or Flaggy Creek Track.

This is a year-round destination, but it is very warm in summer.

For further information, contact the ranger, ph: (03) 6071 2604.

MT SAMARIA STATE PARK

Large granite boulders, tumbling waterfalls and rich blooms of wildflowers are what beckons walkers to this park in central Victoria. It lies 13 km north of Mansfield and 130 km northeast of Melbourne.

Early Europeans settled in the countryside

during the mid-1800s, although the rugged plateau did not lend itself well to grazing cattle, ultimately being favoured by loggers.

Extensive logging was carried out in the 1920s on the large stands of messmates, stringybarks, peppermint and other gum trees to support the booming housing industry. The mills didn't last long due to the difficulty of hauling the timber out of Samaria, and most had closed by the time the Depression hit. Ruins of an old sawmill and tram tracks are still evident today. Fortunately the park was declared in 1979 and the logging ceased.

Mt Samaria Road cuts through the centre of the park and halfway along, not far from the road, is the ruins of the Spring Creek Sawmill. Mounds of old sawdust and old kilns are all that remain, but there is a camping area nearby.

The eastern side of the park can be accessed from Mansfield via the Maroondah Highway and Blue Range Road. The western side can be approached from the Midland Highway.

Camp grounds with toilets can be found at Samaria Well at the northern tip of the park, Wild Dog Creek Falls Campsite in the central area, and Camphora Campsite near the south.

An 800 metre walk is required to reach the camp site near Wild Dog Creek Falls and a further hike is necessary to reach the falls themselves. An overnight hike can take you from this camp site, along the Wileman Walking Track, to the Camphora Campsite, before taking in the delights of Back Creek Falls and returning along the Mt Samaria Road to the starting point. This moderate walk covers 9 km return.

For further information, contact the ranger, ph: (03) 5761 1611.

NYERIMILANG PARK

Perched on the shores of the Gippsland Lakes less than 10 km northwest of Lakes Entrance, stands Nyerimilang Park, a combination of forest and formal gardens surrounding the historical Nyerimilang Homestead.

The land which now forms the park was purchased in 1884 and the homestead was originally built as a base for the owners' visitors who would take their fishing and hunting holidays in the Lakes District.

The Victorian Government purchased the land in 1976 and it is now available for day use, offering an important historical display and a variety of walks along bush and farmland tracks with magnificent views across the channel and down onto the lakes, making it an ideal place for family picnics.

Tables are provided and there are toilets and facilities for the disabled near the car park.

The best time to visit the park is spring and summer when the magnificent rose gardens surrounding the homestead are in full bloom

The Victorian High Country

and the sun shimmers on the water below.

Accommodation is plentiful at nearby Lakes Entrance or Metung.

For further information, contact the ranger, ph: (03) 5156 3253.

ORGAN PIPES NATIONAL PARK
85 HECTARES

Towering basalt columns formed from volcanic eruptions millions of years ago are today a fascinating sight for the visitors to this Melbourne park, 25 km northwest of Melbourne.

The size of the park is very small by Victorian standards, but within it stands a dramatic group of columns that reach 20 metres high and resemble the pipes of an organ. These basalt pillars were formed when the lava from an ancient volcano flowed through this land, and cooled within it.

The park was originally set up as a conservation exercise and now, after hard work, most of the weeds have been removed and the parkland is covered in native plants such as bottlebrush, wattles, eucalypts and tea-tree.

There is only a picnic area in the Organ Pipes National Park and access to the park is gained via the Calder Highway from Melbourne.

The volcanic waste, formed many years ago, is now of great geological interest and other basalt formations from the same volcanic eruption, such as tessellated pavements, can also be found in the area. Geological information and a self-guided walking trail are found at the park.

For further information, contact the ranger, ph: (03) 9412 4796.

WALHALLA HISTORICAL AREA

Nestled into a deep valley on Stringers Creek, the small township of Walhalla has survived the decline of the gold mining era to emerge as a popular historic tourist town.

Situated in West Gippsland, 184 km from

Melbourne, the small township still has a handful of residents, although most use the town as a weekend retreat. It is, however, still not supplied with electricity and is the only residential town in Victoria without power—generators are used for lighting. But although most of the prospectors left earlier this century, the town has managed to maintain its heritage value, using it to stay alive.

Many old buildings have been restored and there are numerous ruins to be explored, along with the cemetery and mines. Fossicking is still allowed and the nearby rivers provide an excellent playground in summer.

This town also signifies the start of the well-used Alpine Walking Trail which ends at the ACT more than 760 km from this restored gold-mining town.

Walhalla can be reached by travelling on the Walhalla Road via Moe, Erica and Rawson. Camping is permitted at the North Gardens Camping Ground, the old railway station at the other end of town, and at other locations along the Stringers and Coopers creeks, most of which do not have facilities.

The Long Tunnel Extended Mine was operational from 1865 until 1911 and was the fifth richest in Victoria, bringing in 14 tonnes of gold. It is immense, with 8 km of tunnels descending nearly 1 km underground. Guided tours are recommended through the 300 metre opening into the hillside which leads to a large storage area used for the mining equipment. Another mine with a similar name is the Long Tunnel, which extended even further into the ground to an incredible 1120 metres and as one of the richest gold mines in this state, yielded almost 30 tonnes of the popular mineral.

Many other points of interest make this old town worth visiting.

For further information, contact the ranger, ph: (03) 5165 3204 or (03) 5165 6250.

WARBY RANGE STATE PARK
7600 HECTARES

Occupying a small pocket in the northeast of the state, 237 km from Melbourne, the Warby Range State Park offers spectacular views of the snow-capped Alps in winter and a show of wildflowers amid the impressive giant grass-trees in spring.

The infamous bushranger Ned Kelly is believed to have hidden out in this rocky bush-land near Glenrowan during the 1870s, but it is doubtful that he appreciated the beauty of the region. He was more interested in the huge escarpments and valleys which could easily hide a fugitive and his gang.

Today visitors come to the park to see the open woodland forest and the large grass-trees with the thick black trunk and long, green, grass skirt. The specimens in this park are very impressive, many of them measuring over 5 metres in height.

The Hume Highway passes right past this park which is just out of Wangaratta. Camping sites can be found at Wenhams, an open area at the base of Mt Warby in the south of the park. Facilities there include toilets, picnic tables, fireplaces and water. Picnic grounds include Ryans Lookout, Pine Gully and Briens Gorge Falls.

A number of roads in the park allow visitors to take a scenic drive, stopping off at prominent features such as Briens Gorge Falls, which requires only a short walk, Salisbury Falls and Ryans Lookout. Here a tower enables visitors to catch superb views of Mt Buffalo and the surrounding Victorian Alps—a spectacular sight in winter when they are topped with snow.

Spring and winter are the preferred times to visit, when the creeks are flowing.

For further information, contact the ranger, ph: (03) 5721 5022.

WERRIBEE GORGE STATE PARK
375 HECTARES

Popular with rock-climbing enthusiasts, this rugged gorge is only 5 km west of Melbourne, unspoiled by surrounding development.

It is the ruggedness of this park that has enabled it to survive, forming an environmental enclosure within the ever-expanding city, and has remained unchanged for hundreds of years.

The gorge was formed when movement along a fault-line extended the depth of the Werribee River millions of years ago. Today it is a fascination to geologists, who have studied the area and found that it contains ancient glacial deposits and evidence of volcanic activity.

Access to the park is via the Western Freeway to Portland Hills or via the Bacchus Marsh–Anakie road. The park is for day use, with picnic facilities only.

There are 2 main climbing areas and access to these is through private property so permission must be sought before entering. To get there, drive along the Western Highway to Bacchus Marsh and turn left at the Geelong Road. Before the railway line turn right and follow this until it veers left then take the right branch around the golf course which leads to a steep hill. Head for the gravel road then turn right beyond the railway cutting. Pass under the railway bridge and then stop at the first paddock to seek permission from the property's manager. Access to the climbing necessitates a walk through 2 paddocks. Here you will find 2 areas for climbing—the Amphitheatre and the Pyramid.

Walking, and swimming in the Werribee River, are also popular activities in this park.

For further information, contact the ranger, ph: (03) 5367 2922.

A pied currawong in Warby Range State Park

WHIPSTICK AND KAMAROOKA STATE PARKS
2300 HECTARES

The blue and green mallee trees in the Whipstick and Kamarooka State Parks, north of Bendigo, in central Victoria, 175 km from Melbourne, have for over 100 years been producing eucalyptus oil for distilleries.

The vegetation throughout the Whipstick State Park is extremely diverse, featuring the Whirrake wattle, unique to the Bendigo area, and the succulent blue and green mallee which normally thrives in sandy soil, not the rocky, dry soil found in this region.

These plants, and the open woodlands, provide a home for delightful songbirds, such as the bellbird and grey shrike-thrush. Many other birds inhabit the park, including honeyeaters who feed on the succulent wildflowers in spring.

The park is accessed from Bendigo then the Midland Highway to the east or Neilborough Road from the south.

Camp sites can be found at the Notley and Shadbolt Picnic Areas where there are picnic tables, fireplaces and toilets.

Visitors to these parks can walk through the stunted eucalypts and also visit the old distillery sites. The Whipstick and Kamarooka parks have over the years supplied many eucalyptus factories with their raw product to produce the famous Eucy Oil. Harland's Eucalyptus Factory is located north of Loeser Picnic Area in the north of the park where visitors may join a conducted tour, run on Sundays. The distillery has been operating since 1890 and still produces the popular oil and soaps.

For further information, contact the ranger, ph: (03) 5444 6666.

WHROO HISTORIC AREA
500 HECTARES

Pudding machines (equipment used in the mining industry), the Balaclava Hill Open Cut Mine and various other mining ruins are scattered over this small historical area in central Victoria.

The gold mining town of Whroo (pronounced 'roo') lies 190 km from Melbourne. The town was first established in 1853 and many gold diggers found their way north to the small field in the hope of making their fortune. In its heyday, 2100 residents were working the goldfields but by the end of 1857 the population of Whroo had plummeted to 500 with many moving to other more lucrative fields. There is no water in the area, and this hampered the efforts of the workers.

While the small park does not boast restored buildings, as do Beechworth or Walhalla, it was considered significant enough to be proclaimed a historic site in 1982.

To access the park, take the Hume Highway to Seymour, then follow the Goulburn Highway to Murchison and head west to Rushworth. The Rushworth–Nagambie road and Murchison Road intersect within the park area, 7 km from Rushworth.

Camping facilities in this historical area offer toilets and fireplaces. There are also many picnic sites. Extensive camping is available at Lake Nagambie less than 40 km away.

Walking tracks lead all round the park to features such as the Old Pudding Machine, Lewis Homestead and the cemetery. Balaclava Hill, however, holds the most remarkable feature, an open-cut mine where visitors can descend 30 metres into the cut. This mine produced a great wealth of gold and gold prospecting is still allowed in the Whroo Historic Area, with the correct permits.

For further information, contact the ranger, ph: (03) 5856 1434.

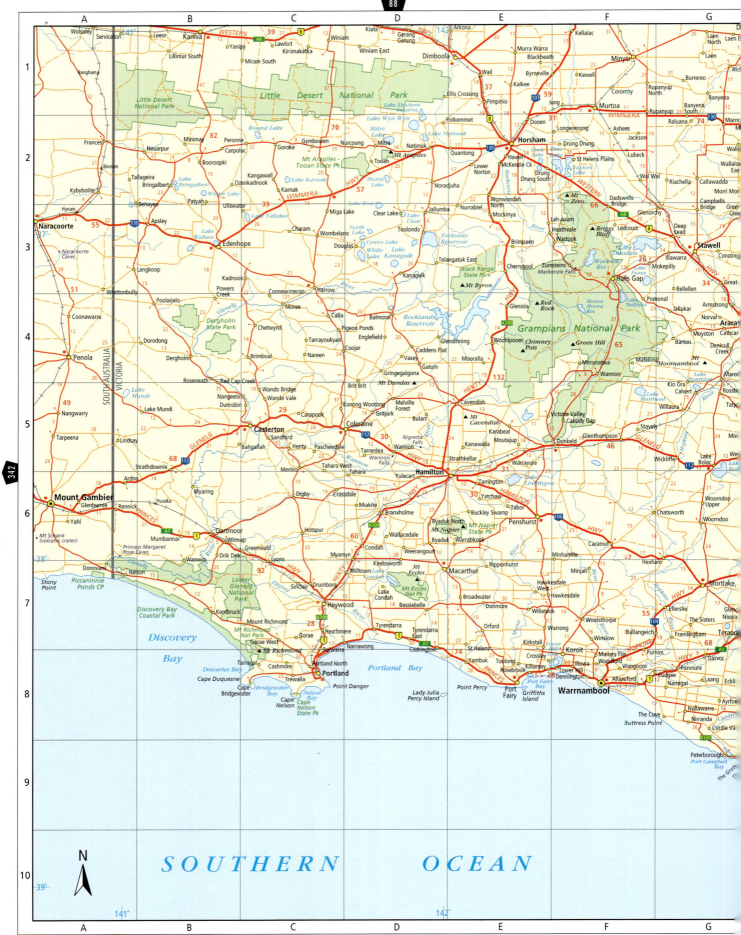

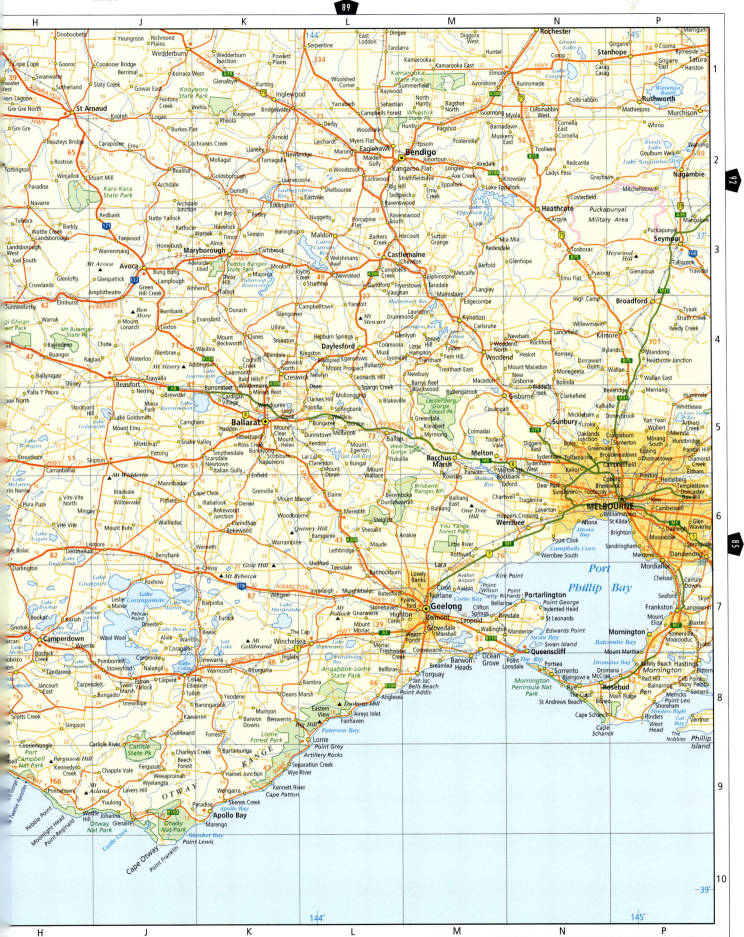

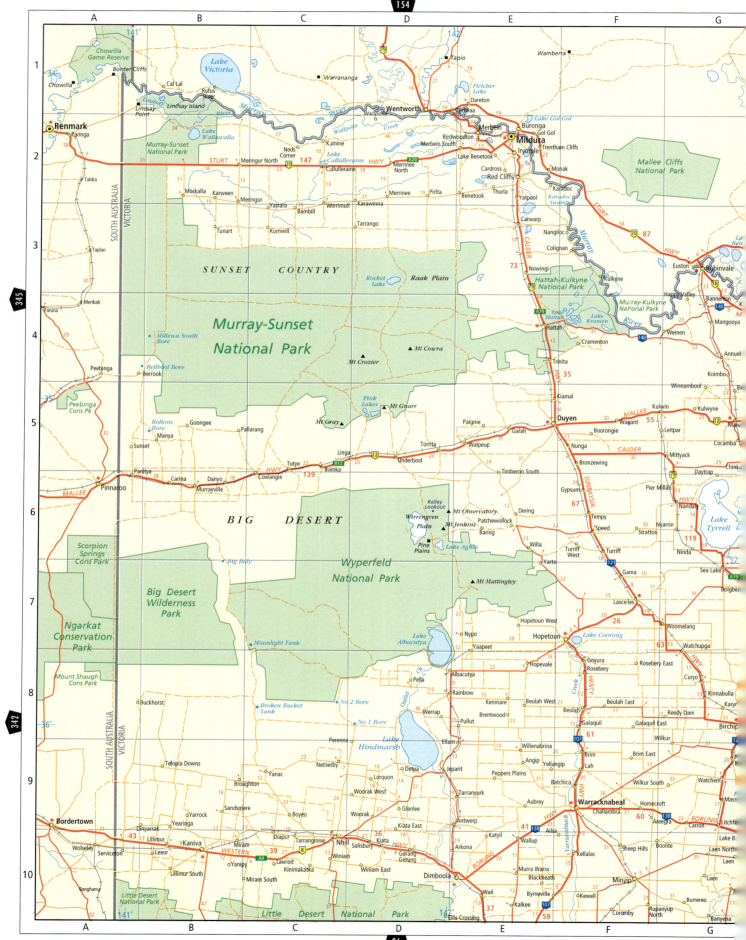

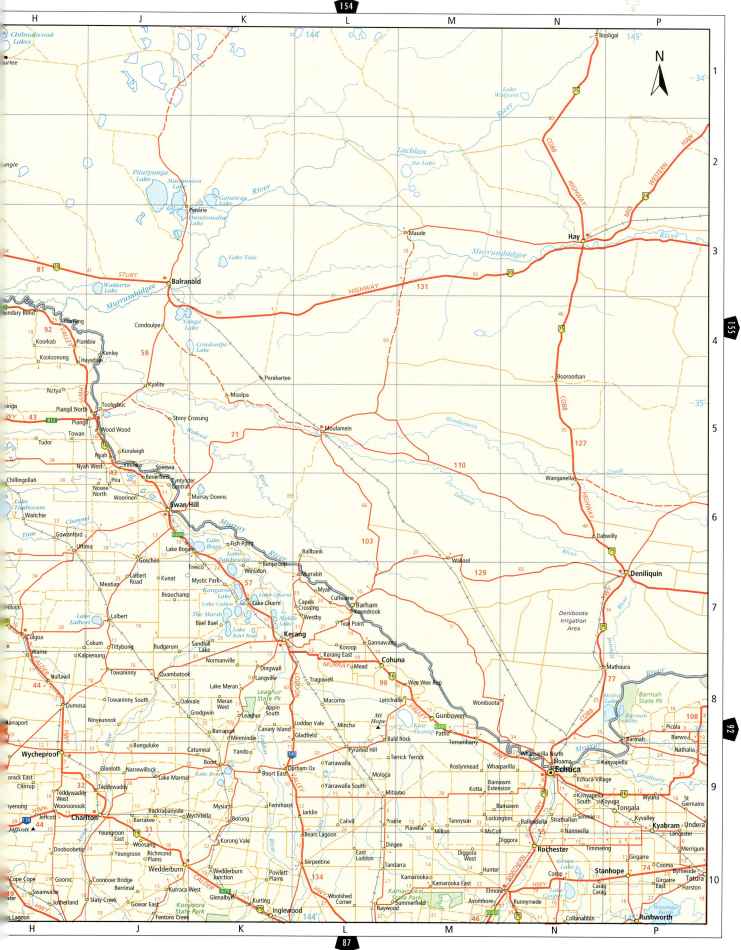

93

92

85

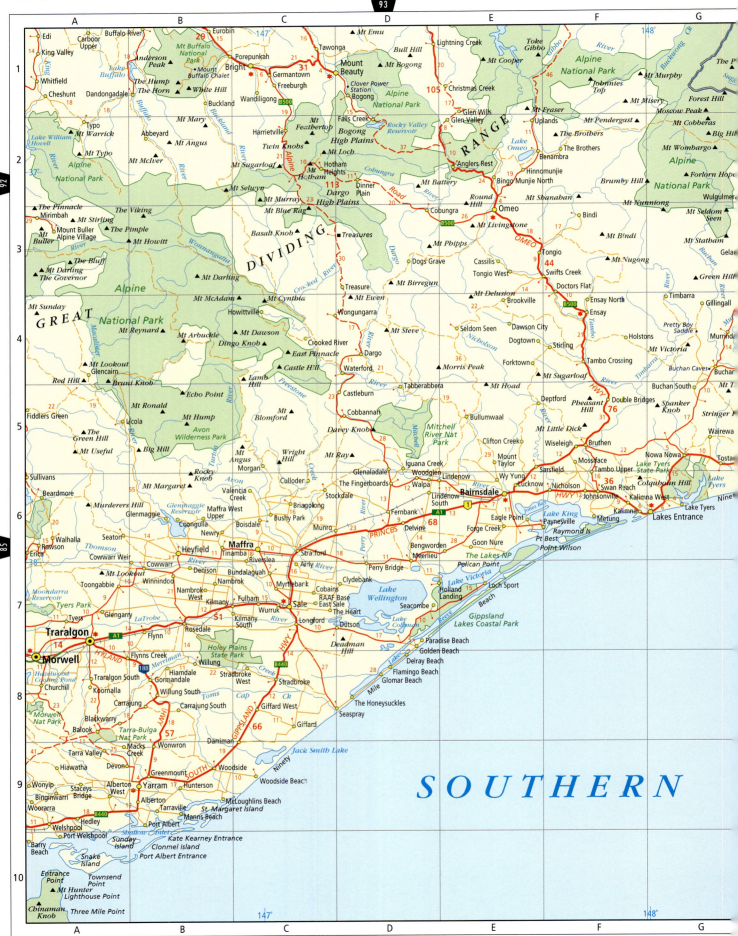

A B C D E F G

Edi
King Valley
Whitfield
Cheshunt
Dandongadale
Typo
Mt Warrick
Mt Typo
The Pinnacle
Mirimbah
Mt Stirling
Mt Buller
Mount Buller
Alpine Village
The Bluff
Mt Darling
The Governor
Mt Sunday
GREAT
Mt Lookout
Glencairn
Red Hill
Fiddlers Green
Licola
The Green Hill
Mt Useful
Sullivans
Beardmore
Walhalla
Rawson
Erica
Tyers Park
Tyers
Glengarry
Traralgon
Morwell
Churchill
Wonyip
Binginwarri
Woorarra
Welshpool
Port Welshpool
Barry Beach
Entrance Point
Mt Hunter
Lighthouse Point
Chinaman Knob
Three Mile Point

Carboor Upper
Buffalo River
Anderson Peak
The Hump
The Horn
Mt Buffalo Chalet
White Hill
Buckland
Abbeyard
Mt Mary
Mt Angus
Mt McIver
The Viking
The Pimple
Mt Howitt
Mt Darling
Mt McAdam
Mt Reynard
Mt Arbuckle
Dingo Knob
Echo Point
Mt Ronald
Mt Hump
Avon Wilderness Park
Big Hill
Mt Margaret
Rocky Knob
Morgan
Murderers Hill
Glenmaggie
Glenmaggie Reservoir
Maffra West Upper
Coongulla
Boisdale
Seaton
Cowwarr Weir
Heyfield
Mt Lookout
Cowwarr
Denison
Toongabbie
Winnindoo
Nambrok West
Kilmany
Rosedale
Flynn
Flynns Creek
Gormandale
Traralgon South
Koornalla
Carrajung
Blackwarry
Balook
Tarra-Bulga Nat Park
Macks Creek
Wonwron
Tarra Valley
Hiawatha
Devon
Staceys Bridge
Alberton West
Yarram
Alberton
Tarraville
Hedley
Sunday Island
Snake Island
Townsend Point

Eurobin
Mt Buffalo National Park
Bright
Porepunkah
Germantown
Freeburgh
Wandiligong
Harrietville
Twin Knobs
Mt Sugarloaf
Mt Selwyn
Mt Murray
Mt Blue Rag
Basalt Knob
DIVIDING
Mt Cynthia
Howittville
East Pinnacle
Castle Hill
Crooked River
Lamb Hill
Blomford
Mt Angus
Wright Hill
Valencia Creek
Briagolong
Bushy Park
Newry
Maffra
Tinamba
Riverslea
Bundalaguah
Nambrok
Fulham
Wurruk
Sale
Kilmany South
Longford
Dutson
Denison
Willung
Hiamdale
Willung South
Carrajung South
Giffard West
Giffard
Darriman
Greenmount
Woodside
Huntterson
Woodside Beach
McLoughlins Beach
St Margaret Island
Manns Beach
Port Albert
Clonmel Island
Port Albert Entrance
Kate Kearney Entrance

Tawonga
Mt Emu
Mount Beauty
Bogong
Falls Creek
Mt Feathertop
Bogong High Plains
Mt Loch
Hotham Heights
Mt Hotham
Dinner Plain
Dargo High Plains
Treasures
Treasure
Mt Birregun
Mt Ewen
Wongungarra
Dargo
Waterford
Castleburn
Cobbannah
Davey Knob
Glenaladale
The Fingerboards
Stockdale
Briagolong
Perry Bridge
Airly
Stratford
Fernbank
Lindenow South
Delvine
Meerlieu
Perry Bridge
Clydebank
Cobains
RAAF Base East Sale
The Heart
Seacombe
Paradise Beach
Golden Beach
Delray Beach
Flamingo Beach
Glomar Beach
The Honeysuckles
Seaspray
Jack Smith Lake
Ninety Mile Beach

Bull Hill
Mt Bogong
Clover Power Station
Alpine National Park
Rocky Valley Reservoir
Cobungra
Mt Battery
Round Hill
Cobungra
Mt Phipps
Dogs Grave
Cassilis
Tongio West
Mt Delusion
Brookville
Seldom Seen
Dawson City
Dogtown
Stirling
Forktown
Morris Peak
Tabberabbera
Bullumwaal
Mt Hoad
Deptford
Clifton Creek
Mt Little Dick
Wiseleigh
Mount Taylor
Iguana Creek
Woodglen
Lindenow
Walpa
Wy Yung
Lucknow
Bairnsdale
Nicholson
Eagle Point
Forge Creek
Goon Nure
Bengworden
Paynesville
Raymond Is
Pt Best
Point Wilson
The Lakes NP
Pelican Point
Lake Wellington
Lake Coleman
Loch Sport
Holland Landing

Lightning Creek
Toke Gibbo
Mt Cooper
Christmas Creek
Glen Wills
Glen Valley
RANGE
Mt Fraser
Uplands
Lake Omeo
Anglers Rest
Benambra
Hinnomunjie
Bingo Munjie North
Mt Shanaban
Omeo
Mt Livingstone
Tongio
Swifts Creek
Doctors Flat
Ensay North
Ensay
Timbarra
Dawson City
Tambo Crossing
Holstons
Mt Sugarloaf
Pheasant Hill
Double Bridges
Bruthen
Mossface
Tambo Upper
Sarsfield
Nowa Nowa
Swan Reach
Johnsonville
Kalimna West
Kalimna
Lakes Entrance
Lake Tyers
Lake Tyers State Park
Colquhoun Hill
Gippsland Lakes Coastal Park

Alpine National Park
Gibbo River
Jobnies Top
Mt Murpby
Moscow Peak
Mt Misery
Mt Cobberas
Big Hill
Mt Wombargo
Alpine National Park
Forlorn Hope
Wulgulmerang
Mt Seldom Seen
Mt Statbam
Green Hill
Buchan Caves
Buchan South
Buchan
Spanker Knob
Stringer
Mt Victoria
Pretty Boy Saddle
Gillingall
Wairewa
Tosta
Lake Tyers

SOUTHERN

© Random House Australia Pty Ltd

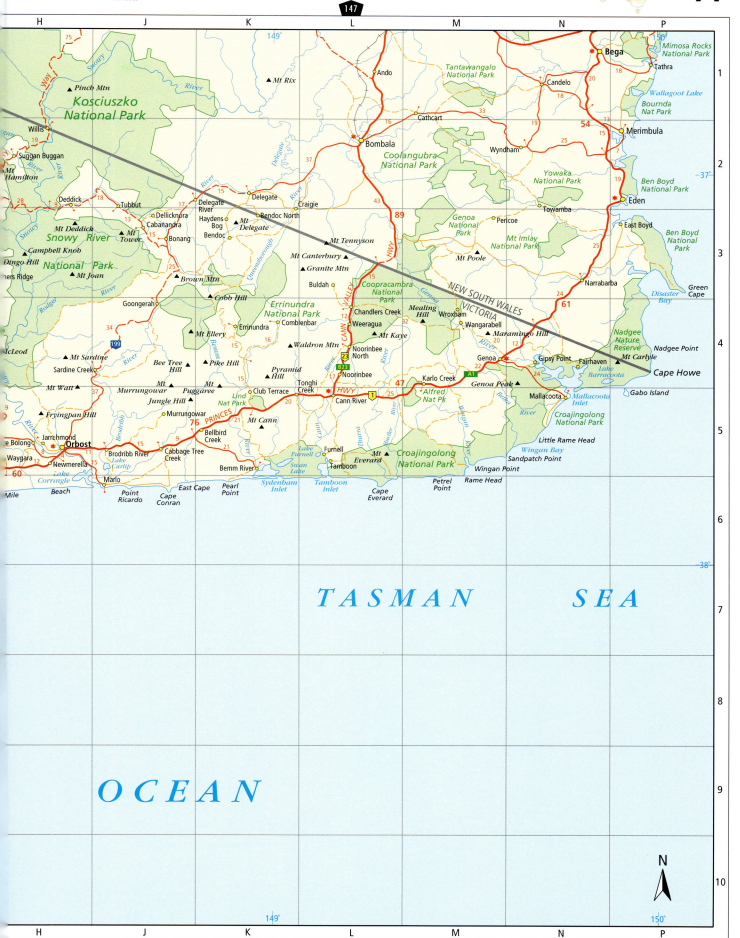

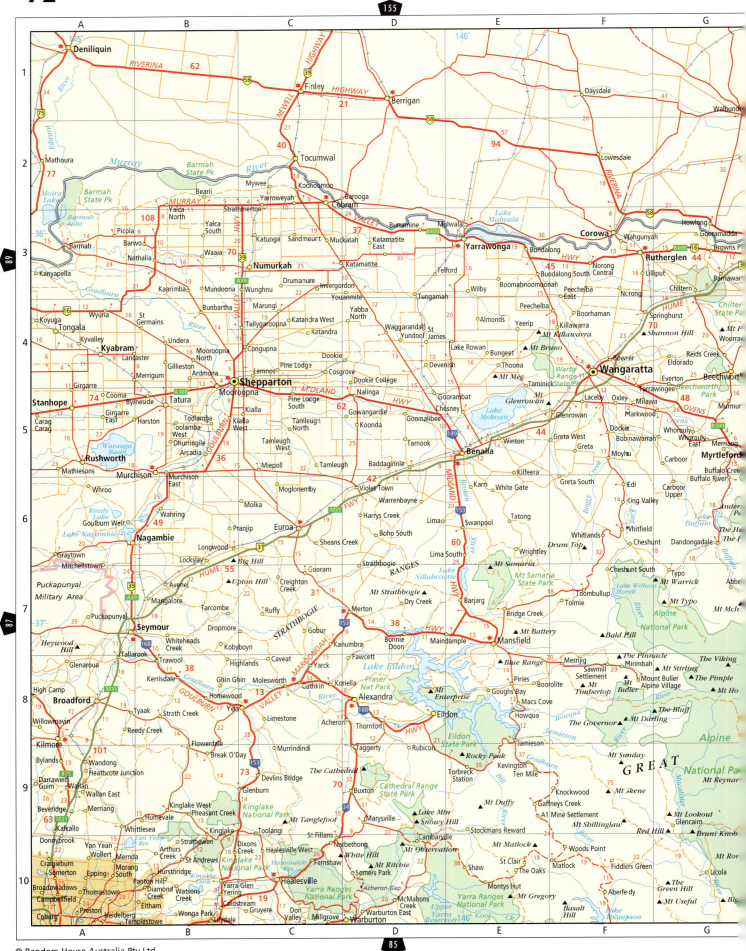

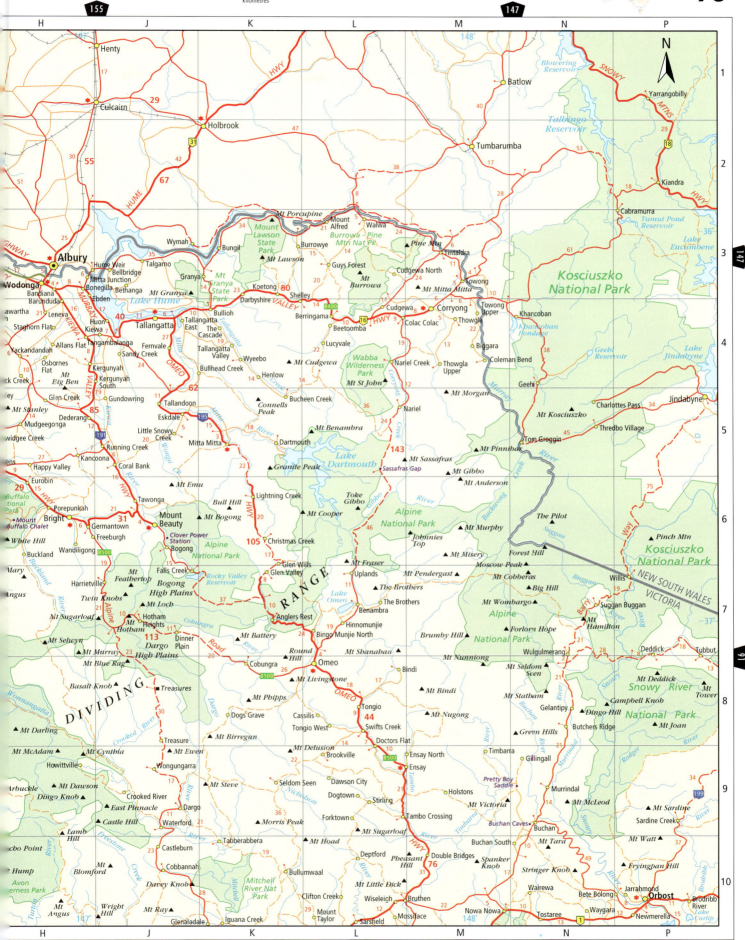

NEW SOUTH WALES

It is fair to say that New South Wales, of all the states in Australia, provides the greatest variety of scenic wonders, diversity of vegetation and opportunities for recreational pursuits. Within the boundaries of New South Wales it is possible to enjoy the true meaning of the Outback, the solitude of a golden beach, the lush growth of a tropical rainforest and the snow-covered mountains of the highest peaks of the continent. No other state can offer such variety.

New South Wales is indeed a wonderland of environmental significance with endless opportunities for those that enjoy the outdoor life. There are World Heritage Listed Areas as diverse as the rainforests of Mt Warning and the lunar landscape of the Walls of China in Mungo National Park. Mix this with the thriving Olympic city of Sydney which is literally surrounded by national parks and compare it to the vast emptiness of Sturt National Park where the kangaroo population far outnumbers the human population and you can begin to understand the boundless opportunities that await the visitor to this great state.

Being the most populated state has ensured the development of some exciting and exhilarating recreational activities. Most national parks in the state are well prepared to satisfy the

needs of its visitors. Within the boundaries of the greater Sydney Metropolitan Area there are several parks that cater specifically for the city-based visitor. Such places as Ku-ring-gai Chase National Park and the world's oldest national park, Royal National Park, are laced with excellent walking trails. These are combined with the various water activities for which Australians are so well known: swimming, canoeing and fishing each provide countless hours of entertainment.

The parks within New South Wales also feature our Aboriginal heritage with excellent art sites found in many of the sandstone caves that are so common in the parks around Sydney. In the Outback, where the summer sun beats down relentlessly, there are artefacts and middens that are the very earliest indications of Aboriginal occupation of a land that has long since changed. Many of our parks also provide a window to our recent European connections. There are blazed trees left by Charles Sturt at

Nelson Beach in Mimosa Rocks National Park

Depot Glen in Sturt National Park, huts in the High Country built by men as tough as nails and even recognition of where it all started for European man at La Perouse. Modern history is also preserved within our parks with one of the greatest engineering feats in the history of mankind, the Snowy River Scheme, literally built within the boundary of Kosciuszko National Park.

New South Wales has set up a large number of national parks. In fact, the recently opened South East Forest National Park now provides a

Mungo National Park

continuous link of parks from the Victorian border to the outskirts of Sydney. It is possible to plan a motoring holiday along the Great Dividing Range that would take easily two weeks to complete if you were to visit every park along this mighty mountain range. The coastal areas are equally well protected under the national park environmental cloak with vast areas of the coastal forests on the far south coast included in the state's park protection. One of the most fascinating places in the country and yet one that still remains little known is the Murramarang National Park just north of Batemans Bay. Here the kangaroos and wallabies are so tame that they are found sleeping on the beaches of Pebbly and Durras. Overseas tourists would flock to see this type of spectacle and yet it remains relatively hidden in a quiet forest area on the south coast.

If your interests include bushwalking in remote areas with breathtaking scenery, it is impossible to ignore the opportunities provided in two of New South Wales' wild and remote parks. The Blue Mountains National Park is just an hour west of Sydney. It has the highest visitor figures of any park in the state and yet to truly enjoy its grandeur it is necessary to pull on a backpack and walking shoes. For those with the time and the energy the walks into the deeply eroded sandstone valleys of the Blue Mountains will provide an enthralling experience. However, it is the Morton National Park inland from Ulladulla on the south coast that provides the most awe-inspiring scenery. Experienced walkers talk of this area as if they have visited another planet. The giant monoliths, sheer cliffs and hidden valleys that very few people have seen, are so unexpected and strange that they will leave their mark on the memory.

Many of the state's national parks are havens for adventure activities. The Blue Mountains are renowned for their adventure sports such as canyoning, rock climbing, abseiling and canoeing. For a real adrenalin rush it is hard to beat abseiling off a 100 metre high sheer cliff face. Some of the country's best whitewater rafting is available in the Nymboida National Park on the north coast, whilst the Shoalhaven River on the south coast, where it passes through Morton National Park is reputed to be one of the toughest whitewater rafting experiences that one can undertake.

But it is the vast opportunities available to the average family that set the parks of New South Wales apart from others. Almost every park has access by conventional vehicles to superb picnic areas, camping grounds and walking trails. Here it is possible to enjoy that great Australianism of having a BBQ lunch whilst the sounds of nature quell the stresses of a busy lifestyle. In many of the parks close to

Sydney there are large clearings where families can be seen each weekend enjoying a game of cricket, kicking a soccer ball or flying a kite.

Many of the parks provide avenues for the new urban explorer in a 4WD to venture into seemingly remote parts with the family or friends to escape the rat race even further. Some parks are acknowledged havens for

A rainforest scene in the Watagan Mountains

sensible 4WD touring where the greatest pleasure comes from pitching a tent beside a crystal clear creek whilst black cockatoos wheel overhead. At night wombats go about their business of foraging along the river bank as excited kids with torches try vainly to keep silent. In the morning the mist rises slowly from the river bed and it is possible to grab a fleeting glimpse of a platypus floating gently on the river's surface. These are typical scenes in Deua and Wadbilliga National Parks.

In the north of the state the parks embrace some of the world's best surfing beaches. Places such as the Seal Rocks area in Myall Lakes National Park, Crowdy Bay and Bundjalung National Parks become a mecca for the surf-loving set in school holidays. However, a visit to these same beaches outside of these times will find deserted beaches that stretch to the horizon. Myall Lakes is renowned for its pure white sands and the dolphins that play in the

surf. Excellent camp sites are found on the shores of the lakes that teem with prawns and it is hard to beat a golden sunset over the lake as you lounge back in a hammock.

It is important to remember, though, that the parks are provided to protect the sensitive, ecologically valuable assets of New South Wales. We need to recognise the importance of these areas and treasure the opportunities to see and enjoy them. At all times, when travelling in a park, be mindful that you play a crucial role in maintaining the park's pristine value. This is easily done by never leaving any rubbish, carrying out that left by other, less-caring people, not disturbing the wildlife or flora and avoiding delicate areas in wet weather.

New South Wales is indeed fortunate to have some of the most spectacular scenery in the country. Its diversity, intricacy and beauty will leave you spellbound. Add to this the increased opportunities to explore and enjoy such areas of beauty and you can begin to realise some of your dreams, whether they be a desire to stand on the summit of Mt Warning as the first rays of a new day reach mainland Australia, or ski across the rooftop of the country on Mt Kosciuszko, tramp through the ancient peat swamps of Barrington Tops or watch an eagle swoop on a joey in Sturt National Park.

NEW SOUTH WALES NATIONAL PARKS AND RESERVES

	Ranger/Park Tel.	Ranger/Information	Camping	Caravan	4WD Access	BBQ/Fireplace	Picnic Area	Marked Walking Tracks	Bushwalking	Kiosk/Restaurant	Fishing	Swimming
1 Bald Rock National Park	(02) 6732 5133	*	*			*	*	*	*			
2 Barrington Tops National Park	(02) 4987 3108		*		*	*	*	*	*			*
3 Ben Boyd National Park	(02) 6495 4130	*	*			*	*	*	*			*
4 Blue Mountains National Park	(02) 4787 8877	*	*		*	*	*	*	*	*		*
5 Boonoo Boonoo National Park	(02) 6732 5133		*			*	*	*	*			*
6 Boorganna Nature Reserve	(02) 6584 2203					*	*	*	*			
7 Booti Booti National Park	(02) 6554 0446	*	*	*		*	*	*				*
8 Border Ranges National Park	(02) 6628 1177	*	*			*	*	*	*			
9 Botany Bay National Park	(02) 9668 9111	*				*	*	*				
10 Bouddi National Park	(02) 4324 4911	*	*			*	*	*	*		*	*
11 Bournda National Park	(02) 6495 4130	*	*	*		*	*	*	*		*	*
12 Brisbane Water National Park	(02) 4324 4911	*	*			*	*	*	*		*	*
13 Broadwater National Park	(02) 6628 1177				*	*	*	*				*
14 Broken Head Nature Reserve	(02) 6628 1177	*	*				*	*				*
15 Budawang National Park	(02) 4887 7270	*					*	*				
16 Budderoo National Park	(02) 4236 0469	*				*	*	*	*			
17 Bundjalung National Park	(02) 6628 1177	*	*	*	*	*	*	*	*			*
18 Bungonia State Recreation Area	(02) 4887 7270	*	*		*	*	*	*	*			
19 Burning Mountain Nature Reserve	(02) 6543 3533	*				*	*	*	*			
20 Cadman's Cottage Historic Site	(02) 9247 8861	*					*					
21 Cathedral Rock National Park	(02) 6657 2309		*			*	*	*	*			
22 Cattai National Park	(02) 4572 8404	*	*			*	*	*	*	*	*	*
23 Cecil Hoskins Nature Reserve	(02) 4887 7270					*	*	*				
24 Cocoparra National Park	(02) 6962 7755	*	*			*	*	*	*			
25 Conimbla National Park	(02) 6331 9777	*				*	*	*	*			
26 Crowdy Bay National Park	(02) 6584 2203	*	*	*		*	*	*	*		*	*
27 Davidson Whaling Station Historic Site	(02) 6495 4130	*					*					
28 Deua National Park	(02) 4476 2888	*	*		*	*	*	*	*			*
29 Dharug National Park	(02) 4324 4911	*	*		*	*	*	*	*		*	*
30 Dorrigo National Park	(02) 6657 2309	*				*	*	*	*	*		
31 Garawarra State Recreation Area	(02) 9542 0666		*			*	*	*	*			
32 Garigal National Park	(02) 4451 3479	*				*	*	*	*	*		
33 Georges River National Park	(02) 9772 2159	*				*	*	*	*	*	*	*
34 Gibraltar Range National Park	(02) 6732 5133	*	*	*		*	*	*	*			*
35 Glenrock State Recreation Area	(02) 4987 3108	*				*	*	*	*		*	*
36 Goulburn River National Park	(02) 6372 3122	*	*			*	*	*	*			
37 Guy Fawkes River National Park	(02) 6657 2309	*				*	*	*	*			*
38 Hartley Historic Site	(02) 6355 2117	*					*			*		
39 Hat Head National Park	(02) 6584 2203	*	*	*		*	*	*	*		*	*
40 Heathcote National Park	(02) 9542 0666	*					*	*	*			*
41 Hill End Historic Site	(02) 6331 9777	*				*	*	*	*	*		
42 Illawarra Escarpment State Recreation Area	(02) 9542 0666	*				*	*	*	*			
43 Iluka Nature Reserve	(02) 6642 0613	*					*	*	*			*
44 Jervis Bay National Park	(02) 4443 0977	*	*		=	*	*	*	*	*	*	*
45 Kanangra Boyd National Park	(02) 6336 1972	*	*		*	*	*	*	*			*
46 Kinchega National Park	(02) 8088 5933	*	*	*	*	*	*					
47 Kings Plains National Park	(02) 6732 5133	*							*			
48 Koonadan Historic Site	(02) 6962 7755	*				=	*	*				
49 Kosciuszko National Park	(02) 6450 5555	*	*	*	*	*	*	*	*	*	*	*
50 Ku-ring-gai Chase National Park	(02) 9457 8900	*	*			*	*	*	*	*	*	*
51 Lane Cove National Park	(02) 9412 1811	*				*	*	*	*	*		*
52 Limeburners Creek Nature Reserve	(02) 6584 2203	*	*			*	*	*	*		*	*
53 Little Llangothlin Nature Reserve	(02) 6732 5133											
54 Macquarie Pass National Park	(02) 4887 7270					*	*	*	*			
55 Mann River Nature Reserve	(02) 6732 5133	*				*	*	*	*			*
56 Maroota Historic Site	(02) 9457 9322	*						*				
57 Marramarra National Park	(02) 9457 9322	*				*		*	*		*	*
58 Mimosa Rocks National Park	(02) 4476 2888	*	*			*	*	*	*		*	*
59 Montague Island Nature Reserve	(02) 4476 2888	*										
60 Mootwingee National Park & Historic Site	(02) 8088 5933	*	*	*	*	*	*	*	*			
61 Morton National Park	(02) 4887 7270	*	*		*	*	*	*	*	*		
62 Mother of Ducks Lagoon Nature Reserve	(02) 6773 7211	*				*	*	*	*			
63 Mt Grenfell Historic Site	(02) 6836 2692					*	*	*	*			
64 Mt Imlay National Park	(02) 6495 4130	*					*	*	*			
65 Mt Kaputar National Park	(02) 6792 4724	*	*			*	*	*	*			
66 Mt Warning National Park	(02) 6628 1177	*				*	*	*	*			
67 Mt Yarrowyck Nature Reserve	(02) 6773 7211					*	*	*	*			
68 Mungo National Park	(02) 5023 1278	*	*	*	*	*	*	*	*			
69 Munmorah State Recreation Area	(02) 4358 1649	*	*	*		*	*	*	*		*	*
70 Murramarang National Park	(02) 4423 9800	*	*	*		*	*	*	*	*		*
71 Muttonbird Island Nature Reserve	(02) 6657 2309	*					*	*	*			
72 Myall Lakes National Park	(02) 4987 3108	*	*	*		*	*	*	*		*	*
73 Nalbaugh National Park	(02) 6495 4130	*					*		*			
74 Nangar National Park	(02) 6331 9777	*					*		*			
75 Nattai National Park	(02) 4677 2873					*	*	*	*			*
76 New England National Park	(02) 6657 2309	*	*			*	*	*	*			
77 Nightcap National Park	(02) 6628 1177	*				*	*	*	*			
78 Nungatta National Park	(02) 6496 1434				*				*			
79 Nymboida National Park	(02) 6732 5133							*	*		*	*
80 Oxley Wild Rivers National Park	(02) 6773 7211	*	*		*	*	*	*	*			*
81 Parr State Recreation Area	(02) 4324 4911	*			*		*	*	*		*	
82 Royal National Park	(02) 9542 0666	*	*			*	*	*	*	*	*	*
83 Sea Acres Nature Reserve	(02) 6582 3355	*					*	*	*	*		
84 Seven Mile Beach National Park	(02) 4423 9800	*				*	*	*	*		*	*
85 Sturt National Park	(02) 8091 3308	*	*	*	*	*	*		*			

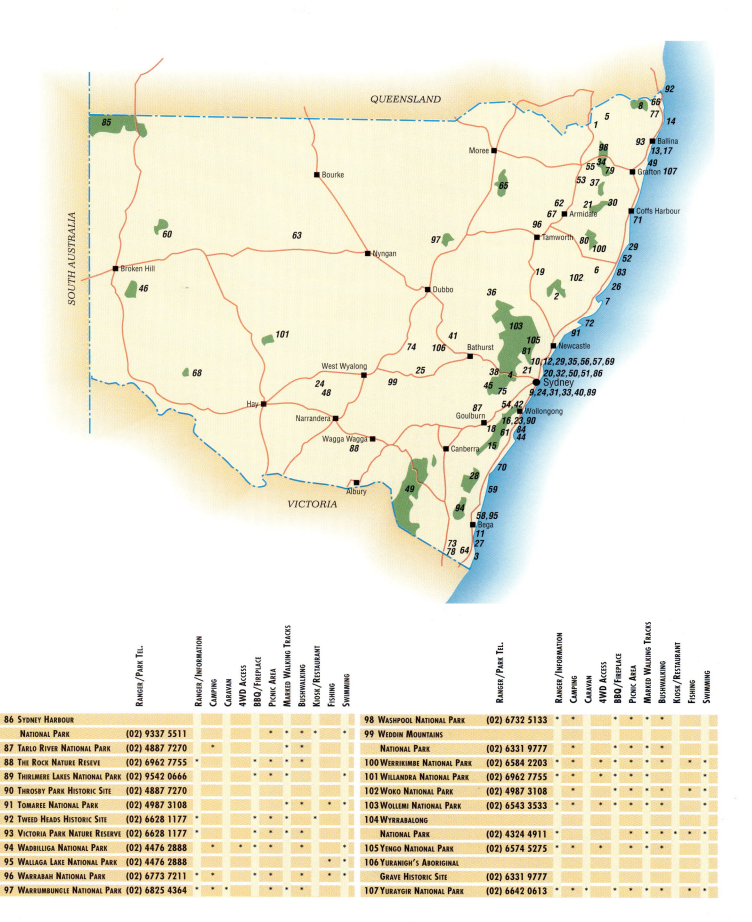

	RANGER/PARK TEL.	RANGER/INFORMATION	CAMPING	CARAVAN	4WD ACCESS	BBQ/FIREPLACE	PICNIC AREA	MARKED WALKING TRACKS	BUSHWALKING	KIOSK/RESTAURANT	FISHING	SWIMMING
86 SYDNEY HARBOUR NATIONAL PARK	(02) 9337 5511					*	*	*	*			*
87 TARLO RIVER NATIONAL PARK	(02) 4887 7270	*				*	*					
88 THE ROCK NATURE RESERVE	(02) 6962 7755	*			*	*	*	*	*			
89 THIRLMERE LAKES NATIONAL PARK	(02) 9542 0666					*	*	*				
90 THROSBY PARK HISTORIC SITE	(02) 4887 7270											
91 TOMAREE NATIONAL PARK	(02) 4987 3108					*	*		*		*	*
92 TWEED HEADS HISTORIC SITE	(02) 6628 1177	*				*	*	*		*		
93 VICTORIA PARK NATURE RESERVE	(02) 6628 1177	*				*	*	*				
94 WADBILLIGA NATIONAL PARK	(02) 4476 2888	*	*		*	*			*			*
95 WALLAGA LAKE NATIONAL PARK	(02) 4476 2888										*	*
96 WARRABAH NATIONAL PARK	(02) 6773 7211	*	*		*	*	*		*		*	
97 WARRUMBUNGLE NATIONAL PARK	(02) 6825 4364	*	*	*		*	*	*	*			
98 WASHPOOL NATIONAL PARK	(02) 6732 5133	*	*		*	*	*	*	*			
99 WEDDIN MOUNTAINS NATIONAL PARK	(02) 6331 9777	*	*		*	*	*	*				
100 WERRIKIMBE NATIONAL PARK	(02) 6584 2203	*	*		*	*	*	*	*		*	*
101 WILLANDRA NATIONAL PARK	(02) 6962 7755	*	*		*	*	*		*			*
102 WOKO NATIONAL PARK	(02) 4987 3108	*	*		*	*	*		*		*	
103 WOLLEMI NATIONAL PARK	(02) 6543 3533	*	*		*	*	*	*	*		*	*
104 WYRRABALONG NATIONAL PARK	(02) 4324 4911	*				*	*	*	*		*	*
105 YENGO NATIONAL PARK	(02) 6574 5275	*	*		*	*	*	*	*		*	*
106 YURANIGH'S ABORIGINAL GRAVE HISTORIC SITE	(02) 6331 9777						*					
107 YURAYGIR NATIONAL PARK	(02) 6642 0613	*	*		*	*	*	*	*		*	*

BARRINGTON TOPS NATIONAL PARK

IN BRIEF

MAP REFERENCE: PAGE 149 J 3

Location 320 km north of Sydney and 30 km west of Gloucester

Best Time Summer and spring; winter is cold and many trails are closed

Main Attractions Great bushwalks, dramatic scenery, 4WD

Ranger Phone NPWS (02) 4987 3108; State Forests, phone (02) 6558 1005; Gloucester Information Centre, phone (02) 6558 1408

Accommodation: The Barrington Country Retreat, phone (02) 4995 9269; Barrington House, phone (02) 4995 3212; Gloucester Caravan Park, phone (02) 6558 1720; Hookes Creek Forest Retreat, phone (02) 6558 5544

Tour Operators: Barrington Outdoor Adventure Centre, phone (02) 6558 2093; Barrington River Lodge, phone (02) 6558 2093; Camp Cobark, phone (02) 6558 5224; Forest Escapes, phone (02) 6558 3197; Great Divide Tours, phone (02) 9913 1395

A cloak of grey mist and a chill wind indicate that at this altitude an early snowfall is possible. A mob of brumbies moves slowly up ahead and disappears into the trees. This scene is typical of the Barrington Tops.

A forest scene in the Barrington Tops

A mountain brush-tail possum

HISTORY

The rugged nature of the Barrington Tops has virtually precluded human exploration of the Tops. Steep gullies, impenetrable vegetation and the freezing cold weather of the higher peaks were not conducive to early settlement. There were at least 4 different Aboriginal tribes that occasionally ventured into the rugged mountains—or the Hunter district as we know it.

European history commenced with timber getting, particularly the prized red cedar that was found in the moist gullies of the lower ranges. Forestry practices grew and most of the trails that exist today were forged during the 1920s. Large sections of the Tops are protected under National Park legislation and in recent times World Heritage status has been granted.

THE PARK'S ATTRACTIONS

A major drawcard of the Barrington Tops is the clean, fresh air. But add to this a vast array of walking tracks, superb scenery and lookouts, magnificent wildflowers and spectacular rainforest, snow gums and peat swamps and it is easy to say that Barrington offers everything. The park covers more than 40 000 hectares that vary from snowplains to impenetrable forests dissected by raging rivers with some wonderful waterfalls. The many different species of flora and fauna over this varied landscape are a feature of the park.

It reaches to over 1500 metres which assures regular snowfalls during winter and even the occasional summer dusting.

The national park is surrounded by vast areas of State Forest which also cater to the tourist with provision of trails, camping and picnic areas.

THINGS TO DO

The Barrington Tops provide a wide variety of activities, the main ones being camping and bushwalking. There is a very good network of walking trails throughout the park. Some are easy short walks whilst others are demanding and involve overnight camps in high altitude areas. If contemplating any type of bushwalking it is essential that you are prepared for very wet and cold weather, even in summer.

Anglers will find trout in the mountain streams but check with local National Parks and Wildlife Service (NPWS) personnel regarding permits and seasons.

The area has always been a mecca for drivers with 4WD vehicles but recent track closures and wilderness declarations have greatly reduced these opportunities. Check with the NPWS and State Forests as to access.

In the lower reaches of the mountains rafting and canoeing are favourite pastimes on the Barrington, Cobark and Gloucester Rivers. There are many tour operators providing guided walks, 4WD tours and canoeing trips. Contact the local Information Centre at Gloucester for details.

ACCESS

Access into the Barrington Tops area is best split into 3 major routes. Vehicle access from the south via Dungog or Gresford leads to the well-known Barrington Guest House and its superb walking trails. This also provides access to the State Forest areas of Chichester Dam and Telegherry Forest Park where excellent picnic and camping facilities are available. Both areas are readily accessible by conventional and 4WD vehicles although caution in wet weather is necessary when some roads may be impassable to conventional vehicles.

From the east, access is via Gloucester to either the Gloucester Tops or further west into the area's highest peaks along the Scone to Gloucester road. A conventional vehicle will access the major camp sites at Gloucester Tops and the State Forest camp site at Polblue Swamp. In winter this road can be closed due to snow and would be dangerous without a 4WD.

If approaching from the west, travel via Scone and Moonan Flat before ascending the range on the Scone to Gloucester road. This is the most direct route to the more remote camp sites around Careys Peak and the Big Hole. Once you leave the Scone road near Polblue camping area it is important that you heed the 4WD only signs and avoid the area in wet conditions. Check with the NPWS before setting out.

CAMPING

There is a wide range of camping opportunities in the Barrington Tops. If you are bushwalking, it is possible to camp virtually anywhere, as long as you are more than 300 metres from a trail or official camp site. For those who wish to camp with their vehicle there are well-maintained camping sites in the southern section, in the Chichester State Forest, at Telegherry Forest Park and Allyn River Forest Park. In the Gloucester Tops region is a well maintained but more restricted camping area. This area is very popular and you should check availability with the NPWS in peak holiday periods.

The camping in the highest region of the Tops is subject to dramatic weather patterns and visitors should be prepared for freezing weather and snow as well as prolonged wet and foggy conditions. The State Forest camping area at Polblue Swamp is excellent. Nearby walking trails and fishing in the creek are just some of the activities that can be pursued. There are camping sites at Junction Hole and the Big Hole which are favoured by the more adventurous bushwalkers and it would be wise to check with the NPWS for availability and access.

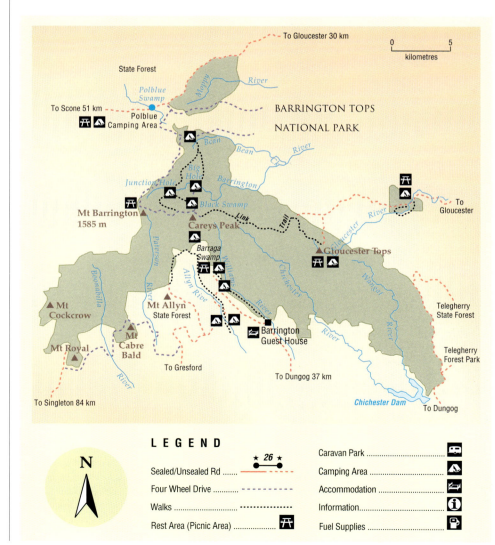

BEN BOYD NATIONAL PARK

MAP REFERENCE: PAGE 147 E 9

Location Far south coast of NSW, on either side of Eden, via the Princes Highway
Best Time Summer, early autumn and late spring
Main Attractions Historic sites, crystal-clear inlets and beaches, beautiful forests
Ranger Phone (02) 6495 4130

Camping: Book through the NPWS, Merimbula, phone (02) 6495 4130

LEGEND

Sealed/Unsealed Rd .... ★ 26 ★	Caravan Park ....
Four Wheel Drive .... - - - -	Camping Area ....
Walks .... ··········	Accommodation ....
Rest Area (Picnic Area) .... 🛆	Information.....................
	Fuel Supplies ....

The park covers an area of 9400 hectares but is separated by Twofold Bay and the town of Eden on the south coast of New South Wales. Each segment provides unique features. The southern section is of major historic interest with Boyds Tower and ruins of the bygone whaling era, while the northern section contains coastal flora and a unique formation known as the Pinnacles. Here fragile sand gullies capped with red clay form an unusual eroded gully off Long Beach.

HISTORY

Ben Boyd National Park was the scene of Australia's main whaling operations. Whaling began in 1828 and continued for 100 years. The 3 Imlay brothers established their commercial and pastoral activities on a scale unknown in the area today. The brothers controlled 100 000 hectares of pastoral land around Twofold Bay. They built a whaling station on the bay and used the port to ship cattle all over the new colony.

In 1843 the economic decline saw an end to the Imlays' reign but a new name came into prominence: Benjamin Boyd. He established a whaling fleet in Twofold Bay which also became the centre of a prosperous shipping trade. Boyd also became a major land owner and left his mark with the construction of Boyds Tower on Red Point. Boyd's business collapsed and he eventually left the area in 1849.

HISTORIC SITES AND WALKS

The history of the area has been preserved by the National Parks and Wildlife Service (NPWS) who are now responsible for the maintenance of Boyds Tower as well as the other historic sites such as the Davidson Whaling Station.

There is an excellent tour of the nearby woodchip mill which is conducted on Thursdays.

There are some great walks in the northern section of the park with a trail leading from Haycock Point to the headland overlooking the mouth of the Pambula River. This walk is 6 km long and you should allow 2 hours to complete it. The 1 km nature trail to the Pinnacles is the best way to see these colourful formations but make sure that you collect the helpful Pinnacle Walk leaflet from the NPWS office in Eden. Another interesting walk is along the beach from Quondolo Point to Haycock Point, a distance of 3 km return.

ACCESS

Access to the northern section is very easy with the park boundary just a few kilometres north of Eden off the Princes Highway. To access the walking trails to the Pinnacles travel 8 km north of Eden and follow the Haycock Point turn-off until the Pinnacles track is seen on your right.

Access to the southern section of the park is found by following the Princes Highway south

Saltwater Bay in the southern section of Ben Boyd National Park

A wonga pigeon in Ben Boyd National Park

from Eden to the Edrom Road. Once on the Edrom road you will find a network of roads that lead to all the major points of interest including the restored Davidson Whaling Station, Boyds Tower, Saltwater Bay, Bittangabee Bay and Green Cape Lighthouse.

Access to both sections of the park is possible in conventional vehicles.

CAMPING

There are no camping facilities in the northern section but basic facilities are provided at Saltwater Creek and Bittangabee Bay with pit toilets and fireplaces. It would be wise to carry your own water to either site. Bookings for camp sites in holiday periods are essential and can be made through the NPWS office in Merimbula.

Camping at the pretty bays of Saltwater and Bittangabee allows plenty of time to fish and explore the beautiful coast.

BLUE MOUNTAINS NATIONAL PARK

MAP REFERENCE: PAGE 148 F 8

IN BRIEF

Location 100 km west of Sydney via the Great Western Highway

Best Time Spring, summer and autumn

Main Attractions Superb lookouts, walking trails, wildflowers in spring; walks, abseiling, rock climbing and canyoning

Ranger Contact the NPWS at the Blue Mountains Heritage Centre at Govetts Leap, phone (02) 4787 8877 or the Visitor Centre at Glenbrook, phone (02) 4739 2950

The NPWS conduct many guided tours under their Discovery program. These include interpretive walks, night-time tours, trips for the kids and talks around the campfire. For details, contact the Blue Mountains Heritage Centre at Govetts Leap, phone (02) 4787 8877

The NPWS also have extensive information on all walking trails

Abseiling, rock climbing and canyoning tours: Contact Blue Mountains Adventure Company, phone (02) 4782 1271

Horse trail rides in the Megalong Valley: Packsaddlers, phone (02) 4787 9150 and Werriberri Trail Rides, phone (02) 4787 9171

Tours of the mountains: Blue Mountains Tour Guides, phone (02) 4751 5946

A view from the Blue Mountains escarpment

a fiery sunset reflect off the giant cliff faces, or dangling precariously on the end of a rope as you abseil down a waterfall into a valley from the Jurassic era.

HISTORY

The sandstone which forms the dramatic scenery was originally deposited by river systems that drained into a coastal plain more than 275 million years ago. Then 50 million years ago the area was uplifted, forming the Great Dividing Range. Volcanoes added to the dramatic scene before the weathering process began to etch the landscape. The deep gorges and towering cliffs of today are the result of this continual weathering action.

The mountains formed a natural barrier to the early settlers in Sydney. A route over the mountains had not been found until 1813 when Blaxland, Wentworth and Lawson stumbled across the only possible route. The rich plains to the west ensured that a rough road was quickly

The Blue Mountains National Park has the highest number of visitors of any park in New South Wales. It is little wonder considering it is virtually in sight of Sydney, being only 100 km west of the Harbour Bridge. It has some of the most spectacular scenery of any of Australia's parks. It is a favourite with many overseas visitors who are as familiar with photographs of the Three Sisters as they are with Uluru.

The visitor to Blue Mountains National Park will be astounded at the raw beauty of the sandstone cliffs and the deep gorges. There are many activities to pursue in the mountains including sitting in an opulent bed and breakfast sipping champagne and watching

The Lost City, Deep Pass in the Blue Mountains National Park

cut into the thick, scrubby bush that clung to the sandstone plateaus. The present-day Great Western Highway follows closely the route of the first coach trail. At Mt York the coach track followed a switchback route down the ridge line to the Hartley Valley. It is possible to follow this track on foot from Mt York, and you will marvel at the ability of the horse-drawn carriages to negotiate the steep grade.

The mountains remained sparsely populated until 1868 when the Great Western Railway opened. This brought the scenic beauty of the mountains within reach of the growing Sydney population and the area was quickly recognised for its tourism value. As early as the 1890s reserves were established to protect the natural areas within the mountains. The Blue Mountains National Park was proclaimed in 1959.

There is a great deal of evidence of Aboriginal occupation in the form of art sites and grinding-stone marks in the sandstone cliffs which have been dated back 14 000 years.

MAJOR ATTRACTIONS

There are a number of activities to occupy you in the Blue Mountains, ranging from simply sightseeing at the many excellent lookouts, to bushwalking deep in the Grose Valley, abseiling off the sheer sandstone cliffs or canyoning and whitewater rafting. Tourism is big in the mountains and there are plenty of options in relation to accommodation and unusual ways to enjoy the natural wonders. A good example is the Scenic Railway with its near vertical drop and the Skyway cable car that stretches across deep, fern-filled gullies.

The most famous attraction in the mountains is the Three Sisters rock formation. Situated within the confines of the town of Katoomba, there is very easy access, parking being the only problem due to the huge number of tourists that flock to the area. For something completely different you could try rock climbing or abseiling on one of the Three Sisters and there are plenty of adventure companies based in the mountains that can assist you in this pursuit.

Bushwalking is another great activity and the park has many wonderful trails. Some are quite easy and include the scenic lookouts while others require a degree of fitness and an overnight camp as they extend into deep river valleys. The National Parks and Wildlife Service (NPWS) have excellent publications detailing the many walks and giving their degree of difficulty and duration.

THINGS TO DO

Around the major towns of Katoomba, Leura and Blackheath there are excellent lookouts accessible by everyone. There is the already mentioned Three Sisters where there are

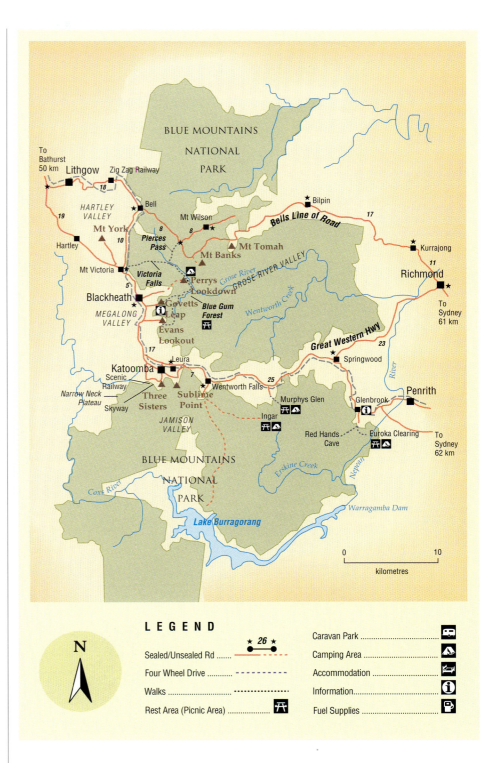

viewing platforms, walks to the base of the rock formations and a well-stocked information and souvenir shop. From Katoomba it is possible to follow the cliff drive which passes several other lookouts over the Jamison Valley as well as some great picnic locations both east and west of Katoomba. Along this route you will find the Skyway and the Scenic Railway. At Leura there are several excellent lookouts over Sublime

Point and these are amongst the best in the park and are within an easy 5 minute walk from the car park.

In the Glenbrook area there are good walks with views over the Nepean River as well as hand stencils to view at Red Hands Cave. Abseiling off the cliffs in this part of the park is also popular and every weekend you will find groups enjoying this exhilarating pastime.

The view from Cahill's Lookout near Katoomba

There are a number of adventure tour companies who can safely take you on abseiling trips off huge cliffs, rock climbing expeditions or canyoning through narrow gorges where waterfalls plunge into deep pools of icy cold water.

West of Katoomba, around Blackheath, there are several roads out to lookouts above the Grose Valley. This is one of the most spectacular regions as the rock faces of the cliffs are several hundred metres high. The better known lookouts include Evans, Govetts Leap, Perrys Lookdown and Victoria Falls. There are several easy walking trails along the top of the escarpment which will occupy at the most 2 hours.

The most renowned walks in the Blue Mountains are those that descend into the Grose Valley from Govetts Leap and Perrys Lookdown. You will need to be fit to tackle the steep trails and you must always be prepared for dramatic changes in the weather. Because the mountains are at quite a high altitude sudden temperature drops and even snowfalls are common. Heavy rain can cut tracks in the valleys and the area should be avoided in this type of weather. There are several walks in the Grose Valley with the Blue Gum Forest being one of the better known attractions. If you are planning a walking trip into the Grose Valley it is suggested that you contact the Heritage Centre at Govetts Leap to obtain maps and advice on your intended walk. It is very wise to let someone reliable know of your intended route and time of return in order to avoid unnecessary searching.

There are some good lookouts off the Bells Line of Road also. These are found a few minutes off the main road at Pierces Pass, Mt Banks and Mt Tomah where there are the excellent high country botanical gardens.

ACCESS

The park lies to the west of Sydney and is best accessed along the Great Western Highway. It stretches in the east from Glenbrook, virtually at the foot of the mountains, to west of Katoomba near Mt Victoria where the road descends onto the western plains. Its northern boundary is the Bells Line of Road where the Wollemi National Park continues northwards and its southern section stretches all the way to Wombeyan Caves, west of Mittagong.

The park has 3 distinct regions: the Glenbrook section covering the lower Blue Mountains down to Lake Burragorang and west to Wentworth Falls; the southwestern section which includes the Jamison Valley and the Three Sisters, and is the most remote area, extending south towards Kanangra Boyd National Park and on to Wombeyan Caves; and the northern section between the Great Western Highway and the Bells Line of Road which includes the Grose Valley and contains some of the best lookouts and walking trails.

CAMPING

It is best to look at each area individually. The Glenbrook section is primarily a day-use area but there is a camping ground at Euroka Clearing. Accessed from the park entrance at Glenbrook it is necessary to book your site and pay a small fee at the Glenbrook Visitor Centre. There are also camping locations at Ingar and Murphys Glen which are accessed off the highway at Wentworth Falls but it is a 5 km walk to Murphys Glen as it is closed to vehicle access. Camping elsewhere in the Glenbrook section is not encouraged.

In the northern section, or the Grose Valley, there is one official camp site at Perrys Lookdown. This is accessed off the Great Western Highway at Blackheath. There are toilets and BBQs but you should bring your own water. This section of the park is very popular with bushwalkers; however, bush camping is permitted in only 2 places in the Grose Valley— Acacia Flat and Burra Korain Flat. In other areas outside the Grose Valley it is possible to bush camp—away from roads and walking trails.

As an alternative there is access off the Bells Line of Road to Burralow Creek where there is a large grassy camping area. The road to this location is gravel and a little rough in places but it does provide car-based camping. It is possible to follow the fire trail all the way up to Kurrajong which makes it a round trip. Look for the track 1 km east of the Fruit Bowl at Bilpin on the Bells Line of Road.

The southern section is much more remote and if you are walking in this area you will need to be very experienced, with overnight bush camping a certainty. Camping within 3 km of Lake Burragorang is not permitted as this is the catchment for Sydney's water supply. It is important to note that, despite their clean and fresh appearance, all streams in the Blue Mountains are polluted with run-off from residential areas on the plateaus. Travellers are strongly advised to boil all water.

Narrow Neck Plateau in the Blue Mountains National Park

BORDER RANGES NATIONAL PARK

IN BRIEF

MAP REFERENCE: PAGE 151 N 2

Location 140 km southwest of Brisbane
Best Time March to November
Main Attractions Walks, wilderness, wildlife
Ranger Phone (02) 6628 1177

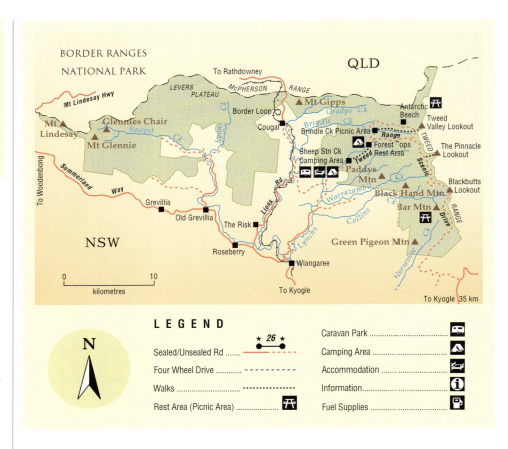

BORDER RANGES NATIONAL PARK

LEGEND

★ 26 ★

Sealed/Unsealed Rd ....
Four Wheel Drive ....
Walks ....
Rest Area (Picnic Area) ....

Caravan Park ....
Camping Area ....
Accommodation ....
Information.........................
Fuel Supplies ....

This unique 30 000 hectares of rainforest wilderness straddles the Queensland–New South Wales border and shares a common boundary with the better known Lamington National Park to the north.

The rugged Border Ranges region was once the centre of tremendous volcanic activity. Throughout time, the plateau has eroded, creating great corridors and deep gullies. A number of prominent pinnacles (volcanic plugs)—The Pinnacle near the Wiangaree escarpment, and Glennies Chair, which protrudes from the slopes of Mt Glennie—have escaped weathering.

For most of this century the forests of the Border Ranges were a major source for the timber fellers who supplied the sawmills in the surrounding district.

THE PARK'S ATTRACTIONS

In the lower parts of the park around Sheep Station Creek, eucalypt forests with an understorey of bracken fern dominate the landscape. This area is home to large numbers of grey kangaroos and red-necked wallabies which can often be seen feeding. Keen-eyed bushwalkers may sight a koala around here during the day.

The Tweed Range scenic drive rises sharply after leaving Sheep Station Creek. The road winds up through the lush rainforest for about 60 km. The gravel road can be comfortably covered in about 2 hours. Because of the park's high rainfall, road conditions are often slippery and drivers should be extremely careful.

Pademelon wallabies inhabit the thick undergrowth here and can usually be seen in the early morning near the forest edge. The potoroo also lives in the damp undergrowth, but is only occasionally seen due to its timid nature.

Upon leaving the Forest Tops rest area, the road winds through cool temperate rainforest which is dominant in the higher areas. Gnarled Antarctic beech trees tower above the ever-moist, moss-clad forest floor. Panoramic views of the Tweed Range can be enjoyed from some of the park's impressive escarpments. Picnic areas and lookouts are studded along the rim of the gigantic ancient caldera of Mt Warning.

Logrunners, scrub-turkeys, white-browed scrubwrens, noisy pittas and whipbirds scratch through the leaf litter on the rainforest floor. Lucky hikers may even get a glimpse of the rare Albert's lyrebird darting across the track. In the canopy above, wompoo fruit-doves, topknot pigeons and the elusive paradise riflebird are more often heard than seen as they squabble over Moreton Bay figs and other ripened fruit.

WALKING

Many old logging trails—some now completely hidden from view by the thick underbrush—crisscross parts of the seemingly impenetrable scrub. Bushwalkers venturing off designated trails should be careful as it is easy to become lost. There are a number of other walking trails ranging from gentle 30 minute return hikes through to a steep 8 km one-way track which joins Sheep Station Creek with Forest Tops. This trail can be walked in about 4 hours.

ACCESS AND CAMPING

The park is situated 140 km southwest of Brisbane. Access is either via Kyogle 35 km to the south, or Murwillumbah 50 km to the east.

Camping in the park is free and permits are not required. There are 2 camping grounds, but because of the steep, winding roads, caravans can only stay at the lower one at Sheep Station Creek. At Forest Tops rest area higher up, there are walk-in sites only. Both have fireplaces, picnic tables, toilets and drinking water.

Bird's nest fern growing in the Border Ranges

The park covers an area of 16 100 hectares and is isolated and remote with very few visitors. This is a true wilderness area with no roads within the park and only limited bushwalking trails. The terrain is extremely rugged and yet beautiful. Visitors need to be particularly well prepared for arduous walking conditions and must carry their own survival equipment.

An orchid butterfly

MAJOR ATTRACTIONS

Peace and solitude await the intrepid walker prepared to endure the hardships of wilderness exploration. The magnificent views from the top of Mt Budawang are often obscured by low cloud or rolling thunderstorms. The deep gorges that roll off the steep sides of the 3 dominating mountains—Budawang, Currockbilly and the Sugarloaf—are generally impenetrable and give rise to the headwaters of the Yadboro River.

The park is often confused with Morton National Park which adjoins the northern tip of the Budawang Park. The two parks are, however, quite different in their topography: Budawang has steep rather than sheer mountainsides and has lush, wet forests.

THINGS TO DO

This is definitely a park for the experienced bushwalker. You will need to be self-sufficient, capable of reading a compass and topographic map and ensure that your proposed walk is reported to the local National Parks and Wildlife Service (NPWS) staff. There is a clearly

marked trail to the top of Mt Budawang from the park boundary but it entails a steep climb of about 1 km. It will take one hour for the return walk.

If you wish to climb the highest peak in the park, Currockbilly, follow the road from Mongarlowe to Charleys Forest. Continue past the trout hatchery and Black Bobs Creek for 500 metres where you will see a gate leading to the rough trail to Currockbilly. This is a very rugged walk suitable only for the very fit and could take up to 2 hours, one way.

Contact the NPWS to inform them of your intentions and for up-to-date information on the weather conditions.

ACCESS

There is only one access road to the edge of the park and no vehicle trails within its boundaries. From Braidwood follow the bitumen road to Mongarlowe to the northeast. Leaving Mongarlowe in a southeastly direction towards the Kings Highway there is a turn-off on your left just out of town. Follow the NPWS signposts through grazing properties, ensuring that you leave the boundary gates as found. In wet weather this track is impassable to conventional vehicles. The track ends abruptly at the base of Mt Budawang at a locked gate and from here there is a walking trail leading to the top of the mountain and the fire tower lookout.

LEGEND

Sealed/Unsealed Rd	★ 26 ★
Four Wheel Drive	
Walks	
Rest Area (Picnic Area)	
Caravan Park	
Camping Area	
Accommodation	
Information	
Fuel Supplies	

There are no designated camping areas or facilities within the park boundary. Remote bush camping is possible but the area has a high rainfall and can be extremely cold in winter.

Hotel and motel accommodation is available in nearby Braidwood. Tombarra Holiday Units are the closest accommodation to the park (phone (02) 4842 2310).

Part of the wilderness that makes up Budawang National Park

BUNDJALUNG NATIONAL PARK

MAP REFERENCE: PAGE 151 N 4

Location 50 km south of Ballina
Best Time Year round
Main Attractions Fishing, swimming, birdwatching, 4WD
Ranger Phone (02) 6628 1177

If you are looking for a tranquil coastal hide-away full of wildflowers, pristine waterways and wide sandy beaches, it's hard to go past the splendour of Bundjalung National Park. This 17 738 hectare wilderness next to the sea is located 50 km south of Ballina in northern New South Wales.

Before white settlement this area was inhabited by the Bundjalung tribe. Today, the only signs of their passing are ancient middens scattered along the banks of the Evans River.

THE PARK'S ATTRACTIONS

Bundjalung is a birdwatcher's paradise. Hundreds of honeyeaters descend to feed on the banksia nectar while both the superb and varie-gated fairy-wrens are commonly seen around camp sites.

Bird life along Bundjalung's coast is prolific, with silver gulls, terns and oystercatchers

A misty morning in Bundjalung National Park

finding rich pickings on its 38 km of beaches and overhead, ospreys, white-breasted sea-eagles and brahminy kites patrol the shoreline.

Egrets, spoonbills, herons and ducks can be seen around the swamps.

The heathland section of the park displays a myriad colours in early spring with purple irises, yellow waxflowers, white daisies and pink boronia among the plants growing here.

Fishing is one of the main attractions at Bundjalung. Bream, whiting, flathead and taylor are the most commonly caught, although a number of other species are landed at various times of the year.

Drivers with 4WD vehicles are permitted on the beach between Black Rocks Rest Area in the central part of the park and Shark Bay, 12 km to the south. To avoid possible mishap, only drive on the sand an hour or 2 before and after low tide. Since many species of seabirds nest in the sand dunes, never drive on the dunes as you can squash eggs and nestlings.

ACCESS AND CAMPING

Bundjalung is easily reached by turning off the Pacific Highway at the National Parks sign which is 3 km south of the small township of Woodburn. The first 5 km of this road is bitumen, the last 13 unsealed and heavily corru-gated in places. Conventional vehicles, includ-ing caravans, will have no trouble in handling the road as long as you take it easy.

There is no charge for camping within the park, and sites don't have to be booked in advance. Facilities at Black Rocks Rest Area include pit toilets, picnic tables, firewood and fireplaces. Drinking water is not available within the park and should be brought in from outside. The nearest place to buy food, fuel and ice is Woodburn 20 km away. Visitors not wishing to rough it can stay at the Woody Head camping ground on the park's southern boundary. Powered sites for vans are not available. Amenities include hot showers, toilets, washing tubs and a small kiosk; phone for bookings on (02) 6646 6134.

LEGEND

Sealed/Unsealed Rd .... ★ 26 ★

Four Wheel Drive .... - - - - - - -

Walks ...: .... ·················

Rest Area (Picnic Area) .... ⛱

Caravan Park .... 🚐

Camping Area .... ⛺

Accommodation .... 🛏

Information .... ℹ

Fuel Supplies .... ⛽

MAP REFERENCE: PAGE 147 E 6

IN BRIEF

Location 100 km southeast of Canberra
Best Time Spring, summer and autumn
Main Attractions Scenery, 4WD, camping, canoeing
Ranger Phone the NPWS office in Narooma on (02) 4476 2888

The 82 926 hectares of Deua National Park cover the mountains inland from the south coast towns of Moruya and Narooma. Primarily a wilderness park, it also provides opportunities for its wilderness areas to be enjoyed by everyone. There are great camping spots beside clear rivers, 4WD trails, fabulous walks, caves, diverse flora and a huge range of wildlife.

The mountains and valleys of the park are of such a rugged nature that they were, for a long time, an impenetrable barrier. However, the early settlers of the Monaro plains needed a stock route directly to the ports at Bega and Eden from where their stock could be shipped to the Sydney market. This led to a stock route being blazed down the steep ridges into the broad valley formed by the Deua River. During the mid-1800s the valley floor was cleared and became an important feeding area for stock.

Deua River, Deua National Park

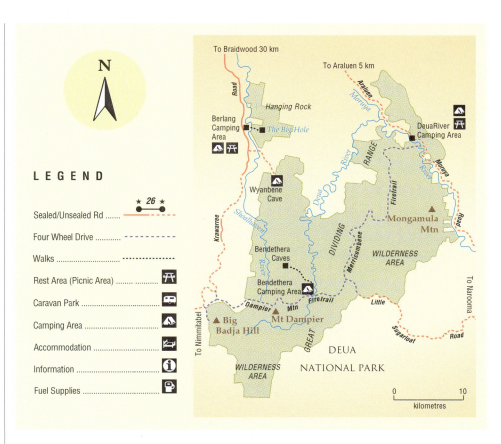

LEGEND

Sealed/Unsealed Rd	★ 26 ★
Four Wheel Drive	
Walks	
Rest Area (Picnic Area)	
Caravan Park	
Camping Area	
Accommodation	
Information	
Fuel Supplies	

THINGS TO DO

Drivers of 4WD vehicles have a number of challenging tracks from which they can enjoy superb views, with one of the best camp sites in NSW waiting at the end of the day in the Bendethera Valley. Whilst the roads are not particularly difficult, all visitors should know how to use their 4WD vehicle in rough terrain. Organised 4WD tag-along tours are conducted by Great Divide Tours (phone (02) 9913 1395).

Amateur and professional speleologists can explore the Bendethera and Wyanbene Caves while remote-country bushwalkers can venture into the rugged southern end of the park.

ACCESS AND CAMPING

The Araluen Moruya Road runs along the Deua River which forms the northern boundary of the park. If approaching from Braidwood head towards Majors Creek and into the Araluen Valley. As an alternative, the Braidwood to Nimmitabel road, often referred to as the Krawarree Road, passes along the backbone of the Great Divide and the western boundary of the park. This provides access to the Big Hole, Wyanbene Caves and 4WD access into Mt Dampier and Bendethera.

From the coast access is via a network of forestry trails out of Moruya which eventually lead to the Bendethera Trail which is 4WD only. Once in the park the trails are the domain of the 4WD and the Bendethera, Merricumbene, Mt Dampier and Minuma Trails provide varying degrees of difficulty. 4WD tracks should not be used in wet conditions.

The few trails that dissect the park have remained open thanks to appropriate management by the National Parks and Wildlife Service (NPWS).

There are established camp sites with pit toilets and BBQs on the Araluen Road at the Deua River Camping Area approximately halfway between Araluen and Moruya. This road is very narrow as it twists along the river bed, but it is accessible to the family car.

On the Krawarree Road from Braidwood the Berlang Camping Area provides picnic and camping opportunities. The Shoalhaven River is nearby and it is a 30 minute walk to the Big Hole. The Big Hole is a result of hillside collapsing into an underground limestone cavern, creating a hole 30 metres across and 90 metres deep.

The Bendethera Valley deep in the heart of the national park provides the best opportunity for camping for those with 4WD vehicles. The valley is reached from either the Krawarree Road via Dampier Trig or from the east via the forests of Dampier State Forest and the Bendethera Trail. There are 2 pit toilets and fire pits provided in the valley which stretches for over 4 km.

KANANGRA BOYD NATIONAL PARK

IN BRIEF

MAP REFERENCE: PAGE 148 E 9

Location 3 hours' drive west of Sydney via Jenolan Caves
Best Time Spring and summer
Main Attractions Wilderness areas, lookouts, walks, 4WD
Ranger Phone the NPWS at Oberon (02) 6336 1972, or at Govetts Leap (02) 4787 8877

Camping: No bookings are taken
Caving: Permits for Tuglow and Colong Caves required in advance from the NWPS

The park is only 3 hours' drive from Sydney and has some of the most spectacular scenery in Australia. Everyone should see the mighty Kanangra Walls at least once in their lifetime.

HISTORY

The Gandangara people were the first inhabitants of this rugged region. European exploration commenced with George Bass, and then Francis Barralier, who were attempting to find a route across the then impassable barrier of the Blue Mountains. Barralier, in 1802, forged his way as far as the Kowmung River which now provides a focal point for many visitors before it flows into the Warragamba catchment. The silver mining, which occurred at nearby Yerranderie, brought a flurry of people to the area before the mines were closed and the easy access from Camden was flooded by the Warragamba Dam in the 1950s. The national park was proclaimed in 1972.

MAJOR ATTRACTIONS

The scenery and the isolation of the area are the major interest points of the park. There are sheer cliffs of several hundred metres and magnificent waterfalls and superb walking trails. There are some great camping spots and the wildlife is plentiful. The park is primarily wilderness, covering 69 000 hectares stretching from Jenolan Caves to Colong Caves.

THINGS TO DO

There are some magnificent walks and views in the park. At the end of the Kanangra Walls Road there are easy, level walking trails leading to several magnificent lookouts over the Walls. There is wheelchair access at this point.

Here you will also find the Waterfall Walk which takes only 30 minutes to the base of the Kalang Falls. The Plateau Walk takes you along the plateau of the Walls, through dense heath which can be very beautiful when flowering in

An abandoned hut in Kanangra Boyd National Park

The beautiful wildflowers of Kanangra Boyd

summer. There are some great views over the wilderness areas. The return walk is approximately 2 km, but could take you up to 2 hours, particularly if you stop and enjoy the scenery.

There are many longer walks in the park which entail overnight camps and you need to be experienced and very fit. These walks commence from Katoomba and wind their way into deep gorges, passing mountains with the evocative names of Cloudmaker, Strongleg, Wild Dog, Stormbreaker and High and Mighty.

The walk out to the top of Morong Falls on the Boyd River is also worth the effort. Follow the Kowmung Trail and turn left before descending the mountainside. Just past the Boyd Crossing there is a trail on your right. This track is closed to vehicles but you can walk the 3 km to the top of the falls where there are magnificent cascades and swimming holes. The walk will take at least one hour.

ACCESS

Despite being a wilderness area, access is quite good. The major route from Sydney is via the Jenolan Caves Road from the Great Western Highway to the caves and then onto the Kanangra Walls Road. This road is 30 km of all-weather gravel but caution in wet weather is needed. You can also approach this road from Oberon or, if you have a 4WD, you would find the route through the Dingo Dell Camping Area and

across the Kowmung River the most interesting.

Around the Walls are mainly walking trails only. 4WD tracks dissect the western side of the park along the Kowmung Fire Trail and near Morong Falls. In the northern section the Six Foot Track on the boundary of the park and the Jenolan State Forest is a shared walking and vehicle track along Black Range. All other access into the very heart of the park is by foot.

CAMPING

There is a vehicle-based camping area on the Kanangra Walls Road at the Boyd River crossing with toilets and BBQs. Accessible by conventional vehicles, it is subject to extreme weather conditions and snow can fall at any time. The Dingo Dell Camping Area, with one pit toilet but plenty of fresh water, is 4WD accessible only and is more proctected from bad weather.

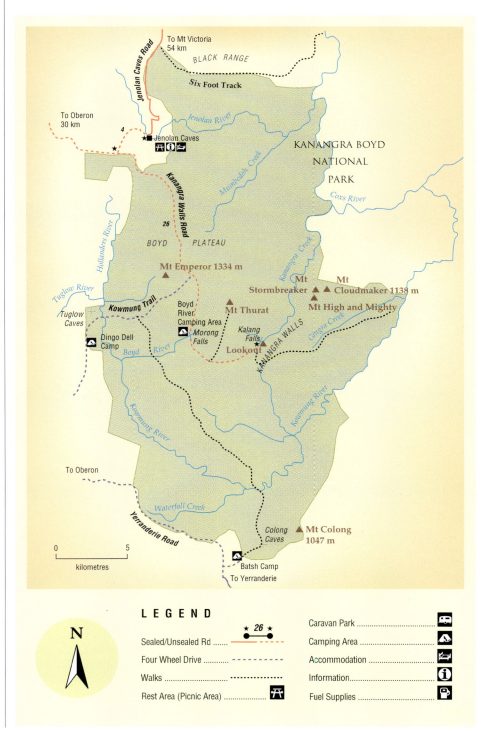

LEGEND

Sealed/Unsealed Rd	★ 26 ★
Four Wheel Drive	
Walks	
Rest Area (Picnic Area)	
Caravan Park	
Camping Area	
Accommodation	
Information	
Fuel Supplies	

KOSCIUSZKO NATIONAL PARK

MAP REFERENCE: PAGE 147 B 6

IN BRIEF

Location About halfway between Melbourne and Sydney; 2 hours' drive from Canberra
Best Time June to September for skiing; summer for bush-walking and camping
Main Attractions Skifields, excellent walks with mountain scenery, 4WD
Ranger Contact NPWS office in Jindabyne, phone (02) 6456 2444

Commercial Tour Operators: Great Divide Tours conduct 4WD tag-along tours in the Victorian section of the Snowy Mountains, phone (02) 9913 1395
Paddy Palin conduct walks, whitewater rafting, horse riding, mountain-bike rides, abseiling and photography tours, phone (02) 6456 2922
Thredbo Centre Activities Desk, phone (02) 6459 4151, offer a variety of tours and activities

Accommodation: Snowline Caravan Park, Jindabyne, phone (02) 6456 2099; Jindabyne Holiday Park, phone (02) 6456 2249; Kosciuszko Mountain Retreat, Sawpit Creek, phone (02) 6456 2224
Camping: Sawpit Creek, phone the NPWS, (02) 6450 5600

There is a daily entry fee into Kosciuszko National Park, per vehicle, or you can purchase an annual pass which also provides access to all other parks in NSW, available from the Gondwana Centre, phone (02) 9337 2777, or from any national park in NSW

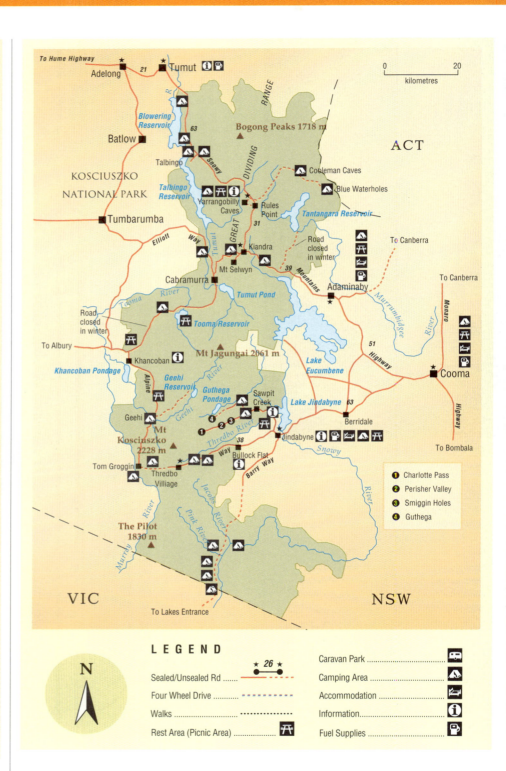

LEGEND

N

Sealed/Unsealed Rd ....
Four Wheel Drive ....
Walks ....
Rest Area (Picnic Area) ....

Caravan Park ....
Camping Area ....
Accommodation ....
Information...........................
Fuel Supplies ....

In terms of size, attractions, activities and grandeur, Kosciuszko National Park is the leader in New South Wales. (Until 1997 the name was misspelt 'Kosciusko'.) At 647 000 hectares it is the largest park in the state. It stretches from the Victorian border all the way to Brindabella Range west of Canberra and sprawls across the highest peaks of the Great Dividing Range. It protects Australia's tallest mountain, Mt

Kosciuszko, which reaches a height of 2228 metres. The park is known primarily for its sensational snow-skiing with world-class ski runs over the winter months. During summer it becomes an idyllic escape for many hundreds of visitors who savour the crisp mountain air and expansive mountain views.

The Snowy Mountains, as they have become known, are the home of Australia's largest

power generating scheme, the Snowy Mountains Hydro-Electric Scheme. It is a massive industrial project that was built at a time when skills needed for such work were unknown in this country.

The park offers 2 faces to its visitors: in winter it is carpeted in snow and is a mecca for skiers from within Australia and overseas. Over

Alpine pools in Kosciuszko National Park (facing page)

summer, the mountains become the ideal place for annual holiday-makers from the cities. During the Christmas period many of the fabulous camp sites beside the rivers and lakes of the mountains are filled to overflowing with campers enjoying the bright blue skies and fresh air. The walking tracks across the main range are visited by numerous walkers awestruck by the uninterrupted views and carpets of wildflowers. Below, in the deep valleys, the lakes created by the Hydro-Electric Scheme and the rivers are full of boats, canoes and anglers. Bushwalkers can explore the wilderness areas which account for more than half of the park and historians will enjoy discovering the huts and homesteads of the high country left by our forefathers.

HISTORY

It is known that the Aborigines visited the mountains at certain times of the year, the harsh winter making it impossible for permanent human habitation. The Aborigines pursued the bogong moth during its mating season, when it travelled in vast numbers across the mountains. This hunt formed an important ceremonial ritual for the Aborigines.

Europeans ventured into the mountains in the early 1800s as graziers searched for better grasslands to feed their stock. It is believed that most of the mountains were explored by these graziers before the first recorded exploration of the mountains by Polish explorer Count Strzelecki who reached the top of Australia in 1840 and named it after Polish patriot Tadeusz Kosciuszko. However, there is a great deal of conjecture as to whether Strzelecki actually reached the summit of Kosciuszko or whether it

Unblemished snow typical of Kosciuszko

Blue Lake in Kosciuszko National Park

was in fact Mt Townsend.

In 1859 there was a minor gold rush at Kiandra, which attracted nearly 10 000 prospectors, but the harsh winters and lack of good gold finds soon ended the Kiandra rush. The lower valleys carried giant stands of timber and this was sought after by the timber getters during the late 1800s and early 1900s. But the environmental significance of the Snowy Mountains had been realised and in 1944 the Kosciusko State Park was established.

In 1949 the Snowy Mountains Scheme began. This was indeed an engineering feat of epic proportions. Five rivers were diverted from an easterly flow to a westerly flow; 145 km of tunnels were bored through solid rock; 17 dams were constructed; 7 power stations established and over 1600 km of roads blazed through some of the most rugged country in the land. This brought enormous economic development to Australia in the form of power generation and irrigation for the Western Plains. However, some are now arguing that the changes to nature will ultimately wreak havoc over our land.

The Kosciusko National Park was proclaimed in 1967 and now there is a mix of commercial ski resorts and wilderness areas stretched across the very rooftop of Australia.

MAJOR ATTRACTIONS

Many enthusiastic walkers make the long trek to the top of Mt Kosciuszko each summer when the winter snows have melted. For others the

glory of walking at high altitudes across fields of wildflowers with endless vistas of mountain ranges is just reward. In the lower altitudes there are equally enthusiastic holiday-makers enjoying sailing, canoeing and fishing on the calm lakes of Eucumbene, Jindabyne and Tantangara. Other visitors will have specific interest in the mighty Hydro-Electric Scheme which reshaped the mountains. There are tours conducted to the power stations and dams. But it is in winter that the Snowies really come alive. Thousands flock to the skifields each winter to enjoy the slopes and the night life in the resorts.

THINGS TO DO

In winter there is primarily one pastime in the park: skiing. The whole of the mountains can be blanketed in metre-deep snow for up to 4 months. There are tremendous opportunities for downhill as well as cross-country skiing. Those intending to do cross-country trails should advise someone of their route and expected time of return. This is most important as sudden weather changes can cause white-out blizzards and many people have died on the slopes.

The park lends itself to a much greater variety of activities during the warmer months. Although the nights can still be extremely cold the days are usually clear and sunny. The scenery at this time is excellent and many bush-walkers prefer this time of year to tackle the many hundreds of kilometres of walking trails that are available. It would be impossible to list all of the tracks that can be walked. It would be best to obtain details of these trails from the National Parks and Wildlife Service (NPWS) office in Jindabyne. The tracks encompass short walks of as little as one hour duration to overnight camp-outs which cover up to 20 km of the mountaintop ranges. If contemplating a long walk overnight ensure that you are totally self-sufficient and ready for the worst, blizzard-style, weather. You will also need to carry your own cooking stoves and fuel as the lighting of fires in higher altitudes is severely restricted.

There are excellent opportunities for canoeing and swimming in the rivers and lakes of the valleys during summer. Trout fishing in season is another major attraction as the rivers and dams are regularly stocked from the nearby trout hatcheries. A permit is required, obtainable from the rangers. Trail riding is a popular activity and is available through a number of horse-riding schools. Whitewater rafting on the mighty Snowy River and other similar adventure sports are readily catered for in the mountains.

The Yarrangobilly Caves and Cooleman Caves are another feature of the Snowy Mountains. The underground majesty of these caves is difficult to rival and there are self-guided tours as well as professional tours. There is even a natural hot spa at Yarrangobilly which can be enjoyed all year round.

The NPWS provide discovery tours and talks during the summer and there are commercial tour operators that can meet your needs.

ACCESS

It takes 6 hours to drive from Sydney to the park or 2 hours from Canberra. You can also fly to Cooma and then drive for an hour to Jindabyne but most people travel by car or coach. The major entry into the park is via the Monaro Highway from Canberra through Cooma and onto Jindabyne.

There are alternative access routes into the park and each of them is spectacular. For those living in the western parts of the state it would be easiest to follow the Snowy Mountains Highway through Tumut before climbing the mountains past Lake Blowering up to Kiandra. At this point it is possible to descend the mountains into Adaminaby and Cooma from where the major ski resorts of Perisher and Thredbo are easily accessed via Jindabyne. As an alternative, from Kiandra follow the Alpine Way to Cabramurra and then along the mountains on their western side to Khancoban. This marks the third possible entry point into the Snowies. For those travelling from Albury or Melbourne this would be an ideal route to follow as it traces the shoreline of the Hume Weir. Khancoban nestles at the foot of the towering mountains and from here you can follow the Alpine Way past Geehi and Tom Groggin to Thredbo, eventually emerging at Jindabyne. This route includes the only remaining gravel section, which is expected to be sealed by 1999.

It is possible to virtually circumnavigate the Snowy Mountains on a good road. However, some sections are closed in winter as the road is subject to heavy snowfalls. During winter all vehicles to the park must carry snow chains and fit them when advised.

CAMPING

There are many opportunities for camping within the park; however, being an alpine area, sudden and severe weather changes are always a possibility. Even in midsummer there is the chance of heavy snowfalls and freezing conditions occuring.

The major camping ground for tents and caravans in the park is at Sawpit Creek. Here you will find toilets, hot showers, fireplaces and even cabins for rent. Bookings need to be made in advance with the NPWS. It is possible to camp anywhere in the park provided you are not in sight of a road or near a watercourse. Some of the better camp sites for the car-based camper are found at Tom Groggin beside the Murray River, near Geehi on the Murray Flats, in the old town site of Ravine or Lobbs Hole below the Yarrangobilly Caves, and at Cooleman Caves on the Long Plain east of Rules Point.

There are commercial camping grounds in Jindabyne and Cooma and a huge number of ski chalets, motels and hotels in both these towns as well as in Thredbo and Perisher Valley. For the avid bushwalker there are countless excellent bush camp sites along the many hundreds of kilo-metres of walks. There are also several old huts scattered across the high country which are ideal refuges in bleak weather but you must not rely on reaching these as bad weather can drastically alter your planned itinerary.

Alpine daisies, a spring feature of the Snowy Mountains

KU-RING-GAI CHASE NATIONAL PARK

IN BRIEF

MAP REFERENCE: PAGE 149 H 8

Location 30 km north of the Sydney GPO
Best Time All year round
Main Attractions Picnic areas, walking tracks, Aboriginal art sites
Ranger Phone
(02) 9457 9322

Kalkari Visitor Centre, phone
(02) 9457 9853
Bookings for the Basin Camping Ground, phone
(02) 9451 3379
Palm Beach Ferry Service, phone (02) 9918 2747

The people of Sydney are literally surrounded by national parks. No other city in Australia has so many national parks so close to its centre. The Ku-ring-gai Chase National Park, covering an area of 15 000 hectares, protects some of the most fascinating and beautiful sandstone escarpment landforms and Aboriginal art sites found in the country.

HISTORY

The original inhabitants of this vast bushland area were the people of the Garigal tribe. It is estimated that the Aborigines occupied this place for at least 10 000 years before Europeans set foot on the shores of Botany Bay.

It was the rugged landscape the Aborigines found so useful for providing shelter and a wealth of food that in some ways prevented European settlement from encroaching. White settlers recognised the environmental importance of the area quite early and proclaimed the national park in 1894.

THE PARK'S MAJOR ATTRACTIONS

The park is primarily a bushwalkers' haven. The outstanding features of the park are really only accessible on foot. These include fascinating deep gullies surrounded by towering sandstone cliffs, Aboriginal rock art sites and magnificent views over the picturesque waterways of Broken Bay. The excellent picnic grounds also attract thousands of visitors each year.

The park has many kilometres of shoreline as it fronts onto the deep waters of Broken Bay and it is a wonderful place to explore by boat. The park completely surrounds the well-known Coal and Candle Creek and Akuna Bay.

In spring and summer the harsh sandstone escarpments above the orange coloured cliffs become a riot of wildflowers.

THINGS TO DO

Apart from swimming and boating, bushwalking is the major activity in the park. There are several walking trails ranging in suitability for the novice to the dedicated bushwalker. It is best to obtain detailed maps of the walks together with interpretive information sheets from the Kalkari Visitor Centre before setting out. It is important to remember that even though the park is very

A kookaburra, often seen in Ku-ring-gai Chase

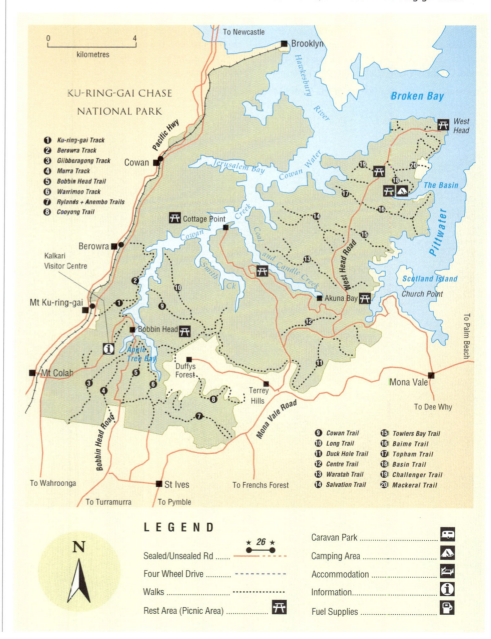

KU-RING-GAI CHASE NATIONAL PARK

1 Ku-ring-gai Track
2 Berowra Track
3 Gibberagong Track
4 Murra Track
5 Bobbin Head Trail
6 Warrimoo Track
7 Rylands + Anembo Trails
8 Cooyong Trail

9 Cowan Trail
10 Long Trail
11 Duck Hole Trail
12 Centre Trail
13 Waratah Trail
14 Salvation Trail

15 Towlers Bay Trail
16 Baime Trail
17 Topham Trail
18 Basin Trail
19 Challenger Trail
20 Mackeral Trail

LEGEND

Sealed/Unsealed Rd
Four Wheel Drive
Walks
Rest Area (Picnic Area)

Caravan Park
Camping Area
Accommodation
Information
Fuel Supplies

close to the heart of the city of Sydney this is still a very remote and wild place. Be prepared for heavy rain and thunderstorms during summer and cool, wet days in winter. The greatest danger to any bushwalker in this park is the possibility of being caught in a wild bushfire. The park was devastated by wildfires in January 1994 and you should heed all fire alert warnings and avoid the area if there is any sign of a bushfire. Never leave a fireplace burning and don't ever leave a cigarette burning in the bush.

At the visitor centre there is a Discovery Walking Trail which is suitable for wheelchair access. A special feature of the park is the Garigal Aboriginal Heritage Walk at West Head. It is only 3.5 km long but allow up to 2 hours to appreciate the culture and heritage of the Aboriginal people who once occupied this land.

The Basin walking track also provides interpretive signs relating to the Aboriginal heritage. The Basin can be reached on foot from West Head Road via a 3 km walking trail; allow an hour each way for the walk. Also from West Head there are several other walking trails that you could explore. These vary in length from 30 minute strolls to lookouts, to all-day journeys through some rugged sandstone country. Maps are available from the visitor centre.

There is a 9 km one-way walk from Berowra to Mt Ku-ring-gai railway station which will take at least 4 hours to enjoy thoroughly. At Bobbin Head there are several other walks, ranging in difficulty and duration from easy to hard, depending on your level of fitness and how much time you have. There are detailed information sheets on the tracks, available from the National Parks and Wildlife Service (NPWS) or the visitor centre.

ACCESS

Access to the park is easy. It is only a 40 minute drive from the Sydney GPO. You can access Bobbin Head within the park either at North Turramurra via Bobbin Head Road or from Mt Colah. Alternatively, access is via Terrey Hills along Coal and Candle Drive to Cottage Point or from Mona Vale along West Head Road to West Head. All of these roads are sealed and suitable for conventional vehicles or bicycles. Each of these access routes passes through fee collection gates and a daily fee per vehicle applies.

If travelling by train you can reach the park from Mt Colah, Mt Ku-ring-gai, Berowra and Cowan stations where walking trails into the park are nearby. Access by ferry is also possible with regular ferry trips to the camping and

picnic area at the Basin leaving from the Pittwater side of Palm Beach. If you have your own boat you can enter the park via any of the many secluded bays along its foreshores. Boat ramps are available at Appletree Bay, Cottage Point and Akuna Bay.

CAMPING

This park is primarily for day visitors. There is only one camping area—at the Basin on Pittwater. It is accessible only by ferry from Palm Beach or a 3 km walk from West Head Road. Bookings through the Information Centre in the park are essential. There are toilets, cold showers and fireplaces but you will need to bring your own fuel.

For the day visitor there are many facilities and opportunities to enjoy the delights of this park. At Bobbin Head there is the Kalkari Visitor Centre which can supply you with all the information you need; it also has an audiovisual display and other exhibits. There are all the usual picnic facilities such as tables, toilets and fireplaces at Bobbin Head, the Basin, West Head, Cottage Point and Akuna Bay. There are kiosks at Bobbin Head, Appletree Bay, Akuna Bay and Cottage Point. Safe swimming can be found at the Basin and Appletree Bay.

The popular Akuna Bay Marina in Ku-ring-gai Chase National Park

MIMOSA ROCKS NATIONAL PARK

IN BRIEF

MAP REFERENCE: PAGE 147 E 6

Location Just north of Bega
Best Time Summer
Main Attractions Camping, water sports, walking
Ranger Phone the NPWS at Narooma, (02) 4476 2888

Located on the far south coast of New South Wales Mimosa Rocks is one of the state's most beautiful coastal parks. The park protects an area of about 5000 hectares.

MAJOR ATTRACTIONS

Being a coastal park, swimming, canoeing, fishing and SCUBA diving are the main activities, but it also has superb scenery and unusual rock formations. You can sunbake, go for long beach walks or just relax in a hammock with a good book. It is often very quiet and deserted. What more could you want?

ACCESS AND CAMPING

The park lies along a 20 km stretch of coast between Bermagui and Tathra. It is off the Princes Highway and it would be best to follow the Tathra to Bermagui road. There are several access routes off this road into the various camp sites and picnic areas. The routes are not linked to each other so it is necessary to loop in and out of each vantage point. The road is gravel but could easily be traversed by conventional vehicles even in wet weather.

The park is split into a northern and a southern section by private land along Wapengo Lake Road. The northern section is accessed by Aragunnu Road which leads to the Mimosa Rocks outcrop. Picnic Point is also accessed via Wapengo Lake Road.

The southern section houses many lovely camp sites with access off the Bermagui–Tathra road to Bithry Inlet and Middle Beach using Haighs Road. Gillards Road leads to Gillards Beach whilst Nelson Lake Road will take you to picnic spots at Nelson Beach, Moon Bay and Wajurda Point.

There are several camping spots; some are accessible by vehicles while others require you to carry your camping gear a short distance. No bookings can be made for the camp sites but apart from the Christmas and Easter holidays it is unlikely that you will find the place crowded.

Camping is permissible along the Aragunnu Road near the beachfront. Facilities are minimal

Mimosa Rocks National Park

with only a pit toilet and rubbish bins. You will need to bring water. The beach and rock platforms are excellent for fishing and swimming.

To find the camping area at Picnic Point, follow the Wapengo Lake Road, which has views over the lake. Make sure you follow the National Parks and Wildlife Service (NPWS) signs as the road passes through private property. Leave all gates as found. The Picnic Point camp site has pit toilets, BBQs and rubbish bins but bring your own water. This area provides access to more great beach fishing spots and the kids will love exploring the many rockpools on the shore.

The next camp site is at Middle Beach off Haighs Road. You will have to carry your gear about 80 metres from the car park to the camping area. There are no facilities and it is quite small but very pleasant as the sound of the waves crashing on the rocks is a great way to drift off to sleep. At nearby Bithry Inlet there is a day-visit area and it is possible to canoe on the quiet waters of the inlet.

Following Gillards Road will bring you to the camp site at Gillards Beach. This is closer to the beach, which stretches into the distance making it a great place to walk, sunbake or surf.

The Nelson Lake Road provides access to the picnic areas of Nelson Beach and Moon Bay. There is no camping in this area. Moon Bay is a lovely, protected, sandy beach which is ideal for young children.

LEGEND

Sealed/Unsealed Rd .... ★ 26 ★

Four Wheel Drive .... ----------

Walks .... ··············

Rest Area (Picnic Area) ....

Caravan Park ....

Camping Area ....

Accommodation ....

Information ....

Fuel Supplies ....

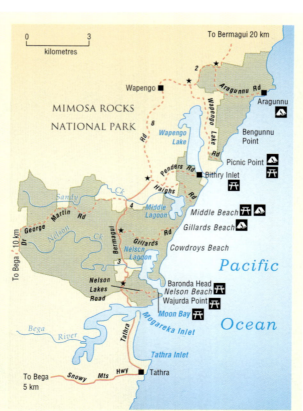

MIMOSA ROCKS NATIONAL PARK

To Bermagui 20 km

Wapengo

Aragunnu Rd

Aragunnu

Wapengo Lake

Bengunnu Point

Penders Rd

Picnic Point

Bithry Inlet

Haighs Rd

Sandy Ck

Middle Lagoon

Middle Beach

Gillards Beach

Martin Rd

Dr George

Nelson

Bermagui

Gillards Rd

Cowdroys Beach

Nelson Lagoon

Pacific

Baronda Head
Nelson Beach
Wajurda Point

Nelson Lakes Road

Moon Bay

Ocean

Bega River

Mogareka Inlet

Tathra Inlet

To Bega 10 km

To Bega 5 km

Snowy Mts Hwy

Tathra

0   3
kilometres

MAP REFERENCE: PAGE 152 D 6

IN BRIEF

Location 130 km northeast of Broken Hill, off the Silver City Highway
Best Time Winter
Main Attractions Aboriginal art sites, Outback scenery, camping, walking
Ranger Phone the NPWS at Broken Hill, (08) 8088 5933

Most of the New South Wales national parks are found scattered along the lush mountain range of the Great Divide, Mootwingee National Park offers a completely different experience. Situated northeast of Broken Hill it has one of the harshest climates in the country.

There are several outstanding Aboriginal art sites at what is known as the Mootwingee Historic Site. The site was permanently reserved in 1967 and the area surrounding the site was protected under national park status during the 1970s.

MAJOR ATTRACTIONS

Mootwingee has a great deal to offer the traveller who has taken the time to travel the vast distances necessary to access the park. There is the colour and grandeur of the real Outback; ancient Aboriginal art sites and ceremonial grounds; the incredible Aboriginal Mootwingee Historic Site, and hidden rockpools amid deep red gorges.

The main features of the park are best seen on foot. There is a good network of walking trails including wheelchair accessible tracks.

At Homestead Creek there are a number of walking trails that will give an appreciation of the region's Aboriginal culture.

The Thaakaltjika Mingkana Walk is only 20 minutes return and is wheelchair accessible. It makes its way into a gorge to a cave with Aboriginal paintings. The Rockholes Loop is a 30 minute walk passing Aboriginal engravings and providing views of Rockholes, Homestead Gorge and the Bynguano Range.

A longer walk for the more energetic is the Homestead Walk. This 3 hour journey goes past craggy cliffs around Homestead Creek and right into the Homestead Gorge with its beautiful Outback colours. There is also the Bynguano route which takes 3 hours and is really for experienced walkers. It affords spectacular views of the gorges along the range.

Mootwingee Gorge to the south of Homestead Gorge is only a 10 minute walk. There is a beautiful rockpool here that is enclosed by red cliffs.

There is also a 10 km vehicle track that passes the ruins of the Rockholes Hotel and unusual rock formations known as Little Dome Rock and Split Rocks.

The Mootwingee Historic Site is found in the park

Unusual rock formations found in Mootwingee National Park

and protects ancient Aboriginal paintings, stencils and engravings that will enthral the visitor. It is necessary to book a tour of the site with the National Parks and Wildlife Service (NPWS) through the Broken Hill office. Tours are conducted on Wednesdays and Saturdays.

ACCESS AND CAMPING

The road from Broken Hill is mostly dry gravel that becomes impassable to all vehicles after rain. Allow at least 2 hours to drive from Broken Hill. The park is also linked to White Cliffs and Tibooburra by road and there are many station gates to close and deep bulldust in places. If planning a trip out here you must check the status of the roads and ensure that your vehicle is in top condition. Always carry extra water and basic spares for your vehicle.

Once in the park there is only one route to follow. It will take you past the various walks and leads to the Mootwingee Historic Site.

There is good camping at Homestead Creek with shade from river red gums. The facilities are basic; people with disabilities are catered for. It would be wise to check availability of sites before leaving Broken Hill.

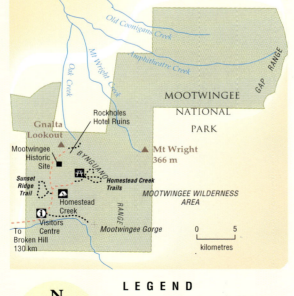

N

LEGEND

★ 26 ★

Sealed/Unsealed Rd ....

Walks ....

Rest Area (Picnic Area) .....

Camping Area ....

Information ....

MORTON NATIONAL PARK

IN BRIEF

MAP REFERENCE: PAGE 147 F 4

Location 20 km west of Nowra, off the Princes Highway
Best Time All year round
Main Attractions Bushwalking, camping, sightseeing, waterfalls, 4WD
Ranger Phone (02) 4423 9800

Coolendel Camping Ground, phone (02) 4421 4586
Fitzroy Falls Visitor Centre, for advice on walks and camping, phone (02) 4887 7270
NPWS Office, Nowra, for advice on trails, phone (02) 4423 9800
State Forests of NSW, for advice on trails through their forests and the camping at Yadboro, phone (02) 4472 6211
Ulladulla Tourist Information, for general information on places and accommodation, phone (02) 4455 1269

This is a park that is relatively unknown and yet it is one of the most spectacular national parks in New South Wales. The park stretches from Fitzroy Falls in the Southern Highlands along the escarpment behind Nowra and Ulladulla to join the Budawang National Park near Braidwood.

HISTORY

To the Wandandian tribe that lived on the coastal plains between Jervis Bay and Ulladulla the towering sandstone cliffs of the Budawang Range were a place of mystery and Dreamtime creatures. There is some evidence of occupation in the form of grinding stones and ceremonial sites but the area generally remained untouched until the early European settlers began their search for red cedar.

Captain Cook sighted and named Pigeon House Mountain which stands tall against the southern horizon of the park. In the northern section where the spectacular scenery was more accessible, the first tourists to visit Fitzroy Falls ventured in on horseback in the late 1800s. In 1938 a large area of the park came under protective state laws and in 1967 Morton National Park was established. The park now occupies an area of over 162 000 hectares.

THINGS TO DO

Bushwalking and sightseeing are the major activities in Morton National Park. Around Fitzroy Falls the spectacular 82 metre falls are well served by easy walking trails. For the more energetic there are longer walks along the escarpment edge with equally spectacular views across the deeply eroded valley. There is a clifftop walk that is relatively flat; about 3 km long, it will take around 3 hours.

There are several great walks around the escarpment behind Bundanoon. These lead to delightful places such as Fern Tree Gully, Fairy Bower Falls and the Glow Worm Glen. For the really fit there is the walk from Long Point Lookout which is a few kilometres out of Bundanoon near Tallong.

A 4WD is needed to explore the trails east of Yalwal, but the popular tracks into the Yalwal Creek and the Shoalhaven River bed are now for bushwalkers only.

The best walks are around Pigeon House and the Castle. The walk to Pigeon House Mountain commences in a small car park 30 minutes inland from Ulladulla. The initial climb is quite steep but then the trail levels out as it crosses the sandstone plateau, followed by a steep and abrupt climb up the volcanic plug at the top

The top of Pigeon House Mountain which rises above Morton National Park

White cockatoos, congregating in the park

of the mountain. The view from the top is magnificent, stretching out to the sea on one side and across the rugged sandstone cliffs of the Budawang Ranges to the west. Allow 4 hours return for this walk and carry plenty of water.

For the truly dedicated bushwalker the trails into the Castle and the Valley of the Gods are simply the best. But you need to know what you are doing, you must be able to read a compass and map, be self-sufficient for overnight camping and carry all your food and water. If contemplating a walk in this area you must notify the local National Parks and Wildlife Service (NPWS) ranger of your intentions.

ACCESS

Due to the size of the park and its rugged nature there are only 3 major routes into the park, each one accessing a different aspect or feature. The easiest snd most popular access is via either Moss Vale in the Southern Highlands or Kangaroo Valley on the south coast. This route leads to the very popular Fitzroy Falls, Belmore Falls, and Gambells Rest near Bundanoon. These access roads are sealed and suitable for conventional vehicles.

Moving further south along the coast to Nowra the park can be entered via a network of gravel forestry trails, usually good. These will take you to the once thriving silver mining town of Yalwal which is now drowned under the Danjerra Dam. Access into the park from here is now restricted as the area has only recently been declared a Wilderness Area but a conventional vehicle will get you to the camp ground at Yalwal.

If you intend to explore further into the park you will need a 4WD or be a keen bushwalker. Another possible route to follow is the Turpentine Road from Nowra towards Braidwood. This dusty, potholed road goes through the park passing the spectacular Tianjara Falls about 30 minutes out of Nowra.

The southern-most entrance to the park is from Ulladulla via Pigeon House Mountain. Again, good forestry roads lead to the edge of the park but any further exploration will have to be on foot due to the rugged landscape.

CAMPING

There is a small camping area at Fitzroy Falls but this is often booked out well in advance. The camping area at Gambells Rest at Bundanoon is quite good. Fees are applicable at these camping grounds.

Camping at Yalwal is available above the dam where there are toilets and BBQs but again this spot gets very busy. There are also commercial camping grounds at Coolendel nearby.

In the southern section there are small camping sites at Blue Gum Flat near Pigeon House, Yadboro Flat, where the road crosses the Yadboro River, and on Long Gully Road. No camp fees apply in this section of the park, but there is no advance booking either.

MT KAPUTAR NATIONAL PARK

IN BRIEF

MAP REFERENCE: PAGE 150 E 7

Location 30 km east of Narrabri, off the Newell Highway
Best Time Autumn and winter
Main Attractions Lookouts, rock formations, 4WD
Ranger Contact the NPWS, Narrabri, phone (02) 6792 4724

This park lies in the northwest of New South Wales near Narrabri. It is dominated by the tall peaks of Mt Kaputar and Coryah at 1520 metres and 1400 metres respectively. These peaks are amongst the highest in the state which will surprise many visitors given their distance from the traditional high country of the Great Divide.

MAJOR ATTRACTIONS

The Nandewar Range was formed by volcanic action some 18 million years ago and the basaltic peaks and rugged nature of the park are all that remain of this once violent landscape. Mt Lindsay was probably a giant volcano. Great walking trails, lookouts and unusual rock formations are the features that attract visitors.

The walking trails vary greatly in length and difficulty. You are best advised to obtain the walking trail pamphlet from the Narrabri office of the National Parks and Wildlife Service (NPWS). Short walks out of Dawsons Spring introduce you to the high altitude vegetation whilst the longer Lindsay Rock Tops walk will take you through snow gum forests and on to bare larval flow rock with commanding views.

In the northern section of the park the road from Narrabri to Bingara passes Sawn Rocks which are oddly shaped, organ-pipe formations of basalt rock. It is a short walk from the picnic area to view the strange rock formations.

There are many different types of animals in the park including the elusive koala, kangaroos, possums, gliders and marsupial mice. Overhead you will see kites and eagles looking for their prey and brightly coloured parrots seeking out the nectar of the flowering gums and grevilleas.

ACCESS AND CAMPING

All visitors must approach the park from Narrabri. It is 30 km over good gravel road to the park entrance and another 20 km of steep, winding road to the main camping grounds. The narrow road prevents caravans from accessing the park but conventional and 4WD vehicles will have no problems.

A small fee, payable on an honour system, applies to the camp sites and no advance bookings are taken. Dawsons Spring provides water, septic toilets, hot showers and wood burning BBQs. It might be wise to bring your own firewood. There are also a few powered BBQs under cover. During school holidays the ranger office at the camp ground is staffed.

At Dawsons Spring there are 2 huts that can be hired. These huts are available for a minimum of 2 nights and accommodate 4 adults or 2 adults and 4 children. You will need to bring your own linen and must book the cabins through the NPWS office at Narrabri.

At Bark Hut, the camping is what is termed as 'off road'. This means you must leave your vehicle in the car park and walk into the camp ground with all your gear. Not an ideal situation for those that use their vehicle to keep the car fridge cold or to power their evening lighting but some people like the feeling of remoteness that is achieved. The amenities block has septic toilets and hot showers.

LEGEND

Sealed/Unsealed Rd ....
Four Wheel Drive ....
Walks ....
Rest Area (Picnic Area) ....
Caravan Park ....
Camping Area ....
Accommodation ....
Information ....
Fuel Supplies ....

Map:

To Moree
Waa Gorge
MT KAPUTAR NATIONAL PARK
Grattai Mtn
To Bingara
Killarney Gap
Sawn Rocks
To Narrabri 30 km
Mt Lindsay ▲ 1373 m
NANDEWAR
Upper Bullana Ck Mt Kaputar 1520 m
The Governor Lookout
Mt Coryah 1405 m
Mt Kaputar Lookout
Dawsons Spring
Green Camp
Eckfords Lookout
To Narrabri 30 km
Bark Hut
RANGE
0   10
kilometres

The craggy Nandewar Range in Mt Kaputar National Park

MAP REFERENCE: PAGE 154 E 3

Location Northeast of Mildura, off the Sturt Highway, in the southwest of the state
Best Time Spring and autumn
Main Attractions The Walls of China and the historic significance of the park
Ranger Contact the NPWS office at Buronga, phone (03) 5023 1278

Mungo National Park is a unique, arid park and part of the Willandra Lakes World Heritage Region which recognises the area's historic and ecological importance. The park covers almost 28 000 hectares 110 km northeast of Mildura.

Lake Mungo, which is now dry, was a huge freshwater lake during the last Ice Age. Evidence of Aboriginal occupation dates back more than 40 000 years ago. The bones of some of the oldest known human occupation of Australia have been found in the Mungo area.

During the 1860s sheep grazing was the major pursuit. The impact of sheep on the fragile landscape is not hard to imagine. The Mungo Station was acquired by the National Parks and Wildlife Service (NPWS) in 1978 and proclaimed a park in 1979.

MAJOR ATTRACTIONS

The major point of interest in the park is the landform known as the Walls of China. This was originally a white sand dune running the full length of the shoreline of the lake bed on its eastern side. Today it forms a strangely weathered lunette of intricately carved coloured sand. The dry lake bed is an archaeological goldmine of bones, middens and artefacts.

THINGS TO DO

There is an informative visitor centre at the park entrance. An inspection of the 1869 Woolshed should be included in your visit. There is a Drive Tour of 60 km around the park which takes you across the lake bed to the Walls of China where the road becomes one-way. This section passes behind the sand dunes and the Belah Camp before providing another access to the Walls of China. The track finally loops to the north and returns to the visitor centre.

There are a number of short walks in the park. The 1 km Grassland Walk gives a good introduction to the flora and fauna of the park. The Foreshore Walk follows the western edge of the dry lake bed and provides a feel for the ancient landscape.

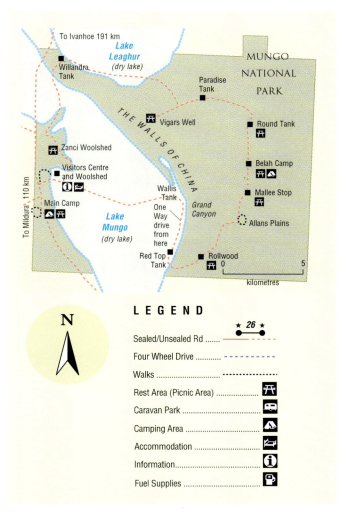

LEGEND

Sealed/Unsealed Rd	★ 26 ★
Four Wheel Drive	----------
Walks	··············
Rest Area (Picnic Area)	⊼
Caravan Park	🚐
Camping Area	⛺
Accommodation	🛏
Information	ℹ
Fuel Supplies	⛽

Other shorts walks to the Walls of China are available around the Drive Tour. The NPWS also conduct guided tours of the park. Contact them for further details.

ACCESS AND CAMPING

Road access is unsealed but open to conventional vehicles. In wet weather it becomes impassable to all vehicles. Similarly with the tracks inside the park. Check the road conditions with local police or the NPWS. There are no services or fuel available in the park so visitors from Mildura would need fuel for at least 300 km.

There are camp sites at the park entrance and at Belah Camp with pit toilets, tables and fireplaces. Bring your own firewood and water.

It is possible to stay in bunk-style accommodation at the shearers' quarters but bookings should be made in advance through the NPWS. Just outside the park there is the independently operated Mungo Lodge (phone (03) 5029 7297) which offers motel accommodation, a restaurant and a golf course.

The arid and fragile landscape of Mungo National Park

MYALL LAKES NATIONAL PARK

MAP REFERENCE: PAGE 149 L 5

Location 230 km north of Sydney via Tea Gardens
Best Time Spring, summer and autumn
Main Attractions Water sports, bushwalking, fishing, 4WD
Ranger Phone (02) 4987 3108

Accommodation and camping: Myall Shores Resort, phone (02) 4997 4495; the NPWS, phone (02) 4987 3108

Information and beach permits: Great Lakes Tourism Office— Free Call, phone 1 800 802 692 or (02) 6554 8799

Water Activities:
Fishing and charter boat tours—Islander Cruises, phone (02) 6555 8525
Houseboat Hire—Luxury Afloat, phone (02) 4997 0307 and Tea Gardens Houseboats, phone (02) 4997 0555
SCUBA diving—Hawks Nest Dive School, phone (02) 4997 0442

Myall Lakes National Park, situated just 3 hours north of Sydney, is one of the most popular parks in the state. It typifies the Australian love affair with the beach, sun and water. During the summer school holidays the place is literally alive with holiday-makers and yet at other times it is easy to have this pristine place to yourself.

HISTORY

The Myall Lakes began to form at the end of the last Ice Age, 8000 years ago. Rising sea water drowned coastal river valleys leaving only a few higher rocky outcrops. Over time the lakes filled with sediment creating their characteristic shallows and the sand dunes formed along the coast as a buffer between the sea and the inland waterways.

Red cedar brought European timber-getters to the area and they virtually stripped the forests of all such trees. During the early 1900s other forestry practices left their mark on the lakes, this time in the form of steam trains. These ran from the mountains around Bulahdelah down to the lake shore at Mayers Point where droghers floated the hardwood logs across the lakes and down the Myall River to Nelson Bay. From there the logs were loaded onto ships for both local and overseas markets.

One of the beautiful areas of Myall Lakes National Park

MAJOR ATTRACTIONS

For most visitors to Myall Lakes the great attraction is the endless stretch of quiet waters on which they can canoe, sail, water-ski or fish. The area is renowned for this type of activity and the nearby beach is one of the most beautiful to be found. Everyone should spend at least some time sitting on the deserted beaches of

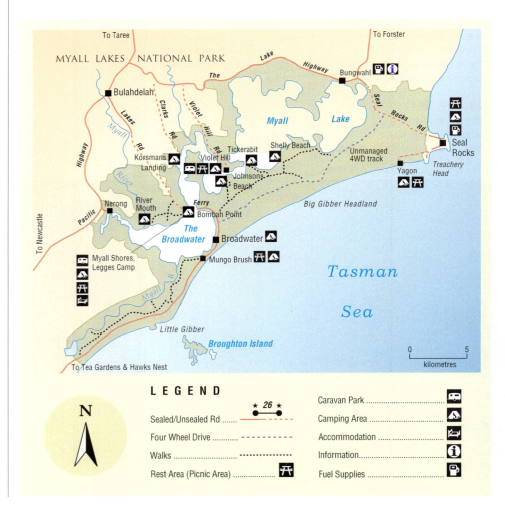

LEGEND

Sealed/Unsealed Rd
Four Wheel Drive
Walks
Rest Area (Picnic Area)
Caravan Park
Camping Area
Accommodation
Information
Fuel Supplies

Myall Lakes watching a pod of dolphins playing happily in the surf.

The park has numerous walking trails spread across its 31 500 hectares. Most pass through its unusual heath-type vegetation which is a riot of wildflower colour during spring.

THINGS TO DO

Myall Lakes is a haven for water sports. Sailing, windsurfing and canoeing are very popular. Water-skiing is permitted but there are strict rules as to proximity to other vessels and people. Regulations applying to all types of boating activities are available from the Maritime Services Board.

Fishing and netting fresh prawns late at night are favourite pastimes of visitors. Bush-walking is well catered for and everyone should experience the unique rainforest trail at Mungo Brush. It takes only 30 minutes to follow but you will be surprised at the unique flora of this coastal rainforest. It is not uncommon to sight koalas on this walk. Longer walks to Johnsons Beach, Tickerabit and Shelley Beach are well marked. You can obtain further information on these trails from the National Parks and Wildlife Service (NPWS) office at Raymond Terrace.

Drivers of 4WD vehicles are also catered for with beach access at designated points along the Mungo Brush Road. Do not traverse any vegetated dunes. It is possible to follow the beach north past the Little Gibber and then travel another 20 km north to the Big Gibber. There is no access to the beaches north of the Big Gibber and onto Seal Rocks as these beaches are important breeding grounds for the little tern. The old sand mining road from Mungo Brush to Seal Rocks is no longer maintained and is very potholed. Certainly not difficult in a 4WD but not recommended in a conventional vehicle. This road is often closed for management purposes so it would be wise to check whether it is open with the local ranger.

Permits for travel along the beach from Hawks Nest are available from the Great Lakes Shire Council at an annual fee. This section of beach has very soft sand and you will need to lower your tyre pressures.

Houseboats are a great way to enjoy the peace of the lakes. They are available for hire from Bulahdelah and at Tea Gardens.

Broughton Island, off the coast, is also within the national park and the fishing in the sea around the island is excellent as is the diving.

ACCESS

Myall Lakes is 230 km north of Sydney and an hour's drive from Newcastle. The main access is via the Pacific Highway to Tea Gardens. From Tea Gardens take the 'Singing Bridge' to Hawks Nest and follow the road north to Mungo Brush.

Deserted sandy expanses in Myall Lakes National Park

Access to the western boundary of the park and the popular Myall Shores Resort is via Bulahdelah and then just 12 km east to Bombah Point. The ferry at Bombah Point may be closed; a call to Myall Shores will confirm this. If you wish to access Mungo Brush and the ferry is closed, you will have to return to Tea Gardens.

If you travel through Bulahdelah and then take the Lakes Way towards Forster you can access the northern end of the park at Seal Rocks.

CAMPING

The NPWS have provided good camping facilities at Mungo Brush with water, toilets and BBQs. The camping beside the Broadwater is superb and for anyone with a canoe or sailboat this is a great place. It is only a short walk over the giant sandhills to the beach but, be warned, the beach is not patrolled or shark netted. This spot gets very busy during the summer and Easter holidays but at other times there is plenty of space.

Myall Shores Resort at Bombah Point provides a commercial camping ground within the national park and it has excellent facilities.

The northern end of the park is served by a new camping ground at Yagon, just out of Seal Rocks. There are limited camping spaces available and all facilities are provided.

There is an alternative camp site at Violet Hill on the western shore of Boolambayte Lake which is accessed off the Lakes Way.

Each of the above camping areas is accessible by conventional vehicles but by following one of the many walking trails in the park you will also find camp sites at Johnsons Beach, Tickerabit and Shelley Beach. Camping fees apply at all of these camp sites. However, you can bush camp anywhere within the park provided you do not disturb any foliage and do not camp within sight of any road.

Casuarina equisetifolia growing in Myall Lakes

OXLEY WILD RIVERS NATIONAL PARK

The Oxley Wild Rivers National Park preserves a number of river gorges that are generally inaccessible. Fortunately, some of the most dramatic features of the park, the waterfalls, are found at the edge of the escarpment where access is easy.

The park covers an area of more than 111 000 hectares, making it one of the largest in the state. It has many boundaries with up to 10 separate river gorges being included in the park. These gorges are separated by farming and forestry land on the higher plateaus.

THINGS TO DO

The waterfalls tumbling off the escarpment into the wild gorges of the many river beds are spectacular. But if you have the energy and the time to explore the deep gullies on foot there are many more excellent rewards: clean, running streams, an enormous variety of bird life and native animals such as wallabies.

The lookouts over Wollomombi, Apsley, Dangars and Tia Falls are all easily accessed by vehicle with easy, short walking tracks to the viewing platforms.

The adventurous bushwalker will also find the park extremely rewarding. There are 2 designated trails into the Macleay River. The first is off the Oxley Highway on Moona Plains Road starting at Budds Mare. The second is at the end of the Raspberry Road. Each entails walks over a few kilometres through hilly terrain which is uphill on the return journey.

Canoeing is possible on the rivers, especially at Georges Junction where access is easiest.

ACCESS AND CAMPING

Travellers can access the park from many different points. The first area would be Georges Creek where the park protects the Macleay River Gorge. Continuing towards Armidale, after climbing the mountain range, you will pass Styx River which also comes under the park control. Just before Styx River, on the left, is the Raspberry Road, at the end of which is a locked gate. Walking from here leads to where the park protects the Macleay River. The Raspberry Road

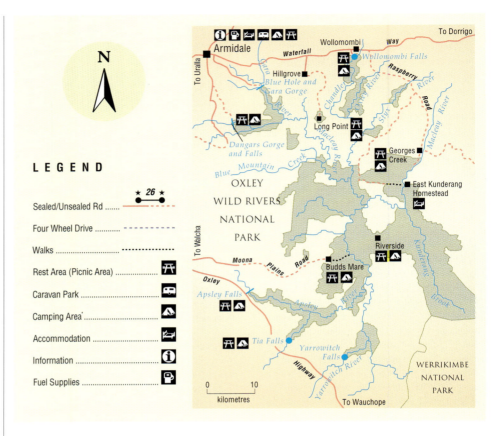

would require 4WD in wet weather.

Further along is the dramatic Wollomombi Falls, one of the highest in the country. As you near Armidale the Castledoyle Road leads to Gara Gorge and Blue Hole where the park takes in the upper reaches of the Macleay River. The Dangars Falls is also found here, 22 km southeast of Armidale along the Dangarsleigh Road.

To access the other major areas of the park it is necessary to travel along the Oxley Highway from Walcha heading east towards the coast. Close to the highway is Apsley Falls on the upper reaches of the Apsley River which has its

entire gorge area included in the park. Continuing eastward it is possible to access Tia Falls a few kilometres further down the highway. After this, there is remote access into the upper reaches of Kunderang Brook via Werrikimbe National Park but this would entail the use of a 4WD and then considerable walking.

Remote camping is permitted anywhere in the park except at designated picnic areas. But as most of the deep river gorges have no vehicle access you will need to backpack all your camping gear. There are many beautiful camping opportunities beside the wild rivers.

Wollomombi Falls in Oxley Wild Rivers National Park

ROYAL NATIONAL PARK

MAP REFERENCE: PAGE 149 H 9
Location 25 kilometres
south of Sydney
Best Time All year round
Main Attractions Extensive
walking trails, picnic areas
and swimming beaches
Ranger Contact the NPWS,
phone (02) 9542 0666 or
the Visitor Centre, phone
(02) 9542 0648

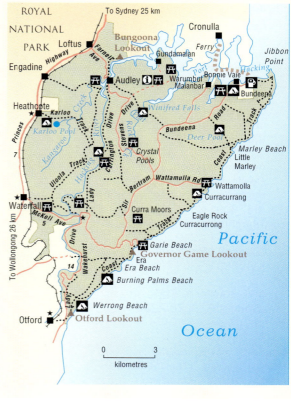

LEGEND

Sealed/Unsealed Rd .... ★ 26 ★
Four Wheel Drive ....
Walks ....
Rest Area (Picnic Area) ....
Caravan Park ....
Camping Area ....
Accommodation ....
Information ....
Fuel Supplies ....

Royal National Park was Australia's first
national park—gazetted in 1879. Originally
called National Park, following Queen
Elizabeth's visit in 1954 the name was changed
to Royal National Park.

Midden sites have been found, as have hand
stencils and other art sites in sandstone overhangs all evidence of the Dharawa tribe's early
occupation of the area.

THINGS TO DO

Bushwalkers will find a huge number of trails to
explore in the 15 000 hectares of the park. The
coast track is the most spectacular but its total
length of 30 km would require an overnight
camp. Fortunately, you can join and leave the
trail at different places and thus see much on a
day walk. Permits are required for overnight
camping, issued from the visitor centre.

The Forest Island walk is 4 km long and
takes 2 hours, going through dense rainforest,

made interesting by interpretive signage. The
Lady Carrington Walk includes visits to the
historic areas of the park along its 9 km length.

The park has many trails dissecting it where
you will see the park regenerating after the

disastrous bushfires of 1994. The National Parks
and Wildlife Service (NPWS) conduct special
interpretive walks into these areas.

Canoes or paddleboats can be hired from
the boat shed near the Audley causeway.
Upstream from the causeway there are several
pleasant picnic spots on the banks of the river.

There are many beaches where swimming is
very popular, as are beach and rock fishing.
Some of the beaches have their own lifesaving
patrols. The more popular beaches are Burning
Palms, Garie, Wattamolla and Bonnie Vale.

ACCESS AND CAMPING

The park can be accessed by car, train and ferry.
Road access is from the Princes Highway at
Loftus via Farnell Avenue or McKell Avenue at
Waterfall. From the south entry is at Otford.

There are walking trails into the park from
the railway stations at Engadine, Loftus,
Heathcote and Waterfall. The ferry service runs
from Cronulla across Port Hacking to
Bundeena, a delightful small settlement.

There is limited camping in the park: the
only developed camping ground is at Bonnie
Vale. Bookings are essential and can be made
through the visitor centre. There is bush
camping or undeveloped sites at various locations including Werrong Beach, Curracurrang,
Winifred Falls, Uloola Falls, North Era, Deer
Pool and Karloo Pool.

A forest scene in the Royal National Park

STURT NATIONAL PARK

IN BRIEF

MAP REFERENCE: PAGE 152 B 2

Location 330 km north of Broken Hill

Best Time Winter

Main Attractions Remote, semi-desert landscape, wildlife, history, 4WD

Ranger Contact the NPWS office at Tibooburra, phone (08) 8091 3308

Accommodation:
Family Hotel, Tibooburra (in true country pub style), phone (08) 8091 3314
Tibooburra Hotel, phone (08) 8091 3310
Granites Motel, phone (08) 8091 3305

4WD Tours: Tri State Safaris, phone (08) 8088 2389

An old tree stump in the Corner Country

The driest, most remote of the New South Wales national parks lies in the far northwest corner of the state and covers an area of more than 310 000 hectares. It is here that the red kangaroo, emu and the wedge-tail eagle reign supreme, where the heat shimmers off the burnt red rock and the mulga bush whistles in the breeze. This is the Outback.

HISTORY

There is ample evidence of Aboriginal occupation in the form of middens and stone relics throughout the vast boundaries of the park. Captain Charles Sturt, after whom the park is named, spent a year in and around the area between 1844 and 1845 in search of the great 'inland sea'.

In 1880 gold was discovered at the granite diggings, which were to become Tibooburra. The gold rush was short lived with small pickings and harsh conditions bringing it to an end by 1890. Pastoralists followed and still remain in the adjoining area. The longest fence in the world, the Dog Fence, was constructed along the borders of Queensland and South Australia and in 1972 the Sturt National Park was established.

MAJOR ATTRACTIONS

The vastness of the Outback is the major attraction of this park. However, once you have ventured into the endless gibber plains you will find there is much more of interest. The park has a huge kangaroo and emu population and there will be ample opportunity to see these magnificent animals at close range. Of equal interest is the evidence of human endeavour, in the form of explorers' camps at Depot Glen and Fort Grey, pastoralists' stations such as Olive Downs and Mt Wood, and the pioneer towns of Milparinka and Tibooburra which regularly record the state's highest temperatures.

A drive through the area after rain will be rewarded with brilliant displays of wildflowers that carpet the harsh landscape in hues of yellow and purple. You might even find good examples of Sturt's desert pea, a brilliant red flower that is synonymous with the Outback.

Take a look at the artists' works in Broken Hill and Silverton and then travel to the Corner Country and see the reality of their interpretation of the landscape: the soft colours of the Outback will leave a lasting impression.

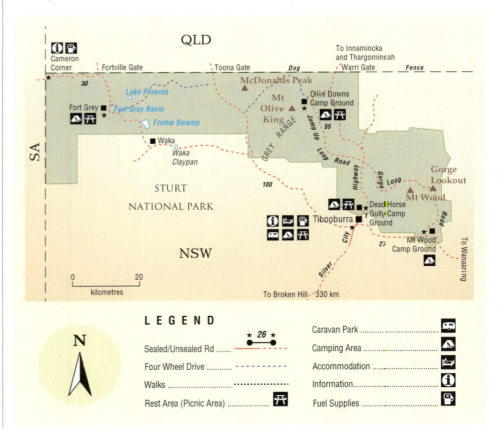

LEGEND

Sealed/Unsealed Rd	Caravan Park
Four Wheel Drive	Camping Area
Walks	Accommodation
Rest Area (Picnic Area)	Information
	Fuel Supplies

THINGS TO DO

Sturt National Park is a very remote and hostile area. Travel in summer is best avoided as the heat is unbearable and the risk of dehydration is very real. The heat will also cause havoc with the proper operation of your vehicle and the flies are intolerable. Autumn through to spring is much more appropriate but expect very cold nights in winter. It can drop below freezing at this time of year.

Before leaving Tibooburra check the National Parks and Wildlife Service (NPWS) office where there is a very informative display depicting local wildlife and other points of interest. Also pick up the relevant brochures detailing the various drives and walking tracks that can be followed.

There is a short walking trail starting in the camp site at Dead Horse Gully just outside Tibooburra. This walk takes you through the unusual granite outcrops unique to this area. There is also a reconstruction of gold mining techniques at Golden Gully for those interested in history.

Short walking trails at Mt Wood and Olive Downs allow the walker to view the surrounding country from the Jump Ups, as the flat-topped plateaus are known, that are so prominent in this section of the park. Spectacular scenery

A brown falcon

and an abundance of kangaroos will dominate your interest on these walks that will take little more than an hour to complete.

At Fort Grey you can walk to the old holding yard constructed by Sturt during his exploration for the inland sea. There is a nearby dry lake that sometimes holds water, the rings of trees around the foreshore showing previous high-water levels.

The park also has a well-mapped drive tour which is self guided with the aid of an information sheet from the NPWS office. The drive encompasses 110 km and takes the visitor via Mt Wood and Olive Downs through what is the prettiest part of the park. You will certainly see huge numbers of kangaroos, emus and eagles. Remember to carry extra water, food supplies and basic vehicle spares on all trips in this remote park.

Part of the Dog Fence, the world's longest fence

ACCESS

The park hugs the corner country of New South Wales stretching from Cameron Corner east to the Silver City Highway and south to Tibooburra. A smaller section continues eastward to Mt Wood. It is a long drive from anywhere to the park through the real Outback. A mixture of bitumen and graded gravel road stretches for 330 km between Broken Hill and Tibooburra, or there is an unsealed route from Bourke and Wanaaring. Both routes are impassable after rain so always check the state of the roads with local police.

A view of the range country in Sturt National Park

CAMPING

Sturt National Park, despite its isolation, caters well for the tourist with 3 well appointed camp sites. Just 1 km out of Tibooburra is the Dead Horse Gully Camp Ground set amongst the huge granite boulders that are typical of the Tibooburra area. Toilets, gas BBQs and water are available. A small camping fee applies with honesty tins on site.

Further north, just outside the old homestead of Olive Downs, is another camp site which provides a beautiful setting amongst the mulga trees below a rocky ridge line. This camp also has toilets and BBQs and there is a short walk to a magnificent lookout over the Jump Up country typical of the northern section of the park.

The other recognised camping area is at Fort Grey on the western fringe of the park just 30 km before Cameron Corner. This is a large level area nestled between low sand hills and surrounded by mulga trees typical of this side of the park. Toilets, gas BBQs and walking tracks are also found here. As with the other camp sites a small fee of just a few dollars applies on an honour system.

Bookings for the camp sites are not possible but the helpful staff in the NPWS office in Tibooburra can advise on numbers currently camping at each location.

At Mt Wood there are also walking trails and lookouts.

The roads to each of the camping sites and picnic areas are generally gravel with some sandy sections. With care they can be traversed in conventional vehicles but after rain a 4WD will certainly be needed. It should be noted that most of these roads are closed to all traffic after persistent rain to avoid damage to the surface.

WADBILLIGA NATIONAL PARK

IN BRIEF

MAP REFERENCE: PAGE 147 D 7

Location Far south coast of
NSW, 80 km from Braidwood
Best Time Summer
Main Attractions 4WD
tracks, the Tuross Falls and
Cascades, remote wilderness
walks
Ranger NPWS in Narooma,
phone (02) 4476 2888

4WD tag-along tours:
Great Divide Tours, phone
(02) 9913 1395

Wadbilliga is a true wilderness park with deep
gorges and a huge variety of flora. The park has
few trails, ensuring that anyone who ventures
into this wild place will certainly have the area
to themselves. The park covers 79 000 hectares
of the mountains of the south coast of New
South Wales, 30 km inland from Cobargo.

HISTORY

The escarpment of the Great Dividing Range
is extremely rugged on the south coast, and
in the area of Wadbilliga National Park it is
particularly wild and remote. It is this terrain
which precluded any major exploration of the
area, apart from the occasional cedar cutter
venturing into the wild gullies during the 1800s.

This ensured that the wilderness qualities
of the area were maintained and these were
eventually recognised with the gazetting of the
park in 1979.

MAJOR ATTRACTIONS

The natural features of this park are its main
attraction—the 35 metre high Tuross Falls, the
4 km long Tuross Gorge and the beautiful Tuross
Cascades. The cascades are easily accessible
but the falls and gorge will require some
difficult walking through dense forest.

Due to the undeveloped nature of the park
its other major attraction is the remote wilderness walks, but you certainly need to be very
experienced and capable of surviving for some
days in often difficult weather conditions.

THINGS TO DO

Bushwalking in remote areas is a major feature
of the park but its lack of walking trails and very
rugged nature ensure that it is not very popular.
Drivers of 4WD vehicles will enjoy touring the
few trails that crisscross the park and the camp
at the Cascades is ideal for those following this
style of recreation. There is a rough walking
trail to the Tuross Falls but it would be best to
contact the National Parks and Wildlife Service

Camping in Wadbilliga National Park

(NPWS) personnel for advice on this trail before
setting out. There is a new access track into a
viewing point above the falls off the Wadbilliga
Track which is found just after crossing the
causeway over the Tuross River at Two River
Plain junction; check with the NPWS for advice
on this track also.

Great Divide Tours is licensed to conduct
4WD tag-along tours along the park's trails; this
is a great way to enjoy the area.

ACCESS

Fortunately, the park, despite being a wilderness area, is not totally inaccessible. Access
along the beautiful valley to the west of Cobargo
to Yowrie provides a pleasant drive through

LEGEND

★ 26 ★	
Sealed/Unsealed Rd	
Four Wheel Drive	
Walks	
Rest Area (Picnic Area)	🏕
Caravan Park	🚐
Camping Area	⛺
Accommodation	🛏
Information	ℹ
Fuel Supplies	⛽

A water dragon, commonly found in Wadbilliga National Park

farmland before entering the thickly forested hills around the Wadbilliga River. This road becomes gradually rougher and would be best attempted in a 4WD vehicle once past the small picnic area on the causeway over the Wadbilliga River.

At this point the track climbs steeply with great views of some sheer granite bluffs before emerging on the high plains of the Great Divide. Here the trail passes through snow gums and heath-covered hills before crossing a deep causeway on the Tuross River and emerging on the good gravel road from Nimmitabel to Countegany.

Access is also possible from Braidwood

which is 80 km north on the Snowball Road. Look for the signs leading to the Cascades Camping Area on the Badja Forest Road. The Cascades is a great place to camp.

The Belowra Road inland from Bodalla also

The proud wedge-tail eagle

climbs the escarpment and follows the boundary that the park shares with the Deua National Park to the north. In dry weather this road would be suitable for conventional vehicles with good clearance.

CAMPING

There are 2 designated camp sites in the park. The Cascades Camping Area on the Tuross Falls Road off the Badja Forest Road has pit toilets, BBQs and picnic tables. There is plenty of fresh water from the Tuross River. This is the best spot to camp as it is right beside the Tuross Cascades where swimming is possible in summer. The last 2.5 km of Tuross Falls Road is really only suitable for 4WD.

You can also camp at the Lake Creek Camping Area which has a bushland setting next to the Wadbilliga River. The facilities here are also fairly basic.

The Wadbilliga Crossing Picnic Area, on the Wadbilliga Road, has tables, toilets and fireplace facilities and plenty of fresh water in the river.

WARRUMBUNGLE NATIONAL PARK

IN BRIEF

MAP REFERENCE: PAGE 148 C 1

Location 27 km west of Coonabarabran in central NSW
Best Time Spring and autumn; avoid school holidays as it will be very crowded
Main Attractions Bushwalks, rugged mountain scenery, 4WD
Ranger Visitor Centre, phone (02) 6825 4364 or the NPWS office, Coonabarabran, phone (02) 6842 1311

Camping: book with visitor centre, phone (02) 6825 4364

Rock climbing permit and access to Burbie Camp: phone (02) 6825 4364

The Breadknife, a well-known landform of the Warrumbungles

This park, situated 27 km west of Coonabarabran, attracts the most visitors to a park outside the major metropolitan area. Over 80 000 people annually visit the Warrumbungles to enjoy the clear mountain air and enjoy the huge range of walking trails that crisscross the mountain range.

HISTORY

Consider yourself lucky that you were not in the area 13 million years ago when this whole region was a mass of very active volcanoes. Tonnes of molten lava spewed from the fissures in the earth's surface creating a covering of several hundred metres of lava. The forces of erosion slowly worked away, creating the valleys and gullies of today's mountain range whilst the volcanic plugs and fissures were slower to weather. These created the impressive land-forms that are so well known in the Warrumbungles today: the Breadknife, Crater Bluff and Split Rock.

The explorer John Oxley ventured into the rugged ranges in 1818 on his second expedition through New South Wales. Other explorers to examine the ranges were Sturt and Thomas Mitchell and following their reports white settlers soon took up holdings around the hills that abut the rugged mountains. The area was proclaimed a reserve in 1953 and reached national park status in 1955. The park now occupies an area of over 21 000 hectares.

MAJOR ATTRACTIONS

Warrumbungle National Park is primarily a bushwalkers' park. There are several walking trails established throughout the park ranging in difficulty from easy, one hour strolls to arduous 2 day treks of up to 15 km.

Rock climbing and abseiling are also permitted in most areas of the park. For those who prefer quieter activities there is a huge bird population with a remarkable number of brightly coloured parrots. The walker who enjoys the crisp mornings of springtime will also be rewarded with a kaleidoscope of wild-flowers on the drier sandstone plateaus.

A spring landscape in Warrumbungle National Park

THINGS TO DO

Bushwalking is the major attraction and there is a huge selection of excellent walking trails. The scenery of the Warrumbungles is a feature of most walks and the well-known Breadknife, a 90 metre wall of solid rock, is one of the best known features of the park.

Upon arrival at the park it is best to check in at the visitor centre where there are excellent displays and all the information and fact sheets you will need to complete your favourite walk. It is here that you could check on current camping availability and access to Camp Burbie if you are going that way.

There are a number of easy, short walks including Whitegum Lookout and Gurianawa Track which are only 1 km long and wheelchair accessible. Other short walks ranging from 1 km to 2 km include Wambelong Nature Track and Burbie Canyon.

For the more energetic there is also a range of very good trails. Fan's Horizon trail from Camp Pincham takes 2 hours return to cover the 3.6 km. It has over 600 steps and provides views of the Grand High Tops area. Split Rock Circuit is more than 4.6 km and it takes 3 hours to complete the arduous walk, including a chain and ladder climb to the top of the southern peak.

The Breadknife and Grand High Tops trail is one of the longer tracks, covering 12.5 km. It is steep but includes the major attractions of the park; allow 5 hours to complete it. From Camp Burbie there are the long Mt Exmouth, Arch and Cathedral walks which are up to 16 km and will require 6 hours of walking. All of these walks are rated as steep.

If you enjoy rock climbing you may pursue this activity in selected areas of the park but you must obtain a permit from the ranger at the visitor centre. No rock climbing is permitted on the Breadknife.

ACCESS

The park is easily accessed by conventional vehicle from either Coonabarabran which is 27 km to the east or Coonamble 57 km to the west. The road through the range is gravel and it would be wise to check with local authorities regarding the condition of the road in wet weather. The southern section of the park can be accessed via Gilgandra, again over a gravel road. The park is primarily a walking trail park and there are limited vehicle trails within the park. The track to Camp Burbie is open to 4WD vehicles only but road conditions should be checked with the ranger beforehand.

CAMPING

There are a number of delightful camp sites within the park. Access to the major camping areas is available from the John Renshaw Parkway which crosses the park from Coonabarabran to Coonamble. Camp Blackman, where caravans and campervans are permitted, has very good facilities with hot showers, septic toilets and powered sites. Camp Wambelong, also popular with families, has pit toilets and tank water. Camp Wambelong and Elongery can be used by large groups and it is not uncommon to find school groups in these spots. If you prefer to avoid large gatherings, check with the ranger as to current bookings for large groups.

Camp Burbie is accessible only by 4WD but you must gain the ranger's permission before using the access trail. In the southern section of the park, accessed from Gilgandra, is Camp Guneemoorco. This is a quiet place beside a creek where basic toilet facilities are provided.

For bushwalkers there are designated camp sites along the longer walking trails but you must register with the ranger and gain permission to camp on these sites in order to avoid overcrowding.

No wood fires are permitted in the park and all cooking must be done on gas BBQs that you bring with you, or on those which have been provided at some camp sites.

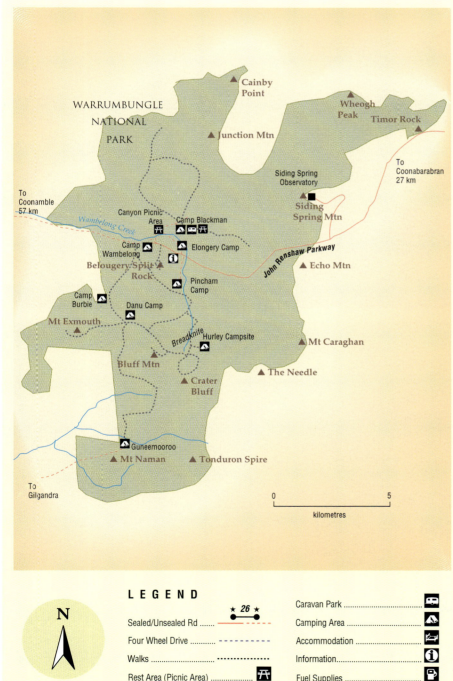

WARRUMBUNGLE NATIONAL PARK

Cainby Point
Wheogh Peak
Timor Rock
Junction Mtn
To Coonabarabran 27 km
Siding Spring Observatory
Siding Spring Mtn
To Coonamble 57 km
Wambelong Creek
Canyon Picnic Area
Camp Blackman
Camp Wambelong
Elongery Camp
Belougery Split Rock
John Renshaw Parkway
Echo Mtn
Pincham Camp
Camp Burbie
Danu Camp
Mt Exmouth
Breadknife
Hurley Campsite
Mt Caraghan
Bluff Mtn
The Needle
Crater Bluff
Guneemooroo
To Gilgandra
Mt Naman
Tonduron Spire
0   5
kilometres

LEGEND

N

Sealed/Unsealed Rd .... ★ 26 ★
Four Wheel Drive ....
Walks ....
Rest Area (Picnic Area) ....

Caravan Park ....
Camping Area ....
Accommodation ....
Information...................
Fuel Supplies ....

WASHPOOL NATIONAL PARK

Wild mountain streams tumble through boulder-strewn gorges, their banks lined with numerous species of delicate ferns and mosses. Overhead, the seemingly impenetrable forest is like a tangled mass, in countless shades of green. Huge bird's-nest ferns, elkhorns and staghorns cling precariously to the branches of ancient forest giants, occasionally crashing to the ground with a mighty thud when their weight becomes too much for their host to bear. On the leaf-littered rainforest floor, fungi of every imaginable shape and size decorate the rotting timber, adding an extra touch of magic to this enchanting world.

This is the Washpool, a 27 700 hectare wilderness which protects the largest area of old-growth, warm-temperate rainforest in New South Wales. Declared a national park in 1983 because of its outstanding natural wonders,

The impenetrable forests of Washpool

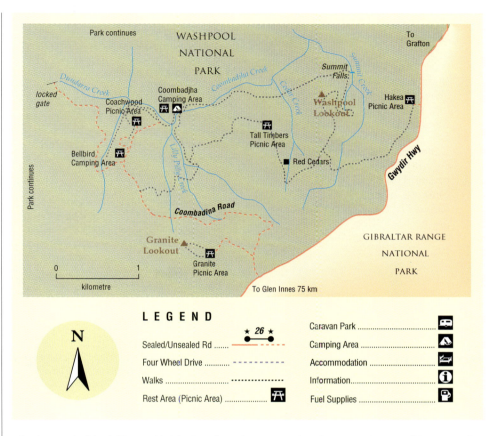

The mountains of Washpool National Park

Washpool has since been given the added status of inclusion on the World Heritage List.

FLORA AND FAUNA

Situated in the high mountain ranges 75 km east of Glen Innes, this isolated rainforest retreat is an ideal year-round destination for anyone wanting to experience the tranquillity of one of Australia's most beautiful national parks.

Much of this unique wilderness lies on an elevated, trackless plateau which in some places rises to 1200 metres above sea level. Numerous species of trees and shrubs clothe its ridges and steep slopes. They include the world's largest remaining stand of coachwood.

Visitors wishing to see a wide variety of wildlife will not be disappointed. The region is one of the richest fauna areas in New South Wales. Currawongs are by far the most vocal of the park's 260 species of birds.

While you are breakfasting, it is not uncommon to see eastern yellow robins, scrubwrens, fantails, Lewin's honeyeaters, crimson rosellas and king parrots within a few metres of your picnic table. You may even catch a glimpse of the elusive lyrebird scratching around the forest edge in search of food. The most intriguing of the park's feathered inhabitants would have to be the large numbers of satin bowerbirds. After constructing an elaborate bower out of fine twigs, the brilliant blue satin male tries to attract a female by placing small blue objects such as straws, feathers and biro tops around the outside of the bower.

Nocturnal animal life in Washpool is extremely interesting, with 3 species of possums being commonly encountered near the camping area. The thick-set mountain brush-tail possum is the easiest to see as they often come around picnic tables in search of food. Ringtail possums are much more shy, but can be spotted with the aid of a good torch in the low trees beside the walking tracks. Sugar-gliders are also present, although their smaller size makes them more difficult to locate. Further up the main vehicle track, near the park entrance, koalas and greater gliders can sometimes be sighted in the tops of tall eucalypts.

GREAT FOR BUSHWALKING

A number of interesting walks within the park range from a pleasant one hour stroll along the banks of Coombadjha Creek to difficult 3 day hikes through the remote parts of this wilderness. Anyone attempting these out-of-the-way treks into the park's interior should be reasonably fit and fully equipped for any emergencies. A compass, topographic maps and wet weather gear are a must.

There is a form near the park entrance where hikers must register their names, the area they are heading to, and the approximate date of return. This precaution allows rangers to know the hikers' general location so they can carry out rescue operations if the party is overdue.

ACCESS AND CAMPING

Washpool is situated on the Gwydir Highway between Glen Innes and Grafton in northern New South Wales. The park is accessible to conventional vehicles. Caravans and trailers should have no trouble negotiating the track into Bellbird Camping Area, but should not attempt the steep descent into the walk-in camp sites at Coombadjha Camping Area. Glen Innes, 75 km to the west, is the nearest main town in which to buy food, fuel and other necessities.

The main camping ground at Bellbird Camping Area has sites screened from each other by tall trees and shrubs to provide privacy from fellow campers. Picnic tables, fireplaces, firewood and toilets are provided. As a bonus, there is a large shelter shed in the middle of the camp ground where campers can cook during wet weather. Washpool is a region of high rainfall, and showers or storms can be expected at any time of the year.

WOLLEMI NATIONAL PARK

IN BRIEF

MAP REFERENCE: PAGE 148 F 5

Location 100 km northwest of Sydney
Best Time All year round
Main Attractions Wilderness area, rock formations, canoeing, swimming
Ranger For more information and to report any planned walks into the park, contact the NPWS, Muswellbrook, phone (02) 6543 3533; Mudgee, phone (02) 6372 3122; Richmond, phone (02) 4588 5247; or Blackheath, phone (02) 4787 8877

Wollemi, at 492 220 hectares, is the second largest park in New South Wales. It is within 2 hours of the busiest city in the country and yet it is primarily a wilderness park. It is an extremely rugged area which defeated most attempts to explore it. The Aborigines inhabited the wild gullies and there is ample evidence of rock art sites to support this. Europeans in the early part of this century found vast deposits of shale which they mined at various sites, the most notable being Newnes and Glen Davis.

In 1994 the Wollemi pine was found deep in the park, the significance of this tree being that it is a direct descendant of the Jurassic period.

MAJOR ATTRACTIONS

The park's major feature is its wilderness value. The intrepid bushwalker will find a fascinating place of hidden sandstone gorges, rock pagodas and fast-running rivers. Being such a vast and uncharted area you will need to be very experienced in rugged trekking and allow a few days for your walks in the area, self-sufficiency being a priority.

There are camp sites at the historic Newnes shale mine site and for those interested in history, this area has plenty to offer. The nearby Glow Worm tunnel, which is actually a disused train tunnel, is within walking distance and is always a great place to spend a few hours.

Canoeing, li-loing and swimming are popular activities in the eastern section of the park on the Colo River.

THINGS TO DO

From Dunns Swamp it is possible to canoe on the quiet waters of the dam where the bird observer will be delighted. From here it is also possible to explore some of the rock pagodas unique to this part of the park. These unusual rock formations create weird twisted shelves amongst the sandstone monoliths, evidence

Tree ferns dwarfed by gums in Wollemi

that the area was once an ocean bed.

The Newnes camping area has equally stunning scenery and there are several walks amongst the ruins and to the Glow Worm tunnel high above the Wolgan Valley. If you are contemplating this walk make sure that you carry drinking water and a torch to light your way in the long, disused train tunnel. Access to the tunnel is also possible from Lithgow following a gravel road for over 25 km to its end where a 3 km walk along the track's original route will bring you to the tunnel entrance.

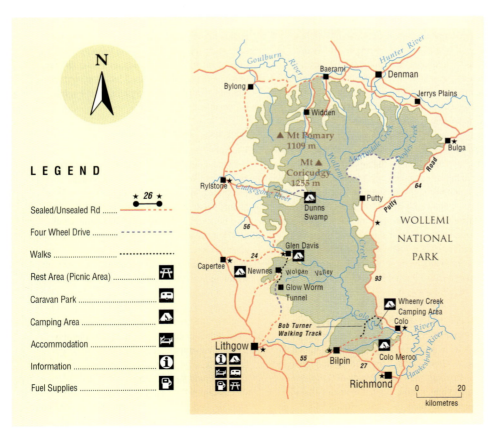

LEGEND

Sealed/Unsealed Rd	★—●—★ 26 ★
Four Wheel Drive	- - - -
Walks	··········
Rest Area (Picnic Area)	🛆
Caravan Park	🚐
Camping Area	⛺
Accommodation	🛏
Information	ℹ
Fuel Supplies	⛽

At Wheeney Creek on the eastern side of the park there are pleasant walks into lush gullies and canoeing on the Colo River. The Bob Turner Walking Track leads to the Colo River. It takes about one hour to reach the river and this track is found off the Putty Road 7 km past Colo Heights.

ACCESS AND CAMPING

Access into the park itself is restricted as it is primarily a wilderness area. Even trails that once existed have now been closed. For the average tourist, it is possible to gain vehicle access only to the park's perimeter; after that it is only for the fit and experienced bushwalker.

The park stretches across the Great Divide from the Blue Mountains near Windsor across to Lithgow and north towards Denman, inland from Muswellbrook. The Putty Road from Windsor to Singleton runs along the park's eastern boundary and provides access to the Wheeney Creek camping area near Colo.

Part of the Bells Line of Road forms the southern boundary and to access the western edge of the park you will need to travel up the Mudgee Road from Lithgow where access into

Newnes, Glen Davis and Dunns Swamp via Rylstone is available.

There are limited developed camp sites. On the eastern side there is camping at Wheeney Creek and Colo Meroo where pit toilets and BBQs are provided. On the western boundary there is a large camping area at the site of the old shale mine at Newnes. This is a pleasant location with plenty of open ground surrounded by towering sandstone cliffs. Dunns Swamp is a beautiful setting on the Narrango Road out of Rylstone where there is a wealth of bird life and many wallabies to keep you company.

BALD ROCK NATIONAL PARK
5451 HECTARES

Tucked away in the thickly forested country between Stanthorpe and Tenterfield along the Queensland–New South Wales border, the huge granite dome of Bald Rock is one of Australia's best kept secrets.

The park has 2 walking tracks, both leading to the top of Bald Rock. The shorter 1.2 km trail is the direct, steep approach, the slightly longer 2.5 km walk is a more gradual climb. Both tracks are shaded most of the way to the base of the rock by stands of eucalypts, mainly stringy-bark and New England blackbutt. White marks have been painted on the rock to make the direct 45 degree climb a little easier to navigate. A trig station at the 1277 metre summit offers 360 degree views of the surrounding terrain. On a clear day the vista to the east stretches as far as Mt Warning and other volcanic plugs on the Tweed Range.

The park is accessible to conventional vehicles and has a camping ground with basic facilities such as pit toilets, tables and BBQs.

The park is a pleasant place to visit at any time of the year, although winters can be very cold.

For further information, contact the NPWS, ph: (02) 6732 5133.

BOOTI BOOTI NATIONAL PARK

Booti Booti National Park is located 250 km north of Sydney, just 10 km south of Forster, on the mid north coast. This is a favourite camping area for those that love the sun, surf and sand. It protects a thin strip of land between the Pacific Ocean and Wallis Lake. Its main attractions are the 11 km long surf beach and the calm waters of Wallis Lake.

Among the many activities that can be pursued here, swimming, fishing and sailing predominate.

There are also excellent walking trails to lookouts at Cape Hawke in the north of the park and Booti Hill in the south. The view from Cape Hawke is excellent, stretching up and down the coast and over the vast lake system of the Myall Lakes.

There are excellent camping opportunities at a place called the Ruins in the southern end of the park where all facilities are provided. It is necessary to book your camp site through the National Parks and Wildlife Service (NPWS). There is also a commercial camping ground at Tiona which is adjacent to the Ruins. There are electric BBQs at Santa Barbara, near the Sailing Club on the lake, and picnic facilities at Elizabeth Beach which is patrolled during holiday periods.

For further information, contact the NPWS, ph: (02) 4987 3108.

Bald Rock, in Bald Rock National Park

BOTANY BAY NATIONAL PARK

Located within the suburban sprawl of Sydney, Botany Bay National Park is easily reached by car or bus. The park protects the entrance to Botany Bay with sections on both the north and south landfalls. Its significance lies in the history of the first landing by Captain James Cook in 1770.

There are historic monuments and a museum commemorating the importance of this landmark. The museum is especially interesting and few would know that the French sailed into Botany Bay as Captain Phillip departed for Port Jackson on 26 January 1788. The museum contains a display of maps, scientific instruments and relics recovered from the French explorers' ships which were eventually wrecked off the Solomon Islands. From the museum there is a good walking trail to the Endeavour Lighthouse with views across the bay entrance to the site of Captain Cook's landing on the southern entrance to Botany Bay.

Captain Cook's Landing Site is reached from the southern Sydney suburb of Cronulla along Captain Cook Drive. A Discovery Centre has been established with information and maps. There are picnic facilities nearby and walking trails along the shoreline and through the unusual heath vegetation that fascinated Joseph Banks. The Towra Point Nature Reserve adjoins the park and protects the home of various migratory birds. If intending to visit the reserve you should contact the National Parks and Wildlife Service (NPWS) in advance, as this is a very fragile area.

For further information, contact the NPWS, ph: (02) 9311 3397 (North), or (02) 9668 9111 (South).

BOUDDI NATIONAL PARK
1200 HECTARES

Another great park close to the major population areas, Bouddi lies 75 km north of Sydney and not far from Gosford. It protects the beaches and forests of the coast immediately north of Broken Bay. A special feature of this park is its Marine Extension over Maitland Bay where all marine life is protected.

Access is via the aptly named Scenic Road from Gosford. Vehicle access leads to Putty Beach where there are picnic tables and limited camping. Walking trails from various access points lead to the secluded beaches of Little, Maitland and Tallow. There is limited camping at Little Beach and Tallow Beach and all camp sites must be booked in advance through the National Parks and Wildlife Service (NPWS). The Maitland Information Centre is staffed on a voluntary basis over weekends and contains information on the park and the famed shipwreck of the paddle steamer *Maitland* after which the bay is named.

For further information, contact the NPWS, ph: (02) 4324 4911.

BRISBANE WATER NATIONAL PARK
11 300 HECTARES

Located 50 km north of Sydney and just west of Gosford, this park stretches from the Newcastle Freeway to the towns of Umina and Woy Woy. The main attractions are the many hundreds of kilometres of walking trails and the Aboriginal art and engraving sites.

The park covers a vast area of rugged sandstone bushland and there are various access

points and places of interest. The Somersby Falls area provides picnic facilities and there is a walking trail to the falls. A few kilometres south of Kariong you will find the Bulgandry Aboriginal Engraving Site which provides some of the best Aboriginal art in the Sydney district. The National Parks and Wildlife Service (NPWS) have descriptive brochures of the engravings and it would be best to obtain these if visiting the site.

The focal point of the park is at Girrakool on the main road from Calga. Here, there are picnic facilities and a number of walking trails. The Great North Walk from Sydney to Newcastle dissects the park and involves an overnight walk. There are several short and longer walks leading off the Great North Walk and it would be best to obtain detailed brochures from the NPWS.

For further information, contact the NPWS, ph: (02) 4324 4911.

BROADWATER NATIONAL PARK
3800 HECTARES

This beautiful national park, 11 km east of the small town of Woodburn, south of Ballina, preserves untouched remnants of northern New South Wales coastal flora. During spring, the heath and wetlands in the park come alive in a blaze of colour. Purple irises, yellow waxflowers, ground orchids, dwarf and heath banksia and red bottlebrush are just a few of the blooms which greet visitors at this time of the year. Bird life is prolific, with numerous varieties of honey-eaters darting in and out of the flowering banksias. White-bellied sea-eagles, red-backed

sea-eagles and the occasional osprey are sometimes seen soaring over the beach looking for fish washed up on the sand.

Aborigines have long been associated with the park, and numerous middens from their former occupancy can still be found along Broadwater's 8 km beach frontage.

Camping inside the park is not permitted, but visitors can put up a tent at Silver Sands Caravan Park at Evans Heads.

The park is a pleasant place to visit throughout the year.

For further information, contact the NPWS, ph: (02) 6628 1177.

CATHEDRAL ROCK NATIONAL PARK
6530 HECTARES

Cathedral Rock National Park, 77 km east of Armidale, is an important refuge for wildlife in the sheep-producing country of the New England Tablelands. Wildlife is abundant in the park and it is easy to identify up to 40 species of birds in the course of a morning's walk.

A diverse range of vegetation can be found within the boundary of the park including eucalypt woodland, banksia heath, swamps and snow gums. There are a number of walking tracks in the park including the 5.8 km Cathedral Rock circuit which weaves its way gently upwards between giant granite boulders to the base of Cathedral Rock. The panoramic views from the top of the rock are spectacular well rewarding the effort in getting there.

There are 2 camping areas: Barokee and Native Dog Creek Rest Area. Both are

accessible to conventional vehicles.

The best time to visit the area is mid to late spring to see the wildflower display.

For further information, contact the NPWS, ph: (02) 6657 2309

CATTAI NATIONAL PARK
424 HECTARES

This is another park located close to Sydney, just 40 km to the west on the banks of the Hawkesbury River. The park is accessed off Wisemans Ferry Road just past Middle Dural and was formerly the Cattai Homestead owned for several generations by the Arndell family.

The homestead still stands and is open for inspection on Sundays and is well worth a visit. The surrounding land covers a broad sweep along the Hawkesbury River with a good camping ground providing excellent facilities including several toilet blocks, shelter sheds and kiosk. Paddleboats and canoes can be hired for use on one of the lagoons within the park or you can swim and canoe on the Hawkesbury River.

There are several short walking trails around the park, some of which provide good views across the Hawkesbury River. It is also possible to hire bicycles or bring your own for a pleasant ride around the bushland setting. There is a daily visitor fee for entry to the park and bookings for the camp site must be made in advance. The gates to the park are closed each evening.

For further information, contact the National Parks and Wildlife Service, ph: (02) 4573 3100.

CROWDY BAY NATIONAL PARK
8000 HECTARES

Crowdy Bay National Park is located 325 km north of Sydney, just 25 km out of Taree. It protects an area of beach front and adjacent heath bush and is a wonderful place for surfing, swimming and fishing.

There is an excellent view up and down the coast from Diamond Head at the northern end of the park. At this point you will find the main camping areas where basic facilities such as pit toilets, tables and fireplaces are provided. Diamond Head and Indian Head rest areas as well as Kylies Beach rest area are good camping spots.

The beach can also be accessed via a gravel road at Mermaid Beach and Fig Tree Beach. Both of these spots are located on a long, sweeping beach between Crowdy Head and Diamond Head. The remainder of the park is low scrubby heath with no vehicle access. Harrington is on the boundary of the park and provides all required facilities and services.

For further information, contact the National Parks and Wildlife Service, ph: (02) 6584 2203.

The forest floor carpeted with wildflowers in Brisbane Water National Park

OTHER PARKS OF INTEREST

DHARUG NATIONAL PARK

Dharug National Park is named after the local Aboriginal tribe that inhabited the rugged sandstone country northwest of Sydney. The park is 75 km from Sydney via Wisemans Ferry. Its chief attraction is the old convict-built Great North Road, which forms its western boundary.

This road was originally constructed in 1827 by convict labour and was once the only route northwards to Newcastle. The first 2 km of the road off the Wisemans Ferry–St Albans road contains the best examples of the engineering feats of the convicts. Here you will see buttressed road edges using cut sandstone blocks that weigh over a tonne. Also, there are sandstone culverts and the fabled hangman's rock where it is said that wayward convicts were tried and punished.

There is a camping ground at Ten Mile Hollow on the convict road where pit toilets and basic fireplaces are provided. The old road is now closed to vehicles and visitors must walk the full length which will take 2 days.

Another camping ground is provided at Mill Creek which can be accessed off the Spencer Road not far from Wisemans Ferry. From this spot there are 2 unmarked bush walks, the longest being 11 km but you need to be an experienced bushwalker and you will have to carry your own water.

There are a number of Aboriginal art sites within the park but the National Parks and Wildlife Service (NPWS) must be contacted in advance regarding access to these sites.

For further information, contact the NPWS, ph: (02) 4324 4911.

DORRIGO NATIONAL PARK
7885 HECTARES

Located 600 km north of Sydney on the Great Dividing Range near Dorrigo, this park has attained World Heritage Listing as it protects a vast area of rainforest. The park has established good walking trails that entice you to enjoy and observe the rainforest and its prolific bird life.

The major attraction of the park is the Skywalk which takes visitors into the treetop canopy to observe this unique ecosystem at close quarters.

There is a nearby Rainforest Centre with theatre, shop and displays. From this point there are 2 great walks that lead into the rainforest: the Lyrebird Walk and the Wonga Walk, the latter being over 5 km in length but well worth the effort. From the Never Never picnic area there are other short walks.

No camping facilities are provided in the park but bush camping is permitted.

For further information, contact the NPWS, ph: (02) 6657 2309.

A scribbly gum growing in Goulburn River National Park

GARIGAL NATIONAL PARK

This is another city based national park. Garigal is found in the heart of the northern beaches suburbs of Sydney and protects the valleys of the upper reaches of the harbour and its feeder creeks. There are various points of access from the surrounding suburban streets on the north shore, the best known access being via Davidson Park under the Roseville Bridge.

The park provides many walking trails that follow the harbour shores around Middle Harbour and Bantry Bay as well as along the various creeks emptying into the harbour. Some of these, notably Deep Creek and Middle Harbour Creek, provide pleasant walks with occasional waterfalls and rockpools. At Davidson Park there are a number of boat launching ramps making this an ideal spot for accessing the harbour. The park also surrounds Narrabeen Lakes where it is possible to fish, swim and canoe. The surrounding sandstone escarpments provide good vantage points for panoramic views of the coast. There are no camping facilities and a fee is charged for access to Davidson Park where there are toilets and BBQ facilities. Walking trail maps can be obtained from the National Parks and Wildlife Service (NPWS).

For further information, contact the NPWS, ph: (02) 9451 3479.

GEORGES RIVER NATIONAL PARK

This park caters to the southern suburbs of Sydney, providing a range of water- and land-based activities. The park is accessed off Henry Lawson Drive at Picnic Point or at the intersection of The River Road and Henry Lawson Drive at Revesby Heights, the latter being the main entrance where a park fee is payable.

A tar sealed road leads through the park past 3 delightful picnic grounds—Morgans Creek, Burrawang Reach and Cattle Duffers Flat. There are toilets, BBQ facilities with wood supplied and boat ramps. This is a great place for a family picnic but the more adventurous will find the boat access to Georges River a great reward as well. Water-skiing, canoeing and fishing are all popular pastimes. For those wanting a quieter time there is a walk-in picnic area at the end of the access road known as Fitzpatrick Park.

For further information, contact the National Parks and Wildlife Service, ph: (02) 9772 2159.

GIBRALTAR RANGE NATIONAL PARK
17 273 HECTARES

The rugged granite country which makes up the Gibraltar Range National Park provides hikers with some of the best wilderness walks anywhere in New South Wales. The park lies 69 km east of Glen Innes on the Gwydir Highway.

Vegetation in the park ranges from heathlands—which are covered in wildflowers during spring—through to towering eucalypt forests.

Wildlife in the park is particularly abundant, with grey kangaroos, red-necked wallabies and swamp wallabies being regularly seen. The endangered parma wallaby is also found in the park, as is the rarely seen tiger quoll. Birds are prolific and include eastern yellow robins, rufous fantails, a multitude of different honey-eaters and the magnificent wedge-tail eagle. Rangers at certain times of the year take visitors on spotlight walks at night to look for some of the park's nocturnal fauna. These include the greater glider, squirrel glider, sugar-glider, brush-tail possum and short-nosed bandicoot.

There is a large camping area at Mulligan's Hut, which is situated 10 km inside the park boundary on the Gwydir Highway. One of the most interesting trails in the park is the 5 km return walk down to Dandahra Falls. The last part of this track is extremely steep, and should be attempted only by fit people.

The best times to visit the park are autumn and spring.

For further information, contact the NPWS, ph: (02) 6732 5133.

GOULBURN RIVER NATIONAL PARK
70 102 HECTARES

This park lies 300 km northwest of Sydney nestled between the towns of Mudgee and Sandy Hollow. It stretches along the twisting bed of the Goulburn River and protects an area of sandstone escarpment and sandy river bed. Access to the park is via Mudgee, Rylstone or Muswellbrook and Sandy Hollow.

The park is relatively undeveloped and there are only a few walking trails, which are not developed. Walking along the sandy river bed is quite easy but the other walks over the rugged escarpment are much more demanding. Camping is restricted to a camp site off Ringwood Road and a 4WD access route to Spring Gully. These camp sites do not have any facilities. There are several rock caves along the river bed and many contain Aboriginal paintings. Therefore, it is important that fires are not lit in these overhangs.

For further information, contact the National Parks and Wildlife Service, ph: (02) 6543 3533.

GUY FAWKES RIVER NATIONAL PARK
46 030 HECTARES

Located 100 km northeast of Armidale, with breathtaking views over rugged gorges and mountain ranges, the Guy Fawkes River National Park is an ideal destination for wilderness seekers. The main feature of the park is the Guy Fawkes River which snakes its way through deep, narrow valleys that are only occasionally penetrated by human visitors.

The vegetation in the park is predominantly open woodland, with cabbage gum, Blakely's red gum, yellow box and broad-leaved stringybark being the main species. In some of the steep, narrow gullies where water gathers, isolated stands of dry rainforest can be found. The

combination of grasslands and closed vegetation has made the park an important refuge for many types of animals. Grey kangaroos, red-necked wallabies, swamp wallabies and walla-roos are normally fairly easy to see, while rarer marsupials like the brush-tailed rock wallaby, potoroo and parma wallaby are also present in small numbers.

There are a number of walking tracks including an overnight 30 km return hike that descends 640 metres to the Guy Fawkes River. Visitors can camp at Chaelundi Rest Area which has basic facilities and is accessible to conventional vehicles.

The best time to visit the park is in spring, although it is pleasant throughout the year.

For further information, contact the NPWS, ph: (02) 6657 2309.

HAT HEAD NATIONAL PARK
6803 HECTARES

Hat Head National Park lies 450 km north of Sydney on the coast from Kempsey. Access is via good roads from Seal Rocks or Crescent Head. This is typical coastal terrain with sweeping beaches, rocky headlands, vegetated sand dunes and swampy heath.

Camping facilities are available at the Hat Head Caravan Park and also at the Hungry Hill Rest Area where there are also picnic facilities. In the northern section of the park, accessed from South West Rocks, is the Smoky Cape Rest Area. Both of these camping grounds are close to the beach where excellent surfing, swimming and fishing opportunities exist. For the energetic, the climb to the Smoky Cape lighthouse affords excellent views up and down the coast. There are good walks around Hat Head that

offer a diverse vegetation cover and unusual coastal rock formations.

For further information, contact the National Parks and Wildlife Service, ph: (02) 6584 2203.

HEATHCOTE NATIONAL PARK
2250 HECTARES

This park lies 50 km south of Sydney on the outskirts of the southern suburbs, adjacent to the Royal National Park. It is primarily a bush-walking park with no road access within its boundaries. Access to the park is found off the Heathcote Road near Engadine and off the Woronora Dam Road which leaves the Princes Highway south of Waterfall.

There are a number of walking trails through the park and the Central Mapping Authority (CMA) map of the Royal National Park is recommended for this purpose. There are no facilities provided in the park; however, bush camping is permitted, but you must obtain a

Dangar Falls near Dorrigo National Park

OTHER PARKS OF INTEREST

Kinchega National Park

permit from the National Parks and Wildlife Service (NPWS) Visitor Centre at Audley if intending to camp in the park. The walking trails follow the sandstone ridges and the deeply eroded creek beds common to this type of country. There are numerous swimming holes and small waterfalls to cool off in during the warmer months.

For more information, contact the NPWS, ph: (02) 9542 0666.

KINCHEGA NATIONAL PARK
44 000 HECTARES

This is an arid park with unique inland water features. It is located 110 km southeast of Broken Hill. Access along a tar sealed road from Broken Hill is available but all other gravel roads within the area become impassable after only a little rain. The town of Menindee is located just outside the park boundary.

The park contains the historic Kinchega Homestead where many artefacts of the bygone wool industry remain.

Visitors to the park can follow the tourist drive around the park where points of interest are marked. Descriptive brochures on these points are available from the information office at Kinchega. The park is bounded by the Darling River which provides many fishing opportunities and delightful camp sites amongst the river red gums. There are two major lakes within the Park—Menindee and Cawndilla. These lakes teem with bird life which makes this place a birdwatcher's delight.

Temperatures in summer are very high and the area is best avoided at these times.

For further information, contact the National Parks and Wildlife Service, ph: (08) 8088 5933.

LANE COVE NATIONAL PARK

Just 11 km north of the centre of Sydney, the Lane Cove National Park lies along the shore of the Lane Cove River. Its main access point is off Fullers Road in the suburb of Chatswood, but there is another entrance off Lane Cove Road just across De Burghs Bridge in the suburb of Ryde.

The park offers some great family picnic areas along the grassy banks of the river. Canoeing on the river and BBQs in the fireplaces provided are just some of the many activities that can be enjoyed. There is a visitor centre and kiosks and plenty of amenities blocks. It is possible to reserve large areas for business or private functions. There are also a number of secluded walking trails for people to enjoy the abundant bird life found along the river valley. There is a certain amount of history associated with the area and this is depicted in various forms in the park.

For further information, contact the NPWS, ph: (02) 9412 1811.

MT WARNING NATIONAL PARK

Located almost on the Queensland border and just 12 km from Murwillumbah, it is impossible not to notice Mt Warning. It is visible to travellers on the Pacific Highway across the Tweed River and swaying cane fields; it beckons to be climbed. This is the first piece of mainland Australia to receive the sun's rays each day. However, its Aboriginal name, which means Cloud Catcher, aptly describes it, as it is frequently enveloped in cloud. Little wonder, considering the peak reaches 1157 metres above sea level.

The park is accessed by a good road from Murwillumbah and the car park is set amidst a lush rainforest. The walk to the summit and return is for the very fit as it will occupy up to 5 hours. It passes through thick rainforest before emerging at the base of the old volcanic plug. The last short climb is steep and a chain rail assists climbers. Viewing platforms have been provided on the summit for the dramatic scene that awaits the intrepid walker. Camping is not permitted in the park; however, commercial camping grounds are found nearby.

For further information, contact the National Parks and Wildlife Service, ph: (02) 6628 1177.

MURRAMARANG NATIONAL PARK

This park is on the south coast of the state just 300 km south of Sydney or 10 km north of Batemans Bay. It follows the coastline from the quiet seaside town of Long Beach all the way to Merry Beach which is near Ulladulla. An attractive feature of the park is the wonderfully tame

An eastern grey kangaroo in Murramarang

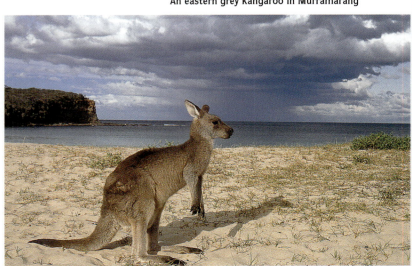

Nothofagus moorei growing in New England National Park (facing page)

eastern grey kangaroos that co-exist with humans in many of the small towns and particularly at Pebbly Beach.

There are several entrances to the park off the Princes Highway. Two major entries are at the northern end via Bawley Point and Merry Beach and in the southern section off the highway near East Lynne to Pebbly Beach and Durras North. The roads through the State Forests to the park are all generally unsealed and caution in wet weather is needed. There are no vehicle tracks in the park itself other than those leading to designated beaches or camping areas. Camping is possible at various locations including Pebbly Beach, South Durras, Depot Beach, Pretty Beach and Merry Beach. Some of these camp sites are commercially operated whilst the National Parks and Wildlife Service (NPWS) also charges camping fees for its sites. The best walk in the park is to the top of Mt Durras, which offers fabulous views up and down the coast and west to the mountains.

For further information, contact the NPWS, ph: (02) 4423 9800.

NEW ENGLAND NATIONAL PARK
30 068 HECTARES

Rugged mountain scenery, swift-flowing streams, lush rainforests and a wide variety of animal life make New England National Park one of the most important areas of biodiversity in New South Wales. The park was placed on the World Heritage List in 1986. It is situated 85 km east of Armidale.

Most of New England National Park is a trackless wilderness that has been penetrated by only a few small groups of well equipped bushwalkers. Excellent panoramic views to the north, south and east can be had from Point Lookout which, at 1564 metres above sea level, is the highest point in the park.

Vegetation in New England is extremely rich and varied, and botanists have identified more than 500 different species of plants. One of the most interesting is the Antarctic beech, which grows just below the often mist-shrouded escarpment at altitudes above 1200 metres. More than 100 species of birds have been seen in the park including crimson rosellas, king parrots, flycatchers, honeyeaters and the superb lyrebird.

Visitors who wish to pitch a tent can camp at Thungutti Rest Area just inside the park entrance. Another camping ground, better suited to caravans, is located at Styx River 2 km from the park boundary.

Visit the park throughout the year, although winters are cold.

For further information, contact the NPWS, ph: (02) 6657 2309.

Nightcap National Park

NIGHTCAP NATIONAL PARK
4945 HECTARES

The park, 34 km north of Lismore, takes its name from the spectacular Nightcap Range which rises in places to 900 metres above sea level. Its southern boundary borders Whian Whian State Forest, which is also good for bird-watching and hiking. Protesters Falls in the Terania Creek section of the park was the site, in the late 1970s, of one of the biggest conservation battles in New South Wales.

A combination of good soils and the highest recorded rainfall in New South Wales has enabled huge brush box, blackbutt and flooded gum to flourish in the wet sclerophyll forest which borders the rainforest. The almost constant damp conditions in the forest allow an incredible array of colourful fungi to grow on the tops and sides of fallen branches strewn across the forest floor.

Bird life is prolific and includes uncommon species such as the Albert's lyrebird, wompoo pigeon and regent bowerbird.

There is a small area for overnight camping (one night only) at Terania Creek.

The park can be visited throughout the year but January–March can be very wet.

For further information, contact the NPWS, ph: (02) 6628 1177.

NYMBOIDA NATIONAL PARK
19 000 HECTARES

Located in the north of the state, inland from Grafton, the Nymboida National Park covers an area of rugged river valley. This park is virtually impenetrable except for those adventurous enough to participate in the exciting sport of whitewater rafting. Access by vehicle is difficult with fire trails leading through Ramornie State Forest, north of the old Glen Innes Road, to the Ramornie Forest Camping Area. There is an equally rough fire trail from the Gwydir Highway, best accessed from Glen Innes, which follows the Narlala Road and Cooraldooral Fire Trail down to the Mann River.

The Mann River merges with the Nymboida River within the park to form a raging torrent that passes through steep-sided valleys clad in thick forest. This is a mecca for whitewater rafting and there are many commercial tour operators out of Coffs Harbour who can take you on a ride of a lifetime. There are no walking trails in the park, so the rivers are the main transport arteries.

For further information, contact the NPWS, ph: (02) 6732 5133 (West), or (02) 6642 0613 (East).

SEVEN MILE BEACH NATIONAL PARK
898 HECTARES

This small park is on the south coast just north of Nowra. Access is easy; by leaving the Princes Highway at Gerringong and following the road to Gerroa you will reach the park after crossing the Crooked River. From the south the park is reached by turning off the Princes Highway north of Nowra and following the signs towards Gerroa, the road follows the coast and the park all the way from Shoalhaven Heads to Gerroa.

There are no vehicle tracks in the park other than one road which leads directly to the beach. However, the beach, with its long sweeping sands, provides a great spot for fishing and surfing. The area is particularly popular during holiday periods. Camping facilities are available

A squirrel glider in Nymboida National Park

at the northern end of the park in Gerroa just at the Crooked River bridge.

For further information, contact the National Parks and Wildlife Service, ph: (02) 4423 9800.

SYDNEY HARBOUR NATIONAL PARK

This must surely be one of the most outstanding national parks in the world. Scattered around what is said to be the most beautiful harbour in the land is a series of national parks that together protect a number of headlands. Access to the various parks is excellent with major roads leading to all areas, and even government bus routes pass right by the many parks.

There are several excellent walking trails around the foreshore, each providing unsurpassed views over the spectacular harbour. The area is dotted with historic fortresses and gun emplacements and this adds to the interest of the park. The park includes North Head and its Quarantine Station, where tours can be arranged, Dobroyd Point near Manly, Middle Head to Bradleys Head and, on the southern side of the harbour, Nielsen Park and South Head. There are also a number of harbour islands included in the park and tours to these can be arranged through the National Parks and Wildlife Service (NPWS).

For further information, contact the NPWS, ph: (02) 9247 5033 or the Quarantine Station, ph: (02) 9977 6229.

A rusting shead stamper on Cells Creek, Werrikimbe National Park

WERRIKIMBE NATIONAL PARK

This is a true wilderness park located on the Great Dividing Range inland from Port Macquarie. It is 500 km north of Sydney with access via Wauchope from the east or Walcha from the west. Once you begin to approach the park the roads become unsealed and the final trails to the edge of the park are difficult in wet weather.

The park features rainforest, heath and alpine forests, snow can fall in winter and high rainfall is common. There are excellent camping opportunities at various locations. On the eastern side of the park camping at Brushy Mountain, Grass Tree and Plateau Beech picnic areas is permitted. Each of these provide picnic shelters and pit toilets as well as BBQ places.

On the western fringe you will find the less crowded camp sites of Cobcroft and Mooraback with fireplaces and pit toilets available at each. Mooraback is the pick of the camping locations thanks to its kangaroo population and access to fresh water.

Walking trails and 4WD tracks are also available in the park, making it enjoyable for everybody.

For further information, contact the NPWS, ph: (02) 6773 7211 (West), or (02) 6584 2203 (East).

WILLANDRA NATIONAL PARK

Willandra was once synonymous with merino wool. The homestead and surrounding flat land became part of the park in 1971. The park is in the west of the state, 64 km northwest of Hillston. Access is via unsealed roads that would be impassable in wet weather. The homestead and other outbuildings have been retained to preserve this part of New South Wales's outback history.

It is possible to stay in the 'Men's Quarters' where bunks and cooking utensils are provided, but bookings through the National Parks and Wildlife Service (NPWS) must be made in advance. Camping is also available near the homestead where water, pit toilets and fireplaces are provided. Remote camping within the remainder of the park is possible for back-packers, but be careful with fire. There are a number of walks in the park with details available from the NPWS. Note that it becomes extremely hot in summer and the area is best avoided at this time. The Merton Motor Trail provides an unsealed road tour of the park for those who prefer this type of travel. The western section of the park has no vehicle access at all and is restricted to bushwalkers only.

For further information, contact the NPWS, ph: (02) 6962 7755.

YURAYGIR NATIONAL PARK

Yuraygir National Park is located on the north coast east of Grafton. It provides excellent fishing and surfing opportunities and is said to contain some of the best beaches in the country. There are several access roads into the various sections of the park. Commencing from the south, Station Creek provides camping and picnic facilities and is accessed off the Pacific Highway 40 km north of Coffs Harbour. The next access is before Grafton and leads to the popular resorts of Minnie Water and Diggers Camp. The town of Wooli is also nearby. Closer to Maclean there is another route into the park which leads to Brooms Head, Sandon River Rest Area and Lake Arragon Rest Area.

Once past Maclean the road to Yamba can be followed. This eventually leads to Angourie where the Mara Creek Picnic Area is found. It is said that the surf beach at Angourie provides some of the best surfing in Australia. With the park providing access to so many fabulous surf beaches it is little wonder that swimming and fishing are priorities for anyone visiting this park. Other activities, such as bushwalking and canoeing, are also popular. Camping fees apply at each of the camp sites in the park and there are a number of nearby commercial caravan parks and motels.

For further information, contact the National Parks and Wildlife Service, ph: (02) 6642 0613.

Australian Capital Territory

NAMADGI NATIONAL PARK

This national park is located 40 km south of Canberra. It is at the northern end of the Australian Alps which run from the Australian Capital Territory through to Victoria. The park boasts a range of vegetation, from broad grassy valleys to snow gum woodlands, and protects a variety of wildlife, such as wallabies, eastern grey kangaroos, lyrebirds, wedge-tail eagles, crimson rosellas, and much more.

The mountainous terrain of the park offers spectacular views from the roads and from the walking tracks. Snow falls are common on the Bimberi and Brindabella Ranges.

The visitor centre, located 2 km south of Tharwa on the Naas/ Boboyan Road, has information on walking tracks and bush camping grounds. It also has interesting displays and a widescreen audiovisual.

For further information, contact the ACT Parks and Conservation Service, ph: (02) 6207 2900.

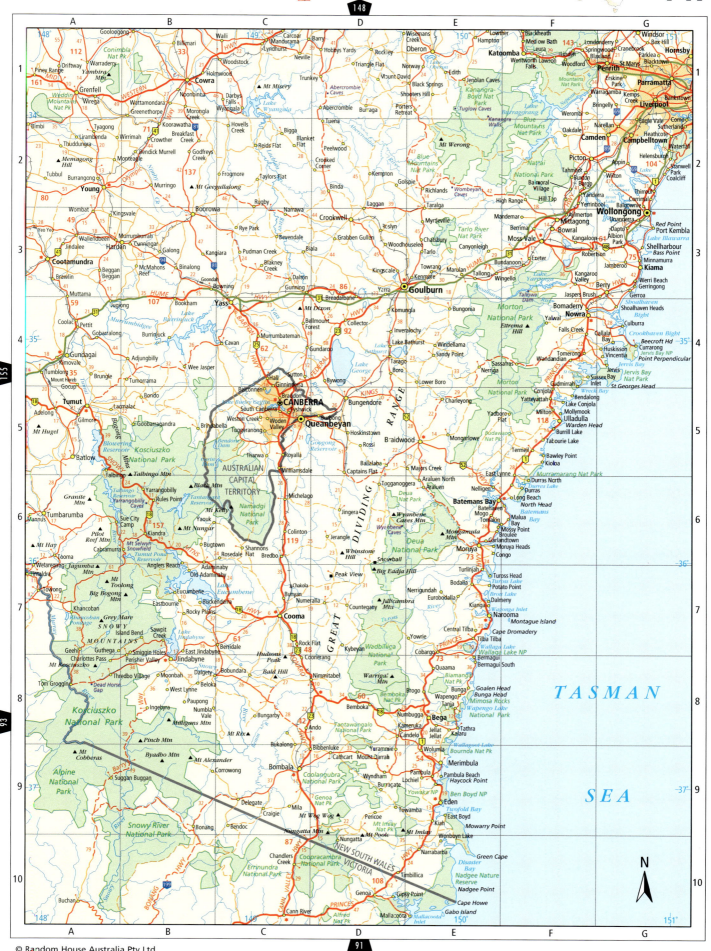

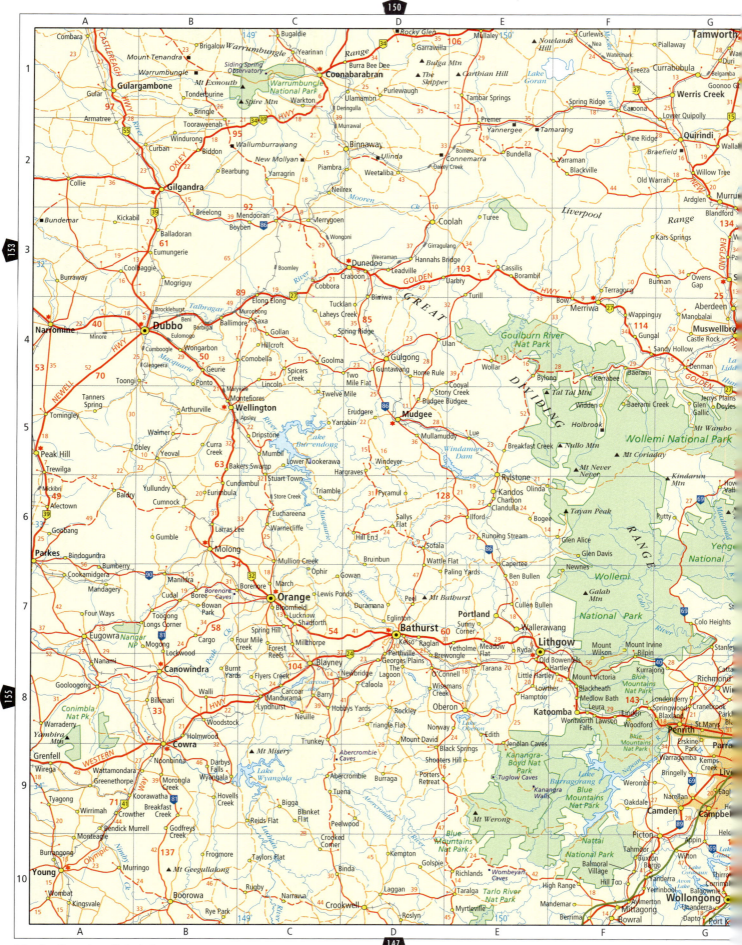

kilometres
0 10 20 30 40 50

H   J   K   L   M   N   P

SOUTH

PACIFIC

OCEAN

TASMAN

SEA

Port Macquarie

Taree

Forster

Maitland

Newcastle

Gosford

SYDNEY

Singleton

Cessnock

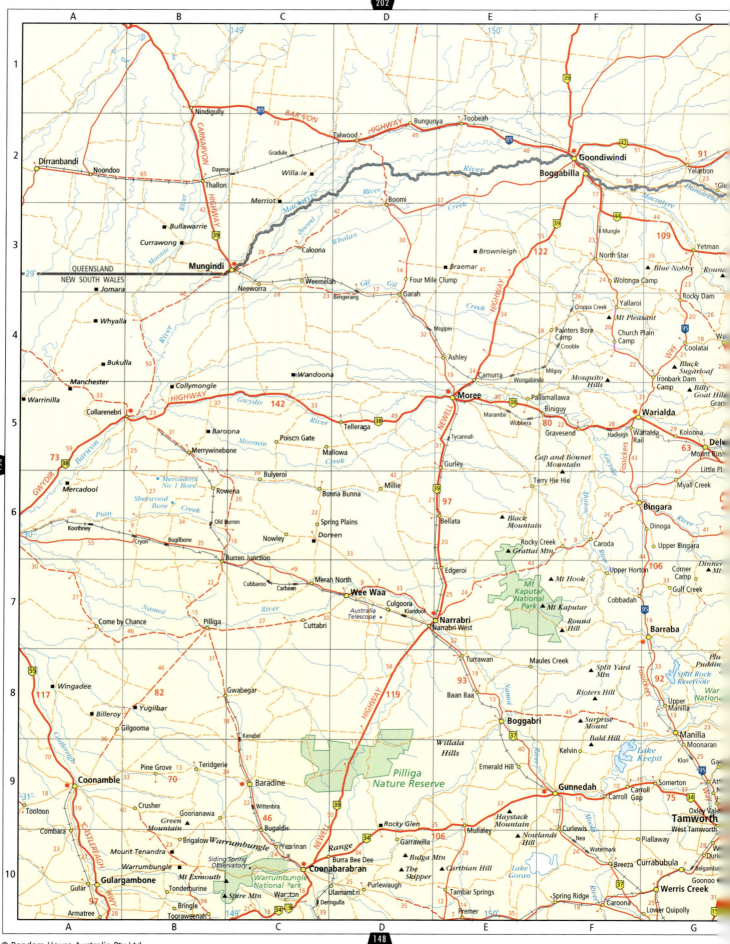

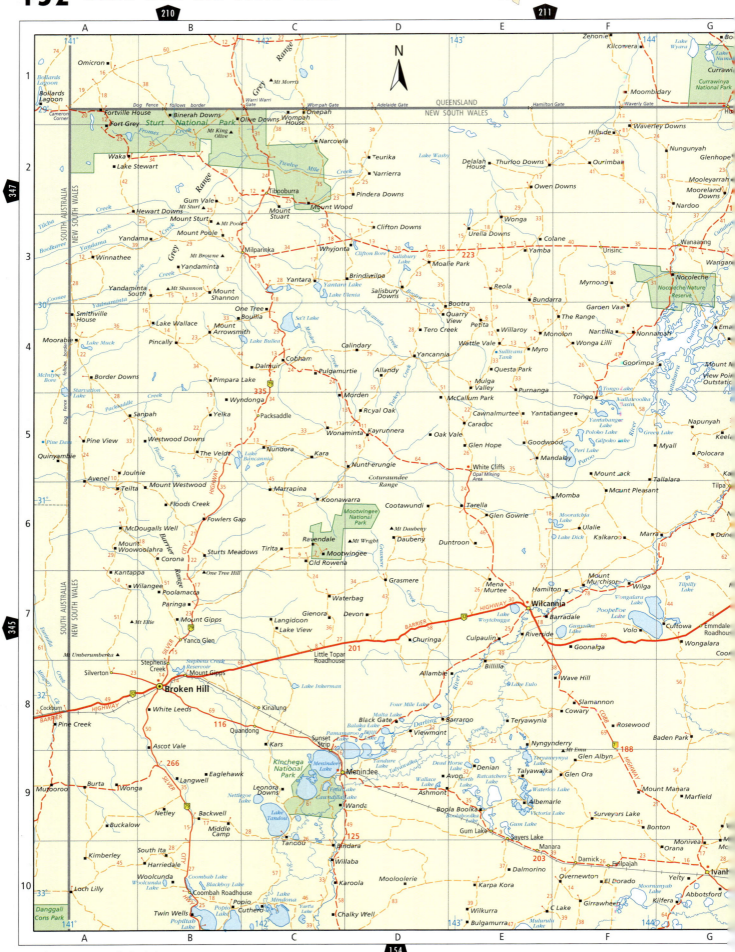

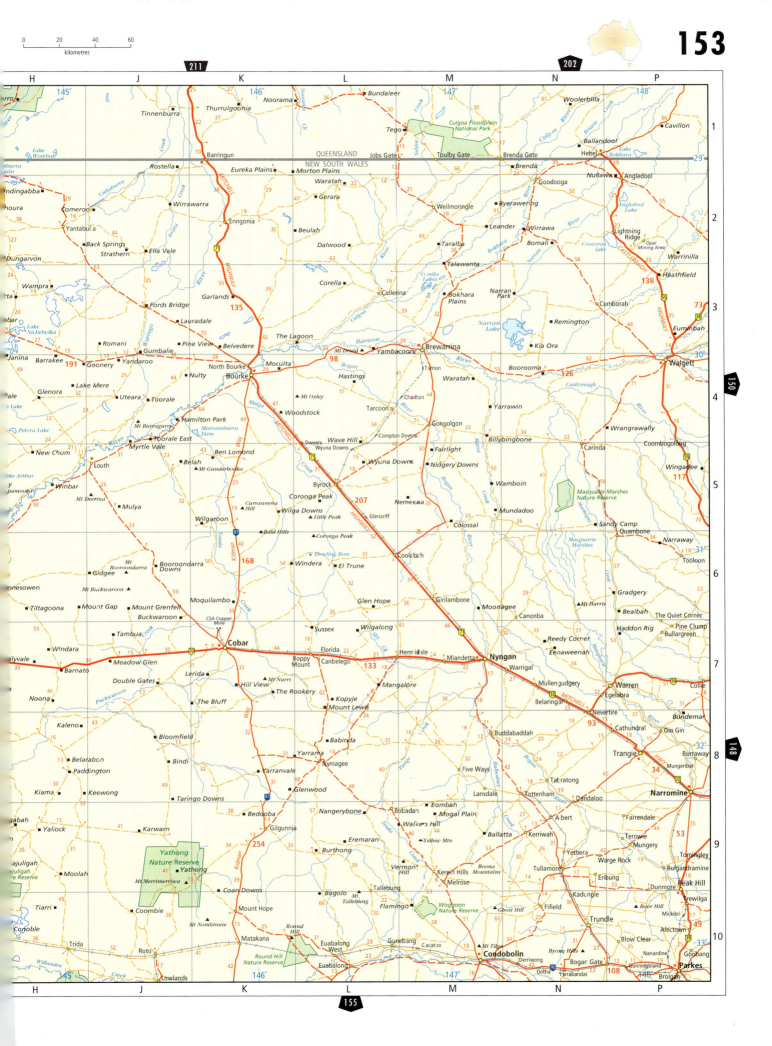

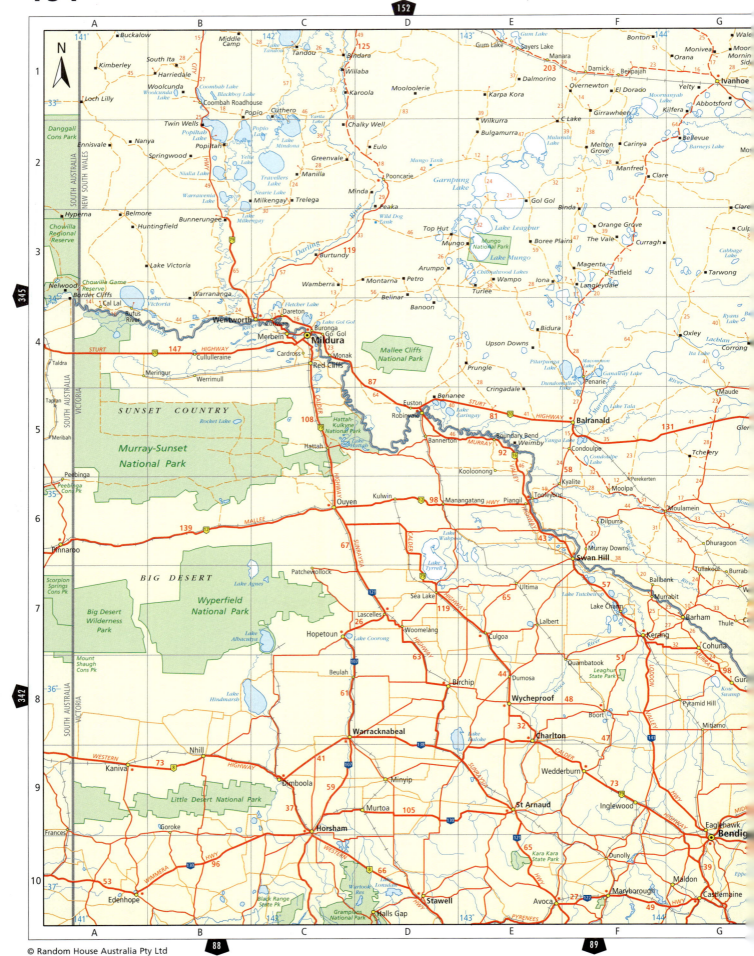

153

kilometres
0 20 40 60

H J K L M N P

Kajuligah Nature Reserve
Tiarri
Conoble
Trida
Coombie
Mt Merrimerriwa
Coan Downs
Bogolo
Mt Tallebung
Tallebung
Melrose
Eribung
Kadungle
Dunmore
Trewilga
Peak Hill
Mickibri
Alectown
Fifield
Trundle
Boor Hill
Goobang
Nanardine
Blow Clear
Byong Hills
Ghost Hill
Mt Tilga
Condobolin
Derriwong
Bogan Gate
Gunningbland
Parkes
Matakana
Round Hill
Euabalong West
Gurebang
Kiacatoo
Oootha
Yarrabandai
Corridgery
Tichborne
Cookamidgera
Daroobalgie
Roto
Euabalong
Mount Hope
Round Hill Nature Reserve
Murrin Bridge
Wallaroi Hill
Fairholme
Warroo
Bedgerebong
Forbes
Lowlands
Willandra National Park
Lake Cargelligo
Wargambegal
Burgooney
Tullibigeal
Banar Lake
Corinella
Bundaburrah
Garema
Cumbijowa
Mulyandry
Moolbong
Ballatherie
Lake Brewster
Mt Bowen
Weja
Winnungra
Bogandillon Swamp
Narang Cowal
Lake Cowal
Wirrinya
Pinnacle Reefs
Driftway
Warraderry
Hillston
Cowl Cowl
Dirrung
Monia Gap
Naradhan
Hannan
Gubbata
Kikoira
Girral
Calleen
Clear Ridge
Marsden
Pullabooka
Piney Range
Yambira Hill
Grenfell
Whealbah
Langtree
Merriwagga
Rankins Springs
Erigolia
Taleeban
Weethalle
Narrah Mtn
Yalgogrin
West Wyalong
Wyalong
Bland
Caragabal
Weddin Mountains Nat Pk
Wirega
Merungle
Goolgowi
Tallimba
Buddigower
Alleena
Yiddah
Quandialla
Bimbi
Bribbaree
Thuddungra
Memagong Hill
Young
Booligal
Gunbar
Mt Cenon
Eurugabah Hill
Tabbita
Warburn
Cocoparra National Park
Bellarwi
Barmedman
Morangarell
Reefton
Narraburra
Tubbu
Burrangong
Wombat
Kingsvale
One Tree
Beelbangera
Binya
Barellan
Moombooldool
Kamarah
Mirrool
Gidginbung
Trungley Hall
Grogan
Milvale
Griffith
Hanwood
Widgelli
Yoogali
Wumbulgal
Murrami
Ardlethan
Uley
Ariah Park
Pucawan
Wallundry
Springdale
Wallendbeen
Jindalee
Hay
Carrathool
Willbriggie
Whitton
Wamoon
Colinroobie
Walleroobie
Cowabbie West
Temora
Combaning
Stockinbingal
Yeo Yeo
Cootamundra
Beggan Beggan
Uardry
Darlington Point
Gogeldrie
Leeton
Yanco
Methul
Mimosa
Sebastopol
Dirnasser
Bethungra
Mt Ulandra
Muttama
Jugiong
Gum Creek
Waddi
Grong Grong
Matong
Ganmain
Marrar
Old Junee
Illabo
Brawlin
Colac
Pettit
Four Corners
Coleambally Irrigation Area
Narrandera
Coolamon
Junee
Eurongilly
Cooba
Gobbaralong
Booroorban
Corobimilla
Sandigo
Galore
Currawarna
Millwood
Downside
Harefield
Mundarlo
Kimovale
Gundagai
Wanganella
Morundah
Birrego
Kywong
Greenvale
Bulgary
Collingullie
Wagga Wagga
Nangus
Brungle
Tumblong
Mt Horeb
Gocup
Tumut
Conargo
Dahwilly
Yulama
Boree Creek
Bullenbong
Uranquinty
Forest Hill
Gregadoo
Borambola
Mt Adrah
Adelong
Gilmore
Morago
Mayrung
Jerilderie
Bundure
Urana
Osborne
French Park
Tootool
The Rock
Milbrulong
Lockhart
Yerong Creek
Mangoplah
Burrandana
Pulletop
Kyeamba
Humula
Westbrook
Batlow
Talbingo
Logie Brae
Berriquin Irrigation Area
Bidgeemia
Urangeline East
Pleasant Hills
Henty
Cookardinia
Umbango
Mt Hugel
Deniliquin
Blighty
Oaklands
Rand
Bulgandry
Alma Park
Walbundrie
Ralvona
Carabost
Tumbarumba
Tuppal
Finley
Osborne Well
Daysdale
Wabonga
Culcairn
Holbrook
Rosewood
Wolseley Park
Mannus
Lankeys Creek
Munderoo
Pilot Reef Mtn
Mathoura
Tocumwal
Savernake
Sangar
Coreen
Lowesdale
Brocklesby
Barrimbuttock
Walla Walla
Gerogery
Woomargama
Granite Mtn
Strathmerton
Barooga
Warragoon
Rennie
Balldale
Hopefield
Burrumbuttock
Mullengandra
Talmalmo
Jingellic
Ournie
Mt Hay
Tooma
Cobram
Mulwala
Merton Vale
Corowa
Buraawannah
Jindera
Bowna
Welaregang
Fintalora
Towong
Khancoban
Moama
Barmah State Park
Barman
Yarrawonga
Rutherglen
Lavington
Thurgoona
Wymah
Burrowye
Corryong
Echuca
Nathalia
Numurkah
Albury
Wodonga
Mt Granya State Pk
Koetong
Berringama
Geehi
Charlottes Pass
Mt Kosciuszko
Rochester
Kyabram
Warby Range State Park
Chiltern State Park
Hume Weir
Tallangatta
Bullioh
Wabba Wilderness Park
Mt Lawson State Park
Burrowa-Pine Mtn Nat Park
Stanhope
Shepparton
Lake Mokoan
Beechworth
Beechworth Park
Bucheen Creek
Dartmouth
Lake Dartmouth
Alpine National Park
Kosciuszko Nat Park
Rushworth
Murchison
Benalla
Oxley
Moyhu
Wangaratta
Myrtleford
Mitta Mitta
Bogong
Mt Cobberas
Waranga Basin
Euroa
Nagambie
Whitfield
Dandongadale
Bright
Mount Beauty
Falls Creek
Alpine National Park
Heathcote
Lake Nillahcootie
Mount Samaria State Park
Mt Buffalo National Park
Hotham Heights
Seymour
Mansfield
Lake Eildon
Mount Buller
Alpine Village
Alpine National Park
Omeo

QUEENSLAND

Tropical rainforests, deserts, melaleuca heathland, granite country, mangrove-lined estuaries, eucalypt forests and beautiful islands bordered by coral reefs combine to make Queensland's national parks system the most diverse in the nation. Covering nearly 4 per cent of the land area, the state's 220 national parks provide homes and protection for many varieties of wildlife including some of Australia's rarest and most endangered creatures.

Queensland's national parks can be divided into 6 geographical regions—the Southeast, Central Coast, Central Highlands, Western Queensland, North Queensland, and Far North Queensland and Cape York. Within each of these areas, the Queensland Department of Environment has endeavoured to preserve as much as possible of the state's very diverse ecosystems.

Queensland's national parks provide homes for nearly two-thirds of Australia's mammals (230 species). Apart from common marsupials such as the grey kangaroo and brush-tail possum, rare creatures like the bilby and the yellow-bellied glider also find a safe refuge in the park system. There are a number of species that are endemic to Queensland, and only found in a few isolated parts of the state. These include varieties of possum such as the Herbert River ringtail, green ringtail. lemuroid ringtail, spotted cuscus and long-tailed pygmy possum. Other mammals that are confined to Queensland's national parks are the extremely rare hairy-nosed wombat, the rufous spiny bandicoot, unadorned rock wallaby, Godman's rock wallaby, Proserpine rock wallaby and Lumholtz tree kangaroo.

Due to the diverse range of habitats in Queensland, over 600 of Australia's 760 species of birds have been recorded in the Sunshine State. They range in size from the country's smallest bird, the weebill, through to the giant southern cassowary, which is restricted to the rainforests of the wet tropics. A number of species are only found in one or two national parks in isolated parts of the state. These include the yellow-billed kingfisher, red-bellied pitta, black-winged monarch, frilled monarch and green-backed honeyeater which are confined to the Jardine River and Iron Range National Parks on the northern tip of Cape York.

Brilliant rainforest species like the catbirds and riflebirds are fully represented within Queensland's national parks. Of the 5 species in these 2 groups, 3 of them—the spotted catbird, Victoria's riflebird and the magnificent riflebird—are confined to the rainforest national parks of the state's tropical north. The other 2 species, the green catbird and paradise riflebird, are found in the temperate rainforests of southeast Queensland and across the border in northern New South Wales.

Approximately half of Australia's species of reptiles and amphibians find a safe home within Queensland's diverse national parks. Of the 303 varieties of skink so far identified, 97 species are endemic only to Queensland.

Apart from providing a protected habitat for wildlife, Queensland's national parks offer visitors numerous opportunities to enjoy the great outdoors. While every park has some particular aspect which makes it special, there are a few places like Fraser Island which abound in a wide variety of things to do.

Coastal national parks are generally the most popular, as they allow you to enjoy water sports while surrounded by the peace and tranquillity of the bush.

Apart from well-known island national parks like Fraser, Moreton and Hinchinbrook,

Blue sea star (*Linckia laevigata*), common throughout the Great Barrier Reef

Queensland has a number of beautiful parks which protect remnants of bushland along its magnificent coastline. Cooloola, east of Gympie, which together with nearby Fraser Island forms Great Sandy National Park, is the southernmost of these coastal gems. Travel another 150 km north along the coast towards Bundaberg and you will reach the small national parks of Burrum River, Woodgate and Kinkuna. Clustered closely together and fringed by casuarinas along the beach, these 3 parks protect important stands of melaleuca woodland, heath country and the fish breeding grounds of the Burrum River estuary.

The residents of Gladstone have the nearby coastal parks of Deepwater and Eurimbula to head for on a weekend, while people from Rockhampton can go fishing and swimming in the beautiful Byfield National Park north of Yeppoon. It's a long stretch up the coast—nearly 240 km—until you reach Cape Palmerston National Park south of Mackay, which is suitable only to 4WD vehicles. Further north is Cape Hillsborough National Park. Although only small at 816 hectares, this tiny piece of paradise offers something for everyone: swimming, fishing, bushwalks or just lazing about in the sun.

Coastal parks become more common the further north you go. People visiting the magnificent Whitsunday Islands, which lie to the east of the sugar town of Proserpine, can also spend a few days exploring Dryander and Conway National Parks. Besides offering good fishing and swimming, these parks protect a number of rare species of fauna and flora that have become endangered as a result of sugar cultivation and cattle grazing in the region.

Situated between Bowen and Ayr, Cape Upstart National Park is an ideal destination for those adventurous types who have a small boat and like a rugged, coastal wilderness with very few people. To the south of Townsville, Bowling Green Bay National Park is an important coastal refuge for thousands of waterbirds that feed off the numerous forms of marine life in the park's mangrove-lined tidal flats. Fishing in the bay is excellent, but swimming should be avoided at all costs because of saltwater crocodiles, sharks and marine stingers.

Edmund Kennedy National Park, halfway between Ingham and Tully, has some attractive beaches for fishing and swimming, but don't forget the insect repellent as the mosquitoes can be very bad during the summer. From Tully to Innisfail, there are a number of very small coastal parks including Kurrimine Beach National Park which are great for swimming or just relaxing in the sun. Probably Queensland's best known coastal national park is the Cape Tribulation section of the Daintree National Park. In this piece of paradise, where the rain-

The eastern yellow robin, often seen in Hinchinbrook Island National Park

forest meets the reef, visitors can wander along kilometres of beautiful beaches, take hikes through the rainforest or cool off in a tidal rockpool by the edge of the Coral Sea.

National parks are important as genetic storehouses for the future. Nearly 50 per cent of the drugs used in modern medicine are derived from plants, many of which are found only in rainforests. Up to 100 different species of trees can be found in a single hectare in North Queensland's rainforest national parks. The unique varieties of flora which thrive in the national parks of central and western Queensland are also extremely important for future research, since many of these plants have become rare as a result of grazing by sheep and cattle.

Australia has been called the driest continent, so the preservation of our waterways is extremely important. National parks and other forested areas not only attract rain, but help to purify it. Brisbane Forest Park acts as a filter for much of the water flowing into Lake Wivenhoe and the North Pine Dam, both of which supply Brisbane and the surrounding areas with most of their water. The small streams which have their beginnings in the high sandstone country of Carnarvon National Park in central Queensland, are not only important for the wildlife that lives there, but also for farmers and graziers outside the park boundary who depend on Carnarvon Range as a watershed for many of

the region's rivers and creeks.

Many of Queensland's national parks have a close association with the state's Aboriginal past. Walk along some of the beaches on Stradbroke, Moreton or Fraser Islands and you will come across piles of sun-bleached pipi shells, known as midden heaps. These sites are the result of thousands of years of Aborigines feasting on shellfish. At Carnarvon National Park, visitors can see well-preserved examples of Aboriginal freehand and stencil art on some of the sandstone overhangs. In some of the state's National Parks, such as the Mossman Gorge section of the Daintree National Park, local Aboriginal people are employed as rangers because of their intimate knowledge of the rugged terrain.

With more and more coastal land being cleared for various types of development, national parks play an important role in saving examples of a quickly vanishing habitat.

Pests, such as feral cats, pigs, foxes and other introduced species which attack the native Australian flora and fauna, are a problem that remains unsolved. Nature lovers need to be vigilant to ensure that the complete biodiversity of Queensland is fully protected. It is hoped that in the near future other suitable areas of land will be acquired by the Queensland Department of Environment to help ensure the preservation of the natural wonders that make up this beautiful state.

	Park	Ranger/Park Tel.	Ranger/Information	Camping	Caravan	4WD Access	BBQ/Fireplace	Picnic Area	Marked Walking Tracks	Bushwalking	Kiosk/Restaurant	Fishing	Swimming
1	Auburn River National Park	(07) 4167 8162	*			*	*	*	*	*			
2	Barron Gorge National Park	(07) 4052 3096				*	*	*	*				*
3	Bellenden Ker National Park	(07) 4067 6304	*	*			*	*	*				
4	Blackall Range National Park	(07) 4145 7301					*	*	*				
5	Blackdown Tableland National Park	(07) 4986 1964	*	*		*	*	*	*				
6	Bladensburg National Park	(07) 4757 1192	*										
7	Blue Lake National Park (Stradbroke Is)	(07) 3224 5641						*	*				
8	Bowling Green Bay National Park	(07) 4778 8203	*	*			*	*	*	*			*
9	Bribie Island National Park	(07) 3408 8541	*	*		*	*	*	*			*	*
10	Brisbane Forest Park	(07) 3300 4855	*	*			*	*	*				
11	Bunya Mountains National Park	(07) 4668 3127	*	*			*	*	*	*	*		
12	Burleigh Head National Park	(07) 5535 3032	*				*	*	*	*			
13	Burrum River National Park	(07) 4122 2455		*	*				*	*			
14	Byfield National Park	(07) 4936 0511		*	*								
15	Camooweal Caves National Park	(07) 4743 2055		*	*		*						
16	Cania Gorge National Park	(07) 4167 8162	*			*	*	*	*	*			
17	Cape Hillsborough National Park	(07) 4959 0410	*	*			*	*	*	*			*
18	Cape Melville National Park	(07) 4069 5777	*	*					*		*		
19	Cape Pallarenda Environmental Park	(07) 4721 2399					*	*	*				*
20	Cape Palmerston National Park	(07) 4951 8788	*		*	*	*				*		*
21	Cape Tribulation National Park	(07) 4098 2188	*		*	*	*	*	*	*			
22	Cape Upstart National Park	(07) 4946 7022	*					*					*
23	Carnarvon National Park	(07) 4622 4266	*	*	*	*	*	*	*				
24	Castletower National Park	(07) 4974 5238	*					*					
25	Cedar Bay National Park	(07) 4098 2188	*					*	*				
26	Chillagoe-Mungana Caves National Park	(07) 4094 7163	*	*			*	*	*				
27	Combo Waterhole Conservation Park	(07) 4658 1761						*					
28	Conway National Park	(07) 4946 7022	*	*	*			*	*	*			
29	Cooloola National Park	(07) 5485 3245	*			*	*	*	*			*	*
30	Crater Lakes National Park	(07) 4095 3768	*				*	*	*				
31	Crows Nest Falls National Park	(07) 4639 4599	*	*		*	*	*	*				
32	Currawinya National Park	(07) 4655 4001	*	*		*	*		*				*
33	Daintree National Park	(07) 4098 2188	*					*	*				
34	Dalrymple National Park	(07) 4087 3388	*										
35	Davies Creek National Park	(07) 4052 3096	*										*
36	Deepwater National Park	(07) 4974 9350	*										
37	Diamantina National Park	(07) 4657 3024	*										
38	Dipperu National Park	(07) 4951 8788	*										
39	Dunk Island National Park	(07) 4066 8601	*			*	*		*				
40	Edmund Kennedy National Park	(07) 4066 8850	*										
41	Eungella National Park	(07) 4958 4552	*	*		*	*	*	*	*			*
42	Eurimbula National Park	(07) 4974 9350	*	*				*					*
43	Expedition National Park	(07) 4627 3358	*						*				
44	Fort Lytton National Park	(07) 3393 4647	*					*					
45	Girraween National Park	(07) 4684 5157	*	*	*			*	*				
46	Glasshouse Mountains National Park	(07) 4494 6630	*					*	*				
47	Great Basalt Wall National Park	(07) 4787 3388	*						*				
48	Great Sandy (Fraser Island) National Park	(07) 4127 9128	*	*		*	*	*	*			*	*
29	Great Sandy (Cooloola) National Park	(07) 5485 3245	*			*	*	*	*			*	*
49	Heron Island National Park	(07) 4972 6055	*										
50	Hinchinbrook Island National Park	(07) 4066 8601	*				*	*	*				*
51	Idalia National Park	(07) 4657 5033	*				*		*				
52	Iron Range National Park	(07) 4060 7170	*						*				
53	Isla Gorge National Park	(07) 4627 3358	*			*	*	*	*				
54	Jardine River National Park	(07) 4060 3241	*			*	*	*	*				
55	Jourama Falls National Park	(07) 4776 1770	*				*	*	*				*
56	Ka Ka Mundi National Park (Carnarvon)	(07) 4984 1716	*			*			*				
57	Keppel Islands National Park	(07) 4933 6595	*										
58	Kinkuna National Park	(07) 4153 8620	*										
59	Kroombit Tops National Park	(07) 4972 6055				*							
60	Lady Musgrave Island National Park	(07) 4972 6055	*						*	*			
61	Lake Broadwater Environmental Park	(07) 4662 2922	*			*	*	*	*				*
62	Lakefield Desert National Park	(07) 4060 3271	*			*	*	*				*	
63	Lamington National Park	(07) 5533 3584	*	*		*	*	*	*				
64	Lawn Hill National Park	(07) 4748 5572	*				*	*	*				
65	Lizard Island National Park	(07) 4052 3096	*						*				
66	Lumholtz National Park	(07) 4776 1700	*					*	*				
67	Magnetic Island National Park	(07) 4774 1411	*					*	*				
68	Main Range National Park	(07) 4666 1133	*	*		*	*	*	*				
69	Mon Repos National Park	(07) 4159 2628	*										
70	Moogerah Peaks National Park	(07) 5563 5041	*					*	*				
71	Moreton Island National Park	(07) 3408 2710	*	*				*	*	*	*	*	*
72	Mt Aberdeen National Park	(07) 4721 2399	*						*				
73	Mt Barney National Park	(07) 5563 5041	*	*				*	*				
74	Mt Hypipamee National Park	(07) 4095 3768	*					*	*				
75	Mt Moffatt National Park	(07) 4626 3581	*				*	*	*				
76	Mt Spec National Park	(07) 4770 8526	*			*	*	*	*				*
77	Mungkan Kanju National Park	(07) 4060 3256	*					*					
78	Murray Falls State Forest	(07) 4066 8804	*				*	*	*				*
79	Noosa National Park	(07) 5447 3243	*					*	*				*
80	North-West Island National Park	(07) 4976 0766	*										*
81	Orpheus Island National Park	(07) 4721 2399	*					*	*				*
82	Peel Island National Park	(07) 3409 9409	*										

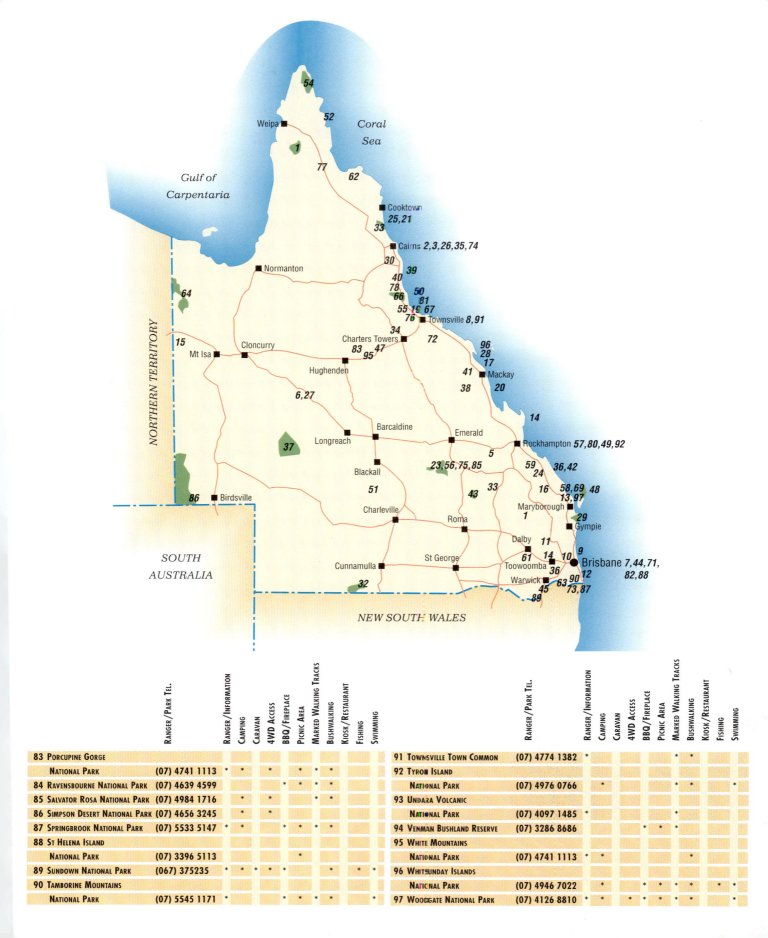

Coral Sea

Gulf of Carpentaria

Weipa

54

52

1

77

62

33

25,21 Cooktown

30

39

40 Cairns 2,3,26,35,74

78
66
50
81
55 19 67
76
Townsville 8,91

NORMANTON

NORTHERN TERRITORY

64

15

Mt Isa   Cloncurry

34

Charters Towers
83 47
95

72

Hughenden

6,27

96
28
17
41 Mackay
38
20

14

Barcaldine   Emerald

Longreach

37

Rockhampton 57,80,49,92

23,56,75,85
5
59
24
36,42

Blackall

51

43

33

16

58,69 48
13,97

Maryborough
1

86 Birdsville

Charleville   Roma

29
Gympie

SOUTH AUSTRALIA

Dalby
11
61 14 10 9
36
Warwick 90 12
45 63 73,87
32
89

Cunnamulla   St George

Toowoomba

Brisbane 7,44,71,
82,88

NEW SOUTH WALES

	Ranger/Park Tel.	Ranger/Information	Camping	Caravan	4WD Access	BBQ/Fireplace	Picnic Area	Marked Walking Tracks	Bushwalking	Kiosk/Restaurant	Fishing	Swimming
83 Porcupine Gorge												
National Park	(07) 4741 1113	*	*		*		*	*	*			
84 Ravensbourne National Park	(07) 4639 4599					*	*	*	*			
85 Salvator Rosa National Park	(07) 4984 1716		*		*			*	*			
86 Simpson Desert National Park	(07) 4656 3245		*		*							
87 Springbrook National Park	(07) 5533 5147	*	*			*	*	*	*			
88 St Helena Island												
National Park	(07) 3396 5113						*					
89 Sundown National Park	(067) 375235	*	*	*	*	*			*		*	*
90 Tamborine Mountains												
National Park	(07) 5545 1171	*				*	*	*	*			*

	Ranger/Park Tel.	Ranger/Information	Camping	Caravan	4WD Access	BBQ/Fireplace	Picnic Area	Marked Walking Tracks	Bushwalking	Kiosk/Restaurant	Fishing	Swimming
91 Townsville Town Common	(07) 4774 1382	*						*	*			
92 Tyron Island												
National Park	(07) 4976 0766		*					*	*		*	
93 Undara Volcanic												
National Park	(07) 4097 1485	*					*					
94 Venman Bushland Reserve	(07) 3286 8686						*	*	*			
95 White Mountains												
National Park	(07) 4741 1113	*	*		*				*			
96 Whitsunday Islands												
National Park	(07) 4946 7022		*			*	*	*	*	*	*	*
97 Woodgate National Park	(07) 4126 8810	*	*	*	*	*	*	*	*		*	*

BRISBANE FOREST PARK

IN BRIEF

MAP REFERENCE: PAGE 203 M 6

Location On Brisbane's western outskirts
Best Time All year round
Main Attractions Bush-walking, birdwatching
Ranger Phone (07) 3300 4855

Camping permit: obtain in advance from the ranger, phone (07) 3300 4855

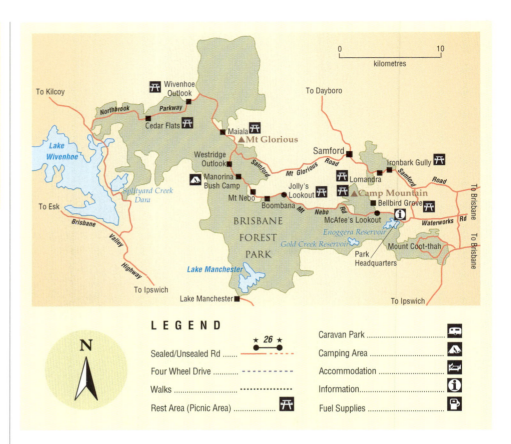

LEGEND

Sealed/Unsealed Rd	★ 26 ★
Four Wheel Drive	
Walks	
Rest Area (Picnic Area)	

Caravan Park	
Camping Area	
Accommodation	
Information	
Fuel Supplies	

The residents of Brisbane are indeed lucky to have this beautiful forest reserve right at their doorstep. The park, covering an area of 28 500 hectares, consists of 4 small national parks, environmental park, state forest and council reserve. A diverse range of habitats are preserved in the park including rainforest, dry eucalypt forest, lakes and creeks.

HISTORY

Brisbane Forest Park was set up in October 1977, when it was decided to amalgamate existing national parks and council water reserves with the surrounding state forests to form one large nature-based recreation park. Aboriginal people lived and hunted in what is now known as Brisbane Forest Park for at least 40 000 years. The swift decline of these gentle people began in 1842 when free settlers began pouring into the Brisbane area. Conflicts over land use quickly arose between the new arrivals and the original inhabitants. Unfortunately, colonial authorities of the day turned a blind eye to the regular shootings and other forms of genocide perpetrated against the Aborigines by the settlers, and by the 1890s the indigenous people had been all but wiped out.

Enjoying a picnic in Brisbane Forest Park

VEGETATION AND CLIMATE

Since elevation, temperature and rainfall within the park vary greatly, vegetation is particularly diverse. At lower altitudes around Bellbird Grove, spotted gums, ironbarks, red mahogany and white stringybark are the main types of large trees, while lilly pilly and weeping bottle-brush grow along the banks of the creek. The spotted gum is the predominant species of eucalypt in the poorer soils on the way up to Mt Nebo. Sydney blue gums thrive in the richer soils around Manorina National Park, as well as large specimens of brush box and tree ferns in the moister gullies. At the top of the range— around 750 metres near Mt Glorious—thick stands of brush box mingle with giant strangler figs, black bean, flame trees and satin ash. In some places the canopy is almost closed, providing shade for cunjevois, lilly pillies, ferns and palms to flourish. Maiala National Park's high rainfall, about 1500 mm a year, is one of the reasons why creepers and vines, like the giant pepper vine and the lawyer vine, or wait-a-while, are common in the rainforest.

GREAT FOR BIRDWATCHERS

Birdwatching is quickly becoming a favourite pastime for visitors to Brisbane Forest Park due to its diverse habitats, close proximity to the city and wide variety of birds. A good place to start looking is in the tall open eucalypt forest at Ironbark Gully. Kookaburras and pied butcher-birds are both common and inquisitive, and will readily land on picnic tables looking for scraps of meat. The unmistakable, melodious call from the pied currawong echoes throughout the forest here at certain times of the year, while the black-backed magpie is regularly seen walking along the ground searching for insects and grubs. If the eucalypts are flowering, the screeching calls from small flocks of rainbow and scaly-breasted lorikeets can be heard throughout the day. More observant bird-watchers will no doubt see some of the less conspicuous feathered inhabitants of Ironbark Gully. These include the black-faced cuckoo-shrike, brown honeyeater, rufous whistler, grey fantail, pale-headed rosella, eastern whipbird and variegated wren.

After a good look around Ironbark Gully many birdwatchers head up to the rainforest at Boombana and Maiala National Parks. Here one may see the beautiful noisy pitta hopping along a rainforest track or catch sight of a regent bowerbird winging its way through the thick rainforest. The rarely seen paradise riflebird also finds a safe refuge along with more common species like rufous fantails and white-browed scrubwrens. One bird call that is difficult to confuse with any other is the sharp whip-like crack from the eastern whipbird. These elusive forest dwellers are more often heard than seen, as they are well camouflaged in the dense undergrowth. Another rainforest species with a distinctive call is the green catbird. When hikers hear this large greenish coloured bird for the first time they mistake it for a cat that has been lost in the forest.

MAMMALS AT NIGHT

The forests around Manorina, Maiala and Jolly's Lookout are great places to look for the park's nocturnal wildlife. Greater gliders, sugar gliders and the endangered yellow-bellied glider are often seen along with more common species like the ringtail and brush-tail possums. Other mammals often sighted include the short-nosed bandicoot and various species of bush rats.

THINGS TO DO

There is much to do and see in Brisbane Forest Park. A good place to start is the park headquarters, where a ranger will provide you with all the necessary information and brochures for an enjoyable stay. Activities range from full-day guided bushwalks to quiet evenings spent spotlighting for wildlife. A unique freshwater wildlife display, restaurant and bushcrafts shop can also be found at the park headquarters.

GREAT FOR WALKING

Walking tracks throughout Brisbane Forest Park vary from easy 30 minute circuits along creek flats, to hard treks across rugged country where a compass is needed to find your way. If you intend doing one of these difficult walks, never attempt it alone, for safety reasons. Always carry plenty of drinking water with you as many of the creeks run dry, especially in summer. An interesting short walk is the Bellbird Grove Turrbal Circuit Trail. A number of signposts along this 1.5 km track describe the day-to-day lifestyle of the Aboriginal people who formerly inhabited the area.

An excellent walking track, which starts at Manorina Bush Camp, winds its way for 3 km, taking about 2 hours, through thick eucalypt forest before reaching the Mt Nebo lookout. Panoramic views over the Samford Valley and onto the coast can be obtained from here.

ACCESS

Brisbane Forest Park lies northwest of the city and can be approached from 2 directions. The first is along Waterworks Road past the suburbs of Ashgrove and the Gap. Shortly after entering the forest you will see a sign pointing to Enoggera reservoir and park headquarters on your left. The road continues to rise gently for a couple of kilometres until you see a sign pointing to Bellbird Grove picnic area to the right. If

Grass-trees and eucalypts growing in Brisbane Forest Park

you keep heading up the mountain for another 10 minutes you will see the turn-off to Camp Mountain picnic area to the right. A further 10 minutes drive brings you to Jolly's Lookout and picnic area which provides fantastic views over the Samford Valley and northern Moreton Bay. The road continues up the mountain past Manorina Bush Camp and Westridge Outlook until it reaches the tiny township of Mt Glorious at the top of the range. A little further on, the road passes Maiala National Park and picnic area to the right before continuing on for another 10 km until it reaches Wivenhoe Outlook. From this lookout one can get fantastic views over Wivenhoe Dam in the country below.

An alternative route from Brisbane city is along Samford Road. This road passes through Ironbark Gully and then the rural village of Samford before beginning its steep ascent up the range and joining the other road not far from Mt Glorious.

CAMPING

There is only one place to camp in the park: the walk-in camping area at Manorina Bush Camp. A permit must be obtained in advance from the ranger. The 19 camping sites are well screened from each other by bushes and tall trees. Due to its popularity and proximity to Brisbane, campers can stay a maximum of 2 nights.

BUNYA MOUNTAINS NATIONAL PARK

MAP REFERENCE: PAGE 203 K 6

IN BRIEF

Location 230 km north-west of Brisbane, via Jondaryan or Kingaroy
Best Time All year round
Main Attractions Wildlife, bushwalks, mountain views
Ranger Phone (07) 4668 3127

Set amidst cool mountain forests 4 hours west of Brisbane, the 11 700 hectare Bunya Mountains National Park is the ideal place to relax. Apart from having the largest stand of bunya pines in the world, waterfalls and a wide variety of wildlife, the park is also a great spot to escape summer humidity on the coast.

Aborigines from the Waka Waka tribes were the first people to venture into these forests. They came to collect the tasty nuts which grew at the tops of the huge bunya trees. Every third year, when there was a particularly heavy crop, smoke signals were sent out to invite tribes to partake in 'bon-ye bon-ye' feasts, held in the mountains.

By the mid-1870s red cedar getters entered the area in search of the 'red gold', and within a few years the giant trees had gone, as had most of the Aborigines, pushed further afield by white settlement. The axemen then turned their attention to the bunya and hoop pines.

A bunya pine in Bunya Mountains National Park

GREAT WALKING TRAILS

There are 9 walking trails in the park, each offering something of particular interest. The scenic circuit track is a delightful introduction to the pleasures of the park. Being just 4 km long, round trip, and with a mild gradient, it is suitable for most people. Once you leave the open spaces around Dandabah to begin this circuit it seems as if you are entering another world. The thick canopy of foliage overhead prevents most of the sun's rays from penetrating through to the forest floor. And in this almost silent place, one could be excused for thinking that the rainforest was almost devoid of life.

The Westcliff track shows another side of Bunya's terrain. On this trail grass-trees are a common sight, their black trunks and bushy crowns of spiky grass giving them a primitive look. Observant hikers may occasionally see red-necked wallabies and swamp wallabies bounding away, although the chances of photographing these animals at close quarters are quite rare. If you are doing this walk in the late afternoon make sure you have a small pocket torch with you as it is easy to trip over protruding tree roots and injure yourself.

ABUNDANT WILDLIFE

King parrots and crimson rosellas gather in the bunya trees near the picnic area in the late afternoon. Flashes of red, blue and green dart through the air. Seeing these birds is often a highlight for park visitors. Please do not feed any native animals as this can harm their health.

Just after dusk, the nocturnal animals begin to emerge. Long-nosed bandicoots, ringtail possums, bush rats and tawny frogmouths are a few of the more commonly encountered creatures. Another animal of the night is the mountain brush-tail possum. Kernels from the black bean tree are a large part of this marsupial's diet, and the forest floor beneath these trees is permanently littered with crunched-up shells.

ACCESS AND CAMPING

The park lies 230 km northwest of Brisbane and can be easily reached by conventional vehicles. There are 2 ways of approaching the park: either along the Warrego Highway through Toowoomba and on to Jondaryan where you turn right, or along the D'Aguilar Highway via Kingaroy.

There are 3 camping grounds in the park but the only one with hot running showers is at Dandabah, near the ranger's headquarters. The other camping grounds are at Burtons Well and Westcott Plain. All of them have toilets, fireplaces and picnic tables. Firewood must be collected outside the park. Permits to camp can be obtained by ringing the ranger.

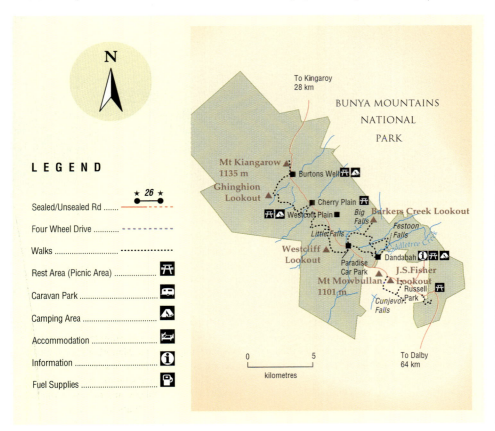

N

LEGEND

Sealed/Unsealed Rd .... ★ 26 ★

Four Wheel Drive ....

Walks ....

Rest Area (Picnic Area) ....

Caravan Park ....

Camping Area ....

Accommodation ....

Information ....

Fuel Supplies ....

To Kingaroy 28 km

BUNYA MOUNTAINS NATIONAL PARK

Mt Kiangarow 1135 m
Ghinghion Lookout
Burtons Well
Cherry Plain
Westcott Plain
Barkers Creek Lookout
Big Falls
Festoon Falls
Little Falls
Saddletree Creek
Westcliff Lookout
Dandabah
Paradise Car Park
J.S.Fisher Lookout
Mt Mowbullan 1101 m
Russell Park
Cunjevoi Falls

To Dalby 64 km

0   5
kilometres

IN BRIEF

MAP REFERENCE: PAGE 204 G 5

Location 115 km southeast of Mackay. 4WD. Roads may be closed in the Wet
Best Time Winter and spring
Main Attractions Birdwatching, fishing
Ranger Phone (07) 4957 6292

This beautiful park south of Mackay covers an area of 7160 hectares and protects a relatively untouched piece of coastal wilderness. Apart from being a great spot for peace and solitude, Cape Palmerston is also an important refuge for many species of birds.

Aboriginal people lived in the region for thousands of years and feasted on a rich diet of shellfish, birds, wallabies, goannas and wild fruits. The first known European to see the area was Captain James Cook, who sailed past in the *Endeavour* on 1 June 1770 and named the headland Cape Palmerston.

VEGETATION IN THE PARK

The flora in Cape Palmerston National Park is diverse and consists of casuarinas behind the coastal dunes, thick stands of mangroves and open eucalypt woodland. The predominant trees in this dry eucalypt forest are ironbarks and the more common gums, while broad-leaved tea-trees and the occasional lilly pilly can be found growing in the moister gullies. There are also grass-trees growing on the grassy slopes near the headland.

THINGS TO DO

A good pair of binoculars should be an essential item of your equipment if you are going to Palmerston as the park has a wide range of birds. You might see a beach thick-knee running along the sand on the beach, while birds of prey include the osprey, white-bellied sea-eagle, whistling kite and brahminy kite. The mangroves attract waders such as egrets, herons, spoonbills and ibises. Mangrove kingfishers and insect eaters, like the spectacled monarch, mangrove gerygone, silvereye and the white-bellied cuckoo-shrike, can be seen darting in and out of the mangroves. There are also good numbers of mud crabs in the mangroves. Finches feed on grass seeds in the more open parts of the park. Often, a small flock of 10 or 20 will rise like a whirring cloud, before flying on another 30 or 40 metres to a new patch of grass. Pale-headed rosellas, rainbow lorikeets and scaly-breasted lorikeets are the most commonly seen parrots in the park, while the dusky honeyeater and beautiful scarlet honeyeater are plentiful when the eucalypts flower.

LEGEND

Sealed/Unsealed Rd ....
Four Wheel Drive ....
Walks ....
Rest Area (Picnic Area) ....
Caravan Park ....
Camping Area ....
Accommodation ....
Information ....
Fuel Supplies ....

Apart from beach walking, visitors can get a great view over the Northumberland Isles from a lookout on the top of Cape Palmerston.

Fishing is also a popular pastime at Cape Palmerston.

ACCESS AND CAMPING

A 4WD vehicle is needed for travel within the park. Turn off the Bruce Highway at Ilbilbie and take the Notch Point road for 4.4 km. Turn left into Greenhill Road and follow the gravel for 2.5 km and then turn left onto wheel tracks. Continue for another 3.5 km until you reach a junction. The left track takes the rough inland route to Cape Palmerston, while the right hand one runs along the beach. Both tracks are about 20 km long but it is easy to become bogged down in beach sand.

Apart from a few tables and fireplaces at Cape Creek camping area there are no other facilities in the park. Visitors should be totally self-sufficient and carry in everything including

Soldier crabs in Cape Palmerston National Park

drinking water. There are 2 other spots for bush camping in the park—at Clarke Bay and Coconut Point. During the wet season—December to March—the roads into the park are often impassable.

There may be marine stingers in summer, so swimming should be avoided then. Remember also to stock up on insect repellent as sandflies and mosquitoes can be a problem during warmer months.

CARNARVON NATIONAL PARK

IN BRIEF

MAP REFERENCE: PAGE 202 D 2

Location 720 km northwest of Brisbane
Best Time Winter and spring; summers can be very hot
Main Attractions Breathtaking scenery, good walking tracks, 4WD
Ranger Phone (07) 4984 4505

Accommodation: Carnarvon Oasis Lodge, phone (07) 4984 4503

Camping: Head Ranger, Carnarvon National Park, via Rolleston, Qld 4702

The rugged, scrub-covered ranges of the isolated Consuelo Tableland in central Queensland are guardians to one of Australia's most spectacular natural gems: Carnarvon Gorge. It is often referred to as the 'down under' version of America's Grand Canyon.

ABORIGINAL HISTORY

The original visitors to this scenic wonderland, the Aborigines, have long since vanished from the area, leaving only their unique artistry behind them. For thousands of years they depicted their way of life and mythical Dreamtime on the undersides of many of the large rock overhangs found throughout the gorge. Careful examination of the paintings—many of them thousands of years old—is needed to obtain the full impact of this stone-age art.

Cathedral Cave, one of the largest rock art sites so far discovered, is approximately 10 km from the camping ground. Boomerangs, spears, emus' feet and goannas are depicted on one side of this large sandstone wall, while on another section the human hand is more commonly featured. Three distinct styles have been used in creating these works of art—free-hand, engraving and stencil. Stencilling was performed by mixing the orche pigment in the mouth with water, then spraying it over an object held flat against the wall.

Another fascinating example of primitive art is the 'Art Gallery'. This stone-age master-piece—which has been carbon-dated at over 4000 years—is 500 metres off the main track.

A NATURAL WONDER

The 223 000 hectares which comprise Carnarvon National Park are only a part of the massive Consuelo Tableland. This predominantly sandstone region rises to 900 metres and is home to 4 of eastern Australia's major river systems.

The park is made up of different sections: Carnarvon Gorge, Buckland Tableland, Ka Ka Mundi, Goodliffe, Salvator Rosa, Mt Moffat, and Moolayember. Although Carnarvon Gorge

Aboriginal relics found in Carnarvon

occupies only a fraction of the park, it is by far the most scenic and easily accessible section.

The main 30 km long gorge was created by the action of water in Carnarvon Creek eroding away the soft sandstone plateau over millions of years. Vertical sandstone cliffs, some up to 200 metres high, rise up from the gorge floor, their colours varying from brilliant whites through to yellow, orange and brown.

Kangaroos playing in Carnarvon National Park

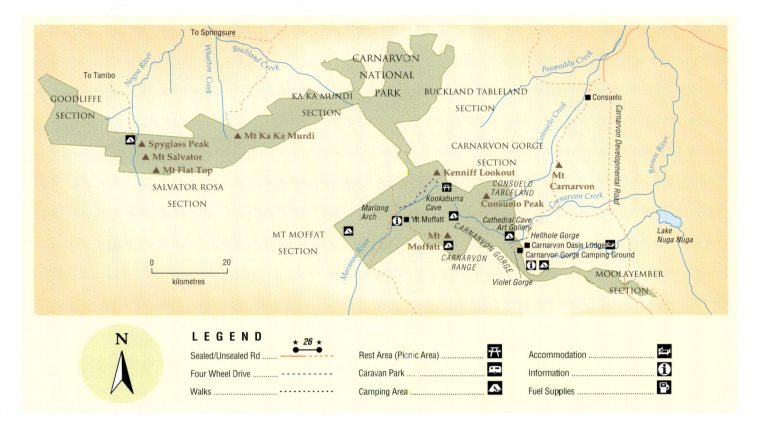

LEGEND

Sealed/Unsealed Rd	Rest Area (Picnic Area)	Accommodation
Four Wheel Drive	Caravan Park	Information
Walks	Camping Area	Fuel Supplies

★ 26 ★

Fine-needled casuarinas cling to the sandy banks along Carnarvon Creek, often competing for space with the weeping bottlebrush. Cabbage-tree palms are common near the creek, while further up the slopes, ironbark, flooded gums and swamp mahogany predominate. Many of these massive eucalypts possess hollowed-out limbs, making them ideal homes for nocturnal marsupials such as possums and gliders.

ABUNDANT WILDLIFE

A wide variety of wildlife can be observed while walking through the gorge. Whiptail wallabies and grey kangaroos are present most of the day, but are more likely to be seen in the early morning when they come out to feed. The clear, shallow waters of Carnarvon Creek are home to the elusive platypus. Sightings of this intriguing creature can occasionally be made from some of the higher banks along the creek.

The diversity of plant life found in the park provides many ideal habitats for the area's prolific birds. Honeyeaters, finches, currawongs, crows and parrots are the most commonly encountered, as well as the occasional sighting of rarer species such as the peregrine falcon.

THINGS TO DO

At least 3 or 4 days should be set aside to visit Carnarvon which is just enough time to explore leisurely the outstanding beauty of the main gorge and the many steep ravines that branch off the gorge.

A well-defined trail which begins near the ranger's headquarters follows the contours of Carnarvon Creek, traversing this picturesque little stream at least 16 times before reaching Cathedral Cave 10 km upstream. This will take about 8 hours for the return walk.

Adventurous hikers can travel a further 15 km into the more remote parts of the gorge. They should be fully self-sufficient and prepared for any emergency over the 2 or 3 days needed for this return trek.

Hellhole Gorge, just 3 km from the camping ground, is the first of the navigable side gorges to branch off the main walking track. Allow 3 hours to explore the gorge well. The sheer 100 metre tall walls of this canyon become narrower the further you go in. Being shaded from sunlight for much of the day, the vegetation is thick and lush. Elkhorns and staghorns cling to the branches of giant eucalypts, while on the ground, a variety of ferns and palms grow in profusion amongst fallen, moss-covered logs.

Violet Gorge is considered one of the most captivating of all the side gorges. Hidden deep within the near vertical walls of this canyon lies the moss garden: a carpet of liverworts and mosses clinging to a large rock overhang. Water cascading from a small stream into a clear rock-pool is the only sound one is likely to hear.

ACCESS

The park is accessible to conventional vehicles although a 4WD vehicle might be necessary to travel over some of the unsealed sections after heavy rain. From Brisbane, the best route is probably via Roma, Injune and Wyseby. The road is good bitumen except for the last 75 km which is dirt. Corrugations might make the ride a little rough in places if the grader hasn't recently been over the road, but they should present few problems for careful drivers.

CAMPING

There are several camping grounds in the park. The main one has a visitor information centre, toilets, cold showers, BBQs and a public phone. Firewood is not available in the park and must be brought in with you. Bushwalkers can also pitch their tent at Big Bend camping area which is 10 km from the nearest car park. The only facility at this spot is a toilet.

Visitors wishing to stay in the park during school holidays should note that the park is often very crowded at these times. Bookings should be made well in advance through the head ranger.

For those not wanting to camp, accommodation is available at the Carnarvon Oasis Lodge just outside the park. There is a general store attached to the Lodge which can also be used by campers.

COOLOOLA—GREAT SANDY NATIONAL PARK

IN BRIEF

MAP REFERENCE: PAGE 203 N 2

Location 200 km north of Brisbane, via the Bruce Highway
Best Time All year round
Main Attractions Water sports, bushwalks, 4WD
Ranger Phone (07) 5486 3160

When the morning sun bathes the massive sandy cliffs of Cooloola on Queensland's east coast, a kaleidoscope of colour springs to life. Earthy shades of mustard, brown, red, orange and yellow mingle with black and white.

The original inhabitants of the area were the Kabi people who lived in harmony with their environment. Their peaceful existence ended in the 1840s when the timber getters arrived and introduced diseases which almost wiped out the tribe. Skirmishes between them and the Kabi occurred regularly from the mid-1860s until just before the turn of the 20th century.

Cooloola, together with the northern half of Fraser Island (see page 174), make up the Great Sandy National Park, although each park is adminstered separately.

RAINFORESTS AND LAKES

One of the many special features of Cooloola is its rainforests which grow in sand. An excellent way to experience the tranquillity of the rainforests is to do the 4.4 km, 2½ hour, return walk to Lake Poona which starts at a picnic area near the main vehicle track.

Lakes are a major feature of the 56 000 hectare park. Nestled high in the dunes, Poona is one of the 5 main perched lakes found in Cooloola. The slight tea-coloured stain in the water is caused by organic particles from the surrounding vegetation. This colour has no effect on the quality of the water.

Apart from a few little grebes and musk ducks Poona is almost devoid of waterfowl. In contrast, other larger lakes such as Cootharaba are slightly brackish and teem with marine life which provides food for many species of birds such as pelicans and sea-eagles.

THINGS TO DO

Surf fishing is very popular at Cooloola, with whiting, bream and flathead among the frequent catches. River fishing is also popular, as is swimming though marine stingers can be a problem when northeasterlies blow.

Canoeing is the best way to explore Noosa River. Canoes can be hired from Elanda Point.

The park has many walking trails and also 4WD tracks.

ACCESS AND CAMPING

There are 2 approaches to the park. Coming from the south you turn off the Bruce Highway near Eumundi and continue to Tewantin and catch the ferry across the Noosa River. From there a gravel track a few kilometres long brings you to the track which leads to the beach. The second approach is from the north: take the Tin Can Bay turn-off at Gympie and continue for about 47 km until the turn-off to Rainbow Beach. 5 km before you reach this small town you will see a national parks sign to the Freshwater camping area.

This is the most developed camp site, but there are other sites on the banks of Noosa River, at Poverty Point and on the Cooloola Wilderness Trail. You can also camp on Teewah Beach between Noosa Shire boundary and Little Freshwater Creek. Sites should be booked in advance with the ranger.

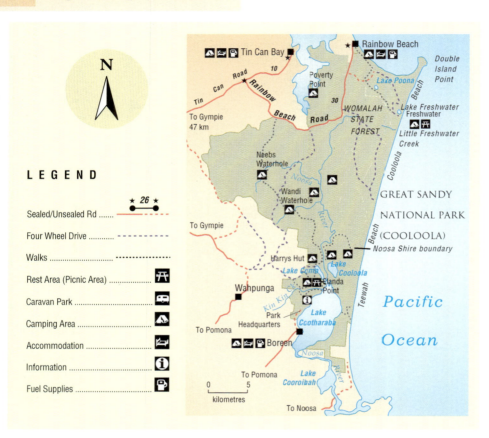

LEGEND

Sealed/Unsealed Rd	★—26—★
Four Wheel Drive	
Walks	
Rest Area (Picnic Area)	⛱
Caravan Park	🚐
Camping Area	⛺
Accommodation	🛏
Information	ⓘ
Fuel Supplies	⛽

The beautiful sand dunes of the Cooloola Section of Great Sandy National Park

IN BRIEF

MAP REFERENCE: PAGE 211 L 9

Location 900 km southwest of Brisbane off the Mitchell Highway. 4WD in the Wet
Best Time Autumn, winter and spring
Main Attractions Birds, lakes, fishing
Ranger Phone (07) 4655 4001

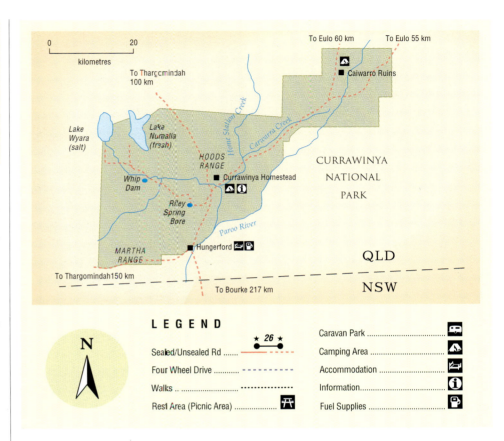

LEGEND

Sealed/Unsealed Rd .... ★ 26 ★	Caravan Park ....
Four Wheel Drive	Camping Area ....
Walks	Accommodation ....
Rest Area (Picnic Area)	Information...........................
	Fuel Supplies ....

N

If you are tired of overcrowded coastal nature reserves and would like to see abundant wildlife, camp under star-studded Outback skies and be awakened by flocks of corellas flying over one of Australia's biggest inland lakes, then the place to go is Currawinya. This 151 300 hectare reserve is a must for anyone who wants to experience peace and solitude in the bush.

Currawinya was gazetted a national park in 1991. For about 130 years, from the 1860s, the land was used to graze sheep. Fortunately, much of the land which was degraded by sheep is starting to regenerate. Relics of this pastoral occupation, including old fencing rails and bottles, are still evident throughout the park.

There are no designated walking tracks in the park and apart from birdwatching most visitors just spend their time relaxing or taking photographs. Fishing is allowed (no permit is required) in the Paroo River but not in the freshwater lakes.

THE LAKES

The semi-arid park was established to protect the area's freshwater lakes, which are an important refuge for inland birds in time of drought. When it rains in Currawinya—which it rarely does—thousands of small ponds and lagoons appear on the claypans between the dunefields. Life explodes virtually overnight as tiny green shoots appear. This profusion of plant life soon buzzes with insects which attract a host of predators, including lizards and birds.

When full, in summer, the seasonal waterholes, lakes and claypans provide a habitat for wetland bird species: royal and yellow spoonbills, greater egrets and ibises are often seen.

In the Dry, bird numbers increase dramatically on the permanent water. Lake Wyara abounds with black swans, pelicans and many duck species, such as the pink-eared, hardhead, black and wood ducks. The lake is a major refuge for the rare freckled duck. In the saline shallows, waders such as sandpipers, godwits, snipes, rails, dotterels, avocets and stilts feed.

Lake Numalla, in the northwest of the park, is a 2200 hectare body of fresh water. It is a great place to cool off during the middle of the day when temperatures often exceed 38°C. During the late afternoon and evening,

hundreds of red and grey kangaroos come down to the lake to drink. Emus are common, too, and it's not unusual to see a family group walking along the water's edge.

ACCESS AND CAMPING

Access to the park is via Cunnamulla/Eulo, Thargomindah or Bourke. The southern side of the park is adjacent to the township of Hungerford. The northern boundary is 60 km south of Eulo. Roads from Eulo, Thargomindah and Bourke are unsealed and can be impassable when wet. 4WDs are recommended. You should check road conditions with the ranger before setting out.

Because it is such a remote park, with no facilities bar a couple of picnic tables, visitors to Currawinya should come well prepared with adequate food supplies and enough drinking water for their stay—about 5 litres per person a day. Vehicles should be in tip-top condition as a breakdown could end up being very expensive.

Camping in Currawinya National Park

Spring, autumn and winter are the best times for a visit as the summer temperatures can get exceedingly hot. At night during June and July the thermometer can fall well below zero, making warm clothes and a good sleeping-bag necessary.

SAFETY HINT

Because of the area's isolation, it may be advisable to inform the local police officer at either Hungerford, on the NSW border, or at Eulo, to the north of the park, of your planned length of stay.

DAINTREE NATIONAL PARK

IN BRIEF

MAP REFERENCE: PAGE 207 L 4

Location The Mossman Gorge section of the Daintree National Park is located 80 km north of Cairns. The Cape Tribulation section starts another 25 km further to the north.
Best Time End of April until October
Main Attractions Bushwalking, birdwatching, 4WD
Ranger Cape Tribulation, phone (07) 4098 0052 ; Mossman Gorge, phone (07) 4098 2188

Daintree River ferry: operates 6 am to midnight, 7 days a week except Good Friday and Christmas Day

The Daintree is a spectacular wilderness of rugged mountain ranges, fast-flowing streams, towering rainforest trees and lush, tangled undergrowth in a myriad shades of green. Cape Tribulation is the only place in Australia where the visitor can experience the splendour of north Queensland's tropical rainforests while being only a stone's throw from the World Heritage listed Great Barrier Reef.

PARK HISTORY

Stretching along the coast from the Daintree River in the south to the Bloomfield River in the north, Daintree National Park is divided into 2 parts: the 56 500 hectare Mossman Gorge section, 80 km north of Cairns, and the 16 959 hectare Cape Tribulation section 104 km north of Cairns. These parks were combined in 1988 to become an important component in the Wet Tropics World Heritage Area.

Cape Tribulation was named by Captain James Cook when his ship, the *Endeavour*, was holed on a reef just north of the cape in 1770. The Aboriginal word for the cape—'Kurranji', which means cassowary—was the name used by the Kuku Yalanji people who had lived in this piece of coastal paradise for thousands of years.

AMAZING MAMMALS

Because of its wide range in elevation—from sea level to more than 1300 metres—the Cape Tribulation area is home to some of Australia's rarest types of mammals. The largest and most spectacular of these is the Bennett's tree-kangaroo. Confined almost entirely to the rainforests of Cape Tribulation and nearby Cedar Bay to the north, this little known marsupial is

A typical rainforest view in Daintree National Park

more often heard than seen when it crashes through the forest canopy.

Another rarely encountered rainforest resident is the Herbert River ringtail possum. Found only at altitudes of 300 metres above sea level, this beautiful black and white possum is sometimes seen at night with the aid of a torch.

GREAT FOR BIRD LIFE

Bird life in both the Mossman Gorge and Cape Tribulation sections is varied and prolific. The large flightless cassowary, which often stands up to 2 metres tall, is occasionally sighted by bushwalkers on rainforest tracks. Never try and get too close to these stocky, helmeted birds as they can inflict serious injuries with their powerful legs. Unfortunately, cassowaries have become rare due to land clearing, and even in protected places like the Daintree, they are threatened by feral pigs which destroy their nests.

Light scratching sounds in the leaf litter on the forest floor usually indicate the presence of chowchillas nearby. These conspicuous 28 cm long birds with their dark brown backs and white and orange neck and chest markings are confined to the Wet Tropics region. The large brush-turkey and the slightly smaller orange-footed scrubfowl are other ground dwellers regularly seen in the park.

At least 6 species of rainforest pigeons inhabit the Daintree. The largest and most impressive of these is the colourful wompoo fruit-dove which spends most of its time in the upper canopy. Other pigeons include the superb fruit-dove and the Torresian imperial pigeon.

THINGS TO DO

Most of the Mossman Gorge part of the Daintree is wilderness which is virtually inaccessible. Anyone trying to hike in this beautiful region should be a fully experienced bushwalker.

One way to enjoy Daintree National Park

ACCESS

The best way to the Mossman Gorge section of the park is to drive north along the Cook Highway for 76 km until you reach Mossman. A 5 km bitumen road connects the town to the picnic ground at Mossman Gorge. To reach Cape Tribulation, go north from Mossman for 28 km until you reach the Daintree River ferry.

From the northern side of the Daintree River the road winds for about 40 km through private land and segments of the national park until it reaches Cape Tribulation. Motorists who want to continue on

Permits for overnight bush camping should be obtained before setting out from the National Parks and Wildlife Service office in Mossman.

There are some beautiful walks in the Cape Tribulation section including the 4 hour return trip from Myall Beach, just south of Cape Tribulation, to Emmagen Creek. Walkers should start this hike on the outgoing tide so they can skirt around the rocks at Emmagen Beach.

At Oliver Creek, near Noah Beach, the very interesting Marrdja Boardwalk winds its way for 800 metres through mangroves and rainforest.

The beautiful beaches north and south of Cape Tribulation are great for swimming from late April until the end of September when marine stingers are absent.

Never swim anywhere near the mouth of a saltwater creek or in the Daintree and Bloomfield Rivers as estuarine crocodiles inhabit these places.

to the Bloomfield River from Cape Tribulation must do so in a 4WD vehicle. This road is often impassable after heavy rain. Drive slowly to avoid hitting wildlife.

CAMPING

Apart from bush camping, there are no facilities for camping in the Mossman Gorge section. The main camping ground in the Cape Tribulation section is at Noah Beach, 8 km south of Cape Tribulation. Toilets, showers and drinking water are provided. Campfires are prohibited in the park, and only fuel stoves should be used. There are a number of private camping areas, hostels and holiday units near the park.

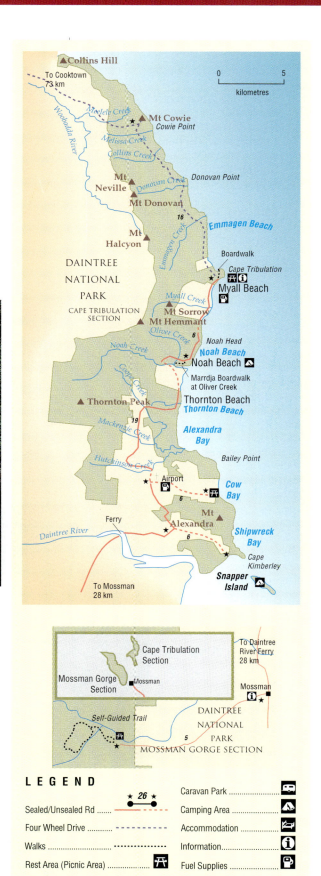

LEGEND

Sealed/Unsealed Rd	Caravan Park
Four Wheel Drive	Camping Area
Walks	Accommodation
Rest Area (Picnic Area)	Information
	Fuel Supplies

EUNGELLA NATIONAL PARK

IN BRIEF

MAP REFERENCE: PAGE 204 F 4

Location 83 km west of Mackay

Best Time April to early November

Main Attractions Rugged rainforest wilderness, waterfalls, wildlife, 4WD

Ranger Phone (07) 4958 4552

Camping: to book a tent or campervan site, phone the ranger on (07) 4958 4552

Towering mountain peaks, deep gorges, tumbling waterfalls and crystal clear streams all combine to make Eungella one of the treasures in Queensland. Situated in the rugged Clarke Range 83 km west of Mackay, Eungella covers an area of 50 800 hectares. The plateau is a meeting point for rainforest species from both the northern wet tropics and the southern Queensland/New South Wales border area. One of Eungella's most appealing qualities is that much of it remains untouched—a trackless wilderness which will be cherished by generations to come.

PARK HISTORY

The word 'Eungella' is taken from a local Aboriginal dialect and means 'land in the cloud'. Anyone who has spent a few days hiking along the more inaccessible regions of this park will agree it has been aptly named. Eungella was gazetted as a national park in 1941.

EUNGELLA'S NIGHT LIFE

Nocturnal creatures in the rainforest are most active during the first 2 hours after dusk when they are on the move to new feeding areas. Probably the first pair of eyes to be caught in your torch beam will belong to a ringtail possum. These gorgeous little animals are fairly abundant in Eungella and feed on a variety of leaves and flowers. Although normally slow moving, the ringtail can become very agile if threatened by a predator. Carpet

pythons, owls and feral cats all prey on this inoffensive marsupial but appear to have little effect on its numbers. Other animals likely to be seen on a night walk include short-nosed bandicoots, bush rats, brush-tail possums, tawny frogmouths and boobook owls.

WALKING TRAILS GALORE

Unless you are contemplating rising before dawn, campers can forget about bringing an alarm clock as the raucous laughter from kookaburras in the camping area will awaken you at first light. A number of reasonably easy walking trails have been constructed around Broken River permitting visitors to share some of Eungella's hidden beauty. A good trail to start off on is the 2.1 km Rainforest Discovery Walk which would take about 1 hour return. This enchanting circuit which begins near the picnic area can be completed by most bushwalkers in little over an hour.

GREAT FOR BIRDWATCHING

Eungella is a paradise for birdwatchers with over 100 species being recorded in the park. Partially eaten Burdekin plums and figs on the forest floor usually indicate the presence of fruit pigeons high in the treetops. Stand still for a while and you will probably hear the unmistakable, loud, guttural calls from wompoo pigeons in the dense canopy. Even though

A king orchid growing in Eungella National Park

they are brilliantly coloured with splashes of purple, green and yellow, wompoo pigeons are normally difficult to locate in the dappled light of the forest.

Small families of white-browed scrubwrens scratch through the leaf litter in their seemingly endless search for worms and insects. Flocks of tiny brown thornbills—one of the most melodious songsters of the Australian bush—add their enchanting chorus to the varied mixture of bird calls reverberating throughout the forest. Other birds likely to be seen while walking include crimson rosellas, regent bowerbirds, emerald doves and rufous fantails.

A DIFFERENT FACET OF THE PARK

To experience another side of Eungella you would have to travel back down the range and turn off just past the small town of Finch Hatton. From here, it is a further 10 km into the Finch Hatton camping area. The last 750 metres of this track is suitable for 4WD vehicles only.

The tropical plants found at this lower elevation are quite different from the subtropical vegetation found at the top of the range. One of the most prominent trees seen on the track which winds up through the gorge is the giant strangler fig. Often the branches of these massive trees come crashing down during storms because of the heavy weight of bird's-nest ferns and elkhorns. Tentacle-like vines hang suspended from the tops of towering red cedars and silver quandongs, their twisted ends disappearing into the profusion of greenery in the forest understorey. Alexandria palms, tree ferns, stinging trees and cunjevois jostle each other for the slivers of sunlight struggling to reach the floor of the rainforest.

One interesting walk in this lower part of the park is the Wheel of Fire Falls Track. Great boulders—worn smooth by the elements—lie scattered throughout Finch Hatton Creek creating miniature rockpools and cascades. Hikers may even catch sight of a platypus swimming in this pristine waterway, although the best place to watch this shy animal is in the higher Broken River section of the park. The tranquil setting at the base of Araluen Falls is an excellent location to stop for lunch and reflect on the magnificence of the gorge. Red-bellied black snakes and carpet pythons often sunbake on the exposed rocks, but they are no problem. The walk would take about 1 hour return.

ACCESS AND WEATHER

From Mackay a good bitumen road meanders through the lush Pioneer Valley, past cane farms and the small sugar towns of Marian, Mirani and Finch Hatton, before ascending the steep Clarke Range to Eungella township. The park's average rainfall of around 2000 mm occurs mainly

A rufous fantail feeding its young in Eungella

between December and March, but heavy down-pours can happen even in winter. Occasionally torrential rain may cause landslides and block the narrow mountain road, isolating the town of Eungella for days on end. A trip to the park during these adverse conditions does have its compensations, however, especially if one is interested in observing some of the delicate mosses, ferns and fungi which only become evident in wet weather. Check the road conditions before setting off on a trip.

CAMPING

The park's 2 camping grounds at Fern Flat and Broken River are located 6 km from the town down a sealed road. Broken River caters for campervans as well as tents, while at Fern Flat there are walk-in tent sites only. Toilets, showers and fireplaces are provided at both places, but being a rainforest area firewood can be a problem. Ideally, it is best to collect enough outside the park boundary before you arrive. Also take a gas cooker as it will be an invaluable aid on those seemingly endless rainy days which are common in Eungella. Eungella can be popular with visitors, so book ahead for a site.

Permits for camping are required for Fern Flats and Broken River sites.

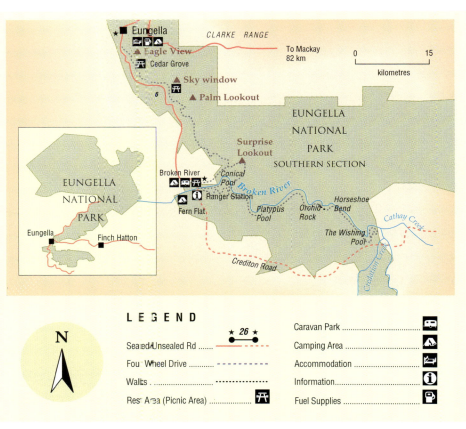

LEGEND

Sealed/Unsealed Rd	Caravan Park
Four Wheel Drive	Camping Area
Walks	Accommodation
Rest Area (Picnic Area)	Information
	Fuel Supplies

GIRRAWEEN NATIONAL PARK

IN BRIEF

MAP REFERENCE: PAGE 203 L 9

Location 260 km southwest of Brisbane via Stanthorpe
Best Time Spring and autumn
Main Attractions Wildflowers, walking tracks
Ranger Phone (07) 4684 5157

Camping: contact the ranger on (07) 4684 5157 for bookings

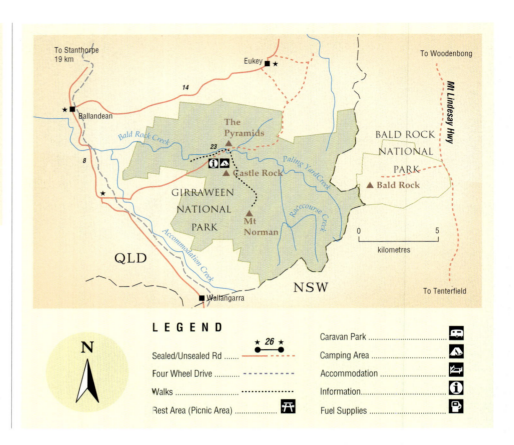

LEGEND

Sealed/Unsealed Rd	★ 26 ★
Four Wheel Drive	
Walks	
Rest Area (Picnic Area)	🏕

Caravan Park	
Camping Area	
Accommodation	
Information	
Fuel Supplies	

When campers reminisce about those frosty mornings spent in the bush huddled around an open fire, or fields of wildflowers bursting into life beneath a brilliant blue sky, they are usually referring to the cool mountainous regions in the southern parts of Australia.

There is, however, one place, even in 'warm, sunny Queensland', where people can experience these normally temperate facets of nature, and that place is Girraween National Park. Situated in rugged granite country 260 km southwest of Brisbane on the Queensland/

Girraween's rugged granite country

New South Wales border, Girraween is a spectacular 11 300 hectare paradise for wildlife, wildflowers and wilderness seekers.

A WEALTH OF WILDFLOWERS

Every year in early spring Girraween becomes a blaze of colour as thousands of wildflowers burst into life. Tufted irises are just one of the many varieties of flowers which thrive in the boulder-strewn park. Ground orchids, daisies, native bluebells, rock roses and pea-flowers are also present, their vibrant hues and delicate textures providing an extra touch of magic to this enchanting floral display.

A WORLD OF INSECTS

Close examination of the thickets of flowering shrubs will reveal a wealth of insect life adorning many of the plants. On some flowers, multi-coloured jewel beetles stand out brilliantly against the sunlight, while on others, small spiders sit camouflaged next to their gossamer-thin webs.

This multitude of tiny creatures provides a rich food source for the many types of insect-eating birds and reptiles. Robins, flycatchers and thornbills as well as small lizards such as the copper-tailed skink and nobby dragon take part in these insect feasts,

FEASTING ON NECTAR

When the red bottlebrush are flowering along the creek, a profusion of honeyeaters are attracted to their nectar-laden flowers. Yellow-tufted honeyeaters, Lewin's honeyeaters, noisy friarbirds, brown honeyeaters, eastern spinebills and red wattlebirds are just a few of the colourful species you can encountered.

At night, the bottlebrush becomes the feeding ground for one of the most delightful little marsupials found in Girraween: the sugar glider. Often, 3 or 4 gliders can be observed in the one tree feasting on the red flowers. Away from the creek, these beautiful animals prefer to dine on the rich yellow flowers of the banksia.

WALKING TRAILS GALORE

There are a number of easy-to-follow walking tracks in Girraween, ranging from the 900 metre link circuit to the 10.4 km trail which weaves its way through the forest to Mt Norman. Allow 6 hours return for the latter. One of the most popular with visitors is the 5 km Junction Track, which starts near the picnic ground and follows the contours of Bald Rock Creek, and takes about 2½ hours return.

Summers in Girraween can be extremely hot, so it is advisable to carry plenty of drinking water if you are thinking of hiking away from

the permanent water in Bald Rock Creek. Note that in midwinter early morning temperatures in the park can often drop to –8°C.

COOLING OFF

A large waterhole in Bald Rock Creek near the picnic area is a great place to go swimming. Depending on the water level, there are also a number of more secluded spots along the creek for cooling off. Sensible precautions, including never diving into these rockpools, will ensure that you will have an enjoyable time.

ACCESS

The park is accessible to conventional vehicles throughout the year. From Brisbane, turn left off the New England Highway 26 km south of Stanthorpe and follow the road for a further 9 km until you reach the park headquarters.

CAMPING

There are 2 large camping grounds at Girraween, one at Bald Rock Creek, the other across the road at Castle Rock Camping Area. Both are well equipped, with hot showers, toilets, tables, BBQ fireplaces and firewood. Due to its popularity, visitors wishing to camp at Girraween during school holidays or long weekends should book up to 12 months in advance.

GREAT SANDY (FRASER ISLAND) NATIONAL PARK

First-time visitors to Fraser Island are often left fumbling for the right adjectives when asked how to describe the beauty and variety of life on this magical sand island off the Queensland coast. Here one can find luxuriant subtropical rainforests growing out of the sand, melaleuca swamps, eucalypt forests, heathland, mangrove-lined estuaries and kilometres of magnificent deserted beaches. Add to this already impressive list the perched dune lakes—including one which is the biggest in the world—fantastic fishing, in both the surf and calm water, and over 230 species of birds, and you will have some idea why this World Heritage listed island has become one of Australia's most visited and best known national parks.

Great Sandy National Park has 2 sections: one is on the northern half of Fraser Island and the other is further south on the Queensland mainland at Cooloola (see page 166). The 2 parks are both part of the Great Sandy Region, but each is adminstered separately.

The *Maheno* wreck on Fraser Island

PRE-EUROPEAN HISTORY

Aborigines from the Butchalla tribe are thought to have inhabited Fraser Island for more than 5000 years. Since the island was extremely rich in food from the sea, lakes and forest, the number of Aboriginal people on the island was relatively high. It has been estimated that nearly 2000 people were living on the island up to the 1830s. Their rapid decline began with the discovery of gold in Gympie in the late 1860s when the island became a quarantine and immigration station for ships bringing in supplies and men to the nearby goldfields. Over the next 40 years, a combination of smallpox, venereal disease, influenza, alcohol and the occasional massacre reduced the numbers of this once proud people to less than 150 individuals. The survivors of this genocide were transported to a number of mainland Aboriginal reserves including Yarrabah near Cairns in 1905.

THE FIRST EUROPEANS

Captain James Cook was the first known European to sight Fraser Island. He named Sandy Cape and Indian Head before continuing north. Matthew Flinders, in his ship the *Norfolk*, sailed by 19 years later and returned in 1802 in another ship, the *Investigator*, to explore more of Fraser's sandy coast.

THE ELIZA FRASER STORY

The Great Sandy Island became a household name in the fledgling colony with the rescue of Eliza Fraser. The drama began on 13 May 1836

The Aquarium Pools, beautiful rockpools on Fraser Island, Great Sandy National Park

when a ship called the *Stirling Castle* struck a coral reef off the northern tip of Cape York Peninsula. The captain, James Fraser, and his pregnant wife Eliza, managed to escape in a longboat with the 16 other passengers and crew. Over the next 6 weeks Captain Fraser steered the longboat back towards the Moreton Bay settlement nearly 2000 km to the south. With dwindling fresh water and virtually no food, the longboat was beached at Fraser Island so the crew could look for supplies. The entire party was quickly rounded up by members of the Butchalla tribe who kept Mrs Fraser captive for nearly 7 weeks. During that time Captain Fraser and a few others died while the remaining crew members managed to escape and walk south towards Moreton Bay. Once the authorities learned of Mrs Fraser's fate, an expedition was formed to rescue her. Within 10 years of her lucky escape, the Great Sandy Island, as it was formerly known, was being called Fraser Island.

TIMBER FELLING

The logging of Fraser Island's beautiful forests began in the early 1860s and continued until all commercial cutting ceased in 1992. During the first 70 years of operations, bullock drays hauled the timber out of the forests to loading points on the coast. Giant satinay (turpentine) trees *(Syncarpia hillii)*, were one of the favourites of the loggers due to their rot-resistant qualities in

salt water. Many of the largest specimens were sent to Egypt for the construction of the Suez Canal in the 19th century.

WORLD WAR II

Fraser Island became a base for the famous Z Force commando units during World War II. Thousands of soldiers trained on the island, preparing themselves in Fraser's rainforests

and mangrove-lined coast for battling the Japanese in similar conditions on the Pacific Islands. Today, a few rusted relics of the war years can be found on the west coast.

HOW FRASER WAS FORMED

Running 120 km from north to south, and 25 km across at its widest point, Fraser is the largest sand island in the world. Covering an area of

GREAT SANDY (FRASER ISLAND) NATIONAL PARK

Wooden ramps near Happy Valley make driving downhill on sand easier

165 280 hectares, the island is part of the Great Sandy Region which was formed over millions of years from eroding sandstone in the Great Dividing Range. Rivers in northern New South Wales washed this sand out to sea, where it was picked up by ocean currents and transported north along the coast. The northerly dispersion of sand was, and still is, stopped by rocky outcrops such as Indian Head. The sand piled up over thousands of years forming dunes and beaches. Seeds, carried by birds and ocean currents, germinated in the sand, providing a layer of vegetation to stabilise the dunes.

THE SANDS OF TIME

Fraser is formed from many different types of sand, including the white oceanic sands which make up most of the island's mass. Much of this sand contains concentrations of heavy minerals such as rutile, zircon and ilmenite. The beaches on the eastern side of Fraser are continually changing due to the action of waves pounding against the shore. Winds and tides form and reform sandbars, gutters and small bays along the coast. During periods of violent cyclonic weather there can be dramatic changes to the shape and slope of the eastern beaches.

THE COLOURED SANDS

Fraser is also famous for its coloured sands which are similar to those found in the southern section of Great Sandy National Park at Cooloola on the mainland. One of the most striking examples of these coloured sands can be seen at the 'Cathedrals' on the eastern beach. Also known as the Teewah Sands, the coloured sands were formed over countless thousands of years from decaying vegetation leaching down into the sand. Shades of yellow and brown are the dominant colours, although rusty reds and orange can also be seen at certain levels. Dig down to any great depth on Fraser and you can see that the coloured sands form much of the underground mass of the island.

PERCHED DUNE LAKES

There are more than 40 perched dune lakes on Fraser including the world's largest, the 200 hectare Lake Boomanjin. These lakes have some of the purest drinking water found anywhere in the world. Some are crystal clear with white sandy bottoms, while others have a reddish colour which comes from humus staining from decaying vegetation such as tea-trees growing near the lake. The reddish stain has no effect on the drinking qualities of the water.

The water is so pure in the lakes that only 3 species of small fish live in them. Tortoises are quite common in some of the lakes, especially Lake Bowarrady. In the past, many visitors hand-fed the tortoises in this lake, but these days this practice is frowned upon as it could upset the animals' natural feeding patterns.

ABUNDANT FRESH WATER

Apart from the dune lakes the island has a number of freshwater streams which flow consistently throughout the year. In many respects the sand on Fraser acts like a large sponge, with rain falling on the island being held in a large underground water-table. The biggest stream on the island is Eli Creek, which flows onto the eastern beach a few kilometres south of the *Maheno* wreck. At numerous other places along the beach fresh water bubbles out of the sand, providing visitors with easy access to good drinking water. None of this water has to be boiled as the sand filters out any impurities.

GREAT FOR FISHING

For more than 70 years visitors have been travelling to Fraser Island to experience its fantastic fishing. At the height of the season, between July and October, hundreds of anglers from around Australia gather on the surf beaches of the island's east coast to try their luck and skills against the huge schools of taylor which migrate up the coast. Pilchards are the preferred bait for these great fighting fish, although they have been known to bite on virtually anything when in a feeding frenzy.

Other fish found on the east coast beaches include silver bream, jewfish and golden trevally. In the calm waters on the western side of the island whiting, flathead, bream and a few other species of fish can be caught throughout the year. Anglers can gather their own bait by either digging for bloodworms or pumping up yabbies from the sandflats at low tide. Nimble-fingered anglers with good eyesight can even try to catch some of the big sand worms which are common on the eastern surf beaches. The best way to do this is to place some stale fish or meat (the smellier the better) in an onion bag and drag it slowly over the sand. When the worm sticks its head up through the sand, bend down, holding a small piece of meat in your fingers, and try to grab the worm when it attaches itself to the meat. More often than not you will miss, but it's fun trying.

Another good form of bait which can be easily gathered along the surf beaches is the pipi. These little triangular shaped shellfish bury themselves a few centimetres under the sand, but can easily be found by dragging your toes along the beach. Apart from being used as bait, pipis can be cooked over an open fire and eaten from the shell or boiled and used in stews or other camp-cooked meals. Mud crabs are also present in good numbers around the mangrove-lined estuaries on the western side of the island, although you will probably need a small boat to get to the places where you can drop your crab pots.

A MECCA FOR 4WDs

Since there are no formed roads on Fraser, a 4WD vehicle is necessary if you want to explore the island. It is best to keep tyres deflated to around 175 kPa (25 psi), although you may have to drop them back to 140 kPa (20 psi) if you get stuck in soft sand. Due to the popularity of the island, accidents on the inland sandy tracks are becoming all too common. Never drive too fast on these tracks, particularly around blind corners. Always carry a spade in your vehicle to dig yourself out of bogs. During prolonged dry spells some of the inland tracks are difficult to negotiate due to the soft sand. Try to keep your beach driving within 2 hours either side of low tide. Apart from being better for your vehicle, since you won't have to drive through salt water, it is less destructive on the foredunes.

A Great Place to Go Walking

Apart from walking along Fraser's beautiful beaches, there are numerous forest hiking trails in the central and southern parts of the island.

One excellent track to start out on is the 6 km Lake Birrabeen to Central Station walk, which would take about 2½ hours one way. Birdwatchers will love this track as it meanders through a wide variety of the park's vegetation including banksia heathland, eucalypt woodland and finally rainforest around Central Station. During late winter and early spring, the heath country around the lakes becomes alive with the many varieties of colourful wildflowers that carpet the ground.

Although rainforest covers only about 5 per cent of the island—approximately 8000 hectares—it is extremely interesting and home to a wide variety of fauna and flora.

A short walking track at Central Station (25 minutes one way) follows the crystal clear Wanggoolba Creek past towering brush box, hoop pine, white beech, ribbon wood and strangler figs. Both the piccabeen palm and the shorter walking-stick palm reach up for the sunlight, entangled in an understorey of tree ferns, vines and decaying branches. Uncommon rainforest dwellers such as the noisy pitta, emerald dove, white-headed pigeon and wompoo pigeon are sometimes sighted here. Two very conspicuous birds on this trail are the rufous fantail and the eastern yellow robin. Often these birds will fly within a few metres of walkers to 'check out the intruders' before flying back into the forest.

Don't Feed the Dingoes

Fraser is probably the best place in Australia to see wild dingoes at close quarters. While in most other parts of the country they have interbred with domestic dogs, the dingoes on Fraser are a pure strain. People who feed them or leave scraps lying around are interfering with the dingoes' ability to hunt their natural prey.

Island Access

Fraser is approximately 190 km north of Brisbane. The island can be reached by a number of methods including vehicular barges,

Dingoes still roam wild on Fraser Island in Great Sandy National Park

passenger launches, aircraft or private boats.

A 4WD vehicle is essential for driving on the island. If you don't have your own they can be hired at Hervey Bay, Rainbow Beach, the Sunshine Coast and Brisbane.

People bringing a vehicle to Fraser must get a vehicle access permit and attach it to their car windscreen. The permit is valid for one month. Unregistered vehicles are not permitted on Fraser Island.

Normal road rules apply for beach driving, and motorists should use their indicators to show oncoming vehicles which side they are going to pass them on.

Transport to the Island

There are 4 vehicular barges which service Fraser Island.

On the southern end of Fraser a barge operates between Hook Point and Inskip Point near Rainbow Beach. There is no need to make a booking for this barge.

From Hervey Bay, barges to Wanggoolba Creek and Kingfisher Bay depart from River Heads. The barge to Moon Point leaves from Urangan boat harbour. Bookings are required for the 3 Hervey Bay barges.

Visitors who arrive by light aircraft will land either at Toby's Gap which is managed by the Queensland National Parks and Wildlife Service (NPWS), or at Wanggoolba Creek which is managed by the Eurong Beach Resort. Landing permission and entry permits are needed for private aircraft before arrival.

A number of commercial tour operators run 4WD day trips and 2 to 3 day camping safaris to the island from Brisbane, the Sunshine Coast, Hervey Bay and Rainbow Beach. For more information contact your nearest office of the Queensland Government Travel Centre.

Camping and Accommodation

The Queensland National Parks and Wildlife Service has camping grounds at Lake Boomanjin, Central Station, Lake Allom, Waddy Point, Wathumba, Lake McKenzie and Dundubara. Facilities in these places include toilets, picnic tables and showers (except for Lake Allom). Lake McKenzie and Dundubara are the only places suitable for caravans or camper trailers.

Visitors are allowed to camp at most spots along the coast unless signs indicate that camping is prohibited. Always make sure your toilet is dug to a depth of 40–60 cm and at least 50 metres away from the high-tide mark. Never bury your rubbish; take it out with you, so that Fraser will remain a pristine wilderness.

Visitors to the island who don't wish to camp can find motel type accommodation at Happy Valley, Eurong, and Dilli Village.

If you want to try a bit of real luxury in one of Australia's most awarded resorts for environmental awareness, you can't go past Kingfisher Bay on the western side of the island. Apart from excellent food and accommodation, visitors can go birdwatching and do other nature tours at the resort.

HINCHINBROOK ISLAND NATIONAL PARK

IN BRIEF

MAP REFERENCE: PAGE 207 M 8

Location Off the Queensland coast between the towns of Ingham and Cardwell
Best Time May to October
Main Attractions Great walks, wilderness
Ranger Phone (07) 4066 8601

Hinchinbrook Ferries: phone (07) 4066 8270

Camping permits: Queensland Department of Environment, phone (07) 4066 8601

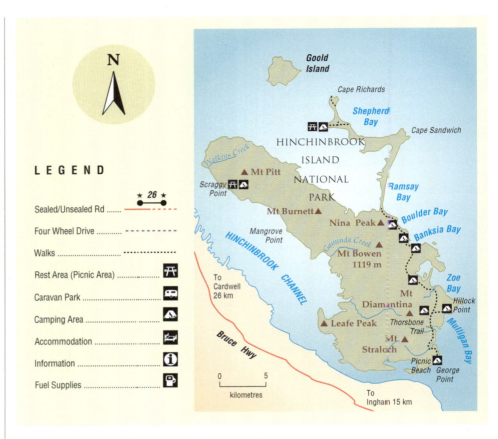

LEGEND

Sealed/Unsealed Rd	★ 26 ★
Four Wheel Drive	
Walks	
Rest Area (Picnic Area)	
Caravan Park	
Camping Area	
Accommodation	
Information	
Fuel Supplies	

Pristine rainforests, isolated sandy coves, mountain peaks and mangrove-lined estuaries are just a few of the facets which harmonise perfectly to make Hinchinbrook Island a magnet for nature lovers and wilderness seekers from around the world. Covering an area of 39 000 hectares, Hinchinbrook is Australia's largest island national park and a refuge for many endangered species of plants and animals.

ISLAND HISTORY

The Bandyin Aboriginal tribe lived on Hinchinbrook for thousands of years, but today the only visible signs of their former occupation are a number of middens and stone fish-traps scattered around the coast. The island, which is separated from the mainland by the Hinchinbrook Channel, was declared a national park back in 1932 because of its natural beauty.

EXTENSIVE HABITATS

The western coastline of Hinchinbrook is covered with extensive stands of mangroves which many botanists consider to be the richest and most diverse in Australia. These almost impenetrable saltwater forests provide a safe haven for a vast number of creatures both great and small including the dangerous estuarine crocodile. Commercial crocodile hunting after World War II drastically reduced the population of this ancient reptile and by the late 1960s they were nearly extinct. Since they became protected in the early 1970s crocodile numbers have built up again around Hinchinbrook and hikers should be aware of their presence in mangrove estuaries or tidal lagoons.

Seagrass beds around the coast of Hinchinbrook provide a home for the endangered dugong. These harmless marine mammals need sanctuaries like Hinchinbrook to ensure their survival.

A giant green tree frog (*Litoria infrafrenata*) found on Hinchinbrook Island

The picturesque coastline of Hinchinbrook Island

Numerous types of fish, crabs and molluscs thrive in the rich marine environment and provide wading birds such as herons, egrets and oystercatchers with a year-round supply of food. The absence of vehicles on the island has been particularly beneficial to some waders, like the beach thick-knee which has all but disappeared from mainland beaches.

RAINFOREST AND MOUNTAINS

Much of the interior of Hinchinbrook is covered with thick tropical rainforest. The island's high rainfall has allowed a diverse array of lush vegetation to flourish. Huge rainforest trees reach up to the sunlight, their tentacle-like buttress roots anchoring them firmly to the forest floor. Palms, tree ferns and tangled vines all jostle for space beneath the tree canopy, while on the ground fungi of various shapes and colours burst into life after rain. One of the most important trees found in Hinchinbrook is the strangler fig. Apart from the figs on this tree being one of the prime sources of food for fruit pigeons and other birds, they are also eaten by flying foxes, possums and native rats.

Wherever you go on Hinchinbrook you will be within sight of Mt Bowen, the highest peak on the island. Rising to 1119 metres, this spectacular rainforest-covered mountain is usually shrouded in clouds.

GREAT FOR WALKING

Hinchinbrook has some of the best walking trails in Queensland including the 32 km Thorsbone Trail which runs from Ramsay Bay to George Point. This for experienced walkers only, and there are no facilities along the way. Allow yourself at least 4 days to complete this beautiful trail which has been described as the north Queensland equivalent of Tasmania's famous Cradle Mountain Walk.

ACCESS

Hinchinbrook is situated off the Queensland coast between the towns of Ingham and Cardwell. Most visitors to the island travel there by boat from the small town of Cardwell. Hinchinbrook Ferries runs a return service to the island for day visitors as well as for campers who want to be picked up at the southern end of the island.

CAMPING

Campers who come to Hinchinbrook should be well prepared for bush camping and bring everything they are likely to need. Only fuel stoves are permitted on the island. Food supplies can be picked up in Cardwell before setting off. Remember to pack insect repellent, sunscreen, a small medical kit, wet weather gear and a hat.

Camping permits are a must and should be booked well in advance. For details, ring the Queensland Department of Environment.

If you intend to go swimming remember that marine stingers are found in the waters around Hinchinbrook Island from mid-October to March and that crocodiles may be encountered throughout the year.

LADY MUSGRAVE ISLAND NATIONAL PARK

IN BRIEF

Location 52 nautical miles northeast of Bundaberg
Best Time November to March for birds and turtles
Main Attractions Diving, bird and turtle watching
Ranger Phone (07) 4976 0766

Lady Musgrave Island is a true coral cay which evolved from a buildup of broken coral, sand and floating debris. It was first charted in 1820 by Philip Parker King, and later recorded in the journals of the HMS *Fly* in 1843.

Guano miners arrived on the island in the 1890s to extract the rich bird droppings. The miners introduced goats which were finally eradicated in 1974, and plant life has slowly return to its original state.

Lady Musgrave is part of the Capricornia Cays National Park which is made up of a number of islands comprising the Capricorn/Bunker Group. The island also falls within the Great Barrier Reef Marine Park and the waters off its eastern end are classified as Marine National Park 'B' Zone. The waters may be used for recreational purposes but nothing may be removed (no fishing or collecting of shells etc).

WILDLIFE

Although it comprises only 14 hectares, Lady Musgrave is an important seabird-nesting site. Between October and March, thousands of black noddy terns make their small nests in the branches of the pisonia trees.

Other species such as the bridled tern, black-naped tern and silver gull lay their eggs in rock crevices or in the sand just above the high-water mark. White-breasted sea-eagles and lesser frigatebirds patrol the island waters as egrets, oyestercatchers and bar-tailed godwits scour the tidal shallows for food.

Between mid-November and the end of January, green and loggerhead turtles arrive on Lady Musgrave's beaches to nest. Up to 20 turtles a night may drag themselves up on the dunes above the high-water mark. After methodically digging out a hole with her back flipper, the female lays up to 120 eggs, then covers them with sand and returns to the sea.

GREAT FOR DIVING

Lady Musgrave is surrounded by a coral lagoon almost 8 km in circumference. The turquoise waters of this aquatic wonderland are home to more than 1000 varieties of brilliantly coloured fish and 200 species of coral. Visibility is excellent for snorkelling and SCUBA diving.

ACCESS AND CAMPING

Unless you arrive in your own boat, the only way to reach the island is on the *Lady Musgrave*, a high-speed catamaran which leaves Bundaberg 4 times a week. It caters for day trippers, and also for campers who want to be dropped off and picked up at a later date. To book, and for information on fares and times, ring (07) 4152 9011.

The only facility for campers on Lady Musgrave is a toilet. You must bring your own water containers which should be filled with fresh water before you leave the boat. There is no fresh water on Lady Musgrave. Include enough emergency supplies for an extra few days on the island in case bad weather delays the boat. A gas cooker is also a must as fires are not allowed. For bookings ring the National Parks Office, phone (07) 4972 6055.

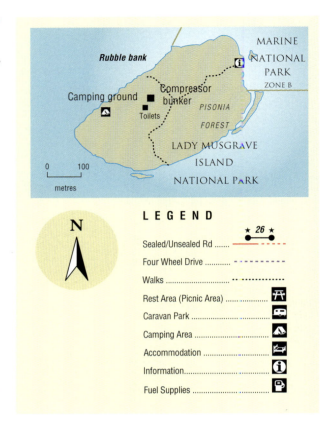

LEGEND

★ 26 ★

Sealed/Unsealed Rd	
Four Wheel Drive	
Walks	
Rest Area (Picnic Area)	
Caravan Park	
Camping Area	
Accommodation	
Information	
Fuel Supplies	

Lady Musgrave Island, a pristine coral cay

IN BRIEF

MAP REFERENCE: PAGE 207 J 2

Location 300 km northwest of Cairns. 4WD is preferable
Best Time May to October
Main Attractions Great fishing, camping, nature watching
Ranger Phone
(07) 4060 3271

A vast sweep of plains covered in sun-bleached yellow grass and dotted with low spindly trees, along with the mud-brown castles of termites, is the overwhelming dry season landscape of Lakefield National Park in far north Queensland. Cut by a myriad rivers, this flat land during the wet season becomes more water than land and near the coast coalesces into an inland sea. As the Dry begins the rivers retreat to within their richly forested banks and eventually dry up to become long stretches of still billabongs and life-saving waterholes.

Lakefield is Queensland's second biggest national park, covering 537 000 hectares north of Laura all the way to the sea at Princess Charlotte Bay. The Normanby River makes up much of the eastern boundary, while the Bizant, Morehead, Hann, North Kennedy and Kennedy Rivers flow in a northerly direction through the park to the coast.

A HOST OF WILDLIFE

Lakefield attracts thousands of birds making the area a birdwatcher's delight. As well as the 180-odd species of birds recorded, there are 18 species of mammals and 38 species of reptiles.

A number of species of ducks, including whistling ducks, shelducks, Pacific black ducks and grey teal, along with the strikingly marked magpie-goose and other species of waterbirds, gather in their thousands on the waterholes as the ephemeral pools and streams dry up.

Out on the open plains kori (Australian) bustards, brolgas and sarus cranes can be seen, but it is the richly coloured black-necked stork (jabiru) that, when seen, takes the accolades.

The main mammals seen are the numerous agile wallabies on the open plains, but feral pigs are also common—and a pest.

All the rivers are home to crocodiles and there are both the timid and harmless fresh-water crocodile as well as the much larger and very dangerous estuarine crocodile.

In the evening the colonies of fruit bats that can be found along the waterways awake and take to the air looking for a feed of blossom or fruit. They can be noisy and smelly.

Smaller, insect-eating bats are often seen flitting through the light of the campfire.

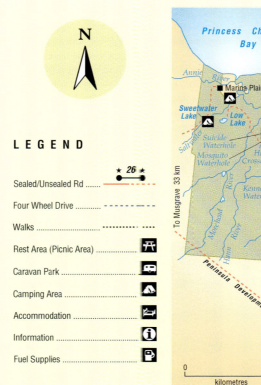

LEGEND

Sealed/Unsealed Rd	★ 26 ★
Four Wheel Drive	
Walks	
Rest Area (Picnic Area)	
Caravan Park	
Camping Area	
Accommodation	
Information	
Fuel Supplies	

FISHING

Lakefield is one of the few parks in Queensland where fishing is allowed, and the prize fish is, of course, the mighty barramundi. There are some top spots to catch fish with a number of places suitable to launch a boat. No fishing is allowed between 1 November and 1 January and a bag limit of 2 fish a day applies. You are not allowed to take more than 5 fish from the park.

ACCESS AND CAMPING

Access is restricted to the dry season, April to November, but after a 'good' Wet the park may be closed until May.

The best access is via Laura on the main road north from Cairns and while a conventional vehicle could go this way in a good year, the country really demands a 4WD.

The main road through the park runs north from Laura past the ranger stations of New Laura and Lakefield and then west out of the park to the small tourist stop of Musgrave. A high-clearance vehicle is required and a 4WD is preferable.

Another, lesser, 4WD road runs from Cooktown, via Battlecamp, to enter the park east of Old Laura.

There are many camp sites available in Lakefield with most of them located on the larger waterholes.

An excellent camp with toilets, fireplaces and tables is located at Kalpowar Crossing, not far from the Lakefield Ranger Station.

Other top spots, although with fewer facilities—or none—are Twelve Mile Waterhole, Mick Finn Waterhole or the Hann Crossing.

Termite castles, typical of the park's terrain

LAMINGTON NATIONAL PARK

IN BRIEF

MAP REFERENCE: PAGE 203 N 8

Location 85 km southwest of Surfers Paradise
Best Time All year round
Main Attractions Rainforest walks, wildlife, waterfalls
Ranger Phone (07) 5544 0634

Accommodation: O'Reilly's Rainforest Guesthouse, phone (07) 5544 0644

Camping permits: phone the ranger, (07) 5544 0634

The mist-shrouded valleys and lush rainforest-covered ridges of Lamington National Park have been silently beckoning nature lovers and travellers for over 80 years. One can quickly find oneself totally absorbed in this seemingly time-less world of huge strangler figs, vines, mosses and bubbling streams.

A regent bowerbird in Lamington National Park

HISTORY OF THE PARK

Apart from being the most popular national park in Queensland, Lamington is also one of the oldest, having been gazetted in 1915. The park gets its name from Lord Lamington who was the governor of Queensland from 1896 to 1902. Unfortunately the governor will not go down in history as one of Queensland's early nature lovers as he marked his once-only visit to this mountainous region by shooting a koala.

The park owes much of its existence to the dedication of Robert Collins, who campaigned tirelessly throughout the 1890s and early 1900s to have the area protected from logging. Collins died 2 years before his dream was realised, although the fight was carried on by one of his strongest supporters, Romeo Lahey. It seems ironic that it was Lahey, whose family owned one of Queensland's largest timber mills at the time, who led the final push to have the 20 200 hectare wilderness declared a national park.

A RAINFOREST WILDERNESS

A wide range of vegetation can be found within the park. Huge brush box, tulip oak, giant stinging trees and buttress-rooted Moreton Bay figs are just a few of the many species which thrive here. The permanent moisture of the rainforest encourages the quick growth of mosses and ferns. These are usually seen growing along creek banks and in wet gullies, or clinging tenaciously to the sides of tree trunks.

Fungi, of many intriguing shapes, are also stimulated by the wet conditions, adding colour-ful splashes to an otherwise lush, green environ-ment. Various types of epiphytes such as staghorns, elkhorns and bird's-nest ferns clutch giant host trees. Orchids can also be seen growing on the trunks and branches of some trees. They vary immensely in shape, colour and size from tiny, delicate whites through to the large yellow flowers of the king orchid.

Gnarled Antarctic beech trees thrive in the

The Canopy Walk, 15 metres above the ground in Lamington National Park

higher parts of the park that are more than 1000 metres above sea level. Scientists believe these beech forests, which are often shrouded in mist, indicate that the Lamington Plateau was once much cooler. The lower sections of the park are dominated by eucalypt woodlands, grass-trees and other dry vegetation.

Abundant Wildlife

Having such a wide range of vegetation, it is little wonder Lamington is regarded as one of the most important refuges for wildlife in south-east Queensland. On the lower slopes of the park both the red-necked wallaby and whiptail wallaby are often seen. Other marsupials found in the drier eucalypt forest include the common brush-tail possum, sugar glider, greater glider and the rare brush-tailed phascogale.

Rainforest species include the red-necked pademelon, mountain brush-tail possum, ring-tail possum, both the short- and long-nosed bandicoots and the endangered tiger quoll. Reptiles are also abundant, among them large rainforest skinks and beautifully patterned snakes such as the carpet python.

Lamington is renowned as a birdwatcher's paradise. Some of Australia's rarest and most colourful species are found there including the noisy pitta, crimson rosella, king parrot, Albert's lyrebird and regent bowerbird.

Whipbirds, logrunners, white-browed scrubwrens and brush-turkeys can be seen scratching through the undergrowth on the forest floor, while in the canopy above, colourful wompoo pigeons, brown cuckoo-doves and the paradise riflebird compete for the forest's soft fruits.

Walks and Waterfalls

The well-marked system of trails in Lamington provides hikers with some of the best walks in Australia. These can vary from pleasant, 2 hour jaunts to 3 day hikes over parts of Queensland's roughest terrain. One interesting way of viewing the park's many wonders from above is via the rainforest canopy walk. Here visitors can stroll across a suspension bridge dangling 15 metres above the forest floor. This provides hikers with a chance of coming face-to-face with some of the brilliant birds which live in the dense canopy.

Morans Falls Track (a 6 km return walk through some of the park's diverse vegetation) is an ideal trail to begin your Lamington adventure. The track begins about 800 metres from the ranger station and winds its way down through the spectacular rainforest. After periods of heavy rain the track becomes very slippery in places and is home to hundreds of leeches! The sound of roaring water is the first indication you are nearing Morans Falls. Plunging 80 metres down a sheer cliff face into a rockpool surrounded by vegetation, the falls are

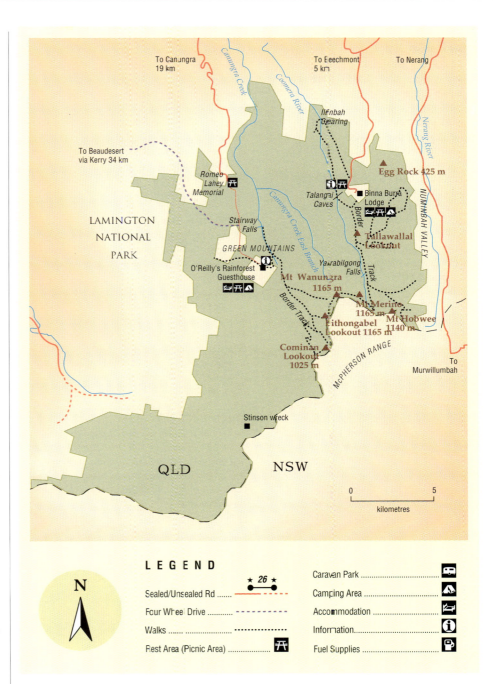

a spellbinding sight. Allow about 3 hours walking time for the return trip.

Access

Lamington is situated 120 km south of Brisbane and 85 km southwest of Southport on the Gold Coast. The park is accessible to conventional vehicles as good bitumen roads go all the way up to the camping ground and O'Reilly's Rainforest Guesthouse. The final 45 km of the trip from the small town of Canungra is the most exciting part of the journey as the road winds past small farms before snaking its way up around extremely sharp S-bends.

Camping

Since Lamington is such a popular spot for camping, permits need to be booked well in advance. The steep winding road makes it unsuitable for caravans and only unpowered sites are available. Showers, toilets, picnic tables, drinking water and fireplaces are provided, but campers should bring in their own firewood as collection of wood within the park is prohibited. For information and camp site bookings call the ranger.

Visitors who don't feel like roughing it can be pampered at O'Reilly's Rainforest Guesthouse or Binna Burra Mountain Lodge.

LAWN HILL NATIONAL PARK

How would you like to go for a swim in a creek full of crocodiles while enjoying the warm emerald-green waters of one of Australia's most pristine waterways? If it appeals, take the plunge and head up to Lawn Hill National Park in far northwest Queensland.

Luckily, the crocodiles in Lawn Hill Creek are the friendly variety, more interested in a good meal of fish than the dangling feet and arms of human intruders.

HISTORY

Aboriginal habitation at Lawn Hill goes back some 17 000 years. The Waanyi people hunted and fished there until the 1930s when missionaries 'removed them' to Mornington Island.

There are still a large number of middens in the park where the Waanyi feasted on mussels that they gathered in the creek. At Rainbow Dreaming and Wild Dog Dreaming art sites, the typical freehand ochre paintings of these former inhabitants can be seen on some of the rock overhangs.

The area around Riversleigh has a World Heritage listed fossil deposit with the remains of prehistoric mammals and reptiles.

UNTAMED BEAUTY

Located 400 km northwest of Mt Isa, near the Northern Territory border, Lawn Hill National Park is slowly becoming a mecca for nature lovers from all over Australia.

The dominant feature of this sprawling 262 000 hectare wilderness is Lawn Hill Gorge, which cuts its way through the rugged sandstone plateaus of the Constance Range. The 60 metre walls of the gorge, which rise up almost vertically, were formed over millions of years by the water in the creek eroding the sandstone.

ABUNDANT WILDLIFE

Besides crocodiles, the park is a haven for an amazing variety of wildlife, including more than 135 species of birds and 36 different types of mammals. Snakes and lizards, also plentiful, are often observed sunning themselves in the early part of the day.

Early mornings in Lawn Hill are particularly

Lawn Hill Creek and the gorge it has carved out

beautiful, with the calls of countless parrots, kookaburras and magpies.

Nights in Lawn Hill often have a magical touch, sitting around a campfire after a good meal listening to the sounds of the Australian bush. The croaking of frogs mingles with the high-pitched shrills of little bats. Occasionally, the distinctive 'woof-woof' call of a barking owl will pierce the darkness. Dingoes are common throughout the park as well, and their long, drawn-out howling can provide that extra-special touch to a night in the great outdoors.

THINGS TO DO

There are 20 km of walking tracks in the park. The 7 km return walk (about 3 hours) to the upper gorge is a good one as it passes through a wide variety of diverse habitats. Take your canoe or inflatable boat (or hire one from the camping ground or from Adels Grove) as many peaceful hours can be spent paddling along the creek.

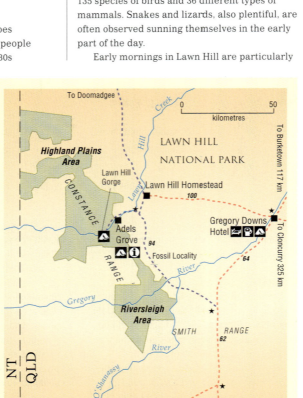

LEGEND

Sealed/Unsealed Rd .... ★ 26 ★
Four Wheel Drive ....
Walks ....
Rest Area (Picnic Area) ....
Caravan Park ....
Camping Area ....
Accommodation ....
Information ....
Fuel Supplies ....

A freshwater crocodile, a harmless species found in Lawn Hill National Park

.ACCESS

Reaching Lawn Hill is an adventure in itself. The gravel roads in this region can be hard on conventional vehicles. During the wet season, December to March, access in and out of the park can be cut for weeks at a time, making it imperative to come prepared with enough provisions for an extended stay. Check on the roads before setting out.

CAMPING

At least 3 or 4 days should be spent in Lawn Hill to fully appreciate it. The camp sites have toilets, showers and fireplaces, but collecting firewood within the park is strictly prohibited. The nearest place to buy fuel is Gregory Downs Hotel, 100 km east of the park. Mt Isa, 400 km to the southeast, is the best spot to buy food and other essentials. For weather information and permits contact the ranger. There is also a private camp site 10 km away at Adels Grove.

IN BRIEF

MAP REFERENCE: PAGE 203 L 8

Location 116 km southwest of Brisbane. 4WD recommended

Best Time All year, but spring and autumn are the best

Main Attractions Walking tracks, mountain views

Ranger Phone (07) 4666 1133

Main Range National Park, long renowned as one of the finest bushwalking areas in southeast Queensland, is quickly becoming a mecca for wilderness lovers from all over Australia.

Aboriginal people lived in and around Main Range for thousands of years. The first white man to venture into this thickly forested region was Allan Cunningham in 1827. He was searching for a pass across the Dividing Range, which today is aptly named Cunninghams Gap. A memorial to this intrepid explorer can be seen at the top of the range beside one of the walking tracks. While sheep and cattle runs were taken up on both sides of the 'Divide', the only activity inside this mountainous region was a small amount of logging on the accessible slopes.

SCENERY AND FANTASTIC VIEWS

Situated 116 km west of Brisbane, the park stretches for 40 km along the Great Dividing Range from Kangaroo Mountain in the north to Wilsons Peak on the Queensland/New South Wales border. An extensive range of vegetation, including rainforest, eucalypts and grass-trees, can be found throughout its 10 500 hectares. Fauna is also extremely varied because of the geographic location of the park—the rugged landscape providing a safe sanctuary for the many species which have become rare as a result of land clearing.

One of the best places to take in the grandeur of Main Range is from Governors Chair lookout, a 150 metre walk up from the car park in the Spicers Gap section of the park. Governors Chair, so named because it was a favourite spot with visiting governors, is a large rock sitting on the edge of the cliff face. Walkers should be careful when approaching the brink of this precipice as there is little indication of the sudden drop. The panorama from this point is outstanding, with breathtaking views of mountains and valleys stretching to the New South Wales border.

WILDLIFE AND WALKING TRACKS

A 4 km, one hour's stroll along the dense Box Forest Track, which follows the banks of West Gap Creek, is a great way to observe the park's wildlife. Along the walk shiny black land mullet—the largest member of the skink family—can often be seen sunning themselves on fallen logs. Striking red-bellied black snakes are also at home along the creek. Although venomous, these beautiful reptiles will not strike unless they are provoked.

Hundreds of scaly-breasted and rainbow lorikeets feed ravenously on the blossoms of the red bottlebrush, screeching as they fly from tree to tree.

On the Mt Cordeaux trail—a 7 km return hike which starts from the Cunningham memorial and takes about 2½ hours—hikers will experience some of the most exhilarating views in southeast Queensland.

ACCESS AND CAMPING

The park headquarters is located just off the Cunningham Highway 116 km west of Brisbane. The nearest main town is Warwick, 45 km to the west. 4WD is recommended to access the park.

Fording a stream in Main Range National Park

There are 2 camping areas in Main Range, both with toilets, picnic tables, drinking water and fireplaces. Neither camping area requires sites to be booked.

The park's main camping area at West Gap Creek lies just off the main highway across from the ranger station.

Spicers Gap camping area, which is the quieter of the two, can be reached via the Moogerah Dam road which branches off the Cunningham Highway 5 km west of Aratula. From the highway, it is 6 km to the junction with Spicers Gap road.

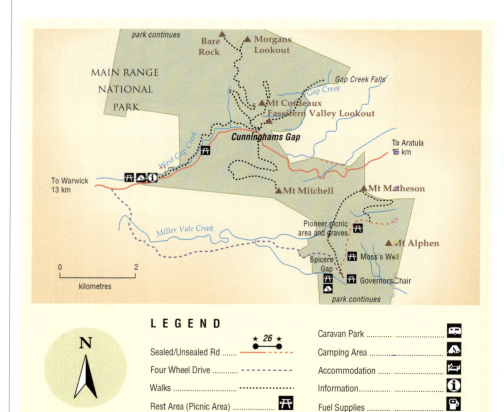

LEGEND

Sealed/Unsealed Rd	★ 26 ★
Four Wheel Drive	- - - - -
Walks	•••••••
Rest Area (Picnic Area)	🏕
Caravan Park	
Camping Area	
Accommodation	
Information	
Fuel Supplies	

IN BRIEF

MAP REFERENCE: PAGE 203 N 6

Location 40 km across Moreton Bay from Brisbane. 4WD only
Best Time All year round
Main Attractions Fishing, driving, swimming
Ranger Phone (07) 3408 2710

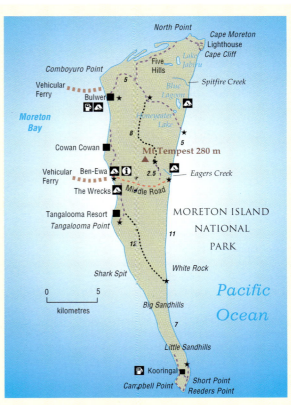

LEGEND

Sealed/Unsealed Rd	★ 26 ★
Four Wheel Drive	
Walks	
Rest Area (Picnic Area)	🏕
Caravan Park	🚐
Camping Area	⛺
Accommodation	🛏
Information	ℹ
Fuel Supplies	⛽

Locating unspoilt wilderness close to our ever-expanding cities is becoming increasingly difficult. There are, however, a few pockets where the march of civilisation has passed by—one of these is Moreton Island National Park. This haven, only 40 km east of Brisbane, is only a short barge trip from the mainland.

Shell middens scattered around Moreton's coastline are evidence that the island was inhabited by Aborigines for at least 2000 years.

The Cape Moreton lighthouse was built in 1857 on a high headland at the northeast end of the island. This beautiful old lighthouse—the oldest in Queensland—is still in operation.

The eastern side of Moreton is part of the migratory route of the magnificent humpback whales on their annual journey along Australia's east coast. The Tangalooma whaling station was closed in 1962, and the numbers of humpbacks has steadily increased. There are daily whale watching tours which operate out of Tangalooma resort in late winter and early spring.

SANDHILLS AND LAKES

Covering an area of 17 000 hectares, Moreton is a wedge-shaped island 38 km long and 9 km across at its widest point. Apart from the rocky

headland in the north of Cape Moreton, the island is made up almost entirely of sand. The world's tallest sandhill at 280 metres, Mt Tempest is situated in the centre of Moreton and can be easily climbed via a 2 hour return walk.

There are several freshwater lakes including beautiful Blue Lagoon perched among dunes on the northeastern side of the island. Nearby Honeyeater Lake is a great place for birds.

A MECCA FOR 4WDs AND ANGLERS

A 7 km sandy track winds its way up to the camping ground at Eagers Creek. Once on the ocean beach you can either head north to Cape Moreton or south to Reeders Point. Never drive on the dunes, as this damages the fragile environment and might also destroy birds' nests.

Many visitors come to Moreton for the great fishing. Flathead, bream, whiting and trevally are found throughout the year while taylor are common during winter.

ACCESS AND CAMPING

There are 2 barges doing the 2 hour crossing to Moreton. The *Combie Trader* (ph: (07) 3203 6399) lands on the beach near Bulwer, while the *Moreton Venture* (ph: (07) 3895 1000) lands further south near the Tangalooma wrecks. Since there are no formed roads, the island is suitable for 4WD vehicles only. There is a fee for vehicles (including passengers) and also a landing fee (valid for one month) for driving on the island. Contact the ranger for details.

There are 5 National Parks camping grounds on Moreton. Facilities include fireplaces, toilets and cold showers. You can also bush camp at most other places around the coast. Food, fuel and ice can be purchased at the small township of Bulwer and at Kooringal, although it is best to bring sufficient supplies with you.

A tranquil beach on Moreton Island National Park

SIMPSON DESERT NATIONAL PARK

IN BRIEF

MAP REFERENCE: PAGE 210 A 3

Location On the Qld/NT and Qld/SA borders. 4WD only
Best Time April to October
Main Attractions Desert landscape, remote camping
Ranger Longreach, phone (07) 4658 1761; Charleville, phone (07) 4654 1255

The Simpson Desert stretches across the corners of 3 states: Queensland, South Australia and the Northern Territory. The Simpson Desert National Park in Queensland is, at 550 000 hectares, the biggest national park in that state and is bounded by the Northern Territory/Queensland border in the west and the South Australia/Queensland border in the south. Much of its eastern boundary is the old rabbit-proof fence that has since fallen into disrepair.

The parallel lines of dunes in this section of the desert are much wider apart than they are further west. The inter-dune valleys are flat and dotted with acacia and hakea scrub, often bordering a claypan that in times of heavy rain can be full of water, attracting a wide variety of wildlife. In the western section of the park is the first of the glistening expanses of salt lakes. The dunes are clothed with spinifex and canegrass which give ample cover for a large number of small reptiles, mainly lizards.

Dingoes are often seen, as are wedge-tail eagles soaring on the thermals.

HISTORY

This remote desert country was one of the last areas in Australia to be explored by Europeans.

Charles Sturt in 1845 had named Eyre Creek. In 1861, John McKinlay crossed Eyre Creek and in 1883 Charles Winnecke surveyed much of the eastern section of the desert. In 1884, Augustus Poeppel established the corner point of the 3 states and surveyed the Northern Territory/Queensland border.

Later that same decade a 240 km-long section of the vermin-proof fence was built from the South Australia/Queensland border north and about 25 km west of Eyre Creek to stop the rabbits—all to no avail. In 1996, however, with the release of the calicivirus disease, it would appear that the rabbit plague has ended.

The route taken by travellers from Birdsville is along much of the QAA Line which was cut in the late 1950s during the exploration for oil.

For most travellers the Queensland park is either the first or the last section of park they journey through on their crossing of the desert from Dalhousie in South Australia. (See Witjira National Park, page 334.)

A salt pan in Simpson Desert National Park

ACCESS AND CAMPING

4WD is essential for this park. A permit is needed to enter and camp in the park, which is available from the Queensland National Parks and Wildlife Service in Longreach, or Charleville. It is also essential to check road conditions with the ranger before setting off.

The only access allowed to this park is, from Birdsville, via the road out to Big Red and then onto the QAA Line to the border and then south to Poeppel Corner.

Camping is allowed beside the track, but probably the most popular camp site is either at the eastern boundary of the park or at Poeppel Corner itself. Because wood is scarce, a gas stove is recommended.

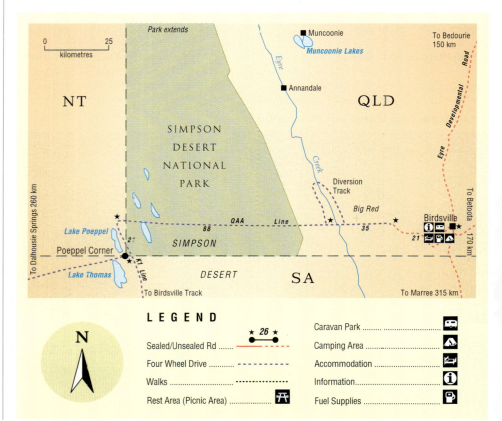

LEGEND

Sealed/Unsealed Rd	★—26—★
Four Wheel Drive	
Walks	
Rest Area (Picnic Area)	🍽
Caravan Park	
Camping Area	
Accommodation	
Information	ℹ
Fuel Supplies	

N

SUNDOWN NATIONAL PARK

IN BRIEF

MAP REFERENCE: PAGE 203 K 9
Location 250 km southwest of Brisbane
Best Time Spring and autumn
Main Attractions Rugged wilderness, wildlife, 4WD
Ranger Phone (07) 6737 5235

Sundown National Park was created in the late 1970s from parts of Glenlyon, Nundubbermere and Ballandean sheep stations. Around the turn of the century these 3 large properties had sections carved off them and sold as smaller leasehold blocks. A combination of drought, hard financial times and the rugged terrain made these properties uneconomic and they were eventually turned into national parks.

Copper, tin and arsenic were mined in the northern part of Sundown in the Red Rock area but very little wealth was gained from the low-grade ore. Abandoned mine shafts and a contaminated treatment plant remain in this part of the park and visitors should keep well away.

Sundown's rugged terrain of steep gullies, eroded ridge tops, gorges and creek flats make the park a mecca for wilderness seekers. The southern boundary of this 16 000 hectare park hugs Roberts Range.

The Severn River which flows through Sundown National Park

RIVER VIEWS

Sundown's most striking feature is the Severn River. At most times of the year the Severn is a series of large rocky waterholes in its upper reaches. During prolonged periods of heavy rain, however, it becomes a raging torrent. Torrential downpours upstream from the park can cause the river to rise within an hour or two.

FLORA AND FAUNA

The park has a wide range of vegetation: in the northern part of Sundown eucalypts such as yellow box and stringybark are the dominant species, while in the southern sections silver-leaved ironbark, white box and cypress are more often seen.

Grey kangaroos, red-necked wallabies and swamp wallabies are common. The beautiful brush-tailed rock wallaby has been decimated by foxes and from competition with feral goats. The numerous fallow deer are also a pest.

More than 130 species of birds have been recorded in the park including various types of finches, parrots, honeyeaters and hawks.

THINGS TO DO

There are no designated walking tracks in the park but it is enjoyable walking along the banks of the Severn River or up one of the many narrow gorges. Summers can be unbearably hot during the day so carry plenty of drinking water with you. In midwinter the early morning temperatures can drop to –6°C .

ACCESS AND CAMPING

Sundown lies 250 km southwest of Brisbane and 75 km southwest of Stanthorpe. Apart from 4 km of gravel, a good bitumen road runs all the way to the southern part of the park. The northern section near Rats Castle is accessible only to 4WD vehicles, by turning off the New England Highway at Ballandean.

The Broadwater camping area has toilets, fireplaces, firewood, drinking water and a wood-fired heater to provide hot showers. There are 2 pit toilets at Burrows Waterhole but no facilities at either Reedy or Rats Castle Waterholes.

SUNDOWN NATIONAL PARK

Jibbinbar Mountain

❶ Reedy Waterhole
❷ Burrow's Waterhole
❸ Donovan's Waterhole
❹ Rats Castle
❺ The Hell Hole
❻ Turtle Waterhole

Red Rock Waterhole

Mt Lofty

Red Rock Falls

Sundown Mine
Beacroft Mine

QLD

Mt Donaldson
Mt Donaldson 1038 m

NSW

❼ Blue Waterhole
❽ Channel Waterhole
❾ Wallaby Rocks Waterhole
❿ Red Cliff Waterhole
⓫ Permanent Waterhole

To Ballandean 10 km
Sundown

RANGE

ROBERTS

Broadwater Camping Area
Entrance
To Stanthorpe 75 km

LEGEND

N

★ 26 ★
Sealed/Unsealed Rd ....
Four Wheel Drive ....
Walks ....
Rest Area (Picnic Area) ....

Caravan Park ....
Camping Area ....
Accommodation ....
Information ....
Fuel Supplies ....

WHITSUNDAY ISLANDS NATIONAL PARK

IN BRIEF

MAP REFERENCE: PAGE 204 G 3

Location Off the
Queensland coast between
Bowen and Mackay
Best Time Winter, spring
and autumn
Main Attractions
Snorkelling, swimming,
relaxing
Ranger Phone
(07) 4946 7022

Boat hire:
Whitsunday Escape, phone
(07) 4946 5222
Whitsunday Rent-A-Yacht,
phone (07) 4946 9232

Diving operators:
Whitsunday Magic Dive
Centre, phone
(07) 4946 7074

Water taxis:
phone (07) 4946 9499

LEGEND

Sealed/Unsealed Rd	Caravan Park ....
Four Wheel Drive	Camping Area ....
Walks	Accommodation ....
Rest Area (Picnic Area)	Information....................
	Fuel Supplies ....

Azure blue seas, white sandy beaches, forest-covered slopes, abundant wildlife and isolated camping spots are just some of the more inviting aspects of a trip to the Whitsunday Islands National Park. These sparkling gems are part of the Cumberland and Northumberland Island groups which lie off the Queensland coast between Bowen and Mackay.

PRE-EUROPEAN HISTORY

The Whitsundays are known as continental islands since they once formed part of the mainland. About 6000 years ago sea levels rose, drowning valleys and forming islands out of mountain peaks on the coastal range.

Aboriginal people lived on many of the larger islands, such as Hook, Whitsunday and Lindeman, and traded with other tribes on the mainland. With an abundance of fish, crabs, dugong, wallabies, birds, yams and wild fruits, the diet of these island people was both varied and nutritious.

THE WINDS OF CHANGE

British history around the Whitsundays began on 3 June 1770 when Captain James Cook sailed through the islands on his voyage of discovery up the Queensland coast. Cook noted favourably in his charts that the islands abounded in good, safe anchorages and named them the 'Whitsundays' after the day on which they were first sighted. Over the next 100 years numerous other sailors landed on the islands to replenish their supplies. Commercial exploitation of the Whitsundays' timber, fish and wildlife began in the latter half of the 19th century.

A few settlers living in the adjacent mainland communities established small sawmills on a number of the islands to cut hoop pine, while others started hunting dugong for their oil or gathering trochus shells for the mother-of-pearl button industry.

A TROPICAL WONDERLAND

There can be few more beautiful sights in nature than to sit on a near-deserted beach in the Whitsundays and watch the setting sun disappearing over the horizon. A place where you will be lulled to sleep under a star-studded sky by the gentle sounds of the sea lapping against the sand. Often the tranquil silence will be broken momentarily by the familiar 'mopoke' calls of a nearby boobook owl, or the mournful wailing sounds of a brush stone-curlew searching for its mate.

SNORKELLING AND DIVING

The lure of swimming among the colourful coral and fish in the Great Barrier Reef Marine Park is one of the main attractions that entice thousands of people every year to the Whitsundays. Visitors can either go out with one of the many professional diving outfits based at Airlie Beach, or bring their own snorkel, mask and fins with them for snorkelling around the islands. Due to their proximity to the mainland, visibility is not as good on the fringing reefs around some of the islands as it is on the outer reefs further off the coast.

The variety of coral and beautiful fish inhabiting the reef areas is simply staggering, and it's easy for divers and snorkellers to become spellbound when they first enter this amazing underwater world. Currents around some of the islands are very strong, so make sure you don't drift too far. For safety sake, *never* go snorkelling or diving alone, always swim in pairs or with a group.

An aerial view of the beautiful Whitsunday Islands

Access

Unless you arrive in your own boat, the best way to visit the Whitsunday Islands is to book with one of the many travel agencies operating in the region. Water taxis, and various types of power and sail boats operating out of Airlie Beach, transport visitors to and from the different island camp sites.

Camping

Visitors to the Whitsundays have a wide choice of islands to camp on although many of them are isolated and difficult to reach. Covering an area of 10 930 hectares, Whitsunday Island is by far the largest, and offers the best camping facilities in the Whitsunday group. At Whitehaven Beach on the east of the island, a spectacular white, sandy beach stretches for 6 km along the coast. The largest camping ground on Whitsunday Island is located at Dugong Beach, on the western side, where up to 40 people can stay at any one time. Other islands with facilities include North Molle (Cockatoo Beach) and Thomas Island (Sea Eagle Beach).

If you prefer solitude and wilderness, you could try Crayfish Beach on Hook Island. This camping spot is for a maximum of 2 people.

Other great places for bush camping include Geographers Beach on Henning Island—great for views and forest walks, and Princess Alexandria Bay on Lindeman Island. Apart from Whitsunday Island and North Molle, drinking water must be taken with you to the islands in the Whitsunday group. Adequate food supplies for your stay, plus 2 extra days' emergency rations in case the weather delays your departure, should be taken with you. A medical kit which has vinegar to treat marine stings should be included with your camping gear.

Hardy Reef, one of the most northerly of the Whitsunday reefs

OTHER PARKS OF INTEREST

AUBURN RIVER NATIONAL PARK
389 HECTARES

The Auburn River runs through this small national park situated 42 km southwest of Mundubbera. The park protects open eucalypt forests and a few pockets of dry rainforest. The main types of vegetation along the river include the various species of leptospermums and callistemons. When the red flowers of the weeping bottlebrush are in bloom, the melodious calls from hundreds of honeyeaters can be heard near the river. These include the brown, scarlet, white-plumed, yellow-faced and blue-faced honeyeaters and the little friarbird. Silver-leaved ironbark and forest red gum clothe most of the park, with the occasional bottle tree scattered in between.

Grey kangaroos and red-necked wallabies are sometimes seen, but these animals are generally shy and won't permit close approach.

There are no formed walking tracks in the park, and hikers should take note of various landmarks to ensure they can find their way back to camp.

Basic facilities for campers, including toilets, picnic tables and BBQs, are available in the park. Drinking water is not available and should be brought in with you.

The best time to visit the park is during the spring and autumn.

For further information contact the ranger, ph: (07) 4122 2455.

BLACKDOWN TABLELAND NATIONAL PARK
23 800 HECTARES

This wilderness park in central Queensland, 160 km west of Rockhampton, straddles a rugged sandstone plateau that has an average elevation of about 800 metres. With a much higher rainfall and cooler climate than the surrounding district, the park has a number of species of fauna that are unique to the plateau. These include a trapdoor spider, a lizard and a Christmas beetle.

Until 1971, when the forestry department built a road up to the plateau to allow timber extraction, very few visitors apart from the occasional stockman had been there. Most of the plateau is covered in thick stands of tall sclerophyll forest, while lilly pillies, tree ferns and cabbage-tree palms line the tributaries of Mimosa Creek.

Due to bone deficiency in the soil, macropods such as wallabies and kangaroos are virtually absent from the park. There are, however, large numbers of sugar gliders and greater gliders as well as other tree dwelling mammals.

Birds are abundant, and king parrots, currawongs, kookaburras and wrens are often seen.

There are a number of good walking tracks, and swimming holes to cool off in at Blackdown, but hikers should keep away from cliff edges as they are often crumbly. Camping is permitted at South

Mimosa Creek, but visitors should be self-sufficient. Conventional vehicles can reach the park.

The park is enjoyable throughout the year, but the winters can be cool.

For further information, contact the ranger, ph: (07) 4927 6511.

BLUE LAKE NATIONAL PARK (STRADBROKE ISLAND)
500 HECTARES

Blue Lake National Park occupies only a small part of the 33 km long Stradbroke Island, a tranquil backwater only one hour by vehicular ferry from Brisbane.

The park is situated just off the Trans Island Road, about 10 km east of the small settlement of Dunwich, where members of the Noonuccal tribe of Aborigines, who first inhabited the island, can still be found.

Twelve barges a day service the island, leaving from the bayside suburb of Cleveland, in Brisbane, and landing an hour later at Dunwich. For bookings, ring (07) 3286 2666. Good bitumen roads connect Dunwich with the other 2 small settlements of Amity and Point Lookout.

Visitors to the park with conventional vehicles can stop at the car park just off the bitumen road and walk along the 2 km winding sand track to the lake. It takes about 30 minutes one way. People with 4WD vehicles can get to the lake along the sandy track. A 4WD is needed for beach driving.

Blue Lake National Park is a haven for many unique species of vegetation as well as a great place to search for some of the island's wildlife. In the early mornings you may sight grey kangaroos, agile wallabies and swamp wallabies grazing near the lake. Echidnas and koalas can occasionally be seen. Birds are prolific, especially when the banksias are flowering in spring.

Camping is not allowed inside Blue Lake National Park but there are plenty of other places on the island. There are 8 caravan parks on Stradbroke, all with good facilities, and beach camping is permitted along certain parts of the coastline; the ranger comes to collect the fees.

Fishing is one of the main attractions for visitors to Stradbroke with year-round catches of bream, whiting, flathead and trevally. For more than half a century this relaxing pastime has enticed visitors, many of whom built fibro shacks and settled permanently around Amity and Point Lookout.

For further information, contact the ranger, ph: (07) 3227 7111.

BOWLING GREEN BAY NATIONAL PARK
55 300 HECTARES

This important park 28 km south of Townsville preserves the rugged Mt Elliot wilderness plus coastal mangrove-lined estuaries between Cape Cleveland and Cape Bowling Green. The huge granite mass of Mt Elliot, which rises to a height of 1342 metres, is the dominant feature of the park. Vegetation around the Mt Elliot section is mainly dry eucalypt forest consisting of popular gum, ironbark, Moreton Bay ash and bloodwood.

A number of creeks run down the eastern side of Mt Elliot, one of the most important being Alligator Creek which flows past the well laid-out camping area near the park's entrance. This beautiful creek is great for swimming in and for observing many of the park's birds which come down to the water to drink, or to feast on the nectar of the weeping bottlebrush which grows on the sandy banks.

Mammals are abundant in the park with the agile wallaby and grey kangaroo often seen throughout the day. After dark, brush-tail possums, rufous rat-kangaroos, short-nosed bandicoots and white-tailed rats are often encountered by visitors on a spotlight walk.

Winter and spring are the best times during which to visit the park.

For further information, contact the ranger, ph: (07) 4778 8203.

BRIBIE ISLAND NATIONAL PARK
4770 HECTARES

This beautiful seaside national park fronts on to Pumicestone Passage and covers nearly a third of Bribie Island. It is situated 65 km north of Brisbane.

Fishing and boating in the calm waters of the

Bribie Island National Park

passage are the main attractions that entice visitors to the park. Bait, such as yabbies and worms, can be pumped up at low tide or bought from one of the bait and tackle shops on the southern part of the island.

Vegetation in the park is a mixture of eucalypt forests, banksias, heathlands and mangrove-lined estuaries. Bird life is prolific and includes many types of honeyeaters, lorikeets, birds of prey and waterbirds. The tidal mudflats are an important feeding ground for migratory waders which spend up to 6 months of the year at Bribie. Between late July and early September, the park bursts into life with numerous varieties of wildflowers carpeting the heath country. These flowers in turn attract a multitude of insects which become a constant food supply for wrens, flycatchers and other insectivores.

Unless you wish to walk, a 4WD vehicle is necessary for travelling within the park.

Camping is permitted at a number of places on the beach, but facilities are spartan to non-existent.

The park is a pleasant place to visit at any time of the year.

For further information, contact the ranger, ph: (07) 3408 8451.

CAPE YORK PARKS
Cape Melville National Park
36 000 HECTARES

This park is in two sections, the main section being centred around Cape Melville which is 2180 km north of Brisbane. It is the easternmost cape of Bathurst Bay, on the east coast, north of Cooktown.

Much of the Melville Range is protected in this remote park and the range itself is made up of a mass of large, black, lichen-covered granite boulders piled on top of one another. Vine scrub and even a small patch of rainforest grow in this harsh habitat but the area is best known for the endemic fox-tailed palms that are found around the base of the range.

Access is via a tortuous 4WD track from Cooktown that is only passable in the dry season, and even then takes a full day for the 180 km trip.

Camping is possible just outside the park's western boundary on the beach. It can be a very pleasant spot to stay for a while and the fishing is great, but the sandflies can be atrocious. Water is available from a delightful stream which babbles out from between giant boulders about 3 km from the beachside camping area. No facilities are provided and you must be self-sufficient.

May to October is the best time to visit the park. For further information, contact the ranger at Cooktown, ph: (07) 4069 5777.

Iron Range National Park
36 600 HECTARES

The area protected by the Iron Range National Park, situated north of Cooktown, contains the largest area of lowland rainforest in Australia and for much of its expanse is still in a pristine state. The park takes in a convoluted and segmented area of land, interspersed with conservation areas and Aboriginal land. The area of protected land is far greater than the park itself, with much of it almost completely inaccessible.

The area is of worldwide significance because of its rich and varied

Iron Range National Park

wildlife. Many birds and even a few species of mammal, the most noteworthy of which are the spotted cuscus, the grey cuscus and the spiny-haired bandicoot, which are found nowhere else, call these dense, tall forests home. More than 10 per cent of Australia's butterflies are found here, with 25 species unique to the area. As well, over 320 species of plants have been found in this region, of which 10 per cent are new or undescribed.

Access is limited to the road which heads east from the main Weipa road to the small hamlet of Portland Roads and the Aboriginal community of Lockhart River.

Access is by 4WD only.

A number of tour operators, especially those that specialise in birdwatching, organise trips into the area. You can fly into Lockhart River and be picked up or travel by 4WD to the park.

Two camping areas are located within the rainforest, close to the main access track. Pit toilets and fireplaces are provided and water comes from the creek. Another camping area, probably the park's most popular, is located on the coast at Chili Beach, just south of the village of Portland Roads.

A permit is required and a fee is payable to camp in the park.

The best time to visit the park is April to November.

For further information, contact the ranger, ph: (07) 4060 7170.

For information on organised trips contact the Far North Queensland Promotional Bureau, ph: (07) 4051 3588.

Jardine River National Park

The Jardine River National Park is located 2640 km north of Brisbane. The 2 reserves that lie on the park's northern and southern boundaries protect the complete catchment area of

the Jardine River, the biggest perennial river in Queensland. The old Overland Telegraph Line Track is the park's western boundary and much of the eastern coast is part of the Great Barrier Reef Marine Park.

The centrepiece of the park is the river itself. Near the track which gives access to the western side of the park there is some fantastic camping on the southern or northern banks of the river.

The Eliot River is one of the Jardine's major tributaries and along its course there are some very pleasant waterfalls, the main one being Indian Head Falls. Nearby is probably the most popular camping area on Cape York Peninsula, but the river, with Canal Creek and Twin Falls close by, is a mecca for travellers.

An access track through this southern reserve area leads to the coast at Captain Billy Landing where you can also camp.

The best time to visit the park is May to October.

For further information, contact the ranger at Heathlands, ph: (07) 4060 3241.

Lizard Island National Park
1012 HECTARES

Lizard Island, located 1820 km north of Brisbane, is probably better known for its premier tourist resort, its game fishing, the marine research centre and its proximity to one of the Great Barrier Reef's best dive sites, the Cod Hole, than it is as a national park. But the park takes up most of the island and the Great Barrier Reef Marine Park surrounds it.

Captain Cook landed here in 1770 when he was trying to find an escape route through the reef and the view today from the lofty peak of the island is as grand and as perfect as it was when Cook climbed it to look for a safe passage through the reef.

While you can stay in the unbridled luxury of the Lizard Island Lodge, expect to pay top dollar for the privilege.

You can also camp in the very small camping area located just back from the beach on Watsons Bay. It is an idyllic camp made even better by the crystal-clear safe waters nearby. Drinking water from a hand pump and a picnic table are located here.

You must be self-sufficient and the only fuel allowed is charcoal beads. The walk from the airstrip is about 1 km so if you are loaded down with unnecessary gear it is a long one.

The best time to visit the park is March to November.

For further information, contact the Department of Environment, Cairns, ph: (07) 4052 3096. To book at Lizard Island Lodge, ph: (07) 4060 3999.

Mungkan Kaanju National Park
457 000 HECTARES

This park is located 2270 km north of Brisbane. It covers 2 sections of land separated by a narrow strip between its northern boundary of the Archer River and the southern boundary of the Coen River.

Much of the region is in a pristine state and consists of vast areas that each year are flooded by the wet season rains. Riverine rainforest stretches along most of the river banks while the swamps and streams are alive with birds and are home to numerous crocodiles.

Access to the western section (Archer Bend) is not allowed, while the eastern section (Rokeby) has a ranger station and a couple of camping areas located on either the Archer or Coen Rivers. Access is permitted only during the Dry and then only by 4WD.

The best time to visit the park is April to October.

For further information, contact the ranger at Rokeby, ph: (07) 4060 3256.

CANIA GORGE NATIONAL PARK
3000 HECTARES

The park is located 12 km north of Monto. A narrow gorge with spectacular sandstone cliffs up to 70 metres in height is the main feature of this beautiful park. Vegetation on the escarpment at the top of the gorge is predominantly dry eucalypt forest, while the sheltered side gullies leading down into the bottom of the gorge consist mainly of dry rainforest, piccabeen palms and tree ferns.

Many varieties of birds are found throughout the park including kookaburras, pied butcherbirds, magpies and honeyeaters in the drier sections and eastern yellow robins, crimson rosellas and superb blue wrens in the more shaded parts of the gorge. Mammals include brush-tail possums, rock wallabies and bandicoots.

There are a number of easy trails through the gorge, one of the most interesting being the 3.2 km return walk to The Overhang and will take about 1¼ hours. This track starts near the picnic area, passes over Three Moon Creek then winds its way through eucalypt forest until it forks at Bloodwood and Dragon Caves. The vivid colours on the sandstone walls of these caves are spellbinding with hues of orange, red and yellow. Camping is not permitted inside the park, but there is a private caravan park nearby. For bookings, phone (07) 4167 8188.

For further information, contact the ranger, ph: (07) 4167 8162.

CAPE HILLSBOROUGH NATIONAL PARK
830 HECTARES

This small coastal national park, about 40 km northeast of Mackay, helps to preserve remnants of flora that were once common in the surrounding areas that have been cleared for farming. Dense pockets of lowland rainforest, vine forest, eucalypt forest and small patches of heath make this biologically diverse park a haven for wildlife. Steep rainforest-covered hills plunge almost vertically to a number of rocky headlands that are connected to each other by wide sandy beaches.

There are a number of interesting walking trails including the 6 km return track to Smalleys Beach. Allow between 3 and 4 hours for this. The Hidden Valley circuit, a 1.4 km self-guided walk through the lowland rainforest, is a good way to begin exploring the park and will take about 1 hour return. Bird life on this track is abundant, and it's easy to count up to 30 different species in a one-hour walk. Robins, flycatchers, fruit pigeons and scrub turkeys are common in the rainforest while various types of seabirds, waders and birds of prey are often seen on the beaches.

Swimming is excellent during winter but should be avoided between October and May because of the deadly marine stingers that may be present. Camping is permitted.

For further information, contact the ranger, ph: (07) 4959 0410.

CHILLAGOE-MUNGANA CAVES NATIONAL PARK
1873 HECTARES

The park is situated 210 km west of Cairns. The Chillagoe–Mungana cave system is a colossal outcrop of limestone covering an area approximately 60 km long and 6 km wide. These awesome towers of limestone encompass some of Australia's most unusual cave systems, in that they are predominantly on the surface. Thousands of years of deep weathering and erosion have sculpted caverns, chambers and passageways beneath these mountains of stone.

The largest part of this unique national park is Royal Arch Cave, which covers an area of 1514 hectares. More than 1.5 km of passages wind through its labyrinth of tunnels and lofty caverns. White limestone curtains drape the

Donna Caves, Chillagoe–Mungana Caves National Park

walls, while stalactites resembling giant chandeliers hang from the ceiling. Both Donna and Trezkinn caves are electrically lit, the former considered the prettiest of them all.

Rock wallabies, wallaroos and other wildlife abound in the vicinity of the caves. Birds are abundant, too, with over 70 species found within the boundary of the park.

Camping is permitted near Royal Arch Cave.

The best time to visit the caves is winter and spring.

For further information, contact the ranger, ph: (07) 4094 7163.

CONWAY NATIONAL PARK
23 800 HECTARES

Lowland tropical rainforest covers much of this coastal peninsula national park which is situated 36 km east of Proserpine. The Conway Range, which forms the backbone of the park, rises to more than 550 metres in places before it drops steeply to the shores of the Whitsunday Passage.

The park is largely undeveloped and protects a wide range of flora and fauna. Apart from lush rainforest, hoop pines can be found growing on the exposed ridges while mangroves and pandanus palms are the dominant types of vegetation found around much of the coast. Conway is a refuge for the rare Proserpine rock wallaby which has the most restricted range of any Australian rock wallaby. Other animals found in the park include the echidna, both the short- and long-nosed bandicoots, native rats, brush-tail possums and ringtail possums. Birds of prey like the osprey, white-bellied sea-eagle, whistling kite and brahminy kite can be seen in reasonable numbers around the mangroves and beaches in the park.

There are a couple of excellent walking tracks at Conway including the 6.4 km Mt Rooper circuit which passes through a large cross-section of the park's diverse environments. This will take about 3 hours for the complete circuit.

Winter and spring are the best times to visit the park.

For further information and details on camping, contact the ranger, ph: (07) 4946 7022.

CRATER LAKES NATIONAL PARK
980 HECTARES

Two separate parks, Lake Barrine (490 hectares) and Lake Eacham (490 hectares) are now combined in the Crater Lakes National Park which lies 70 km southwest of Cairns. Both lakes, which are only a few kilometres from each other, are the result of explosions which occurred millions of years ago due to volcanic heating of water trapped under the ground.

A 5.14 km circuit track follows the edge of Lake Barrine passing through lush rainforest. Many species of butterflies including the magnificent blue Ulysses can be seen along this trail, as well as the colourful Boyd's forest dragon. The clear blue waters of Lake Barrine are also home to the saw-shelled tortoise, while water dragons and the large amethystine python are sometimes found around the edge of the lake.

A 2.8 km track runs beside Lake Eacham giving visitors an opportunity to see some of the rare wildlife such as the musky rat-kangaroo and the 100-odd species of birds which live in the surrounding rainforest. The lake is also a great place for swimming. There are well laid-out picnic areas around both lakes but camping is prohibited.

Autumn, winter and spring are the best times to visit the park.

For further information contact the ranger, ph: (07) 4095 3768.

DEEPWATER NATIONAL PARK
4090 HECTARES

Deepwater, 130 km southeast of Gladstone, is a haven for both anglers and nature lovers. The park encompasses a wide variety of terrain including paperbark swamps and open forests of wattle, banksia and cabbage palms. But it is Deepwater's 10 km of near perfect beaches that most people come to enjoy. Fishing is generally good most of the year, especially from Wreck Rock and Middle Rock on the outgoing tide. Bait such as pipis and sea worms can be gathered along the beach.

Sea turtles visit Deepwater each year from late November until mid-February to lay their eggs. Loggerhead turtles are the main species that nest there, followed by the green and flatback turtles. Bird life in the park is diverse and includes many varieties of honeyeaters, figbirds, scrub turkeys, wrens, tawny frogmouths, brahminy kites and sea-eagles.

A 4WD vehicle is essential for travelling through the park. There is a well laid-out camping ground at Wreck Rock and sites should be booked in advance during peak periods.

Dunk Island National Park

Autumn, winter and spring are the best times to visit the park.

For further information, contact the ranger, ph: (07) 4976 0766.

DIPPERU NATIONAL PARK
11 000 HECTARES

This park, 120 km southwest of Mackay, protects tracts of brigalow/belah scrub which has become scarce in the surrounding grazing lands due to clearing. Other types of vegetation found at Dipperu include dry eucalypt forest and small clumps of vine thicket. Bird life at Dipperu is prolific, which is the reason nature lovers visit the park. Permanent waterholes scattered throughout Dipperu provide homes for thousands of waterbirds. Jabirus, white-faced herons, jacanas, ducks, spoonbills, plovers, greater egrets and brolgas are just some of the many types of waders which make this park an ornithologists' delight. The permanent lagoons also attract finches, doves pigeons, parrots and birds of prey. Mammals include black-striped wallabies, grey kangaroos, rufous rat-kangaroos and the occasional northern quoll.

During the wet season, which can last from December to March, the waterholes can spill across the country making travel in and out of the park difficult even in a 4WD vehicle.

Camping is permitted, but visitors must be self-reliant as there are no facilities in the park.

Winter and spring are the best times to visit the park.

For further information, contact the ranger, ph: (07) 4951 8788.

DUNK ISLAND NATIONAL PARK
730 HECTARES

Thick rainforest grows almost to the water's edge on Dunk Island, making it one of Australia's most beautiful island national parks. The island, which lies 4 km off the coast of South Mission Beach near the town of Tully, was joined

OTHER PARKS OF INTEREST

to the mainland before rising sea waters separated it thousands of years ago. A steep ridge which forms the backbone of the island rises to a height of 271 metres at Mt Kootaloo. Dunk receives some of the heaviest rainfall in Australia, which makes the island's lush vegetation amongst the most diverse in the wet tropics.

Rainforest birds are in abundance, although many of them are easier to hear than to see in the thick forest. Insect life is also prolific in this pulsating world of greenery, with multi-hued beetles and dragonflies clinging to leaves and branches while butterflies like the brilliant blue Ulysses flitter through the canopy.

There are a number of excellent beaches around the island, although the presence of marine stingers in the summer months can make swimming dangerous. Camping is permitted on the island.

Winter and spring are the best times to visit the park.

For further information, contact the ranger, ph: (07) 4066 8601.

EURIMBULA NATIONAL PARK
7830 HECTARES

This beautiful park southeast of Gladstone, about 20 km from Agnes Waters, protects a complex display of coastal vegetation including mangroves, paperbark swamps, eucalypt forest and rainforest. The first European visitor to the park was Captain Cook in 1770, when his ship, *Endeavour*, dropped anchor in what is now known as Bustard Bay.

Bush birds in the park include scrub turkeys, numerous species of honeyeaters, wrens, tawny frogmouths, nightjars, figbirds, kingfishers and brahminy kites. With various types of seabirds inhabiting the beach, and waders in Eurimbula

Creek, the park is an ideal destination for birdwatchers.

At most times of the year conventional vehicles can reach the park, but after periods of heavy rain a 4WD vehicle may be necessary. Campers should be totally self-sufficient, and camp well back from the frontal dunes to lessen the chance of erosion.

There are a number of short walks, including a 360 metre trail which provides panoramic views over much of the park. Swimming is excellent from May until October, but dangerous box jellyfish may be present during the summer months.

Winter and spring are the best times to visit the park.

For further information contact the ranger, ph: (07) 4976 0766.

EXPEDITION NATIONAL PARK
104 000 HECTARES

With towering sandstone walls up to 100 metres high, Robinson Gorge is the most breathtaking and accessible part of Expedition National Park, which lies 120 km north of Taroom. This rugged wilderness straddles Expedition Range in central Queensland, and is an important refuge for some of the region's fauna and flora that has been greatly affected by land clearing outside the park boundary.

Vegetation in the park consists of bottle-brush, cabbage-tree palms and forest red gums along the creeks, with dry eucalypt forest on the escarpment above. The gorge, which is 12 km long, is a great place to look for birds. King parrots, figbirds, friarbirds rainbow lorikeets and brown honeyeaters are just a few of the more common species seen regularly. Whiptail wallabies, echidnas and the occasional brush-tailed rock wallaby also live in the gorge.

Keen-eyed bushwalkers may even come across Aboriginal paintings under some of the sandstone overhangs in the gorge. Never touch any of these priceless works of art as they are easily damaged.

Camping is permitted at Starkvale Creek. All supplies, including sufficient drinking water, should be brought in with you. Access is by 4WD vehicles only.

Winter and spring are the best times to visit the park. For further information contact the ranger, ph: (07) 4627 3358.

GLASSHOUSE MOUNTAINS NATIONAL PARKS
698 HECTARES

The Glasshouse Mountains National Parks, situated 75 km north of Brisbane, off the Bruce Highway, consist of 4 small mountainous national parks: Coonowrin (113 hectares), Beerwah (245 hectares), Tibrogargan (291 hectares) and Ngungun (49 hectares). These mountain peaks, which were given the name Glasshouse Mountains by Captain James Cook in 1770, are the eroded remains of a giant volcano which erupted in the area 20 million years ago.

The flora is mainly a mixture of predominantly dry eucalypt forests, narrow gullies of piccabeen palms and rainforest and heath vegetation on the summits. Since much of the surrounding area has been cleared for farming, these small parks have become a refuge for koalas, brush-tail possums, echidnas and rare birds like the peregrine falcon.

Bushwalking is the main attraction for visitors, with rough trails leading up to the top of most peaks. Mt Ngungun is the easiest to climb (about 2 hours return), while Mt Tibrogargan (about 3 hours return) should be attempted only by the reasonably fit.

There are no camping facilities in the parks.

Autumn, winter and spring are the best times to visit the parks.

For further information, contact the ranger, ph: (07) 4194 6630.

HERON ISLAND NATIONAL PARK
16.8 HECTARES

Situated in the Capricorn–Bunker group of islands on the southern edge of the Great Barrier Reef, Heron is an isolated coral cay 70 km northeast of Gladstone. The Queensland National Parks Department controls two-thirds of the island as part of the Capricorn Cays National Park, while the remainder is shared by a tourist resort and marine research station.

Together with other similar islands in the area, Heron is an important breeding ground for thousands of migratory seabirds. Between

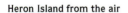
Heron Island from the air

A flock of black-naped terns at Heron Island National Park

November and March, the branches of pisonia trees, pandanus trees and casuarinas, which constitute the bulk of flora on the island, strain under the weight of nesting seabirds.

White-capped noddy terns are the dominant species, but there are also thousands of black-naped terns, roseate terns, bridled terns and silver gulls. Thousands of noisy wedge-tailed shearwaters also breed there, constructing their nests by burrowing into the ground.

Turtles visit Heron to lay their eggs from November to March, with many of these large marine mammals being tagged by scientists living at the research station. The clear waters around the island make conditions excellent for diving and snorkelling as the reef abounds in countless varieties of colourful fish.

Camping is not permitted on Heron, although visitors can stay at the island's resort.

The park is a great place to visit throughout the year. For further information, contact the ranger, ph: (07) 4927 6511, or the resort, ph: (07) 4978 1388.

IDALIA NATIONAL PARK
144 000 HECTARES

Set in the Gowan Ranges 100 km west of Blackall in central Queensland, Idalia National Park is a rugged wilderness park that is visited by very few people.

The endangered yellow-footed rock wallaby finds a safe refuge in the park. Many of these beautiful marsupials have been radio-collared for scientific research as their population has been devastated by feral animals such as foxes and goats.

Idalia takes in the headwaters of the Bulloo River, along with many of the creeks which eventually drain into the Barcoo River.

There is a wide range of vegetation in the park including river red gums along the creeks, silver-leaved ironbark, poplar box, Dawson gums, mulga scrub and lancewood.

Western grey kangaroos, red kangaroos, wallaroos and black-striped wallabies are also found in good numbers.

Idalia is a great place for birdwatchers, with white cockatoos, mallee ringnecks, mulga parrots, wedge-tailed eagles and finches in reasonable numbers.

Visitors intending to camp in the park should have a reliable 4WD vehicle and be totally self-sufficient. All drinking water must be brought in with you.

Winter and spring are the best times to visit the park.

For further information, contact the ranger, ph: (07) 4657 5033.

ISLA GORGE NATIONAL PARK
7800 HECTARES

This rugged national park at the eastern end of the central highlands in the Dawson Range, 55 km north of Taroom, gets very few visitors. However, it is a great spot for self-reliant campers who prefer peace and quiet.

Aborigines from the Jiman tribe used to live near the park's western boundary, and some excellent examples of their rock art can still be found on the undersides of sandstone over-hangs. Much of the sandstone in the gorge has been eroded by time, giving rise to bizarre formations that often look as if they have been sculpted by hand.

Flora consists mainly of various types of eucalypts, brigalow, grevillea, golden banksia and bottle trees. Bird life is quite varied, with wedge-tailed eagles, peregrine falcons and little eagles often seen soaring in the thermals. When the banksias and grevilleas are flowering down in the gorge, numerous species of honeyeaters—including the brown, spiny-cheeked and blue-faced—can be seen darting in and out of the trees.

Descending into the gorge can be quite dangerous due to loose rubble and should be undertaken only by experienced bushwalkers. Bush camping is permitted.

Winter and spring are the best times to visit the park.

For further information, contact the ranger, ph: (07) 4627 3358.

KA KA MUNDI NATIONAL PARK
38 500 HECTARES

This remote national park (about 120 km southwest of Springsure), and now part of Carnarvon National Park, protects a diverse array of plant communities including briga-low, bonewood and softwood scrubs. Popular box, silver-leaved ironbark, thickets of acacia trees and bottle trees provide a home and food source for many species of fauna.

The park gets its name from Mt Ka Ka Mundi, a 400 metre high peak which rises above the rugged sandstone escarpment. Aboriginal people once lived in the area and many of their paintings can still be found in well sheltered rock overhangs throughout the park.

Being a wilderness area, with no facilities, campers should come well prepared for any emergencies. A 4WD vehicle is essential to reach the park. During the wet season, from December to March, the surrounding black soil plains may become impassable, blocking access to the park for weeks on end. There is a pleasant area for bush camping at Bunduncudoo Springs.

Wildlife which may be sighted in the park includes king parrots, birds of prey, fig-parrots, grey kangaroos and red-necked wallabies. Snakes and lizards are common.

Spring and autumn are the best times to visit the park.

For further information, contact the ranger ph: (07) 4984 1173.

KINKUNA NATIONAL PARK
13 300 HECTARES

Kinkuna, 22 km southeast of Bundaberg, is a magnificent coastal wilderness which protects a large number of vanishing plant and animal communities. The park is totally undeveloped, having none of the normal facilities such as drinking water, fireplaces, tables and toilets.

The beautiful 8 km sea beach which sweeps along the park's eastern boundary is surely one of the most picturesque in southern Queensland. Since vehicles can't go any further south than the mouth of Theodolite Creek on Kinkuna's southern boundary, the sand is a delight to walk on. When the tide recedes, a series of shallow pools often forms along sections of the beach. These pools are a great place to observe the small marine creatures that are temporarily trapped until the tide comes in.

A loggerhead turtle in Mon Repos Environmental Park

Birds of prey such as white-breasted sea-eagles and the osprey are often seen along the beach.

A 4WD vehicle is necessary for visiting Kinkuna National Park.

Autumn, winter and spring are the best times to visit the park.

For further information, contact the ranger, ph: (07) 4126 8939.

LUMHOLTZ NATIONAL PARK
124 000 HECTARES

This large national park west of Ingham preserves a wide range of vegetation, from open eucalypt forests through to dense rainforest. Most people visit the more accessible Wallaman Falls section in the southern part of the park. Here, one can be awed by nature's handiwork and marvel at the spellbinding sight of Wallaman Falls tumbling out of the mist-enshrouded rainforest before plunging 305 metres into a large fern-lined pool below. With rainfall in excess of 2000 mm a year, much of the park seems to be continually damp during the wet season, which lasts from November to March.

Bird life is prolific in both the rainforest and adjacent eucalypt forest in the western part of the park. Pied currawongs, golden whistlers, pale-headed rosellas, flycatchers and tawny frogmouths are common in the drier country, while the northern logrunner, whipbird, golden bowerbird, Lewin's honeyeater and Victoria's riflebird can be seen in the rainforest. Mammals in the park include pademelons, green ringtail possums, long-nosed bandicoots and the fawn-footed melomys.

Camping in the park is permitted. March to October is the best time to visit the park.

For further information, contact the ranger, ph: (07) 4776 1700.

MON REPOS ENVIRONMENTAL PARK

At Mon Repos, a small stretch of beach 15 km east of Bundaberg in southern Queensland, visitors are privileged to witness an age-old ritual which has few rivals in the animal world.

Between late November and the end of January, huge loggerhead turtles emerge from the sea at night and drag themselves up on the sand. After slowly scraping away any loose sand with her flippers, the female then digs a vertical, pear-shaped egg chamber. When this part of the operation is complete, up to 150 eggs, the size of a ping-pong ball, are deposited over a 15 minute period. With her strength nearly depleted, the turtle covers the egg chamber and returns to the sea. The 1 km long beach where the turtles nest is strictly patrolled by National Parks' rangers and other volunteers who take visitors on guided walks to watch the egg-laying spectacle.

Visitors can stay at the adjacent Turtle Sands caravan park, which has both powered and unpowered sites and cabins for rent.

Late November until the end of January is the best time to visit the park. For further information, contact the ranger, ph: (07) 4159 1652, or Turtle Sands caravan park, ph: (07) 4159 2340.

MOOGERAH PEAKS NATIONAL PARK
676 HECTARES

This small national park, 16 km southwest of Boonah, consists of a number of mountain peaks that are isolated from each other by cleared farming land. They include Mt French (579 metres), Mt Edwards (632 metres), Mt Moon (784 metres) and Mt Grenville (770 metres). These peaks are volcanic in origin, being all that remains of a volcano which erupted over 20 million years ago.

The vegetation clothing these mountains is mainly dry eucalypt forest, including spotted gums, grey gums and stringybark. Lizards are often seen in this area, in particular the common blue-tongue lizard and bearded dragon. The quick moving eastern brown snake is also at home on these peaks, and bushwalkers should be aware of this deadly reptile's presence, particularly in summer.

There is a rough bush track up to the summit of Mt Edwards (3 hours return), and to the top of Mt Grenville (4 hours return). The sheer cliff faces on Mt French make this an ideal destination for rock climbers from all over southeast Queensland.

There are toilets and picnic facilities at Mt French, but camping is not allowed. Autumn, winter and spring are the best times to visit the park. For further information, contact the ranger, ph: (07) 5563 1579.

Noosa National Park

MT BARNEY NATIONAL PARK
11 500 HECTARES

This rugged wilderness park, 130 km southwest of Brisbane, provides hikers with some of the best bushwalking in southeast Queensland. Mt Barney is a large dome-shaped granite mountain with very little vegetation on the summit. Visitors intending to hike in this area should take plenty of water to drink and carry a small medical kit for any emergencies.

Most of the park is open eucalypt country consisting of native apples, grey gums and spotted gums. River she-oaks, weeping bottlebrush, silky oak and sandpaper figs line many of the creeks that flow down from the higher parts of the park. Here you will find the brilliant azure kingfisher, red-browed finches, figbirds, pale-headed rosellas and many types of honeyeaters. Swamp wallabies are often encountered in the thick undergrowth in the vicinity of these creeks, while red-necked wallabies and grey kangaroos can be seen on the more exposed slopes.

Bush camping is permitted inside the park although it is essential to book a permit in advance from the ranger. Visitors can also stay at the adjacent Yellowpinch camping reserve which is operated by the Beaudesert Shire Council, phone (07) 5540 5111.

Winter and spring are the best times to visit the park.

For further information, contact the ranger, ph: (07) 5463 5041.

MT HYPIPAMEE NATIONAL PARK
360 HECTARES

Even though it is only a small park, Mt Hypipamee, about 100 km southwest of Cairns, houses some of the most diverse fauna found anywhere in Australia. Take a walk with a powerful torch at night and you can find up to 7 species of possum feeding in the dense foliage. The green ringtail and coppery brush-tail are most commonly seen, but with patience and luck you may even spot the Herbert River ringtail, lemuroid ringtail or the strikingly marked striped possum.

The main feature of the park is an ancient 'volcanic pipe' or crater 70 metres across, whose vertical granite walls drop 58 metres from the rainforest-covered rim down to a greenish coloured lake 82 metres deep.

Another spectacular sight in this beautiful high altitude park is Dinner Falls, which plunges out of the often mist-enshrouded rainforest onto a boulder-strewn creek below.

Birds such as the spotted bowerbird, Victoria's riflebird and various species of colourful fruit pigeons are just a few of the more than 200 species recorded at Hypipamee.

The park is also one of the few places where you can find the rarely seen Lumholtz tree-kangaroo. There are no camping sites in the area.

Winter and spring are the best times to visit the park.

For further information, contact the ranger, ph: (07) 4095 3768.

MT SPEC NATIONAL PARK
7224 HECTARES

Mt Spec, 61 km north of Townsville, is part of the Paluma Range National Park which includes the nearby Jourama Falls section a short distance to the north. Rising to a height of 1000 metres above sea level, the top of Mt Spec is often covered in dense clouds.

Vegetation in the park changes dramatically from eucalypt forests of ironbarks, bloodwoods and popular gums on the lower slopes through to hoop pines and thick rainforest scrub at higher altitudes. With an annual rainfall of over 2800 mm on the summit, many species of colourful fungi can be found clinging to fallen branches rotting on the forest floor.

Birds are prolific in the thick rainforest, including the brilliant Victoria's riflebird and noisy pitta. Many birdwatchers come to the park to try and spot the golden bowerbird which builds the largest bower of all the bowerbird species.

Visitors can stay in the beautiful camping ground at Paradise Waterhole beside Big Crystal Creek, a great place to cool off in the hot summer months. Campers should book well in advance; contact the ranger.

Autumn, winter and spring are the best times to visit the park.

For further information, contact the ranger, ph: (07) 4770 8526.

NOOSA NATIONAL PARK
477 HECTARES

Surrounded by the Pacific Ocean on one side and intense seaside development on the other, Noosa National Park, set beside the holiday town of Noosa, is a pocket of tranquillity in one of Australia's fastest growing holiday areas. Its

Springbrook National Park (see page 200)

OTHER PARKS OF INTEREST

Curtis Falls in Joalah, Tamborine Mountains National Parks

very existence is owed to the foresight of Noosa's settlers who declared the area a town reserve back in 1879.

Vegetation in the park is a mixture of rainforest, open eucalypt forest, wallum heathlands, pandanus palms and grasslands. Wildflowers bloom in the wallum areas in spring. Fruit pigeons, eastern yellow robins, rufous fantails, satin bowerbirds and crimson rosellas are found in the rainforest, while various species of honeyeaters and wrens inhabit the wallum heathlands.

Mammals in the park include the short-nosed bandicoot, common ringtail possum, brush-tail possum and native rats.

There are a number of walking tracks including one which winds its way up to 147 metre high Noosa Hill. The beaches around the park are excellent for swimming.

Camping is not permitted inside the park.

The park is a great place to visit throughout the year.

For further information, contact the ranger, ph: (07) 4147 3243.

SPRINGBROOK NATIONAL PARK
2954 HECTARES

Gentle mountain streams, gnarled Antarctic beech trees, dense rainforest and plunging waterfalls combine to make Springbrook one of the most enticing national parks in southeast Queensland. Set on a 900 metre high plateau in the Gold Coast hinterland, 29 km west of Mudgeeraba, the park is a haven for many species of wildlife which have become endangered in the surrounding areas due to land clearing.

Springbrook has the second highest rainfall in Queensland, averaging up to 3000 mm a year. There are a number of waterfalls in the park, with the most spectacular being the magnificent Purling Brook Falls. Plunging more than 100 metres straight down into a lush rainforest-lined gorge, these falls are best viewed after a few days of heavy rain. A 4 km return walk, which will take about 1½ hours, starts at the top of the plateau and weaves its way to the bottom of the falls.

Birds such as the eastern yellow robin, rufous fantail, satin bowerbird and whipbird are commonly seen along this track. The harmless carpet python and sluggish land mullet (the largest member of the skink family) can also be seen here.

There is a small camping area adjacent to the Gwongorella picnic area.

The park is a pleasant place to visit throughout the year.

For further information, contact the ranger, ph: (07) 5533 5147.

ST HELENA ISLAND NATIONAL PARK
75 HECTARES

Alluring when seen from afar, the thickly vegetated cliffs of St Helena belie the island's dark and troubled history. Certainly, St Helena, 8 km from the mouth of the Brisbane River, was never an island paradise for the hundreds of convicts who spent their last days there toiling under subhuman conditions imposed on them by the prison officials of the day. The first convicts transported to St Helena arrived on the brig *Prosperine* in 1886. Under the watchful eyes of their guards, the prisoners were forced to construct their own jail. The waters of Moreton Bay were renowned for sharks, and prisoners knew that once on the island there was little chance of escape.

When the prison doors finally closed in 1932, nature quickly took over the island, concealing its cruel memories under layers of tangled scrub and vines. The extensive ruins on the island are now being restored by the National Parks Department and they give a fascinating insight into the prison conditions of the time. Day visitors can reach the island on regular tourist launches—Adai Cruises, (07) 3260 7944, leaves from Breakfast Creek, and Cat-o-Nine-Tails, (07) 3396 3994, leaves from Manly—but camping is prohibited.

The park can be visited throughout the year.

For further information, contact the ranger, ph: (07) 3396 5113.

TAMBORINE MOUNTAINS NATIONAL PARKS
620 HECTARES

There are 7 small parks which are combined to form Tamborine National Parks, situated 75 km south of Brisbane. One of the parks, 'Witches Falls', is the oldest national park in Queensland, being gazetted in 1908. The other 6 parks are Joalah, Palm Grove, Macdonald Park, Zamia Grove, The Knoll and Cedar Creek. These small national parks help to preserve remnants of the area's original rainforests and eucalypt forests.

Various types of birds including crimson rosellas, eastern whipbirds, Lewin's honeyeaters and satin bowerbirds can be observed in the thick rainforest, while black-faced cuckoo-shrikes, magpies, kingfishers and noisy miners are common in the dry eucalypt forest.

Palm Grove (118 hectares), has an excellent walking trail—1 hour return—which weaves its

way through a thick stand of piccabeen palms. Other trees seen on this track include the yellow carabeen, strangler figs and black beans. At Macdonald Park (12 hectares), there is another interesting walk through thick

Fishing in Woodgate National Park

rainforest festooned with vines, staghorns and bird's-nest ferns. This will take about 45 minutes for the return walk.

Visitors who feel like a swim should head to Cedar Creek (230 hectares) and cool off in one of the beautiful rockpools at the base of Cedar Creek Falls. Camping is not permitted.

The park can be visited throughout the year.

For further information, contact the ranger, ph: (07) 5545 1171.

UNDARA VOLCANIC NATIONAL PARK
65 000 HECTARES

Considered by many scientists to be a geological masterpiece, the lava tubes in the park, which is 40 km east of Mt Surprise and 261 km southwest of Cairns, were formed more than 190 000 years ago when a huge volcano erupted on the Mcbride Plateau, spewing millions of tonnes of molten lava into the surrounding countryside. Much of this bubbling mass flowed along dry

river beds, forming a hard crust on the surface as it cooled. The boiling lava underneath continued to surge below this hardened exterior, creating hollow tubes as it drained away. These natural pipes are by far the largest in the world, weaving their way across savanna country for nearly 160 km.

Animal life in the park is prolific and includes wallaroos, rock wallabies, grey kangaroos and brush-tail possums. Birds are plentiful with red-tailed black cockatoos, kingfishers and pale-headed rosellas being just a few of the more common species seen. Five species of bats live inside the lava tubes along with millipedes, spiders and snails.

Visitors can either camp in the park or stay in beautifully refurbished railway carriages at Undara Lodge, phone (07) 4097 1411.

Winter and spring are the best times to visit the park.

For further information, contact the ranger, ph: (07) 4097 1485.

WOODGATE NATIONAL PARK
5500 HECTARES

Bounded by the blue Pacific to the east and the tranquil Burrum River to the south, Woodgate National Park, situated 7 km north of the small township of Woodgate and 60 km south of Bundaberg, is a coastal gem often overlooked by travellers.

With its wide variety of habitats, Woodgate National Park harbours numerous species of birds. When the banksias are flowering, both the rainbow and scaly-breasted lorikeets feed ravenously on the succulent nectar of the yellow brushes.

The broad expanse of beach at Woodgate is no doubt the park's greatest attraction. A wooden ramp, designed to protect the dunes from unnecessary erosion, leads on to the soft sand near the camping area. Vehicles can traverse the beach for about 7 km north of the camping ground, to a point where another wooden ramp leads up to the small village of Woodgate.

Both the shallow waters off the beach and the Burrum River are excellent for fishing and swimming. Yabbies, which are good bait for whiting, bream and flathead, can easily be pumped up from the sand at low tide.

Depending on the condition of the sandy track, a 4WD vehicle may be necessary to negotiate the last 5 km to the camping area. As there are only 16 sites booking should be made in advance from the ranger.

The park is a beautiful place to visit at any time of the year.

For further information, contact the ranger, ph: (07) 4126 8810.

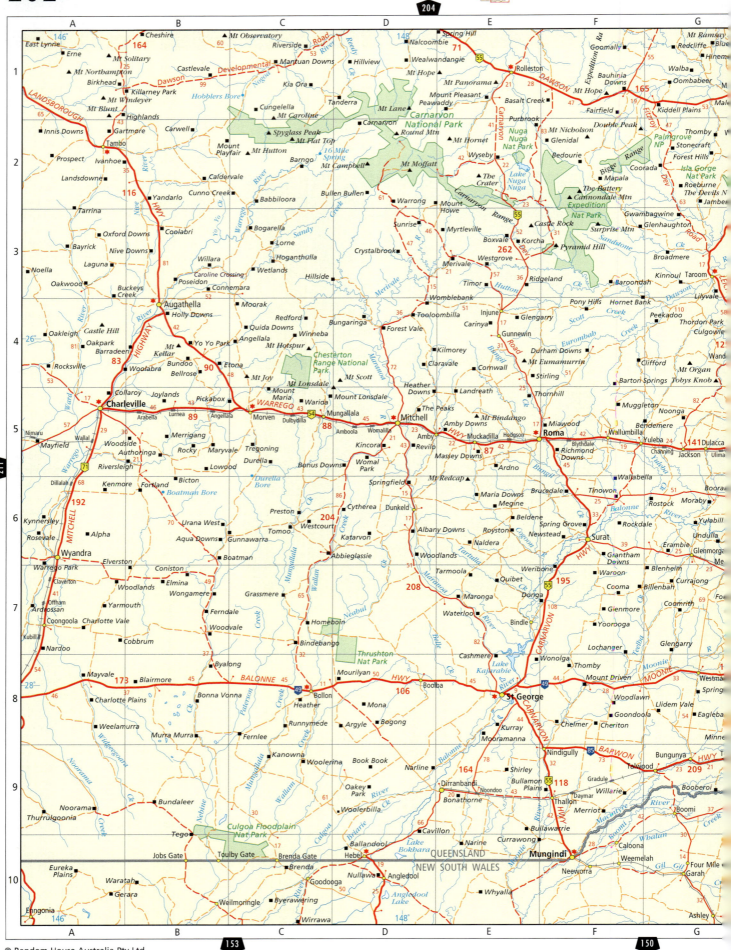

N

0   20   40   60   80   100
kilometres

150
152
20
22
24

GREAT
Round Reef
are Reef
Bugatti Reef
Hunt Reefs
Edgell Reefs
Bax Reef
Robertson
Reefs
Packer
Reefs
Boulton Reef
ays

Credlin Reefs
Stevens Reef
Creal Reef
Cumberland
Islands
Warland Reef
Calder Island
Cole Reefs
outh Cumberland
Is National Park
Gable Reefs
BARRIER
Scawfell
Island
Chauvel Reefs

iscus
ast
Penrith Island
Prince Reef

Prudhoe Island
Double Is
Pompey Reef
night Is
Munster
Island
Beverley
Group
Nat Park
Heralds Reef Prong
REEF
almerston
Digby
Island
Curlew Is
Heralds Prong No. 3
erston NP
Middle Island
North East Island
Nat Park
Heralds Prong No. 2
Thomas Cay
vonga Point
Percy
Isles
South Island
Nat Park
Swain Reefs
ill Island
Hill Nat Pk
Duke
Islands
Northumberland Isles
uila Is
Wilo
Duck Is
Bamborough Island
Gannett Cay
Point
Marble Island
High Peak Island

ew
Long
Island
Quail Island
Broad
Sound
Cheviot Island
Great Barrier Reef Marine Park
Stanage
Price Mtn
Leicester Is
Cape Townshend
(Mackay-Capricorn Section)
Broad
Sound
Collins
Is
Townshend Island
rence
Tortila
Reef Point
ewport
Pen
Shoalwater
Bay
Pearl Bay
Rosewood
Island
Shoalwater Bay
Perforated Point
algi
Double Mtn
Warginburra Peninsula
x
Military Training Area
Cape Clinton
Ogmore
Banksia
Freshwater Bay
Glenprairie
Mt Phipps
Cliff Point
Mt O'Connell
Conical
Mtn
Cape Manifold
BRUCE
Mt Atherton
Marlborough
Princhester
Byfield
Stockyard Point
104
HWY
Kunwarara
Byfield National Park
The Oaks
Water Park Point
Balmoral
Corio Bay
Rossmoya
Capricorn
Canoona
Nth Keppel Is
Cooberrie
Nat Park
Milman
Yeppoon
Coast
Yaamba
Mt Etna Caves
Kinka Bay
Ridgelands
The Caves
Great Keppel Island
Waroula
Cawarral
Tanby
Parkhurst
Emu Park
Dalma
Rockhampton
Keppel Sands
Black
Mtn
Gracemere
North West Is
Broomfield Reef
Foleyvale
Stanwell
Kabra
Gavial
Wilson Island
Sorrel Hills
Midgee
Broadmount
Cape Keppel
Capricorn
Boulcombe
Port Alma
Heron Island
Group
Gogango
Westwood
Bajool
Mt Barker
Mast Head
One Tree Island
145
Duaringa
Windah
Curtis
Island
Fitzroy Reef
oulbura
HWY
Mount
Morgan
Raglan
Is Nat Park
Polmaise Reef
Llewellyn Reef
Grantleigh
Mt Helen
Epala
Black Head
Boult Reef
15
106
Ambrose
South End
Eunker
Hoskyn Islands
omoboolaroo
Dululu
Mount Larcom
Facing Island
Group
Fairfax Islands
Wowan
Cedric Mtn
East End
Yarwun
Lady Musgrave Island
Cooncel
Mt Alma
Gladstone
Vimy
Lancefield
Burua
Boyne Island
Richards Point
reek
Rannes
Mt Redshirt
Stirrat
Benaraby
Bustard Point
Kokotungo
17
Jooro
Fry
Calliope
Middle Island
Koomba
Goovigen
39
102
Barmundoo
Turkey Beach
araba
Jambin
Koonkool
Bindawalla
Castle
Tower
Nat Pk
Eurimbula
Nat Park
Seventeen Seventy
a Park
Callide
Amys Peak
Wietalaba
Bororen
Agnes Water
cliffe
Blue Hills
Callide Coal Mine
and Power Stn
Nagoorin
Round Hill
Deepwater Nat Park
Hinemoa
Callide Dam
Miriam Vale
Lady Elliot Island
babeer
Biloela
Kroombit Tops
National Park
Ubobo
Colosseum
Taunton
Great Barrier Reef Marine Park
Banana
Thangool
Littlemore
Rosevale
Fu es Beach
(Mackay-Capricorn Section)
Scoria
Many Peaks
Kotenan
lowmead

kilometres

0 20 40 60 80 100

H   J   K   L   M   N   P

SOUTH

PACIFIC

OCEAN

CORAL

SEA

Great Barrier
Reef Marine Park
(Cairns Section)

Great Barrier Reef Marine Park
(Central Section)

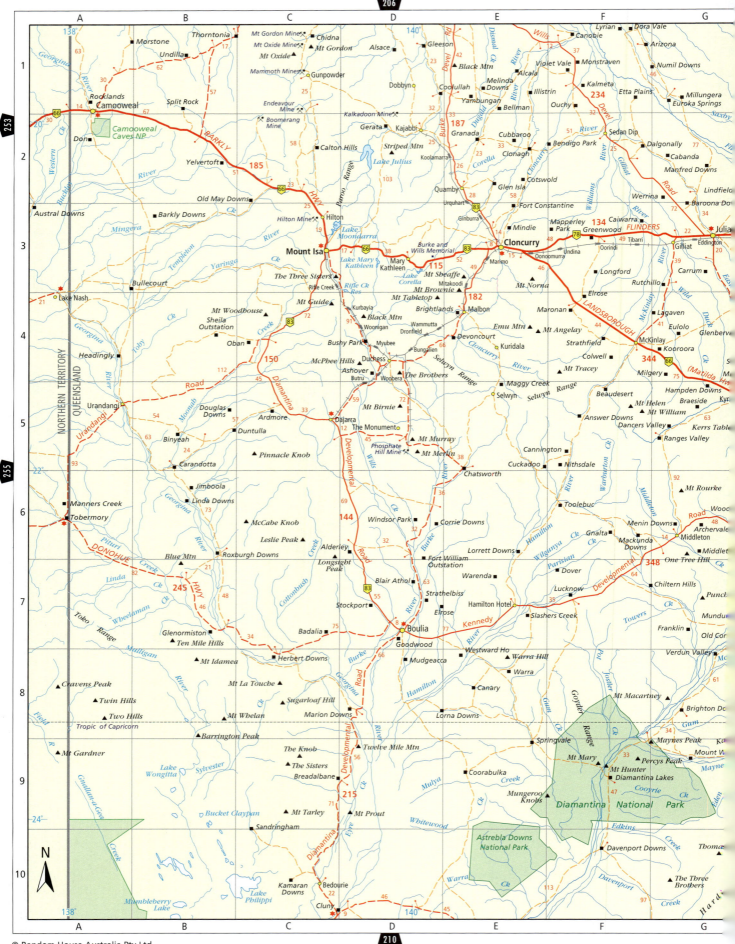

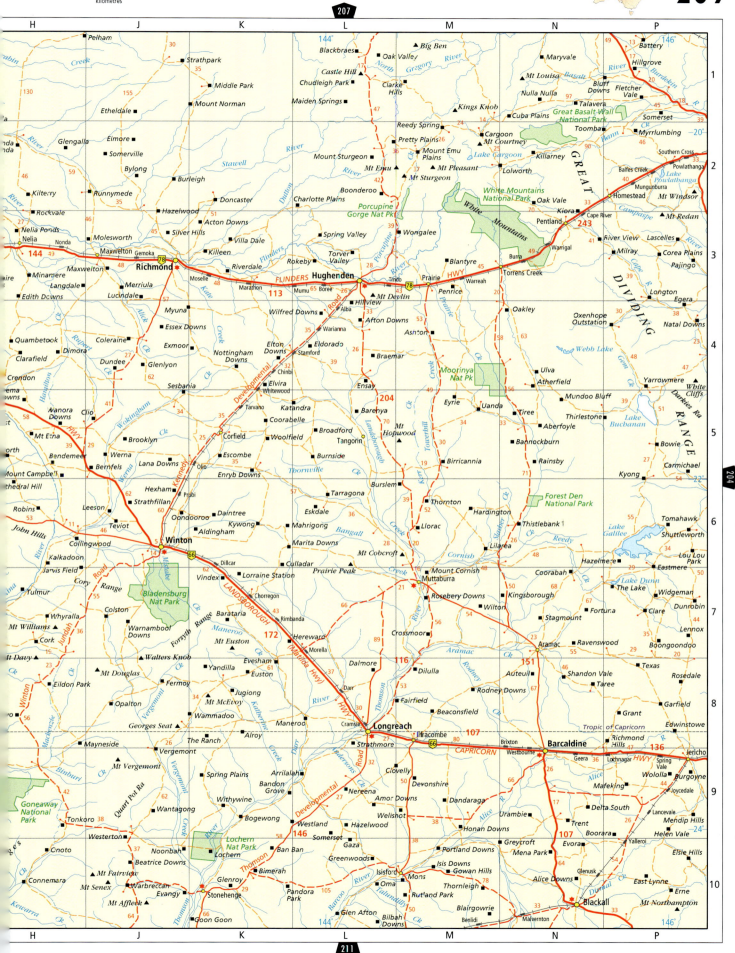

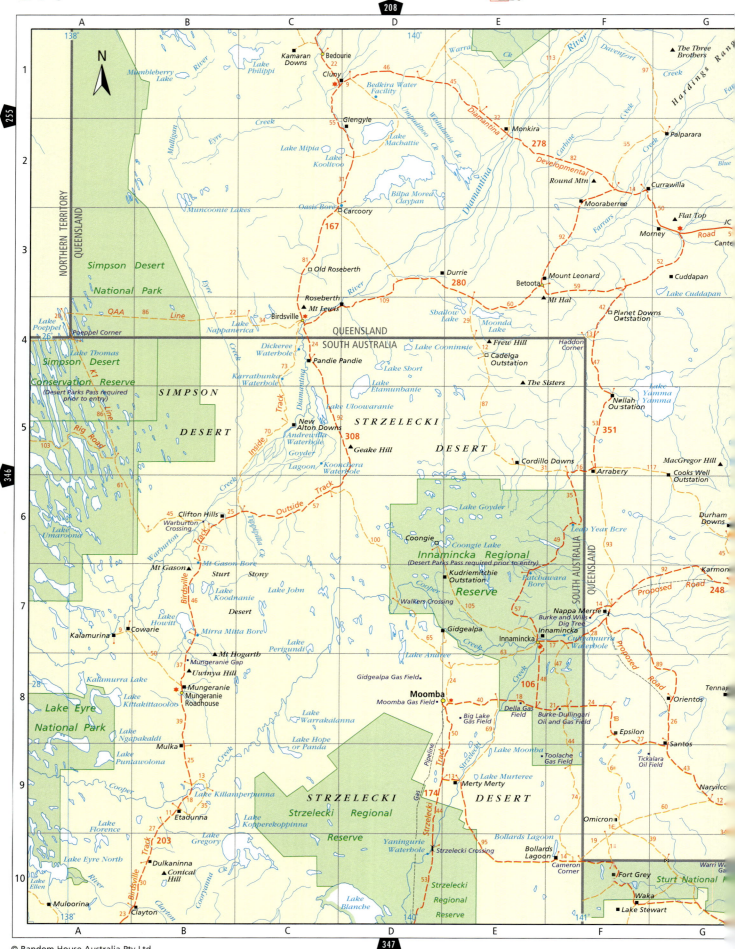

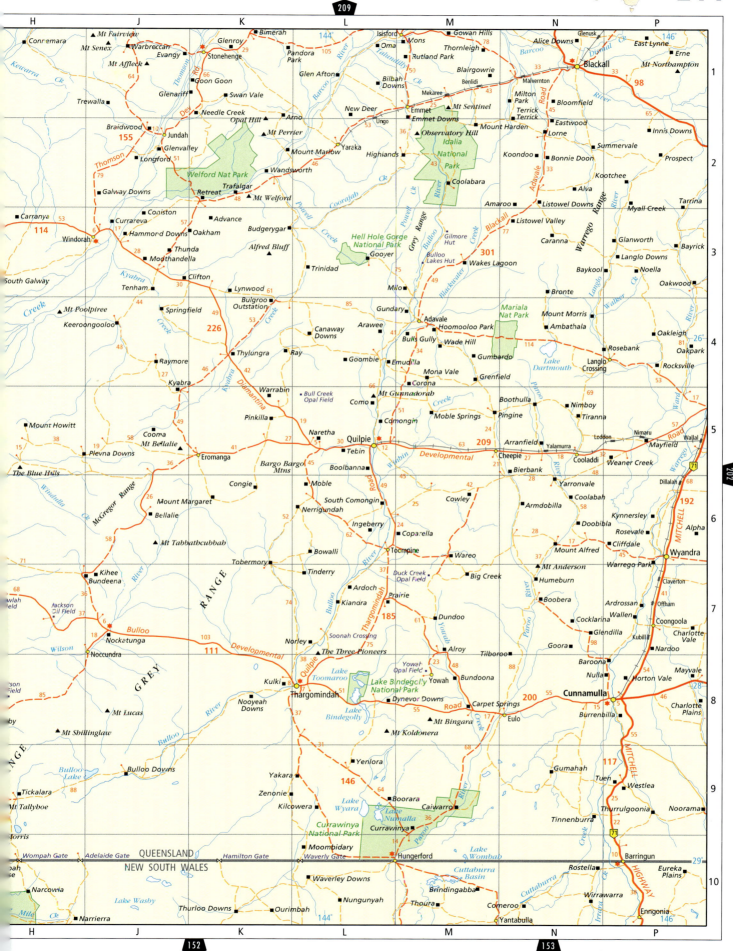

kilometres

0 20 40 60 80

TORRES   STRAIT
Orman Reef
Warrior Reefs
Mabuiag Island
Sassie island
Badu Island
Moa Island   Ashmore Reef
Cook Reef   Long Reef   Yule Entrance
West Island
Hawkesbury Island   North Torres Reef
                     South Torres Reef
Hammond Island   North West Reef
Thursday Island   Wednesday Island
Friday Is   Horn Is
Prince of Wales Is   Mt Adolphus Island
                            Cape York
ARAFURA   Possession Is   Albany Is
             Nat Park   Somerset
Cape Cornwall Dayman Is
             Bamaga   Womer Cay   CORAL   SEA
Injinoo Aboriginal Community
Van Spoult Head   Turtle Head Island
Crab Island   Sharp Point
SEA   Vehicular   Shadwell Peak
            Ferry   Furze Point
                                 Ussher Point   Olinda Entrance
Vrilya Point   Left Hill   Orford Bay
                                 Orford Ness   Parsons Reef
CAPE   False Orford Ness   Maclennan Cay
                                 Bosanquet Hill   Onslow Reef   Pandora Entrance
                    Holby Hill
                    Wizard Reef Boydong Cays
YORK   Captain Billy Landing   Great Detached   BARRIER
        Heathlands Messum Hill   Thrush Reef   Reef
                    Red Cliffs   Forwood Reef   Three Reefs
                    Middle Peak   Shelburne   Cockburn
                                  Bay   Reef   Five Reefs Star Reef Yule Detached Reef
Cullen Point   Conical Hill Round Point
Mapoon   Cape Grenville   Job Reef
Aboriginal Community   Home Islands
          Agnew   Laurel   Mason Reef   Martha Ridgeway
PENINSULA Bramwell   Reef   Nomad Reef   Reef
          Bertiehaugh   Bolt Head   Black Rocks
Pennefather River   Temple Bay   Great Barrier
          Batavia   Mosquito Point   Reef Marine Park
          Outstation   Fair Cape   Quoin Island   Lagoon Reef (Far Northern Section)
Duyfken Point Andoom   Huxley Hill   Carron Hill
          Weipa   Moreton Telegraph Weymouth Bay   Long sandy Reef
          Napranum   Station   Portland Roads   Second Small Reef
Albatross   Joyce   Cape Weymouth
Bay   Sudley   Hill   Cape Griffith
PENINSULA   Batavia Downs North Pap   Iron Range NP
                                 Lloyd Is
Boyd Point   Iron Range   Lockhart River Aboriginal Community
Pera Head   Cape Direction   Bligh Reef   REEF
Thud Point   Tor Hill
False Pera Head   Merluna   Iguana Mtn   Osborne Reef Franklin Reef   CORAL
                                 Jacks Knob   New Reef
                    Wenlock   Night Island
Warbody Point   (ruins)   Bobardt Point   Tijou Reef
Wallaby Island   Wolverton   Cone Peak   SEA
          Aurukun   Archer River   Whale Hill   Celebration Reef
          Aboriginal Community   Roadhouse   Cape Sidmouth
          Archer Bend   Friendly Point   First 3 Mile Opening
          National   Birthday Mtn   Campbell Pt Ogilvie Reef
          Park   Campbell Mtn   Round Mtn
                    Rokeby National Park   Creech Reef
                    Rokeby   Hay Is   Noddy Reef
          Merapah   Double Hill
Cape Keer-weer   Coen Aerodrome Colmer Point Magpie Reef
                    Mt Croll   Roberts Point Rooda Reef
                    The Twin Humps Hedge Reef   Wilson Reef
                    Mt White   Claremont Point Corbett Reef
                    Coen   Silver Plains Reef   Davie Reef Tydeman Reef
                                    Old Silver   Eden
Christmas Point   Plains   Reef
                    Foxs Lookout   Flinders Group Stanley Is
                                    Nat Park   Flinders Is   Cape Melville
                    Yarraden   Bathurst Head Bathurst   Twin Peaks
                    Pollappa   Princess Charlotte Bay   South Warden
                    Strathburn   Beabey Hill   Reef
                    Lily Vale   Bathurst Head Barrow Pt   Mid
Old Strathgordon   Wakooka   Red Pt   Reef
                    Marina Plains   Outstation   Cape Bowen   Howick Is
New Strathgordon   Murdoch Pt   Howick Group NP
                    New Bamboo   Brown Peak
Pormpuraaw   Lakefield   Flat Top Hill
Aboriginal Community Musgrave   Breeza Plains Black Hill   Munburra
                    Glen Garland   National   Outstation   Kalpowar   Mt Norkwa
                    Strathmay Strathaven   Park   Lakefield   Starcke Nat Park
Wallaby Island   Dixie   Lakefield
                                   Outstation   National Park Starcke
                    New Dixie   Glenrock Eldersile
                    Kalinga   Hann River   Mt Jack
                                    Roadhouse   Lakefield National Park Battle Camp

kilometres
0 10 20 30 40 50

The Northern Territory is still classed today as a remote destination. To reach the capital, Darwin, and other areas of the Top End you may have to travel by road from anywhere between 3000 km and 4500 km, and maybe further. That, to say the least, is an enormous distance to travel when you are on holiday. Remote destinations in the Northern Territory are normally accessed by overland travellers and those with unlimited time. Alternatively, visitors fly into the Northern Territory and then access destina-

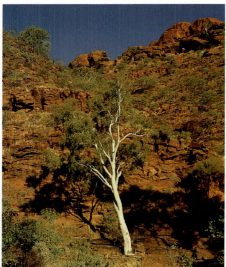

A eucalyptus tree growing in Watarrka National Park

tions by rented vehicle or tour company. More than three-quarters of the parks and reserves have direct, sealed road access.

The overwhelming majority of the more popular destinations are encompassed within national parks and reserves which cover barely 2 per cent of land within the 1 346 200 square kilometres of surface area in the Northern Territory. Almost 60 per cent of land in the Northern Territory has been handed back to the indigenous population in the form of freehold title and these areas are not normally accessible without a permit, which may be difficult to obtain. The remainder of the country is utilised by pastoral leases or is harsh, uninhabited desert area.

Over the past 20 years the Northern Territory Government, through its Parks and Wildlife Commission, has set about proclaiming and promoting a series of national parks that are user friendly. All parks are managed with the assistance of the traditional Aboriginal owners. Only two parks within the Northern Territory—Kakadu and Uluru–Kata Tjuta—are managed by outside interests, namely the Australian Nature Conservation Agency which has its headquarters in Canberra.

The best time to visit the north is from May

to October. A very mild winter prevails in Central Australia around Alice Springs, and cool nights and warm days may be experienced in the Top End around Darwin and Katherine.

The Northern Territory has a diverse ecology. From the absolute wetlands of the far north to the semi-arid woodland forests and grassy plains of the Barkly Tableland, to the dry arid zone of the south where the red sand dunes are interspersed with mountain ranges and rocky outcrops. The one thing that is plentiful in the Northern Territory is water. During the monsoon months from October through to May the northern half of the Northern Territory is deluged with rainwater. This time is known as the Wet. Plant growth is prolific and grass may reach 3 metres in height. Then comes the drying off period known as the Dry. Grass fires, spontaneous or deliberate, clear the dried grasses during this period and leave the countryside black and burnt. Then early morning dew provides the sustenance for regrowth and so the whole process starts all over again. Late summer rains in the southern half, although not consistent, fill up the dry watercourses and there are many waterholes that remain a permanent water supply to the wildlife of this area. The desert blooms after rain but soon dries off due to the very warm weather. Central Australia has a very good underground water supply which, incidentally, flows from Papua New Guinea by means of an aquifer—a watercourse under the earth's crust. This provides moisture for the plant growth throughout this region.

National parks are set aside to preserve the environment which has evolved through time into an ecological phenomenon. They also provide access to the environment by all humans and animals. Kakadu encompasses the virtues of wetlands and prolific bird life, of escarpments and rainforest pockets, of giant rivers with barramundi sport fishing for the enthusiast or crocodile viewing, of isolated billabongs for that tranquil repose, or of soothing waves crashing upon a beach of the Arafura Sea. Ancient Aborigines left their mark of stylised art upon the rock faces of this park and today you may be guided to these places by a traditional owner of the land. To the north Gurig National Park beckons the visitor with access by sea, air or 4WD vehicle for remote camping, pristine white sand beaches and a colourful history. Over on the western side of the Territory, Window on the Wetlands gives an insight into the nature of the Adelaide River plains while Litchfield National Park caters for bushwalking, swimming and to a lesser extent bush camping with 4WD access. In and around Darwin all the beaches are classed as coastal reserves and are managed as such. Within the city limits Holmes Jungle provides the visitor

Rainbow Valley Conservation Park

with a walk through a monsoon rainforest. The Territory Wildlife Park near Berry Springs has a wonderful display of marsupials, birds, reptiles and nocturnal animals. The visitor should set a whole day aside to experience this very well presented park. South of Darwin, Manton Dam for waterskiing, Daly River for fishing, Tjuwaliyn (Douglas Hot Springs) for swimming, Butterfly Gorge and Umbrawarra Gorge for bushwalking and swimming all give the holiday-maker time to relax and enjoy the good weather.

The town of Katherine caters for visitors to Nitmiluk (Katherine Gorge) National Park where commercial operators ply the waters of the gorge with their pontoons showing the visitors the wonders of this ancient gorge. In the Wet, when the river is a raging torrent, the gorge may be accessed by thrill-seekers in a jet boat. A number of walking tracks give the experienced bushwalker the opportunity to get the feel of nature's forces at work in this gorge. Katherine River Low Level Recreation Reserve is an ideal place to have a picnic while on the other side of the river a bubbling hot spring can soothe away the tensions of travel.

West of Katherine, along the Victoria

Highway, the traveller has access to parts of Gregory National Park by bushwalking tracks and picnic places. A section of this park is set aside with rough tracks for access by 4WD vehicles only and leads to regions for remote camping. Keep River National Park on the Northern Territory border has a marvellous display of ancient rock art.

Elsey National Park and Mataranka Thermal Springs are there for the weary traveller to recharge the batteries with a relaxing swim in the thermal pool or by canoeing and fishing on the Roper River.

The Devils Marbles Conservation Reserve, south of the goldmining town of Tennant Creek, is a good place to camp overnight as it is secluded yet only a short distance away from the main highway. Davenport Range National Park to the southeast of Tennant Creek is accessible, because of its rough tracks, by 4WD vehicle only and caters for remote camping. It also has a biological diversity which is unique to the area.

Alice Springs is the centre for tourism in Central Australia. This town's population of 26 000 may double in number during the winter months. From this jumping-off point the visitor may travel to a number of national parks to experience the unique flora and fauna of this region. The West MacDonnell National Park—which encompasses the Larapinta (bushwalking) Trail, the Alice Springs Telegraph Station, Simpsons Gap, Standley Chasm, Ellery Creek Big Hole, Serpentine Gorge, Serpentine Chalet, the Ochre Pits, Ormiston Gorge, Glen Helen Gorge, Redbank Gorge and Tylers Pass Lookout—is a park with a magnificent array of canyons, cliffs and ridges, ancient hills and valleys, permanent waterholes and sandy creek beds. Here you may indulge yourself with outdoor activities such as bushwalking, swimming, nature study or just relaxing. The new Alice Springs Desert Park which opened in early 1997 is home to more than 400 desert animals and also has thousands of native plants on display. Visitors are encouraged to use this park as an introduction to the region's network of park and reserves.

Six parks of this region cater for 4WD vehicles only: Palm Valley, Finke River Gorge, Chambers Pillar, N'Dhala Gorge, Ruby Gap, and the Mac Clark (Acacia Peuce) Reserve. There are commercial tour operators based in Alice Springs with 4WD vehicles for hire. Gosse Bluff, a comet crater some 130 million years old, and Henbury Meteorite Craters give an insight into the astrophysical happenings on earth eons ago. Take a walk up and over the rim of Kings Canyon in Watarrka National Park and you may feel empathy with the area's early inhabitants.

Ayers Rock and the Olgas, Uluru and Kata–Tjuta, whichever name you call these towering monoliths, cause all to stand in awe of them. Icons for the whole of Australia, they are as amazing to the indigenous inhabitants of this land as to the thousands of visitors who make their way to this sacred place.

Whatever your schedule may be on your visit to the national parks of the Northern Territory, take time to explore and enjoy this ancient land. It will be impossible to see it all on one holiday so choose your destinations carefully and make the most of your time in the north.

Although the destinations within the Northern Territory are remote, modern technological services such as mobile phones, Eftpos, credit cards, fax and the Internet are all available from major towns and fuel stops along the Stuart, Victoria, and Barkly Highways.

#	Park	Ranger/Park Tel.	Ranger/Information	Camping	Caravan	4WD Access	BBQ/Fireplace	Picnic Area	Marked Walking Tracks	Bushwalking	Kiosk/Restaurant	Fishing	Swimming
1	Alice Springs Desert Park	(08) 8951 8711	*					*	*		*		
2	Alice Springs Telegraph Station Historic Reserve	(08) 8951 8211	*					*					
3	Arltunga Historic Reserve	(08) 8951 8211	*					*	*				
4	Barranyi National Park	(08) 8975 8711									*		*
5	Berry Springs Nature Park & Territory Wildlife Park	(08) 8988 6000	*				*	*	*				*
6	Casuarina Coastal Reserve	(08) 8947 2305	*					*	*				*
7	Chambers Pillar Historic Reserve	(08) 8951 8211		*	*		*	*					
8	Corroboree Rock Conservation Reserve	(08) 8951 8211						*	*				
9	Cutta Cutta Caves Nature Park	(08) 8973 8888	*				*	*	*		*		
10	Darwin Botanic Gardens	(08) 8999 5535	*				*	*	*		*		
11	Davenport Range National Park (proposed)	(08) 8962 2140	*	*		*	*						*
12	Devils Marbles Conservation Reserve	(08) 8951 8211	*	*	*				*	*			
13	Emily & Jessie Gaps National Park	(08) 8951 8211						*	*				
14	Elsey National Park	(08) 8975 4560	*	*	*			*	*		*	*	*
15	Ewaninga Rock Carvings Conservation Reserve	(08) 8951 8211					*	*	*				
16	Finke Gorge National Park	(08) 8951 8211	*	*		*	*	*	*	*			*
17	Fogg Dam Conservation Reserve	(08) 8988 8009	*					*	*				
18	Gregory National Park	(08) 8975 0888	*	*	*	*	*	*	*	*	*	*	*
19	Gurig National Park and Cobourg Marine Park	(08) 8984 3585	*	*		*		*				*	*
20	Henbury Meteorite Craters Conservation Reserve	(08) 8951 8211		*			*	*	*				
21	Holmes Jungle National Park	(08) 8947 2305						*	*	*			
22	Howard Springs Nature Park & Hunting Reserve	(08) 8983 1001	*		*			*	*	*	*	*	*
23	Illamurta Spring Conservation Reserve	(08) 8951 8211				*				*			
24	John Flynn's Grave Historic Reserve	(08) 8951 8211											
25	Kakadu National Park	(08) 8938 1100	*	*	*	*	*	*	*	*	*	*	*
26	Keep River National Park	(08) 9167 8827	*	*		*		*	*	*			
27	Leaning Tree Lagoon Nature Park	(08) 8999 5511											
28	Litchfield National Park	(08) 8976 0282	*	*	*	*	*	*	*	*			*
29	Mac Clark (Acacia Peuce) Conservation Reserve	(08) 8951 8211		*						*			
30	Manton Dam Conservation Reserve	(08) 8999 5511	*			*						*	*
31	Mary River Crossing Conservation Reserve	(08) 8999 5511	*	*			*	*				*	*
32	N'Dhala Gorge Nature Park	(08) 8951 8211	*	*		*	*	*	*				
33	Nitmiluk (Katherine Gorge) National Park	(08) 8972 1886	*	*	*		*	*	*	*			*
34	Olive Pink Flora Reserve	(08) 8999 5511	*										
35	Rainbow Valley Conservation Reserve	(08) 8999 5511	*	*		*				*			
36	Ruby Gap National Park	(08) 8951 8211	*	*		*				*			
37	Ryans Well Historic Reserve	(08) 8951 8211	*			*							
38	Tennant Creek Telegraph Station Historic Reserve	(08) 8951 8211	*							*			
39	Tnorala (Gosse Bluff) Conservation Reserve	(08) 8951 8211	*			*			*	*			
40	Trephina Gorge Nature Park	(08) 8951 8211	*	*		*	*	*	*	*			
41	Uluru–Kata Tjuta National Park	(08) 8951 8211	*			*	*	*			*		
42	Umbrawarra National Park	(08) 8973 8770		*		*	*	*					*
43	Watarrka (Kings Canyon) National Park	(08) 8951 8211	*	*	*	*	*	*	*	*	*		
44	West MacDonnell National Park	(08) 8951 8211	*	*	*	*	*	*	*	*	*		*

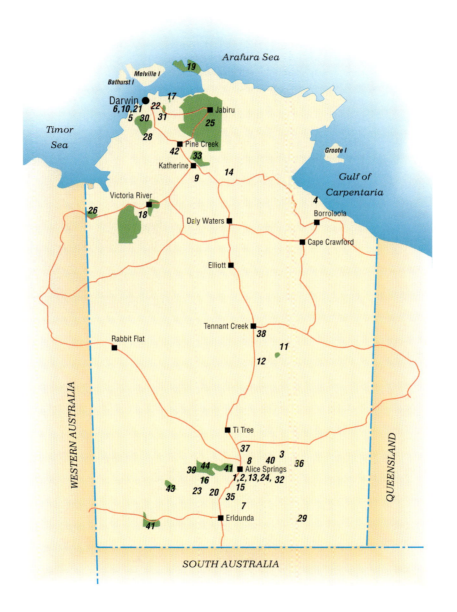

Arafura Sea

19

Melville I
Bathurst I

17

Darwin
6,10,21   *22*
5   *30*   *31*   ■ Jabiru
28   *25*

Timor
Sea

42   ■ Pine Creek
33
Katherine ■
              9   *14*

Groote I

Gulf of
Carpentaria

Victoria River
26   *4*
         18   Borroloola ■
         Daly Waters ■

                                    Cape Crawford ■

                    Elliott ■

Rabbit Flat ■   Tennant Creek ■
                              38
                                    11
                              12

WESTERN AUSTRALIA

QUEENSLAND

              ■ Ti Tree
                    37
              8 *40* *3*
39 *44* *41*   *36*
      16   Alice Springs ■
                1,2,13,24, *32*
43   *15*
      23 *20* *35*
                    7
              ■ Erldunda   *29*
41

SOUTH AUSTRALIA

ARLTUNGA HISTORICAL RESERVE

IN BRIEF

MAP REFERENCE: PAGE 255 J 6

Location 110 km east of Alice Springs along sealed Ross Highway for 70 km and gravel road for 40 km

Best Time Beginning of April to late October

Main Attractions Historical mining reserve, fossicking, walking trails, tours, informative Visitor Centre

Ranger Visitor Information Centre, cnr Gregory Terrace and Hartley Street, Alice Springs, phone (08) 8952 5800

Born out of the gold rush to Central Australia in 1887, Arltunga became the first town of this region and supported a population of up to 3000. Today its population could be less than 10.

The discovery of alluvial gold in a dry creek bed downstream of an area known as Paddys Rockhole, in the East MacDonnell Ranges, drew some 500 Australian miners from the southern states of Australia. These hardy fortune seekers were able to travel by rail to where the track ended at Oodnadatta in South Australia. They had then to make their way, often on foot, over the last 600 km through arid land to reach their destination at Arltunga in the Northern Territory. Here the miners experienced very harsh conditions and deprivations: there was barely enough fresh food and water to survive on. When you visit the White Range Cemetery you will see the headstones of those souls who will never leave this dry and desolate place. However, help for some of the miners was on its way in the form of an enterprising family who travelled overland all the way from Queensland in their horse-drawn wagon. They established a small farm, known as the Garden, near Arltunga and traded fresh fruit and vegetables for gold.

Mining activities eventually ceased around 1913 and a number of families took up pastoral lands. Some of their descendants are still working the properties today. In recent years some of the old buildings and mining equipment in Arltunga have been carefully restored and are open to the public to explore. The reserve has been set up to show the way in which the early European miners and settlers lived, together with their frenetic activities brought on by gold lust.

Gold mining near Arltunga has had a resurgence in recent years, with mining activities in the White Range to the immediate east of the reserve.

HOW TO GET THERE

The reserve is located 110 km east of Alice Springs and is accessible by conventional vehicles. The first 70 km along the Ross Highway is sealed and then a formed gravel road takes the traveller the rest of the way.

WALKS AND MINE TOURS

By following the walking tracks you can explore the Old Police Station, ore battery, cyanide works, mine workings and residential areas. The walk will take about one hour. Rangers conduct tours to the Joker Mine on a regular basis from April through to September. To take part in a tour, you should check with the rangers or at the Visitor Information Centre in Alice Springs. For these tours you will need to bring a torch. By climbing down into some of the mines, you will get a idea of the hardships that the early miners had to endure. These days just their ghosts remain. In some caves you may find clusters of small bats which will be unperturbed by your visit.

OTHER ATTRACTIONS

The Arltunga Historical Reserve has a modern visitor centre that gives an introduction to the area. The centre presents static displays, slide shows and the opportunity to find some gold for yourself. An old Two Stamp Battery is activated by the ranger on duty at the centre and you will be able to see how gold was won in the days gone by.

Picnic facilities with shade shelters are located at the Visitor Centre and at the Old Police Station. Commercial camping is available at the Arltunga Outback Tourist Park.

On the eastern border of the Arltunga Reserve there is a fossicking reserve, where, with the proper fossicking permit, the visitor may search for alluvial gold. The permit is available from the Department of Mines and Energy in Alice Springs, and strict conditions apply.

Arltunga Police Station

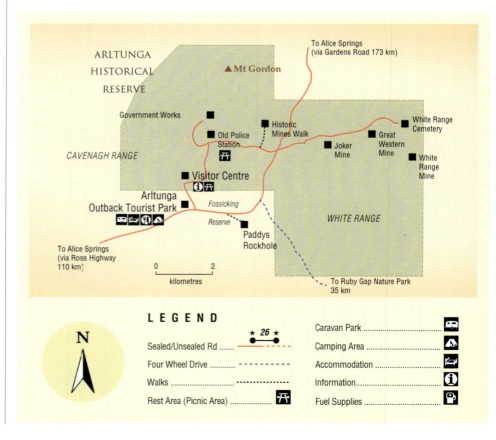

LEGEND

Sealed/Unsealed Rd	Caravan Park	
Four Wheel Drive	Camping Area	
Walks	Accommodation	
Rest Area (Picnic Area)	Information	
	Fuel Supplies	

MAP REFERENCE: PAGE 255 H 3

Location 160 km south of Alice Springs along the Old South Road. Access is by 4WD only
Best Time April to end of October
Main Attractions Towering sandstone pillar, walking trail, beautiful desert scenery, bush camping
Ranger Visitor Information Centre, cnr Gregory Terrace and Hartley Street, Alice Springs, phone (08) 8952 5800

Towering 50 metres above the low sand dunes on the western edge of the Simpson Desert, Chambers Pillar (known to the Aborigines as Itirkawara, the Gecko Ancestor) beckons all travellers throughout these arid lands. Standing out from the dunes as it does, it is a good place from which to take a bearing on a journey.

The first European to set eyes upon this pinnacle of sandstone was the intrepid overland explorer, John McDouall Stuart, who, on his attempt to cross the Australian continent in 1860, saw the column of sandstone and named it after one of his sponsors, James Chambers. The latter, a cartage and mail contractor, land speculator and businessman—reputed to begin his accounts at 6 am of a morning with a bottle of whisky and to finish both before breakfast—turned a little capital into a fortune. He was the first person to send Stuart out to the north of South Australia to find new pastoral lands.

John McDouall Stuart, born in Scotland in 1815, emigrated to Australia in 1838. His first explorations were in the company of Charles Sturt in the years 1844 to 1846. Then in 1858 William Finke financed the first of 6 northern expeditions in which Stuart finally reached the north Australian coast and the Arafura Sea in 1862. Stuart and William Kekwick, who accompanied Stuart on his last 4 expeditions, passed by Chambers Pillar and used it as their marker in Central Australia. Until the railway line was built, the Pillar was an essential point of reference for travellers, many of whom carved their names on it. Modern-day graffiti has continued, with one of the latest additions being a drawing of Halley's Comet made in 1986.

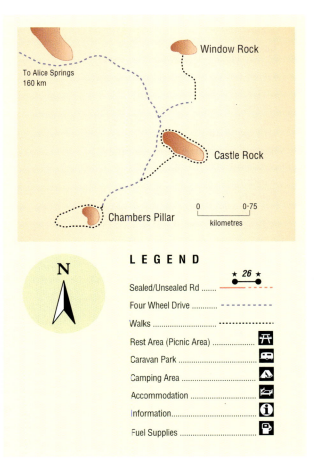

To Alice Springs 160 km

Window Rock

Castle Rock

Chambers Pillar

0   0·75
kilometres

N

L E G E N D

★ 26 ★

Sealed/Unsealed Rd ....
Four Wheel Drive ....
Walks ....
Rest Area (Picnic Area) ....
Caravan Park ....
Camping Area ....
Accommodation ....
Information...............................
Fuel Supplies ....

Chambers Pillar soars out of the Simpson Desert

ABORIGINAL SIGNIFICANCE

Aboriginal Dreamtime legend states that the powerful Gecko Ancestor was disgraced after violating their strict code of marriage and was banished into the desert where he turned into the pillar. His wife turned into the nearby Castle Rock with her back towards him in shame.

ACCESS

Chambers Pillar Historical Reserve is 340 hectares and access is via the Old South Road, 160 km south of Alice Springs past Maryvale Station. Access is by 4WD vehicle only as the road is not sealed and dunes and river beds are crossed. Commercial tours to Chambers Pillar operate out of Alice Springs and information on these tours is available from the Visitor Information Centre in Alice Springs.

WALKS AND CAMPING

A walk to the base of the Pillar has been constructed which will take about ½ hour return. Please do not vary from this walking track as the surrounding sandstone country is very fragile. Picnic tables, BBQs and toilets are provided. Bush camping is allowed and a nominal fee is charged using an honour system of placing the amount due in a box at the site.

DAVENPORT RANGE NATIONAL PARK

MAP REFERENCE: PAGE 253 K 10

Location There are 4 access points to this park which lies 500 km northeast of Alice Springs and 251 km southeast of Tennant Creek. 4WD access recommended

Best Time Beginning of April to late September

Main Attractions Remote bush camping, biodiversity, bush-walking

Ranger Parks and Wildlife Commission, Alice Springs, phone (08) 8951 8211

Tucked away on the eastern side of the central Northern Territory, southeast of Tennant Creek and northeast from Alice Springs, this remote area represents the biological inter-zone between the northern woodland savannah and the arid inland of Central Australia.

The Davenport Ranges denote the boundaries between the traditional lands of the Aboriginal groups of the Warumungu, Alyawarre and Kaytetye. In more recent times missionaries came to this area, followed by the pastoralists who took up vast tracts of grazing land. The miners came next, digging for wolfram, gold, copper, tin, bismuth and scheelite. Wolfram, used in the hardening of steel and in the production of armaments, enjoyed good prices up to the end of World War II. The mining decline began after the war ended and mining ceased by the late 1960s. Today pastoral properties and Aboriginal land trusts form the borders of the national park.

The Davenport Range National Park has a rugged, remote atmosphere. The diversity of the fauna and flora of this park is centred along the many permanent waterholes that are found along the watercourse of the Frew River which cuts through the park. This river supports 7 species of fish, small inland crabs, 44 species of birds (a prime nesting area for budgerigars) and desert mice, antechinus, dunnarts, spectacled hare-wallabies, northern nail-tail wallabies, black-footed wallabies, euros, kangaroos and dingoes. Feral cats, feral donkeys and cattle also inhabit the park and their removal is proving an onerous task.

The Davenport Range National Park is remote and unstaffed. Please make sure that you are well prepared and that you carry all the necessary supplies, first aid equipment and vehicle spares. Remember to let someone know of your travel destination and expected time of return and do not forget to advise of your return. All natural and cultural resources in the park are protected. Please take all your litter with you.

CAMPING

Camping is only allowed at Old Police Station Waterhole, but picnic facilities along the Frew River Loop Track have been provided. There are no other facilities inside the park, so please come well prepared.

ACCESS

A 4WD vehicle is required to access the park and Old Police Station Waterhole. There are 4 access roads to this national park. The first is from Barkly Homestead Roadhouse on the Barkly Highway via Epenarra Station, a distance of 166 km; the second comes from Tennant Creek via Bonney Well on the Stuart Highway, Kurundi Station and Epenarra Station, a distance of 251 km. You can also come from Alice Springs via the Sandover Highway, Ammaroo Station, Murray Downs Station, an approximate distance of 496 km; or also from Alice Springs via the Stuart Highway, Barrow Creek, Taylor Creek, Murray Downs Station, an approximate distance of 500 km. The Stuart Highway and the Barkly Highway are sealed roads. The remainder of the access roads are gravel roads and bush tracks. Drive carefully in this remote country. All access roads are signposted.

An alternative access to Old Police Station Waterhole turns off the Taylor Creek access

Old Police Station Waterhole

road about halfway between the abandoned Pioneer Mine and Bull Creek Bore. This very demanding 17 km track, known as the Frew River Loop Track, should only be attempted by experienced drivers.

THINGS TO DO

Old Police Station Waterhole is a permanent waterhole. Only the depth varies with the amount of rain that has fallen. Swimming is a favourite pastime as well as canoeing, but this is rather limited.

The river and ranges offer excellent bush-walking opportunities. There are no marked tracks, however, and walkers must be experienced and well prepared. Birdwatching and night-spotting of native fauna are also popular.

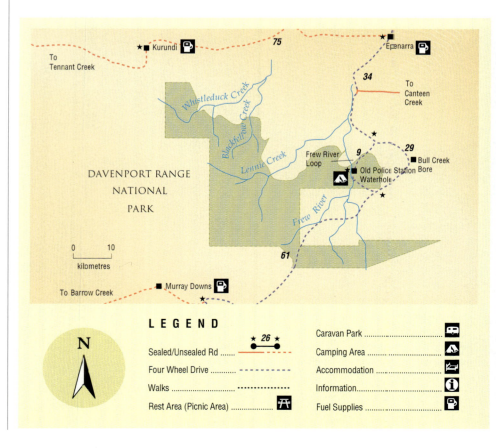

To Tennant Creek

Kurundi

75

Epenarra

34

To Canteen Creek

Whistleduck Creek

Blackfellow Creek

Lennie Creek

DAVENPORT RANGE NATIONAL PARK

Frew River Loop

9

29

Old Police Station Waterhole

Bull Creek Bore

Frew River

61

0   10
kilometres

To Barrow Creek

Murray Downs

LEGEND

N

Sealed/Unsealed Rd .... ★ 26 ★	Caravan Park ....
Four Wheel Drive	Camping Area ....
Walks	Accommodation ....
Rest Area (Picnic Area)	Information ....
	Fuel Supplies ....

IN BRIEF

MAP REFERENCE: PAGE 254 F 7

Location 138 km west of Alice Springs along Larapinta Drive. Access is by 4WD only

Best Time Between March and October

Main Attractions Ancient cabbage palms in Palm Valley, 4WD track along Finke Gorge, Aboriginal culture, walking trails and camping

Ranger Visitor Information Centre, cnr Gregory Terrace and Hartley Street, Alice Springs, phone (08) 8952 5800

This national park covers an area of some 46 000 hectares of the oldest watercourse in the world, the Finke River, and includes the spectacular and amazing Palm Valley, which follows Palm Creek, a tributary of the Finke River.

The river starts its journey in the West MacDonnell Ranges and meanders over the plains, cutting through the Krichauff, Waterhouse and James Ranges. It is the longest river in Central Australia: after about 400 km the river has a floodout (where the waters spread out and dissipate into the sand) in the Simpson Desert close to the Northern Territory border with South Australia. It most likely feeds the artesian waters of Dalhousie Springs and Purnie Bore which are located in the northern part of South Australia and which are accessible along the popular 4WD Simpson Desert crossing route.

Palm Valley, in the Krichauff Range, is world renowned for the red cabbage palms that grow prolifically along the creek bed. Its water supply comes from the porous Hermannsburg Sandstone ridges. Weathered away over eons, these ridges now form a huge water storage tank. This has enabled life forms which belong to a wetter era still to flourish in the valley.

The park holds special significance for the Western Arrernte Aboriginal group. Their forefathers resisted with force the arrival of Ernest Giles, the first European explorer to this region. Giles discovered Palm Valley with its unique growth of palms. The present growth of the palms, *Livistona mariae*, is estimated to be around 300 years old and scientists believe that palms have existed here for up to 20 000 years.

Pastoral activities in the area flourished around the turn of the century. Cattle were an easy alternative food source for the Aborigines and a police station was built at Boggy Hole in order to prevent cattle stealing. Nearby the Lutheran Mission of Hermannsburg was established in 1877 and very gradually European civilisation encroached upon this timeless land.

ACCESS

Access to all aspects of this park is by 4WD only. The soft sands of the Finke River make for slow going along the river bed tracks. Once into Palm Valley there are rocky sections which need careful negotiating.

Access to the Finke Gorge river track is via Hermannsburg and Ellery Creek. Careful sand driving techniques are required and the 4WD traveller must have the ability to deflate and inflate tyres. A wheel track leads 10 km from Hermannsburg to Ellery Creek. From there it is 19 km of river driving to Boggy Hole where bush camping is allowed but there are no facilities. After Boggy Hole the track winds in and out of the river for 68 km to the Ernest Giles Road and onto Watarrka National Park. You can take an 11 km detour to Illamurta Springs where a police station once stood.

The Visitor Information Centre in Alice Springs can provide details of tours to the park.

THINGS TO DO

The Palm Valley section of this park offers a modern camping ground with flush toilets, solar showers, wood BBQs and picnic areas. During

Boggy Hole on the Finke River

the winter rangers give campfire talks.

There are a number of walking tracks. The Kalaranga Lookout Walk is 1.5 km and takes 45 minutes return. It is an easy climb with spectacular views of a rock amphitheatre surrounded by rugged red sandstone cliffs. Look out for the black-backed wren that nests here.

The Mpaara Walk is longer at 5 km and 2 hours return. It will give you an insight into Western Arrernte Aboriginal mythology.

For a short walk among the palms, take the Arankaia Walk of 2 km, 1 hour return.

A longer walk, the Mpulungkinya Walk at 5 km and 2 hours return, takes you up through the valley and returns along the ridge top.

Always remember to carry at least one litre of water per hour's walk.

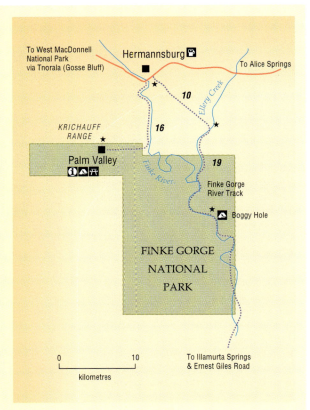

LEGEND

★ 26 ★	
Sealed/Unsealed Rd	
Four Wheel Drive	
Walks	
Rest Area (Picnic Area)	
Caravan Park	
Camping Area	
Accommodation	
Information	
Fuel Supplies	

To West MacDonnell National Park via Tnorala (Gosse Bluff)

Hermannsburg

To Alice Springs

10

16

KRICHAUFF RANGE

Palm Valley

Ellery Creek

Finke River

19

Finke Gorge River Track

Boggy Hole

FINKE GORGE NATIONAL PARK

0 10

kilometres

To Illamurta Springs & Ernest Giles Road

GREGORY NATIONAL PARK

IN BRIEF

MAP REFERENCE: PAGE 250 D 9

Location 175 km southwest of Katherine on the Victoria Highway. Roads may be closed after heavy rain
Best Time May to September
Main Attractions Rugged scenery, history, excellent bushwalks and camping, remote 4WD tracks
Ranger Timber Creek, phone (08) 8975 0888, or Bullita, phone (08) 8975 0833

Several commercial tour operators conduct fishing and crocodile spotting trips on the Victoria River: enquire at Timber Creek, phone (08) 8975 0888, and Victoria River Roadhouse, phone (08) 8975 0744 where fuel and supplies are also available

The Northern Territory's largest waterway, the mighty Victoria River, has, over millions of years, carved into the Top End landscape like a jagged knife, creating majestic cliffs, gorges and towering red escarpments.

Centred around the most scenic of the Victoria River region's natural attractions is the Gregory National Park. Measuring 10 500 square kilometres, this is the Territory's second largest park after Kakadu.

HISTORY

Explorer and surveyor, Augustus Charles Gregory, was the first European to explore the area in detail during his 1855–6 expedition to look for good pastoral land in the region. He, in fact, reported that he had found 'some of the finest grazing lands in Australia', and as a result, through the late 1800s, stock routes and cattle stations began to spring up everywhere around the Victoria River landscape. There are many stories of extreme hardship, of confrontations with local Aborigines, cattle rustling and acts of sheer courage that add to the intrigue and appeal of the area.

WHAT TO SEE

Some of the best gorge and escarpment scenery in the northern section of the park can be found just off the main road near the Victoria River Crossing. The Escarpment Walk, 2 km west of the crossing, and Joes Creek Walk, 10 km west of the crossing, each offer some magnificent cliff, gorge and escarpment views. You should allow one hour return for the Escarpment Walk,

which is an easy to moderate walk. The Joes Creek Walk, with hundreds of tall *Livistona* palms along the way, is particularly appealing. Aboriginal art is also found on cliff faces along the trail. This is an easy to moderate walk, and you should allow 1½ hours for the return.

The Kuwang Lookout, 57 km west of the crossing, is also worth visiting, where a special man-made lookout tower has been erected over-looking the surrounding countryside and Stokes Range. Interpretive information boards have been installed to give an insight into the long Aboriginal association with the area, including Dreamtime legends.

An excellent boat ramp is easily accessible at Big Horse Creek, and for those travellers with a dinghy, the waters here offer great fishing with the prize barramundi being top of the list. A

camping area is located adjacent to the boat ramp, with picnic facilities and pit toilets.

Access further into the park to the old Bullita Homestead, 41 km off the highway (turn off 15 km from Timber Creek), is along a gravel track which, with care, can be covered in a conventional vehicle (caravans are not recommended). Along the way a turn-off to the right (after 33 km) leads to Limestone Gorge—an area of strange, grey dolomite tower karsts and many fine examples of the odd-looking boab trees, whose botanical name, *Adansonia gregorii*, honours Augustus Gregory.

From the car park, a 2 km circuit walk, the Limestone Ridge Trail, leads through limestone outcrops, bloodwood, nutwood and bauhinia trees, hakeas, and flat savannah grasslands—all typical vegetation in this region. This is rated as

The unusual-looking boab tree

an easy walk, and should take about one hour.

The old Bullita Homestead has been restored and opened to visitors. With the help of information boards, you should learn a good deal about the history of the property and the hardships and challenges that faced early settlers in the area. It has been extremely well done.

Camping areas with BBQs and toilets are located at Limestone Gorge and near the Bullita Homestead.

Further into the park is strictly 4WD country. There are 3 old stock routes—Bullita, Humbert and Wickham Tracks (trek notes are available at the beginning of the tracks)—where it is necessary to sign an 'intentions book' detailing your vehicle, occupants and travel plans. You are required also to sign off at the end of the tracks. These old trails are particularly remote and quite rough and challenging in parts. For the adventurous they offer some great 4WD experiences, splendid scenery and lovely, remote camp sites beside rivers and waterholes along the way. There are no facilities at all along any of these 4WD tracks. Make sure you carry enough water, vehicle spares and 2 spare tyres on these tracks.

ACCESS

Gregory, gazetted in 1990, is a park still in the development stage with further trails now being considered. All roads in the area, including the

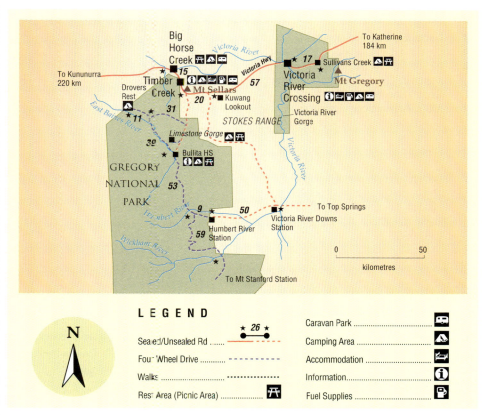

Victoria Highway, may be closed after heavy rains, particularly during the summer wet season, so it would be wise to check with the ranger before setting off on your trip.

The remoteness of Gregory National Park

GURIG NATIONAL PARK & COBOURG MARINE PARK

MAP REFERENCE: PAGE 250 E 2

IN BRIEF

Location 200 km by sea northeast of Darwin, or 570 km by road from Darwin through Arnhem Land. 4WD access only
Best Time May to September
Main Attractions Fishing, beachcombing, remote tropical camping
Ranger Phone (08) 8979 0246

Beach huts: Bookings, Gurig store, phone (08) 8979 0263
Permit required: Contact Gurig Permits Officer, Darwin, phone (08) 8989 3881

When it comes to 'out of the way' parks on the Australian coastline, Gurig is almost as remote as you can get. Accessed through Kakadu and Arnhem Land, the Cobourg Peninsula is found high up in the Northern Territory on a little gnarled finger of land jutting out into the Arafura Sea, some 200 km northeast of Darwin. The peninsula contains the Gurig National Park (220 700 hectares) and the Cobourg Marine Park which is slightly larger.

HISTORY

Home to 4 main Aboriginal clans for thousands of years, the Cobourg Peninsula has been quite used to outside visitors from as far back as the 16th century. Macassans came in from the north fishing, collecting trepang (sea cucumbers, long considered a delicacy in Asia), and searching for pearls. They also collected timber from the area to take back to Macassar. They continued coming into these northern Australian shores until the early 1900s, when the government firstly imposed duties on their harvests and finally in 1906 banned their visits altogether.

LEGEND

Sealed/Unsealed Rd .... ★ 26 ★	Caravan Park ....
Four Wheel Drive .... - - - - -	Camping Area ....
Walks .... • • • • •	Accommodation ....
Rest Area (Picnic Area) .... ⌂	Information ....
	Fuel Supplies ....

A pristine beach on the edge of the Cobourg Marine Park

In the 1800s the British also arrived at Cobourg, with the peninsula named by Lieutenant King in 1818. There then followed the establishment of a defence settlement, Fort Wellington, on the north side of the peninsula, and in 1838 Captain Gordon Bremer was commissioned to set up what was planned to be the first major European settlement in the Northern Territory's Top End. The Victoria Settlement began in an idyllic setting in Port Essington, one of the world's largest natural harbours. Time, however, proved this to be an ill-fated venture by people who were unsuitably prepared for life in such a hot, remote and unforgiving part of the world. The lack of a good fresh water supply, the heat, humidity, plus severe problems with disease and basic supplies, as well as a cyclone that did enormous damage to the fledgling settlement, all contributed to a disastrous venture. The settlement was abandoned in 1849, with 80 people having lost their lives. Some 20 years later the site of present-day Darwin was eventually chosen to replace the settlement.

Today the area is owned by the local Aboriginal people (following a successful land claim lodged in 1976) and is managed by them in conjunction with the Parks and Wildlife Commission of the Northern Territory.

The national park was established in 1981, and to control and protect the local marine life, the Cobourg Marine Park, the Northern Territory's largest aquatic reserve, was established in 1983.

ATTRACTIONS

Gurig's main attractions are its remoteness, its pristine white sandy beaches ideal for beachcombing (where it is likely you'll have entire stretches to yourself), its tropical setting, beautiful sunsets, and, importantly for most who come here, the superb fishing. Many come thousands of kilometres each year simply to fish for mackerel, coral trout, queen fish, snapper and the prize barramundi. Fishing from the beach or off the settlement's long jetty is rewarding, but to enjoy fishing to the full at Cobourg, a small aluminium dinghy would give you access to the nearby coral reefs and offshore islands.

Swimming is not recommended because of marine stingers, stonefish and saltwater crocodiles. Abundant in these waters are the large leatherback and green turtles which come ashore to lay eggs in the sand. Dugongs (sea cows) are also found grazing in the sea. The occasional wide-horned buffalo, Javan rusa deer, Timor pony or Bali cattle can still be seen in nearby bushland.

Using a small boat launched from outside the Ranger Station at Black Point, visitors can reach the site of the old Victoria Settlement, where eerie crumbling ruins of the main buildings and structures still lie in the bush as a melancholy reminder of the settlement's unfortunate past.

ACCESS

The Cobourg Peninsula is 570 km from Darwin, travelling first on the Arnhem Highway through Kakadu National Park to the East Alligator River (304 km). These are good, sealed roads. From here to the park—266 km—a 4WD vehicle is required and you should allow 5 hours. Crossing the East Alligator River at Cahill's Crossing (be aware of tide times) the track passes through picturesque green wetlands and billabongs backed by the huge Arnhem escarpment. The Oenpelli and Murgenella Aboriginal communities are passed along the way, as well as extensive sections of tall kentia and Cobourg Peninsula palms. The road into the park is closed during the wet season.

There is limited access allowed through Arnhem Land into the park (currently only 15 vehicles at any one time) and an access permit from the Parks and Wildlife Commission of the Northern Territory is required. It is advisable to book your time 3 or 4 months ahead, longer if possible, particularly if you want to go during the peak times of June, July or August. A permit will cover the specific days of your visit. Camping fees are applicable.

It is possible to fly in to a local park airstrip or to come by sea (there are safe anchorages available).

CAMPING

The camping area in the park is at Smith Point among tall casuarina trees and tropical vines. These sites are spaced out well apart from each other and are situated 100 metres from the beach. The setting is quite idyllic. There are toilets, BBQs and cold showers—all bush camping, there is no power. Generators are allowed in a special area.

Self-contained beach huts with their own aluminium dinghy and 15 hp motor are also available. Bookings for these are made at the Gurig store.

The small store operates restricted hours and is located at Black Point adjacent to the Ranger Station. Limited basic supplies, water and fuel are available here.

The Cobourg Peninsula is a remote area and travellers should prepare accordingly, bringing all necessary supplies, water, a first aid kit and vehicle spares. No caravans or motor bikes are allowed in the park.

A forest in Gurig National Park

KAKADU NATIONAL PARK

IN BRIEF

MAP REFERENCE: PAGE 250 F 5

Location 147 km southeast of Darwin along the Stuart and Arnhem Highways, and 149 km northeast of Katherine. Some park roads 4WD only
Best Time April to October
Main Attractions Scenic gorges, waterfalls, wetlands, bush-walking, fishing, photography, birdwatching, Aboriginal art, camping
Ranger Headquarters Bowali Visitor Centre, open daily 8 am to 5 pm, P.O. Box 71, Jabiru, NT 0886, phone (08) 8938 1100

Gagudju Cooinda Lodge, phone (08) 8979 0145; motel, camping and caravan facilities, fuel, food and general supplies

Jabiru Tourist Centre, phone (08) 8979 2548 for tours

Kakadu Holiday Village, phone (08) 8979 0166 for tours to all parts of the park

Kakadu National Park is not only Australia's biggest national park measuring almost 20 000 square kilometres, but is unquestionably one of the country's national treasures.

Towering over the park's wetlands is the huge 500 km long Arnhem Land escarpment which was created about 2 billion years ago. Everywhere you look in this ancient landscape you are left with a feeling of majesty and awe. Its natural geological features, including rock formations, huge and powerful waterways, towering cliffs, spectacular waterfalls and quiet, peaceful streams and lagoons, as well as its diverse wildlife, extensive, and in many cases unique, plant life, together with some of the country's best Aboriginal art galleries, all add up to a truly magnificent area.

The value of Kakadu's treasures is also reflected in the park's World Heritage listing. Whilst most other places on this exclusive international register qualify for either their cultural or natural significance, Kakadu was selected for both. Amongst our parks around the country, Kakadu is a jewel in our national crown.

ABORIGINAL HISTORY

A large portion of this magnificent park in the Top End of the Northern Territory is owned by Aboriginal people (the Gagudju Association) who have maintained strong personal and spiritual links with these traditional lands for at least 60 000 years. Current investigations may reveal that this period of Aboriginal occupation could even extend over 100 000 years.

Kakadu's Aboriginal art sites are also of world significance, and Ubirr Rock has been added in its own right to the World Heritage listing for its cultural, anthropological and archaeological value. Ubirr Rock, together with the other significant art sites in the park at Nourlangie, Nanguluwur and Anbangbang, give the whole area an historical aura unmatched anywhere else in the country.

The many art galleries found in the park on cliffs, rock faces and in large natural rock shelters, record Aboriginal history, culture and beliefs. They also record the visits of Macassans who came from the north to fish, gather trepangs and search for pearls. Visits by the Dutch, and later the British, shown with their ships, axes and firearms, all feature in Kakadu's ochre art galleries.

OTHER HISTORY

The East Alligator, South Alligator and West Alligator Rivers were named in 1818 by surveyor Phillip Parker King, who mistook the many crocodiles he saw along the river banks for alligators. The explorer Ludwig Leichhardt, leader of the first land-based expedition to the area, was the first European to stand on the Arnhem Land escarpment. This happened during his epic, 15 month, overland trek from Moreton Bay in Queensland in 1845.

The first stage of Kakadu National Park was proclaimed in 1979, and in 1981 it was World Heritage listed. The park was subsequently extended in various stages and now occupies

The escarpment overlooking Kakadu National Park

19 799 sq km. The park is leased back to the Commonwealth and is managed by a specially selected board of management where the traditional owners are represented.

Within the park boundaries special title exclusions apply to the Ranger, Jabiluka and Koongarra mineral leases.

Today Kakadu is drawing visitors from around Australia and, indeed, from all around the world, at a rate of well over 200 000 people every year, and the number is continually growing. Most come in the Top End's dry season, from April to October, when the climate is almost perfect for exploring and taking in all of the park's attractions. For those few who come during the wet season and are prepared to put up with the heat and humidity, some of the rewards on offer are even more spectacular—the waterfalls are flowing at full strength, the billabongs are full, the area is lush and green everywhere. In contrast, by late in the dry season, much of the bushland is tinder dry and grass fires, lit in the park as part of its management control system, have blackened much of the bushland area. Roads to some of the more remote attractions may, however, be flooded and impassable during the Wet.

Things to Do

Kakadu has some splendid bushwalks leading off from car parks (as well as other cross-country treks) usually incorporating one of the park's many attractions, such as art sites, waterfalls, billabongs, fishing spots, swimming holes, to name a few.

Fishing, birdwatching, photography, exploring and swimming are only some of the activities on offer at Kakadu. This world-class park has something for everyone. To see and enjoy the park properly, allow at least 4 or 5 days (even more, depending on your personal interests). Insect repellent (flies and mosquitoes), a hat and good comfortable walking gear, fishing lines and lures are needed for your camping stay. The following are some of the park's most interesting and scenic areas.

Jabiru

This centre is Kakadu's residential hub. The town, originally built to house workers from the Ranger Uranium Mine, also houses many of those who work in the park. Enquire in the town for permission to look over the mine. Fuel, supplies, a post office, supermarket, a wide range of services and accommodation (including the famous crocodile-shaped hotel, the Gagudju Crocodile Hotel) are all found in the Jabiru township.

Scenic flights over Kakadu can be arranged in Jabiru. They take off from the airport which is 6 km out of town.

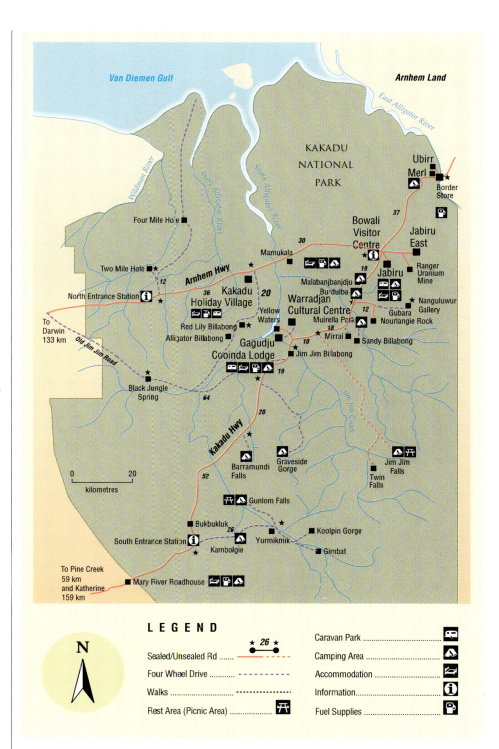

LEGEND

Sealed/Unsealed Rd .... ★ 26 ★

Four Wheel Drive ....

Walks ....

Rest Area (Picnic Area) ....

Caravan Park ....

Camping Area ....

Accommodation ....

Information ....

Fuel Supplies ....

Bowali Visitor Centre and Park Headquarters

Located on the edge of town on the Kakadu Highway, this is certainly worth a visit. Anything you need to know about the park is available: full information, maps, walk trails, road conditions, details of flora and fauna. Morning and afternoon teas and meals are also available. In addition, local souvenirs, Aboriginal art, as well as static and audio-visual displays on the park,

all make this an ideal starting-off place for your Kakadu visit.

Ubirr

3 km north of the Border Store (where fuel and supplies are available) is Ubirr. It is some 40 km from Jabiru and is where the main road crosses the East Alligator River into Arnhem Land, which is accessible only with a permit. Ubirr, reached by sealed road on this side of the river,

KAKADU NATIONAL PARK

is one of the main accessible art sites in the park. A 1 km, easy walking circuit trail leads from the car park. The main art site is also accessible by wheelchair.

There are various art styles here, including the stick-like Mimi figures, some estimated to be up to 20 000 years old, but the more recent, dramatic, X-ray style is the most striking.

Whilst at Ubirr, climb to the top of the rocky escarpment for splendid views out over the Kakadu countryside. You will also get a panoramic vista over the nearby billabongs of the Arnhem wetlands and the huge Arnhem Land escarpment which lies across the East Alligator River. The view from here, particularly around sunset, is quite stunning.

Bardedjilidji

Return to the upstream picnic area near the Border Store where the boat ramps are also located. Here you will find the start of the highly recommended Bardedjilidji Sandstone Walk, which covers 2.5 km. An easy walk, the trail wanders through tall, tropical grasses, amongst oddly shaped sandstone outcrops. You will also encounter tall termite mounds, pandanus, fig and native peach trees,and pass under rocky overhangs, and see some more good examples of Aboriginal art.

Art Sites

Guided walks around most the park's main art sites, some by experienced Aboriginal guides, are held daily—several times a day in the peak winter season. Check the times with the local rangers.

There is an excellent extended bushwalk linking Nourlangie and Nanguluwur art sites. This involves some fairly strenuous climbing, so you need to be quite fit. You should allow between 6 and 8 hours for the return walk. It is important that you sign in with the rangers, and again sign out on your return. A trail map is available from the rangers.

Nourlangie Rock

19 km south of the visitor centre is the Nourlangie Rock, which is an art site of great significance to the traditional owners. The main circuit trail of 1.5 km is a relatively easy stroll of about one hour—most of it is accessible by wheelchair. The main galleries here include some excellent artwork with signboards explaining the figures and the stories behind them. Namarrgon, the Lightning Man, is one of the gallery's most striking figures. Much repainting has taken place both here and at Ubirr, with some of the much older, faded works seen underneath some of the more recent art. Repainting at Aboriginal sites was a traditional practice.

Waterlilies in Kakadu National Park

Nanguluwur Gallery Walk

This easy, 3.4 km return walk—allow 1½–2 hours—through flat, open woodlands is on the western side of Nourlangie Rock and leads to one of the most interesting galleries in Kakadu. Its walls are like pages in a history book illustrating aspects of the lives of Aboriginal people from ancient to modern times. As you stand on the boardwalks here, try to imagine scenes from the lives of the original occupants of the land. In these protected rock shelters evidence of meals of fish, mussels, turtles and wallabies has been found. This was their living room and dining room area.

Jim Jim Falls and Twin Falls

These falls are spectacular in the wet season when water thunders over the top of the Arnhem escarpment and plummets 200 metres to the creek below. Jim Jim is at this time particularly awesome. The pool at the bottom is cold, but ideal to cool off in or to enjoy an invigorating swim. The falls are usually reduced to not much more than a trickle as the dry season progresses. Camping is allowed at Jim Jim where toilets, BBQs and tables are provided. Access to this area is suitable for 4WD vehicles only.

For a great day trip only (no camping), a visit to the nearby Twin Falls is thoroughly recommended. The mostly sandy 10 km track from Jim Jim is slow and winding and will take about one hour in a 4WD vehicle. On reaching the end of the trail at one of the creek's white sandy beaches, it's then into the water—take your inflatable mattress for a great paddle (about 1 km) towards the falls. Look up at the rock faces as you slowly make your way upstream. There are a few rocks to cross over before you reach a lovely sandy beach and the huge, clear, natural splash pool at the foot of the falls.

Yellow Waters

Located virtually in the centre of the park, Yellow Waters is a magnificent billabong on the South Alligator River. A boardwalk extending several hundred metres along the edge of this picturesque waterway is a must for bird-watchers, with a wide variety of waterbirds always in the area. Boat cruises on this beautiful stretch of water, especially for early morning sunrise and late afternoon sunset, are always popular. Fishing for prize barramundi and crocodile spotting are also highlights of time spent at Yellow Waters.

Camping is not allowed here, but just 1 km away is the Gagudju Cooinda Lodge which has motel, caravan and camping facilities, as well as food, general supplies and fuel.

Also located here is the recently opened Warradjan Aboriginal Cultural Centre. This excellent centre gives a good insight into local Aboriginal culture with artefacts and locally produced works of art, including bark paintings, available for sale.

Barramundi Falls (Maguk)

Further south in the park, Barramundi Falls are the next worthwhile stopping-off point. The 4WD track leads 12 km to a small waterfall which tumbles down through the sandstone escarpment into a large, clear pool at the bottom. There are some beautiful swimming spots with sandy beaches along the walking trail to the falls.

Gunlom Falls

Previously known as the UDP Falls, the Gunlom Falls are in the southern section of the park, 37 km off the main Kakadu Highway. The conventional vehicle access road leads to a pretty grassed picnic area with the falls and its large, sandy-bottomed, plunge pool only around

100 metres away. The walk trail to the falls is suitable for wheelchair access. This is a particularly appealing picnic and swimming spot (great also for children) with several different walk trails. When the Gunlom Falls are in flood it is, indeed, a splendid sight.

Fully recommended for those of reasonable fitness is a walk and climb trail to the top of the falls. Allow ½ hour to reach the top. Here there are several small, appealing, rockpools in which to cool off. You can take in the sweeping view from the escarpment, out over the Kakadu countryside, and more immediately, down to the large pandanus-lined splash pool at the foot of the falls. Ludwig Leichhardt is reported to have stood at this very spot during his epic overland journey in 1845.

WILDLIFE

Wallabies, euros, wild black pigs, and even the occasional wild Timor pony are found in the park, as are crocodiles.

Many varieties of large waterbirds, including egrets and jabirus, brolgas, as well as many grass and bushland species of birds, are found in Kakadu. A total of over 300 species of birds has been recorded.

PARK ACCESS

From Darwin go south along the Stuart Highway for 40 km, then turn east onto the Arnhem Highway for a further 107 km to the western park boundary. Soon after entering the park the road leads to the park entrance station manned by national park rangers. An entry fee applies and your permit is valid for 14 days (or multiple entries to the park within the 14 day period).

When coming from the south, turn off the Stuart Highway 90 km north of Katherine at Pine Creek. It is then 59 km to the park boundary. 6 km into the park you reach the southern entrance station where you can obtain your 14 day permit, maps and information notes on the park.

Both of the access routes are good, sealed, all-year-round roads which will only be closed in the most extreme weather conditions. Throughout the park there are a number of other places of interest not detailed here, including Red Lily, Alligator and Sandy Billabongs, Two Mile and Four Mile Holes (all great fishing spots, particularly for barramundi), Graveside Gorge, Koolpin Gorge and Gimbat. Check with the rangers on road conditions— some are 4WD access only. The track between Red Lily and Alligator Billabongs has occasionally been totally washed away.

CAMPING

Kakadu offers some really superb camping experiences—often near waterfalls, billabongs, or with rocky escarpment outlooks. They range from caravan parks (including those at Jabiru, Kakadu Holiday Village and Cooinda), to several formal camping areas also quite suitable for caravans at Merl (near Ubirr), Muirella Park (between Jabiru and Yellow Waters), Mardugal (near Yellow Waters) and at Gunlom Falls. These areas are all equipped with showers, flushing toilets and water, and have facilities for the disabled. A camping fee is charged at these spots. A free camping area with pit toilets only, and quite suitable for caravans, is Malabanjbanjdju (13 km south of Jabiru).

Throughout the park there are a number of other, less developed, tent camping areas, most with toilets, BBQs, but not showers. There are some in more remote locations with no facilities at all. Your park permit allows you to camp in these less developed areas at no extra charge.

In addition to camp sites there are day picnic areas located near many of the main attractions throughout the park, most with BBQs, tables and chairs.

Hotel or motel accommodation is available at Jabiru, Cooinda and at the Kakadu Holiday Village near the South Alligator River.

Warning

Dangerous estuarine (saltwater 'salty') crocodiles inhabit a number of the Kakadu waterways. Do not go into, and be very careful near, the water in these areas—look out for the crocodile warning signs. Many of the popular swimming holes are safe, but if in doubt, check with the local rangers.

The Ubirr escarpment

KEEP RIVER NATIONAL PARK

MAP REFERENCE: PAGE 250 A 10

Location 48 km east of Kununurra and 190 km west of Timber Creek off the Victoria Highway. Park entry is 3 km inside the Northern Territory border
Best Time May to September
Main Attractions Scenery, birdlife, photography, bush-walking, Aboriginal art, camping
Ranger Phone (08) 9167 8827

The nearest supplies of food, fuel and general requirements are at Kununurra. Visitors are advised to call into the ranger station on the way into the park for information on walk trails, camping and Aboriginal art sites.

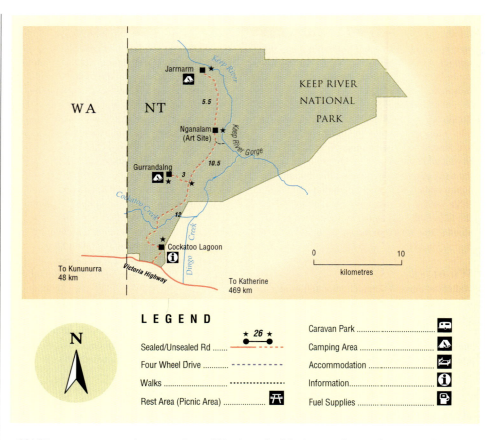

LEGEND

Sealed/Unsealed Rd .... ★ 26 ★
Four Wheel Drive .... – – – – – – – –
Walks .... ••••••••••••••
Rest Area (Picnic Area) .... 🎋

Caravan Park ....
Camping Area ....
Accommodation ....
Information...........................
Fuel Supplies ....

Carved out of ancient limestone, the striking land forms of this quite isolated park are like scenes from a forgotten world. All around the park is evidence of a time when this area was subject to volcanic and glacial activity, geological events that have left strange rock shapes, forms and colours everywhere.

The Keep River region, on the Western Australia/Northern Territory border, is part of the traditional land of the Mirriwung and Gadjerong Aboriginal people whose ancestors have lived here for at least 25 000 years. Evidence of this early occupation can be found in the many rock art and camping sites, shell middens and special ceremonial ritual and initiation sites scattered throughout the park. Within the park boundaries there are still several Aboriginal communities living close to their traditional way of life.

In the days of early European settlement over 100 years ago, the large Auvergne cattle station covered this part of Australia, and the waterholes we see today were used to water cattle along the old Auvergne Stock Route leading to the port of Wyndham.

Today, Keep River National Park is a scenic delight with bushwalking, Aboriginal art, nature and photography amongst its many attractions.

SPECTACULAR SCENERY

The scenery is rugged and spectacular, consisting of features like towering limestone cliffs, natural rock archways, caves, gorges and balancing rocks. Tall bamboo grass, screw palms (*Pandanus* spp.), turkey bush, kapok trees, the beautiful Kimberley rose, desert grevilleas and

wild hibiscus are seen growing everywhere. Old boab trees, completely bare of leaves in the winter, stand like sentinels throughout the park, and tall *Livistona* palms can be seen in deep valleys and clinging to cracks and crevices high on cliff faces.

Cockatoo Lagoon, a permanent waterhole in Keep River National Park

WILDLIFE

In the Cockatoo Wetlands area, soon after entering the park, a walk trail leads to Cockatoo Lagoon and a bird hide in the framework of an old windmill, where visitors can observe a large variety of birds at this permanent waterhole. Over 100 different species have been recorded in the park.

Other wildlife here include rock wallabies, kangaroos, dingoes, as well as a variety of lizards and snakes. At Policeman's Waterhole (a regular resting spot for early police patrols through the region), a saltwater crocodile has made its home. You can try fishing for barramundi in this waterway. Swimming is NOT one of the park's attractions.

ABORIGINAL ART

The major Aboriginal art site is at Cockatoo Dreaming (Nganalam) and is easily accessible (including wheelchair access). Paintings here depict a history of Aboriginal life and include a variety of hand stencils and renditions of animals, serpents, boomerangs, spears and other weapons. Under a large rock overhang, two giant human-like Mirriwung figures in red ochre look down from the rock shelter ceiling. It is also possible to see grooves in the rocks in which Aboriginal artists mixed their ochre paints.

This is an extensive art site containing some 2500 paintings and petroglyphs (engravings), some dating back at least 5000 years. There are a number of smaller art sites to be found throughout the park.

Visitors are asked not to venture into several sacred sites in the park which are fenced off and specially signposted—a fine of up to $20 000 applies to offenders.

CAMPING AND ACCESS

The park, measuring some 700 sq km, was opened in 1985. There are 2 main camping areas (no power) and both have pit toilets, BBQs and picnic tables.

Access to the park and to the 2 camping areas is by a good gravel road quite suitable for conventional vehicles and caravans. Drinking water is available only at one location near the ranger station.

THE WALKS ARE A PHOTOGRAPHER'S DREAM

From each of these camp sites there are walks leading out into the park. The Gurrandalng Walk (1.5 km easy walking with some climbing—allow 1½ hours to look around) and the Nigli Gap Walk (6 km return which is flat, easy walking—allow 2–3 hours to look around) are particularly appealing both in the late afternoon and early morning when the sun brings out the

Nigli Gap in Keep River National Park

deep colours in the many cliffs, gorges and valleys. Strange rock formations in the shape of animal and human heads, castle turrets, lost Aztec-like cities and beehive shapes, similar to the famous Bungle Bungles, can be seen along these trails.

Other walks take visitors through the 4 km long Keep River Gorge and to Policeman's Waterhole (5 km return). Further walking trails are being developed.

OTHER INFORMATION

Bring insect repellent, a hat and good walking shoes.

Although more spectacular during the wet season with flowing creeks, waterfalls and lush green countryside, the area is only accessible during the Dry, when conditions are cooler and less humid.

Keep River National Park is a must for anyone travelling across northern Australia.

LITCHFIELD NATIONAL PARK

IN BRIEF

MAP REFERENCE: PAGE 250 D 5

Location 130 km from Darwin, about 2 hours drive, via Batchelor

Best Time April to October

Main Attractions Tropical wilderness, waterfalls, bushwalks, natural mountain swimming pools, Lost City, large termite mounds, camping

Ranger At Northern Territory Parks & Wildlife Commission, Batchelor, phone (08) 8976 0282

LEGEND

Sealed/Unsealed Rd .... ★ 26 ★

Four Wheel Drive ....

Walks ....

Rest Area (Picnic Area) ....

Caravan Park ....

Camping Area ....

Accommodation ....

Information ....

Fuel Supplies ....

Situated in the Top End of the Northern Territory, Litchfield National Park is claimed by many to be to Darwin what the Blue Mountains are to Sydney, or the Dandenongs to Melbourne. These days, however, Darwinites are having to share more and more this extremely appealing area with southerners and overseas tourists who are making their way there in their thousands. The word is coming back that Litchfield's got the lot, and it's hard to argue against that.

The Finniss Expedition was, in 1864, the first European group to explore this northern Australian region. When a small party led by Fred Litchfield crossed the Tabletop Range, they found beauty and, more importantly to them at the time, settlement prospects for the region. Litchfield himself later returned to settle here, and his descendants still live in the area.

The Tabletop Range area, some 100 km directly south of Darwin, is a tropical wilderness, and until the mid-1980s there was rough access only into what has now been unveiled to

A cycad growing in Litchfield National Park

visitors in their thousands as some of the most spectacular and diverse landscape anywhere. Dry woodlands and forests dominate the huge sandstone plateau which forms the range. Closer to the escarpment, springs give rise to creeks which channel their way into the plateau surface. Where only bare rock remains, the creeks tumble over rapids and swirl through rock pools to descend finally as cascading waterfalls into the deep pools and rainforest valleys below.

Wallabies and brush-tailed possums, along with with blue-winged kookaburras and red-tailed black cockatoos are seen regularly.

ACCESS

Initially only 4WD access was possible into some of the area's attractions, but today, most of the main sections of the park can be reached by sealed road. It is an easy 2 hour drive of 130 km from Darwin, via the green tropical township of Batchelor. There is also a northern park entry via the Cox Peninsula Road, but most of this is gravel road and is a less popular route. These access roads are suitable for all vehicles; however, the rising waters of the Reynolds and Finniss Rivers may cause road closures for short periods during the wet season, which usually lasts from November or December to late March or early April. A rough 4WD track leads from the bottom of the park to the Daly River Road.

CAMPING

Within this 143 000 hectare national park there are 3 main camping areas with BBQs and toilet facilities. These are at Wangi, Florence Falls and Buley Rockholes. There are several other bush camping areas throughout the park. Campers should be fully self-sufficient with adequate food, water, fuel and other requirements. The nearest fuel and supplies are at Batchelor, 24 km from the northeastern park boundary. A small camping fee applies at the main camping areas.

Access for caravans is quite suitable to the 3 main camping areas, but is not advisable for the others.

Some visitors try to see Litchfield in a day, but generally find it is far too rushed. A 2–3 day time period is ideal. Although the park is quite small compared to many other national parks, its numerous features are spread out. It is best to make a base and travel out from there.

WATERFALLS

Litchfield features some magnificent waterfalls, the most spectacular of these being the Wangi, Florence, Tjaynera and Tolmer Falls. Each of these falls is quite different, and depending on the volume of water flowing over, they can be even majestic.

Buley Rockholes are ideal for those wishing to cool off shortly after entering the park. In a series of small, picturesque pools fed by fresh, clean, mountain water cascading from one pool to another down the hillside, this is a spot where you can spend hours without any trouble at all.

Wangi Falls is also a favourite of many visitors as it allows camping within a 100 metre stroll of a lovely, sandy pool set at the foot of the falls. Litchfield has many quite large swimming holes, and Wangi is one of the best.

BUSHWALKS

One of the most popular activities in the park is bushwalking through a wide range of escarpment trails, through tropical rainforest, open savannah grass plains and around numerous water-lily covered billabongs.

These walks range from flat and easy to some quite strenuous trails which often lead to crystal clear pools in which to cool off, refresh, and relax.

At Wangi there is a well-marked walk trail up into the escarpment to the top of the falls. Here, with the assistance in some parts of wooden steps and boardwalks, the trail passes small pools at the top of the falls, through heavy monsoon forest where moist humid conditions are ideal for small, delicate ferns, pandanus and a variety of other palms. The trail, quite steep in parts, winds up one side of the falls, across a bridge at the top, and then down the other side, returning to the main swimming splash pool at the bottom. You should allow ½ hour to the top, a little less coming down.

TERMITE MOUNDS

Another splendid feature in the park is the large termite mounds—some of the best examples of magnetic mounds you will see in the Top End of Australia. These intriguing wedge-shaped mounds dot the landscape like headstones and make the treeless, black soil plains look like a bush cemetery. The mounds, it is believed, face north–south as a temperature control mechanism, with only the thinnest part of the mound exposed to the sun during the hottest time of the day.

Rangers have built a boardwalk-viewing platform and information shelter at the main magnetic termite area. As well as the display boards which give visitors an insight into these tiny, but prolific, builders, rangers also regularly conduct talks here, at the centre, for those interested in hearing more about the mounds and the life and habits of their builders.

OLD HOMESTEAD

Evidence of early pastoralist activity is found at the historic remains of the old Blyth Homestead, which gives a vivid picture of the harsh, isolated and primitive conditions endured by early settlers. It was built by the Sargent family in 1929.

THE LOST CITY

Located 10.5 km along a bush track leading off the main road in the centre of the park, the Lost City is a quite spectacular collection of free-standing sandstone formations which seem to suddenly spring out of an otherwise quite flat countryside. Walking through these unusual towers it is easy to see how they resemble the ruined remains of a city built of stone, many centuries ago. The formations take on an eerie mood in early morning and late afternoon light.

The track into the Lost City is a fairly narrow, single lane trail, the first 8.5 km of which could, in the dry season, be negotiated by a conventional vehicle with high clearance. From there the final 2 km to the end of the trail is most definitely a 4WD high clearance vehicle track only. Many drive to where the track gets rough and then walk the final 2 km—this would take about ½ hour. The effort is worth it; this is one of the hidden 'gems' of Litchfield.

Linking the old Blyth Homestead and the Lost City is a very rough, unmaintained 4WD-only track that has become quite dangerous. Do not attempt to use this trail without checking with the ranger first.

Wangi Falls and its beautiful waterho e

NITMILUK (KATHERINE GORGE) NATIONAL PARK

IN BRIEF

MAP REFERENCE: PAGE 250 F 7

Location Katherine Gorge is 30 km east of Katherine; Edith Falls is 62 km northeast of Katherine, via sealed roads
Best Time April to September
Main Attractions Gorges, waterfalls, scenery, swimming, canoeing, bushwalking, photography
Ranger Katherine Gorge, phone (08) 8972 1886, Edith Falls, phone (08) 8975 4852

Canoes and camping gear hire, phone (08) 8972 3604
Travel North Caravan Park, phone (08) 8972 1253

The Katherine Region of the Northern Territory extends from the Gulf of Carpentaria to the Kimberley. It is known as 'Never Never' country, following the publication of Jeannie Gunn's book, *We of the Never Never*, which described her time in this region in the early 1900s.

The town of Katherine, on the banks of the Katherine River, is the Territory's third largest centre and much of its growth over the years is thanks to its proximity to the spectacular scenic attraction of Katherine Gorge, just 30 km away. Now set within Nitmiluk National Park, Katherine Gorge, with its high cliffs of grey and orange sandstone towering over deep waterholes and lush pockets of rainforest, is one of the Territory's major natural attractions.

Much of the area included within the park boundary is the traditional home of the Jawoyn Aboriginal people. The area abounds with Dreamtime stories and legends. One of these tells of Nabilil, a dragon-like figure, who travelled across the country carrying water and firesticks under his arm. This somewhat evil figure, who named the gorge Nitmiluk, was eventually killed as he travelled through it, and the water he carried was spilt, forming the Katherine River, thus giving life to the birds and animals which continue to thrive in the area today.

NITMILUK—THE PARK

The park areas owned today by the local Jawoyn people have been leased back to the Northern Territory Government to be managed under a board of management by the Parks and Wildlife Commission. Nitmiluk National Park—180 352 hectares—has 2 main sections: the Katherine Gorges section in the south, and the Edith Falls section in the northwest. Both have sealed road access all year round.

Wildlife in the park include blue-winged kookaburras (kingfishers), butcherbirds and bowerbirds, wallabies, kangaroos, bandicoots and freshwater crocodiles. The vegetation, particularly around waterways, is dense and tropical, with ferns, figs, paperbarks and pandanus seen along the banks.

Barramundi fishing is popular in the Katherine River.

Water is available at both main park centres.

THE GORGES

In the Gorges Sector there is not just one, but 13 spectacular gorges formed by the Katherine River cutting its way approximately 12 km through the Arnhem Land plateau. Many believe the best way to see these quite awesome gorges, with their cliff faces towering in some sections 100 metres above the water, is from a boat or canoe on the river.

From the Water

Tour boat cruises operate from a base at the entrance to the gorge, where canoes are also available for hire. If you have limited time, join a boat tour (ranging from one hour to a full day) which will take you through 1, 3, up to 5, of the lower gorges. These tours are a lot of fun and often include time for a swim along the way.

If you can spare the time, however, and you enjoy canoeing, then this is a canoeist's paradise. Launching areas are available at the entrance to the gorges and, with special ranger permission, it is possible to undertake extended canoeing trips and camp out in designated areas in the 5th, 6th and 9th gorges well upstream. Bring your own canoe, or hire one, but either way a permit must be obtained from the ranger as authorities are keen to control activity in the gorges and currently limit the number of permits to 40 on any one day.

Canoes and tour boats are restricted during the wet season when the river is subject to flooding and becomes dangerous.

During the dry season, rocky outcrops separate the waterways between gorges. If travelling by tour boat it is simply a matter of getting out of one boat and making your way on a walkway 50 metres or so over the rocks into another boat waiting on the other side. Canoeists or kayakers will need to carry their craft over the rocks at the end of each gorge section.

Private powerboats are not allowed from 1 June to 31 August.

Bushwalking

Bushwalking here at Nitmiluk is another very popular activity, with both short and long walks available. To gain an immediate feeling for the grandeur of Katherine Gorge, on arrival take a short, relatively easy, walk along the river bank and up onto the escarpment to a gorge lookout

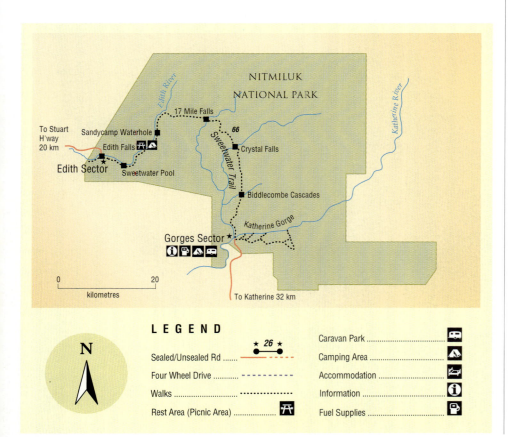

To Stuart H'way 20 km

NITMILUK NATIONAL PARK

Edith River
17 Mile Falls
Sandycamp Waterhole
Edith Falls
Edith Sector
Sweetwater Pool
Sweetwater Trail
66
Crystal Falls
Biddlecombe Cascades
Katherine Gorge
Katherine River
Gorges Sector
To Katherine 32 km

0   kilometres   20

LEGEND

★ 26 ★

Sealed/Unsealed Rd
Four Wheel Drive
Walks
Rest Area (Picnic Area)

Caravan Park
Camping Area
Accommodation
Information
Fuel Supplies

N

(approximately 1.5 km each way—allow one hour return). This splendid vantage point looks out over the Katherine River and valley up towards the lower gorge. It gives visitors an opportunity to gauge the magnitude of what lies ahead of them.

Other walks along the river or, for the more energetic, up and along the gorge escarpment, are very scenic. Make sure you take a camera along and plenty of film. In all there are 10 organised and marked walk trails (most requiring quite good levels of fitness) extending from 1.5 km to 66 km each way (1 hour to 5 day treks). The longer trails mean you will need to camp along the way. Camping gear is available for hire and camping permits are obtained from the Park Visitor Centre. Guided walking tours and walking trail maps are also available. Look out for some well preserved Aboriginal art sites along many of the trails.

From the Air

Another option to see the gorge is by helicopter—an exhilarating ride through the gorge system. Flights, from 15 minutes to 30 minutes, are available throughout the year.

Camping and Other Information

The main camping area at Katherine Gorge is at the Travel North Caravan Park. This caravan park offers a full range of facilities, including powered or unpowered sites, and a kiosk for food, drink, supplies and fuel.

There is a swimming area adjacent to the picnic grounds.

Ranger slide shows are held at the Visitor Centre daily at 7.30 pm during peak season.

EDITH FALLS SECTOR (LELIYN)

This delightful area of Nitmiluk National Park is accessed via the Stuart Highway north of Katherine (42 km). Turn off to the east, then travel a further 20 km, all on sealed road, to the car park and camping area.

Walking Trails

From the car park you can take a short walk of around 100 metres through tall shady trees. This will bring you to the edge of a large, open pool fringed with eucalyptus and pandanus palms. The lower section of a series of permanently flowing waterfalls spills into the far side of the pool. This is an ideal swimming hole.

A scenic 2.6 km Leliyn Loop walk and climb trail (moderate fitness level required—allow 1½ hours return) leads from here to the top of the escarpment on one side of the falls, across the stream by a bridge at the top, and down the other side. The trail takes in a series of small cascades some delightful crystal clear pools and the Upper Edith Falls which are bigger than

Nitmiluk from the air

those seen below. These upper pools are ideal places to cool off along the way. There are several splendid lookouts, including the panoramic Bemang Lookout which provides good views of the falls, pools and surrounding countryside. In the Wet Edith Falls are among the most spectacular to be found anywhere.

An additional walk (for those who are reasonably fit) can be undertaken from the top and leads another 3 km upstream to Sweetwater Pool (allow 3–4 hours return).

For the real walking enthusiast the Sweetwater Trail is really only the beginning (or end) of a trail approximately 66 km long that links the Katherine Gorge Sector with Edith Falls. Walking the Sweetwater Trail, and the 5 days camping trail, must be organised with the ranger—some hard walking and climbing, together with spectacular scenery, will be experienced on this trek.

Camping

The Edith Falls camping area has toilets, cold showers, BBQs, tables and shady picnic area, but no power. Generators are allowed. A kiosk is located on site.

Katherine Gorge from the water

ULURU–KATA TJUTA NATIONAL PARK

Uluru (Ayers Rock) and Kata Tjuta (the Olgas) stand as symbols of mystery and mystique in the heart of the Australian continent. Revered by both the Aboriginal culture and the European Australian culture, these massive protrusions of sedimentary rock serve as totemic symbols.

Around 600 million years ago the movements of plates in the earth's crust forced the layers of conglomerate into a mountain-building event. Since then extreme weathering, firstly through the presence of an inland sea and a wetter climate, and secondly by the sun, wind and less frequently rain, has taken place. At one stage the level of the surface around Uluru was 90 metres below the present-day level. Then some slight warping in the earth's crust took place to bring the desert sands to their present-day levels.

Uluru stands some 340 metres above the surface of the plain while Kata Tjuta rises to 600 metres. Both these land forms are remnants of a landscape more than 100 million years old and their uppermost levels were part of a much more extensive land surface. It is believed that the 36 individual domes of Kata Tjuta may once have been a single dome many times the size of Uluru. The weathering continues today as shown by the 'flaking' or exfoliation of Uluru, where, due to expansion and contraction of the rock, parts fall down to the plain below where they disintegrate.

ABORIGINAL SIGNIFCANCE AND MODERN HISTORY

The evidence presented by archaeologists suggests that the Aboriginal people of this part of Australia have lived here for at least 22 000 years. Aboriginal people know that the landscape of Central Australia has been part of their culture since the beginning.

The Aboriginal people of this area call themselves by the collective name of Anangu ('we

The thorny devil, also known as a moloch

people'). The Anangu are made up of 3 main groups: the Yankunyjatjara, the Pitjantjatjara and the Ngaanyatjara. The network of language, kin and religious inter-relationships which unite the Anangu extends over a large territory. This network ties the traditional owners of Uluru in with places as far afield as Kings Canyon, Papunya, Port Hedland, Kalgoorlie, Ceduna, Yalata, Maralinga and Alice Springs. Fundamental to the Anangu way of life is the Tjukurpa which provides the explanations for the origins of life, of all living things, and of the features of the land. The Tjukurpa is Aboriginal law and only available to those who are initiated into the law.

The first European explorer to this area was Ernest Giles, who in 1872 registered the name of Mt Olga for the Aboriginal site of Kata Tjuta. Olga was the queen of Würtemberg in Europe. Then came W.E. Gosse who, in 1873, gave the monolith its English name in honour of the then Chief Secretary of South Australia.

Over the next 50 years there was very little intrusion into this southwest corner of Central Australia by Europeans. During the early 1930s pastoral activity commenced. Mining exploration took hold in the wake of Harold Lasseter's fabled reef of gold. Even before roads existed in this part of the world Michael Terry travelled here by an early version of a 4WD vehicle.

Needless to say, when the Anangu encountered the intruders on their land, the interaction between them and the Piranypa' (the term the Anangu used for all non-Aborigines) became more frequent and more violent. The Anangu continued to lead their natural nomadic life.

LEGEND

Sealed/Unsealed Rd .... ⋆ 26 ⋆

Four Wheel Drive ....

Walks ....

Rest Area (Picnic Area) .... 🏕

Caravan Park .... 🚐

Camping Area .... ⛺

Accommodation .... 🛏

Information .... ℹ

Fuel Supplies .... ⛽

Uluru, the world's most famous monolith (facing page)

ULURU–KATA TJUTA NATIONAL PARK

Uluru rising out of the plain

ACCESS

All major airlines in Australia offer either direct or connecting flights to Connellan Airport at Ayers Rock Resort, the town that services the national park. The longest flying time from the most distant capital city, Brisbane, is 4½ hours.

It is 465 km from Alice Springs by car along the sealed Stuart and Lasseter Highways and all the roads within the park are sealed. Access from Alice Springs via Larapinta Drive and the Mereenie Loop Road is open to conventional vehicles. Approximately 200 km of this road is an unsealed formed gravel road and careful driving techniques are advised. 4WD access to Uluru may be enjoyed by taking a journey down the bed of the Finke River from Hermannsburg in the dry season.

However, government borders crisscrossed their land, making life very difficult for them when they had to deal with different governments and differing policies.

Tourism to this part of Australia started in the late 1940s and by the mid-1970s over 50 000 visitors a year were tramping over and around Uluru. Sites of religious significance were being desecrated by uninformed and unthinking visitors which distressed the Anangu immensely. In 1976 the Northern Territory Land Rights Act came into being and the Anangu commenced a claim for Uluru–Kata Tjuta to protect their traditional lands. This legal battle took 9 years and on 26 October 1985 the Anangu and the Uluru–Kata Tjuta Land Trust accepted freehold title to their lands. Immediately thereafter an area encompassing Uluru and Kata Tjuta was leased back to the Commonwealth Government as a national park. The park is managed on a co-operative basis by the Australian Nature Conservation Agency and the traditional owners through the Uluru Board of Management on which the traditional owners have a majority representation.

ECOLOGICAL VALUES

Plants and animals evolve as a result of their environment, with many factors, such as soil types, the influence of fire, the abundance or lack of water, and how organisms interact with one another, playing a part. Traditional knowledge enabled the Aboriginal people to harvest efficiently an enormous range of natural resources which sustained them throughout the ages. Today the Anangu are still passing on their knowledge to the next generation, and, in a more limited way, teaching visitors to Uluru–Kata Tjuta National Park to understand and appreciate their way of life.

In the years since the national park was established, over 400 species of plant life, 22 species of mammals, 150 different bird groups and many reptiles and frogs have been recorded. Visitors are likely to see only a fraction of these. Those, however, who take the time to walk the various tracks that have been provided for visitor enjoyment will be rewarded by seeing how arid land flora and fauna survive.

In 1987 Uluru–Kata Tjuta National Park was inscribed on the World Heritage List by the United Nations. It is also one of 12 Australian Biosphere Reserves.

ABORIGINAL MYTHOLOGY

At the time of the Creation when ancestral beings performed deeds, a big, flat, sand hill turned to stone and became Uluru. The Kuniya, the carpet snake people, camped here by the base of the rock.

One day the Liru, the venomous snake men, attacked the camp of the Kuniya. A powerful woman, Pulari, wishing to protect her newborn child, spat out the essence of death and killed many Liru. Kulikudgeri, the fierce warrior of the Liru, slew a young warrior, but the mother of the young warrior struck Kulikudgeri on the nose with a digging stick and he ended up dying in agony.

Many of the geographic features of Uluru now mark these ancient beliefs and may be seen by the visitor whilst walking along the circular path around Uluru. These features are Ngaltawadi—the Digging Stick, Tapudji—Little Uluru, Mutidjula—Maggie Springs, Putta—Marsupial Pouch, Djudajabbi—Cave of the Women, the Sound Shell—Mala people.

Kata Tjuta (the Olgas), is the home of Wanambi, the mythical snake with long teeth, a mane and a long beard.

The Kangaroo Tail, a rock feature on the side of Uluru

ACCOMMODATION

There are no accommodation or camping facilities within the national park. The township of Ayers Rock Resort (formerly Yulara) was built in the early 1980s to service the needs of the tourist industry to Uluru. Today it supports a workforce of over 2000, with visitor numbers reaching another 1000 at any given time. Five establishments provide services from luxury accommodation through to budget rooms, with a total of 750 rooms available. A further 224 beds are provided in dormitory-style accommodation. An established camping ground within the resort has 204 caravan sites 500 tent sites, 20 coach sites and 14 air-conditioned log cabins.

There are 12 restaurants and eating establishments, 4 bars, a take-away bottle shop and an entertainment centre.

The Visitor Centre within the confines of the resort has an informative display and museum of Aboriginal culture and local geology, plant and animal life. Tour bookings, information, videos to watch or buy and a wide range of books and souvenirs are also available. Close by is the Shopping Square. Here you will find a variety of shops including a bank, newsagency, post office, travel agency, gift shop, photo supplies and a supermarket with fresh food. On the side of the Square is a cafe which is open from early till late and a bakery which is open during daylight hours.

THINGS TO DO

Do not try to see everything on your first day. There is too much to take in and a leisurely time spent in this national park is well worth the effort.

Climbing Uluru

For safety and cultural reasons the Anangu prefer that visitors do not climb the rock. However, visitors who do decide to climb should remember that very hot conditions can lead to heat stress or even death. On an extended walk carry 1 litre of water with you for every hour of walking. You should only climb along the route that has the safety chain. The climb is 1.6 km return and should take about 2 hours. If you are suffering from a heart condition, breathing difficulties or vertigo, do not attempt the climb.

Walking Tracks

There is a walk around the base of the rock, the Uluru Circuit Walk, which is 9 km long and should take around 4 hours.

Liru Walk goes from the main car park to the Ranger Station, National Park Visitor Centre and Maruku Arts and Crafts. This is a distance of 2 km and should take about ½ hour one way.

The Kata Tjuta Valley of the Winds Walk is 6 km. Allow 3 hours return.

Olga Gorge Walk is shorter about 2 km and one hour return.

Bookings and information on guided walks are available at the Ranger Station.

There are many tours departing from Ayers Rock Resort including Aboriginal culture, helicopter and plane flights, motorcycle tours and nature-based tours. There are also full day, extended and specialist charter tours available. For more information contact the Visitor Centre at Ayers Rock Resort.

There are more than 50 tour operators conducting business out of Alice Springs so you should find something to suit you. Those visitors who only want a short stay at Ayers Rock Resort may choose from day and overnight tours from Alice Springs to Ayers Rock Resort and Uluru–Kata Tjuta National Park.

It is important to note that Uluru and Kata Tjuta are areas of special significance to Aboriginal people and, as sacred sites, consist of women's places and men's places. These sites are cared for by members of the appropriate gender who extend privileges to the other sex. However, some of the sites are

Among the boulders at Kata Tjuta

'too strong' in religious terms and mixed visits are totally forbidden according to Tjukurpa Law. When walking around the base of Uluru the visitor will see signs which clearly mark where access is closed to the public.

While the opportunity for photography is great especially at sunrise and at sunset, the Anangu do not like to be photographed. They ask that the visitor respect their culture and do not film them or take photographs of their important spiritual areas. If in doubt, you may obtain guidelines from any of the visitor centres or hotel reception areas.

WATARRKA (KINGS CANYON) NATIONAL PARK

MAP REFERENCE: PAGE 254 E 7

IN BRIEF

Location 302 km southwest of Alice Springs along the sealed Stuart Highway and the unsealed Ernest Giles Highway

Best Time Between April and November

Main Attractions Scenic landscape, diverse fauna and flora, Aboriginal culture, walking trails, camping

Ranger Visitor Information Centre, cnr Gregory Terrace and Hartley Streets, Alice Springs, phone (08) 8952 5800

Kings Canyon Resort, phone (08) 8956 7442

Tours operate from Alice Springs; for more details contact the Visitor Information Centre in Alice Springs, phone (08) 8952 5800

The geological features of Kings Canyon are like no other in the Northern Territory. Set in the George Gill Range and forming part of the Watarrka National Park, this geological masterpiece evolved over millions of years. Jointing caused fractures within the sandstone layers of the George Gill Range and Kings Canyon was created. As the sandstone cracked and fractured large boulders were left on the surface while some fell into the newly formed ravines. The rectangular-shaped boulders on the surface eventually weathered to become 'beehive-like' domes. These sandstone structures are now called the Lost City. In the bottom of the ravines fractured boulders still remain where they help preserve water levels in times of drought.

The upheaval of the landscape has left a valley with vertical sandstone cliffs. The porous sandstone collects water like a sponge during rain periods and slowly filters it through to the base of the ravine where the moist crevices act as a refuge for many plants and animals. When it does rain the desert blooms and over 600 plant species, of which more than 60 are rare or relicts from a bygone era, use the retained moisture from the canyon floor to survive.

Reptiles are a common feature in this park, and 64 varieties from the mighty desert perentie to the smallest skink have been recorded. Yabbies and other forms of acuatic life are found in the waterholes, while bird life is prolific.

HISTORY

The Luritja group of Aboriginal people are believed to have had ancestral connections with this part of Central Australia for 22 000 years. Ernest Giles and his party of explorers found life-saving water here in 1872. Giles named the site Kings Canyon after one of his expedition companions. The George Gill Range he called after one of his sponsors.

In 1894 the famous Horn Expedition passed through on the first biological examination of Central Australia. The members of the expedition were amazed at the biological richness which they discovered at the base of the range.

The Watarrka National Park was declared in 1983 and the land handed back to the Luritja people. Today these people live in small groups within the park boundaries and have a strong

Kings Canyon in Watarrka National Park

voice in its management. They also operate tours that give visitors an insight into their culture. Much of the adjacent land surrounding this park has been handed back to the traditional owners. Watarrka is the Luritja name for an acacia species.

ACCESS

Watarrka National Park and Kings Canyon are accessible by conventional vehicles by way of 3 different routes. From Alice Springs along the Stuart and Ernest Giles Highways it is 302 km. A slightly longer route of 327 km follows along Larapinta Drive and the Mereenie Loop Road from Alice Springs via Hermannsburg. Access from Uluru is 279 km on a sealed road, while the other 2 routes have sections of formed gravel road; careful driving techniques are advised. Always carry at least 20 litres of water and sufficient spares and spare tyres as the distances between service outlets are great.

Commercial tour operators service Watarrka National Park from Alice Springs on a regular basis. Please contact the Visitor Information Centre in Alice Springs.

ACCOMMODATION

Kings Canyon Resort, located 7 km from the canyon, and within the national park boundaries, has been designed to blend into the environment and to complement the beauty of the surrounding wilderness. The facilities include 96 hotel rooms, 60 serviced caravan sites and fully grassed camping grounds with shared amenities. Hotel rooms are air conditioned and leisure facilities include a restaurant, cocktail bar, public bar, cafe, 2 swimming pools and a tennis court. There is a daily air service from Alice Springs and Uluru, a souvenir shop and a fuel outlet.

WALKS IN THE PARK

The Kings Creek Walk is a 1.3 km one-way walk which should take one hour to complete. It meanders up Kings Creek to a lookout vantage point. This walk is suitable for families and there is also wheelchair access for the first 700 metres. The walk starts from the car park.

A longer walk is the Kings Canyon Walk. This is a 6 km return walk which should take 3–4 hours. The best time to do this walk is in the early morning or late afternoon. Photographic opportunities are best after midday along this walk. After an initial climb which is moderately hard but safe, this walk offers spectacular views from the canyon rim. Along the way the visitor may wander through the eroded domes of the Lost City and walk down into the Garden of Eden on the canyon floor to be amongst the lush vegetation and cool, clear, rockpools. A well-constructed boardwalk with safety rails makes

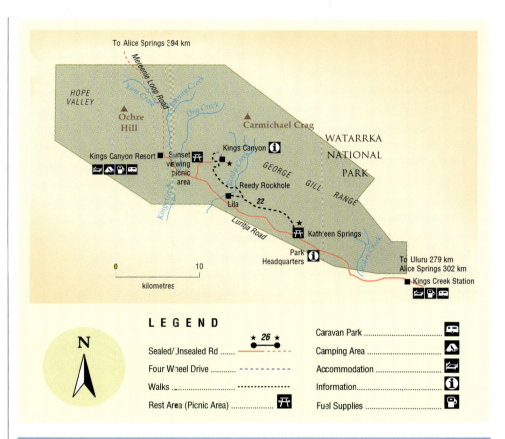

The sheer sides of Kings Canyon

the descent and ascent in and out of the canyon a pleasure. Once you are beyond the canyon the signposted track follows the contours of the range for a gentle descent. Emergency radios are located along the Kings Canyon Walk and at the Kings Canyon car park. Please use them to contact rangers in an emergency. Access to this walk is from the car park.

A delightful walk of 2.6 km return and 1½ hours, the Kathleen Springs Walk leads to a beautiful spring-fed waterhole. This is an easy walk which is suitable for families and has wheelchair accessibility.

The Giles Track is an overnight walk traversing the top of the George Gill Range from Kathleen Springs to Kings Canyon, a distance of 22 km, with an entry point at Reedy Creek and an exit at Lila. Please contact the rangers at the park headquarters for a map and more information before attempting this walk.

WEST MACDONNELL NATIONAL PARK

IN BRIEF

MAP REFERENCE: PAGE 254 F 6

Location This park stretches from the fringe of Alice Springs township westwards for 220 km

Best Time All year round, summer temperatures may reach mid 40s. Larapinta Trail may be closed between October and April

Main Attractions Numerous scenic gorges and waterholes, walking trails, swimming, hiking, camping, cycling and scenic drives, Aboriginal culture

Ranger Visitor Information Centre, cnr Gregory Terrace and Hartley Streets, Alice Springs, phone (08) 8952 5800 Commercial Tour operators service the park from Alice Springs. For details contact the Visitor Information Centre, phone (08) 8952 5800

Ellery Creek Big Hole

The MacDonnell Ranges, reaching heights of over 1500 metres above sea level, span some 400 km east to west across the centre of Australia, and include the town of Alice Springs. They encompass many of the natural features of this land. The ranges are a mixture of granite, quartzite, limestone, sandstone and siltstone, thrust up, bent, squeezed and folded by the internal forces of the earth about 2200 million years ago. Extreme weathering over the millennia has eroded about 2000 metres from the top of the ranges. Since their initial appearance, Central Australia has also been covered by an inland sea as fossil evidence found in some of the valleys of the MacDonnell Ranges testifies.

LEGEND

Sealed/Unsealed Rd	Rest Area (Picnic Area)	Accommodation
Four Wheel Drive	Caravan Park	Information
Walks	Camping Area	Fuel Supplies

HISTORY

In more recent times, 20 000 to 30 000 years ago, the early Aboriginal Australians travelled throughout these lands pursuing their nomadic lifestyle. More recently still, less than 140 years ago, European explorers passed through the MacDonnell Ranges. Then came the pastoralists, the telegraph line, the miners and eventually a township was created to accommodate the various interests of a stationary society. Today Alice Springs, a 20th-century town, caters for a number of diverse cultures.

MAJOR WONDERS OF THE PARK

In 1994 the West MacDonnell National Park was established to encompass all the parks and reserves within the MacDonnell Ranges to the west of Alice Springs and to facilitate the building of the Larapinta Trail a world-class bushwalking trail which, when completed, will follow the backbone of the ranges for about 220 km.

The natural features of the park are linked by the Larapinta Trail. This walking trail starts at the Alice Springs Telegraph Station and continues on to Simpsons Gap, Standley Chasm, Ellery Creek Big Hole, Serpentine Gorge, Serpentine Chalet, the Ochre Pits, Mt Giles, Ormiston Gorge, Glen Helen Gorge, Mt Sonder, Roma Gorge, Redbank Gorge, Tylers Pass, Mt Razorback and Mt Zeil. About half of the trail is open to the public from March to October. The trail should be completed by the year 2000.

ACCESS

All the features in the park are accessible by conventional vehicle or with a tour operator, with the exception of the mountains and Roma Gorge (still under development and 4WD access only). Namatjira Drive which services the park is sealed as far as Glen Helen Gorge, 130 km. Beyond that point a formed gravel road runs west. Corrugations can be a problem at times and careful driving techniques are advised.

A WEALTH OF ACTIVITIES ON OFFER

The park has facilities to entertain both young and old. Please ensure that you are well versed with the harsh summer or mild winter conditions of Central Australia. You must carry water with you wherever you go. All walkers have to register with the nearest ranger station before setting off on a major walk. Most of the waterholes are extremely cold and care must be taken not to stay in the water too long, otherwise hypothermia may set in. Good walking shoes, a hat and sunscreen are essential for all outdoor activities. Access to these facilities is by car, or you can take a tour with one of the many tours operators in Alice Springs.

Alice Springs Telegraph Station

This is the start of the first section of the Larapinta Trail, just 4 km from the town centre by walking or cycle path. There are historic buildings, surrounded by shaded picnic areas. This is a great place to relax.

Simpsons Gap

This is the first of many gaps which bisect the MacDonnell Ranges. Here you may be lucky enough to have the opportunity to see black-footed rock wallabies at dusk.

Some of the walks in Simpsons Gap include the Ghost Gum Walk which starts from the Visitor Information Centre and gives interesting information on the ghost gums of Simpsons Gap. It is about ½ hour return. The Cassia Hill Walk is a 500 metre walk from the Cassia Hill parking area, while a longer walk, the Woodland Trail, is an easy 17 km return walk to Bond Gap for which you should allow about 8 hours.

Free gas BBQs are available in the shady picnic area of Simpsons Gap.

Enjoy a different approach to Simpsons Gap by cycling along the sealed bicycle path which runs for 17 km from Flynns Grave (7 km out of Alice Springs on the Larapinta Drive). Detailed information about the bicycle track may be obtained from the Visitor Information Centre.

Standley Chasm

Midday, when the sun is directly overhead, is considered to be the best time to visit this narrow gap in the ranges. A nominal entry charge to the chasm applies. There are walks through and beyond the chasm, and there is a picnic area. This is traditional Aboriginal land and the kiosk and tea room are managed and staffed by the traditional owners.

Ellery Creek Big Hole

This is a large, permanent waterhole, about 90 km out of Alice Springs along Namatjira Drive. It is popular with locals and tourists alike. The banks of Ellery Creek Big Hole are shaded by tall river red gums (*Eucalyptus camaldulensis*) and this is a lovely spot for a picnic. There are tables and toilets provided and camping is allowed, for which a nominal fee applies.

The folded layers of the MacDonnell Ranges

WEST MACDONNELL NATIONAL PARK

Serpentine Gorge

This gorge is a an important refuge for a number of rare plant species and home to a special species of Central Australian fish. From the car park there is a 1.3 km woodland walk to the entrance of the gorge. To the right of the gorge is the start of a 15 minute walk which takes you to a lookout with spectacular views of the surrounding ranges and bluffs. The entrance of the gorge is normally blocked by a body of water. However, in drier times access is possible up to the far end of the gorge where a narrow fissure cuts through the range. Please do not swim in this part of the gorge.

Serpentine Chalet Bush Camping

The chalet represents an earlier tourism venture which failed. Today bush camping facilities are provided for travellers in conventional vehicles and further on for 4WD travellers. Several short walks offer visitors a chance to experience the remoteness of the ranges.

The Ochre Pits

Aboriginal culture is on display here and signs explain the various uses of ochre by the Aboriginal people. A 300 metre path provides easy access for all visitors, and there is a 3 hour return bushwalk to the base of the ranges.

Ormiston Gorge and Pound

This is one of the most spectacular gorges in Central Australia, and insight into the geological features of this region may be enjoyed. The gorge is renowned for its walking tracks.

The Waterhole is an easy 10 minute return walk; Ghost Gum Lookout an easy ½ hour return walk; Ghost Gum walk is a moderate ½ hour loop; Pound Walk, a moderate 2–3 hour loop; Bowmans Gap, a moderate 1–2 day return walk; and Mt Giles which is a difficult 2–3 day return walk.

There is a visitor centre at the gorge, and camping and caravan sites are available. A nominal fee applies for these.

Glen Helen Gorge

The Finke River, the oldest watercourse in the world, cuts through the West MacDonnell Ranges at Glen Helen Gorge. Through the gorge on the south side of the ranges is a series of fascinating rock formations known as the Organ Pipes. Glen Helen Lodge is a former pastoral station, which has a kiosk from which fuel and drinks are available.

Redbank Gorge

The road west from Glen Helen is a formed gravel road but it can become very corrugated at times. Redbank Gorge lies a further 20 km along this road and 5 km in on the graded access road. From the car park to the entrance of the gorge is a pleasant 25 minute walk along the tree-lined creek. Redbank Gorge is a narrow cleft in the ranges which forms a series of waterholes. Climbing through the gorge is possible but only the very fit and adventurous should attempt this.

There is a woodland camping area about halfway along the access road. Picnic tables, sandy tent pads, toilets, wood BBQs and free gas BBQs are all part of this camping area; there is a nominal camping fee for these facilities.

Tylers Pass

This is not so much a pass as a road up and over the lower part of the ranges. At the summit of the pass a lookout and shaded rest area, with interpretive signs, give a sweeping vista of the surrounding country and the magnificent Gosse Bluff Comet Crater. Tylers Pass is the most westerly feature of the park and is situated 187 km from Alice Springs.

You may exit the park here and continue on to Gosse Bluff, Hermannsburg Mission and Palm Valley in the Finke National Park. The road is a formed gravel road and careful driving techniques are advised. It is 125 km from Hermannsburg to Alice Springs of which about 100 km are sealed.

Ellery Creek

ALICE SPRINGS DESERT PARK

The Alice Springs Desert Park opened early in 1997 and is becoming a world-class attraction. Set with the spectacular backdrop of the MacDonnell Ranges and just 10 minutes from the centre of Alice Springs, the park shows the various landforms, animals and plants of the Central Australian deserts. In addition it highlights the traditional use and management principles of the desert regions by the Aboriginal people.

Some 400 animals are housed in the park with many rare and endangered species on display. A multitude of native plants are presented in their habitats. This habitat-based approach places the park on the forefront of environmental displays world-wide.

It is intended that visitors use this desert park as an introduction to their visit to other national parks and reserves in this region.

The main features of the park include a visitor centre with a series of interactive galleries and displays. A huge glass window looks out on the MacDonnell Ranges. Three separate habitats depicting varying environments have been created along a 1.6 km loop track. The aviaries feature hundreds of bird species from the tiniest finch to the big red-tailed black cockatoo while there are more than 350 species of plants on display. The park claims the largest desert nocturnal house in the world which showcases those animals which live underground, and a walk-through exhibit features kangaroos and emus. The Aboriginal guides present Dreaming stories connected to the park, and there is a nature theatre with specially trained birds of prey soaring above their handlers.

The park also offers other facilities including a restaurant and kiosk, souvenir shop, shaded rest areas with water fountains, extensive car and coach parking, rest facilities for coach drivers, wheelchair access and an education centre for schools and specialist groups.

The park is open every day of the year from 9 am to 9 pm except for Christmas Day. A visit of at least 3 hours is recommended.

For further information, contact the park, ph: (08) 8951 8788.

ALICE SPRINGS TELEGRAPH STATION HISTORICAL RESERVE

In August 1872 the Overland Telegraph Line was completed, linking Adelaide to Darwin and the rest of the world. Twelve telegraph stations spanned the distance across the continent. The Alice Springs Telegraph Station was built near a waterhole in the river bed which was named Alice Springs after the wife of Charles Todd, the man who was responsible for building the telegraph line. The spring in the river is known

Alice Springs Telegraph Station

as Thereyurre by the Arrernte Aboriginal group on whose land the telegraph station was built.

Isolation and loneliness were a factor in the early days of the station. In 1886 with the discovery of 'rubies' (really garnets) and then gold at Arltunga in 1887, the pressure on the station staff was so great that the township of Stuart (later to be renamed Alice Springs) was declared 4 km south of the station.

Today the telegraph station is fully restored and furnished with relics of the past. Picnic tables and coin-operated BBQs set in shaded lawn surroundings make a popular venue for locals and tourists alike. Guided tours of the buildings of the historical precinct are conducted throughout the year.

Access to the reserve is by sealed road or by commercial tours. There is also a 4 km walking and cycle track that connects the town to the telegraph station. Section One of the Larapinta Trail through the West MacDonnell National Park starts from here. For more information, contact the Visitor Information Centre in Alice Springs, ph: (08) 8952 5800.

CASUARINA COASTAL RESERVE

This reserve is located just 17 km from the centre of Darwin, in the northern suburbs (off Tower or Lee Point Roads). The park contains some of the city's most popular beaches and picnic areas. The area also includes some historic World War II artillery observation posts which provide graphic reminders of the area's wartime involvement.

It has long stretches of white sandy beaches (ideal for swimming and fishing) fringed by casuarina and palm trees, stretching from Lee Point in the north to Rapid Creek in the south. There is a free beach (nude bathing is allowed)

in the northern section of the park.

Particularly appealing are the attractive Dripstone Cliffs and sections of paperbark trees and monsoon vine thickets. Exploring the coastline's rockpools and tidal flats at low tide,

The Dripstone Cliffs in Casuarina Coastal Reserve

as well as walking or bike riding along the cliff top access trails, are all popular activities here. Carry drinking water on any extended walks in the reserve. The area is also a great favourite for those who like to enjoy the colourful Top End sunsets. People often bring picnic teas here to sit and watch the sun go down.

The reserve is home to a wide variety of bird life, including ospreys, sea-eagles, cormorants and gulls.

The reserve is for day visits only—camping is not allowed. It is accessible by conventional vehicles and is open and worth a visit at any time of the year. Swimming, however, in the summer is not recommended because of the presence of stingers (box jellyfish).

For more information, contact Parks and Wildlife Commission of Northern Territory, ph: (08) 8989 5511.

CORROBOREE ROCK CONSERVATION RESERVE

This unique limestone formation juts out of the surrounding landscape, 46 km east of Alice Springs along the sealed Ross Highway. Every land feature in Central Australia is connected with a sacred tradition of the Arrernte people. This group of Aboriginal people was broken up into small groups and the myths, beliefs, songs and ceremonies were entrusted to a few initiated men in each group who had personal links to these land features. Corroboree Rock, known as Antanangantana, had a sacred cave where sacred objects were kept. The name 'corroboree' was given to the rock because of the European belief that initiation rites were held here. Anthropologists disagree on whether the rites took place here. As the fame of this unique rock spread after the Europeans first came to this country, it was visited by unscrupulous men who destroyed the sacred objects, and the traditions of an age-old religion were lost forever. Today there is an interpretive walk around the rock, while wood BBQs and toilets are provided. Camping is allowed. For more details, contact the Visitor Information Centre in Alice Springs, ph: (08) 8952 5800.

DEVILS MARBLES CONSERVATION RESERVE
1827 HECTARES

These fascinating spherical or egg-shaped granite boulders, often balanced precariously on top of one another, are the main feature along the Stuart Highway between Alice Springs and Tennant Creek. The shape of these boulders was fashioned by weather as the boulders originally had joint fractures at right angles. Over the millennia the edges have been eroded and eventually weathered to rounded edges leaving this spectacular natural phenomenon.

The Devils Marbles are situated on either side of the road 122 km south of Tennant Creek along the sealed Stuart Highway. Bush camping facilities are provided which include shaded

picnic tables, fireplaces and toilets. There is ample parking for caravans. A nominal camping fee applies.

An easy walking track with interpretive signs is situated on the western side on the access road. There are also many informal walking tracks where the visitor may wander through the boulders for a chance at that quintessential photograph. Clusters of fairy martin nests are found attached to the underside of the boulders. Sometimes you may be lucky enough to spot a spiny-tailed gecko or a sand goanna. Zebra and painted finches abound and clumps of spinifex have taken root in the crevices between the boulders.

The Devils Marbles is a registered Aboriginal sacred site and visitors are asked to respect the cultural heritage of the area. For more details, contact the Tennant Creek Regional Tourist Association, ph: (08) 8962 3388.

ELSEY NATIONAL PARK
13 840 HECTARES

Elsey National Park is located 7 km east of the township of Mataranka, which is approximately 100 km south of Katherine on the Stuart Highway. The park includes the upper reaches of the Roper River with the main attraction being the Mataranka Thermal Springs. The

(08) 8975 4544) with motel-type accommodation and a caravan park (powered and unpowered sites) is located adjacent to the thermal springs.

The usually serene waters of the Roper River are ideal for fishing, swimming, canoeing and small powerboats with up to 10 hp motors. A launching area is located next to the resort.

There is a grassed caravan and camping area along the river at 12 Mile Yard. No power is available, but it has toilets, showers (with facilities for the disabled), hot water, BBQ and boat launching facilities.

There are pleasant bushwalks along the riverine foreshore, including an easy 1.5 km botanical walk (allow ½ hour) and a 4 km each way (allow 2 hours return) easy trail that leads to the picturesque Mataranka Falls, a good swimming area. There are several day picnic areas along the river.

Adjacent to the thermal pool is a replica of the old Elsey Homestead made famous by Jeannie Gunn in her book, *We of the Never Never*. Graves of some of the main people in the book are located at the old Elsey Cemetery.

All the roads are suitable for conventional vehicles, but some temporary closures may occur during the wet season. The best time to visit is May to October. For more information, contact the ranger, ph: (08) 8975 4560.

Humpys erected near the Elsey Homestead in Elsey National Park

warm 34°C swimming pool, which is wheelchair accessible by a boardwalk, is set amongst tall paperbark and *Livistona* palms. It is a real oasis attracting visitors all year round, and the waters are said to have therapeutic values. The Mataranka Homestead Tourist Resort (phone

EWANINGA ROCK CARVINGS CONSERVATION RESERVE

On the desert fringe, just 35 km out of Alice Springs along the Old South Road, the small Ewaninga Reserve protects some of the most accessible and enduring petroglyphs (rock carvings) in Central Australia. This clump of low hills is tattooed with the shallow engravings in the sandstone, giving a valuable link and insight into the way that an earlier culture lived. Much of the meaning of the petroglyphs is sacred to the Arrernte Aboriginal people and these secrets may only be shared with initiated Arrernte people. The custodians of Ewaninga, however, are happy to give visitors access to the site but ask that they respect the carvings and do not interfere with them.

The low hills are set adjacent to a small claypan which fills with water when the rains come and which attracts wild birds and game. The early nomads lived here in the times of plenty, left their mark on the rocks and then moved on in the drier time.

The reserve is accessible by conventional vehicle along a graded, formed gravel road.

Picnic tables and a toilet are provided. A walk through the hills is marked by interpretive signs. Camping is not allowed in the reserve. For more information, contact the Visitor Information Centre in Alice Springs, ph: (08) 8952 5800.

FOGG DAM CONSERVATION RESERVE

Built in the 1950s to provide a store of water for the short-lived rice plantations nearby, the area, since rice growing ceased, has developed into an internationally acclaimed wildlife sanctuary, for bird life in particular.

The dam wall, on the Adelaide River floodplains, serves to retain a permanent wetland environment which attracts birds in their thousands all year, with an even greater build-up towards the end of the dry season (August to November) when other billabongs in the area have started to dry up. The dam wall, which extends around 500 metres across the wetland, also provides an excellent vantage point to watch and photograph the birds. Although it is possible to drive across the dam wall, many take their time and walk. On the other side there is a superb viewing tower which serves as a hide and gives a marvellous view over a wide area of the dam. There are separate, well-signposted, walk trails and boardwalks (including wheelchair access) extending some 3.5 km which lead through rainforest and wetlands lined with paperbark trees. This is easy walking; take your time and allow at least 2 hours. Amongst bird life here are egrets, pygmy-geese, jabirus and magpie-geese.

Rangers are always on hand ready to assist visitors. During the dry season they also conduct night walks using torches to show the wide diversity of nocturnal wildlife—the mammals, harmless water pythons and birds which are commonly found around the dam.

The park is 52 km east of Darwin along the Arnhem Highway. It is accessible by conventional vehicles all year round. Best times are early morning and late afternoon. Because of saltwater crocodiles there is no swimming. Come prepared for walking and bring a picnic and drinking water. There are toilets, but no camping is allowed. For more information, contact the Parks and Wildlife Commission of the Northern Territory, Head Office, ph: (08) 8989 5511 or Fogg Dam Office, ph: (08) 8988 8009.

Fogg Dam is famous for its bird life

HENBURY METEORITE CRATERS CONSERVATION RESERVE
16 HECTARES

The Aboriginal translation for these pockmark indentations on the earth's surface is 'Sun, Walk, Fire, Devil Rock'. Whether or not this cosmic event, some 4700 years ago, was witnessed by the Aboriginal people then living in the area is unknown. The Henbury Meteor, travelling at an accelerating speed of around 40 000 km per hour and weighing several tonnes, disintegrated before impact and formed 13 craters at the Henbury site. The rock fragments that have been found consist mainly of metals and are incredibly heavy. One of the fragments, being about the size of a football, weighed 46 kg. The largest of the craters is about 180 metres across and 15 metres deep.

The craters are located 145 km south of Alice Springs along the Stuart and Ernest Giles Highways. The first 132 km is sealed and the remaining 13 km is formed gravel road which can be slippery after heavy rain. There is an informative loop walk trail across a crater-pitted plain resembling a small scale moonscape. The easy walk, about 1 km, leads around the rim of the main crater; there are signboards along the way. The reserve is accessible all year round and the best time to visit it is from April through to September. Early in the morning or late in the afternoon when the shadows created by the sun clearly define the craters is the best time for taking photographs. Wood BBQs, picnic tables and toilets are provided. There is no water available and camping is not allowed. For more details, contact the Visitor Information Centre in Alice Springs, ph: (08) 8952 5800.

ILLAMURTA SPRINGS CONSERVATION RESERVE

Tucked away in the James Ranges, this small conservation reserve is perhaps the most peaceful and quiet of all the reserves in Central Australia. The presence of a natural spring provides a habitat for aquatic plants which are survivors from an earlier age.

The reserve also protects the ruins of the old police station which served the area between 1893 and 1912. This police station was set up to counter Aboriginal resistance and cattle killing when pastoralists moved into the area. When the cattle killing waned the station was used as an administration centre and food was also distributed from there.

Illamurta Springs is known by the Western Arrernte people as Kunnea, the Snake Python Dreaming. A number of stone artefacts have been found in the area providing evidence of a long occupation here.

The reserve is located 192 km west of Alice Springs along the Ernest Giles Highway and is accessible by 4WD vehicles only. The reserve is for day use only, but camping facilities are provided at nearby Ilpurla Community. For more details, contact the Visitor Information Centre in Alice Springs, ph: (08) 8952 5800.

MAC CLARK (ACACIA PEUCE) CONSERVATION RESERVE

This remote conservation reserve lies out on the hard, harsh gibber plains which run in the corridors between the sand dunes. On the western fringe of the Simpson Desert and 185 km along the track between Allambi Station and Old Andado Station is a signpost that guides you 6 km to the Mac Clark (Acacia Peuce) Conservation Reserve. Mac Clark was a former pastoralist of Andado Station who perished when his light aircraft crashed in the desert.

Acacia peuce, also known as waddy-wood, are trees that thrive in this extreme climate

OTHER PARKS OF INTEREST

where summer temperatures average 40°C and rainfall is less than 150 mm. These trees grow up to 17 metres tall and may live for up to 500 years. About 1000 trees are protected in this reserve. This site is only one of 3 sites in the world where *Acacia peuce* is found. The other 2 sites are in Queensland. In earlier years the waddy-wood was cut down to build stockyards and shelters even though this wood is so hard that nails cannot be driven into it.

Access is by 4WD vehicle only. As you are on private leasehold property, please remember to stay on established tracks, leave gates as you found them and slow down around areas where

Aboriginal petroglyphs in N'Dhala Gorge

cattle are grazing. This reserve has no facilities and no camping is allowed. For more details, please contact the Visitor Information Centre in Alice Springs, ph: (08) 8952 5800.

N'DHALA GORGE NATURE PARK

N'Dhala Gorge, known as Irlwentye (Eel-oon-ja) by its Aboriginal custodians, is an important site for the Eastern Arrernte people. It is also a site of world significance as it contains close on 6000 petroglyphs (rock carvings). These carvings are estimated to be between 2000 and 10 000 years old. Some of the carvings have special relevance to the totemic beliefs of the modern-day custodians and relate back to a story of the Caterpillar Dreaming.

The park is also the refuge for several rare plants, including the Hayes wattle and the peach-leafed poison bush.

This shady gorge is accessible from the Ross Highway and lies 90 km by road from Alice Springs. The last 11 km are accessible by 4WD vehicles only. There is a small camping area, and toilets are provided. A walking track leads into the gorge and is the start of the comfortable one hour return walk in the sheer-sided gorge.

Rainbow Valley

There are interpretive signs along this track explaining the significance of the petroglyphs.

Ross River Homestead, which is situated 11 km back along the track into N'Dhala Gorge, has motel accommodation and camping facilities, a restaurant and fuel supplies. For more details, contact the Visitor Information Centre in Alice Springs, ph: (08) 8952 5800.

RAINBOW VALLEY CONSERVATION RESERVE

This dominating scenic bluff lies within the James Range. The rainbow-coloured bands in the sandstone cliffs are caused by water. Thousands of years ago, when Central Australia experienced wetter conditions than the present, the red iron of the sandstone layers was dissolved and drawn to the surface in drier periods. The minerals in the soil formed a dark red surface layer with exposed, leached white sand layers below.

The reserve has also been the traditional land of the Southern Arrernte Aboriginal people where they lived in their nomadic state up to the late 1950s. Evidence of this occupation can be found throughout the reserve in the form of petroglyphs (rock carvings and paintings) and stone implements. Today artists and photographers delight in reproducing the effects on Rainbow Valley caused by light in the late afternoon and at sunset.

Picnic tables and toilets are provided and camping is allowed at a nominal fee. There is no water. Due to the fragile environment of

Rainbow Valley please take care where you walk.

The valley is situated 75 km south of Alice Springs along the Stuart Highway and 22 km west from the turn-off along a sandy road. Access to the reserve is recommended by 4WD but by using skilful driving techniques access is possible by conventional vehicle. Commercial tours operate out of Alice Springs to Rainbow Valley. For more details, please contact the Visitor Information Centre in Alice Springs, ph: (08) 8952 5800.

RUBY GAP NATURE PARK

On the far eastern perimeter of the MacDonnell Ranges, the Hale River scours a path through these rugged ranges on its way to the Simpson Desert where it dissipates into the sand near the Allitra Tableland. The Hale River, known as Lira Altera by the Eastern Arrernte Aboriginal group, has its headwaters in the Harts Ranges and has cut impressive gorges through the Amarata Foothills. Ruby Gap is one of the more accessible gorges and from here the river continues onto Glen Annie Gorge.

The park is situated 150 km east of Alice Springs and access is via the Arltunga Historical Reserve and Ranger Station. A high clearance 4WD vehicle is absolutely essential to gain access. Only experienced drivers should attempt to drive to the end of the track. It is advisable to stay on the existing track and not to venture into the river bed as there are areas of quicksand. During the summer months heavy rains may cause the track to Ruby Gap to become impassable.

The names Ruby Gap and Glen Annie Gorge are attributed to the explorer David Lindsay, who in 1886, found bright pink gemstones in the Hale River and mistaking these high quality garnets for rubies started the first mining rush to Central Australia.

You can bush camp in Ruby Gap Nature Park, which also incorporates Glen Annie Gorge, but there are no facilities. For more details, contact the Visitor Information Centre in Alice Springs, ph: (08) 8952 5800.

TJUWALIYN (DOUGLAS HOT SPRINGS) NATURE PARK

In a delightful tropical setting amongst tall paperbark trees and pandanus palms, the hot artesian springs are the attraction here. The hot water, around 60°C, comes to the surface in a pool adjacent to the camping area. Do not swim here; however, about 200 metres downstream from the spring pool, the water is ideal and delightfully warm. A few metres further down it becomes quite cool where it mixes with the waters of the Douglas River. A popular pastime involves moving across the small sandy stream from hot to cool and back again. The waters here are said to have therapeutic qualities and some people come for weeks, or even several months, to sit and swim daily in the steam.

There are short, easy ½ hour walk trails beside the river and billabongs and through the surrounding countryside. Bird life is quite prolific and bandicoots and flying foxes can be seen and heard at night.

There is a large camping area suitable for caravans. It has pit toilets, BBQs, tables and drinking water, but no power. Camping fees apply.

The turn-off to the park from the Stuart Highway is 145 km north of Katherine and 172 km south of Darwin. It is 38 km off the Stuart Highway. The last 7 km are unsealed but usually in good condition. Conventional vehicle access is possible except in the wet season when the roads are often closed. The best time to visit is May to October. For more information contact the Parks and Wildlife Commission of Northern Territory, Katherine Office, ph: (08) 8973 8770 or Head Office, ph: (08) 8989 5511.

TNORALA (GOSSE BLUFF) CONSERVATION RESERVE
4759 HECTARES

Thundering through the stratosphere at an unbelievable speed, a piece of cosmic rock, possibly a comet, and about 600 metres across, collided with the earth right in the centre of Australia. The continent was at that time still part of the supercontinent known as Gondwanaland, and it is very likely that no living thing witnessed this momentous event. About 130 million years later the early Aboriginal Australians named this crater Tnorala and wove their totemic Dreamtime stories into the fabric of their culture.

In 1872 the explorer Ernest Giles saw this crater from a distance and thinking that it might be a row of hills, named it Gosse Bluff after P. H. Gosse, a friend and a member of the Royal Society.

Today Tnorala Conservation Reserve has been handed back to its Aboriginal traditional owners who manage it in conjunction with the Parks and Wildlife Commission of the Northern Territory.

The best access to Tnorala is via Namatjira Drive and Tylers Pass, west from Alice Springs. This road is sealed for 130 km to Glen Helen and then there are 68 km of formed gravel road which can be corrugated at times. The view from Tylers Pass is magnificent. Access by 4WD vehicle is recommended. Camping is not allowed in the reserve. Before you go please check with the Parks and Wildlife Commission on (08) 8951 8211 regarding the need for permits to access the park.

TREPHINA GORGE NATURE PARK
1770 HECTARES

This nature park is noted for its massive quartzite cliffs and its sandy creeks which are lined with river red gums. Two gorges dissect the East MacDonnell Ranges: Trephina with its wide vista, and John Hayes Rockhole with its narrow aperture carved out through time by the flow of water. The waterholes attract a diversity of bird life as well as marsupials and macropods such as black-footed rock wallabies.

Tnorala viewed from Tylers Pass lookout

Camping sites are provided with picnic tables, free wood, free gas BBQs and drinking water at Trephina Bluff and Trephina Gorge. At John Hayes Rockhole there are picnic tables and toilets but no drinking water. From Trephina Gorge there are 2 very pleasant one hour return walking tracks: the Trephina Gorge Walk and the Panorama Walk. A longer ridge-top walking track has also been made for the more experienced walker. This walk links Trephina Gorge with John Hayes Rockhole and you should allow 6½ hours one way. Along these walks you may see a wide range of bush food such as the native fig or the very tasty wild passionfruit.

The park is accessible by conventional vehicles and lies 85 km east of Alice Springs along the Ross Highway. When you have turned off onto the Trephina Gorge access road, look out for the side road that leads to the biggest ghost gum tree in Central Australia. For more details, contact the Visitor Information Centre in Alice Springs, ph: (08) 8952 5800.

WILDMAN RESERVE

This reserve takes in a significant proportion of the extensive Mary River Wetlands. Located 170 km from Darwin off the Arnhem Highway, it provides excellent opportunities for visitors to experience a tropical wetland environment.

Fishing is extremely popular, particularly at Shady Camp and North Rockhole, where the highly sought-after barramundi are regularly caught. There are boat ramp facilities as well as toilets, picnic and camping facilities at each location. Bring your own drinking water, insect repellent and all supplies you might need.

There are 2 private wilderness lodges in the reserve offering full accommodation and fishing tour facilities. Couzens Lookout is an excellent vantage point to view the Mary River and extensive areas of attractive red waterlilies. Walking and birdwatching are popular activities here with a huge number of waterbirds found along the waterways and billabongs. Be wary of saltwater crocodiles throughout this region.

Roads in the Wildman Reserve are gravel but suitable for conventional vehicles except during the wet season when flooding may cause road closures.

North Rockhole in the Wildman Reserve

Located at Beatrice Hill, 60 km from Darwin between the turn-offs to Fogg Dam and Wildman Reserve, is the Window On The Wetlands Visitor Centre. This excellent complex has been set up to give visitors an overview of the Northern Territory's wetlands. It has informative displays, computer touch screens and a video room, all designed to provide historic background, details of local wildlife and their habits, seasonal changes, and much more. The best time to visit the Wetlands area is from May to October. For more information, contact the Visitor Centre, ph: (08) 8979 8904, or the Wildman ranger, ph: (08) 8981 5386.

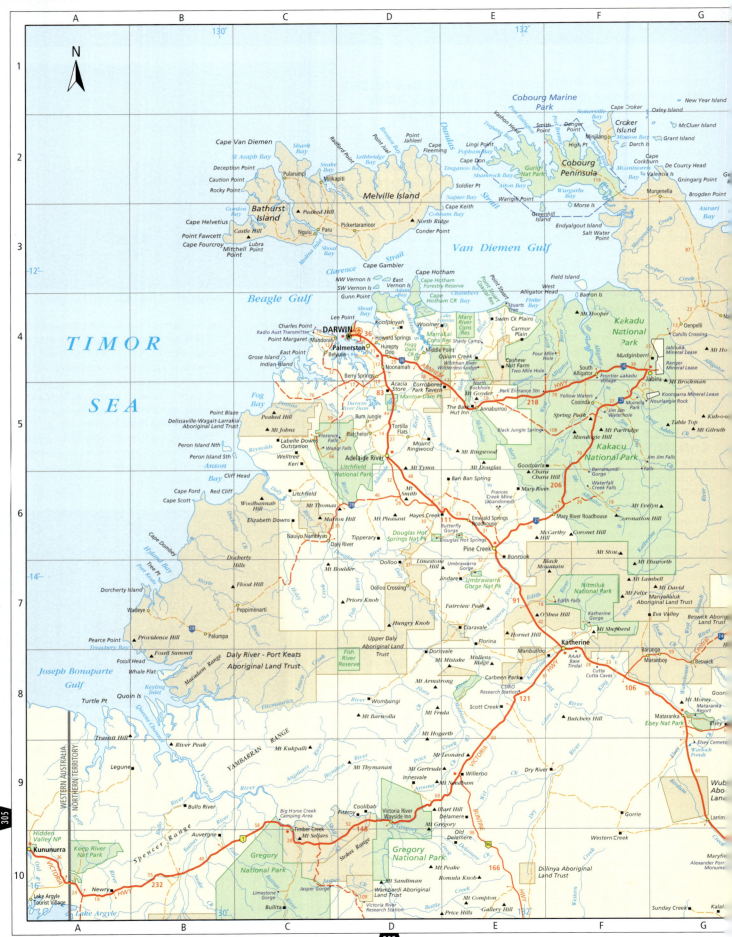

H   J   K   L   M   N   P

134°   136°   138°

ARAFURA SEA

1

Rimbija Is
Cape Wessel

Wessel
Islands

2

Marchinbar Island

Stevens Island
Guluwuru Island
Truant Island

Cuthbert Point
Braithwaite Point
Junction Bay

Nth West
Crocodile Island
Drysdale Island
Reragala Island
Islands

3

Hawkesbury Point
Skirmish Point
False Point
Cape Stewart
Rabuma Is
Howard Island
Mooroongga Is
Elcho Island
Galiwinku
Point Napier
Inglis Island
Cunningham Islands
Alger Is
The English Companys
Bromby Islands
Cape Wilberforce

−12°

Maningrida
Milingimbi
Ramingining
Castlereagh Bay
Probable Is
Flinders Pt
Mallison Island
Arnhem Bay
Melville Bay
Boney Point
Bremer Island
Nhulunbuy
Yirrkala

Gove Peninsula

4

Gapuwiya
Cape Arnhem
Road
416
Arnhem
Frederick Hills
Port Bradshaw
Mt Alexander
Wanyanmera Point

ARNHEM LAND

Central
109
MITCHELL RANGE
Camburinga Village
Point Alexander
Mt Caledon
Caledon Bay
Cape Grey
Bald Point

5

116
Shadforth Hills
McKay Hills
Arnhem Land
Trial Bay
Point Arrowsmith
Wardarlea Bay

−14°

Aboriginal Land Trust
PARSONS RANGE
Mt Fleming
Mt Ramsay
Julma Bay
Cape Shield
Isle Woodah
Nico¹ Is

6

Mt Jean
Mt Weir
Mt Marumba
Bulman
24
Mt Ranken
BATH RA
Morgan Is
Blue Mud Bay
Burney Is
North Point Island
North East Isles
Hawk Island

Mt Stretton
Road
78
Black Mountain
Cape Barrow
Bickerton Island
Chasm Is
Winchelsea Island
Bacchus Hill

Mt Catt
Mt Leane
Miliyakburra
Alyangula
Umbakumba

Mountain Valley
Mainoru
Mt Bray
305
Whamett Bluff
Mt Furner
Three Graces
Snowden Peak
157
Rantyirrry Point
Tasman Point
Sandy Hill
Groote Eylandt
Angurugu
Bluff Hill
Ilyungmadja Point
Dalumbu Bay

7

Mt Karmain
Mt Bagster
Mt Phillip
Boomerang Hill
Numbulwar
South Point
Ungwariba Point
Cape Beatrice

Mt James
Urapunga
Ngukurr
Edward Island
Nyinpinti Point

8

Moroak
Mt Elanor
Roper Bar
2
70
St Vidgeon
Port Roper
Warrakunta Point
GULF OF

Price
20
184
Yutpundji-Djindiwirritj Aboriginal Land Trust
18
Roper
44
Port Roper
Limmen Bight
Maria Island
Marra Aboriginal Land Trust

Mt Mueller
Mt Forrest
Mt Hughes
CARPENTARIA

9

Mt Davidson
Mt Kelly
Mt Eliza
107
Sir Edward Pellew Group

Hodgson Downs
Mason Bluff
The Four Archers
West Island
Barranyi Nat Park
Watson Is
North Island
Cape Vanderlin

Hodgson River
153
Nathan River
Rosie
Bing-Bong
Sth West Island
Centre Is
Vanderlin Island

Alawa Aboriginal Land Trust
34
Batten Point
Port McArthur
Wurralibi Aboriginal Land Trust

10

Nutwood Downs
King Ash Bay
Manangoora

103
Borroloola
21
Mt Featherto
26
Narwinbi Aboriginal Land Trust
Greenbank

−16°

Mt Joe
Bauhinia Downs

134°   136°   138°

H   J   K   L   M   N   P

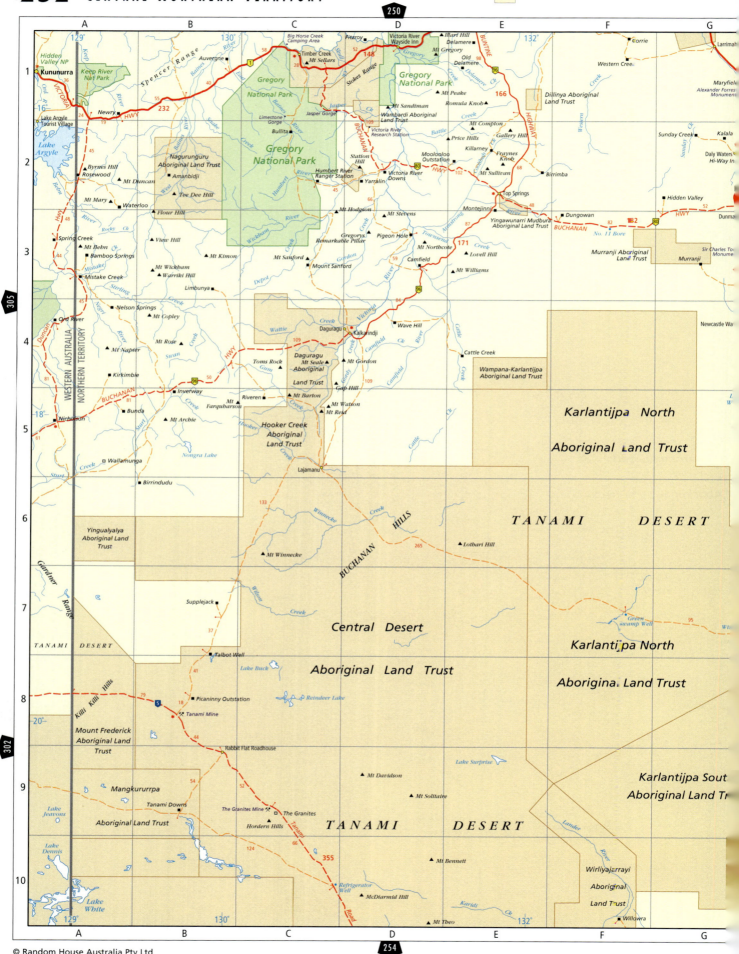

A   B   C   D   E   F   G

305

302

129°   130°   132°

Hidden Valley NP
Kununurra
Keep River Nat Park
Spencer Range
Auvergne
Big Horse Creek Camping Area
Timber Creek
Mt Sellars
Fitzroy
Victoria River Wayside Inn
Hart Hill
Delamere
Mt Gregory
Corrie
Western Creek
Larrimah

1

Lake Argyle
Newry
Gregory National Park
Gregory
Jasper
Jasper Gorge
Mt Sandiman
Mt Peake
Romula Knob
Old Delamere
Dillinya Aboriginal Land Trust
Maryfield
Alexander Forrest Monument
Lake Argyle Tourist Village
Bullita
Limestone Gorge
Wambardi Aboriginal Land Trust
Victoria River Research Station
Mt Compton
Price Hills
Gallery Hill
Sunday Creek
Kalala
Daly Waters Hi-Way Inn

2

Byrnes Hill
Rosewood
Nagurunguru Aboriginal Land Trust
Amanbidji
Gregory National Park
Humbert River Ranger Station
Station Hill
Yarralin
Victoria River Downs
Killarney
Mt Sullivan
Fraynes Knob
Top Springs
Birrimba
Mt Duncan
Mooloolo Outstation
Hidden Valley

Mt Mary
Waterloo
Tee Dee Hill
Flour Hill
Mt Hodgson
Mt Stevens
Montejinni
Yingawunarri Mudbura Aboriginal Land Trust
Dungowan
No. 11 Bore
HWY
Dunma

3

Spring Creek
Mt Bebn
Bamboo Springs
View Hill
Mt Kimon
Mt Sanford
Gregorys Remarkable Pillar
Pigeon Hole
Mt Northcote
Lovell Hill
Mt Williams
Camfield
Murranji Aboriginal Land Trust
Murranji
Sir Charles Todd Monume
Mistake Creek
Mt Wickham
Warriki Hill
Mount Sanford

Nelson Springs
Limbunya
Mt Copley
Mt Rose
Ord River
Daguragu
Kalkarindji
Wave Hill
Newcastle Wa

4

Mt Napier
Suan
Toms Rock Gum
Daguragu
Mt Seale Aboriginal Land Trust
Mt Gordon
Cattle Creek
Wampana-Karlantijpa Aboriginal Land Trust

Kirkimbie
Inverway
Mt Barton
Gap Hill
Karlantijpa North

5

BUCHANAN
Riveren
Farqubarson
Mt Watson
Mt Reid
Aboriginal Land Trust
Nicholson
Bunda
Mt Archie
Hooker Creek Aboriginal Land Trust

Wallamunga
Lajamanu

Birrindudu

6

Yingualyalya Aboriginal Land Trust
Winnecke
HILLS
TANAMI DESERT
Mt Winnecke
Lotbari Hill
BUCHANAN
Gaidner Range

7

Supplejack
Central Desert
Green swamp Well
Karlantijpa North
TANAMI DESERT
Talbot Well
Aboriginal Land Trust
Lake Buck
Aboriginal Land Trust

8

Killi Killi Hills
Picaninny Outstation
Reindeer Lake
Tanami Mine
20°

Mount Frederick Aboriginal Land Trust
Rabbit Flat Roadhouse
Lake Surprise
Karlantijpa Sout
Aboriginal Land Tr

9

Lake Jeavons
Mangkururrpa
Tanami Downs
Mt Davidson
Mt Solitaire
Lake Dennis
Aboriginal Land Trust
The Granites Mine
The Granites
Hordern Hills
TANAMI DESERT
Lander
Wirliyajerrayi Aboriginal Land Trust

10

Lake White
Refrigerator Well
McDiarmid Hill
Mt Bennett
Karidi
Mt Theo
Willowra

129°   130°   132°

A   B   C   D   E   F   G

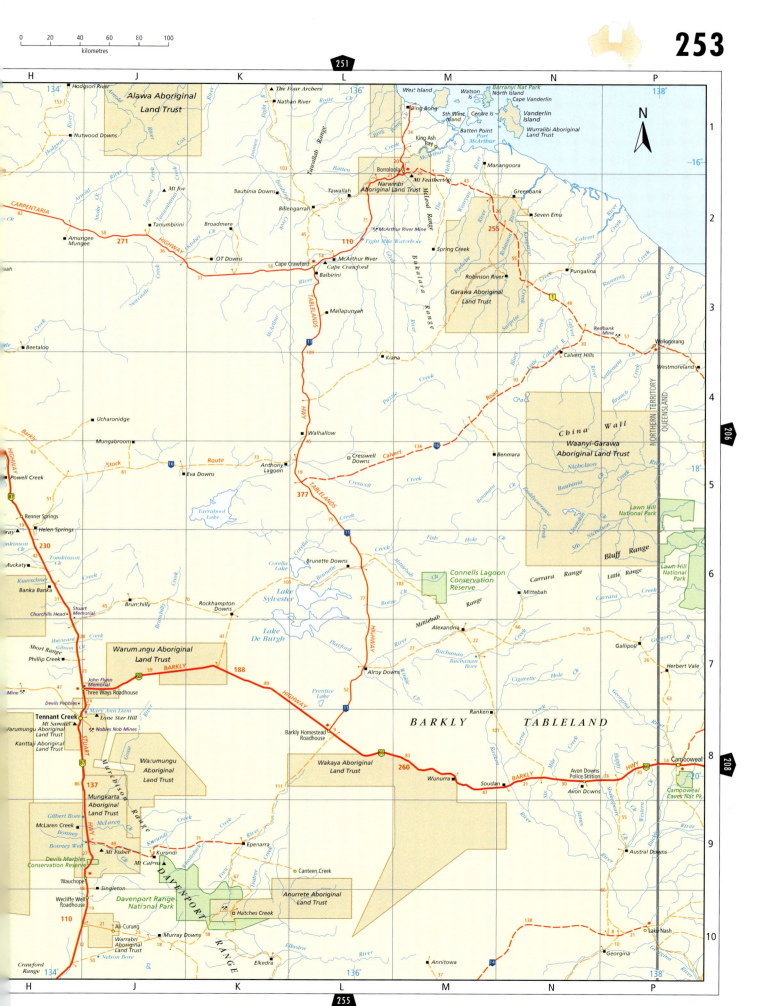

Alawa Aboriginal
Land Trust

The Four Archers
Nathan River

Hodgson River
153
134°

Nutwood Downs

West Island
Bing Bong

Watson Is
North Island

Barranyi Nat Park
Cape Vanderlin

82

Mt Joe

Borroloola

King Ash
Bay

Batten Point
Port
McArthur

34

Centre Is

Vanderlin
Island

Wurralibi Aboriginal
Land Trust

-16°
138°

CARPENTARIA

Bauhinia Downs

Tawallah

Narwinbi
Aboriginal Land Trust

Mt Featherton

Manangoora

Greenbank

Ck

103

51

43

Seven Emu

Billengarrah

271

Amungee
Mungee

58

HIGHWAY

36

Broadmere

Tanumbirini

110

7°

McArthur River Mine

McArthur River

Spring Creek

255

26

Robinson River

Pungalina

OT Downs

Cape Crawford

14
Cape Crawford

Balbirini

McArthur River

Garawa Aboriginal
Land Trust

Robinson River

1

48

Calvert Hills

37

Mallapunyah

Bukalara Range

30

Redbank
Mine

57

Wollogorang

Westmoreland

Beetaloo

Kiana

93

China Wall

Waanyi-Garawa
Aboriginal Land Trust

NORTHERN TERRITORY
QUEENSLAND

206

Ucharonidge

Mungabroom

Walhallow

Cresswell
Downs

134

16

Benmara

Nicholson

Bluff Range

Lawn Hill
National Park

-18°

Powell Creek

63

Stock

Route

81

16

73

Eva Downs

Anthony
Lagoon

19

45

Calvert

Creswell

TABLELANDS

377

Creek

Fish Hole Ck

Bambinia

Badikwarrana

Chanson

Little Range

Lawn Hill
National Park

87

51

Renner Springs

19

230

Helen Springs

42

Tomkinson Ck

Muckaty

Kuerschner

Banka Banka

31

Churchills Head

45

Brunchilly

70

Tarrabool
Lake

75

11

Brunette Downs

Corella
Lake

101

Lake
Sylvester

Brunette

Rockhampton
Downs

103

77

Connells Lagoon
Conservation
Reserve

Carrara Range

Mittebah

Carrara Range

Little Range

135

Short Range

Hayward Creek

Phillip Creek

41

Lake
De Burgh

Playford

Mittiebah

Alexandria

22

Gregory R

Gallipoli

Herbert Vale

Warumungu Aboriginal
Land Trust

59

BARKLY

188

89

HIGHWAY

52

Alroy Downs

Buchanan

Buchanan
Bore

72

Cigarette Hole Ck

26

John Flynn
Memorial

87

Three Ways Roadhouse

24

Prentice
Lake

11

Ranken

Georgina R

63

Tennant Creek

Mt Samuel

Mary Ann Dam
Lone Star Hill

Nobles Nob Mines

Barkly Homestead
Roadhouse

9

BARKLY TABLELAND

101

Devils Pebbles

Warumungu
Aboriginal
Land Trust

Kanttaji Aboriginal
Land Trust

87

137

86

Murchison Range

Warumungu
Aboriginal
Land Trust

Mungkarta
Aboriginal
Land Trust

Wakaya Aboriginal
Land Trust

260

66

83

Wunurra

111

47

Soudan

BARKLY

Avon Downs
Police Station

Avon Downs

21

30

HWY

66

14

Camooweal

Campoweal
Caves Nat Pk

-20°

208

McLaren Creek

Gilbert Bore

Bonney

Bonney Well

McLaren

49

Mt Fisher

Kurundi

71

Epenarra

STUART

HWY

Kurundi

Mt Cairns

67

Canteen Creek

Anurrete Aboriginal
Land Trust

James River

55

Western Ck

Austral Downs

Devils Marbles
Conservation Reserve

Wauchope

Singleton

Wycliffe Well
Roadhouse

110

21

Ali-Curung

DAVENPORT RANGE

Davenport Range
National Park

Hatches Creek

138

Lake Nash

8

Georgina

Warrabri
Aboriginal
Land Trust

50

Nelson Bore

18

58

Murray Downs

Elkedra

Elkedra

River

136°

Annitowa

37

14

138°

Crawford
Range

134°

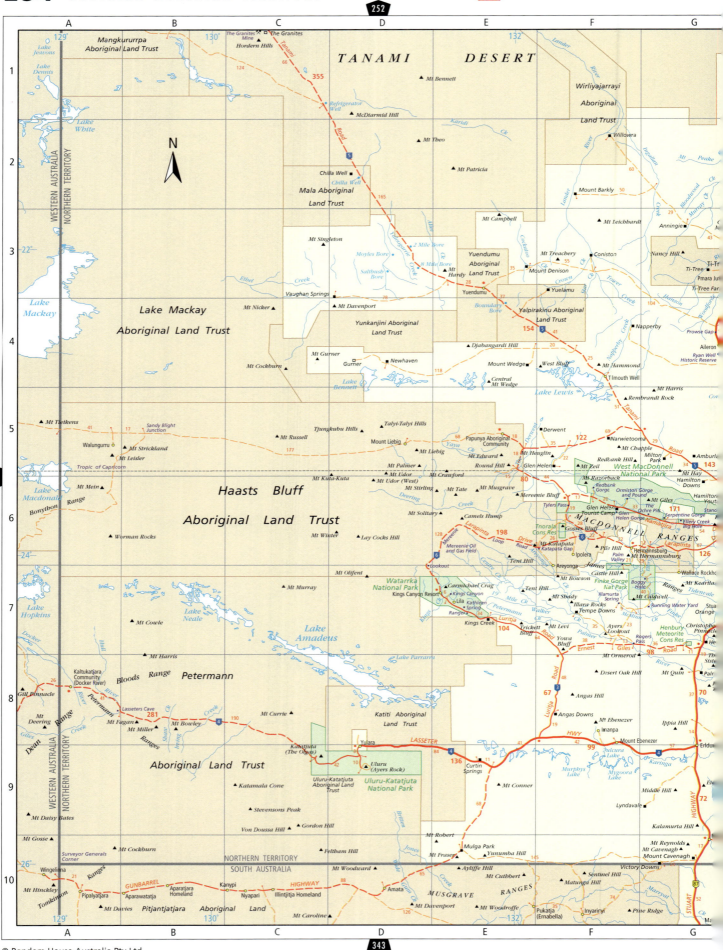

253

kilometres
0 20 40 60 80 100

H J K L M N P

1
134° Wauchope
Singleton
Wycliffe Well Roadhouse
110
DAVENPORT RANGE
Davenport Range National Park
Ali-Curung
Warrabri Aboriginal Land Trust
Murray Downs
Canteen Creek 136°
Hatches Creek
Anurrete Aboriginal Land Trust
138°

2
Crawford Range
Narrow Creek
Mt Guynne
Neutral Junction
87 30
Elkedra
Elkedra River
Annitowa
14 HWY
331
Lake Nash
Georgina
8
21
Georgina River
Headingly

3
Stirling
Wilora
Mt Tops
Alyawarra Aboriginal Land Trust
RANGE
Ammaroo
Corella Bore
Gregory Bore
Nyngan Bore
Weepita Bore
Ooratippra
SANDOVER
Argadargada
Urandangi
22°
93
Manners Creek

4
Central Mt Stuart Historical Reserve
Anmatjere Aboriginal Land Trust
Mt Ocy
Angarapa Aboriginal Land Trust
Arlparra
Utopia
Woola Downs
Mt Harper
Cedan Peak
Mount Skinner
Atartinga
246
Derry Downs
Mt Michael
MacDonald Downs
Arapunya
Lucy Creek
Anatye Aboriginal Land Trust
Tarlton Downs
PLENTY HWY
101
Marqua
Tobermory
17

5
SANDOVER
14
PLENTY
Wallaby Knob
Mt Bleechmore
Gemtree Roadhouse
Bushy Park
Mt Strangways
Coles Hill
Yambah
12
67
Waite River
Delmore Downs
Delny
South Point
Dneiper
Mendip Hill
Table Hill
Alcoota
Black Point
Conical Hill
Harts Range Police Station
12
Entire Point
Red Tank
Huckitta
Tent Hill
Prossers Bore
Jinka
Mt Saintbill
Baikal
Jervois
PLENTY
485
Atula
Mt Winnecke
Mt Tietkens
Mt Woods
Mt Wooldridge
Mt Reinecke
Mt Barrington
Cravens Peak
Twin Hills
Two Hills

6
Scrub Hill
Eald Hill
Randalls Peak
Pinnacles Bores
The Garden
Amalindum
Claraville
Cogblan
Mt Long
Mt Powell
Mt Emma
Indiana
Ambulbinya Peak
Christmas Dam
Atnetye Aboriginal Land Trust
Mt Knuckey
Mt Gardner
Tropic of Capricorn
Alice Springs
Undoolya
Emily and Jessie Gap Nat Pk
Ruby Gap Nature Park
Glen Annie Gorge
Atnarpa
Ross River
MACDONNELL RANGES
No. 4 Bore
Lake Caroline
24°

7
Ewaninga Rock Carvings Cons Res
Mt Ooraminna
Santa Teresa Aboriginal Land Trust
Santa Teresa
Mt Guenevere
Mt Pellinore
Ringwood
Limbla
Mt Kathleen
Numery
Casey Bore
Post Hill
Birch Hill
Pmere Nyente Aboriginal Land Trust
O'Neill Point
Lake Valerie
Simpson Desert National Park

8
Deep Well
Mt Brunonia
Allambi
Rodinga
Mt Rodinga
Fergusson
Range
Fletcher Hill
Prominent Pillar
Parakeelia Peak
Mt Peachy
Hugh River
Mt Burrell
Maryvale
Mt Madigan
Rodinga
Mt Charlotte
Bundooma
Mt Triodia
Depot Hill
Mt Casuarina
Engoordina
Point Eremophila
Marshall Bluff
Mac Clark (Acacia Peuce) Cons Reserve
North Bore
Hubbard Hill

9
Chambers Pillar Historical Reserve
Idracowra
Mt Santo
Mt Humphries
Horseshoe Bend
Colson Pinnacle
Mt Rumbalara
Rumbalara
Mt Musgrave
Tonys Lake Dam
Andado
Old Andado
Yalura Hill
SIMPSON DESERT
Simpson Desert National Park
Lilla Creek
Mt Gordon
Finke
Mt Day
Peebles Bore
Mt Peebles
New Crown
Pmer Ulperre Ingwemirne Arletherre Aboriginal Land Trust
Waggon Claypan Dam
Anacoora Hill
Lake Poeppel
Poeppel Corner
QAA Line
210

10
134°
Tieyon
Mt Andersen
Abminga
Mt Beddome
Mt Daniel
Duffield
Charlotte Waters
Bloods Creek
Witjira National Park
Mt Dare
Horse Hill
Mount Dare
Mt Apperda
Dakota Hill
NORTHERN TERRITORY
SOUTH AUSTRALIA
136°
French Line
Dalhousie Line
Simpson Desert Regional Reserve
Purni Bore
Approdinna Attora Knolls
Lake Tamblyn
Lake Thomas
Simpson Desert Conservation Park
138°
26°

NORTHERN TERRITORY / QUEENSLAND

208

346

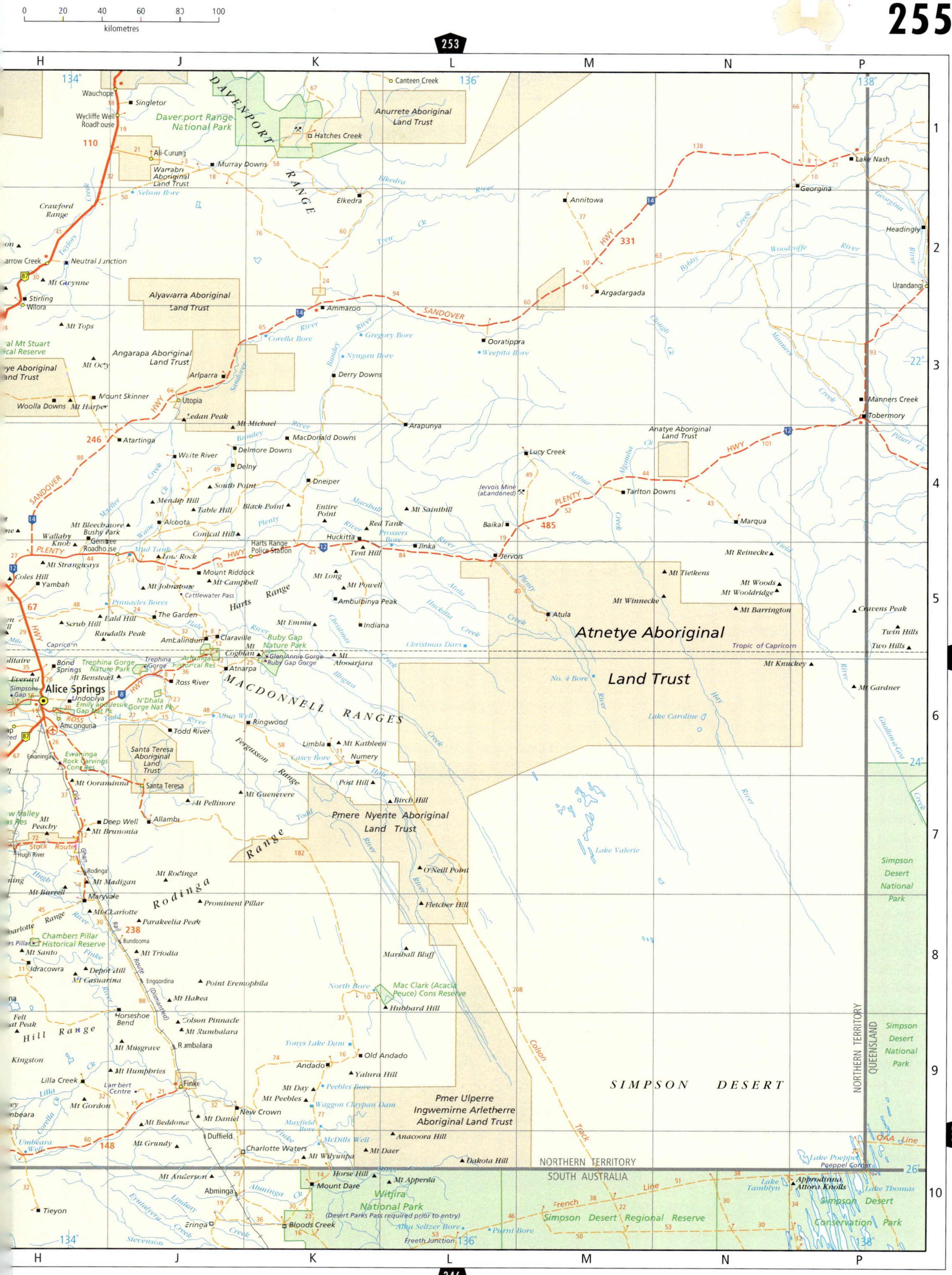

WESTERN AUSTRALIA

One of the first things visitors to Western Australia notice is space—measuring well over half the size of Europe this state is huge by any standard and the feeling of spaciousness is ever present for travellers right around the state. In addition, wherever you go, everything seems to be of large proportions, such as the iron ore, diamond and gold mining operations, the Ord River irrigation scheme, the extensive red sand dune outback desert country, and some of the northern river systems.

Whilst Western Australia's total area of over 2.5 million square kilometres is around one third of the Australian continent, it is in real contrast to the size of its population. Western Australia has only 1.6 million people—less than 10 per cent of the national total—and of these, 90 per cent live down in the southwestern corner of the state, including a little over 1 million people in the state capital, Perth.

Scenery in the west is full of variety, contrasts and surprises, with many of its landscapes like no other place in the country.

In the north the vast Kimberley region, dominated by its wet and dry seasons, is home to some of Australia's largest rivers, beautiful, untouched inland and coastal wildernesses, hundreds of uninhabited islands and magnificent gorge country spread out across its central and northern regions. In many respects, this area can be classified as one of the nation's last undeveloped frontiers.

A little further south, the Pilbara region has become synonymous with Australia's huge North-West Shelf natural gas and oil drilling operations, as well as its massive iron ore mines. These exist alongside the spectacular, colourful and dramatic gorges of the Hamersley Ranges, and the sheer beauty and tranquillity of the inland oasis of Millstream—a unique, lush eco-system in an otherwise hot, dry, spinifex landscape, a relic of thousands of years ago when the oceans covered much of the Australian continent.

The beautiful coral reefs extending several hundred kilometres along the Ningaloo coastline near Exmouth are claimed by many to be even better than those of the Great Barrier Reef. At Ningaloo there is the added advantage of easy accessibility with much of the reef just a couple of kilometres, and in some places only a hundred metres, off the coast.

To the south of the state the countryside changes again. Inland lie Mt Augustus (the world's largest monolith), the rich Western Australian goldfields and the state's famous wildflower regions. For many years, Western Australia has been known as 'the Wildflower State', and in springtime, particularly in the southwest corner, it is not hard to see why. Even the north of the state can, depending on

SCUBA diving in Ningaloo Marine Park

rainfall during late summer and autumn, in some years be a blaze of colour in early spring.

Throughout the state there are some 15,000 different plant species to be found. About half of these, including delicate orchids and a wide range of banksias, are endemic to Western Australia. Spring flowering starts early in the

Kimberley and Pilbara, in July and August, while in the south September and October, and even November in the deep south, are the best months to view the wildflowers. Each year the reputation of Western Australia's wildflower show draws thousands of visitors both from around Australia and the world.

The lower southwest of the state, is in most respects, a complete contrast to the open spaces of the north and the inland desert regions. It is like another world with its lush growth, tall mountain ranges of the Stirlings and Porongorups, and some of the best rugged coastal scenery of granite rocks and limestone cliffs to be found anywhere. The magnificent tall timber country found in this corner of Western Australia is home to majestic stands of karri, jarrah, marri and tingle trees, some measuring over 80 metres high and up to 1000 years old.

When thinking about a trip to Western Australia, consideration about the weather should be high on the planning list.

In the north the Kimberley and much of the Pilbara are subject to an annual wet season where it is not uncommon for up to 2 metres of rain, and occasionally more, to fall in just 3 or 4 months, and barely a trace for the rest of the year. Such dramatic climatic conditions pose enormous pressures on road systems. At some stage during the Wet, road travel can come to a halt. However, the Wet, usually lasting from

A kangaroo in Cape Range National Park

December to March, offers visitors a landscape scenery that can only be described as awesome. When roads to scenic areas are closed, light plane and helicopter flights cater for the increasing numbers of people coming to see the grandeur of the mighty Fitzroy, Ord and other rivers flowing many kilometres wide. Huge waterfalls thunder over the escarpments, and lakes, billabongs, creeks and lagoons dominate the landscape in a way that cannot even be imagined by visitors during the dry season. Certainly the weather conditions from May to September are more hospitable and road travel can be assured, but towards the end of the Dry, when the countryside is mostly brown, many waterways have virtually dried up, major rivers are just a chain of waterholes, and spectacular waterfalls reduced to a trickle, it is easy to understand why wet season visits are becoming as popular as dry.

Similarly in the south, many visitors come during the September/October wildflower season when the weather can still be quite cool and changeable, and then often miss out of the delightful summertime attractions, particularly around the southwest corner's coastal strip when conditions are generally splendid for bushwalking, swimming, diving, sailing, canoeing, and sightseeing.

Visitors who are aware of the seasonal variances, try to go back to areas in a different season from when they were there last time—few are ever disappointed by their return visit.

From a glance at a map of Australia, it is easy to see why much of the geology, flora and fauna found in the west is so different from that seen elsewhere around the country. Western Australia is cut off from the east by extensive areas of desert, including the Nullabor Plain, Gibson, Great Victoria and Sandy Deserts. This barrier has allowed the natural attributes that make Western Australia so different to flourish.

Another outcome of the West's isolation can be seen in its wildlife. It shares with the rest of Australia the hardy, well-travelled kangaroos and emus, but many of its other animal species, and even some bird life, has evolved quite differently from those found in the east. Some of its less adaptable wildlife, including quokkas, bettons, native mice and the state's fauna emblem, the numbat, is found nowhere else.

Geologically speaking, the Western Australian landscape has some of the world's most ancient formations. In terms of human population, recent studies deem that Aboriginal occupation, particularly in some northern regions, may date back well over 100 000 years. Western Australia has thousands of ancient Aboriginal art sites and other areas of significance, many of which are included in national parks and reserves where they are being protected and preserved, and as importantly, made available to visitors to experience this significant part of Australian history.

In European terms, the West's coastal regions were subject to the Dutch and French exploration long before any real interest was taken in eastern Australia. The earliest recorded visit to our shores is thought to have taken place on 25 October 1616 when Captain Dirk Hartog on the Dutch trading ship *Den Eendraght*, sailed past what are now known as the Zuytdorp Cliffs at Shark Bay (the Australian mainland's most westerly point). He landed and erected a post with a pewter plate from the ship's galley at Point Inscription, on what was named Dirk Hartog Island. All of this was over 150 years before Captain Cook made his 1770 epic journey of discovery to Australia's east coast. Permanent European settlement of Western Australia did not take place until the British set up Albany on the state's south coast in 1826. This was followed, in 1829, by the establishment of the Swan River Settlement which later became the state capital of Perth. Unlike most other early Australian cities, Perth was colonised by free settlers; convicts were brought into the settlement many years later to overcome labour shortages.

Much of Western Australia's early history is documented in national park booklets which are available to visitors from rangers and Conservation and Land Management (CALM) offices throughout the state.

In all, the state has in excess of 175 000 kilometres of roadways. When travelling throughout Western Australia today, visitors quickly become used to very long stretches of road between points of interest—particularly in northern and inland regions. Fortunately, all the state's major roads are now sealed and the majority of its minor roads are either sealed or generally good gravel. With much less traffic than is experienced in Australia's eastern states, driving to Western Australia's attractions is an uncrowded, enjoyable adventure.

One thing that the state does have in common with other Australian regions, however, is the forethought that has gone into both the location and development of its national parks and reserves. Strategically placed around both the state's extensive 15 000 km coastline and vast outback regions. the parks offer visitors a wonderful sample of some of Western Australia's best scenic and natural attractions.

Extending from its mostly cool climate southwest regions over 3000 km to its hot tropical north, and even out into the desert heartland of the state, the national parks system

The boab tree (*Andersonia gregorii*)

covers a wide variety of climates, landscapes, wildlife and, importantly, for visitors, a vast choice of things to see, do and experience.

The size of the state and distances involved, together with the quite dramatic seasonal changes that occur in the various regions, often means visitors will need to make several visits, perhaps at different times of the year, to take in all the attractions and features of Western Australia's national parks.

WESTERN AUSTRALIA NATIONAL PARKS AND RESERVES

#	Park	Ranger/Park Tel.	Ranger/Information	Camping	Caravan	4WD Access	BBQ/Fireplace	Picnic Area	Marked Walking Tracks	Bushwalking	Kiosk/Restaurant	Fishing	Swimming
1	Alexander Morrison National Park	(08) 9652 7043											
2	Avon Valley National Park	(08) 9574 2540	*	*			*	*					
3	Badgingarra National Park	(08) 9652 7043						*	*				
4	Beedelup National Park	(08) 9776 1200					*	*	*				
5	Bell Creek	(08) 9193 1411		*									
6	Blackwood River Conservation Park	(08) 9756 1101		*								*	*
7	Boorabbin National Park	(08) 9021 2677											
8	Bridgetown Jarrah Park	(08) 9756 1101	*					*					
9	Brockman National Park	(08) 9776 1200				*							
10	Canning River Regional Park	(08) 9405 0700						*	*	*			*
11	Cape Arid National Park	(08) 9075 0055	*	*	*	*		*	*	*		*	*
12	Cape Le Grand National Park	(08) 9075 9022	*	*	*			*	*	*		*	*
13	Cape Range National Park & Ningaloo Marine Park	(08) 9949 1676	*	*	*	*	*	*	*	*		*	*
14	Collie River	(08) 9725 4300	*	*									*
15	Collier Range National Park	(08) 9143 1488											
16	D'Entrecasteaux National Park	(08) 9776 1107	*	*		*	*	*	*	*		*	*
17	Drovers Cave National Park	(08) 9652 7043		*			*	*	*				
18	Dryandra Woodland National Park	(08) 9881 1113	*	*			*	*	*				
19	Drysdale River National Park	(08) 9168 0200		*		*							
20	Eucla National Park	(08) 9071 3733											
21	Fitzgerald River National Park	(08) 9835 5043	*	*		*	*	*	*	*		*	*
22	Forrestdale Lake Nature Reserve	(08) 9334 0333						*	*				
23	Francois Peron National Park	(08) 9948 1076	*	*		*	*		*	*		*	*
24	Frank Hann National Park	(08) 9076 8541											
25	Gibson Desert Nature Reserve	(08) 9334 0333				*							
26	Gloucester National Park	(08) 9776 1200	*				*		*	*	*		
27	Golden Valley Tree Park	(08) 9731 6232	*				*		*	*			
28	Goongarrie National Park	(08) 9021 2677											
29	Gooseberry Hill National Park	(08) 9298 8344											
30	Greenmount National Park	(08) 9298 8344											
31	Hassell National Park	(08) 9841 7133											
32	John Forrest National Park	(08) 9298 8344	*				*	*	*	*			*
33	Kalamunda National Park	(08) 9298 8344						*	*				
34	Kalbarri National Park	(08) 9937 1192	*				*	*	*			*	*
35	Karijini (Hamersley Range) National Park	(08) 9189 8157	*	*	*		*						*
36	Karri Gully	(08) 9756 1101					*	*					
37	Kennedy Range National Park	(08) 9943 0988	*				*	*					
	Kimberley Parks												
38	- Geikie Gorge National Park	(08) 9191 5121	*				*	*	*	*			*
39	- King Leopold Range Conservation Park	(08) 9191 5121	*	*				*	*				
40	- Mitchell Plateau	(08) 9168 0200		*				*	*				*
41	- Parry Lagoons Nature Reserve	(08) 9168 0200											
42	- Tunnel Creek National Park	(08) 9191 5121	*				*	*	*				
43	- Windjana Gorge National Park	(08) 9193 1411	*	*	*		*	*	*				
44	Lane-Poole Reserve	(08) 9538 1001	*	*			*	*				*	*
45	Leeuwin-Naturaliste National Park	(08) 9752 1677	*				*	*	*			*	*
46	Lesmurdie Falls National Park	(08) 9298 8344	*						*				
47	Lesueur National Park	(08) 9652 7043	*						*				
48	Marmion Marine Park	(08) 9448 5705	*									*	*
49	Millstream-Chichester National Park	(08) 9184 5144	*	*		*	*	*	*				*
50	Migenew-Coalseam Conservation Park	(08) 9921 5955	*	*				*	*				
51	Mirima-Hidden Valley National Park	(08) 9168 0200	*					*	*	*			
52	Moore River National Park	(08) 9561 1044											
53	Mt Augustus (Burringurrah) National Park	(08) 9943 0527	*	*		*	*	*	*	*			
54	Mt Frankland National Park	(08) 9840 1027	*					*	*	*			
55	Mt Hart Homestead	(08) 9191 4645											
56	Nambung National Park	(08) 9652 7043	*			*		*				*	*
57	Neerabup National Park	(08) 9561 1004											
58	Ningaloo Marine Park	(08) 9949 1676	*	*		*			*			*	*
59	Peak Charles National Park	(08) 9076 8541	*										
60	Porongurup National Park	(08) 9853 1095	*				*	*	*	*			
61	Purnululu (Bungle Bungle) National Park	(08) 9168 7300	*	*		*		*	*	*			
62	Rowley Shoals Marine Park	(08) 9192 1036											
63	Rudall River (Karlamilyi) National Park	(08) 9143 1488	*			*							
64	Scott National Park	(08) 9758 1756										*	*
65	Serpentine National Park	(08) 9390 5977	*	*			*	*	*	*			
66	Shannon National Park	(08) 9971 1988	*	*	*		*	*	*	*			
67	Shark Bay Marine Park	(08) 9948 1208		*		*						*	*
68	Shoalwater Islands Marine Park	(08) 94485705										*	*
69	Silent Grove	(08) 9193 1411	*										
70	Sir James Mitchell National Park	(08) 9771 1988											
71	Stirling Range National Park	(08) 9827 9230	*	*	*		*	*	*	*			
72	Stockyard Gully National Park	(08) 9652 7043					*	*	*				
73	Stokes National Park	(08) 9076 8541	*	*		*	=	*	*			*	*
74	Sue's Bridge	(08) 9756 1101	*									*	*
75	Swan Estuary Marine Park	(08) 9448 5705										*	*
76	Tathra National Park	(08) 9652 7043											
77	"The Hills Forest, Mundaring"	(08) 9295 2244	*	*					*	*			
78	Torndirrup National Park	(08) 9844 4090										*	*

National Park	Ranger/Park Tel.	Ranger/Information	Camping	Caravan	4WD Access	BBQ/Fireplace	Picnic Area	Marked Walking Tracks	Bushwalking	Kiosk/Restaurant	Fishing	Swimming
79 Tuart Forest National Park	(08) 9752 1677	*				*		*				
80 Walpole–Nornalup National Park	(08) 9840 1026	*	*	*	*	*	*	*			*	*
81 Walyunga National Park	(08) 9571 1371					*	*	*	*			*
82 Warren National Park	(08) 9776 1207	*				*					*	*
83 Watheroo National Park	(08) 9552 7043							*	*			
84 Waychinicup National Park	(08) 9341 7133	*				*		*	*		*	*
85 West Cape Howe National Park	(08) 9844 4090	*	*		*	*		*	*		*	*
86 William Bay National Park	(08) 9840 9255	*			*	*	*		*		*	*
87 Wolfe Creek Crater National Park	(08) 9168 0200											
88 Yalgorup National Park	(08) 9739 1067	*			*	*	*	*			*	*
89 Yanchep National Park	(08) 9561 1004	*			*	*	*	*		*	*	*

BURRINGURRAH (MT AUGUSTUS) NATIONAL PARK

IN BRIEF

MAP REFERENCE: PAGE 300 F 2

Location 1100 km north of Perth; 450 km east of Carnarvon via Gascoyne Junction, and 350 km northwest from Meekatharra
Best Time April to September
Main Attractions View world's largest rock, climbing and walking
Ranger National park rangers are based at the Tourist Resort from June to September, phone (08) 9943 0527

Accommodation, supplies and fuel: Mt Augustus Outback Tourist Resort, phone (08) 9943 0527

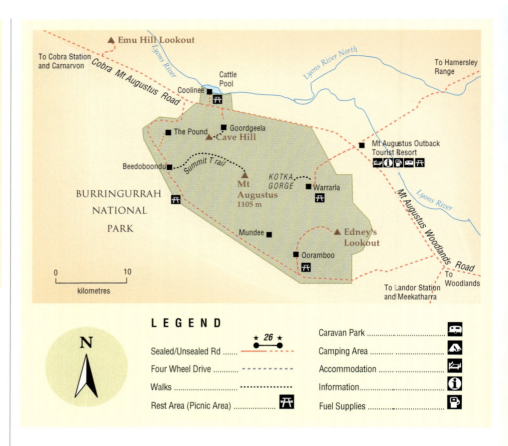

LEGEND

Sealed/Unsealed Rd ....
Four Wheel Drive ....
Walks ....
Rest Area (Picnic Area) ....

Caravan Park ....
Camping Area ....
Accommodation ....
Information............................
Fuel Supplies ....

Located some 450 km east of Carnarvon in Western Australia's Upper Gascoyne region, Mt Augustus has been called a 'sleeping giant' who is only now 'being awakened and discovered' by visitors who are coming in their thousands to see 'the world's biggest rock'.

The *Guinness Book of Records* describes Mt Augustus as the 'world's largest rocky outcrop', more than twice as big as Uluru (Ayers Rock) and millions of years older. Unlike Uluru, which is bald and has virtually no vegetation on

Aboriginal art in Burringurrah National Park

Mt Augustus, the world's largest rock

it, Mt Augustus is covered with small, shrubby trees, grasses and spinifex.

HISTORY

Discovered by explorer Francis Thomas Gregory in 1858 and named after his brother, Augustus, this monocline—a tilting strata of rock—stands 706 metres above the surrounding plain, and is about 16 km long and 5 km across.

The local Aboriginal tribal name for Mt Augustus is Burringurrah. Their Dreamtime story tells of a boy called Burringurrah who broke Aboriginal law during his initiation and, as a punishment, was speared and his body fell in the shape of the mountain as we see it today.

Burringurrah National Park was established in 1989 and has a total area of 9168 hectares.

CLIMB TO THE TOP

When the explorer Gregory came through here in 1858, his diary records he spent 'two hours of heavy toil' climbing to the mountain summit from where, in the clear air at the top of this dominant landmark, he was able to take bearings on other hills more than 160 km away.

Today one of the main attractions at Burringurrah is still the climb to the top. Be warned, however, that this strenuous climb is some 6 km each way and is for only the fit and healthy. Rangers advise allowing 5 to 6 hours for the return trek, and always to carry drinking water. Whilst there are now 2 clearly marked summit trails, neither is easy and should not be tackled if you are in any doubt about your ability to make the climb.

OTHER WALKS AND CLIMBS

Elsewhere around the mountain, the rangers have developed a number of trails to points of interest, including Edneys Lookout, where Edney, an early cattle rustler in the area, kept watch for the police.

In addition, there are several Aboriginal art sites, including ancient petroglyphs (rock engravings), waterfalls, caves, several splendid stands of stately ghost gums, and picnic sites.

Each of these locations is accessed from a well-maintained 49 km gravel driving track which circumnavigates the mountain. A delightful picnic spot is found at nearby Cattle Pool—a permanent waterhole lined by large, white river gums—on the Lyons River which runs past Mt Augustus. The waterhole attracts a variety of waterbirds, and is a pleasant place for a swim.

Scenically the mountain has some dramatic faces, particularly the cliff section on its northern side. Photographically there are moody images to be recorded as the rock changes colour, especially in the early morning and towards sunset.

Over 100 different bird species, including honeyeaters, emus and bustards, have been recorded in the park and in springtime the area is carpeted in colourful everlasting daisies.

ACCESS

Access is by gravel roads from either Meekatharra in the southeast or Carnarvon in the west. Except after heavy rain, these roads and all tracks within the park are accessible by conventional vehicles.

ACCOMMODATION

Camping is not allowed in the park, but a full range of accommodation—camp sites through to cabins and motel-style rooms—is available at the Mt Augustus Outback Tourist Resort located just outside the national park, 5 km from the mountain. Basic food supplies, water and fuel are available at the resort. Allow 3 or 4 full days in the region to see all the park has to offer.

CAPE ARID NATIONAL PARK

Mt Arid

Situated on Western Australia's south coast 120 km east of Esperance, this 280 000 hectare park features remote sweeping beaches, clear blue seas, rocky headlands and kilometres of sandplain and heathland vegetation. Grey granite cliffs and inland hills are features of the landscape in the park. Mt Ragged, part of the Russell Range in the northern sector of the park, is, at 594 metres, the most dominant peak.

This area was extensively explored by the French. In 1792 Bruni D'Entrecasteaux in 1792, named Esperance after one of the ships in his fleet when he took shelter in the bay. He was also responsible for naming Cape Arid and the Recherche Archipelago.

During the 1800s several overland expeditions tackled the arduous route connecting eastern and western Australia. These included the expeditions of Edward John Eyre in 1841, John Septimus Roe in 1848 and John Forrest in 1870. The graziers followed, settling around Thomas River and Pine Hill. However, it was the finalising of overland telegraph line between Adelaide and Albany in 1877 that really opened up the area.

In a deep valley near Mt Arid can be found the grave of Will Ponton, one of the early settlers. The remains of John Baesjou's homestead which was built in 1905 and destroyed by fire in the mid-1920s, can still be seen today.

THINGS TO DO

Throughout the park there are a number of walk and climb trails including a quite strenuous 3 km return Mt Ragged to Tower Peak trail, which gives extensive views over the countryside. This will take about 2 hours. This northern section of the park is 4WD country and attracts only a limited number of visitors.

The most popular section of the park is its southern coastline, with its long, clean beaches, ideal for fishing and swimming. Commercial fishermen wait along the WA south coast for the huge annual salmon migration.

There are walk trails (including the popular Tagon Coastal Walk of around 7 km which takes about 4 hours return) around picturesque headlands where it is often possible to spot whales, Australian sea lions and the New Zealand fur seals. Other animal life found in the park includes bush rats and western brush wallabies. Watch out also for the rare Cape Barren geese around the coastal headlands Bird life in the park is quite prolific with over 150 recorded species.

In springtime the colour in the heathland is vibrant with wildflowers and several species of orchids can be found on and near Mt Ragged.

In a 4WD vehicle with tyre pressures lowered, it is possible to drive, with care, along extensive sections of the park's beaches. However, be careful to watch the tides.

ACCESS

Access to the park is on gravel roads suitable to conventional vehicles.

When travelling from Esperance, it is advisable to call in and get up-to-date notes and track information from the ranger based just inside the park on the western side at Thomas River. Information can also be obtained from the Department of Conservation and Land Management (CALM)'s District Office in Dempster Street, Esperance. With fires that occasionally sweep through the area and the spread of dieback which, in places, seriously threatens vegetation, roads and walk trails are changed from time to time.

CAMPING

There are 3 main camping areas in the park: at Thomas River, Seal Creek and Mt Ragged. Each of these has toilets, BBQ and picnic facilities. There are numerous other pleasant places, particularly along the coast, which also make great camp sites. Campers must be totally self-sufficient, however, as there is no drinking water or other supplies in this quite remote park. Firewood is scarce and it is advisable to bring gas cooking appliances. The nearest main supplies are in Esperance. A small camping fee applies in the designated camping areas.

LEGEND

Sealed/Unsealed Rd .... ★ 26 ★

Four Wheel Drive .... - - -

Walks .... ·······

Rest Area (Picnic Area) .... 🏕

Caravan Park .... 🚐

Camping Area .... 🏕

Accommodation .... 🛏

Information .... ℹ

Fuel Supplies .... ⛽

Map: Cape Arid National Park showing Pine Hill, Mt Symmons, Tower Peak, Mt Ragged 594 m, The Diamonds Hill, Price Hill, Balladonia Road, Gora Road, Fisheries Road, Merivale Road, Telegraph Line Road, To Esperance 120 km, To Israelite Bay 16 km, To Point Malcolm 4 km, Thomas River, Poison Creek, Seal Creek, Jorndee Creek, Sandy Bight, Cape Pasley, Mt Arid, Arid Bay, Tagon Bay, Tagon Point, Cape Arid, Southern Ocean

MAP REFERENCE: PAGE 299 M 8

IN BRIEF

Location 40 km east of Esperance on the south coast of Western Australia
Best Time Spring, summer and autumn
Main Attractions Coastal and granite outcrop scenery, swimming, bushwalking, fishing, and 4WD
Ranger Phone (08) 9075 9022

Massive rocky outcrops, long stretches of pristine, white sandy beaches and clear aquamarine water are the outstanding features of this attractive park near Esperance.

An impressive chain of granite peaks, including Mt Le Grand, Frenchman Peak and Mississippi Hill, rises above the undulating heath-covered sandplains that extend over most of the park's 32 000 hectares. Some of the caves and tunnels in the rocky outcrops are of interest to bushwalkers and modern day explorers.

Cape Le Grand was named in 1792 by the French explorer Bruni D'Entrecasteaux.

VEGETATION AND WILDLIFE

The sandplains support a wide variety of plant life, with wildflowers in spring (including several different species of banksia) making an especially colourful show.

Almost tame kangaroos are another special attraction as they come in close looking for food at the camp sites. Tiny honey possums are sometimes observed getting nectar from banksia flowers, and small, southern brown bandicoots can be seen by torchlight at night.

Be on the lookout for Australian sea lions and New Zealand fur seals in the bays or lazing on rocky foreshores. In deeper water, southern right whales are often spotted.

THINGS TO DO

Bushwalking is one of the park's most popular activities. Numerous walk trails range from just a few hundred metres to an extremely scenic 15 km coastal track which winds from Le Grand Beach in the west via Hellfire Bay, to Rossiter Bay on the eastern side of the cape. Allow about 4 hours one way for this walk. A guide map is available from the ranger based in the park.

A special signposted Le Grand Heritage Trail (2 km) has recently been set up taking in some of the park's most scenic areas and historic landmarks. The walk is also a photographer's delight with picturesque bays, tall granite headlands and outcrops and expansive beaches. This walk would take about 1½ hours.

Fishing is also popular here. There are boat

launching facilities at Lucky Bay; small boats can also be launched off Le Grand Beach. Salmon black bream and whiting and larger species of fish such as mulloway, sharks and blue groper are amongst the regular catches.

Swimming in the warmer months is a highlight of a Cape Le Grand visit.

CAMPING

There are camping areas at Lucky Bay and at Le Grand Beach. These are cleared, well-organised camp sites with septic toilets and showers. There is very little firewood available and campers should use a portable gas stove for cooking. A camping fee applies.

ACCESS

Access into the park is by an all-weather sealed road from Esperance. Within the park most main roads are also sealed. There are also several, usually good condition, gravel sections. All are accessible by conventional vehicles.

For those with 4WD vehicles there is a beach access track into the park from Esperance. It

Cape Le Grand National Park

leads from Wylie Bay to Le Grand Beach and if taken with care, lowering tyre pressures for soft beach sand travel, it is a picturesque and rewarding way to make your way to the cape. It is about 20 km on the beach and you should allow ¾ hour for the trip.

LEGEND

Sealed/Unsealed Rd	★ 26 ★
Four Wheel Drive	- - - - - -
Walks	....
Rest Area (Picnic Area)	🏕
Caravan Park	🚐
Camping Area	⛺
Accommodation	🛏
Information	ℹ
Fuel Supplies	⛽

CAPE RANGE NATIONAL PARK & NINGALOO MARINE PARK

IN BRIEF

MAP REFERENCE: PAGE 306 B 7

Location 400 km north of Carnarvon, off the Great Northern Highway
Best Time March to October
Main Attractions Superb coral reef, great fishing, diving & 4WD
Ranger Exmouth, phone (08) 9949 1676

Bay View Resort, Coral Bay, phone (08) 9942 5932
Dive Shops: Coral Bay, phone (08) 9942 5940; Exmouth, phone (08) 9949 1201
Exmouth Tourist Bureau, phone (08) 9949 1990
Fisheries Department of WA, phone (08) 9220 5333
Milyering Information Centre, phone (08) 9949 2808
Yardie Creek Tours, phone (08) 9949 2659

Fishing in Ningaloo Marine Park

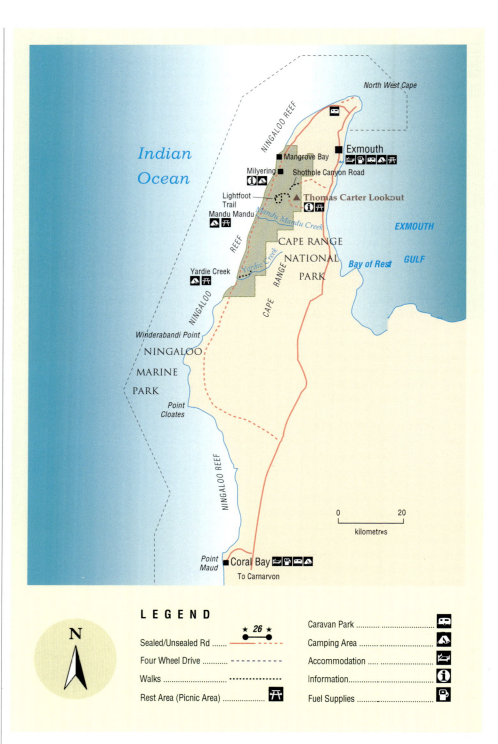

Suddenly out of the blue it appears, dwarfing everything with its size and presence; the largest fish in the world, the biggest shark in the sea, growing to over 10 metres in length with a mouth so big it seems it could swallow a small car. Quite quickly it draws level and you realise you need to swim flat out just to keep up with this languidly moving animal. Then the whale shark, *Rhincodon typus*, dips its head and slowly swims down to the dark depths from where it had appeared.

This great animal of the marine world, more than any single thing, has put the Cape Range National Park and the adjoining Ningaloo Marine Park on the world stage as it is the only place where you can be guaranteed a swim with the biggest of the world's sharks. It is an experience available to all and one that should be achieved in everyone's lifetime.

HISTORY

Cape Range National Park, covering 50 581 hectares, was founded in 1969 and takes up much of the west coast and the spine of land

that is known as North West Cape. A narrow strip of coastal reserve runs north from the northern boundary of the park to near the very tip of the Cape. South of Yardie Creek, where the national park ends, the land is at present pastoral lease, but the marine park, which takes in all the water from the eastern tip of North West Cape south to Amherst Point, also includes all the land west of the main Exmouth road as a management area.

CAPE RANGE

This forms the backbone of North West Cape and is cut by many spectacular gorges, the most famous of which is Yardie Creek Gorge in the southwestern end of the park.

This rugged country is home to the rare black-striped rock wallaby and you'll often see them at Yardie Creek. Elsewhere on the less rugged country red kangaroos and stockier built euros, or hill wallaroos, are very common. In

LEGEND

Sealed/Unsealed Rd
Four Wheel Drive
Walks
Rest Area (Picnic Area)
Caravan Park
Camping Area
Accommodation
Information
Fuel Supplies

fact, so common, that driving on the main north–south track around sunrise or sundown is decidedly hazardous.

Walking Trails

There are some excellent walks in the park, from long stretches of beaches, to rugged walks across the range country.

The 2–3 hour, 7 km Lightfoot Trail, on the east side of the range, is a beauty. This trail, accessible from the end of the vehicle access on the Charles Knife Road, traverses some rugged and broken country, giving good views and an idea of what the oil exploration teams had to contend with when searching for oil in the region in the 1950s. This trail is marked by rock cairns, and a brochure is available from the Department of Conservation and Land Management (CALM).

Another walking trail—about 10 km—leaves from the car park near the Thomas Carter Lookout and heads north to the picnic area at the end of the vehicle access track called the Shothole Canyon Road. The walk will take about 3 hours.

On the western side of the range there are a couple of short walking trails. One heads up along Mandu Mandu Creek from a point inland from the camping area of the same name, and will take about 2 hours return. The second walk, at Yardie Creek, is the most popular trail on the coast. It is possible to head inland on either side of the creek, but the north side has a recognised walking trail which is a little easier to follow. It is about 2 km long and will take 1½ hours for the return walk. In the early morning or evening you may be able to spy the elusive black-striped rock wallaby on the southern cliffs of Yardie Creek Gorge. You will also see many of the 154 species of birds that have been recorded in the area. These include birds of prey such as the white-bellied sea-eagle, brahminy kite, osprey and spotted harrier.

Yardie Creek Boat Cruise

A boat cruise on Yardie Creek is great and really is the best way to see the gorge and its wildlife. Yardie Creek Tours have the only powered craft allowed on Yardie Creek and tours are run most days of the tourist season. Private boats are only allowed without motors, making a canoe the best option by far!

Ningaloo Reef

This coral reef is magnificent and in places is only 100 metres offshore, although for most of its length it is a kilometre or so out to sea. The fishing is great and the diving superb.

Being a park there are many areas where fishing is not allowed and you need to see the information centre in the park, or the dive

A whale shark in Ningaloo Marine Park

shops at Exmouth or Coral Bay for the areas where activities are permitted.

Even with such intensive management the choices are endless and you won't be disappointed. The Fisheries Department of WA can also provide information on the fishing requirements and the bag limits for the marine park.

The waters of the reef provide not only a home for a myriad fish but also for the dugong and turtles, the latter being commonly seen at places like Turquoise Bay where many come to shore to nest between October and February each year.

At other times of the year manta rays congregate in large numbers feeding on the plankton that also attracts the whale sharks. All in all this is an area that is hard to beat.

ACCESS AND CAMPING

The park is easily accessible via the good bitumen road that heads north off the Great Northern Highway and leads to the small town of Exmouth, or to the holiday hamlet of Coral Bay. Both have a range of accommodation and camping as well as all supplies, tours and other necessities.

From Exmouth the road heads north and then south, turning from bitumen to a good dirt surface. For all the way the road hugs the coast and a few kilometres inside the national park is the Milyering Information Centre. This is a top spot to start your visit to the area. Obtaining a camping permit here opens up a number of excellent camp sites dotted along the coast, and most of these are small and secluded, being tucked away close to the beach.

The camping ground at Yardie Creek is a little bigger than most and is located a short distance back from the creek and the beach.

South of Yardie Creek and north of Coral Bay is 4WD territory and the camping is not so regulated, but you need permission from the land owner.

Sunset along Cape Range National Park

D'ENTRECASTEAUX NATIONAL PARK

IN BRIEF

MAP REFERENCE: PAGE 298 C 9

Location 20 km west of Walpole, 30 km south of Pemberton, off the Vasse Highway
Best Time September to April
Main Attractions Fishing, coastal scenery, sand dunes, swimming, remote beaches, photography, and 4WD
Ranger Department of Conservation and Land Management, Pemberton Regional Office, phone (08) 9776 1107

Stretching about 130 km along Western Australia's southern coastline, D'Entrecasteaux National Park is long and quite narrow, covering some 115 000 hectares of diverse and mainly untouched country. Located between Walpole and Augusta it has huge sand dunes, limestone cliffs and long, white, sandy beaches. Inland there are lakes, wetlands, the Shannon, Donnelly and Warren Rivers, areas of heathland and tracts of tall karri and jarrah forest.

Wildlife here includes a small number of quokkas, chuditch, ringtail, brush-tail and pygmy possums, wallabies and bandicoots, while southern right whales migrate along the coast.

Point D'Entrecasteaux was named in honour of Bruni D'Entrecasteaux, who led a French scientific expedition along the coast of Western Australia in 1792.

In 1990 archaeological studies were carried out in Lake Jasper in the park's northern sector. Divers found Aboriginal artefacts, trees and grass-tree (blackboy) stumps deep underwater, and ancient camp sites dating from 40 000 years ago when the Aboriginal Minang people lived in the region.

DONNELLY BOAT LANDING

This picturesque picnic and camping site with BBQ and toilet facilities has a boat launching ramp. It also has good fishing and swimming. A lovely stretch of water leads 11 km to the river mouth with spectacular limestone cliffs and a beautiful beach.

YEAGARUP LAKE

This is one of a several lakes that lie behind the coast's dune system. It is a pleasant spot for a swim, a picnic or camping with BBQ and toilet facilities. From here you can walk into the Yeagarup Dunes. A 4WD-only track leads from the lake to the coast (about 10 km—30 minutes).

A view of D'Entrecasteaux's rugged coastline

MT CHUDALUP

This is a huge granite outcrop 188 metres high. A quite steep, 1 km walk and climb trail leads to the summit. From here there are good views to the coast, over heathland and tall timber forests. Allow 1½ hours for the return walk. There are BBQ and picnic facilities at the car park.

WINDY HARBOUR AND SALMON BEACH

Windy Harbour (conventional vehicle access) and Salmon Beach (4WD only near Point D'Entrecasteaux are picturesque spots: good for photography, fishing and swimming (but be careful of rips at Salmon Beach). There are caravan park facilities—showers, toilets, BBQs and grassed sites—and a small settlement at Windy Harbour.

BROKE INLET

This is an extensive, shallow lake, and the area around is good for walking and birdwatching and fishing. The photographic opportunities in the early morning and at sunset are excellent.

ACCESS AND CAMPING

Several conventional access trails lead off the Vasse Highway, Windy Harbour Road and South-Western Highway to the park's main features. There are also rough, narrow and sandy 4WD tracks going to various sections of the park and to the coast, mostly to great fishing spots.

There are a few designated camping areas with basic facilities, but there are also many appealing bush camping spots, particularly for 4WD enthusiasts. No supplies are available in the park—bring all your requirements, including water. The nearest fuel and supplies are at Pemberton, Northcliffe and Walpole.

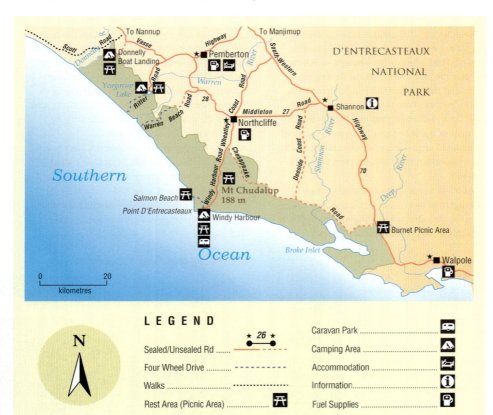

LEGEND

Sealed/Unsealed Rd ....
Four Wheel Drive ....
Walks ....
Rest Area (Picnic Area) ....

Caravan Park ....
Camping Area ....
Accommodation ....
Information...................
Fuel Supplies ....

IN BRIEF

MAP REFERENCE: PAGE 300 D 10

Location 5 km east of Jurien and 255 km north of Perth. 4WD access only
Best Time August to October
Main Attractions Caves and wildflowers
Ranger Phone (09) 9652 7043

Lying on Western Australia's coastal limestone belt, this park takes its name from the drovers' stock route that passed through here in the 1800s. When a rail line was opened in 1894, the trail was no longer needed, and was largely reclaimed by the bush. In 1955 a petroleum exploration company rediscovered many of the caves and sinkholes scattered throughout the region.

The park was officially declared in 1972 to help protect the caves, the fossil deposits of prehistoric mammals found here and the plant life surrounding them. This is an area full of interesting caves and has a true diversity of plants and wildflowers.

THE CAVES

The park, which is a small one at about 2681 hectares, is still a virtual wilderness area. It has only one main track—a single lane, sandy 4WD-only trail—leading in a north–south direction through its centre. While the whole limestone area here is riddled with caves, sinkholes, crevices and rock depressions, the trail leads to the most interesting ones.

Driving into the park from the south, Drovers Cave is the first to be reached, just 1.3 km inside the park boundary. The cave is around 50 metres off the track on the right-hand side surrounded by dryandra woodland. The cave is considered to be suitable for exploration only by experienced speleologists and access into it is barred by a door. Those wanting to explore the cave should contact the ranger.

A further 1 km north is Hastings Cave. This is an interesting cave open to the public to explore with a torch but a great deal of care is needed. A feature here is the huge beehives that hang like curtains over the entrance to the cave.

Visitors should be careful not to antagonise the bees. The cave faces north—it is best to photograph the entrance in the morning.

900 metres further north there is a track heading to one of the region's many sinkholes—like a manhole in a pavement—leading to an underground cave.

For the next 2.6 km north, the track becomes quite narrow with dense banksia foliage on either side. It ends at Moorbe Cave. probably the most interesting accessible cave in the park. The cave was once a hive of activity when a small operation was set up to mine the bat droppings, well over a metre thick. The evidence of that operation— timber structures and the old train track carriage rails used to haul the droppings to the surface—is still there. It is possible to climb a couple of hundred metres down into this cave system. However, only experienced cavers should proceed beyond that point.

Other caves in this north section of the park include the Old River Cave and Mystery Cave.

PLANTS AND ANIMALS

Wildflowers are a real attraction in the park with several varieties of banksia and wattles, as well as parrot bush, smokebush, one-sided bottlebrush, purple flag, curry flowers, native violets, and the twining old man's beard all growing here. Ripe quandong fruit can be found in the park around October.

Bustards, western grey kangaroos, emus and honey possums all inhabit in the park.

BUSHWALKING AND CAMPING

Bushwalking in the park is fairly restricted because of the very dense scrub. In addition, the area's many sinkholes and limestone crevices and cavities make it quite dangerous except for the most experienced.

Whilst camping is not prohibited in the park, there are, because of the ground conditions, no nice, easily accessible sites. It would be better to bush camp outside the park, or to arrange accommodation at nearby Jurien on the coast, which has a full range of hotel, motel and caravan park facilities.

Carry all your own supplies into the park, including water, and take a good tick repellent.

ACCESS

Access to the park is off the sealed Jurien Road. The turn north into the park is 5 km east of Jurien. The national park entry sign is 50 metres along the sandy access track. There are absolutely no facilities in the park.

Banksias growing along the tracks in the park

DRYSDALE RIVER NATIONAL PARK

IN BRIEF

MAP REFERENCE: PAGE 305 L 3

Location Northern Kimberley, 580 km west of Wyndham off the Gibb River–Kalumburu Road. 4WD access only
Best Time May to September
Main Attractions Remote camping in a pristine environment
Ranger Kununurra, phone (08) 9168 0200

In a region dominated by rugged mountain ranges, cliffs and escarpments, the Drysdale River National Park is not only the largest park in the Kimberley, it is also one of the most remote, encompassing the spectacular Carson Escarpment. This unbroken line of cliffs is one of the Kimberley's largest features, stretching from the central plateau area to the northern coast at Cape Londonderry.

Europeans have made little impact on this wild and remote area but for thousands of years Aboriginal people have lived here, as testified by the numerous art galleries along the cliffs.

In 1901 the government surveyor, Fred Brockman, led a party through this unexplored region, following the Drysdale River and the escarpment before heading east back to Wyndham. Some of the nearby area was taken up for cattle grazing, but in the 1950s the Aboriginal community at Kalumburu took it over and has been running it ever since. The rest of the country was deemed too rugged for anything else but a park, which is what it now is.

A RUGGED ESCARPMENT

While the Carson Escarpment is the dominant feature of the park, the Carson and Drysdale Rivers provide a delightful, cool change from the monotonous plains. They are a verdant habitat for birds, mammals and reptiles. The rivers harbour a surprising number of fresh-water fish with over 26 recorded species.

There are a number of gorges and some magnificent waterfalls in the park, including Morgan, Falls on Palmoondora Creek and Solea Falls on the Drysdale River itself.

The park covers 448 264 hectares, with the Drysdale River flowing north–south through its centre and forming the southwestern boundary. Uninhabited Aboriginal land lies to the east, and Aboriginal-owned pastoral leases to the north.

WALKING AND CANOEING

There are no walking trails in this remote park but for the well-experienced and prepared bushwalker there are some excellent wild areas to visit. For the well-equipped canoeist the rivers provide a wonderful way to explore this

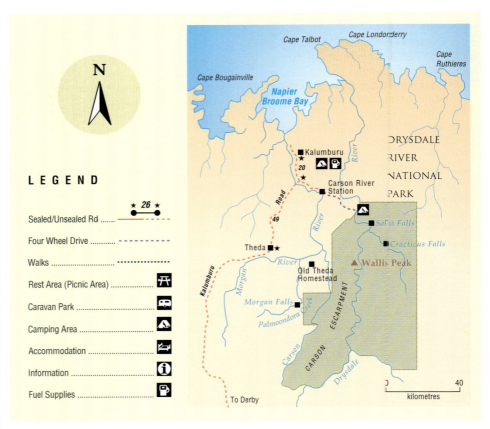

LEGEND

Sealed/Unsealed Rd .... ★ 26 ★

Four Wheel Drive ....

Walks ....

Rest Area (Picnic Area) ....

Caravan Park ....

Camping Area ....

Accommodation ....

Information ....

Fuel Supplies ....

The Drysdale River

park, especially at the beginning of the Dry.

The most common excursion is to Solea Falls, and requires experience and being well equipped. The walk, or the canoe–walking trip, takes a good 2 days from the camping site upriver to the falls and back again. Late in the Dry the river is more a series of waterholes, so forget the canoe.

From the camp site there are plenty of short, easy walks along the river to enjoy. Small wallabies, colonies of flying foxes and any one of the 129 varieties of birds, along with water monitors and large goannas, may be seen.

ACCESS AND CAMPING

Access to this vast park is limited to one track that leaves the main Kalumburu road 20 km south of the Kalumburu community. This track crosses the Aboriginal-owned Carson River Station and permission is needed before entry. Phone the manager on (08) 9161 4330 before heading that way. A small fee is also payable.

The track is sandy in places and is 4WD access only. It leads to the only camping area in the park and is fairly well signposted. At the camp site there is shade from the trees and water from the river—it is a delightful spot.

IN BRIEF

MAP REFERENCE: PAGE 299 H 8

Location 180 km northeast of Albany and 240 km west of Esperance, on the south coast of Western Australia
Best Time September–May, June–July for whales
Main Attractions Scenery, wildflowers, bushwalking, fishing, photography, 4WD
Ranger Phone (08) 9835 5043 or fax (08) 9835 5045

The area now known as the Fitzgerald River National Park was described by early Australian explorer Edward John Eyre in June 1841 as 'a wretched and arid looking country'. Some years earlier in 1802, Matthew Flinders, when exploring the southern coastline, had held a similar opinion when he named the area's 3 dominant mountains West, Mid and East 'Mt Barren'.

Today this park, named after Charles Fitzgerald RN (Governor of WA from 1848 to 1855), is one of Australia's largest and botanically most significant national parks. It was gazetted in 1978 by UNESCO as a World Biosphere Reserve.

Measuring 329 039 hectares, the park contains beautiful scenery, including rocky coastal headlands, sweeping white sandy beaches, rugged mountains and picturesque river inlets. Two rivers, the Fitzgerald and the Hamersley, cut deeply through the landscape.

FLORA AND FAUNA

The park is rich in flora with 1784 different plant species recorded, of which 75 are found nowhere else in the world. The wildflowers are particularly colourful in late spring and early summer. Top of the list is the royal hakea (*Hakea victoria*)—a tall, hard and prickly plant with green, yellow and red scallop-shaped leaves—followed by the unusual qualup bell (*Pimelea physodes*), colourful grevilleas and rare weeping gums.

The 52 km Hamersley Drive Heritage Trail in the eastern sector of the park has short marked walks which allow you to view the plants.

A number of rare animals, some originally thought to be extinct, live in the park. One of these is the dibbler, a small speckled marsupial mouse. The bird life is also prolific with owls, sandpipers, penguins, albatross and rare ground parrots making up a few of the 184 recorded species.

WALKS AND OTHER ATTRACTIONS

As much of the park is not accessible by vehicle because of the nature of its terrain, its many walk trails are a great way to enjoy the park's attractions. A few of the shorter, well signposted trails which offer splendid scenic views are Mt Maxwell (only 100 metres long), Point Ann Heritage Trail (1.5 km—allow 45 minutes), West Beach Point (about 2 km—allow 1 hour) West Mt Barren (3 km—allow 1½ hours) and East Mt Barren (4 km—allow 2 hours).

Fishing both along the coast and in river inlets is popular, with salmon amongst the species regularly caught.

There are delightful beaches and bays along the foreshore, but be careful of the rips that occur along this strip of coastline.

Keen photographers will appreciate the rugged coastline around Point Ann, which is the start of the rabbit-proof fence built in 1904–5 and which originally extended 1164 km north to Meekatharra. The headlands and foreshore around Mylies Beach and the spongelite at Twertup also make excellent photographic subjects.

This coastline is popular as a viewing place for southern right whales. Point Ann and Four Mile Beach are both ideal vantage spots, particularly during June and July. Seals and dolphins can be seen playing in the waves.

ACCESS AND CAMPING

Roads in the park are gravel and earth formed but conventional vehicle access is available to

Point Ann in Fitzgerald River National Park

most of the main attractions. However, a 4WD vehicle will open up more of the park and the access to Fitzgerald Inlet, Trigelow Beach, Quoin Head and Whalebone Beach is 4WD only.

There are basic camping facilities with toilets and free gas BBQs at Quoin Head, Point Ann, Fitzgerald Inlet and Hamersley Inlet. Bring all supplies including water. No camp fires are allowed. The nearest fuel and supplies are at Ravensthorpe, Jerramungup, and Bremer Bay.

LEGEND

Sealed/Unsealed Rd
Four Wheel Drive
Walks
Rest Area (Picnic Area)

Caravan Park
Camping Area
Accommodation
Information
Fuel Supplies

FRANÇOIS PERON NATIONAL PARK

IN BRIEF

MAP REFERENCE: PAGE 300 B 4

Location The park entrance is 4 km north of Denham on the road to Monkey Mia. It is 835 km north of Perth. Access beyond the Peron homestead is 4WD only

Best Time April to October

Main Attractions Coastal scenery and fishing, bush camping

Ranger Based in Denham, phone (08) 9948 1076

Nowhere around Australia is there a more spectacular view of the Red Centre meeting the sea than here in Shark Bay. Known as the Outback Coast, this is where the huge red sand dunes which spread across much of inland Australia come to a halt as they melt into the ocean.

Both the peninsula and the 52 500 hectare park were named after François Péron, a French naturalist who visited Shark Bay in 1801 and in 1803. A sheep station, set up in the 1880s, operated until 1990 when it was purchased by the WA state government to establish the park.

AN OLD HOMESTEAD EXPERIENCE

The old Peron homestead and outbuildings in the park have been opened up to the public with information signs erected to give visitors an insight into early life here. Also a feature at the homestead is an old hot water artesian bore, which is still in operation today. The water is pumped up from 390 metres into a specially built 'hot tub' and shallow splash pool. Visitors are free to make use of these during their visit.

FLORA AND FAUNA

It is mostly arid vegetation that thrives here: wattles, hakeas, grevilleas and myrtles. The purple Shark Bay daisy creeper is seen everywhere.

A variety of sea and land birds are seen within the park, including fairywrens, finches, grasswrens and wedgebills. Euros and other small wallabies are quite numerous as are rodents and lizards. Also quite abundant are the thorny devils which feed almost solely on ants.

The waters off Peron are home to thousands of dugongs (sea cows), turtles, dolphins and manta rays, which can often be seen from headlands around the peninsula.

A wildlife conservation venture known as Project Eden is well under way in the park. The

The overflow from an artesian bore near the Peron homestead

project's aim is to eliminate feral animals (cats and foxes among others) and reintroduce to the area of the now rare bandicoots, bettongs and rodents which once thrived here.

ACCESS AND CAMPING

Access to the old homestead, approximately 6 km into the southern section of the park, is along a well-maintained sand/earth formed road which leads off the sealed Denham to Monkey Mia Road. This access is suitable for conventional vehicles, but travel further into the park is 4WD only. A sign at the gate leading north from the homestead requests drivers to lower tyre pressure to assist travel along the sandy tracks and on the edge of numerous claypans (called birradis), and also to impose less impact on the environment. Don't try to drive across claypans as you are likely to get bogged.

Camping is permitted within the park and there are a number of waterfront locations which are perfect. Big Lagoon, a large but fairly shallow lagoon where the sea has covered a stretch of claypans creating inland bays, has camp sites right on the water's edge.

Further north, where the red sand dunes dramatically slide into the sea, ocean-front camp sites are located on the western side of the peninsula at Gregories, Bottle Bay and South Gregories. Across the cape on the eastern side is another delightful bush camping spot right on the waterfront at Herald Bight.

There are only limited facilities at any of these camp sites, with fireplaces and pit toilets at some locations. Campers must be fully self-sufficient bringing all supplies and water with them. It is preferable to use a gas stove as wood is very limited.

All camping areas offer easy access to the water and many people bring small car-top dinghies to launch from the beach. There is good fishing by boat or from the beach all year round with snapper, bream, kingfish, mackerel and whiting the choice catches.

LEGEND

Sealed/Unsealed Rd .... ★ 26 ★

Four Wheel Drive .... – – – –

Walks .... ••••••••

Rest Area (Picnic Area) ....

Caravan Park ....

Camping Area ....

Accommodation ....

Information ....

Fuel Supplies ....

IN BRIEF

MAP REFERENCE: PAGE 302 C 8

Location 1540 km northeast of
Perth, via Meekatharra and
Wiluna. 4WD access only
Best Time Winter
Main Attractions Remote
desert landscape, wildflowers
after local rain
Ranger Kalgoorlie, phone
(08) 9021 2677

The Gibson Desert is just one of the deserts that stretch across the vast expanses of central Australia and inland Western Australia. Here in the western half of the continent the Great Victoria Desert changes imperceptibly into the Gibson Desert, which merges into the dunes of the Little Sandy and the Great Sandy Deserts.

Covering 1.9 million hectares of this vast area, the Gibson Desert Nature Reserve takes up a smallish section in the southern area of the Gibson Desert. The reserve includes Mt Everard in the Browne Range, and takes in the Young Range and the Alfred and Marie Ranges as well as several salt lakes and pans, the largest of which is Lake Newell in the east of the park.

Lake Cohen in the north of the park is an ephemeral freshwater lake that when it has water, is alive to the sounds of hundreds, if not thousands, of nesting birds.

HISTORY

The area has long been the wandering grounds for the local Aboriginal groups. However, it was not until 1873 that the region was explored by Ernest Giles, who named the desert in honour of one of his companions who had died. Giles' route is across the northern section of the reserve, while the route of David Carnegie, an English earl who won a fortune in gold before turning his hand to gold exploration, passes from south to north. He named the spectacular McPhersons Pillar in the north of the reserve.

The area was left to its own devices until Britain wanted a place to detonate atomic bombs and try out inter-continental ballistic missles. Len Beadell was called in to survey a series of roads through the desert. Between 1955 and 1964 he and his Gunbarrel Road Construction Party opened up more than 2.5 million square kilometres of desert country and graded over 6500 km of track in the area.

Everard Junction, a track junction in the southwestern region of the reserve, was named by Len Beadell when he surveyed and constructed the Gunbarrel Highway in the late 1950s. The junction is the joining point of the east–west Gunbarrel and the southern end of the north-running Gary Highway, also built and named by Beadell.

RARE WILDLIFE

Since the reserve's dedication in 1977, the Department of Conservation and Land Management (CALM) of WA have carried out a number of surveys in the desert, discovering important populations of rare or endangered native animals. While the lesser stick-nest rat has slipped into oblivion—its demise almost certainly due to feral cats and foxes that roam this arid environment—other animals such as the long-tailed dunnart have a secure stronghold in the Young Range. Other small marsupials include the mulgara, the wongai ningaui, the spinifex-hopping mouse and the beautiful dalgytes or bilbi.

ACCESS AND CAMPING

A 4WD is essential in this remote region. The easiest access is from Wiluna 350 km to Carnegie Homestead, and then another 240 km along the Gunbarrel Highway from this station outpost. You can get fuel, limited repairs and supplies at Carnegie, as well as camp in pleasant surroundings or stay in air-conditioned dongas. Phone (08) 9981 2991 for more details.

From the east, access is via Warburton, 253 km east of Everard Junction. Once again, camping, fuel and limited stores are available at the Warburton Roadhouse, phone (08) 8956 7656.

Only in the south, close to Everard Junction, do you pass through low, rocky range country. As you head north along the Gary Highway the country is low, undulating sand country.

There are no dedicated camping areas, but many people choose to camp close to the track near Mt Everard, further north near Charlies Nob, or further north again near Lake Cohen. This last spot is ideal if there is even a hint of water in the normally dry bed of the lake.

The Gunbarrel Highway

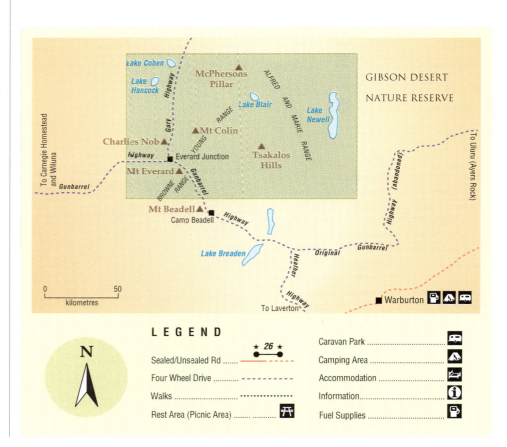

LEGEND

Sealed/Unsealed Rd ....
Four Wheel Drive ....
Walks ....
Rest Area (Picnic Area) ....

Caravan Park ....
Camping Area ....
Accommodation ....
Information.......................
Fuel Supplies ....

JOHN FORREST NATIONAL PARK

IN BRIEF

MAP REFERENCE: PAGE 298 C 4

Location 26 km east of Perth
Best Time All year round—
wildflowers best in spring
Main Attractions
Bushwalking, wildflowers,
picnics, bike riding and horse
riding, bush camping
Ranger Phone (08) 9298 8344

more than an average level of fitness.

These trails lead to such attractive park features as the Hovea Falls (2 km return—allow ¾ hour), Gauging Weir (500 metres return—allow 20 minutes), and National Park Falls (3 km return—allow 1½ hours), all of which are usually flowing in winter and spring. The trail along Jane Brook to Rocky Pool is a 7 km return walk, and will take around 3 hours. These are great places to cool off, particularly in summer.

A special favourite of most walkers is the more extensive John Forrest Heritage Trail—around 5 km each way (mostly quite easy walking)—which retraces a section of the old eastern railway line, including the Swan View Tunnel built in the 1890s. From the main picnic area you can pick up this trail in either direction, towards the tunnel or Hovea Falls.

Bike riding, particularly mountain biking, is extremely popular in the park. There are a series of challenging trails as well as easier ones often leading to scenic park attractions. No competitive riding is allowed and riders are asked to keep off trails set aside for walking.

Special trails have also been established for horse riders. These tracks meander through delightful sections of bushland well away from the crowd. Horses must keep to designated tracks and not eat or trample the vegetation.

PICNIC AREAS

Throughout the park there are a number of pleasant picnic spots, all with BBQs, tables and toilet facilities, including disabled access.

Surrounding the centrally located tea rooms are rock gardens built by sustenance workers during the 1930s depression. These cultivated native gardens lead down to the brook which has been dammed to create a attractive pool area. A tavern and restaurant, together with shelter areas which have been set up at various points, enable visitors to enjoy the park at any time of the year.

FLORA AND FAUNA

The park is set in a jarrah forest, still largely in its natural state.

In the spring, thousands come to John Forrest National Park just for the wide variety of wildflowers. These include delicate orchids, kangaroo paw, melaleucas, bottlebrush and wattles. There are also plenty of banksias, red gums, wandoo, paperbarks, zamias and the attractive grass-trees (balgas).

Over 100 species of birds have been recorded, ranging from the tiny splendid wren to the large wedge-tailed eagle. 23 species of native mammals have been sighted including western grey kangaroos, wallabies, bandicoots and echidnas, and more than 20 species of reptiles. Look out for a variety of lizards sunning themselves on granite outcrops.

ACCESS AND CAMPING

Access to the park is by a good sealed road up the Darling Escarpment 10 km from the Perth suburb of Midland. There are 3 entrances leading off the Great Eastern Highway.

Bush camping is permitted within the park, but application must be made to the park ranger. Water is available in the main facilities area of the park.

LEGEND

Sealed/Unsealed Rd ....
Four Wheel Drive ....
Walks ....
Rest Area (Picnic Area) ....
Caravan Park ....
Camping Area ....
Accommodation ....
Information ....
Fuel Supplies ....

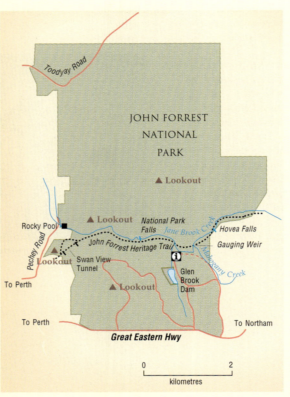

JOHN FORREST NATIONAL PARK

▲ Lookout

▲ Lookout
National Park Falls
Jane Brook Creek
Hovea Falls
Gauging Weir
Rocky Pool
Pechey Road
John Forrest Heritage Trail
Lookout
Swan View Tunnel
To Perth
▲ Lookout
Glen Brook Dam
Mahogany Creek
To Perth
To Northam
Great Eastern Hwy
Toodyay Road

0   2
kilometres

Grass-trees, also known as balgas or blackboys

Sheltered in Western Australia's Darling Range Escarpment just 26 km east of Perth, this park has been a long-time favourite for 'Perthites', as well as visitors to the state. Not vast, at 2676 hectares, the park has a variety of attractions.

It was established in 1898 and, as such, is the nation's second oldest after Sydney's Royal National Park. Initially known as Greenmount National Park, its name was changed to John Forrest National Park in 1947 in recognition of Lord Forrest, one of WA's accomplished explorers and state premiers (1890–1901).

ACTIVITIES

Walking is one of the park's major features. Most of the park's scenic attractions are found along its many walk trails, most of which are quite easy, ranging from a couple of hundred metres to several kilometres. None requires any

MAP REFERENCE: PAGE 300 C 6

Location 167 km north of Geraldton, 1 km from Kalbarri town
Best Time All year although it can be hot in summer. The cool months are best for walking
Main Attractions Scenic gorges, bushwalking, photography, water sports
Ranger Phone (08) 9937 1192; assistant ranger, phone (08) 9937 1178

From a small stream hundreds of kilometres inland in Western Australia's Upper Gascoyne region, the Murchison River fed by an extensive catchment area, quickly builds to be one of WA's most significant waterways. The path it cuts through a gorge that extends some 80 km in the centre of the park together with spectacular coastal cliffs near the river mouth, combine to form the magnificent centrepieces of Kalbarri National Park.

The area—186 000 hectares—has immense appeal to bushwalkers, photographers, anglers, canoeists and wildflower enthusiasts.

THE COAST

Red Bluff, a huge, rocky headland standing at the end of a splendid surfing and swimming beach, is the beginning of a section of coastline of cliffs, outcrops and inlets which is compared with scenery found along Victoria's Great Ocean Road. The ocean here has carved out massive chunks of the soft limestone, leaving remnant cliff formations, resilient island rocks, a natural bridge formation and unusual shapes such as Mushroom Rock. There is also a beautiful beach at the foot of Eagle Gorge and colourful layered sands and silts at Rainbow Valley.

From Red Bluff a sealed road leads along the clifftop with pull-ins to main points of interest. Towing caravans to these clifftop vantage points is not recommended.

A popular activity for those of reasonable fitness is a breathtaking clifftop walk. Some people start at Red Bluff for a 12 km (about 6 hours) hike one way south to Natural Bridge. Others drive to Eagle Gorge for an 8 km (3–4 hours) trek to Natural Bridge. Take drinking water, and arrange to be picked up at the end. Beware of large waves at sea level and unstable, crumbly rocks on the cliffs.

THE RIVER GORGES

Over millions of years the Murchison River has carved some spectacular scenic red and white banded gorges and escarpments through the countryside. At each of the main vantage points mentioned below there are picnic facilities—tables and toilets—while at the Loop and at Z Bend, free gas BBQs are supplied.

The Loop: There are several lookouts accessed by moderately easy (approximately 1 km each way) walk trails, with some stairs. Here the river does an almost 360 degree switchback loop and is the location of Natures Window Lookout—a natural rock arch which frames a view of the winding river. A splendid Loop Walk Trail for those of reasonable fitness leads down the slope and around the loop and back up again—this is 7 to 8 km (allow between 3 and 4 hours).

Z Bend: An easy walk trail of 500 metres leads to a high rocky clifftop lookout which overhangs the river 100 metres below. It is possible to climb down the steep slope from here to enjoy a swim in the river pools directly below.

Hawks Head and Ross Graham Lookout: These are other locations offering splendid gorge views. From the Ross Graham car park it is only a short, easy walk down to the river

For keen bushwalkers amd bush campers there are 2-day hikes from Ross Graham Lookout to Z Bend or another 2 days from Z Bend to the Loop. Be prepared to get wet crossing the river in sections. Make sure you notify the ranger before setting out, and carry all necessary water.

A cliff face showing the coloured layers of sand

WATER SPORTS

Rafting and canoeing—for the experienced only—are popular, especially after heavy rains when the river is deep enough to navigate.

ACCESS AND CAMPING

Access to the park's attractions is on gravel roads leading off the sealed road into Kalbarri.

As there are no formal camp sites in the park, most visitors use as a base the thriving fishing and tourist township of Kalbarri, just outside the park. An ideal length of time to explore the area is between 3 and 4 days.

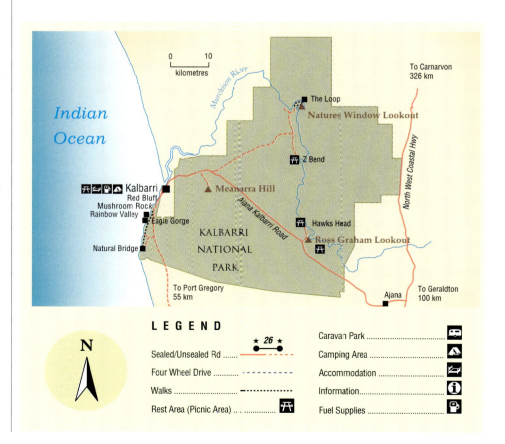

LEGEND

Sealed/Unsealed Rd ....
Four Wheel Drive ....
Walks ....
Rest Area (Picnic Area) .. ..

★ 26 ★

Caravan Park ....
Camping Area ....
Accommodation ....
Information.....................
Fuel Supplies ....

KARIJINI (HAMERSLEY RANGE) NATIONAL PARK

IN BRIEF

MAP REFERENCE: PAGE 307 H 8

Location 310 km from Roebourne and 285 km from Port Hedland
Best Time May to October
Main Attractions Scenic gorges, waterfalls and pools, bushwalking, swimming, wildflowers, photography
Ranger Phone (08) 9189 8157 or fax (08) 9189 8104

Set in the heart of Western Australia's inland Pilbara, the extensive Karijini National Park features breathtakingly beautiful scenery with a wide variety of plants and wildlife.

Originally called the Hamersley Range National Park, the park now takes its name from the region's traditional owners, the Panyjima, Innawonga and Kurrama Aboriginal people, who call the area Karijini.

The first European here was the explorer Francis Thomas Gregory in 1861. He named the range after Edward Hamersley, the sponsor of his expedition. It remained largely untouched until the mining magnate, Lang Hancock, began mining blue asbestos in Wittenoom Gorge in 1943. The mine eventually closed in December 1966. Today Wittenoom is almost a ghost town.

The Hamersley Range is, however, busier than ever with nearby Tom Price, Paraburdoo, Pannawonica and Newman producing millions of tonnes of high-grade iron ore each year. In the centre of all this is Karijini National Park measuring 627 445 hectares, and visited by over 50 000 people every year.

BUSHWALKING

Most of the park's attractions are in its northern sector, while much of the southern section is inhospitable, with hot, dry countryside, little vehicle access, and not much to attract walkers. However, the northern area is a bushwalker's delight with marked trails ranging from a couple of hundred metres up to around 9 km. The following are short, mostly easy walks leading to some of the spectacular features:

Oxers Lookout—150 metres each way. An amazing natural lookout where 4 gorges join, with a sheer 100 metres drop down to the river
Joffre Falls—around 150 metres return. This is a curved waterfall forming a natural amphitheatre which is spectacular after rain.

Porcupine grass growing alongside ghost gums

Gorge Rim Walk—about 1 km (allow 1 hour). It follows the rim of the gorge between Circular Pool Lookout to Dales Gorge car park, with some wonderful views along here.
Fortescue Falls and nearby Fern Pool—around 400 metres each way to the falls (allow ¾ hour return plus swimming time). A certain degree of fitness is needed for this climb trail down to the beautiful falls and spring-fed pools, which are perfect for a swim.

There are more extensive walk/climb trails that range from just an hour or 2 to full day ventures. Water should always be carried on any extended walk.

WILDFLOWERS AND WILDLIFE

Sections of the Hamersley Range, especially in late winter and early spring, can be extremely colourful while eucalypts and porcupine grass grow on the plateaus. and ridges.

Bird life is varied, particularly around waterholes. Animals include kangaroos, the rare Rothschild's rock wallaby, bats and dingoes. There are numerous native rodents, marsupials and reptiles living in the park. Look out for small and large red soil termite mounds.

ACCESS AND CAMPING

All park roads are gravel and suitable for conventional vehicles and caravans. Access is via Tom Price from the south and Roebourne in the north. If you are on the Great Northern Highway, turn off at Auski Roadhouse in the eastern sector of the park.

The 3 main camping and caravans sites are Joffre, Weano and Fortescue. Each site has pit toilets, picnic tables and free gas BBQs. Camping is not allowed elsewhere. Joffre and the visitor centre also have water.
Warning: Keep clear of the piles of asbestos tailings in Wittenoom Gorge and Yampire Gorge to the north of the park.

Map:

KARIJINI NATIONAL PARK

To Roebourne
To Port Hedland
Wittenoom Road 65
Roy Hill
Wittenoom
Weano Camping Area
Oxers Lookout
Joffre Falls
Kalamina Falls
Joffre Creek
Falls 13 6
Joffre Road 26
Joffre Camping Area
Mt Vigors 1160 m
Entrance Station
Entrance Station
Marandoo Road
Dry Weather Only
Tom Price Nth Rd
To Tom Price
Nanutarra
Wittenoom Road 24
Gorge Road 24
Fortescue Camping Area
Circular Pool
Fortescue Falls 10
Vampire Gorge 19
Juna Downs 11
Visitors Centre (seasonal)
Auski Roadhouse
Great Northern Highway
Northern
41
0   20
kilometres
To Newman

LEGEND

To Tom Price 26

Sealed/Unsealed Rd ....
Four Wheel Drive ....
Walks ....
Rest Area (Picnic Area) ....

Caravan Park ....
Camping Area ....
Accommodation ....
Information ....
Fuel Supplies ....

N

Location 260 km northeast of Newman and 420 km east of Marble Bar. 4WD only
Best Time June to August
Main Attractions Remote camping, bushwalking, nature, photography
Ranger Based at Karratha, phone (08) 9143 1488

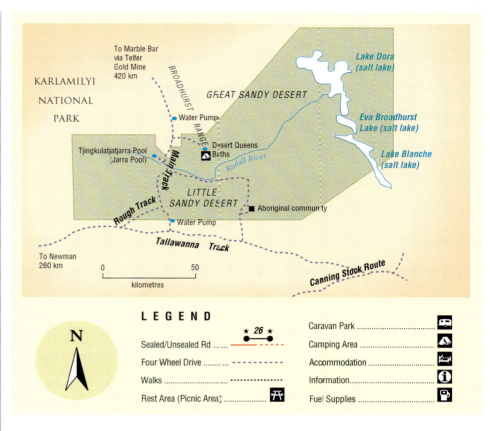

LEGEND

Sealed/Unsealed Rd	★ 26 ★
Four Wheel Drive	
Walks	
Rest Area (Picnic Area)	

Caravan Park	
Camping Area	
Accommodation	
Information	
Fuel Supplies	

Situated 420 km east of Marble Bar in Western Australia's Great and Little Sandy Deserts, Karlamilyi National Park is about as remote and lonely as you can be anywhere in Australia.

The Martu, Western Desert people, have lived in this area for thousands of years. The 2 sizable Aboriginal communities who continue to live within the park boundaries do so largely in their own traditions, with strong ties to the land and little outside influence. There are some 28 registered Aboriginal sites, including rock art areas, within the park boundaries.

The park, proclaimed in 1977, took its English name from William Rudall, a government surveyor who explored this area between 1896 and 1898. Karlamilyi is little changed today. It is a hot, dry desert region with no visitor facilities. A park of 156 459 hectares, there is not even a national park sign. This is strictly 4WD country with tracks in the park being unmaintained, corrugated, sandy and, in some sections, quite slow and rocky.

RUGGED DESERT BEAUTY

Although much of the park is red sand dunes, spinifex and even some salt lake sections, the real appeal is the spectacular breakaway country in the Broadhurst Range, brought about by glacial action millions of years ago. Tall, colourful cliffs, valleys, sandstone and quartzite plateaus, and eroded pinnacle shapes can be found, as well as picturesque waterholes.

The best of these natural waterholes is Desert Queens Baths. At the end of a slow, rough trail about 18 km off the park's main track, is the camp site near the entrance to the gorge which houses Desert Queens Baths. Allow around 1½ hours each way along this trail. Access to the baths is then by a relatively easy, rock hopping, unmarked trail up the creek bed, around 1 km from the car park—about ½ hour each way. Desert Queens Baths are really a series of rockpools cradled by tall, orange-red gorge walls. It is possible to swim and climb from one pool to another in this delightful spot.

Along the Rudall River, which generally flows only after cyclonic downpours, are several attractive waterholes which make ideal camp sites. Small creeks flow into the main river and located on one of these is Tjingkulatjatjarra ('Jarra') Pool, a lovely spot to camp and cool off.

Walking in the park is delightful, but go prepared. There are no marked trails. Do not walk alone and always carry water.

FAUNA AND FLORA

In the park dingoes can be seen, and heard howling at night. Single wild camels, or herds of up to 30 or more, are seen quite regularly. There are also kangaroos, native mice, rock wallabies and wild donkeys. Bird life is concentrated around the waterholes with over 72 recorded species including honeyeaters, diamond doves budgerigars, and mistletoe birds.

Around the waterways, tall stands of coolibah, river gums, acacias, bloodwoods and paperbarks line the banks. Whispering desert oak trees are seen out on the sandplains.

Desert wildflowers are particularly appealing with golden grevilleas, callistris, hakeas and Sturt's desert pea being among the most colourful.

ACCESS AND CAMPING

Access from the north is via the Telfer Gold Mine (Newcrest Mining), but you must seek permission to use this road (phone (08) 9158 6200 or fax (08) 9179 8679).

From the south, travel northeast from Newman via the Tallawanna Track which leads past the southern park boundary. Access into the Aboriginal communities is not encouraged.

It is advisable to travel with a minimum of 2 vehicles in this remote area. Radio contact is also strongly advised. The nearest supplies are at Newman and Marble Bar—you will need to be totally self-sufficient for the entire return trip.

There are no formal camping areas—just look around. The park may well be all yours!

Wild camels in Karlamilyi National Park

LEEUWIN–NATURALISTE NATIONAL PARK

IN BRIEF

MAP REFERENCE: PAGE 298 A 7

Location 261 km south of Perth to Cape Naturaliste, 324 km south of Perth to Cape Leeuwin
Best Time October to May
Main Attractions Coastal and forest scenery, fishing, swimming, limestone caves, bushwalking, diving, 4WD
Information Phone Department of Conservation and Land Management on (08) 9752 1677 (Busselton) or on (08) 9757 2322 (Margaret River)

Cape Leeuwin Lighthouse is open for inspection Tuesday to Sunday 9.30 am to 3 pm
Cape Naturaliste Lighthouse tours are available Thursday to Tuesday 9.30 am to 4.00 pm
Fuel, water and general supplies are available at Dunsborough, Margaret River township and Augusta.

Accommodation: Camping— Boranup and Conto Camping Areas, contact CALM at Margaret River, phone (08) 9757 2322
Cowaramup Bay—Gracetown Caravan Park, phone (08) 9755 5301
Hamelin Bay Caravan Park, phone (08) 9758 5540
Smiths Beach—Canal Rocks Beach Resort/Smiths Beach Chalets, phone (08) 9755 2116
Yallingup Beach Caravan Park, phone (08) 9755 2164

Fishing licences for cray and abalone fishing:
Dept of Fisheries, Perth (08) 9482 7333, Augusta (08) 9758 1266 or Busselton (08) 9752 2152

In the far southwest corner of Western Australia some 300 km south of Perth is a small coastal strip between 2 horn-like capes which jut out into the Indian Ocean. This area is host to a rough, most dramatic coastline and, underground, to some of the smallest, most delicate formations to be found anywhere.

HISTORY

This unique corner of the Australian continent which stretches from Cape Leeuwin in the south to Cape Naturaliste, about 120 km away to the north, is known as the Leeuwin-Naturaliste Ridge, a 600 million year-old geological formation of granite, capped by limestone and sand dunes. It is around 40 km from the ridge to the sea, a vast expanse of what was originally sea bed and debris.

Aboriginal occupation of the area has been dated to around 40 000 years ago with bones, implements and other evidence found at sites, including caves, throughout the region.

The earliest recorded European account of the area is a mention in 1622 of 'Leeuwin's Land' in the log of the Dutch East India Company ship *The Leeuwin*, which had sailed across the Indian Ocean in the prevailing 'Roaring Forties' winds before turning north to Java.

A second reference was made by J.P. Poereboom, who, in 1685, anchored in what is thought to be Flinders Bay. He also was the first to write a description of Aboriginal culture. Many explorers followed, including Matthew Flinders. who named Cape Leeuwin in 1801, and Nicholas Baudin from whom Hamelin Bay, Cape Naturaliste and Geographe Bay got their names.

Over the past 150 years the area has been known at different times for its sealing and whaling, grazing and pastoral leases, fishing and timber industry and, more recently, for its world class vineyards.

THE PARK TODAY

Covering an area of 19 700 hectares this long, thin park—the Limestone Coast— is a popular holiday destination for West Australians. They are attracted by the sheltered bays and beaches, good fishing, dramatic wind-swept coastal scenery, limestone caves, jarrah and karri forests, excellent surfing and the local wineries.

ALONG THE COAST

The coastal strip is a bushwalker's delight with many short, easy trails, as well as other longer, more demanding treks. Roads lead to the main scenic attractions and from many of the car parks, walk trails head off along clifftops and beaches, through heathland and limestone and granite outcrops. Some popular spots are:

Cape Naturaliste

Sealed roads lead to the lighthouse built in 1903 (an excellent vantage point to look out over the cape and Geographe Bay), and to Sugarloaf

A limestone cave near Margaret River

Quininup Falls

Rock (a rough exposed section of coastline featuring a tall, pyramid-shaped rock). Watch out for dangerous waves when walking around the rocky shoreline. A 4WD track leads from near the lighthouse to the coast, good for surfing and fishing. A 3 km walk trail (allow 1 hour each way) connects the lighthouse with Bunker Bay, a picturesque spot on the northern end of the park. This is a good choice for a picnic, swim, or for snorkelling and fishing. Toilets and tables are provided.

Yallingup

This popular holiday destination, particularly in summer, is a real favourite for surfers keen to tackle the huge rolling swells. A caravan park and wide range of other accommodation are available here. There are also toilets and picnic facilities.

Smiths Beach

A popular surfing spot along an extensive stretch of clean, sandy beach, this is also good for swimming. Fishing from the rocks and along the beach is a favourite sport. There is a caravan park and other chalet and unit accommodation 200 metres from the beach.

Canal Rocks

A series of rocks extend into the ocean from the headland, making a natural canal. This is a good

LEGEND

★ 26 ★

Sealed/Unsealed Rd .... ——— ———

Four Wheel Drive .... - - - - -

Walks .... ••••••••

Rest Area (Picnic Area) .... 🏕

Caravan Park ....

Camping Area ....

Accommodation ....

Information........................

Fuel Supplies ....

LEEUWIN–NATURALISTE NATIONAL PARK

Ellen Brook

fishing spot, but dangerous for swimming. A walkway and bridge lead out into the rocks to view the canal and see the power of the ocean as it surges through the passageways. There is a protected boat ramp here.

Cowaramup Bay (Gracetown)

A lovely scenic bay, this has a good lookout on the right before reaching the town. Fishing is popular here and when the swells are right, some excellent waves for surfing come in across the bay. There are picnic facilities, toilets and a caravan park in the town opposite the bay.

Prevelly Park

Located at the mouth of the Margaret River, just outside the park, this area is famous for its magnificent surfing. The annual 'Margaret River Classic' attracts top surfers from all around the world. There are headlands and vantage points from which to watch the surfers. Canoeing here is a popular pastime. The Margaret River is a lovely pristine waterway with plenty of bird life.

Hamelin Bay

Set in a protected bay behind Hamelin Island and the surrounding reef, this pretty bay is especially popular with families and anglers. The swimming is good and there are some excellent diving and snorkelling areas. A boat ramp is available for launching small craft. The long beach is ideal for walking, while a climb to the headland gives nice views. There is a caravan park beside the beach.

Last century, Hamelin Bay was used for exporting karri timber. In its heyday, the port had a jetty catering for 5 ships and heavy moorings for 4 more ships in the bay. The rotting stumps of the jetty can still be seen in the water, and where the old timber yard once stood is now the camping area.

Cape Leeuwin

This is the point where the Indian and the Southern Oceans meet, with the impressive Leeuwin Lighthouse right on the cape. In 1895, during the building of the lighthouse (opened 1896), a spring was tapped to provide fresh water for the workers. The spring water was carried along a narrow wooden channel to the wooden water wheel. This rudimentary system was used until 1928. Since then, salt deposits have steadily encrusted the wheel, virtually encasing it in stone.

Flinders Bay

In July 1986 this was the site of one of the biggest and most successful whale rescues ever carried out in Australia. For 2 days and nights the Department of Conservation and Land Management (CALM) officers, townspeople, tourists, and many other volunteers, laboured in freezing cold conditions to save 114 stranded false killer whales, each measuring between 2 and 5 metres long. Altogether 96 of the whales were saved and eventually herded out of the bay into deep water. A memorial to the rescue has been set up near Town Beach at Augusta.

Whale Watching

The annual whale migration to and from Antarctica can be seen close up along the Leeuwin-Naturaliste coastline. Both humpback and southern right whales swim past these shores in July on their way to northern breeding grounds and southwards between October and November. The southern right whales are often seen lazing about in some of the shallow bays along the coast. Part of this behaviour is to enable adult females to give birth, then nurture their young in the shallows away from the danger of predators, particularly sharks, in the deeper waters. The best vantage points to see the humpback whales are Cape Leeuwin, Cape Naturaliste, Gracetown Lookout at Cowaramup Bay, and around Sugarloaf Rock. It is estimated that 3000 to 4000 humpbacks make their way along this coast each year.

Fishing

With the warm Leeuwin Current running off-shore from this coastline, the fishing from the beach, off rocks and over reefs in small boats is excellent all year round. Good catches of skippy, dhufish, snapper, whiting, school and gummy sharks and flathead are regularly made.

During late summer and early autumn when the Australian salmon make their migratory run up the coast to around Perth and then back again fishing activity around the beaches and headlands can be quite hectic. There are a number of commercial salmon fishing teams operating with large nets, boats and tractors along the beaches during peak season.

Abalone and cray fishing are popular in a number of bays—licences are needed for these.

Other Water Sports

The coastline offers many great diving spots in protected bays around the islands and reefs.

Fourteen ships are known to have sunk during storms and after hitting reefs around Hamelin Bay. A dive trail has been established which takes in 4 of those which are still visible.

Sailing and windsurfing are also popular summertime attractions along the coastline.

INLAND
Boranup Forest

Boranup Forest is the largest known karri forest growing in limestone sands, and covers 3200 hectares. It is around 100 kilometres from Western Australia's other main forest areas where the trees are usually found growing in red clay loams. Boranup was mostly clear-felled between 1882 and 1913 by one of the state's first big timber companies. This was set up to cut sleepers to build part of the Adelaide to Melbourne railway. By 1913 most timber from the area had been cleared and the last mill in the area closed. Remnants of the old mills destroyed by fire some years ago can still be seen at Karridale.

The karri forest has since regenerated with most trees (some up to 60 metres high) now less than 100 years old. Grass-trees (balgas) also grow quite prolifically in this region.

There is a pleasant, tall timber drive through the forest, and the Boranup camping area, set in the bush, is quite basic with BBQs, tables and toilet facilities, but no water. It's a great place to enjoy the forest and birds. At night armed with a torch, you should look out for possums.

Caves

Beneath the sweeping landscape of the park lies an intriguing underground world containing stalagmites and stalactites. Over the years, fossils of long-extinct marsupial lions, Tasmanian tigers, a shark, koalas, and even the remains of a gigantic wombat-like creature the size of a horse (dated around 37 000 years ago) have been found here. The cave systems are among the oldest and most valuable archaeological sites in Australia.

The extent of this underground limestone system is extraordinary with over 360 caves having been discovered in the park. They range from narrow tunnels to enormous caverns measuring over 14 km long.

Whilst most caves are accessible only to experienced speleologists, 4 of the most spectacular are open to the public with regular guided tours. These are Yallingup Cave, to the north of the park, Mammoth and Lake Caves in Boranup Forest, and Jewel Cave in the south near Augusta. While there are fine examples of large formations, including some beautiful shawls, there are also some of the bizarre and mysterious helictites—curious formations which twist, bend and curl in all directions.

In addition there are 2 adventure caves in Boranup Forest: self-guided experiences where no lights are provided. Take a torch and wear strong footwear and old protective clothing—they are a lot of fun, but care must be taken. Experienced cavers should contact the ranger for access to other caves in the area.

OTHER ATTRACTIONS

Whilst travelling between various sections of the park, you will encounter other notable features: numerous wineries, cheese factories, craft shops, galleries and studios making anything from gumnut ornaments to jewellery, pottery and furniture. In recent years this area has developed a name for its cottage industries.

Most wineries open their cellar doors for both tasting and bottle sales, while the galleries, studios and factories often have demonstrations of their craft and samples for sale.

A visit to the old Ellensbrook Homestead, situated near the mouth of the Margaret River, is also popular. Ellensbrook was built in 1857 by Alfred Bussell for himself and his young wife, Ellen. The building has now been restored by the National Trust and is open to the public.

WILDLIFE AND WILDFLOWERS

Animals found here include western grey kangaroos, brush-tail possums, honey possums and fat-tail dunnarts. There is a wide range of seabirds, as well as wedge-tailed eagles, kites and the red-tailed tropic bird. In all, around 200 species of birds have been recorded.

The wildflowers are particularly colourful around headlands and in low heath areas in spring and early summer. Acacias, tiny orchids, coastal daisy bush, wattles, cocky's tongue, banksias and one-sided bottlebrush are all found in the park.

ACCESS AND CAMPING

Roads to all of the main areas in the park are either sealed or good gravel. In addition there are several 4WD tracks to remote coastal areas, where the fishing and surfing can be good.

Apart from the Boranup camping area (mentioned above), the Conto camp ground—located off Caves Road, south of Prevelly Park near the coast—offers secluded sites for individuals and families, and larger areas for groups. Wood BBQs, drinking water and toilets are provided. The area is set among peppermint woodlands which offer shelter from the winds..

There is another camp site located nearby at Point Road which also has tables, BBQs and toilets. No water is available.

In addition, there are a number of caravan parks in the surrounding area, including Dunsborough, Margaret River township and Augusta—all of these make good bases from which to explore nearby sections of the park.

Leeuwin Lighthouse

MILLSTREAM–CHICHESTER NATIONAL PARK

IN BRIEF

MAP REFERENCE: PAGE 306 G 6

Location 150 km south of Roebourne (along the road to Wittenoom, 180 km away)
Best Time May to September
Main Attractions Bushwalking, boating, fishing, enjoying nature
Ranger Phone (08) 9184 5144, fax (08) 9184 5146

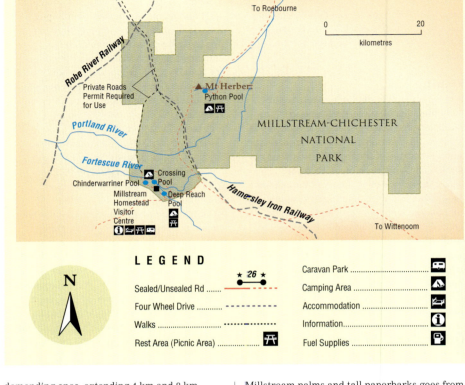

LEGEND

N

Sealed/Unsealed Rd .... ★ 26 ★
Four Wheel Drive ....
Walks ....
Rest Area (Picnic Area) ....

Caravan Park ....
Camping Area ....
Accommodation ....
Information...
Fuel Supplies ....

Natural freshwater springs, ivory-coloured waterlilies, crystal clear pools surrounded by tall cotton palms—all hidden away in a corner of a hot, and parched landscape: the Millstream section of this national park is a true oasis. Incorporated in the same park is the Chichester Range. a sparsely vegetated, arid region littered with weathered, rust-coloured rocks. The park, set up in 1982, is a area of beauty and contrast.

This arid-tropical region is the traditional home of the Yinjibarndi Aboriginal people. The first European to discover Millstream was the explorer Francis Thomas Gregory in June 1861. By 1865 the first pastoral lease had been taken up in the district, running 55 000 sheep. The old Millstream Homestead, built in 1914, now serves as the visitor centre for the park.

The park, straddling the Fortescue River, covers 200 000 hectares. Millstream is part of a underground reservoir or aquifer covering 2000 square kilometres.

Things to Do

In the northern section of the park is Python Pool, a permanent waterhole set at the base of a tall cliff in the Chichester escarpment. There are a number of popular walk trails including a short (600 metre—allow one hour), relatively easy track to Mt Herbert, and several more

The cliffs at Deep Reach overlook Crossing Pool

demanding ones, extending 4 km and 8 km cross-country along sections of old camel trails.

In the south, the popular walks which set out from the Millstream Homestead Visitor Centre, are somewhat easier. The Homestead Walk (750 metres, about ½ hour return and accessible to wheelchair users), is a stroll through the homestead grounds, amongst tall palms (with date palms planted by cameleers) and paperbarks. It winds past the waterlily-covered Chinderwarriner Pool. This ancient ecosystem was cut off when the inland seas receded.

A more extensive 6.8 km, 2 hour walk (the Murlunmunyjurna Track) through riverine vegetation, groves of wattle with the unique

Millstream palms and tall paperbarks goes from the old homestead to the nearby Crossing Pool.

Swimming in the permanent waterholes is popular, although the water is quite deep and cold. Boating— rowboats, canoes and windsurfers but no powerboats—is also a great way enjoy the waterways.

The 2 drives around Millstream take in Deep Reach Pool, Crossing Pool and the Cliff Lookout.

Fauna and Flora

Animal life in the park includes mammals such as rock rats, native mice, kangaroos, wallabies and a colony of several thousand fruit bats.

The more unusual birds found here include bustards, bush stone-curlews and dollarbirds.

Wildflowers include the prolific Sturt's desert pea and mulla-mulla.

Access and Camping

The roads are gravel and suitable for conventional vehicles. With the exception of the Millstream Circuit Drive, they are suitable for caravans, but can be closed after heavy rainfalls.

Shady bush-style camping areas with pit toilets are provided at Crossing Pool, Deep Reach Pool, and in the north at Snake Creek near Python Pool. Gas and wood BBQs (wood supplied) are located at Crossing Pool and Deep Reach Pool. Generators are allowed and drinking water is available at the visitor centre, but there are no other supplies in the park. The nearest fuel and supplies are at Roebourne.

IN BRIEF

MAP REFERENCE: PAGE 298 B 2

Location 245 km north of Perth via the Brand Highway
Best Time September to May
Main Attractions Pinnacle shapes, bushwalking, swimming, fishing, wildflowers in spring, 4WD
Ranger Phone(08) 9862 7043

When during the 17th century Dutch sailors first sighted strange shapes on the Western Australian coastline, they believed these were the remains of an ancient lost city. What they were actually looking at are known today as the Pinnacles. These unusually shaped limestone columns, numbering about 150 000, are the centrepiece of Nambung National Park. They have been sculpted into wierd forms: some look like tombstones, others are round and pointed, still others sharp and jagged.

Ranging from a few centimetres up to nearly 5 metres high, the Pinnacles protrude from golden yellow sands and sparse coastal scrub. Formed by the interaction of water, quartz, sand and limestone, the pinnacle shapes are estimated to be only between 10 000 and 30 000 years old— quite young in geological terms.

THE PARK'S ATTRACTIONS

There is a one-way loop track of about 5 km through the pinnacles area which is suitable for conventional vehicles but not caravans. There are places to park so you can explore the pinnacles area on foot. Leading from the Ranger Station there is a 500 metre loop walk that passes by hundreds of pinnacles with names such as the Seal, Koala, and Two Nuns. It takes in a splendid lookout with views over the area and to the coast 3 km away.

Photography is a popular activity in this unusual area. There are some eerie, moody scenes here, particularly in the early morning and late afternoon.

The white and red sand deserts, as well as the Painted Desert, are spectacular sand dune areas worth exploring. Inform the ranger before setting out on foot to explore these remote sections, and always carry drinking water.

On the coast, Kangaroo Point and Hangover Bay have toilets and picnic facilities (there are also a shelter and gas BBQs at Hangover Bay).

The Pinnacles

Both are popular fishing spots—taylor, herring and whiting are regularly caught here. The beautiful beaches along this section on the coastline are ideal for swimming and walking.

FLORA AND FAUNA

This mainly sand dune and sandplain country supports a wide variety of plants, including acacias, myrtles, casuarinas and banksias. The area has many wildflowers which are a picture during spring.

Emus and grey kangaroos are found in the park as well as a variety of reptiles, including bobtail skinks and snakes. Over 90 species of birds have been recorded here.

ACCESS

The main northern access road into the park from the nearby town of Cervantes, and the tracks to Kangaroo Point and Hangover Bay, are all suitable for conventional vehicles, although the last 6 km into the Pinnacles can be corrugated.

A great 4WD experience can be enjoyed by coming into the park from the south, along a sandy (including some beach sections) trail with some rough, rocky sections leading from Lancelin on the coast some 70 km away—allow 3 hours for this section. The trail passes through the small, shanty fishing villages of Wedge Island and Grey along the way.

This alternative route allows visitors from Perth a 4WD experience, returning to the city via the sealed Brand Highway, or vice versa. Commercial Pinnacles tours with the optional 4WD round trip experience operate from Perth.

This is a day visit park only; there are no camp sites. Open fires are not permitted in the park but there are free gas BBQs supplied for picnics. The nearby town of Cervantes (17 km from the Pinnacles) has a variety of motel and caravan park facilities, as well as fuel and other supplies. Many use this centre as a base for their Nambung visit.

N

LEGEND

Sealed/Unsealed Rd	★ 26 ★
Four Wheel Drive	- - - - - - -
Walks	············
Rest Area (Picnic Area)	⛱
Caravan Park	🚐
Camping Area	🏕
Accommodation	🛏
Information	ⓘ
Fuel Supplies	P

To Badgingarra

0   5
kilometres

Cervantes

Thirsty Point

Hansen Bay

Cervantes Islands (Nature Reserve)

Nambung Bay

Kangaroo Point

Hangover Bay

Indian Ocean

Buller Island (Nature Reserve)

Wittell Island (Nature Reserve)

Green Islands (Nature Reserve)

NAMBUNG NATIONAL PARK

The Springs

▲ Pudding Hill

Private Property

Nambung River

Kinchella Pool

▲ Green Hill

White Desert

Red Desert

Pinnacles Desert

Frederick Smith Creek

ⓘ ▲ The Pinnacles
One way loop

▲ Limey Lookout

▲ North Hummock

Painted Desert

South ▲ Hummock

Little Painted Desert

Grey ★

35

PURNULULU (BUNGLE BUNGLE) NATIONAL PARK

MAP REFERENCE: PAGE 305 N 7

IN BRIEF

Location 3000 km north of Perth via Broome; 110 km north of Halls Creek and 250 km south of Kununurra. 4WD only

Best Time May to September; the park is closed 1 January to 31 March

Main Attractions Spectacular ranges, beehive-shaped domes and magnificent gorges

Ranger Ranger Base, Three Ways (during the Dry), phone (08) 9168 7300, or Kimberley Regional Office, CALM, Cnr Konkerberry & Messmate Way, PO Box 942, Kununurra, WA 6743, phone (08) 9168 0200, fax (08) 9168 2179

Alligator Air, phone (08) 9168 1333
East Kimberley Tours, phone (08) 9168 2213
Heliworks, phone (08) 9169 1300
Kingfisher Aviation, phone (08) 9168 1620

The dusty track that leads 80-odd kilometres from the Great Northern Highway to the Purnululu National Park which contains the Bungle Bungle Range is definitely 4WD and it is planned to stay that way. It is so bad that it is strongly suggested that you don't take trailers or vans, although a good off-road trailer will get you there and back.

The Bungle Bungle Range is so close to the major round-Australia highway that it is hard to imagine that it was not until the mid-1980s that this unique, magical place was 'discovered'; it soon became known around the country and the world. It is only when you get within a few kilometres of the Bungle Bungle massif that you first see it. Even then it is not the huge domes that are so typical of the Bungles, but great, banded cliffs that glow fire red in the late afternoon sun, that you first notice.

HISTORY

Aboriginal people know the area as Purnululu and have lived in the region and used its resources for generations.

The surrounding country was first opened up to European graziers in the late 1800s. However, by the time the Ord Dam was built in 1967, the land was so badly eroded that the government resumed the leases in order to implement an erosion control program throughout the Ord River catchment area.

Hidden from prying eyes and known to just a handful of Aboriginal people, cattlemen and the occasional mineral exploration crew, it was not until 1982, when a television film crew happened upon the starkly beautiful range and the unique, beehive-shaped domes that dot the surrounding landscape, that it was brought to the country's attention. Shown on television, the area soon became a destination for adventurous travellers.

Proclaimed in March 1987, the park is today managed by the Department of Conservation and Land Management (CALM) together with the local Aboriginal people, a number of whom are employed as rangers within the park.

Taking up a triangular shape of country, the national park and its adjoining conservation park covers 320 000 hectares, with its southern and southeastern boundaries being the Ord River and a section of the Panton River.

A NATURAL WONDER

Scientists tell us that this place is a geological masterpiece, with the range rising from the flat surrounding plain as a great bulk of weather-worn sandstone. Around its southern edge the beehive-shaped domes dominate the landscape, at first being small outliers of the main range, then becoming more and more dense as they crowd up to the massif, as if trying to swamp it.

Around the western edge of the deeply fissured plateau the walls rear up steeply in great cliffs and the domes are not so apparent.

Once a great marine deposit formed over 350 million years ago during the Devonian Era, it has been eroded and worn down by countless wet seasons to form its present structure of domes, high cliffs and sheer-sided gorges.

The orange bands on the rocks are of silica, while the black bands are lichen, and beneath this seemingly tough, but in fact fragile exterior, lies a core of white sandstone.

In amongst its sheltered shaded gorges away from the heat of the sun, delicate ferns can be found, while pools of water last late into the Dry. Several plants have only recently been recorded for the first time in WA and includes a hitherto undescribed species of *Livistona* palm.

In fact, it is the various species of palms that are the most distinctive vegetation on and close to the range. The flat plains surrounding the fortress of rock are clothed in a sea of grass and spinifex, dotted with spindly bloodwoods and snappy gum, along with flowering hakeas and grevilleas.

ACCESS AND CAMPING

Access is limited to the western and south-western section of the Bungle Bungle massif.

There is only one route into the park and this leaves the main highway about 110 km north of Halls Creek, the closest main town.

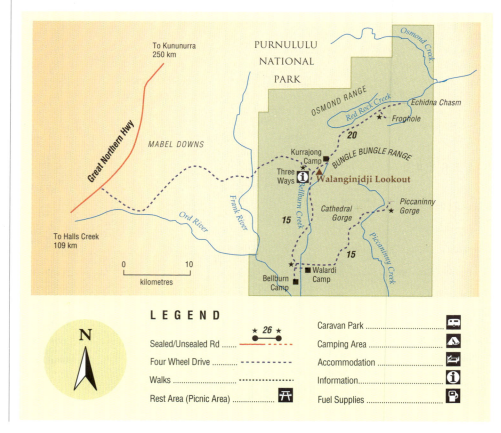

LEGEND

N

Sealed/Unsealed Rd	Caravan Park ....
Four Wheel Drive	Camping Area ....
Walks	Accommodation ....
Rest Area (Picnic Area)	Information ....
	Fuel Supplies ....

The track in is rough, and 51 km from the bitumen the intersection known as 'Three Ways' is reached. A ranger base and an information shelter is situated nearby. From this point it is just 5 km north to Kurrajong Camp or 16 km south to Walardi Camp.

Both camps have toilets, water, fireplaces with wood provided and separate areas for those with generators and those without.

To camp, it is best to buy a Purnululu Pass which combines an entry pass and a camping permit for a 7 night stay.

Tented accommodation with all meals is also available at the exclusive Bellburn Camp operated by East Kimberley Tours.

A number of tour operators from Kununurra fly into the park where camping accommodation, transport and so on can be provided. See below for details.

CATHEDRAL GORGE AND PICCANINNY GORGE

Located about 6 km east of the Walardi Camp is the car park and access track to Cathedral and Piccaninny Gorges.

If there is any one gorge to go to while in Purnululu it is Cathedral Gorge. The walk is an easy to moderate stroll along the bed of Piccaninny Creek, past domes of striped rock to where a tributary joins. Following this creek you are soon hemmed in by steep striated walls of sandstone. Suddenly, as you round a corner, you enter the 'Cathedral' and it is breathtaking. A small amphitheatre dips down to a dark, tranquil pool of water, while all around the rock rears upwards to the sky. Only by craning your neck backwards can you see the touch of blue above. It is a magical place, so take your time. You should allow about 2 hours for the return walk.

The walk to Piccaninny Gorge continues along Piccaninny Creek but is really an overnight walk of 30 km return. Make sure you let the ranger know before setting out on this one.

ECHIDNA CHASM, FROGHOLE AND MINI PALMS

The car park and access trails for these gorges are located about 15 km to the north of Kurrajong Camp.

Echidna Chasm is an easy to moderate 2 km walk—allow about 2 hours—and as you penetrate deeper and deeper into the gorge it becomes narrower and narrower, until it is only an arm's width apart with the walls towering upwards for over 100 metres.

Froghole is an easy walk of 1.5 km but you should allow about 1½ hours, while the walk to Mini Palms is a harder 3 km jaunt, which could take 2½ hours.

An aerial view of the Bungle Bungle Range

A FLIGHT NOT TO MISS

To get a full appreciation of the Bungles you really need to see it from the air. Flights are available in helicopters and the booking office for Heliworks is on the airstrip not far from Walardi Camp.

Light aircraft operated by Alligator Air or Kingfisher Aviation fly over the range from Halls Creek and Kununurra. While the flight is cheaper from Halls Creek, you miss out on flying over Lake Argyle and the Argyle Diamond Mine.

STIRLING RANGE NATIONAL PARK

MAP REFERENCE: PAGE 298 F 9

IN BRIEF

Location 330 km southeast of Perth, and 75 km north of Albany

Best Time October and November are best for wildflowers, spring and autumn are best for bushwalking. It is usually hot in summer and cold and wet in winter

Main Attractions Wildflowers, bushwalking, mountain scenery, photography

Ranger Phone (08) 9827 9230

Information Shelters tell visitors about plant, bird and animal life and guide them to places which may be of greatest interest.

Stirling Range Caravan Park, phone (08) 9827 9229

Note: Walk trails to Mt Hassell and Mt Trio have recently been closed because of the spread of dieback.

Looking for all the world like islands rising from a flat sea floor, the blue, many peaked outline of the Stirling Range, when seen from a distance, stands tall, mysterious and alone. Coming closer the blue hues around its imposing shapes begin to fade, but the intrigue of this truly dominant landmark in the southwest corner of Western Australia is only enhanced. If possible, allow yourself at least a few days to take in fully the attractions of this scenic and florally quite spectacular park.

HISTORY

It is believed that Aboriginal occupation of this area, about 330 km southeast of Perth, dates back around 40 000 years. Dreamtime legends relate the forming of these mountains to the ancient Kangaroo People who lived in this area. The story tells of a male kangaroo, a female and their joey. Every day the male kangaroo went off in search of food, but instead of hunting he would spend time having fun with his friends, and every day he would return to camp with nothing. This happened again and again. Very angry and tired of having no food, the female herself went to hunt and, finding plenty, she brought it all back to camp where she and the joey had a feast. When the male returned, again empty handed, and found they had feasted and there was none left for him, he became very

angry. He picked up a spear and threw it at his wife hitting her in the heart. She fell down dead. The husband raced off into the bush. The young joey, who had watched what happened, also became angry and took off to chase his father. When he found him they had a terrible fight and the joey killed his father. The body today forms the mountain range and the knees of the dead kangaroo sticking up in the air form the peaks. Even today, many people call this range 'the sleeping beauty', but this is more due to the fact that the shape of the mountain, when viewed from the south, resembles the sleeping outline of a woman, than having anything to do with the ancient Aboriginal legend.

In geological terms, the peaks and summits of the range were once part of a shallow tidal sea with sediment deposited on the granite lowlands around 1000 million years ago. After the sea receded, the area of the range sank. The surrounding land then gradually eroded back to basic granite and the range, under extreme pressures and temperatures, was slowly uplifted in folds and tilted rock strata. Years of erosion by rain, wind and sun produced the Stirling Range as we see it today. Chester and Red Gum Passes mark the courses of rivers that flowed south during the early stages of formation. Ripple marks can still be seen on exposed rock in the range. Its upper layers are quartzite and sandstone overlying shales and slates, while the lower plain surrounding the range is formed of granite.

Contrary to common belief, the Stirlings' Bluff Knoll (1073 metres) is not WA's tallest peak. This honour lies with Mt Meharry (1245 metres) in the Hamersley Range in the state's northwest.

In early European exploration, Matthew Flinders had given the name of Mt Rugged to the eastern massif in 1802, and explorer Ensign Dale made a trip in 1832 into the area to survey the country and look for some particular Aboriginal bush foods known to be found in the region. It was not, however, until WA's first Surveyor-General, John Septimus Roe, passed through here in 1835 that the range took on a real identity when he named it after Captain James Stirling, the first governor of the fledgling Swan River Colony (Western Australia). 'The Stirling Range burst on our view in great magnificence as we rounded the crest ... the whole extent of the conical summits were spread before us,' Roe wrote in his journal.

The real value of the Stirlings was not realised, however, until 1843, when botanist James Drummond began a study over a number of years of the botanical riches that have lured visitors here ever since.

As early as the 1920s the recreational potential of the ranges was recognised with the formation of the Stirling Range Tourist

STIRLING RANGE NATIONAL PARK

To Cranbrook
Salt River Road
STIRLING
Ranger's Residence
RANGE
To Amelup
Stirling Range Caravan Park
Formby Sth Rd Road
Drive
Ridge Walk
Ellen Peak
Bluff Knoll 1073 m
Mt Success
Stirling Range
Mondurup Peak
Moingup Springs Camping Area
Success Ridge Track
Pillenorup Track
Pillenorup Swamp
Quarberwardup Lake
Two Mile Lake
Red Gum Pass Road
Young River
Kalgan River
Woogenilup Road
Pass
Nth
Woogenilup Road River
Chillinup Road
Chester Pass Road
To Kojunup
Mt Barker
To Albany
To Albany

▲1 Mt Magog 856 m
▲2 Talyuberlup Peak 783 m
▲3 Toolbrunup Peak 1052 m
▲4 Mt Hassel

0 — 10
kilometres

LEGEND

Sealed/Unsealed Rd .... ★ 26 ★

Four Wheel Drive ....

Walks ....

Rest Area (Picnic Area) ....

Caravan Park ....

Camping Area ....

Accommodation ....

Information ....

Fuel Supplies ....

The Stirling Range

Association, and regular outings into the range were made in those years.

THE STIRLINGS TODAY

Surrounded by a farming plain which stands 200 metres above sea level, the abrupt form of the Stirlings has over a dozen summits reaching up over 750 metres with Bluff Knoll standing supreme in the east at 1073 metres. Measuring some 65 km long, around 20 km wide, and laid out in an east–west direction, this 115 671 hectare national park is one of Western Australia's premier parks. Its scenic and botanical attractions draw visitors in their thousands each year (approximately 60 000 per annum at 1996).

The general vegetation and terrain around the mountain range is thick, often prickly, scrub covering much of the lower slopes. This gives way to rough stony sections with sparse growth in the higher parts.

THINGS TO DO
The Stirling Range Drive

This 42 km drive trail (Stirling Range Drive), which runs through the centre of the park, is one of the best mountain drives to be found any-where in Australia. The winding trail follows closely James Drummond's 1843 footsteps as he began discovering some of the floral and scenic beauties the region has to offer.

The trail can be driven from either direction, but it is recommended that you travel from west to east to make the most of the picturesque mountain views along the way. Particularly appealing views of the range can be seen from the marked lookouts near Mondurup Peak and Mt Magog.

For those interested in wildflowers, Stirling Range Drive is magnificent. Over 1500 different species have been found throughout these ranges. The area is not laid out with carpets of flowers like those found elsewhere in the

state, rather the flowers are found in the low, scrubby, quite prickly heathland. The drive trail, a wide, generally good gravel road with a few corrugated patches, is one that should be taken very slowly with plenty of stops to see wildflowers at their best. A walk of just a few metres off the road into the bush often reveals many colourful blooms, sometimes small and low to the ground, that cannot be seen from the roadway. It is not uncommon to find half a dozen or more different varieties of flowers within a few square metres.

Flora

Travelling through the park, many visitors realise that not only are these ranges like islands in a descriptive sense, they are also ecological islands which provide a climate and conditions very different from those of the surrounding lowlands. Amongst the huge variety of plants found in the park, there are

STIRLING RANGE NATIONAL PARK

The road to Bluff Knoll

Bushwalking

The whole of the Stirling Range is a mecca for bushwalkers, with a variety of marked trails leading from car parks, plus over 100 km of other park management trails, ideal for walking and exploring some of the more remote sections of the park. Advice and full details of these latter tracks should be obtained from the ranger. Some of the formal walk trails include:

Mt Magog (856 metres)—an 8 km return trail, allow 3–4 hours. This is a hard, energetic, climb for the fairly fit, with lovely views. Note: there is no formal path for the final 1 km to the mountain summit.

Mt Talyuberlup (783 metres)—a 3 km return walk, allow 2 hours. The huge, rocky spires and caverns along this moderately demanding climb trail make it interesting and quite exciting.

Mt Toolbrunup (1052 metres)—allow 3 hours. This is accessed off Chester Pass Road. This is a

Bluff Knoll

60 that are endemic to the range and not found anywhere else in the world.

The following are a few of the wildflowers for which the Stirling Range is renowned.

Blueboy *(Stirlingia latifolia)* is common along road verges and flowers prolifically in spring, especially in a season after fire.

Scarlet banksia *(Banksia coccinea)* is a brilliant, scarlet red dome-shaped banksia which flowers October to December. It can be seen along Stirling Range Drive and several other places in the park.

Stirling Range banksia *(Banksia solanderi)*, with its purplish-bronze candle-shaped flowers and large irregular jagged leaves, is found on higher peaks in the range. There are good specimens on the edge of the roadside 1 km west of the Talyuberlup picnic area. They are found only in the Stirlings.

Mondurup bell *(Darwinia macrostegia)* is an elegant, white, variegated bell-shaped flower with crimson veins which is seen on the hillside near the Mondurup Lookout. In all there are 10 different species of mountain bells found in the park, only one of which is known to grow outside of the Stirling Range. Each one occurs in a well-defined area, either on one particular peak, or several peaks, or in the valleys between the peaks.

Slender banksia *(Banksia attenuata)* has bright yellow flowers. Seen along Stirling Range Drive, it was highly prized by Aborigines for the large amount of nectar found in its flowers.

Many varieties of small delicate orchids are also found in the Stirling Range (over 123 in all), often in areas which, not long ago, were subject to fire.

Trees in the Stirlings include the wandoo, or white gum, seen along creek beds, jarrah and Albany blackbutt. The colourful flowering gums and WA Christmas tree, which blooms from November to January, all make a delightful show.

Another fascinating plant is the black gin *(Kingia australis)*. It is distinguished from the somewhat similar-looking grass-tree plants *(Xanthorrhoea platyphylla)* by its silver green leaves and drumstick-like flowerheads. Both of these plants respond well after fire.

The disease dieback is, unfortunately, rife in a number of areas in the Stirlings. Caused by an introduced microscopic fungus and spread through the movement of soil, it is a major threat to many of the plants found in the park. It kills plants by invading and rotting their roots, thereby inhibiting water intake—banksias are particularly susceptible. Rangers ask that visitors keep to formed roads, stay out of closed areas, and clean vehicles, and even shoes, before entering the park.

hard, energetic climb trail, and is regarded by many to be the best in the park. There are excellent 360 degree views from the summit—the dramatic rocky outcrops are particularly scenic.

Bluff Knoll (1073 metres)—6 km return, allow 3 hours. Situated in the eastern section of the park, this peak is the highest in the Stirling Ranges. A reasonably hard, energetic climb trail leads to the summit. This trek is by far the most popular of all walks/climbs in the park. Because it is the highest, most visitors consider it to be a must! The view at the top is spectacular and quite breathtaking; the rough, rocky outcrops from the sheer clifftop lookout make the effort well worthwhile.

Ridge Trail—20 km, 2 to 3 days. This is for the real enthusiast, a quite hard and demanding ridge trail which climbs up from the base of the range to Ellen Peak in the east and winds along the top of the ridge to Bluff Knoll and ends at the Bluff Knoll car park. This is only for the fit and experienced. One or 2 nights' camping out on the ridge is required. Walkers must register with the ranger and obtain trek notes before setting out.

There are, in addition, quite a number of much easier wildflower and scenic walks ranging from a few hundred metres to 5 km setting out from near the Stirling Range Caravan Park.

On all walks it is advisable to carry water. If possible, don't walk alone, but, if you do, make sure someone knows where you have gone.

Walking in the park is usually quite hot in summer. It is much more pleasant in spring and autumn. For safety reasons, visitors are advised not to enter the bush or to use bushwalk trails on days of extreme fire danger.

Climbs are also not recommended in wet or windy conditions. The Stirling Range is one of just a few places in Western Australia where snow is occasionally encountered in winter. It usually melts within a few days, but at all times of the year climbers should be prepared for sudden cold changes, particularly if they are on the higher peaks.

Abseiling

Several sections of the Bluff Knoll rock faces have been set aside for the abseiling enthusiast or those just beginning. Abseilers must consult the ranger and register their intentions before setting out.

Photography

Photographers keen on wildflowers and rugged mountain scenery should come prepared with plenty of film. If you are able to do so, always carry your camera on all walks/climbs—your photos will make the effort worthwhile.

WILDLIFE

Bird life in the park is quite prolific (130 species in all have been recorded) including western rosellas, splendid wrens, golden whistlers, several different robins, red-capped parrots and malleefowl. It is not uncommon to see wedge-tail eagles riding the thermal air streams high above the range.

The Stirling Range as a dramatic backdrop

Animals which live in the park but are only rarely seen include the honey and pygmy possums, quokkas and black-glove wallabies. Western grey kangaroos are often seen in the early morning and late afternoon. There are several varieties of reptiles, including poisonous snakes, as well as spiders and frogs, but these are rarely encountered.

CAMPING

At strategic places throughout the park a number of picnic areas have been set up with free BBQs, tables and toilet facilities.

Adjacent to the ranger's office is the Moingup Springs camping area which provides individual sites, free gas BBQs and toilets. This is the only formal camping area in the park and many visitors who have come prepared for camping use this as a base for exploring the park. The area is suitable for caravans, but there is no power. Full park information, notes,

plant and bird lists and walk trail brochures are available from the ranger based here. Limited drinking water is also available.

Backpack camping is also permitted along the park's extended (management) walk trails. Please advise the ranger before setting out on any of these. Log books to record your plans (including route, estimated time of return, etc.) are located at Moingup Springs camping area and at Bluff Knoll picnic site.

On the northern edge of the park on Chester Pass Road, the Stirling Range Caravan Park provides the luxury of powered sites and hot showers for those looking for a little more comfort at the end of an energetic day. They also have on-site vans, chalets and cabins.

ACCESS

All roads leading into the park, and the main tracks within, are either sealed or quite good gravel and suitable for conventional vehicles and caravans. If staying in the park or the nearby caravan park it is advisable to leave your van there and travel through the park with just your vehicle. It would be much more manoeuvrable on some of the narrower, winding, sections of roadway.

There are no optional 4WD tracks available to visitors.

STOCKYARD GULLY NATIONAL PARK

A series of caves, linked by an ancient watercourse that carved its way underground through rolling limestone hills, is the central feature of this small and little-known national park hidden away in the hinterland of Jurien Bay, some 280 km north of Perth. It is a wilderness area of 2000 hectares and is accessible only by 4WD.

The Stockyard Gully Cave area was originally part of the Old North Road which ran between Perth and the Geraldton region. The trail was, in its heyday in the late 1800s, a busy stock route and supply trail. It was used to take sheep and cattle to Perth as well as to transport farm equipment and supplies northwards by bullock drays and by camels with their Afghan drivers. The area that became known as Stockyard Gully provided good feed and water for sheep and cattle along the stock route.

THE CAVES

Bring a torch, because the highlight of a visit here is to wander along a sandy creek bed through 3 underground caves linked by open sections of creek bed. From the car park the walk trail leads to the creek bed and then along the sand to the entrance to Stockman's Cave. Once inside, the cave meanders around several corners. Turn off your torch about 100 metres in and listen for the bats. This cave is around 300 metres long.

Middle Cave, a much shorter cave, is next, followed by Cook's Cave, named after a traveller, James Cook, who died in the cave in 1886. His body is buried above the caves.

Between each of the caves, continue to walk and climb (over and under fallen tree branches and rocks) along the creek bed to the next cave. The caverns are up to 10 metres wide in parts and 5 or 6 metres high, although some sections are narrower and lower—watch your head.

In winter time there is often water flowing along the creek bed and after a lot of rain the caves fill to the ceiling and are dangerous. In summer, however, the creek bed is usually dry.

The trail eventually ends 100 metres or so into Cook's Cave, where large boulders make the going quite tough. It is advised that only experienced cavers (speleologists) should

consider proceeding beyond this point. The creek bed cave trail extends for around 1 km and you need to come back the same way. Allow at least 2 hours for the return trip. With a little rock hopping and climbing, the trail is suitable for anyone of average fitness.

The underground stream winds its way to the coast, 20 km away. It is believed that the stream resurfaces about 7 nautical miles off the coast in the bottom of the ocean.

Watch out for nesting owls, as well as for stalagmites and stalactites in the caves, and for bees and their honeycomb veils which can be seen around the cave entrances.

WILDFLOWERS

Wildflowers are extensive in the area, including many fine examples of the splendidly colourful *Banksia sphaerocarpa*. Also to be found in Stockyard Gully are some large, ancient species of *Macrozamia*, cycads, which are believed to be over 1000 years old.

ACCESS AND CAMPING

Access from the sealed Jurien Road is via Cockleshell Gully and Grover Roads (both gravel roads) to a 4WD only trail: Gould Simpson Road, which is sandy and rocky. This

Looking out from a cave in Stockyard Gully

leads to the park and caves, approximately 5.5 km away.

There is no camping allowed in the park. However, it is a delightful spot for a picnic and a day outing. There are no facilities provided and you should bring your own drinking water. Just outside the southern section of the park, off Grover Road, there is a grassy bush camp site at Three Springs. Here, natural spring water bubbles to the surface into small pools set amongst shady trees.

Alternatively, the nearby township of Jurien has a full range of hotel, motel and caravan park accommodation available.

Bring a tick repellent as there are quite a few ticks in the area. This is a very quiet and unique place—take time to enjoy it.

N

LEGEND

Sealed/Unsealed Rd	★ 26 ★
Four Wheel Drive	
Walks	
Rest Area (Picnic Area)	
Caravan Park	
Camping Area	
Accommodation	
Information	
Fuel Supplies	

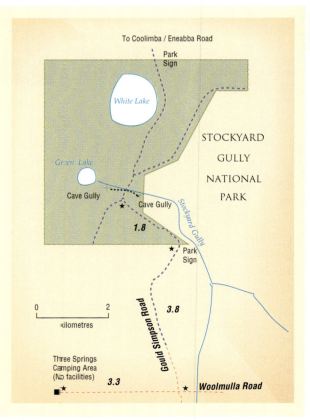

To Coolimba / Eneabba Road

Park Sign

White Lake

STOCKYARD GULLY NATIONAL PARK

Green Lake

Cave Gully

Cave Gully

Stockyard Gully

1.8

Park Sign

Gould Simpson Road

3.8

0   2
kilometres

Three Springs Camping Area (No facilities)

3.3

Woolmulla Road

WALPOLE-NORNALUP NATIONAL PARK

IN BRIEF

MAP REFERENCE: PAGE 298 D 10

Location Centred around the town of Walpole, 120 km west of Albany
Best Time September to May
Main Attractions Tall timbers, coastal scenery, canoeing, swimming, fishing, photography, 4WD
Ranger Phone (08) 9840 8263

Karri trees

Magnificent tall timber country, featuring huge karri and tingle trees as well as pristine rivers, waterfalls and long expanses of unspoilt coastline, give this park (430 km south of Perth) some quite superb scenic attractions.

The tall, buttressed red tingle trees that are endemic to the area were, no doubt, growing here in 1627 when the Dutch navigator Pieter Nuyts first saw the region. However, only a relative few now remain.

The 40 km of Southern Ocean coastline contained in the 18 000 hectare park include spectacular granite headlands, wide, clean, sandy beaches, extensive sand dunes, heath-clad slopes and tightly sheltered coves. The park's central feature is the almost landlocked basin, the Nornalup Inlet, fed from either side by the Frankland and Deep Rivers. Leading off this inlet further inland is the picturesque Walpole Inlet where the town of Walpole is located—once a timber town, now a holiday and tourist centre. There are numerous reminders in the area of Walpole's timber background, including the old saw pit near Rest Point.

FLORA AND FAUNA

Along many of the scenic drive tracks and walk trails a wide variety of wildflowers is found. The area is famous for its many small orchids as well as the brilliant red Albany bottlebrush and the beautiful red flowering gums.

The forests and coast support an abundance of bird life, while there are species of reptiles and amphibians that are found only in this area.

BUSHWALKING

Bushwalking in this extensive park is excellent. Trails range from just a few hundred metres to over 30 km, including sections of the extensive Bibbulmun Track, which winds its way over 600 km from Perth to Walpole. There are also trails through the untouched Nuyts Wilderness (named after the Dutch navigator). For safety reasons there is a registration book to sign in and out, and water must be carried.

SCENIC DRIVES

There are a number of quiet bushland tracks leading through forests, to hilltop lookouts, waterfalls, mountain pools, rivers and the coastal strip. Most popular among these are the Circular Pool Road, Peaceful Bay, Conspicuous Beach Road, and in the far western section, a trail leading to the beautiful beach at Mandalay.

The Valley of the Giants drive trail features huge karri and red tingle trees, some measuring 16 metres in circumference and several hundred years old. At the main car park and picnic area, a boardwalk, with wheelchair access, meanders around and even through the old trees. A superb, 600-metre, loop tree-top walk enables visitors to 'walk amongst the leaves' up to 40 metres above the forest floor. It is suitable for assisted wheelchairs.

WATER SPORTS

The long expanses of the Frankland and Deep Rivers, as well as Irwin Inlet and Rest Point in Walpole Inlet are popular with canoeists. The picnic spots and car parks along the rivers and inlets offer easy canoe access.

There are many places in the park from which you can swim or fish.

ACCESS AND CAMPING

A conventional vehicle will get you around the park. There is also a 4WD access track west from Peaceful Bay, and to Bellanger Beach and the Blue Holes.

There are well-organised camping areas with toilets, BBQs and tables. Bush camping is also allowed, and there are picnic areas with BBQs and tables. On the banks of Walpole Inlet, the Rest Point Caravan Park has all amenities in a waterfront setting (phone (08) 9840 1032).

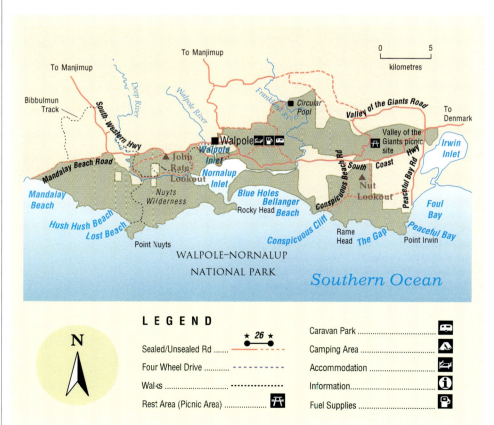

WALPOLE-NORNALUP NATIONAL PARK

Southern Ocean

L E G E N D

Sealed/Unsealed Rd ....
Four Wheel Drive ....
Walks ....
Rest Area (Picnic Area) ....

Caravan Park ....
Camping Area ....
Accommodation ....
Information.......................
Fuel Supplies ....

WILLIAM BAY NATIONAL PARK

IN BRIEF

MAP REFERENCE: PAGE 298 E 10

Location 70 km west of Albany and 52 km east of Walpole on WA's south coast
Best Time September to May; winter for stormy seas and dramatic photography
Main Attractions Coastal scenery, swimming and fishing, photography, 4WD
Ranger Phone (08) 9840 9255

This attractive park covers 1867 hectares along Western Australia's southern coastline and features heathland, karri forest and around 10 km of beautiful beaches and headlands.

THE COAST

A feature of the coastal strip, the granite rocks, cliffs and headlands tower up to 50 metres out of the water, some of which extend 100 metres or so out to sea. The beaches have clean, white sand and the protruding boulders make a picturesque sight.

Fishing is a real drawcard with good catches of salmon, mulloway, herring and whiting. It is particularly popular during the annual Australian salmon migration along the coast in late summer and early autumn.

Greens Pool, which is on the ocean front and is the most popular section of the park, offers an excellent large, clear pool of calm water for swimming. It is well protected from the waves of the Southern Ocean behind a barrier of granite rocks which act as a reef across the bay.

A well thought-out viewing platform and walkway giving visitors extensive views out over the coastline includes wheelchair access. There are toilet facilities (also with wheelchair access) near the car park. This bay is a popular family beach and picnic area.

Another favourite for many visitors is the charming Elephant Rocks area which lies around the headland from Greens Pool and only

Elephant Rocks

a few hundred metres from another car park.

In Elephant Rocks there is a delightful beach nestled in a small cove full of granite rocks which, for all the world, look like the round forms of elephants. When the sea is rough, this little bay, with its waves surging in and out around the huge boulders, is quite a sight.

Madfish Bay, about 2 km away, is also an attractive spot. It has a granite island which provides shelter to a small cove making it ideal for swimming and fishing.

This whole coastline is also especially appealing to photographers. Stormy skies and

rough seas, mainly seen during winter, only enhance its photographic possibilities.

ELSEWHERE IN THE PARK

High rolling sand dunes behind the beach and attractive inland areas of heathland are the main features of the countryside. Colourful wildflowers are found here late in the spring. Permanent streams and water seepage areas throughout the heathlands support scattered thickets of stunted peppermint trees, and there is a small, but quite spectacular, stand of 60 metre tall karri trees growing on the protected side of Tower Hill. There is a small section of petrified forest caused long ago when shifting sand buried tall trees. The subsequent movement of sand has exposed the remains of the tree trunks, now solid and petrified.

In the western section of the park, Parry Inlet is a breeding ground for waterfowl and is a popular birdwatching area.

ACCESS AND CAMPING

Access to the main section of the park is via sealed and gravel roads which are suitable for conventional vehicles. A 4WD track off the South Coast Highway leads to Lights Beach, a good fishing spot, on the far side of Madfish Bay in the eastern extremity of the park.

No camping is allowed in the park, although a camp ground is located at Parry Beach, just outside the park's western boundary. There are some delightful picnic spots in the park.

Map

To Walpole · South · Coast · Highway · To Denmark

WILLIAM BAY NATIONAL PARK

Parry Inlet
Parry Road
William Bay Road
Tower Hill
Madfish Bay Road
Greens Pool
Elephant Rocks
Edward Point
Madfish Bay
Lights Beach
Lights Road
William Bay
Parry Beach Camping Area

Southern Ocean

0 — 3 kilometres

LEGEND

N

Sealed/Unsealed Rd .... ★ 26 ★
Four Wheel Drive ....
Walks ....
Rest Area (Picnic Area) ....

Caravan Park ....
Camping Area ....
Accommodation ....
Information ....
Fuel Supplies ....

IN BRIEF

MAP REFERENCE: PAGE 304 G 7

Location 146 km east of Derby via Gibbs River Road
Best Time May to September
Main Attractions Spectacular gorge, canoeing and bird-watching
Ranger Derby, phone (08) 9193 1411

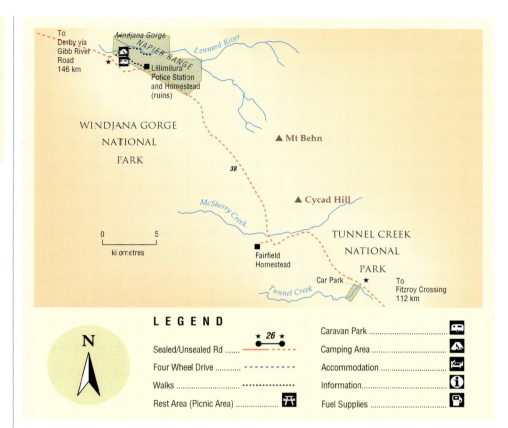

LEGEND

N

Sealed/Unsealed Rd	★ 26 ★
Four Wheel Drive	– – – – –
Walks	··········
Rest Area (Picnic Area)	🏕

Caravan Park	
Camping Area	
Accommodation	
Information	
Fuel Supplies	

Paddling a canoe on the still waters of Windjana Gorge, or walking below the towering walls beside the water's edge where the Lennard River has carved its way through the Napier Range are both equally delightful ways to enjoy this small but impressive park. At times, around sunset, the walls of the gorge light up in a vivid display of fire red rock that rears up from the flat plains, providing an unforgettable sight.

HISTORY AND LEGEND

Steeped deep into the psyche of the local Aboriginal people, the Bunaba is the legend that the gorge was formed by the Rainbow Serpent, Ungeroo, and the gorge and its waterholes were an important source of food and spirit children.

With the opening up of the Kimberley in the 1880s, Lillimilura Homestead was established just a few hundred metres east at the base of the limestone range. In 1894 Pigeon, or Jandumurra as he was known to his people, killed a police officer at Lillimilura and then attacked and killed a group of settlers as they tried to pass through the gorge, and these events made the gorge the centre of attention. Jandumurra's story came to an end in 1897 when he was tracked down and killed near Tunnel Creek. A visit to Tunnel Creek, also a national park, is worth it for a look at the fossil reef.

Already by 1897 the first geologist to visit the gorge, E. G. Hardman, discovered the bones of an extinct wombat-like animal, *Diprotodon australis*. Today the gorge and the surrounding range is considered a classic example of geology in that the various deposits of a Devonian barrier reef are so well portrayed.

Only a small park, Windjana Gorge National Park stretches along the Napier Range for a short distance; the gorge carved out by the Lennard River is its centrepiece.

PLEASANT WALKS

Probably the most popular walk in the park is the one that follows the eastern wall of the gorge through to the northern side of the range. This 3.5 km walking trail, one way, is an easy walk that for the most part stays in the shade of the thin strip of vegetation that lines the river.

Birds flit through the bush while waterbirds cruise the still water or stalk the muddy edges for a feed. Noisy corellas call the place home, as does a large colony of fruit bats. If you are quiet, there is a good chance of seeing a few freshwater crocodiles sunning themselves beside their favourite waterhole. These timid, shy creatures retreat into the water at the slightest disturbance and are not a threat to humans. The walking time is approximately 1 hour each way.

A short 'Savannah Walk' does a loop from near the camping ground, and will take about ½ hour while a longer walk heads east along the base of the Napier Range for 3 km (one way) to the ruins of Lillimilura Homestead and police station. You should allow 1 hour each way for this walk.

ACCESS AND CAMPING

Windjana Gorge is located 20 km east of the Gibb River Road, the turn-off being 126 km east of Derby, the closest town. Fitzroy Crossing is 150 km east. For the last half of the route, whichever way you come, the road is generally good dirt but it can be cut up just after the Wet, and corrugated and dusty at the end of the Dry.

A pleasant camping area is located a short distance away from the river, the gorge and the vertical wall of the range. There are toilets, showers, water and fireplaces, with wood being available from the ranger. A separate camping

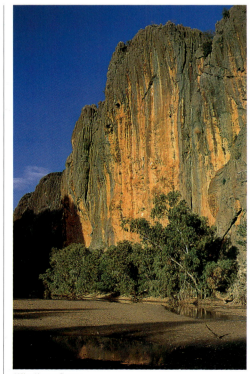

Windjana Gorge

area is provided for those with generators. A fee for camping is payable to the rangers who are based at the gorge.

OTHER PARKS OF INTEREST

CANNING RIVER REGIONAL PARK

Situated 10 km from Perth right on the doorstep of residents living in the suburbs of Cannington, Ferndale and Wilson, this attractive, winding parkland stretches either side of the Canning River. This is a tributary of Western Australia's Swan River which flows into the ocean at Fremantle.

The area is a summer playground for people of all ages. Many come with a picnic simply to sit and enjoy the grassy waterfront and activity on the river. Others bring a canoe to paddle the peaceful waterways and explore some of the river's bays and tributaries. Launching of canoes is easily done at many spots throughout the length of the park. There is a miniature train ride to enjoy or join the anglers who regularly come here, particularly early in the morning or late afternoon. Mulloway and bream are among a variety of fish regularly caught.

There is a bike and walk trail along the water's edge, extending the length of the park—an easy trail of around 6 km which should take about 2 hours.

There are BBQs, picnic tables, shelter sheds and toilet facilities at a number of locations along the river bank. There are also playgrounds for the kids and some safe swimming areas. Local guides conduct escorted walks including some concentrating on birdwatching and plant life, or even frog watching—remember to bring a pair of rubber boots.

No camping is allowed.

The main access is off Leach or Albany Highways, or Nicholson Road.

For further information, contact the Department of Conservation and Land Management, ph: (08) 9405 0700.

COLLIER RANGE NATIONAL PARK

This remote national park in the southern Pilbara region lies 155 km south of Newman and 245 km north of Meekatharra. The range, situated between the upper reaches of the Ashburton and Gascoyne Rivers, is a mixture of low hills and high ridges with some dramatic cliff faces.

There are no formal roads into this wilderness park and absolutely no facilities are provided. The access is 4WD only and is achieved through private station properties off the Great Northern Highway—always seek permission to use these tracks. The southern boundary of the park is located near the Kumarina Roadhouse on the Great Northern Highway, 225 km north of Meekatharra.

The vegetation is dominated by mulga and spinifex and attractive white eucalyptus line the creeks. Colourful wildflowers include areas of Sturt's desert pea and large sections of purple mulla-mullas.

The wilderness of the park offers a remote 4WD experience, bushwalking (no formal trails) and bush camping (no designated areas). Rangers request that visitors use gas cooking appliances to reduce the risk of fire. Ensure you carry vehicle spares, water and a first aid kit in this remote area.

For further information, contact the ranger at Karratha, ph: (08) 9143 1488.

FORRESTDALE LAKE NATURE RESERVE
245 HECTARES

Located just 23 km from the centre of Perth, Forrestdale Lake was formerly known as Jandakot Lake. To local Aborigines, 'Jandakot' means 'place of whistling eagle (or kite)'. According to tradition, this lake is home to a powerful Waugal, or Dreamtime rainbow serpent.

Today the reserve is a wildlife sanctuary and birdwatcher's delight. This is particularly so in late summer: its waters begin to dry up and contract and the area teems with waders and waterfowl feasting on the abundant food in the shallow waters. It is estimated that the lake supports over 10 000 waterbirds at various times during the year (with 72 species having been recorded), some migrating thousands of kilometres from Siberia each year. Seventy-four different species of bush bird have also been sighted here. The reserve is one of WA's most important conservation reserves and is on the Register of the National Estate.

Apart from the bird life, other varieties of wildlife include the endangered quenda (southern brown bandicoot), 15 species of reptiles, long-necked tortoises and 7 different species of frogs. These live in and around the lake.

Banksias, acacias, WA Christmas trees, fringed lilies and paperbarks line the lake foreshore.

Cycling is a popular pastime. There is a concrete cycleway which winds through Skeet Memorial Park in the reserve and along a gravel track further around the lake foreshore.

There is a pleasant 6 km walk trail around the lake. It is mostly flat, easy walking and takes 1½ to 2 hours for the circuit. Watch out for tiger snakes along the way—these are highly venomous.

This is a park for day use only: bring a picnic and enjoy it by the lake. There are tables, toilets and picnic shelters, and a playground for the children in Skeet Memorial Park.

For further information, contact the Department of Conservation and Land Management, ph: (08) 9334 0333.

KENNEDY RANGE NATIONAL PARK
141 660 HECTARES

The Kennedy Range, an eroded plateau in the outback of WA, is located 800 km north of Perth and 160 km east of Carnarvon. It is breakaway country on a large scale with the range measuring nearly 200 km long and, in parts, up to 25 km across.

The elaborate branched gorges and towering sandstone cliffs rise up like battlements over 100 metres high from the flat surrounding plain. This mass of craggy, white-orange, brown and even black cliff faces are a remnant of the land surface that elsewhere has been eroded away.

There are a number of activities to be enjoyed by visitors here, including walking, photography, exploring the canyons and gorges, wildflowers in spring, birdwatching, and outback camping. Gemstones can be found

Kennedy Range National Park

here, as well as ancient marine fossils embedded in rocks around the range. Early morning light on the east face of the range is particularly appealing for photography.

The main access is from the east side of the range north of Gascoyne Junction. These roads are gravel (suitable for conventional vehicles) but can be slippery, or even closed, after heavy rain.

There are basic camping facilities: pit toilets and wood BBQs. Wood is scarce, so bring your own or gas cooking equipment. There is no drinking water, and the nearest fuel and supplies are at Gascoyne Junction, 60 km away. The area is remote and travellers must be totally self-sufficient.

Access into the western side of the range, which also includes some lovely breakaway country, is strictly 4WD through private station properties—seek permission first.

The whole area can be extremely hot in summer: 45˚C plus is common. The best time to visit is from May to October.

For further information, contact the ranger at Gascoyne Junction. ph: (08) 9943 0988.

KIMBERLEY PARKS
Geikie Gorge
3136 HECTARES

The most visited park in the Kimberley, Geikie Gorge National Park has as its centrepiece the gorge where the mighty Fitzroy River cuts through the Geikie Range and the area immediately around it.

The gorge has been cut through an ancient barrier reef and is over 14 km long. The walls of the gorge are scoured white by the annual wet season floods that often see water 10 to 12 metres above the dry season level.

Freshwater crocodiles are common along the length of the gorge, while the fish found here include the barramundi as well as many common saltwater species such as rays and sawfish.

Mammals include the rare rock wallaby and more commonly the agile wallaby and the euro. Birds number well over 100 species.

No camping is allowed but an information shelter and picnic sites are provided and other facilities include toilets, water, gas BBQs and access for disabled people. A number of short walking trails head either upriver to the gorge or downriver through the narrow strip of riverine forest.

The main attraction of this park is the boat tours that cruise the gorge 3 times a day. They are not to be missed. During the dry season private boats and canoes are permitted access to the gorge after 4.30 pm; however you must notify the rangers before launching your boat.

The park is closed during December to

March. Located in the southern Kimberley, 280 km north from Derby, it is an easy 22 km drive from Fitzroy Crossing by conventional vehicle.

For further information contact the ranger at Fitzroy Crossing, ph: (08) 9191 5121. During the Dry, contact the ranger at Geikie Gorge, ph: (08) 9191 5112.

King Leopold Range

As the name suggests, this park takes in a great swath of the King Leopold Ranges from near the coast to 200 km inland. It includes the upper reaches of the Lennard River and the Lennard River Gorge and the lower section of the Isdell River together with Bell Gorge, probably the most spectacular gorge in the Kimberley.

The area has hardly been studied but it doesn't matter—it is such a stunningly rugged range it can't fail to impress.

It is located in the central Kimberley, and access is via the Gibb River Road from Derby. Camping is allowed at the Silent Grove camping area or along Bell Creek. The turn-off to Silent Grove and Bell Gorge is 204 km northeast of Derby and the camping areas are 20 and 30 km respectively off the main road. Access to these areas is by 4WD.

The camping areas are well set up with water, BBQs, rubbish bins, toilets, showers and fireplaces, while wood is provided. The Silent Grove camping area also has non-generator and generator sites.

A camping fee is payable.

Accommodation at the Mt Hart homestead, which is inside the park, can be arranged by phoning (08) 9191 4645 beforehand. Access by vehicle to the homestead is via the Gibb River Road—170 km—and then turn west and head along a 4WD track for 50 km. You can fly in as well. Mind you, at the homestead you are a long way from either Bell or Lennard River Gorges.

Exploring the gorges or just relaxing in the cascading pools is what this park is all about. If there is any one gorge you visit in the Kimberley, make it Bell Gorge! The best time to visit is from May to September.

For further information, contact the ranger in Derby, ph: (08) 9193 1411; at Silent Grove, RFDS callsign 6DE.

The Fitzroy River flowing through Geikie Gorge

Mitchell Plateau

This area, although not a dedicated park, deserves to be one! It is managed by the Department of Conservation and Land Management (CALM).

The most striking feature of the plateau is the predominance of the palm, *Livistona eastonii*, amongst the open eucalypt forest. In places they form clusters and quite dense stands. Apart from that, the region is one of a very few in WA that has all its complement of native mammals and if you are lucky your camp may be visited by a northern quoll, or you may see a small endemic rock wallaby, known as a monjon, hopping off through the rocks and grass.

Located in the northern Kimberley, access is off the Kalumburu road, 580 km north of Derby, where a rough track heads northwest, crosses the King Edward River (good for camping) and heads to the main camping area near Mitchell River Falls, 82 km from the main road.

Expect water at either camp site, sparse shade and little else, except for a helicopter at the Mitchell River falls camp site offering flights over the falls and surrounding area. It is a great way to experience this fabulous place.

Better still, fly one way and walk the other to the falls. It's about an hour walk each way and while not particularly easy, it is worth it. The falls, and the waterholes above the falls, are fabulous. You may come across some Aboriginal art in the area—look but don't touch!

The best time to visit the region is from April to October.

For further information, contact the ranger at Kununurra, ph: (08) 9168 0200.

Varanus tristis, the freckled monitor lizard

Parry Lagoons Nature Reserve

If you love looking at great mobs of birds, then Parry Lagoons Nature Reserve, just out of Wyndham, is the place to go to during the Dry.

Located in northeast Kimberley on the floodplain of the mighty Ord River and the much smaller Parry Creek, during the Wet this area coalesces into an inland sea, drying up as the Dry progresses, into green grassed floodplains dotted with large waterholes and billabongs.

Access is via a 4WD track off the main Wyndham road, 20 km south of the town.

Camping is not allowed; however, information panels and bird hides have been erected. The best time to visit is from May to November.

For further information, contact the ranger at Kununurra, ph: (08) 9168 0200.

Tunnel Creek

This is one of the great natural wonders of the Kimberley. An 800 metre long natural tunnel has been cut through the Napier Range, 20 km east of Windjana Gorge, by Tunnel Creek. In the 1890s it was where Jundumurra, an Aboriginal also known as Pigeon, hid out from the white man's law. The hideout served him in good stead for a number of years until it was finally discovered by the police.

The walk through the tunnel is a wet one and pretty dark, so you need bathers and a good torch. You are never really far from seeing light, though, as the roof has caved in halfway through and this is always a good spot to stop and soak in the atmosphere of this unique place. The far end is delightful, so take your time and don't hurry back.

The creek is in the southern Kimberley and access is via a reasonable dirt road suitable for conventional vehicles from either Derby (165 km) or Fitzroy Crossing (130 km).

Camping is not allowed, but an information board and toilets are provided.

The best time to visit is May to November as the creek is not accessible during the Wet.

For further information contact the ranger at Derby, ph: (08) 9193 1411.

LESUEUR NATIONAL PARK

26 987 HECTARES

This park, centred on Mt Lesueur, about 245 km north of Perth, is one of the richest flora areas in Australia, perhaps even in the world, with 200 of its 900 different plant species so far recorded having special conservation significance. The park includes a number of plants which are unique to this region, including the rare pine banksia (*Banksia tricuspis*).

The park has a diversity of landforms from salt lakes to coastal dunes, heathlands and laterite ridges which help to explain the huge variety of flora.

The formation of the park in 1992 happened quite rapidly after a proposal to mine the area's extensive, but low grade, coal reserves and to develop a power station was stopped.

The prolific bird life is also a result of the diverse landforms and habitats. Fairy-wrens, thornbills, Carnaby's black cockatoos, western rosellas and wedge-tail eagles feature amongst the over 120 species recorded. There is also a variety of possums, bats and kangaroos, while the region is renowned for its diverse reptile population, with lizards and snakes among the most commonly seen.

There are no camping or any other facilities in the park, so make sure you always carry your own water. Bush ticks are common and a tick repellent is advisable.

Except for the main park access track, all of the old vehicle trails in the park have been closed in recent years due to the spread of dieback; so the best way to explore the area is on foot. Make use of the many walk trails which crisscross the park to the best areas.

The access track, off Cockleshell Gully Road near Jurien Bay, is for 4WD vehicles only.

For further information, contact the ranger, ph: (08) 9652 7043 or (08) 9651 1424.

MIRIMA (HIDDEN VALLEY) NATIONAL PARK

1800 HECTARES

Located just 2 km from Kununurra in the East Kimberley region of Western Australia, Hidden Valley is a mass of twisted valleys and eroded sandstone gorges within a broken, strangely sculpted range. With permanent waterholes and plenty of shelter here, this was once a popular meeting place and corroboree ground for the Miriuwung Aboriginal people. There are rock paintings and engravings, and look out also for grooves in the rocks above Lily Pool where the Aborigines once sharpened their hunting axes and spears.

Today this is the Kimberley's most visited national park. The area is a photographer's delight, particularly in early morning and late afternoon when the richness of the sun's rays bring out the deep textures in this eroded landscape. There is also much bird and animal life, while the unusual shaped boab trees also grow here, clinging to the cliff walls.

There are many walking trails throughout the valleys and leading into the hilltops—most are short, between 500 metres and 1 km and quite easy, although care is needed with loose, brittle rocks along the tracks. The ridge-top trails also involve climbing over some crumbly rock faces. Allow 1 hour return for the main Didbagirring climb trail. There is also an easy 1 km nature trail.

Mirima has often been referred to as the 'Mini Bungle Bungles', as it has sections where the rock formations resemble the beehive shapes for which the Bungle Bungles have become famous, although Mirima's are not as spectacular.

There are picnic facilities, tables, toilets and an information shelter, but camping is not allowed in the park. The Hidden Valley Caravan

Mirima (Hidden Valley) National Park

Park—one of a number in Kununurra—is located adjacent to the park. For bookings, ph: (08) 9168 1790.

The best time to visit is between May and October.

For further information, contact the Department of Conservation and Land Management (CALM) in Kununurra, ph: (08) 9168 0200.

PORONGURUP NATIONAL PARK
2401 HECTARES

Located 50 km north of Albany, the Porongurup Range, measuring 12 km long and up to 670 metres high, is largely made up of huge, bare, granite domes, cliffs and balancing boulders. The area has great appeal to rock climbers. It is also popular for walking, with a variety of trails up to 5 km long and ranging from easy to quite strenuous. Walkers should carry water on these climbs, and it is necessary to watch out for snakes in summer.

Photographers enjoy the sight of sheer cliffs, round rock shapes, tall karri trees and wildflowers (500 different species) found throughout the park, especially in spring and early summer.

For birdwatchers, there are wedge-tail eagles soaring overhead in the updrafts created by the peaks, as well as scarlet and yellow robins, western rosellas, tree-martins, rufous treecreepers and black cockatoos. Among the mammal wildlife brush-tail possums, western grey kangaroos and brush-tail wallabies are common.

There is a scenic drive through the northern section of the park giving excellent views of the rocky outcrops.

The picnic facilities in the middle of the park near 'Tree in the Rock' have free gas BBQs, tables and chairs, and toilets, all of which have wheelchair access.

No camping is allowed in the park, but the Porongurup Range Tourist Park (ph: (08) 9853 1057) and other accommodation is located at Porongurup, just 2 km away with a shop and tearooms located nearby.

Access is by sealed and gravel roads suitable for conventional vehicles. This is a park that has something on offer all year; October to December are best for wildflowers.

For further information, contact the ranger, ph: (08) 9853 1095.

SERPENTINE NATIONAL PARK
635 HECTARES

Centred around Serpentine Falls in WA's Darling Escarpment, this small national park has been a popular outing spot for the people of Perth since the late 1890s. The area has a long association with the Nyungar Aboriginal people

who hunted, fished and lived in this area for thousands of years.

The park stretches up the granite slopes of the Serpentine River, and in winter the falls become a cascade of white water pouring into a swirling rockpool at the base. Many people come here in midwinter just to see the falls in full flow. However, in summer, the Serpentine Falls is a popular swimming spot as the Falls Pool, a large granite waterhole, is ideal for all ages. Most people bring a picnic and enjoy it on

Karri trees in Shannon National Park

the grassed picnic area shaded by lovely tall eucalyptus. BBQs, tables, toilets and water are all available. Camping is allowed, but visitors must check with the ranger first.

Bushwalking is another popular activity, mostly following the short, easy walks along the river from the picnic area. There are several more challenging trails up into the hillsides— the ranger can provide details.

The park has 2 rare eucalypts: the salmon white gum which is found at the base of the escarpment, and the butter gum which grows higher up. The wildflowers are another drawcard, particularly in the spring. They are at their best during September and October.

The park is 55 km southeast of Perth and 26 km south of Armadale via good sealed roads. It is open 9 am to 6 pm daily.

For further information, contact the Department of Conservation and Land Management (CALM), ph: (08) 9390 5977.

SHANNON NATIONAL PARK
53 500 HECTARES

Located some 358 km south of Perth in WA's southern forest region, Shannon National Park is largely a virgin wilderness area of untouched

forests, wetlands, sand dunes and swamps. It is in the middle of the southwest's tall timber country, but Shannon has more to offer than just tall trees.

Based around the old abandoned timber town of Shannon (now a camp ground), the national park has what many describe as a kaleidoscope of 'ecotypes': it has old growth and regrowth karri forests as well as biologically rich heathlands and wetlands. Some forest areas have never been touched and so, like some sections of the Southern River basin, are still in a pristine state.

The whole Shannon area is a bushwalkers' delight. The Bibulmun Track, WA's premier bushwalking trail (from Perth to Walpole) leads through the park. Other trails include the Shannon Dam Trail (3.5 km) which winds through towering karri and marri trees, thickets and swamp area. This is mostly an easy trail with the first 1.5 km suitable for wheelchairs.

The Rocks Loop Trail (5.5 km) climbs through rocky outcrops to a lookout over the Shannon townsite. Only a reasonable degree of fitness is needed, and you should allow 2 hours. There are many old logging trails ideal for walking—ask the ranger for a map.

Swimming and canoeing are popular in the Shannon Dam, particularly in summer. Trout fishing is also popular in the Shannon Dam and River, while there is a golf course at the old Shannon townsite.

The main camp ground has BBQs, hot showers and toilet facilities. Backpack bush camping is also allowed throughout the park. Make sure you always carry water.

The best time to visit the area is from October to May.

The old townsite of Shannon is 53 km south of Manjimup, but there are fuel and supplies at Quininup which is 20 km away. The park's main areas are accessible by conventional vehicle.

For further information, contact the ranger, ph: (08) 9771 1988.

STAR SWAMP BUSHLAND RESERVE
100 HECTARES

This small reserve, located 15 km northwest of Perth, is adjacent to the coast suburb of Watermans. The area, which contains a 1.4 km heritage walk trail (with wheelchair access) and several more kilometres of bush tracks, has both historic and natural significance. Information signs have been installed along the heritage trail pointing out items of interest.

Star Swamp, a natural permanent waterway fed from the underground watertable and located in the western section of the reserve, is home to many waterbirds and supports a variety of animals and reptiles.

The area has a diverse history: during the mid-1800s it served as a timber reserve. It was an orchard and pastoral lease (1869–70), a camel quarantine station (1890s), a cattle stock route watering hole (from the late 1800s to early 1900s), dairy cattle grazing land (early 1900s), a market garden (1915), a marl quarry used for sealing limestone roads (1919), a sanitation disposal site (1920s and 30s) and a base for the 10th Light Horse Division during World War II.

Walking, enjoying wildflowers and bird-watching are all popular activities in this rich and diverse city bushland.

No camping is allowed in the reserve, but pleasant, grassed picnic facilities are located beside the main lake.

Walking access to the reserve can be gained from several car parks off the suburban streets which surround the reserve. The reserve is open all year round, but the best time for wild-flowers is in the spring.

For further information, contact the Heritage Council, ph: (08) 9221 4177.

STOKES NATIONAL PARK
10 700 HECTARES

Centred around Stokes Inlet on the WA south coast 86 km west of Esperance, the main section of the park is accessible by a good gravel road leading off the South Coast Highway.

The tranquil, protected waters of the inlet are ideal for sailing, windsurfing and swimming. Take care, however, of shallow areas and some rocky sections. Fishing in the inlet and along the ocean beaches is excellent, especially for salmon, King George whiting and black bream in the inlet.

Walking along the shores of the inlet and its kilometres of untouched beaches is also a popular activity here at Stokes. A ridge-top heritage trail with information signs along the way (1.5 km) offers lovely views over the inlet and surrounding areas. Fresh mussels can be found on the rocks along the banks of the inlet.

A 4WD trail (Farrels Road), off the South Coast Highway, leads to the remains of the old Fanny Cove Homestead and its accompanying giant Moreton Bay fig tree.

The area contains heathland, paperbark trees around the inlet and swamp areas which support a variety of waterbirds, including migratory waders.

Two main camping areas, with pit toilets and BBQs, are located at the end of the main park access road on the shores of the inlet. Other more remote camping areas, accessible by 4WD, are located on the coast at Skippy Rocks and Fanny Cove.

There is no water or supplies or any other facilities in the park and visitors should be totally self-sufficient. The best time to visit the park is during the months of September to April.

For further information, contact the ranger, ph: (08) 9076 8541.

TORNDIRRUP NATIONAL PARK
3906 HECTARES

Located just 10 km south of Albany on the edge of the Southern Ocean, this picturesque national park contains some sections of coastline which are the roughest in WA. The park, situated across Princess Royal Harbour from Albany, is one of the state's most visited parks, with around 250 000 visitors each year.

The area is a delight for bush-walking, both cross-country and around the park's many spectacular bays and headlands. There are both short and long walks with well laid-out trails available. Places not to be missed by visitors are the Gap, Natural Bridge, Blowholes, Stony Hill and Salmon Holes—all are extremely dramatic and very scenic places.

The area is a photographer's delight, so take plenty of film. The heath-lands give a colourful wildflower display in spring. Fishing is also popular in some of the more protected coastal sections, and in Frenchmans Bay, but be extremely careful on rocks and headlands. There are designated climbing areas: check with the ranger.

With good sealed roads leading to all main areas, access is suitable for conventional vehicles. There is no camping in this park, but for day visitors, there are numerous locations to enjoy a picnic whilst taking in some of the spectacular views.

Other nearby attractions just outside the park boundaries are the old Quarantine Station and the Whaleworld Museum.

For further information, contact the ranger, ph: (08) 9844 4090.

WALYUNGA NATIONAL PARK
1800 HECTARES

Centred around a picturesque section of the Swan River some 40 km north of Perth along the Great Northern Highway, this park, accessible by good sealed roads, is a popular picnic spot all year round.

Many people enjoy bushwalking along the banks of the river and on the short cross-country tracks. There is an Aboriginal heritage

Torndirrup National Park

walk (an easy walk, 1 km each way—allow 1 hour) with en route information boards. There is also a more demanding Walyunga Heritage Trail with some climbing required (around 10 km—allow 3 hours) which follows part of the old survey track taken by Lord John Forrest back in 1877–8. This trail starts and finishes at the car park, and, if river levels are low, it can be crossed to take in an additional section (approximately 10 km, and a reasonable level of fitness is needed—allow 3 to 4 hours) which includes a climb to Walyunga Lookout, with good views out over the Swan Valley.

During the spring a good range of wild-flowers can be seen along these trails. Trees to be seen include jarrah, wandoo, flooded gum and marri.

In winter the river is a raging torrent and is popular with canoeists trying their skills in the white water. Canoe access is available from the car park or at many places along the river. This section of river is part of the annual Avon Descent course, and there are good vantage points along the river bank to watch the power boats and canoeists in this event, held in early August each year.

Wildlife in the park includes waterfowl, kingfishers, parrots, geckoes, lizards, echidnas, kangaroos and black-gloved wallabies.

There are excellent picnic facilities near the river with free gas BBQs, tables, chairs and toilets. Camping is allowed, but you must make arrangements with the ranger. Swimming is popular in summer.

This park is popular all year, but the walks can be hot in summer. The best time to view the wildflowers is in the spring.

For further information, contact the ranger, ph: (08) 9571 1371.

WEST CAPE HOWE NATIONAL PARK
3517 HECTARES

West Cape Howe is another small but scenic coastal park covering just over 20 km of WA's southern coastline. Located 30 km west of Albany, it can easily be explored in a day trip using Albany as a base.

For those with more time, the park has some delightful camping spots around the coastline. These are all strictly bush camping areas, with absolutely no facilities provided, except at Shelley Beach where there are basic toilets. Bring all your supplies, including water and a gas stove—no open fires are allowed.

This is essentially a 4WD park with the only conventional vehicle access via Lower Denmark and Hortin Roads, and quite good gravel tracks to Shelley Beach. All the other trails are hilly, sandy, and often quite narrow 4WD tracks, requiring low tyre pressure.

Coastal scenery is a real feature with clean, sandy beaches and some dramatic headlands of granite and limestone. The dark cliffs of Cape Howe, WA's most southerly point, are formed of dolerite—a black igneous rock which was squeezed up in molten form from deep below the earth's surface.

There are no formal walk trails, but along the coast there are some good beaches and headlands to explore. Shelley Beach in summer, with the prevailing easterly winds, is a popular hang-gliding spot. The take-off zone is from the lookout car park. For experienced rock climbers, West Cape Howe offers some challenging climbs, but you should check with the ranger. There is good fishing from the rocks and beaches with salmon, mulloway, herring and whiting regularly being caught. Beware of big waves around headlands. Shelley and Dunsky beaches are also popular for SCUBA diving and snorkelling, but be wary of strong rips which sometimes occur.

There is a variety of plants and wildlife. The swamp areas contain some of the carnivorous Albany pitcher plants and there is a small area of karri forest near the main park entrance.

The best times to come are during the spring and summer.

For further information, contact the ranger, ph: (08) 9844 4090.

YANCHEP NATIONAL PARK
2842 HECTARES

Established in 1905, Yanchep is Western Australia's second oldest park and one of the most popular day outing destinations from Perth, with over 250 000 visitors each year.

Located 51 km north of the city on the all-sealed Wanneroo Road, the park, on the Swan coastal plain, features a picturesque setting around a natural lake (Loch McNess) with plenty of grassed, shady areas ideal for picnics and children's games. Free gas BBQs are provided, as well as tables and chairs and toilets, all of which have wheelchair access. There is a shop and the old Tudor-style Yanchep Inn located near the car park.

Extensive landscaping has taken place in the park giving visitors easy viewing access to wildflowers and a variety of trees and plants. The area also has a wide range of wildflowers growing naturally in the bush.

There are a number of pleasant, easy walk trails, several with wheelchair access, giving opportunity for birdwatching and photography of wildlife, old World War II bunkers and scenic lake and bushland subjects. Some trails have en route information signs installed. Huge, old paperbarks lean over the trail which leads around the lake.

Situated near one of the main car parking areas is a well set-out koala sanctuary which allows visitors to see the animals at close range. The original koala colony came from Victoria in the 1930s. Twin koalas were born here in 1996 which adds to the attraction.

Kangaroos and emus roam the park, while black swans and ducks are a relaxing sight around the waterways.

Rowing boats and paddle boats to use on the lake are available for hire, and there is a golf course on site. Rangers provide a series of guided walks in the park, including to several of the park's limestone caves.

The park is a favourite for family and group outings particularly as there are ovals available for social sports.

The park is a pleasant place to visit all year round, but camping is not allowed.

For further information, contact the ranger, ph: (08) 9561 1004.

A koala in Yanchep National Park

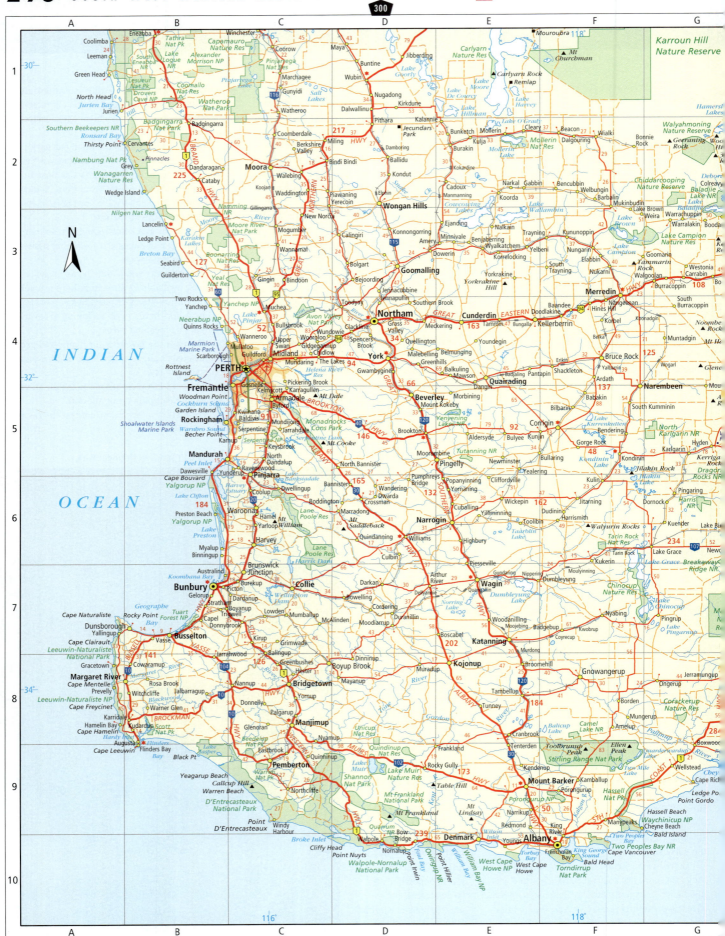

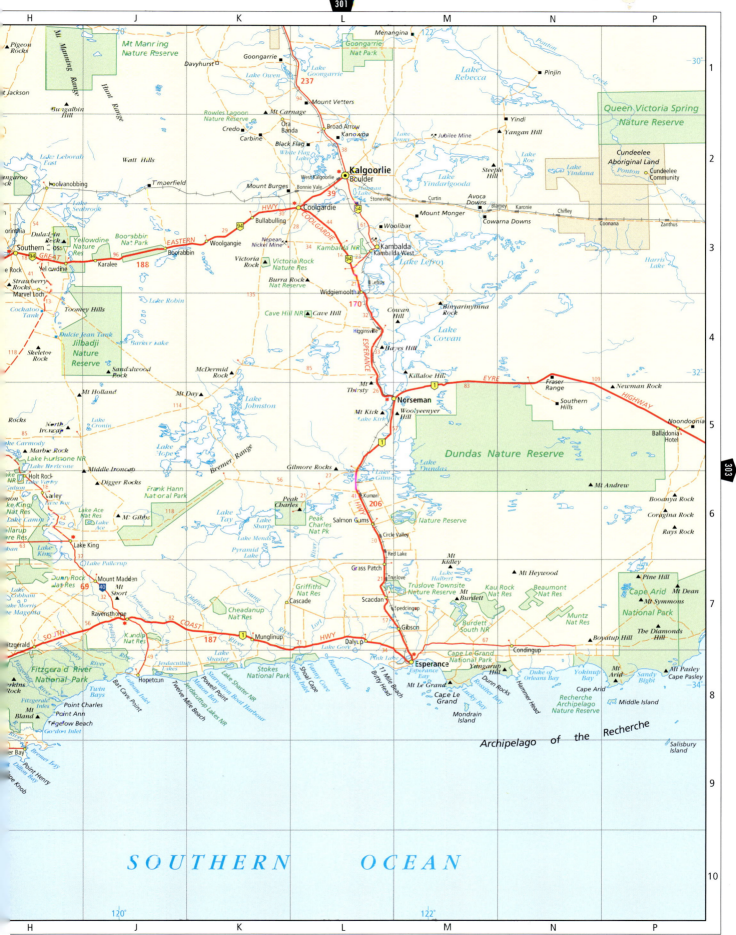

306

INDIAN

OCEAN

SHARK BAY

Scale

302

303

LITTLE SANDY DESERT

Lake Disappointment
Durba Hills

1

Mundiwindi

Weelarrana

Savory Creek

24°

120° 122°

Bulloo Downs

Kunderong Range

Tunnel Creek

Ashburton River

Lofty Range

42
57
151

Mt Vernon

71

Mt Bedford

Tangadee

Collier Range

Collier Range National Park

52

Yanneri Lake

Terminal Lake

Lake Wilderness

Kumarina Roadhouse
Beyondie
Wonyulgunna Hill

White Lake

Lake Sunshine

Lake Aerodrome

Striped Lake

2

33

Mulgul

Bremner Creek

63

North River

Gascoyne River

Ten Mile Lake

Mt Essendon

3

Mingah Springs

47

Three Rivers

Middle River

25

Gascoyne River

Mt Davis
Mt Salvado

Carnarvon Range

Canning Stock Route

Glenayle

Brassey Range

Lake Bremner Lake Keene

Neds Creek

Lake Gregory

Lake Nabberu

Earaheedy

Granite Peak

Mt Moore

Lake Buchanan

Lake
Mt Archie
Bodie Bodie Range
Fenne Range

Mt Nossiter
Keatland Hills

3

Bryah

94

Doolgunna

Mt Fraser
Peak Hill

256

New Springs

Mt Patterson

Verscher

Lake King Range

Lake Teague

Carnegie

Linke Lakes

128

Lake Bedford

Mt Lancelot

4

47

Diamond Well

Cunyu

Lorna Glen

Wongawol

Charles Wells Ck

Gunbarrel Highway

Lake Carnegie

26°

Karalundi
Mooloogool

Munarra

5

Killara

Paroo

Yandil

Jundee

Millrose

Wellington Range

Princess Ranges

Windidda

Mt Elisabeth

Prenti Downs

Point Katherine

183

Sherwood

Meekatharra

49

Wiluna

Millbillillie

Ngangganawili

Lake Violet

Lake Way

46

176

Von Treuer Tableland

Lyell Brown Bluff
Holroyd Bluff

Lake Wells

5

38

Hillview

Murchison Downs

Mt Lawrence Wells

Barwidgee

5C

Polelle

Gabanintha

Youno Downs

90

Lake Way

Wanjarri Nature Res

Worganoo

De La Poer Range Nature Reserve

De La Poer Range

6

Yarrabubba

108

Mt Townsend

57

165

Mount Keith

Albion Downs

88

Farquharson Tableland

Ernest Giles Range

72

190

Gidgee

40

Yeelirrie

Mt Mann

Nackeroal Range

Erlistoun Ck

Cosmo Newbery Hill

Warburton Road

28°

Coola Downs

78

Barrambie

Lake Mason

52

Kaluwiri

Lake Miranda

Yackabindie

15

Banjawarn

Lake Darlot

35

Bandya

Cosmo Newbery

Mt Shenton

Yamarna

78

Point Salvation

7

Booylgoo Spring

Agnew Mine

Leinster Downs

95

Cosmo Newbery Aboriginal Land

Wondinong

Black Range

Windsor
Anketell

157

109

Sandstone

21

Depot Springs

130

Black Hill

Leinster

Agnew

20

33

Melrose

44

Weebo

Teutonic

131

Erlistoun

Laverton Downs

White Cliffs

Mt Crawford

52

Laverton

Mount Weld

Merolia

7

Atley

Dandaraga

50

Pinnacles

38

Mt Clifford

98

Mt Clifton

Nambi

Windarra

Mount Margaret

Challa

Windimurra

92

Lake Noondie

Maynard Hills

Black Range

Ida Valley

70

Sturt Meadows

Lake Raeside

67

Mt George

Mertondale

86

8

Yuinmery

Bulga Downs

Termoola

Leonora

19

Mount Weld

Mount Margaret

Yuanji Downs

Poison Rocks

61

Youangarra

Ray Rocks

Cashmere Downs

Trainers Rocks

45

Perrinvale Outcamp

Copperfield

33

Malcolm
Minara

Melita

Glenorn

50

Yundamindra

Mount Remarkable

Lake Carey

Mount Celia

Hope Campbell Lake

303

9

Lake Barlee

Lake Barlee

Walling Rock

13

Jeedamya

Morapoi

Kookynie

Lake Raeside

Mendleyarri

Menangina

Edjudina

Lightfoot Lake

Lake Minigwal

Diemals

37

Riverina

46

Menzies

237

Goongarrie

Lake Marmion

Lake Goongarrie

Goongarrie Nat Park

Karrour Hill Nature Reserve

Pigeon Rocks

Mt Manning Range

Johnson Rocks

Mt Manning Nature Reserve

Davyhurst

Pontoy Creek

Pinjin

30°

10

Mount Jackson

Bungalbin Hill

Hunt Range

Kurt Range

Rowles Lagoon Nature Reserve

Mt Carnage

Ora Banda

Mount Vetters

Broad Arrow

Yindi

Lake Rebecca

Queen Victoria Spring Nature Reserve

Hamersley Lakes

120° 122°

H J K L M N P

0   25   50   75   130
kilometres

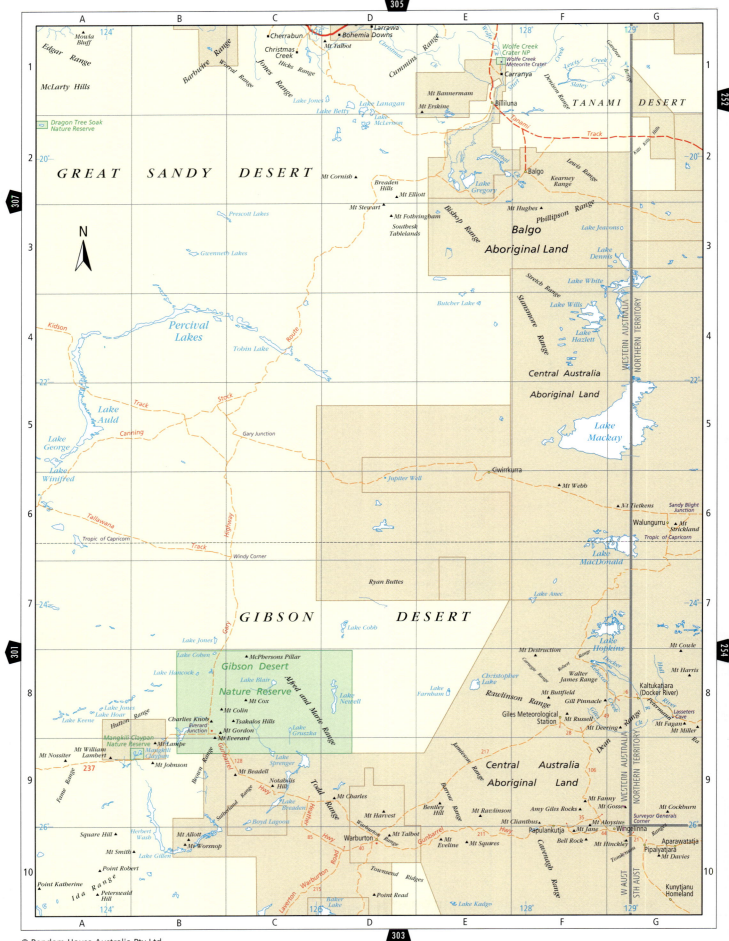

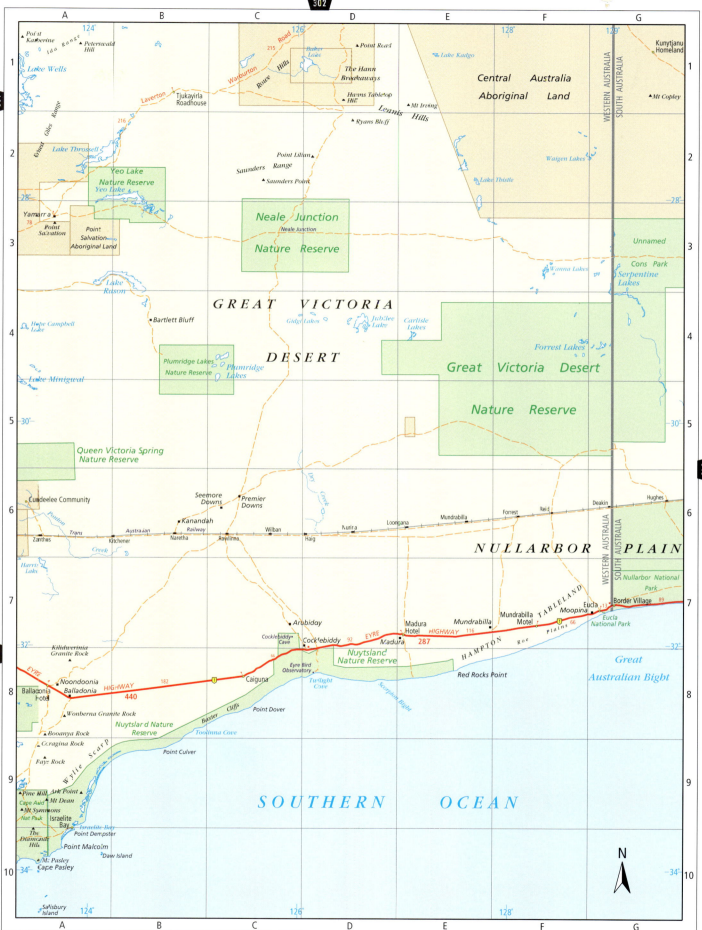

INDIAN OCEAN

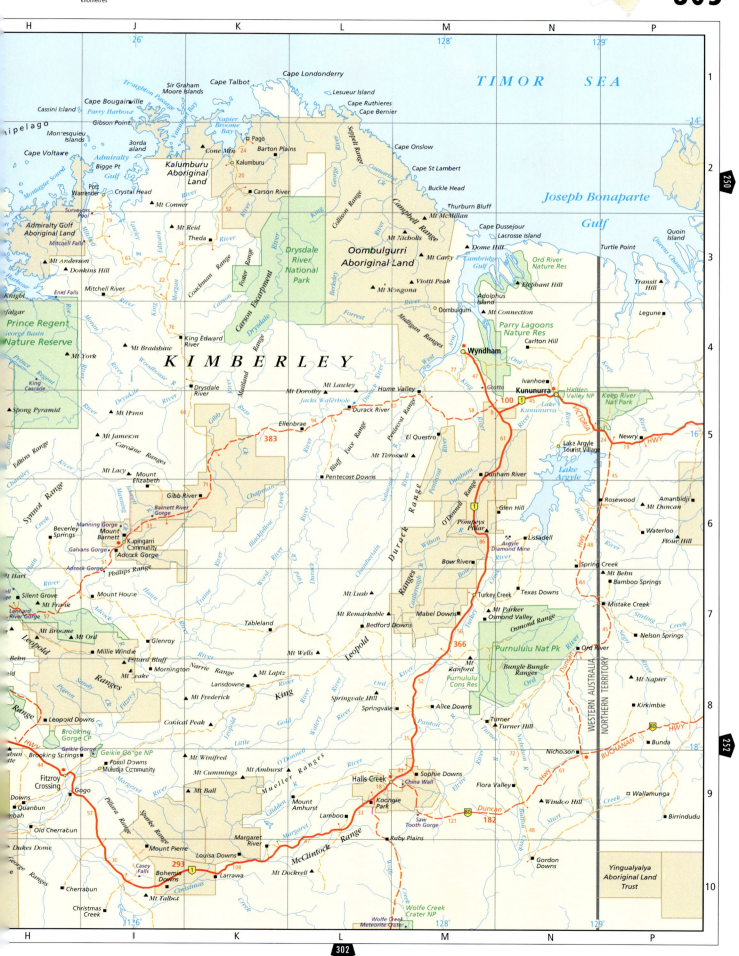

0 20 40 60 80 100
kilometres

H   J   K   L   M   N   P

120°

Rowley Shoals
Marine Park

122°   James Price Point
       Quondong Point
       Cape Boileau

Point Coulomb
Nat Reserve

Mt Jowlaenga
Mount Jowlaenga

112

Mowanjum
Community

Yeeda

Willare Bridge
Roadhouse

Kilto   Ck
                    56   NORTHERN   188   40
Roebuck
Roadhouse   19
                                                    Manguel Creek   Udialla
Cable Beach   25
Broome   10   Roebuck Plains   -18

Gantheaume Point   28
Entrance Point

Roebuck Bay

Thangoo   30   GREAT

Bush Point

Cape Villaret

Gourdon Bay

Cape Latouche Treville
Port Smith

51

Frome Rocks

Dampier
Downs

False Cape Bossut

Lagrange Bay
Cape Bussot   Lagrange

Babrongan Tower

Sandy Lake

Mowla Bluff

Admiral Bay
Geoffroy Bay
Cape Jaubert
Desault Bay
Cape Missiessy

Frazier
Downs

Mt Collins

Edgar
Range

Beach   Nita Downs
                                                   McLarty Hills
251
Anna Plains   142

Shovel Lake

HWY
Mile   Dragon Tree Soak
                                    Nature Reserve

Eighty Mile Beach   Mandora
                     45   Sandfire
                           Roadhouse

Eighty

Poissonnier Point   Cape Keraudren
Breaker Inlet

44   291   49
NORTHERN

Kidson

Track

-20°

Spit Point

Pardoo   50   Pardoo
                Roadhouse

Port Hedland

De Grey   53   GRE-1
20   30
Strelley   Goldsworthy

De Grey

Shay Gap

Isabella Range

42   45   Coongan
            Warralong
Carlindi   Muccan   Yarrie
Wallareenya   Callawa

Tabba Tabba   Lalla Rookh   55   Eginbah   Warrawagine

124   16   Bamboo Creek

26   Carawine
Marble Bar   9   Gorge
Comet Mine

Gregory   Range

Yilgalong

Creek

Lake
Waukarlycarly

Private

Road   Patterson Range
                    Telfer Mine

Throssell Range

Kidson

Track

-22

302

261   Abydos
              Pilga   103   Corunna
                              Downs
Woodstock   Woodie Woodie

Pinga   Hillside

95   Eamboo
               Springs   40   Nullagine

NORTHERN   Mt Isdell
                            Creek
Mulga Downs   Coolbro

Wittenoom   RANGE   Bonney
                          Downs
Aaski Roadhouse
Vampire Gorge   42   Noreena Downs
Fortescue
Fortescue Falls   37   60   Mt Divide
RANGE   Marillana   Mt Hodgson   Tongolelo
Juna Downs   HWY   78   Roy Hill
212   131   Yandicoogina   38   Balfour
Mt Mebarry   Downs
                                                         Taliawana
Opthelmia   Ethel Creek
Spearhole   Range

Mt Newman   Jigalong
Newman   Kalgan   Carranilla Creek   Billinnooka
Capricorn   Walgun   Robertson
Roadhouse   Range
42   55   Jigalong
                                Aboriginal   Jigalong
Sylvania   Land

Robertson
Range

Mt Connaughton

Patterson Range

Broadhurst   Range

Rudall

Rudall River

National Park

Lake
Dora

Eva Broadhurst Lake

Lake
Blanche

Lake
George

Lake
Winifred

Harbutt
Range

McKay Range   Runton Range

Tropic of Capricorn

Emu Lake

Kunderong Range
Turee Creek   Prairie
               Downs
River

Tunnel
Creek   Bulleo Downs   Weelarrana
              Lofty   Range
151   120°

Mundiwindi

LITTLE   SANDY   DESERT

Lake
Disappointment

Durba
Hills

Savory

122°

-24°

H   J   K   L   M   N   P

SOUTH AUSTRALIA

Think of South Australia and lovers of the outdoors will immediately think of such places as the Flinders Ranges, the Simpson Desert, the spectacular coast south of Robe in the far southeast, or the cliffs lining the Great Australian Bight where the flat plains of the Nullarbor Plain plunge into the rolling swells of the Southern Ocean. There are a host of other localities, but they have one thing in common—all the areas are protected by some form of park or reserve, thereby ensuring that these magnificent natural delights will remain pristine and available for future generations to use and love as we do.

Covering more than 980 000 square kilometres, the state takes up about one-eighth of the Australian continent and has the dubious record of being the driest state in the driest continent on earth. Over 80 per cent of the state receives less than 250 mm of rain a year and none of that is received on a regular basis. Much of it comes in sudden storms after months, or even years, of little or no rain, transforming the country. Regular desert travellers will know the joy and lushness these rains bring, and while access along the main roads such as the Birdsville, Strzelecki and Oodnadatta Tracks may be cut for a week or more, the rains put life and vigour back into the country. In such years travelling in these remote regions is a real bonus. Only in the southeast can rainfall be considered predictable and in this area amongst the rolling hills and flat plains the state takes on a different face—a more gentle one.

With more than 17 per cent of South Australia protected in the shape of a park or reserve, the state can boast one of the most dynamic and forward-thinking reserve systems in the country.

Much of the remote north is protected in Regional Reserves where economic activity such as cattle grazing or oil and gas production can go on, while at the same time the region remains open and accessible for travellers. These areas, managed by the national parks department in consultation with the land owners or lessees, include the Simpson Desert Regional Reserve and the Innamincka Regional Reserve, and to visit them for recreational purposes you require a Desert Parks Pass—a unique South Australian invention. But it works, and works well, keeping access open to these vast desert lands while preserving the landscape and its vegetation and wildlife. Of course there is a price to pay and an annual pass costs around

$60, but this pass gives you access to a vast region of northern South Australia and, while you can't go anywhere and everywhere you'd like, the choice of routes across the desert or places to camp are wide and varied.

Other reserves, for example those found in the far northwest of the state, are remote with few if any tracks cutting across them. Other parks, such as the UnNamed Conservation Park, are surrounded by Aboriginal land or by Department of Defence land and you require a permit from either or both to visit these parks. The best place to start organising a trip into these remote regions is with the national park regional offices. Such a trip is not for the family car or for the inexperienced 4WD driver. Set your sights on something not so remote for your first or even second and third outback trips.

Much of South Australia is flat, with only 20 per cent of the landmass being over 250 metres above sea level. The highest peak, St Mary Peak in the Flinders Ranges, reaches the slightly dizzy heights of just 1170 metres. Closer to Adelaide and acting as a tallish backdrop to the city, Mt Lofty comes in at 726 metres and is the highest peak in the Mt Lofty Ranges.

These two ranges, the Flinders in the north and the Mt Lofty Ranges in the south, cut through the heart of the state from Cape Jervis, 100 km south of Adelaide, to Mt Hopeless on the fringes of the desert country, 650 km north of the capital. It's not surprising, given the proximity of both ranges to the city and the more densely populated part of the state, and the fact that much of South Australia is relatively flat, that these two ranges have more than their fair share of parks and reserves.

Around Adelaide parks and reserves crowd close into the outer suburbs offering locals and visitors alike a wide range of recreational activities and a chance to commune with nature. Some of these city parks, such as Belair National park, are dotted with recreational facilities such as tennis courts, footy ovals and a

small golf course, while other parks are ideal for rock climbing. Then again there are parks and reserves which make great venues for easy walks along well marked trails, such as Cleland Conservation Park. It takes in the summit of Mt Lofty and offers a number of walking trails, as well as having one of the best Australian wildlife zoos in the country.

Further afield, along the southern coast of the Fleurieu Peninsula but still within 100 km of the city, larger parks offer a quieter, more natural experience, which makes them popular with walkers, anglers and surfers.

For long distance walkers there is the Heysen Walking Trail that stretches from Cape Jervis through most of the parks in the southern ranges, past Adelaide, and into the Flinders Ranges. For those keen and tough enough to tackle this world recognised walking trail, it takes them from the gentle climes of the vineyard clad Mt Lofty Ranges, all the way north to near Blinman in the central Flinders Ranges.

The Flinders Ranges have some of the best

Knob-tailed gecko at home in the Simpson Desert

The spectacular Flinders Ranges

known attractions of South Australia and it is within the ragged battlements of these desert ranges that one can really experience the Outback—and do it with ease and in comfort. While Mt Remarkable National Park in the far south of the Flinders and the Gammon Ranges National Park in the far north offer two vastly different experiences and landscapes, it is the Flinders Ranges National Park centred around the magnificent Wilpena Pound that is the epitome of the whole area. This is an impressive park and one that should be on everyone's list of places to visit. You can stay at the delightful resort or in the well-serviced caravan park on the edge of Wilpena Creek, or head bush and camp in any one of a number of delightful places along the edge of a creek tucked into the ranges, with just the birds and the kangaroos for company.

No mention of South Australia would be complete, though, without a reference to the wild coastline, much of it protected in a number of parks and reserves.

Down on the 'toe' of Yorke Peninsula there is Innes National Park, which is one of the state's top surfing, fishing and diving meccas. It's a magical place for a summer holiday, with the beach at Pondolowie Bay ranking with the best.

Over on Eyre Peninsula there are the Lincoln National Park and Coffin Bay National Park, as well as a host of other parks dotted along the coast. The great attraction of these areas is not only their beautiful white sandy beaches, rugged headlands and cliffs and blue water, but also the lack of people.

Then there is Kangaroo Island, much of which is protected in national parks and reserves, with Flinders Chase National Park taking up all the western end of the island. Not only is there fabulous scenery, history, great fishing and surfing, but the Seal Bay Conservation Park offers one of the greatest wildlife experiences in the country. The seals—really Australian sea lions—laze on the beach uncon-cerned about the humans wandering past.

The mighty Murray River also has its parks, with the Coorong National Park at the Murray Mouth being one of the great wetland regions in Australia. Down through the southeast the story is much the same: wild, windswept beaches and freshwater lagoons and swamps, all playing host to waterbirds in their thousands.

Of course, if you are a SCUBA diver, then the small reserves around Ewen Ponds or Piccaninnie Ponds would be the place to head for. These are world-class diving sites—the crystal clear water seeping from the surrounding limestone offering one of the world's greatest underwater experiences.

That's typical of this state and what it has to offer: hidden jewels tucked in amongst its vastness. Luckily for us and our children most of them are protected in the parks and reserves that dot South Australia. Explore and enjoy—here is a lifetime of adventure to be had with South Australia's parks.

	Ranger/Park Tel.	Ranger/Information	Camping	Caravan	4WD Access	BBQ/Fireplace	Picnic Area	Marked Walking Tracks	Bushwalking	Kiosk/Restaurant	Fishing	Swimming
1 Acraman Creek Conservation Park	(08) 8625 3144	*			*				*		*	*
2 Bakara Conservation Park	(08) 8595 2111	*							*			
3 Bascombe Well Conservation Park	(08) 8688 3177	*			*				*			
4 Beachport Conservation Park	(08) 8735 6053	*			*			*	*		*	*
5 Belair National Park	(08) 8278 5477	*	*	*		*	*	*	*			
6 Belt Hill Conservation Park	(08) 8735 1177											
7 Black Hill Conservation Park	(08) 8204 9234	*				*	*	*	*			
8 Bool Lagoon Game Reserve	(08) 8764 7541	*	*	*		*	*	*	*			
9 Brookfield Conservation Park	(08) 8595 2111					*		*				
10 Butchers Gap Conservation Park	(08) 8735 1177							*	*			
11 Calpatanna Waterhole Conservation Park	(08) 8688 3177	*			*				*			
12 Canunda National Park	(08) 8735 6053	*	*		*	*	*	*		*		
13 Cape Bouguer Wilderness Protection Area	(08) 8553 2381								*			
14 Cape Gantheaume Conservation Park	(08) 8553 8233	*	*				*	*				*
15 Cape Torrens Wilderness Protection Area	(08) 8553 2381	*			*				*			
16 Chowilla Game Reserve & Regional Reserve	(08) 8595 2111	*	*	*		*	*	*	*		*	*
17 Cleland Conservation Park	(08) 8281 4022	*				*	*	*	*	*		
18 Clements Gap Conservation Park	(08) 8648 5310					*		*				
19 Clinton Conservation Park	(08) 8648 5300	*			*							
20 Cobbler Creek Recreation Park	(08) 8204 9234							*				
21 Coffin Bay National Park	(08) 8688 3111	*	*	*	*		*	*	*		*	*
22 Coorong National Park	(08) 8575 1200	*	*	*	*	*	*	*			*	*
23 Corrobinnie Hill Conservation Park	(08) 8575 1200	*			*				*			
24 Danggali Conservation Park	(08) 8595 8010	*	*		*				*	*		
25 Deep Creek Conservation Park	(08) 8552 3677	*	*		*		*	*	*		*	
26 Dingley Dell Conservation Park	(08) 8735 1177							*				
27 Dutchman's Stern Conservation Park	(08) 8648 5310	*	*				*	*				
28 Flinders Chase National Park	(08) 8559 0048	*	*	*		*	*	*	*	*	*	
29 Flinders Ranges National Park	(08) 8648 4244	*	*	*	*		*	*				
30 Franklin Harbour Conservation Park	(08) 8204 9234	*									*	*
31 Furner Conservation Park	(08) 8735 1177	*					*	*				
32 Gammon Ranges National Park	(08) 8648 4829	*	*						*	*		
33 Goose Island Conservation Park	(08) 8648 5300	*										*
34 Hallett Cove Conservation Park	(08) 8207 3999							*				*
35 Hambidge Conservation Park	(08) 8207 3999	*			*				*			
36 Hincks Conservation Park	(08) 8688 3172	*			*				*			
37 Innamincka Regional Reserve	(08) 8648 4244	*	*		*			*	*	*	*	*
38 Innes National Park	(08) 8854 4040	*	*	*	*	*	*	*	*	*	*	*
39 Kellidie Bay Conservation Park	(08) 8757 2261								*			
40 Kelly Hill Conservation Park	(08) 8559 7231	*			*	*	*	*	*	*		
41 Kyeema Conservation Park	(08) 8552 2677	*							*			
42 Lake Eyre National Park	(08) 8648 4244	*			*				*			
43 Lake Gairdner National Park	(08) 8648 4244	*			*							
44 Lake Gilles Conservation Park	(08) 8648 4244	*			*				*			
45 Lake Robe Game Reserve	(08) 8735 1177	*									*	
46 Lake Torrens National Park	(08) 8648 4244	*			*				*			
47 Laura Bay Conservation Park	(08) 8625 3144	*			*						*	*
48 Lincoln National Park	(08) 8688 3177	*	*	*	*		*	*	*		*	*
49 Little Dip Conservation Park	(08) 8768 2543	*			*				*			*
50 Loch Luna Game Reserve	(08) 8595 2111	*										
51 Morialta Conservation Park	(08) 8204 9234	*				*	*	*	*	*		
52 Mt Brown Conservation Park	(08) 8648 5310	*						*	*			
53 Mt Remarkable National Park	(08) 8634 7068	*	*	*		*	*	*	*			
54 Murray River National Park	(08) 8595 2111	*	*	*	*		*	*			*	*
55 Naracoorte Caves Conservation Park	(08) 8762 3412	*	*	*		*	*	*	*	*		
56 Newland Head Conservation Park	(08) 8552 3677	*			*				*		*	*
57 Ngarkat Conservation Park	(08) 8757 2261	*	*		*				*			
58 Nullarbor National Park and Regional Reserve	(08) 8625 3144	*	*	*	*				*			
59 Onkaparinga River Recreation Park	(08) 8207 3999					*	*	*	*		*	*
60 Para Wirra Recreation Park	(08) 8204 9234	*				*	*	*	*	*		
61 Piccaninnie Ponds Conservation Park	(08) 8735 1177	*						*				*
62 Point Labatt Conservation Park & Aquatic Reserve	(08) 8625 3144											
63 Pureba Conservation Park	(08) 8688 3177	*			*				*			
64 Ravine des Casoars Wilderness Protection Area	(08) 8553 2381								*			
65 Seal Bay Conservation Park & Aquatic Reserve	(08) 8559 4207	*	*				*	*	*	*	*	*
66 Simpson Desert National Park	(08) 8648 4244	*	*									
67 Sir Joseph Banks Group Conservation Park	(08) 8688 3177	*							*		*	
68 Spring Gully Conservation Park	(08) 8648 5300	*							*			
69 Strzelecki Regional Reserve	(08) 8648 4244	*			*							
70 Tallaringa Conservation Park	(08) 8688 3177	*			*							
71 Tatanoola Caves Conservation Park	(08) 8734 4153	*				*	*		*			

311

	Ranger/Park Tel.	Ranger/Information	Camping	Caravan	4WD Access	BBQ/Fireplace	Picnic Area	Marked Walking Tracks	Bushwalking	Kiosk/Restaurant	Fishing	Swimming
72 Telowie Gorge Conservation Park	(08) 8648 5310		*		*	*	*	*				
73 UnNamed Conservation Park	(08) 8625 3144				*							
74 Venus Bay Conservation Park	(08) 8625 3144	*	*		*			*			*	*
75 Waldergrave Island Conservation Park	(08) 8688 3172										*	
76 Warrenben Conservation Park	(08) 8648 5300	*							*			
77 Winninowie Conservation Park	(08) 8648 5310	*							*			
78 Wirrabarra Forest Reserve	(08) 8648 5300	*				*	*	*				
79 Witjira National Park	(08) 8670 7835	*	*						*			
80 Yellabinna Regional Reserve	(08) 8688 3177	*	*						*			
81 Yumbarra Conservation Park	(08) 8625 3144	*	*						*			

CANUNDA NATIONAL PARK

IN BRIEF

MAP REFERENCE: PAGE 342 F 8

Location 390 km southeast of Adelaide via the Princes Highway
Best Time Summer
Main Attractions Wild, spectacular coast, fishing, beach driving, wildlife, 4WD
Ranger Southend, phone (08) 8735 6053

Caravan parks:
Carpenter Rocks, phone (08) 8738 0035
Millicent, phone (08) 8733 3947
Southend, phone (08) 8735 6034

Pounded by winter gales ripping across the Southern Ocean, the southeastern coast of South Australia has one of the most wild, untouched coastlines on the continent. In summer the gales abate, but big surf still rolls in, curling onto long stretches of white sand or breaking in an explosion of foam onto the many headlands that dot this ragged, indented coast.

Canunda National Park is the largest coastal park in this region, taking up 9358 hectares of coast that is dominated by large sand dunes and, in the north of the park, rugged limestone cliffs that look down on small, reef-strewn bays. The southern section of the park backs onto the shallow waters of Lake Bonney.

WALKING TRAILS

In the north of the park close to Southend a number of short walking trails give travellers an opportunity to experience this park first-hand.

The Khyber Pass Walk starts at a car park, accessible by the family car, on the Bevilaqua Ford track, and is only a short stroll to a spectacular area of sand dunes known as the Khyber Pass.

From the Cape Buffon lighthouse a trail, known as the Seaspray Walk, takes visitors along the edge of the cliffs for about 1.5 km. It is a dramatic introduction to the forces that have shaped this section of coast.

The Seaview Walk is a 4 km extension to the Seaspray Walk and takes about 2 hours for the return trip. Halfway along this section of walking track a lookout has been provided which gives great views of the coast. In fact, if you are feeling particularly energetic you can walk for a couple of hours along the cliffs past Eddy Bay, Stanway Point, Abyssinia Bay and Boozy Gully and the views overlooking Cullen Bay and Sweep Rocks to McIntyre Beach.

The Jetty Walk and the Coola Outstation Walk are 2 other short walks of less than 1 km each that can be accessed from Southend.

At the Southend end of McIntyre Beach there is a large Aboriginal shell midden. A number of these middens can be found scattered along the coastline indicating where the original inhabitants of the area gathered to feast on the bounty of the sea.

For the keen angler the coast can provide good catches of salmon, mulloway, flathead and the occasional shark.

WILDLIFE

Nature watchers may sight some of the world's rarest birds, including the orange-bellied parrot and the hooded plover, as well having the chance to see those magnificent birds of prey, the white-bellied sea-eagle and the swamp harrier. Penguins and seals are also regular visitors along this coast and can often be spied resting on a quiet beach.

Offshore the larger sea mammals, including

Animal tracks on a sand dune in Canunda National Park

The deserted sand dunes of Canunda National Park

the southern right whale and the minke whale, pass by on their regular migrations to and from Antarctica, while dolphins are also commonly seen in the bays.

ACCESS AND CAMPING

Access by conventional vehicles is limited to Cape Buffon and Boozy Gully in the north of the park, which is reached from the seaside enclave of Southend, as well as to Oil Rig Square in the central section of the park, which is easily at hand from the township of Millicent.

For those with a 4WD the complete park is accessible by following the orange marker posts that lead through the park from Southend to Carpenter Rocks in the very south of the park. This route can be challenging and you need to deflate your tyres to 110 kPa or around 16 psi just to get through. Ensure you stick to the track! You can always find a section of beach or a small bay that you can have to yourself.

In the north of the park there are a number of camping spots close to Southend. Oil Rig Square has water and toilets, although it can be a very exposed site. Number Two Rocks, in the southern section of the park, also has toilets. A permit, available from the ranger, is required to camp in the park. There are caravan parks in Millicent, Southend and Carpenter Rocks.

LEGEND

Sealed/Unsealed Rd	★ 26 ★
Four Wheel Drive	
Walks	
Rest Area (Picnic Area)	
Caravan Park	
Camping Area	
Accommodation	
Information	
Fuel Supplies	

COFFIN BAY NATIONAL PARK

IN BRIEF

MAP REFERENCE: PAGE 344 C 9

Location 625 km west of Adelaide, via Port Lincoln
Best Time October to April
Main Attractions Spectacular coastal scenery, good fishing, safe swimming, surfing, 4WD
Ranger Coffin Bay, phone (08) 8685 4047

Accommodation:
Caravan Park, Coffin Bay, phone (08) 8685 4170
Siesta Lodge, Coffin Bay, phone (08) 8685 4001

General Store:
Coffin Bay, phone (08) 8685 4057

This is a park of extremes. On one side of the great T-shaped peninsula are the placid protected waters of Coffin Bay, an ideal place for the family and the kids to swim, sail a boat or to fish for whiting. On the opposite side of Coffin Bay Peninsula, along its southwestern coast, the surf generated from great Southern Ocean swells pounds the coast continuously.

On land too there are extremes. In places, sterile white sand swamps all living things in its endless march in front of the prevailing winds. This barren landscape of big dunes and highly mobile sand is at odds with the protected bays and enclaves that are often backed by a thick woodland of black tea-trees. These trees sometimes form dense stands of mature trees up to 10 metres in height but in more exposed areas they can be stunted by wind and salt to remain as low bushes. In summer and spring their profusion of creamy white flowers play host to a variety of insects and birds. In other parts of the park she-oak woodlands and low swampy areas covered in samphire hold sway and while there are many walks that take in these areas it is the coast that attracts most people.

Of course, such a wild untamed area has other attractions as well and for those who love birds the beaches, headlands, rich shallow coastal waters and scrub-covered sand ridges provide a rich and bountiful habitat. The endangered hooded plover can often be seen in summer tending well-camouflaged eggs just above the high tide mark. Ospreys can also sometimes be spotted searching for food or resting on a high vantage point overlooking a favourite fishing area. Rock parrots nest in the scrub above the cliff-lined beaches and shearwaters skim the nearby waters. Stilts, gulls and oystercatchers parade along the shallows, and in the nearby scrub dozens of bush birds, including the western whipbird, can be seen.

HISTORY

The Nauo Aboriginal tribe was once the inhabitants of the area around Coffin Bay. Shell middens around the coast are a reminder of their lifestyle.

Matthew Flinders was the first European to see this coast as he sailed past in 1802 on his great circumnavigation of Australia. He named Point Whidbey on the southwestern tip and sailed on, but not before naming the bay after his friend, Sir Isaac Coffin.

The area was colonised in the 1840s and signs of these pioneering times in the form of rough fences and yards are dotted here and there. The early graziers shipped their hard-earned bales of wool from Morgans Landing, on the northwestern coast of Coffin Bay. But the drifting sands, thick scrub and bare limestone outcrops, along with mineral-deficient pastures, beat the pioneer sheepmen who turned to horses which could survive in this tough region. Today descendants of these horses still roam the park, but in ever-dwindling numbers.

The park takes up the whole of the Coffin Bay Peninsula, its 30 380 hectares of sand and limestone country covered mainly with mallee, tea-tree and she-oak scrub.

WALKING

There are a number of walking trails in the park, most of which follow old vehicle tracks. The beaches too make an ideal venue for a walk.

From near the car park area at Yangie Bay there is a very short walk of just 300 metres to the Yangie Lookout or a longer 1.5 km Kallara Nature Trail walk that takes about 40 minutes. Other walks from here include the one hour or so, 5 km walk to Yangie Island or to Long beach, the latter requiring information from the ranger before setting out.

Other walks of up to 6 km can be had from the Black Springs camping area along the beach or south to Black Rocks.

In the Whidbey Wilderness area there are a number of walks. For those who want a short walk of less than one hour that has as a reward some spectacular coastal scenery, the 3 km trail to Sudden Jerk Lookout, on the southern headland of Misery Bay, can't be beaten.

Overnight walks include a 26 km walk south along the Whidbey Trail or a 24 km walk to the west coast at Boarding House Bay.

FISHING

The fishing is superb no matter where you try.

The protected bay beaches and bays within the large expanse of Coffin Bay are a mecca for

LEGEND

Sealed/Unsealed Rd ...... ★ 26 ★
Four Wheel Drive .... - - - - -
Walks .... ·········
Rest Area (Picnic Area) ...... ⛩

Caravan Park .... 🚐
Camping Area .... ⛺
Accommodation .... 🛏
Information....................... ℹ
Fuel Supplies .... ⛽

Avoid Bay at Coffin Bay National Park

King George whiting, one of the most delectable feeds available. Garfish, trevally, flathead and salmon are also caught.

The jetty at Coffin Bay is good for whiting, trevally and tommy ruff.

Boats can be launched at the Coffin Bay township and can be hired or chartered.

Along the wilder coast you can fish the lines of surf on the beach or try your luck off the rocks. Salmon, snapper whiting and a wide variety of reef fish, including big blue groper, can be caught.

ACCESS

Access to Coffin Bay is easy and on good roads from the main Flinders Highway. The township is just 50 km from the biggest town on Eyre Peninsula, Port Lincoln.

The ranger station is just through town as you enter the park. A road leads west for about 12 km then splits, one road heading another 6 km to Point Avoid on the storm-tossed southern coast and the other, 3 km north to the protected Yangie Bay. That's as far as conventional vehicles can go.

From near Yangie Bay a series of soft, sandy 4WD tracks head west to Seven Mile Beach, Morgans Landing, the Pool camp ground, Sensation Beach and Point Sir Isaac.

The Whidbey Wilderness area in the far southwestern section of the park has no access for vehicles.

CAMPING AND ACCOMMODATION

There is a fair range of camping and accommodation in nearby Coffin Bay township. The local general store has tourist information, as well as supplying all your daily requirements in food and fuel.

In the park you are only allowed to camp at Yangie Bay, Black Springs, Morgans Landing and at the Pool along the protected northern beaches. Along the wilder southern coast the only places where camping is allowed are at Avoid Bay and Sensation Beach

Walkers, obviously, have a wide choice of where they can go, but they should be well equipped before setting out on extended walks in this region as there is no surface water.

COORONG NATIONAL PARK

MAP REFERENCE: PAGE 342 B 7

Location 140 km southeast of Adelaide

Best Time Late spring and summer

Main Attractions Fine fishing, wildlife, spectacular coastal scenery, 4WD

Ranger Meningie, phone (08) 8575 1200

Salt Creek Visitor Centre, phone (08) 8575 7014

IN BRIEF

An old fence line in Coorong National Park

Protected from the rolling surf of the Southern Ocean by a narrow strip of sand dunes known as the Younghusband Peninsula, the Coorong is a series of shallow lagoons, with an average depth of less than 3 metres. These stretch south from the lakes that are part of the mouth of the Murray River. This chain of lagoons gets progressively shallower and saltier the further they are from the river mouth, providing a rich habitat for hundreds of thousands of birds that include pelicans, swans and waders.

It's a place that you would hardly call beautiful or spectacular, but it does have a strange attraction, an untamed feeling about it. At times southern storms blast across the area, whipping sand and water into a stinging frenzy, while at other times hardly a breeze stirs the water as the sand and sea bake in the sun.

HISTORY

The name Coorong originates from the local Aboriginal name of 'kurangh', which means 'long narrow neck of water'. In the past the area was a rich hunting and gathering ground for the Tanganekald tribe of people who had lived in this region for more than 40 000 years.

The first Europeans took up land in the area in the 1840s and in the 1850s Chinese immigrants who had landed in Robe, headed north

along the old bullock dray road and set up a garden and supply area at what became known as Chinamans Well.

The first camping reserves were established in the northern Coorong in 1901 and the national park was established in 1966. The national park and the adjoining game reserve stretch for 130 km along the coast taking in 46 800 hectares of land and water.

WALKING TRAILS

There are any number of walks that can be done, with a choice of wandering the surf-swept beaches of the ocean to the shores of the placid lagoons that make up the Coorong lakes.

At the northern end of the Coorong you can take a 30 minute, 1.6 km walk to the first barrage that helps hold the salt water back from Lake Alexandrina. This barrage, known as

Tauwitchere Barrage, is well over a kilometre long and stretches between the mainland and a small island where waterbirds abound.

The Lakes Nature Trail is a 3 km, one hour self-guided walk that starts at the car park located 2 km south of Salt Creek where the Loop Road heads off from the highway.

FISHING

The ocean beaches are a surf fisherman's delight and there is excellent fishing for mulloway, whiting, flathead, salmon and shark. The Murray Mouth itself is a top spot for mulloway.

The Coorong proper is ideal for those with a small boat and there are a number of boat launching ramps located along the mainland side of the Coorong. These shallow waters are can get rough if a storm brews up. They also demand careful navigation because of sandbars.

In the lagoon mullet abound as well as bream, salmon and flounder.

Fishing is not permitted within 150 metres of the barrages.

BIRDS GALORE

The Coorong is a birdwatcher's paradise with over 200 species of birds being recorded. The shallow waters of the lake and the variety of habitat make this one of Australia's most important wetlands and the area has international significance as migratory birds fly in from as far away as Siberia to summer here.

The lakes regularly support over 120 000 waders, a large population of Cape Barren geese during summer, as well as a large number of breeding pairs of black swans.

A Pelican Nursery

North of Salt Creek and just offshore from Jacks Point a group of islands play host to a large breeding colony of pelicans. Up to 4000 birds make the Coorong the single biggest pelican breeding area in Australia.

Made famous by the publication of Colin Thiele's children's book, *Storm Boy*, and the subsequent film, the islands and the waters up to 150 metres offshore are a prohibited area.

A walking trail leads from the car parking area at Jacks Point for a short distance to a viewing point overlooking the island sanctuary.

ACCESS

Camping areas, picnic spots and points of interest on the mainland side of the park are accessible via conventional vehicles and a mix of bitumen and gravel roads.

Access tracks across the dunes to the ocean beach are well marked and, apart from the 42 Mile Crossing accessed from a point 18 km south of Salt Creek, are strictly 4WD. All vehicles must stay on the marked routes.

The best area to drive along the beach is just above the waterline at low tide. Tyre pressures need to be deflated to 125–150 kPa or 16–20 psi. At times, especially in early summer, the ocean beach track may be washed away and the sand particularly soft. Take special care!

The route north along the beach from Tea Tree Crossing is closed from 24 October to 24 December each year to protect the endangered hooded plover.

Be aware that it is 100 km or so from Tea Tree Crossing—the northernmost access track to the beach and one that is only open in summer as it crosses a stretch of lagoon—to the Murray River mouth.

Drive only on the marked tracks through the dunes to camping areas and if you have to park on the beach, do not block the traffic.

Access to the lakes, lagoon and the eastern side of the Younghusband Peninsula is by boat and there are a number of boat ramps located on the mainland side of the park or at Goolwa and Hindmarsh Islands.

CAMPING AND ACCOMMODATION

There are plenty of places to camp that can be accessed by car, 4WD or boat. You will require a camping permit and these are available from the national parks office in Meningie, the Salt Creek Visitor Centre or at a number of other local outlets.

The Old Melbourne Road winds in and out of the park from the southern boundary to near Salt Creek and gives access to a number of pleasant camping spots.

In the northern section of the park good camping can be found at Mark Point, Long Point and Pelican Point, although they lack any shelter and are a little exposed.

Other camping spots exist at the beach crossing points of 42 Mile Crossing, 32 Mile Crossing and Tea Tree Crossing.

For drivers of 4WDs there are any number of camping spots to be found along the ocean beach, anywhere between the high tide and the low water mark. There are also designated bush camping spots behind the first line of dunes: look for a tall, green-topped post.

With a boat you can really experience the wilderness aspect of the Coorong by camping along the eastern edge of the Younghusband Peninsula.

For those wanting a bit of comfort, there are caravan parks and motels close by at Meningie or a little further south at Kingston.

Noonameena House, situated on a low cliff top in the heart of the park, offers 3 bedroom accommodation for up to 8 people. Located just 9 km from Meningie the house has great views of the Coorong and the dunes of the Younghusband Peninsula. Contact the national parks office in Meningie for details.

The shallow waters of the Coorong

FLINDERS CHASE NATIONAL PARK

IN BRIEF

MAP REFERENCE: PAGE 342 B 2

Location On Kangaroo Island, 270 km southwest of Adelaide
Best Time Late spring and summer
Main Attractions Coastal scenery, wildlife, fishing
Ranger Rocky River, phone (08) 8559 7235

Accommodation: for details of all places mentioned, contact the ranger at Rocky River, phone (08) 8559 7235
Ferries:
SeaLink, phone 13 1301;
Kangaroo Island Fast Ferries, phone 1 800 626 242 (overnight from Port Adelaide)

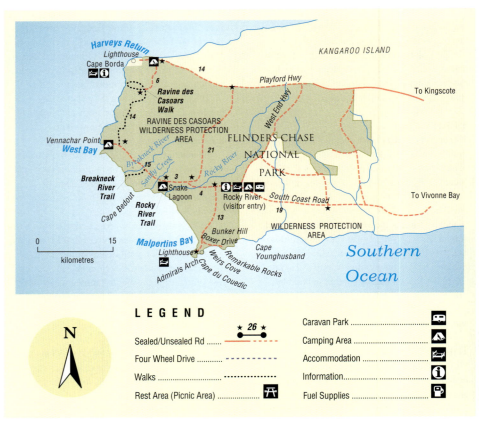

It's the view, through Admirals Arch, of a wild, turbulent Southern Ocean pounding a rocky inlet on the far western coast of Kangaroo Island that is the indelible impression of Flinders Chase National Park. That, and the wildlife.

HISTORY

The park consists of 73 841 hectares of wild virgin scrub and bush country on the far western end of Kangaroo Island, including the whole western coast from Cape Borda in the north to Cape du Couedic in the south. Because of its undisturbed nature and its wide variety of habitats and fauna, it is one of South Australia's most important parks.

WILDLIFE

The wildlife in the shape of kangaroos laze around the park headquarters area at Rocky River and create quite a stir when they come into a picnic shelter looking for a cool shady spot to lie down or just maybe, a scrap of food, which no one is allowed to give them—of course!

Emus may also be on patrol, often a little less discreet, snatching food from people.

Other wildlife thrive in this vast park that takes up around a quarter of the island. Free from competition from rabbits and foxes, Cape Barren geese, emus, koalas, ringtail possums and platypus have been introduced and have not only settled in but have expanded their realm to take up so much of the island that the koalas and possums are considered by many to be reaching plague proportions.

Over a dozen species of mammals are native to the park including tammar wallabies, southern brown bandicoot, the Australian sea lion and the New Zealand fur seal.

A number of reptiles live in the park including Gould's sand goanna, a handsome monitor lizard that reaches 1.6 metres in length. Black tiger snakes and copperhead snakes can also be seen but these should be left well and truly alone.

There are nearly 200 species of birds found in the park with yellow-tailed black cockatoos, Cape Barren geese and emus being the most commonly seen birds. The rare western whipbird and the glossy black cockatoo may also be sighted on occasion.

WALKING TRAILS TO SUIT ALL

At Cape du Couedic there is a short walking trail of 15 minutes or so, down to view the seals that frolic in the waters below the low cliffs and the fantastic Admirals Arch where the sea has cut through the headland.

At Remarkable Rocks a walking trail of about 1 km, which would take between 30 minutes and one hour, goes from the car park up and around the fantastic shapes of seemingly delicately balanced boulders, sitting on top of a large granite dome.

The Rocky River walking trail leads about 1.5 km from the camping area at Snake Lagoon to the mouth of the river where the river tumbles over a small waterfall to the beach. Allow an hour or so for this very pleasant walk.

The Sandy Creek walking trail and the Breakneck River walking trail follow their respective streams through Sugar Gum forest to the coast, taking about one hour for the 3 km Sandy Creek walk and 2 hours for the 6 km Breakneck River walk.

The Ravine des Casoars walk in the northern section of the park is a moderate to hard walk of 7 km to the west coast and some impressive coastal scenery. You should allow around 3 hours for the return walk.

Longer walks through the wilderness areas of the park are possible by those who are well equipped and experienced.

FISHING AND DIVING

Kangaroo Island is known for its great fishing and the far western end of the island, with its many isolated bays and rocky headlands, is one of the best areas.

At West Bay the rock fishing is fantastic, with heavy line and gear being the order of the day to deal with the big blue groper and large red snapper that can be caught there. Sweep, whiting and rock cod are also to be found.

Up north at Harveys Return snapper and sweep can be caught from the rocks and whiting and salmon off the beach, while down the southern end of the island, once you get to water level, there is good fishing for sweep, groper and rock cod from the rocks or whiting and salmon off the beaches.

For SCUBA divers this is virtually an untouched coast restricted by poor access and often wild seas. A number of wrecks have occurred along this coast including that of the *Loch Vennachar*, a 250-foot clipper which disappeared in 1905 and was finally discovered in 1976 a kilometre north of West Bay. A grave of an unknown sailor can be seen just up from the beach at West Bay.

Harveys Return on the northern coast is a little more protected, and once you've got down to the bottom of the cliffs there is some quite pleasant snorkelling.

ACCESS

Access to Kangaroo Island is via a large ferry from Adelaide which is normally an overnight trip arriving at the 'capital' of Kingscote, or by SeaLink ferry from the nearest point on the mainland, Cape Jervis, to the small, eastern end town of Penneshaw. This latter trip takes just an hour or so and is the cheaper alternative.

From Penneshaw, Flinders Chase National Park is down the other end of the island, 150 km away, either on bitumen or excellent dirt roads.

The park headquarters is located at Rocky River on the South Coast Road.

Within the park most roads are good dirt, and the many points of interest are accessible in the family car.

CAMPING AND ACCOMMODATION

At Rocky River there is a well established camping and caravan area with showers, toilets and limited supplies. Accommodation is also possible at the old Rocky River homestead.

At Cape Borda, in the northwest of the park and the island, there is also accommodation in the old lighthouse keeper's quarters. Here you have a choice between the original stone buildings of the light keeper, and the more modern relieving keeper's quarters. Just a short distance away at Harveys Return, where stores were once landed for the lighthouse and staff, there is a small camping area, the only facility being toilets.

The old light keeper's house at Cape du Couedic, in the far southwest of the park, is available to stay in.

West Bay, on the far western end of the island, has toilets and water and is an ideal spot to camp. Snake Lagoon, passed on the way to West Bay from Rocky River, is also a good bush camping spot where there are toilets and water available.

Bushwalkers have a wider choice of bush camping spots to select from.

Entry fees and camping fees apply. If you are staying and touring the island an 'Island Pass' will work out cheaper and more convenient.

The rocky coastline of Flinders Chase National Park

FLINDERS RANGES NATIONAL PARK

MAP REFERENCE: PAGE 345 K 2

IN BRIEF

Location 460 km north of Adelaide

Best Time April to October, early spring is best for wildflowers

Main Attractions Great camping, remote mountain scenery, wildflowers

Ranger Wilpena, phone (08) 8648 0048; Oraparinna, phone (08) 8648 0047

Accommodation:
Wilpena Pound—motel, caravan park, store, fuel, phone (08) 8648 0004
Prairie Hotel, Parachilna, phone (08) 8638 4606

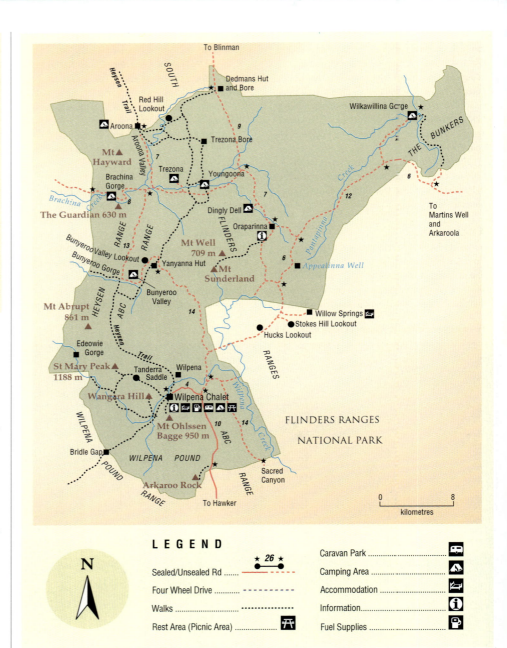

LEGEND

Sealed/Unsealed Rd .... ★ 26 ★

Four Wheel Drive .... - - - - - - - -

Walks .... · · · · · · · ·

Rest Area (Picnic Area) .... 🏕

Caravan Park .... 🚐

Camping Area .... ⛺

Accommodation .... 🛏

Information .... 🛈

Fuel Supplies .... ⛽

Sunrise! There is nothing quite like it when you are sitting on top of a relatively low peak looking out at the craggy tops of the Heysen Range, just one of the many minor stretches of range that combine to form the Flinders Ranges. The changing light colours the mountains with varying hues of blue, then pink, gold and yellow, before they take on their daytime appearance of raw-coloured rock and the dull green of the native scrub.

At sunset the ranges are etched in darkening blues as the sky above and behind them changes from cobalt blue to rich golds and reds, then finally to purple just as the light fades.

Often kangaroos—mainly stockily built euros in this part of the range, but sometimes tall, powerful red kangaroos—grace the landscape, feeding and taking little or no notice of visitors admiring the view.

All around, as far as the eye can see, is the Flinders Ranges National Park. To the south the great battlements of the northeastern wall of Wilpena Pound and the highest point in South Australia, St Mary Peak, dominate the vista, while between our viewpoint and the Heysen

Following a creek bed in the Flinders Ranges

Range, 3 km away to the west, the lower, smoother peaks of the ABC Range cut across the scene.

For many people this spectacular region of semi-arid mountain country is their first experience of the Australian Outback and what a grand introduction it is. From the great Australian artist Sir Hans Heysen who 'discovered' these ranges in the 1930s to the latest artists, who with both brush and camera have tried to capture the changing moods and magic of these mountains, the Flinders have enchanted all who see them.

No other comparable area of Australia has had so many glossy coffee-table books produced on it as these ranges that stretch 300 km from

near Gladstone in the relatively well-watered parts of the state, north to the low hill of Mt Hopeless on the edge of the Strzelecki Desert. But it is the central Flinders, around the unique geological structure of Wilpena Pound, that the ranges take on their grandest and most distinctive character.

HISTORY

The Flinders were, long before the coming of the white man, an important area for the Aboriginal nomads of Australia. The relatively well-watered ranges with their more permanent waterholes, rich vegetation and bountiful game were in stark contrast to the surrounding arid plains.

The Flinders Ranges stand in sharp contrast to the arid plain

The Adnyamathanha people, or 'Hill People' as they are called today, have left a rich heritage behind in the art sites that dot the region.

While Matthew Flinders was the first European to see the ranges on his circumnavigation of Australia in 1802, and after whom the great sweep of mountains is named, it was Edward John Eyre in 1839 and 1840 who opened the area up for settlement. Other explorers and surveyors followed but it was the pioneer pastoralists searching for rich grazing and farming land were responsible for the development of the region.

Two doctors, the Browne brothers, opened the area up around Wilpena Pound and the Aroona Valley just to the north.

In 1970 the government bought Oraparinna Station and a national park was founded to the northeast of Wilpena Pound. In fact, since the early 1950s, the Pound has had a tourist resort located at the Wilpena Creek entrance, and the Pound itself had been declared a reserve. In 1972 the new national park was amalgamated with the Pound and 4 years later the park was enlarged. In 1988 Wilpena Station, which took in much of the eastern flank of the Wilpena Pound Range, was included in the park which now covers 92 746 hectares.

WILPENA POUND

Wilpena Pound is still the major attraction and the centrepiece of the Flinders Ranges National Park, attracting most of the visitors and the acclaim.

Taking its name from the early settlers' name for a stock enclosure, the name Wilpena is said to mean in the local Aboriginal dialect,

'a cupped hand', which is a magnificent description of this huge natural amphitheatre. Nearly 5 km wide and 11 km long, the rolling pine-clad grassland inside the Pound sweeps up on its edges to the lofty craggy peaks of the all-encircling Wilpena Pound Range, that on the very outside plummet to the surrounding plains.

There are only 2 exits from the Pound. One, in the north, through Edeowie Gorge is narrow and rock and cliff strewn, while the other follows the gum-lined Wilpena Creek through a steep-sided valley on the eastern side of the Pound.

In the early days this was the main access route for the horse-drawn drays that hauled the wheat from this most northerly grain growing area to the shipping port of Port Augusta, 160 km southeast. This road was washed away in a big flood in 1914 and today the route along Wilpena Creek is still the main access into the heart of the Pound, but is used only by walkers.

All the facilities that Wilpena has to offer are located close to this entrance around the gum-lined beauty of Wilpena Creek.

Few people would come to this area and not take at least a short stroll through the gap carved by Wilpena Creek. Ancient, giant red gums tower over the track and crowd the rocky, often reed-shrouded creek bed, making the walk a shady delight, especially welcome after a long walk across rocky ridges or sun-scorched open plains.

The shorter walks take you into the old homestead and then up the ridge on a short but steep climb to Wangara Lookout. The return walk of 2 to 3 km will take between 1 to 2 hours, depending on your fitness and how long you

stop to admire the view over the Pound.

From the entrance into the Pound there is also an hour long walk along a nature trail and a more strenuous walk of about 2 hours to the lookout on top of Mt Ohlssen Bagge.

Longer walks of a day or more can take you south to Bridle Gap or north to Edeowie Gorge, while a circuit route via the heart of the Pound and Cooinda Camp can take you north to Tanderra Saddle and the top of St Mary Peak. From there it is south along the battlements of the range back to the starting point at Wilpena Creek.

Part of the long-distance Heysen Walking Trail cuts through the park entering at the southern end of the Pound via Bridle Gap and heads north from Wilpena Creek along the ABC Range to the Aroona Valley and out of the park to Parachilna Gorge and beyond. You can enjoy this trail for a day, a week or even longer, but you need to be experienced and well equipped for the extended forays.

SACRED CANYON

One of the best Aboriginal art sites in the Flinders is Sacred Canyon. This small chasm is located just outside the park proper but is only accessible via a good dirt road that heads off the main Blinman road just north of the Wilpena Pound Resort turn-off.

A brief walk from the car park along a tree-lined creek brings you to the short narrow canyon. There are rock engravings, or petroglyphs, which can be seen on the sheer rock faces on both sides of the canyon. This ancient form of Aboriginal art includes animal tracks, circles and other symbols.

FLINDERS RANGES NATIONAL PARK

AROONA VALLEY

The picturesque Aroona Valley tucks in beside the northern peaks of the ABC Range, but it is the Heysen Range immediately to the west that dominates the scene. The ruins of the Aroona homestead are perfectly situated to make the most of the view, but the pine and mud walls of one of the buildings and a few scattered remains of rock and lime testify as to how hard life was here back in the boom days of the late 1800s.

The Heysen Walking Trail passes by the ruins and you can enjoy a short or long stroll along that or along the nearby creek. Another walking trail leads out to Red Hill Lookout, a 7 km, 1½–2 hours, return trip, while the walk to Trezona Bore leads east to the very headwaters of Brachina Creek where the bore is located. Instead of returning the same way, a 14 km round trip, you can head south along the creek to the main road near the camping area of Trezona. From there you can complete the circuit back to Aroona by following the road and Brachina Creek west to the track that leads to the Aroona camp site and ruins. All up, this is a 25 km walk and takes over a day. But with a car shuffle you could make it a long day walk of about 16 km.

BRACHINA GORGE

Where the Brachina Creek cuts its way on a meandering course through the Heysen Range it forms one of the most delightful features in the area. Gums line the creek which often has a slow trickle of water running along it. In places, quite large pools, protected by a rugged bluff or group of shady trees, provide a permanent water source for the screeching corellas, twittering doves or brightly coloured parrots that call the area home. In the evening small roos and wallabies come down to join the bird life in a drink.

While there are no designated walks as such, a stroll along the creek is a must and for those who feel energetic a climb of one of the nearby peaks will give a grand view of the gorge and the surrounding mountains.

This really is a delightful place.

A TOP SCENIC DRIVE

One of the best drives in the place is to take the Yanyanna Hut–Bunyeroo Valley road in the early morning. It is especially colourful after rain when the wildflowers bloom. Once you are off

Grass-trees are a distinctive feature of the park

the main Blinman road red kangaroos are very common and as you get closer to the main range and the hills begin to crowd in, euros and western grey kangaroos will be seen.

The views are fantastic, with the pine-clad hills rolling away to the sheer bluffs of the Heysen Range. If you want to make a day of it, head up to the Prairie Hotel in Parachilna for lunch and then in the evening head back taking the Moralana Scenic Drive to Wilpena. This 36 km drive, although out of the park, gives great views of the western walls of Wilpena and in the dying light of day they are just fabulous.

WILKAWILLINA GORGE

Located in the very northeast of the park is Wilkawillina Gorge where the Mt Billy Creek has cut its way through the Bunker Range.

There is a camping ground located close to the vehicle track end and a walk of about a kilometre will take you into the gorge proper.

The peaks of the Flinders Ranges

This part of the Flinders is much drier than the Wilpena side but water can often be found in the heart of the gorge. As well, there are fewer travellers in this region and you may have the place to yourself.

ACCESS

You can travel all the way from Adelaide to the resort at the entrance to Wilpena Pound on the bitumen via Wilmington and Quorn (400 km), while the slightly shorter way (370 km) through Orroroo and Jamestown has a 50 km section of good dirt road south of Hawker. The latter route also misses out on some of the delightful range country between Melrose and Quorn.

Elsewhere, good dirt roads suitable for the family car lead through the park to all the points of interest. Only after occasional severe rains or floods are any of the roads closed, and then generally only for a short time.

CAMPING

At Wilpena Pound there is a well-established caravan park with all facilities and a motel complete with general store, fuel outlet, ranger base and information centre. This place does get crowded at holiday times so it is best to book well in advance.

Apart from this well set-up camping ground there are also a number of places to camp.

There is some very pleasant camping in the Aroona Valley, with the main camping area just to the east of the Aroona homestead ruins having toilets and water available.

Further east along the headwaters of Brachina Creek at Slippery Dip, Trezona and Youngoona, bush camping areas have been established and while all have toilets, you will need to take your own water.

Camping areas are also located at Dingly Dell on the Blinman road 30 km north of Wilpena Pound, along the main road through Bunyeroo Gorge, just north of the Pound proper but 27 km by road from the resort, and at Wilkawillina Gorge in the far

northeast of the park.

Our favourite area, though, for camping is along Brachina Gorge where a good dirt road leads from the Aroona Valley through the Heysen Range to exit the park where the western ramparts of the rugged range country meet with the flat plains of the desert country surrounding the great salt lake of Lake Torrens.

There is a host of small camp sites along Brachina Creek that are ideal for a vehicle or two, but there are no facilities, so you need to be well prepared.

No matter where you camp a fee is payable but bush camping is a little cheaper than at the camping ground at Wilpena Pound.

GAMMON RANGES NATIONAL PARK

IN BRIEF

MAP REFERENCE: PAGE 347 K 10

Location 750 km north of Adelaide, and 110 km east of Leigh Creek
Best Time May to September
Major Attractions Rugged mountain country, remote bushwalking, 4WD
Ranger Balcanoona, phone (08) 8648 4829; Hawker, phone (08) 8648 4244

The Flinders Ranges take on a more inhospitable character as they strike further north into the heart of our dry continent. Just before they peter out into a series of low hills, they put on one last great effort in a maze of twisted landforms, steep-sided gorges and rugged, weather-worn bluffs. Known as the Gammon Ranges, its periphery was explored back in the late 1800s, but it wasn't until 1947 that the Gammons were crossed by Europeans.

Much of the area was first proclaimed a park in 1970, then 15 years later it reached its present size of 128 228 hectares. A convoluted shape, the park is centred on the Gammon Ranges and Mainwater Pound, with a thick arm running off to the east across flat plain country to the shores of Lake Frome.

The park's southern boundary is Aboriginal land, while to the north is the Arkaroola–Mt Painter Wildlife Sanctuary, a private concern that offers travellers an even better glimpse of this wild northern region of the Flinders Ranges.

A couple of 4WD tracks cut through the park from just north of Balcanoona to historic Grindells Hut, then north to Mainwater Well and the ruins of Yadnina, to exit the park on the northwestern side where a reasonable station track can take you south to the main Copley road or north to Arkaroola.

The heart of the park, around the Plateau, the main spine of the Gammon Ranges themselves and Mainwater Pound and the creek of the same name, is really the realm of the adventurous and experienced bushwalker.

For the not so adventurous there are a couple of shorter walks through Weetootla Gorge in the southeast of the park (9 to 10 km—about 2–3 hours); from Yadnina to the ruins of the Illinawortina homestead (6 km—

Sturt's desert pea blooms throughout Gammon Ranges National Park

1½–2 hours) or along the Illinawortina Creek to the homestead (15 km—5–6 hours).

From Italowie Gorge in the south of the park a number of walking tracks lead north into the rugged range country. The McKinlay Basin walk is a 16 km return trek, while the walk to McKinlay Springs is a little shorter at around 14 km, and up to 6 hours, return.

Take plenty of water with you; this is a remote area and the trails are unmarked.

ACCESS

Once you leave Copley, 570 km north of Adelaide, the dirt begins and while it can be rough in places it is passable by a normal car. It's just over 100 km from Copley to the park headquarters at Balcanoona.

The slightly shorter route from Adelaide is via Yunta, but over 340 km of that is dirt—but good dirt for most of the way.

CAMPING

On the way from Copley the main road passes through Italowie Gorge, a popular bush camping spot and accessible by conventional vehicle. There are other designated bush camps, including Weetootla Gorge, Grindells Hut and Loch Ness Well, 7 km, 26 km and 31 km from the park headquarters respectively.

Further north at Mainwater Well is probably the best bush camping spot in the park accessible to vehicle-based campers. At the old Yadnina Outstation, not far from Mainwater Well, bush camping is also allowed.

The stone homestead beside Grindells Hut can be rented but you need to provide your own bedding and food. Phone the ranger for details.

The resort at nearby Arkaroola, (phone (08) 8648 4848), has a range of accommodation, or you can camp. A popular place to stay, it also has supplies and fuel. There are some interesting drives and excellent walks in the region, while scenic flights over the area can be arranged through the resort.

LEGEND

N

Sealed/Unsealed Rd ...... ★ 26 ★
Four Wheel Drive .... - - - - -
Walks ....
Rest Area (Picnic Area) ..... ⛏

Caravan Park .... 🚐
Camping Area .... ⛺
Accommodation .... 🛏
Information .... ℹ
Fuel Supplies .... ⛽

MAP REFERENCE: PAGE 347 N 3
Location 1045 km north of Adelaide, via Lyndhurst and Innamincka
Best Time April to October
Main Attractions Cooper Creek, Coongie Lakes, camping, 4WD
Ranger Innamincka, phone (08) 8675 9909; Hawker, phone (08) 8648 4244

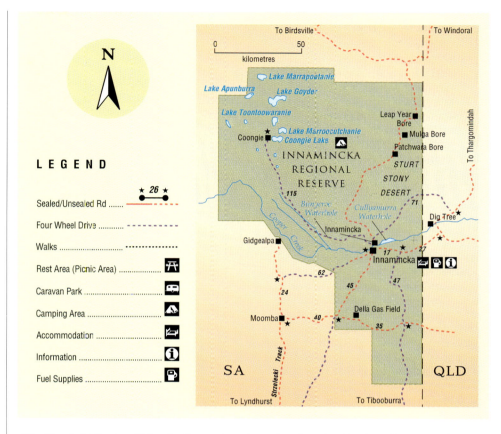

LEGEND

Sealed/Unsealed Rd	★ 26 ★
Four Wheel Drive	- - - - -
Walks	....
Rest Area (Picnic Area)	🏕
Caravan Park	🚐
Camping Area	⛺
Accommodation	🛏
Information	ℹ
Fuel Supplies	⛽

The Cooper Creek and the Coongie Lakes complex of northern SA make up one of the great wetland areas of Outback Australia. Surrounded by harsh gibber plain and the sand ridges of the Strzelecki Desert, the Cooper brings life and vitality to this arid region. In the good years water fills the Coongie Lakes creating an oasis that brings fish, birds and animals.

While the creek may stop flowing in drought years, many of the waterholes remain. Cullyamurra Waterhole is the biggest and deepest waterhole in Central Australia—one that has never been known to dry up.

Charles Sturt was, in 1845, the first European in the region. However, it was the ill-fated journey of Burke and Wills in 1860 that etched the region into history and the Australian psyche. The monuments to their struggle and where they died are scattered along the creek.

Established in 1972 the Innamincka Regional Reserve protects much of Cooper Creek, Coongie Lakes and several surrounding lakes.

ACCESS

From Adelaide the best way to the tiny outpost of Innamincka is via Lyndhurst, where the bitumen ends, and then up the good dirt roads of the Strzelecki Track and Moomba Gas road for 450 km.

Queenslanders have less than 200 km of dirt road from around the Jackson Oil Fields, west of Thargomindah, to the Cooper Creek outpost.

These 2 routes are generally passable in a coventional vehicle.

From Broken Hill in NSW there are a number of routes, the most popular being via Tibooburra and Cameron Corner to the Moomba road and north to Cooper Creek. There is about 450 km of varying dirt along this route and, while you could do it in the family car, a 4WD is recommended. Note that there is no fuel available between Innamincka and Marree on the Strzelecki Track.

While the main roads described above are public roads, all other tracks in the area require a SA Desert Parks Pass, which is also necessary for camping.

CAMPING

Along Cooper Creek or out at Coongie Lakes you will find some of the best camping spots in Central Australia.

The Cullyamurra Waterhole, 15 km northeast from Innamincka, is one such, while there are a number of top spots west of the township, along the creek.

At Coongie Lakes there is an excellent camp but here wood fires, generators, power boats and dogs are prohibited. Indeed, at all the popular camping areas firewood is nearly non-existent so you should use a gas or fuel stove.

The Town Reserve at Innamincka itself, a popular spot for campers and vanners, does not require the Desert Parks Pass. Here the river and its gum trees are delightful.

Accommodation is available at the Innamincka pub, phone (08) 8675 9901, or at the Innamincka Trading Post, phone (08) 8675 9900, where all fuels and supplies are also available.

Camels resting in the Coongie Lakes region

INNES NATIONAL PARK

MAP REFERENCE: PAGE 342 A 2

IN BRIEF

Location 300 km west of Adelaide on Yorke Peninsula
Best Time Late spring and summer; winter is good for salmon fishing
Main Attractions Fishing, surfing, diving, great coastal scenery, pleasant camping
Ranger Innes NP, phone (08) 8854 4040; Stenhouse Bay, phone (08) 8854 4084

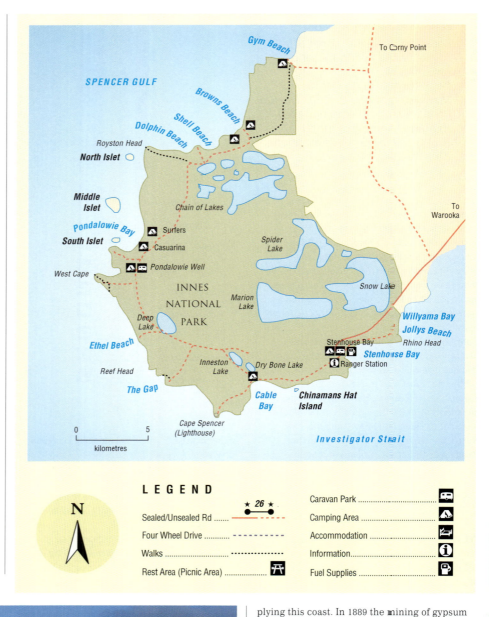

LEGEND

★ 26 ★	
Sealed/Unsealed Rd .... ●━━●━━●	Caravan Park ....
Four Wheel Drive .... - - - - - - -	Camping Area ....
Walks .... •••••••••	Accommodation ....
Rest Area (Picnic Area) .... ⊼	Information................................
	Fuel Supplies ....

The drive from the entrance gate deeper into the park is a beauty. The road climbs a low hill and as you crest the peak the coast suddenly leaps into view. Small bays and low headlands crowd each other along the southern coast while in the background the lighthouse and tall cliffs of Cape Spencer look over it all. Just offshore is Chinamans Hat Island, but the eyes are always drawn further out to sea, where Little Althorpe and Haystack Islands lead to the dominating cliffs and lighthouse on top of Althorpe Island. It's a grand view and inspires most people.

From this point the road swings north, passing the turn-off to the old mining complex of Inneston and tracks that lead to headlands and bays, before coming to the camping area at Pondalowie Bay.

The park extends further north covering the 'toe' of Yorke Peninsula, 9100 hectares in total.

A BRIEF HISTORY

Before the Europeans arrived, the Narrangga tribe of Aborigines inhabited this region.

In 1802 Matthew Flinders sailed past and during the 1830s sealers and whalers were

Cape Spencer Lighthouse

plying this coast. In 1889 the mining of gypsum began at Marion Bay and a plaster factory was built at Inneston in 1916.

In 1969 the park was gazetted soon after the discovery of a population of rare western whip-birds amongst the dense thickets of mallee which cover much of the area away from the coast and the salt lakes.

In 1979 the park was extended to its present size. Some of the lakes have been excluded from the park as they are still a source of gypsum.

The hamlet of Stenhouse Bay, once the outlet for the gypsum, is now the entrance gate and the location of the park headquarters.

REEFS AND RUGGED HEADLANDS

This wild coast is protected in most places by sheer high cliffs that in places rear 100 metres or more out of the sea. Probably the best spot to experience such a dramatic scene is at the Gap, where there is a parking area, and a short walking trail leads to the top of the cliff. Here there is a spectacular view of the headland of Reef Head to the north and Cape Spencer to the south. Reefs dot the sweep of sea and most days these are covered in white water as great swells from the Southern Ocean break on the rocks.

Just to the north of the Gap a very steep walking trail, that takes about 30 minutes each way, leads down to a small protected beach tucked in close to the cliffs. It's a magic spot, ideal for swimming and snorkelling.

Further north another vehicle track leads west to the cliffs above Ethel Beach. Once the wreck of a small ship, the *Ethel*, sat forlornly on the beach, but the ravages of salt and pounding surf have collapsed its remains into a pile of rusted steel. The *Ethel* is one of a number of wrecks that scatter this coast.

A DELIGHTFUL BAY

A more delightful bay than Pondalowie Bay, or Pondy as it is referred to by most locals and lovers of the area, would be hard to find. Only a few tantalising glimpses of it are possible as you approach—as you walk onto the beach from between the dunes its full grandeur hits you.

Off to your right a wide sweep of sparkling white sand runs away to the east and north, while to the west the beach continues a short distance until it reaches a low rocky headland. Joined to the point by a strip of rocky reef is South Islet and at low tide you can wade quite

easily out to this 'island'. Tucked into this southern corner are the most protected waters of the bay, ideal for young kids or to launch and anchor a boat. Further out is Middle Islet and north again, just off Royston Head, is North Islet.

When the swell is up big walls of water run between the 2 southern islands and bring a near-perfect wave to the far eastern shore of the bay. At those times the word gets out and the surfers crowd each and every blue-green wall as it peaks and curls onto the glittering white sand.

Around the bay there is pretty reasonable fishing, made even better if you have a small boat. The same can be said about the snorkelling or diving, but with a good boat the islands and reefs that dot the coast outside the bay beckon. One word of warning: 'outside' can be a dangerous place as the area is rarely calm.

A WEALTH OF WILDLIFE

While western grey kangaroos are seen in the park, it is the bird life that is outstanding.

A walk through the scrub will often result in a chattering group of western whipbirds being seen, the main reason this park was formed in the first place. While there are many smaller parrots and bush birds through the thick scrub, it is along the coast and on the islands that the birds really attract the eye. That magnificent bird of prey, the osprey, can be seen flying and at times nesting on rocky pinnacles along the coast. Rock parrots also call these stark cliff edges home and in the more secluded spots common terns and Caspian terns can be found

nesting. Along the rocky, more protected shores pied and sooty oystercatchers strut across the shallows, while around the shoals of the inland lakes dotterels, plovers and waders can be spied fossicking for a feed.

ACCESS AND CAMPING

Access to the park gate at Stenhouse Bay, 300 km west of Adelaide, is by good bitumen road. Once inside the park the main roads are all good dirt, with only a number of the minor roads leading to some points of interest being of a poorer standard.

There are a number of small camping spots dotted around the coast. In the north there is Gym Beach, while on the very southern side there is the Cable Bay camping area. Shell Beach and Browns Beach are both north of Royston Head and are good if you are fishing.

Surfers camping area, on the very eastern side of Pondalowie Bay, is the one to go for if you are into surfing.

By far and away the most popular is the large camping ground located on the southern end of Pondalowie Bay itself. This site, with toilets, is suitable for vans.

An entrance and camping fee is payable as you enter the park, though bookings are not generally required.

Some accommodation is also available within the park. Contact the ranger for details.

The general store, located close to the entrance to the park, can supply basic food requirements as well as fuel.

Gym Beach, in the north of Innes National Park

LAKE EYRE NATIONAL PARK

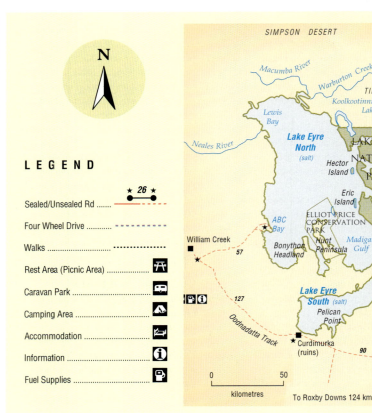

LEGEND

Sealed/Unsealed Rd	★ 26 ★
Four Wheel Drive	
Walks	
Rest Area (Picnic Area)	
Caravan Park	
Camping Area	
Accommodation	
Information	
Fuel Supplies	

It is the sheer vastness of the glittering white, harsh bed of the lake that first impresses. Walking out on its often fragile soft crust, many people are overwhelmed by it. Fear and loathing are the feelings of some, while others have a sense of insignificance as they are dwarfed by their surroundings.

This is an extreme environment—in fact, it is probably the harshest spot on the Australian continent. Take a close look at the lake's salt-encrusted, heat-reflecting surface. Other living creatures have wandered out here—small lizards, centipedes, moths, assorted bugs, even scorpions—and died!

A Giant of a Lake

Lake Eyre, at over 8000 sq km, is the largest salt lake in Australia and the largest saltpan in the world. Surprisingly, it has water in it more than it does not, but the lake is so vast that for years many believed that any sightings of water were purely a mirage.

The rivers that feed this vast inland lake system come from far away in southwest Queensland, the southern Northern Territory and northeastern South Australia, the catchment taking up nearly 20 per cent of the Australian landmass. There are the 2 giants of the inland, the Cooper Creek and the Diamantina River, and a number of lesser rivers such as the Hamilton, Neales and Macumba, and it takes a good flood down a couple of them, or all of them, to get the lake anywhere near full. In the last 150 years the lake has filled to capacity only 3 times, the most spectacular being in 1974 when the water was up to 10 metres deep. It was close to being full in 1989 and has had a fair amount of water even more recently.

While it is a salt lake, after an initial flood the water is fresh and birds in their thousands, mainly

pelicans, gulls and ducks, feed on the myriad small fish that are washed into the lake and then breed. As the water dries the lake becomes more and more salty. The fish die and then many of the birds.

The Lake Eyre National Park covers 1 225 000 hectares of the lake and the adjoining Tirari Desert which lies to the east of the lake. It is one of the driest areas in Australia and its

Sunset over Lake Eyre

southern arm, Lake Eyre South, is the lowest point on the mainland, being over 15 metres below sea level. People have swum, fished, boated and sailed, even skied on the lake, but for most it is seeing the lake and soaking up the atmosphere that is the attraction.

Access

For the normal family car only the southern end of Lake Eyre South, which is not in the park, is accessible and this is just off the Oodnadatta Track, 90 km west of Marree.

A 4WD track leads 40 km north and west from Muloorina homestead to the southeastern shore of the lake. Muloorina is 55 km north of Marree.

Another 4WD track leads east from a point on the main road 7 km south of William Creek, 57 km to the western shores of the lake. There is no public access into the Elliot Price Conservation Park that takes up all of the Hunt Peninsula in the southern area of the park.

A SA Desert Parks Pass is required for access and camping in Lake Eyre National Park.

Camping

Anywhere near the lake is not the greatest of places to camp—it's that sort of environment. The best spot to camp is at Muloorina Bore, not far from the homestead, from where you get permission to camp. Only gas fires can be used.

It is the wild coastline and the fishing and diving that attract most people to this park.

WATER SPORTS

For the energetic a rough trail of about 10 minutes leads down the cliffs on the western side of Wanna Cove giving access to a short section of wave-washed rocks that in calm weather is a good spot to cast a line for sweep, salmon and groper.

A 4WD track from Sleaford Mere heads west behind the dunes to Wanna, leading to many popular surf fishing spots.

Another 4WD track leads east to West Point and Memory Cove, the latter named by Matthew Flinders in 1802 when 8 of his men drowned while surveying the coast. Flinders erected a memorial to them at Memory Cove.

Shore diving is popular but access to the water can be a problem with a climb down the cliffs and back up again. A better plan is to launch a boat up at Taylors Landing and to fish and dive the nearby coast from there. This is a pleasant sandy cove, tucked in between 2 limestone headlands.

WALKS

There are many pleasant walks in this park, either along the beaches or along the clifftops where you may find an access track to a small secluded cove, that you will have, almost definitely, all to yourself.

In the north of the park, west of Spalding Cove, a number of circuit tracks lead along the coast as far as Woodcutters Beach and then inland to places such as Flinders Monument, with magnificent views of Port Lincoln and the nearby islands.

There is a road to the cliffs overlooking Wanna Cove that ends just before the cliff edge. A short walk west takes you to the rocky edge. The view from there is awe inspiring.

Overlooking Proper Bay and Lincoln National Park

ACCESS AND CAMPING

A sealed road leads south from Port Lincoln. Entry and camping permits to the park are available from the park entrance. A good dirt road heads east into the park and about 6 km from the main road divides, with the left hand route heading along the coast to Cape Donington, while the right hand route leads south to Wanna Beach, Cape Catastrophe and Memory Cove.

Car-based camping is allowed at a number of spots, mainly on the more protected northern and northeastern coasts.

Memory Cove, accessible via 4WD, is the most southerly camping area with toilets and water. A permit and key are required for entry. These are available from the Visitor Information Centre in Port Lincoln.

Further north along the eastern coast, at Taylors Landing, there is a well set-up camping ground even suitable for vans. You can launch small boats from this spot as well.

Around the protected waters of Spalding Cove and Surfleet Cove on the northern coastline there are many very pleasant camp sites, with the camping area at Surfleet Cove having toilets and being suitable for vans.

Donington Cottage is available to rent, contact NPWS in Port Lincoln.

LEGEND

★ 26 ★

Sealed/Unsealed Rd ....

Four Wheel Drive ....

Walks ....

Rest Area (Picnic Area) ....

Caravan Park ....

Camping Area ....

Accommodation ....

Information ....

Fuel Supplies ....

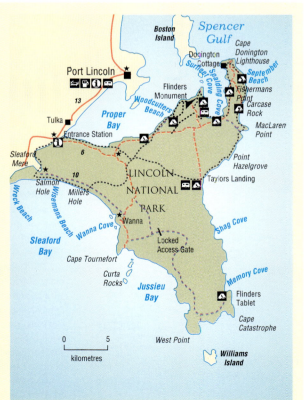

Spencer Gulf
Boston Island
Cape Donington Lighthouse
Dogington Cottage
Surfleet Cove
September Beach
Port Lincoln
Flinders Monument
Fishermans Point
Woodcutters Beach
Spalding Cove
Carcase Rock
13
MacLaren Point
Tulka
Proper Bay
Entrance Station
6
Point Hazelgrove
Sleaford Mere
Taylors Landing
10
LINCOLN NATIONAL PARK
Salmon Hole
Millers Hole
Wrek Beach
Wisemans Beach
Wanna Cove
Wanna
Shag Cove
Sleaford Bay
Cape Tournefort
Locked Access Gate
Curta Rocks
Memory Cove
Jussieu Bay
Flinders Tablet
Cape Catastrophe
0   5
kilometres
West Point
Williams Island

MT REMARKABLE NATIONAL PARK

IN BRIEF

MAP REFERENCE: PAGE 345 H 5

Location 260 km north of Adelaide via the Main North Road
Best Time Spring
Main Attractions Bushwalking, magnificent gorges, camping
Ranger Mambray Creek, phone (08) 8634 7068

The park consists of 2 sections: the area around Alligator Gorge and the area around Mt Remarkable. Alligator Gorge is a great defile slashed through the mountains of the southern Flinders Ranges. This is where the Flinders Ranges begin to take on their jagged, harsh Outback character, and is a division between the well-watered southern sections of the state and the drier interior. It is the gorge and the creek it feeds that are the main attractions of this park.

The area receives a relatively good rainfall. This, combined with the variety of country, means the region has a diversity and abundance of flora that other areas of the Flinders Ranges lack. The park is rich in wildflowers and the birds that feed on them. Red kangaroos forage on the plains and euros and the delightful but rarer yellow-footed rock wallaby use the rougher, steeper country as a home base.

EXPLORING THE PARK

Unlike most gorges in Australia, you enter Alligator Gorge from above, down a set of steep steps.

From the base of the steps you can take a 15 minute walk upstream to an area known as the Terraces where the creek is a series of large steps, or you can head downstream for 5 minutes or so to the Narrows. Most times there is a trickle of water in the gorge and it is cool and pleasant. Ferns hide in the coolest, dampest sections of the ravine, while just metres away only plants that can survive heat and an infrequent water supply are at home on the rocky slopes.

One of the better, longer walks is from Alligator Gorge to Mambray Creek, a 13 km, 5 hour walk each way.

Another walk taking in the delights of the gorge is the Ring Route which is a 7 km, 4 hour

The ruins of a homestead in Mt Remarkable National Park

walk from the Terraces further upstream to meet with the Ring Route. From there you can head south, to Blue Gum Flat where it is a short walk back up to the gorge car park.

Walks can also take you up onto the Battery Ridge where there are impressive views overlooking the western plains and the headwaters of Spencer Gulf.

Mt Remarkable is a spectacular backdrop to the delightful hamlet of Melrose and the most accessible walking route to the 960 metre peak is from the main road just north of the town centre. This is a steep, 8 km, 4 hour walk but has fabulous views of the surrounding country.

The Mambray Creek camping area in the very southwest of the park is also the start of a number of walking trails. From here you can walk to Alligator Gorge or take to the Battery Ridge via Pine Flat and Hidden Gorge. This circuit walk of 13 km takes around 5 hours and leads you down narrow valleys and gorges densely clothed in native pine.

There are a number of other walks that take in some of the more rugged, drier sections of the park and are best suited to those experienced and equipped for such conditions.

ACCESS AND CAMPING

Access to Alligator Gorge is via a good dirt road from the pretty town of Wilmington, 15 km away.

Mt Remarkable itself is accessible from Melrose, 24 km south of Wilmington.

The Mambray Creek camping area is accessible from Highway 1. Mambray Creek, with its water and shady red gums, is a popular spot where you need to book in advance with the ranger, and also obtain a permit.

It is the park's only designated site, but there are a number of bush camping sites. Some of these have water.

Campfires are banned from 1 November to 30 April and at times all fires, including gas fires, are banned.

LEGEND

Sealed/Unsealed Rd .... ★ 26 ★

Four Wheel Drive .... – – – –

Walks .... ·············

Rest Area (Picnic Area) ....

Caravan Park ....

Camping Area ....

Accommodation ....

Information ....

Fuel Supplies ....

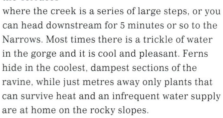

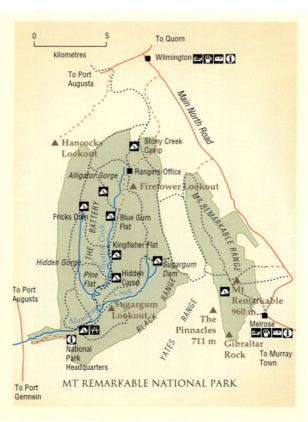

MT REMARKABLE NATIONAL PARK

The Murray River National Park is made up of 3 distinct sections of floodplain spread along the Murray River from above Renmark to just north of Loxton in the heart of the Riverlands of eastern South Australia.

The park protects not only the natural wonders and rich wildlife of the place but the signs of past inhabitants. The Aborigines of the Erawirung tribe extended over much of this rich hunting country. There are middens, canoe trees, ceremonial rings of stone, along with burial sites, stone chips and tools, throughout the park.

Charles Sturt was the first European to explore this section of the river in 1830 and by the 1840s the river was an accepted route for the overlanding of cattle between New South Wales and Adelaide. The first stations were taken up a short time later and the paddle-steamer trade began between these outlying posts of civilisation and the coast in 1853.

Most of the properties raised cattle or sheep, but some, such as the one that included Katarapko Island, ran horses for much of the time. Along the river and across the islands the giant red gums were cut first for fuel for the paddle-steamers, and then for railway sleepers for an expanding network of railways.

In 1968 Katarapko Island and 2 other islands were dedicated as conservation parks, while the national park was founded in 1991.

The Katarapko section covers 8905 hectares of river flats and is the largest, while the Bulyong Island and the Lyrup Flats sections cover 2382 and 2000 hectares respectively.

Fishing, camping, birdwatching, canoeing and cruising on a houseboat are popular pastimes. The Kai Kai Walking Trail in the central part of the Katarapko section, along the banks of Katarapko Creek, takes about 15 minutes, but bushwalks can be enjoyed throughout the park. There are boat launching facilities in a number of places, except in the Lyrup Flats section.

CANOEING AND HOUSEBOATING

Both the Katarapko and Bulyong Island sections are popular with canoeists, with a map-cum-

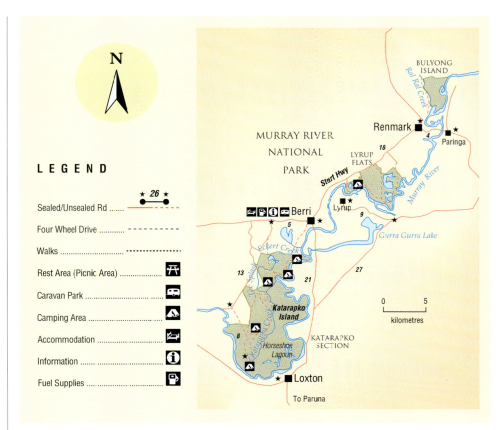

LEGEND

Sealed/Unsealed Rd	★— 26 —★
Four Wheel Drive	- - - - - - - -
Walks	··············
Rest Area (Picnic Area)	⛱
Caravan Park	🚐
Camping Area	⛺
Accommodation	🛏
Information	ℹ
Fuel Supplies	⛽

canoe guide being available for each area. The canoeing is very pleasant and trips of up to 4 days can be done in the Bulyong Island area, incorporating Ral Ral Creek and the Murray, while 1 or 2 day trips can be planned in the Katarapko section of the park.

A stately red gum

All 3 sections of the park offer pleasant places on the Murray for houseboats to pull up and enjoy the solitude. There are guides available for the whole length of the river.

ACCESS AND CAMPING

Access to the Katarapko section is off the Sturt Highway, west of the township of Berri, 180 km from Adelaide. The main access point is off the Katarapko Crescent–Winkie Road where dirt roads lead to numerous camping sites along Katarapko Creek and the Murray River.

Lyrup Flats is located upstream from Berri with the Sturt Highway giving good access to an all-weather dirt road that leads to a number of large camping areas and tracks that head to smaller individual camps along the river.

Bulyong Island, just upstream from Renmark, is a popular spot and while it doesn't have any designated camping areas, camping is possible at many points along the river. The 150 Link Reserve, which basically borders the Murray River, allows camping within 30 metres of the water's edge, but often access is across private land, so permission is required.

Canoeists or houseboats can normally pull up and use the banks anywhere, but in the Katarapko section they are required to use the designated camping spots, marked on the bank.

Camping permits, available from the ranger, are required when camping in the park.

NGARKAT GROUP OF CONSERVATION PARKS

IN BRIEF

MAP REFERENCE: PAGE 342 B 9

Location 250 km southeast of Adelaide, via Pinnaroo or Bordertown
Best Time Spring
Main Attractions Wildflowers, wildlife, desert environment, 4WD
Ranger Tintinara, phone (08) 8757 2261

Four adjoining parks, Scorpion Springs Conservation Park, Mt Rescue Conservation Park, Mt Shaugh Conservation Park and Ngarkat Conservation Park, (the largest), take in 262 700 hectares and a veritable sea of undulating mallee scrub and heath-covered sand plains. Adjoining these parks, across the border in Victoria, is the Big Desert Wilderness and Red Bluff Nature Reserve.

ACCESS

Access to the heart of the parks is easiest off the main dirt road that runs through the park from Pinnaroo in the north to Bordertown in the south, both towns being on major highways.

Other access points, from Tintinara and Keith in the southwest, and from near Lameroo in the north, are also possible, but these routes are only passable to a conventional vehicle as far as the boundary of the park, where the route becomes a 4WD track.

A number of 4WD tracks, especially the one along the border fence, give good access to the more remote sections of the park. Much of the Border Fence track is one way only—from north to south!

The speed limit along any tracks in the park is 40 kph and the green markers guide you to various points of interest in the parks. Make sure you observe the 'Tracks Closed for Vermin Control' signs.

CAMPING

Pleasant caming spots within the park include Box Flat, Bucks Camp, Comet Bore, Pertendi Hut, Pine Hut Soak, Rabbit Island Soak and Scorpion Springs.

Please remember that many of these localities are the only source of water around for any thirsty wildlife, so don't camp too close to the water points.

There are no facilities, so come prepared and take all rubbish out with you.

Much of this region sees very few travellers and is remote, so carry ample water.

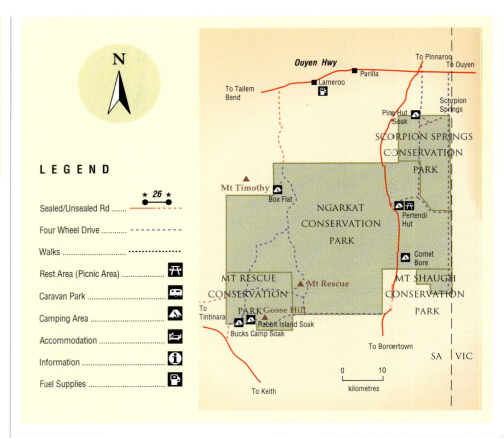

LEGEND

★ 26 ★	
Sealed/Unsealed Rd	
Four Wheel Drive	
Walks	
Rest Area (Picnic Area)	🛆
Caravan Park	
Camping Area	
Accommodation	
Information	ℹ
Fuel Supplies	

Ngarkat Group of Conservation Parks from Red Bluff Nature Reserve in Victoria

For most people travelling the vast flat plains of the Nullarbor there is little to attract the eye. The ribbon of tar that is the Eyre Highway stretches away to the horizon while all around dull coloured saltbush and bluebush spread across a light brown land.

Take any track off to the south, though, and a short distance later you come to where the plain—an elevated plain—plunges directly over 60 metre-high cliffs into the boiling waters of the Southern Ocean. The cliffs stretch for kilometres in each direction along the Great Australian Bight, a section of spectacularly dangerous coast that is the longest in the world without a natural harbour.

WILDLIFE

This coast provides travellers with the opportunity to view one of nature's greatest animals, the southern right whale. They congregate along this wild coast in winter and spring to calve and nurse their young. They are best seen at the Head of Bight, which is just to the east of the park on Yalata Aboriginal Land. Permits are required to visit this area and trips can be arranged from the Nullarbor Roadhouse (hotel/motel), phone (08) 8625 3447, located on the eastern boundary of the park. Helicopter flights are also available from the roadhouse.

A number of Australian sea lion colonies exist along this coast as well and these and the whale breeding area are soon to be protected in a marine national park. Sanctuary zones have been established already to protect the whales at the Head of Bight and the sea lion colonies.

Wildlife is scattered in this arid country where the only reliable water is hundreds of metres underground. While the area once supported a wide variety of small native mammals—at least 32 different species—rabbits, foxes, cats and the common house mouse have seen this variety almost vanish. The southern hairy-nosed wombat has its last great stronghold in this park and the adjoining reserve and they are often seen close to the highway. Western grey and red kangaroos are also common, especially after local rain and can be a problem for anyone travelling at night.

HIDDEN DEPTHS

The terrestrial national park stretches east along the coast to the Western Australian border and approximately 20 km inland. The regional reserve borders the national park and takes in a much larger area to the north and east of the park, with its northern boundary being the Trans Australian Railway Line. In all, both park and reserve cover 2 873 000 hectares of remote country.

These parks protect only part of the Nullarbor Plain which makes up the world's largest semi-arid karst (limestone) landscape, which is characterised by caves and an underground drainage system. These caves are dotted across the region and in recent years a number of these water-filled caves, which can extend for many kilometres underground, have been explored by well-equipped and experienced local and foreign diving teams. Others, such as Koonalda Cave in the northern central section of the park, have long been recognised as some of Australia's most significant and different Aboriginal art sites. The art found deep underground and in total darkness consists entirely of finger markings in the soft limestone.

The underground water found in most of the caves in the region was used by the early pioneer graziers to water their stock and this still continues today outside the park.

ACCESS AND CAMPING

The Eyre Highway gives good access to the park while a number of tracks lead south to the coast and the sheer cliffs.

North of the highway a few 4WD tracks head across the flatness to deserted railway sidings along the railway line.

Camping is possible at any number of places and you are guaranteed not to be disturbed as this is a region that sees few travellers.

A view of the Nullarbor National Park

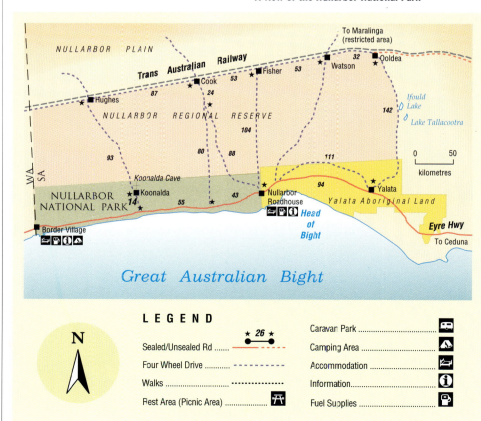

LEGEND

Sealed/Unsealed Rd	Caravan Park
Four Wheel Drive	Camping Area
Walks	Accommodation
Rest Area (Picnic Area)	Information
	Fuel Supplies

WITJIRA NATIONAL PARK, SIMPSON DESERT REGIONAL RESERVE & PARK

IN BRIEF

MAP REFERENCE: PAGE 346 F 2

Location 1360 km north of Adelaide, on the border with Qld and NT
Best Time May to September
Main Attractions Desert landscape, remote camping, warm springs, 4WD
Ranger Hawker, phone (08) 8648 4244

Mt Dare Homestead: accommodation, camping, fuel, phone (08) 8670 7835

Some say there is no finer desert oasis in Australia than the warm waters of Dalhousie Springs located in the far north of South Australia, in the very west of Witjira National Park. Here the contrast between what is some of Australia's most arid desert country and the lush vegetation and life that surround the natural warm baths of Dalhousie Springs is very marked—these springs are unexpected in an arid land.

Located on the western edge of the Simpson Desert, the group of 60 or so springs that make up the Dalhousie group of mound springs comprises the most significant natural outflowings of the vast artesian basin that underlies much of Outback Australia. Originating in the Great Dividing Range, the water flows deep underground, taking possibly millions of years to reach the natural outlets on the southwestern edge of the Great Artesian Basin. Mound springs are so named because the springs that flow from them often form a low hill of natural mineral deposit. (Other well-known natural mound springs include those further south along the Oodnadatta Track, the very reason why the track was put there in the first place.)

HISTORY

A number of Aboriginal tribes included different areas of the Simpson Desert in their tribal lands, but due to the harsh nature of the desert most of their activity was around the margins and along the ephemeral watercourses. Only in good seasons was the heart of the desert used in their wanderings, and today sites and artefacts still remain.

Dalhousie Springs and the permanent water points on the western edge of the desert were of mythological significance as well as an important water source to the Lower Southern Aranda people and the Wangkangurru people.

The desert was first seen by a European when Charles Sturt, in 1845, was pushed back by the large dunes on the eastern edge of the desert around Eyre Creek.

Parrot pea, which flourishes in a desert environment

While Stuart passed close to the area in the early 1860s on his successful expedition to cross Australia, the life-giving waters of the Dalhousie Springs were not discovered by Europeans until

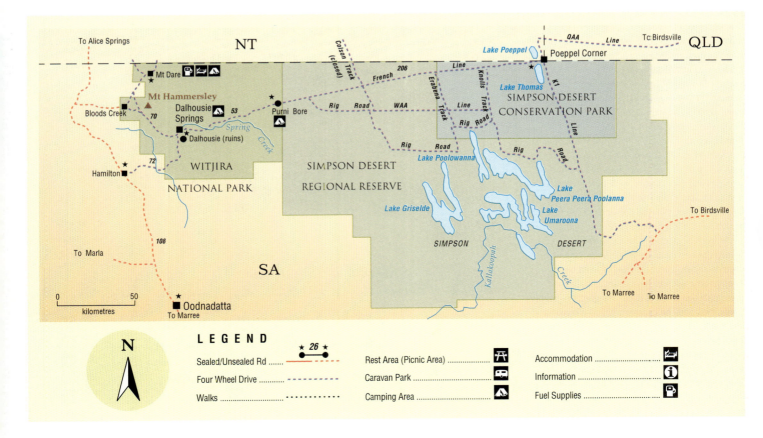

LEGEND

Sealed/Unsealed Rd	★ 26 ★
Four Wheel Drive	
Walks	
Rest Area (Picnic Area)	
Caravan Park	
Camping Area	
Accommodation	
Information	
Fuel Supplies	

the early 1870s and soon after a pastoral lease was taken up around the springs by Ned Bagot. By 1885 a homestead and outbuildings had been built at the southern extremity of the springs.

In 1886 David Lindsay crossed the desert from Dalhousie to a point on the Queensland border, 50 or so kilometres north of the corner post at Poeppel Corner.

In 1936 Ted Colson became the first white man to cross the complete desert from Bloods Creek to Birdsville and return. Cecil Madigan crossed the northern section of the Simpson in 1939 and it was he who nominated the name, Simpson Desert, after his patron Alfred Simpson, President of the SA branch of the Royal Geographic Society.

Interest in the desert was revived in the 1950s when oil exploration began and this continued through to the 1970s. All the tracks across the desert from Dalhousie east are the result of that exploration work, with the French Line being the first access route across the desert in 1963. Part of that work, completed by Dr Reg Sprigg, the head surveyor, included being the first to drive a vehicle across the desert a year before the French Line was put in.

In 1967 the Simpson Desert Conservation Park of 6927 sq km was proclaimed, as was the Simpson Desert National Park of 5552 sq km on the Queensland side of the border. In 1988 the Simpson Desert Regional Reserve of 29 642 sq km was declared linking all 3 parks while the Witjira National Park of 7770 sq km, on the far western edge of the desert, was set up around the same time. Witjira National Park is now managed jointly by the SA Department of Environment and Natural Resources and the Irrwanyare Aboriginal Corporation.

Today, for more than 350 km in an east–west direction, there is a continuous expanse of reserved land, a total of nearly 5 million hectares—the biggest single reserved area within Australia. For details on the Queensland Simpson Desert National Park see page 188.

PLACES TO EXPERIENCE

It is the desert ambience, the peace and the solitude, that are the great memories of a trip to the Simpson Desert parks, but there is more.

The springs around Dalhousie, once you can tear yourself away from the warm water, are worth exploring and the variety of birds to be found here make it memorable. Likewise, Purnie Bore, deeper into the desert, is a real gem and the wetlands created by this bore attracts much wildlife.

The ruins of the old Dalhousie homestead, passed on the way north from Oodnadatta, are always worth exploring. Mound springs dot the area, their presence easily noticeable by the date palms that crowd each and every one. A

relic from the days of the Afghan camel trains, these are another reminder of the history and settlement of this vast desert region.

ACCESS

There are considerable numbers of dirt roads to travel on to get to these parks, no matter what direction you come from.

The area is really the realm of a 4WD, but in good times the tracks from Oodnadatta in the south are passable to a conventional vehicle when driven with care.

The route from Oodnadatta via Hamilton Station homestead and the Dalhousie Ruins is the most popular route covering just 180 km.

Other routes from Marla and Kulgera, on the main Stuart Highway, are also a possibility.

ROUTES ACROSS THE DESERT

From Dalhousie the route across the desert heads east striking the first of the sand ridges just over 50 km east. Purnie Bore is located close to the track just over one ridge and this man-made oasis is a delight.

Thirty-odd kilometres later you reach a track junction and from here you can continue straight ahead along the original French Line to Poeppel Corner, 170 km east, or you can turn south to take your chances with the longer WAA Line or the much longer Rig Road.

The French Line is the roughest track, the WAA Line a good alternative, while the Rig Road

is the easiest. However, all are definitely 4WD routes. From Poeppel Corner you can head through Queensland and the Simpson Desert National Park to Birdsville.

All these routes may be closed after rain. Check with the rangers before setting off.

CAMPING

The old homestead of Mt Dare, in the very north of the park, 70 km from Dalhousie Springs, offers homestead accommodation, camping, meals, fuel, tyres and minor repairs as well as a breakdown service and a cold beer.

The only other designated camping grounds are at Dalhousie Springs and Purni Bore where you can find toilets and water.

Dalhousie is the most popular camp in the whole region, while the camping area at Purni Bore is rather small.

Elsewhere you can camp close to the track on any one of the designated routes across the desert.

DESERT PARKS PASS

To travel, camp or to enter this spread of reserved land in northern South Australia you require a Desert Parks Pass. This includes a good range of maps and booklets and the pass is valid for a year. These passes are available from good map shops Australia-wide, national parks offices in northern South Australia or local general stores.

Sand dunes in the Simpson Desert

OTHER PARKS OF INTEREST

BELAIR NATIONAL PARK

In 1891, Belair National Park became the first national park to be dedicated in SA. The park not only protects one of the few remaining areas of native bushland in the Adelaide Hills, it also includes a range of facilities where visitors can enjoy their choice of activities in scenic surrounds. The Old Government House, built in 1860, is now a museum and open to the public.

Close to the western entrance to the park there is a range of ovals, tennis courts and a golf course. A number of sealed roads head off through the park giving good access to much of it and the facilities dotted along the roads. BBQ facilities abound and walks radiate to all corners of the park.

Playford Lake, close to the developed area, supports good numbers of waterbirds and a 1 km walking trail around the lake is a pleasant way to view the birdlife. Railway Dam on Minno Creek can also be reached by a walking trail that follows the creek and continues upstream, close to the Long Gully picnic area, just one of a few along the road and creek.

The park, which can be enjoyed at any time of the year, is open to day visitors only and an entrance fee is charged.

For further information, contact the ranger, ph: (08) 8278 5477.

BOOL LAGOON GAME RESERVE
2690 HECTARES

Consisting of a series of shallow, saucer-shaped lakes, Bool Lagoon is the largest and one of the most important waterbird breeding wetlands in southeastern Australia. A high natural embankment traps the water, forming the swamp, but the lagoon is also used as a way of controlling floods along Mosquito Creek. This has increased the importance of the reserve as a refuge for birds when much of inland Australia is in the grip of drought.

Large concentrations of brolgas can be seen around the lagoon, the only place in SA where such groups congregate, while the dense tea-tree stands around the main lagoon are an important rookery for up to 10 000 ibis. Of the 75 species of waterbirds recorded in the reserve, 47 species breed here.

The reserve, 370 km southeast of Adelaide, is easily accessible from Naracoorte, travelling on sealed roads.

Camping is possible at the small designated area close to the main lagoon. The best time to visit is during the spring and summer.

For further information, contact the ranger at Naracoorte, ph: (08) 8762 2340, or Mt Gambier, ph: (08) 8735 1177.

CAPE GANTHEAUME CONSERVATION PARK
21 316 HECTARES

This large park is located on the southern coast of Kangaroo Island 190 km south of Adelaide and takes in a wide sweep of wilderness area and spectacular remote coastline. On the park's western boundary is the Seal Bay Conservation Park and the access road. On the eastern edge of the park, around D'Estrees Bay to just north of Cape Linois, is another road, one of the few signs of man in this isolated region. The park headquarters are located at the very northern edge of the park close to Murray's Lagoon.

Murray's Lagoon is the largest lagoon on Kangaroo Island and is an important place for a host of waterbirds, including swans and ducks. The bush provides a habitat for kangaroos, possums, bandicoots and many other smaller animals while along the coast seals and penguins make their home. White-bellied sea-eagles and ospreys are also common on this wild, remote coast.

Bush camping is possible at Murray's Lagoon (depending on the water level), not far from the ranger headquarters, as well as on the east coast south of D'Estrees Bay.

A walking trail from the ranger base around the eastern edge of Murray's Lagoon exists, but any other walks are really for the more experienced and better equipped walker. The walk south to Cape Gantheaume from the furthermost point of road access is an overnight walk at least. The best time to visit the park is during spring and summer.

For further information, contact the ranger at Murray's Lagoon, ph: (08) 8553 8233, or Kingscote, ph: (08) 8553 2844.

CHOWILLA GAME RESERVE
18 400 HECTARES
CHOWILLA REGIONAL RESERVE
75 600 HECTARES

The Chowilla Game Reserve covers floodplain and wetlands along the northern side of the Murray River, directly to the west of the NSW/SA border. The larger Chowilla Regional Reserve takes in surrounding mallee woodland, black oak and bluebush scrubland that stretches to the Danggali Conservation Park further north. Both reserves, 290 km east of Adelaide, make up part of the Bookmark Biosphere Reserve.

Close to the river waterbirds gather in large numbers while in the drier country to the north malleefowl can sometimes be seen.

Access is off the main Renmark–Wentworth road. There is an information centre at the Chowilla Woolshed in the reserve's southwest.

There is a camping area with toilets just to the north of the woolshed and a number of small camp sites, with no facilities, are dotted along the Chowilla and Monoman Creeks. Many of these have easy access to the water. Another camping area with toilets and a boat ramp is located on the southern side of the Murray at the Border Cliffs general store. Only designated camp sites are to be used and a permit is required.

There's good fishing along the river for a wide variety of fish and there is some excellent canoeing in the many side creeks. The birdwatching is also very good and the Old Coach Road gives reasonable access to the floodplain and all it has to offer. Being a game reserve, duck hunting is allowed at certain times of the year. Contact the ranger for details.

The best time to visit is during the spring and summer.

For further information, contact the ranger at Berri, ph: (08) 8595 2111.

Bool Lagoon Game Reserve

DANGGALI CONSERVATION PARK

This large park, taking in the once struggling pastoral properties of Morgan Vale, Canopus, Postmark and Hypurna, is located about 60 km north of the River Murray on the western side of the NSW/SA border, some 360 km east of Adelaide. This vast area of mallee scrubland was the first International Biosphere Reserve classified in Australia under a UNESCO program. This area was deemed important because the mallee lands to the south overlap with the arid land systems to the north.

A couple of drives starting from the ranger base at the old Canopus homestead, one of which is suitable for the family car when driven with care, gives the visitor a fine opportunity to discover all that Danggali has to offer. A 10 km, 3 hour long, walking trail passes through mallee scrub to Target Mark Dam for those with a bit more energy to burn.

Camping permits, available from the ranger, are required to stay in the park and there are many places to put up a tent, with some secluded spots in mallee or black oak woodland near Canopus. You need to bring your own water. Winter and spring are the best times to visit Danggali Conservation Park.

For further information, contact the ranger at Canopus, ph: (08) 8585 8010; or Berri, ph: (08) 8595 2111.

DEEP CREEK CONSERVATION PARK
4500 HECTARES

The Deep Creek Conservation Park stretches along the southern coast of the Fleurieu Peninsula for over 10 km, with only a couple of 4WD tracks, situated at either extremity of the park, reaching the coast. In most places steep cliffs drop into the sea, their bases pounded by the swells of the Southern Ocean. From the lofty ridges back from the coast, each ridge is separated from the other by a steep-sided valley and great views can be had of the coast and across to Kangaroo Island.

The park, about 120 km south of Adelaide, conserves a rich variety of plants varying from the stunted coastal vegetation to the rich ferns and orchids that are found in the moist gullies just a short distance back from the windswept coast.

The Heysen Walking Trail cuts through the park and this can be joined at a number of spots, making a good choice of half-day walks. Deep Creek Cove can be reached by trails from either Trig or Tapanappa camping grounds, the latter being just a little longer walk but through much steeper country. In winter or early spring the 5 km, 3 hour return walk to Deep Creek Waterfall or to the Aaron Creek Cascades are

most certainly worth the effort.

Along the coast there is some excellent fishing for salmon, snapper and sweep, with the Blowhole Beach, accessed by a 4WD track in the very west of the park, being the most popular place to try your luck.

The park offers a number of good camping spots and the vehicle-based camper can choose from sites at Stringybark, Tapanappa, Trig or Cobbler Hill camping grounds, while Eagle Waterhole camp ground is set aside purely for bushwalkers. Camping is only permitted in the designated areas and a permit is required. Spring and summer are the best times to visit Deep Creek.

For further information, contact the ranger, ph: (08) 8598 0263.

DUTCHMAN'S STERN CONSERVATION PARK
3500 HECTARES

The Dutchman's Stern Conservation Park lies to the north of Quorn in the central Flinders Ranges, 370 km north of Adelaide, and protects an area of surprisingly steep and rugged country.

Taking its name from a distinctive bluff that overlooks much of the surrounding area, there are a number of walking trails leaving from the car park located just inside the park and near

the old homestead, which is a legacy of the area's pastoral past.

The vegetation is typical of the southern Flinders, but also supports such magnificent trees as the blue gum and the sugar gum which don't normally grow this far north. The rare and restricted Quorn wattle is also found here.

Western grey kangaroos and euros are common, as are emus and a host of other smaller birds.

The walking trail to the top of Dutchman's Stern takes about 3 hours but the rewards are well worth the effort. Other walking tracks lead deeper into the park, taking up to a full day to complete the round trip. The lookouts situated on the main spine of the ridge not only take in great views to the east but also to the west, and the waters of Spencer Gulf.

Camping is not allowed in the park but a pleasant picnic area is located at the car park. Winter and spring are the preferred seasons for visiting the park.

For further information, contact the ranger at Port Augusta, ph: (08) 8648 5310.

HINCKS CONSERVATION PARK
66 285 HECTARES

Protecting an area of low, mallee-covered dunes, the Hincks Conservation Park is located in the centre of Eyre Peninsula, 90 km north of

The bluff that gives Dutchman's Stern Conservation Park its name

OTHER PARKS OF INTEREST

Port Lincoln and 620 km west of Adelaide.

Open, grassy country, dotted with large white mallee and mallee box, is a feature of the southwestern corner of the park which contrasts strongly with the dunes. In the southeast out-crops of sandstone, known as the Blue Range and Verran Hill, occur, with small, ephemeral swamps around the base of the hill country where creeks flood-out from the peaks.

Over 60 species of birds have been identified in this park while a number of mammals, the most obvious being western grey kangaroos and euros, call it home. Reptiles are very common and include geckos, dragon lizards and snakes.

Nicholls Track is the only vehicle track within the park and this leads into the north-west corner of the park. Normal cars have access during the drier months.

Bush camping and remote bushwalking are possible in this park but adequate food and water must be carried.

The best time to visit is during the spring and summer.

For further information, contact the ranger at Port Lincoln, ph: (08) 8688 3177.

LITTLE DIP CONSERVATION PARK

This small and popular park lies just on the out-skirts of Robe in the southeast of South Australia, 290 km east of Adelaide, and takes in 11 km of windswept coast. It also extends up to 3 km inland in places, protecting a number of small lakes, including Lake Robe, which is the largest in the park.

Aborigines have lived in this region for over 10 000 years and there are a number of middens found along the coast.

Small bays, with white sandy beaches separated by low rugged headlands, are a feature of this park and are a pleasant spot to relax or fish. As the coast is subject to big swells the chances for a swim can be limited.

Conventional vehicle access is possible to Long Gully and to Little Dip beach, but a designated 4WD track gives access to the whole length of coastline. Be warned, though, that you need to take care as the sand is soft.

Camping is permitted at a number of sites including the Gums, Old Man Lake, Long Gully and Freshwater Lake. Long Gully is the only one close to the coast.

The best time to visit the park is from late spring to early autumn.

For further information, contact the ranger at Robe, ph: (08) 8768 2543, or Mt Gambier, ph: (08) 8735 1177.

Grass-trees, or blackboys, growing in Para Wirra Recreation Park (see page 340)

Little Dip Conservation Park (see page 338)

NARACOORTE CAVES CONSERVATION PARK

This small park, 370 km southeast of Adelaide, is now on the World Heritage List because of the discovery of rich fossil beds in Victoria Cave. First found in 1969, this bed of fossils continues to excite as the remains of marsupials and other animals, some of which are extinct, are unearthed. Provision has been made for visitors to view the 'dig'.

Within the park a number of other caves are open to tourists, including Blanche Cave, Wet Cave and Alexandra Cave. There are tours that are conducted daily.

Between November and February thousands of common bentwing bats take up residence in some of the caves which are ideal for breeding and raising young. At dusk the bats leave the caves in search of food, making a spectacular sight which can be viewed by arrangement with the ranger.

The camping ground in the park is well set up with powered sites, shower and toilet facilities. A permit is required before you can camp. The best time to visit is during the spring and summer.

For further information, contact the ranger at Naracoorte, ph: (08) 8762 2340, or Mt Gambier, ph: (08) 8735 1177.

NEWLAND HEAD CONSERVATION PARK
945 HECTARES

The 2 beaches protected by this park offer some of the best fishing in South Australia. Waitpinga Beach and Parsons Beach are 2 of the great salmon fishing spots on the south coast and, situated 105 km from Adelaide, there are nearly always a few fishing people dotted along the coast on any given weekend.

The park stretches a short distance inland but for most visitors the coast with its fishing or surfing are the main attractions. There are plenty of birds in the nearby scrub and there are some pleasant walks along the coast.

Access is off the main Victor Harbour–Cape Jervis road onto the all-weather Waitpinga Beach Road.

Camping is only allowed at the small camp ground, where toilets and water are provided. The best time to visit is in spring and summer.

For further information, contact the ranger, ph: (08) 8552 3677.

PARA WIRRA RECREATION PARK
1409 HECTARES

Covering rolling hills and steep-sided valleys, this park is located just 40 km northeast of Adelaide, making it popular with day visitors wanting to get away from the city at any time of the year.

The main entrance off Humbug Scrub Road leads into the heart of the park, passing a range of sporting facilities such as tennis courts and ovals along the way. Gas BBQs are also dotted around the main roads through the park, while walking trails lead to a number of scenic spots or lookouts. Most of the walking trails range between 2 and 10 km giving a good variety of terrain and distance to enjoy.

Western grey kangaroos are common in the park as are emus. Other birds, especially parrots, abound while smaller bushbirds, such as thornbills, tree-creepers, wrens and honey-eaters can easily be seen.

For further information, contact the ranger in Adelaide, ph: (08) 8281 4022.

PICCANINNIE PONDS CONSERVATION PARK

This small reserve takes up a section of coast in the very far southeast of South Australia about 430 km southeast of Adelaide, just over the border from Victoria. Behind the beach a large reed swamp is surrounded by a dense band of tea-tree and sedge. And, while this combination of water and weed offers birds and a number of frogs a prime habitat, it is in the heart of the swamp that the real jewel of this park lies.

Piccaninnie Ponds is one of the most famous cave dives in the world with the crystal clear water of the ponds being a huge attraction. The Chasm, with its white walls and curtains of algae, is superb, while the Cathedral at the far end is a large cavern accessible to SCUBA divers. You will need a Cave Diving Certificate to dive in these ponds, but a Snorkel Permit can be issued to anyone who wants to sample the underwater delights of this unique place. You are allowed an hour to enjoy the place and bookings must be made 8 days in advance.

The best time to visit Piccaninnie Ponds is in spring and summer.

For further information, contact the ranger at Mt Gambier, ph: (08) 8735 1177.

POINT LABATT CONSERVATION PARK AND AQUATIC RESERVE
30 HECTARES

This small park is located 50 km south of Streaky Bay and 720 km west of Adelaide. It protects the only mainland colony of Australian sea lions in Australia. All the other colonies are on offshore islands.

The aquatic reserve is a prohibited area but there is an excellent viewing point located on top of the cliffs where you can watch the animals on the beach below. It's a good idea to take binoculars and a telephoto lens for your camera.

Access is via good dirt roads from Streaky Bay. As the coastline is spectacular, it is well worth driving slowly. Camping is not permitted in the park.

The best time to visit the area is during the spring and summer.

For further information, contact the ranger, ph: (08) 8625 3144.

SEAL BAY CONSERVATION PARK AND SEAL BAY AQUATIC RESERVE

Seal Bay on Kangaroo Island, 190 km south of Adelaide, must be one of the best places in the world to see and experience sea lions and fur seals at really close quarters. The wide white beach of Seal Bay plays host to dozens of these magnificent animals which are surprisingly tolerant of humans.

Guided tours of the beach with a ranger are

a highlight of any trip to Kangaroo Island. Often, if you are lucky, a young seal will approach you as you sit on the beach—a great experience!

Access to other beaches and bays along the coast from Seal Bay is totally prohibited and there is no swimming, fishing or boating allowed in the adjoining aquatic reserve.

Picnic shelters, gas BBQs and toilets are provided at the Bales Bay visitor area at the eastern end of Seal Bay. Camping is not allowed.

The best time to visit Seal Bay is in the spring and summer.

For further information, contact the ranger at Kingscote, ph: (08) 8553 2844.

TELOWIE GORGE CONSERVATION PARK

This small park protects a significant area of rugged range country in the Southern Flinders Ranges, 30 km northeast of Port Pirie and 255 km north of Adelaide. The diverse habitat of the park ranges from steep ridges to deep, sheer-sided gorges and floodout plains at the base of the range.

The park is home to a small colony of the endangered yellow-footed rock wallaby.

The Wirrabara Forest Reserve provides the eastern boundary of the park along the main spine of the Flinders Ranges and there are a number of walking trails that lead across the range from one reserve to the other. The Heysen Walking Trail also follows the spine of the range before dropping off the peaks down onto the flatter country on the eastern side of the ranges.

The Nukunu Walking Trail is an easy, 30 minute, 1 km return walk into the gorge from the car park, while experienced walkers can head deeper into the gorge. Camping is not allowed in the gorge but walkers can bushcamp just about anywhere in the park, except between 1 November and 30 April which is the fire danger season.

Car-based campers have a small camping area on the northern side of Telowie Creek, just off the access road to the gorge. There are no facilities here except for fireplaces. A camping permit is required. The best time to visit the gorge is in the winter or spring.

For further information, contact the ranger at Mt Remarkable National Park, ph: (08) 8634 7068 or Port Augusta, ph: (08) 8648 5310.

UNNAMED CONSERVATION PARK

2 132 600 HECTARES

This large park covers desert scrub country of the Great Victoria Desert. It is situated north of the Trans Australian Railway with the Western Australia/South Australia border as its western boundary. About 1350 km northwest of Adelaide,

the park is surrounded by Aboriginal land.

Only 2 sandy 4WD tracks cut through the park: the Anne Beadell Highway which runs east–west and which is the main access to the area, and the north–south track north from the railway siding at Cook to Vokes Hill Junction, located in the east of the park. Permits are required to travel both these routes and only well-equipped and experienced four wheel drivers should attempt them.

The park is one of South Australia's most pristine and remote wilderness areas and is home to the Alexandra's parrot and a number of rare mammals. The vegetation is mainly mallee scrub land and spinifex sandplains while stands of marble gums, desert poplars and desert kurrajong provide a delightful change. After rain the desert blooms with a host of brightly coloured ephemerals such as daisies, para-keelya, hakeas and thryptomenes.

Near the border the long chain of vivid white salt pans known as the Serpentine Lakes can be found. These are crossed by the Anne Beadell Highway which gives good access to these remote and interesting landforms.

The best time to visit is winter or spring.

For further information, contact the ranger at Ceduna, ph: (08) 8625 3144.

WALDERGRAVE ISLAND CONSERVATION PARK

This island, just offshore from Cape Finnis, a short distance north of Elliston on the west coast of Eyre Peninsula, helps protect the southern end of Anxious Bay. 640 km west of Adelaide, Waldergrave Island is one of many island conservation parks on the west coast and one of the easiest to get to with safe water for boating and a nearby concrete boat ramp. It is also one of the easiest islands to land on with a well-protected beach near McLaren Point where

sheep and stores were once unloaded during the pastoral days on the island.

There is some excellent fishing around the island and in the protected waters of the bay, with everything from big Australian salmon and blue groper to beautiful King George whiting.

The best time to visit the island is during spring and summer. There are no facilities for camping.

For further information, contact the ranger at Port Lincoln, ph: (08) 8688 3177.

WIRRABARA FOREST RESERVE
7000 HECTARES

Seventy-five per cent of Wirrabara Forest Reserve is in its natural state, the rest being mainly planted with radiata pine. Located on the eastern slopes of the southern Flinders Ranges, 245 km north of Adelaide, the native forest mainly consists of a mixture of red gum, blue gum, long-leaved box, grey box, sugar gum, northern cypress pine and Flinders Ranges wattle. In spring this forest is rich with flowers.

The Heysen Walking Trail cuts through the heart of the reserve, taking in the high point of the Bluff at the very southwestern corner of the reserve and on top of the main ridge of the Flinders Ranges. A number of other walks exist within the park giving access to most of the range country as well as the flatter land along the edge of the reserve.

A couple of short forest drives exist within the reserve, while camping is restricted to the Ippinitchie Camping Area, located just off the main access road towards the reserve's centre.

The best time to visit the reserve is during winter or spring. Bush camping is possible in any suitable place beside the tracks—there are no facilities.

For further information, contact the ranger at Wirrabara, ph: (08) 8668 4163.

Seal Bay Conservation Park

kilometres

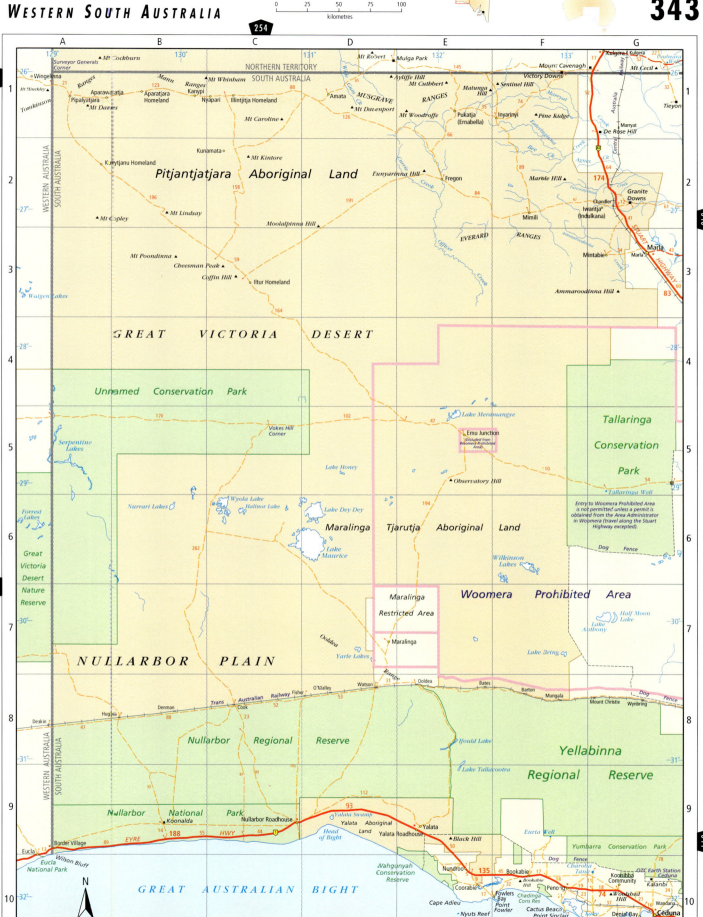

WESTERN SOUTH AUSTRALIA

kilometres

0   25   50   75   100

254

302

303

NORTHERN TERRITORY
SOUTH AUSTRALIA

129°   130°   131°   132°   133°

Surveyor Generals Corner
Wingelinna
Mt Yinckley
Mt Cockburn
Ranges
Tomkinson
Aparawatja
Pipalyatjara
Mt Davies
Mann
Aparatjara Homeland
Kanypi
Nyapari
Illintjitja Homeland
Ranges
Mt Whinbam
Mt Robert
Mulga Park
Amata
MUSGRAVE
Ayliffe Hill
Mt Cuthbert
Matunga Hill
Victory Downs
Sentinel Hill
Mount Cavenagh
Kulgera
Mt Cecil
Ombeara Well
Railway

Mt Davenport
Mt Woodroffe
RANGES
Pukatja (Ernabella)
Inyarinyi
Pine Ridge
De Rose Hill
Tieyon

Pitjantjatjara Aboriginal Land
Kurytjanu Homeland
Kunamata
Mt Kintore
Eunyarinna Hill
Fregon
Currie Creek
Marble Hill
174
Marryat
Chandler
Iwantja (Indulkana)
Granite Downs
Marla
Mintabie
Marla
STUART HIGHWAY
83

Mt Copley
Mt Lindsay
Moolalpinna Hill
EVERARD RANGES
Mimili
Ammaroodinna Hill

Mt Poondinna
Cheesman Peak
Coffin Hill
Iltur Homeland
Officer Creek

Waigen Lakes

GREAT   VICTORIA   DESERT

Unnamed Conservation Park
Serpentine Lakes
Vokes Hill Corner
Lake Meramangye
Emu Junction (Excluded from Woomera Prohibited Area)
Observatory Hill
Tallaringa Conservation Park
Tallaringa Well

Forrest Lakes
Nurrari Lakes
Wyola Lake
Halinor Lake
Lake Dey Dey
Lake Honey

Great Victoria Desert Nature Reserve
Lake Maurice
Maralinga   Tjarutja   Aboriginal   Land
Wilkinson Lakes
Woomera   Prohibited   Area
Half Moon Lake
Lake Anthony
Dog Fence

Entry to Woomera Prohibited Area is not permitted unless a permit is obtained from the Area Administrator in Woomera (travel along the Stuart Highway excepted).

Maralinga Restricted Area
Maralinga
Ooldea
Yarle Lakes
Lake Bring

NULLARBOR   PLAIN
Range
Ooldea
Bates
Barton
Mungala
Mount Christie
Wynbring
Dog Fence

Deakin
Hughes
Denman
Trans   Australian   Railway   Fisher
O'Malley
Watson
Cook

Nullarbor Regional Reserve
Ifould Lake
Yellabinna

Lake Tallacootra

Regional   Reserve

Nullarbor   National   Park
Koonalda
Nullarbor Roadhouse
Yalata Swamp
Yalata Aboriginal Land
Yalata
Yalata Roadhouse
Black Hill
Yumbarra Conservation Park
OTC Earth Station
Koonibba Community
Kalanbi

Border Village
Eucla
EYRE   HWY
188
Head of Bight
Nundroo
135
Bookabie
Charola Tank
Penong
74
Woolshed Hill
Ceduna
Thevenard

Eucla National Park
Wilson Bluff
Nahgunyah Conservation Reserve
Coorabie
Bookabie Hill
Nundroo
Dog Fence
Wandana

N

GREAT   AUSTRALIAN   BIGHT
Cape Adieu
Nuyts Reef
Nuyts Reef Conservation Park
Point Fowler
Fowlers Bay
Point Fowler
Chadinga Cons Res
Cactus Beach
Point Sinclair
Point Bell
Rocky Point
Point Peter
Goat Is
Denial Bay
Laura Bay
Cape D'Estrees
Lake MacDonnell

346

344

WESTERN AUSTRALIA
SOUTH AUSTRALIA

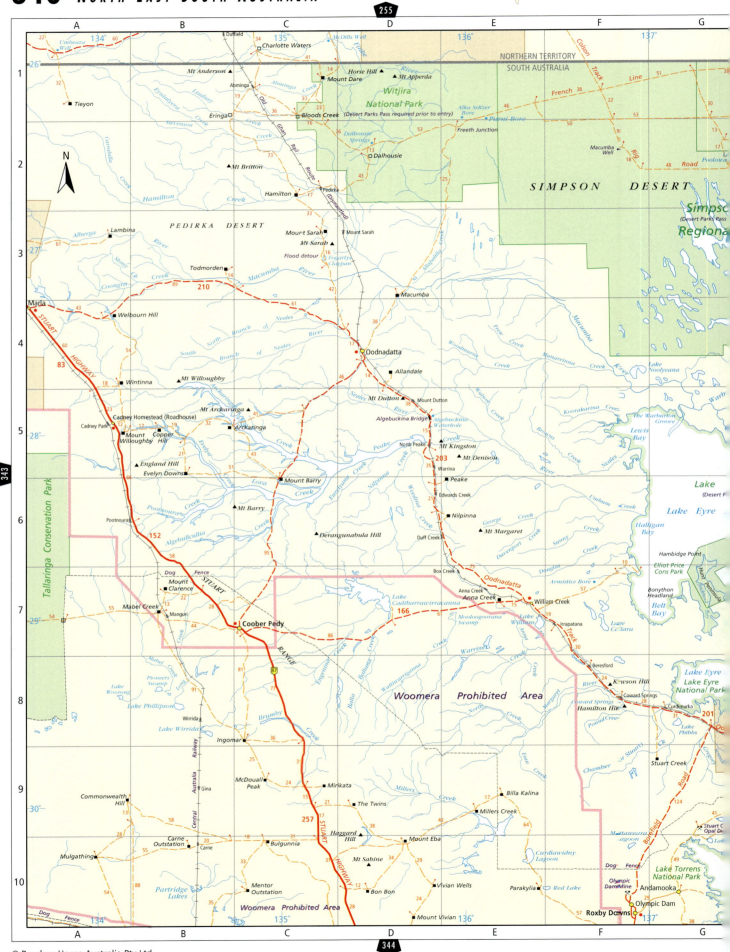

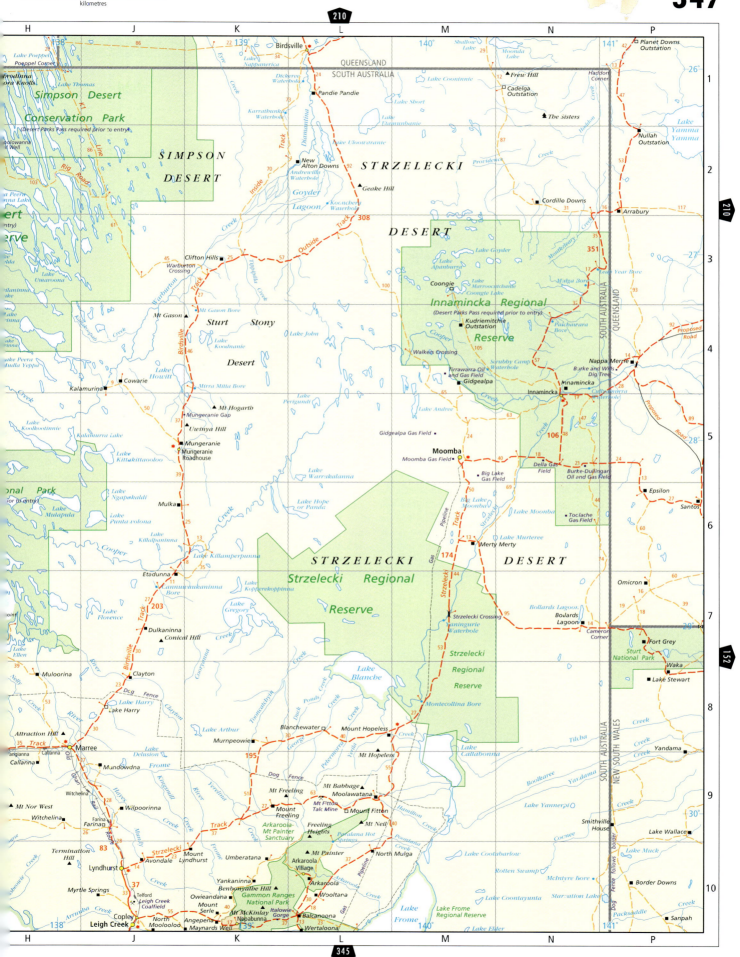

0 20 40 60 80
kilometres

H J K L M N P

1
2
3
4
5
6
7
8
9
10

QUEENSLAND
SOUTH AUSTRALIA

SIMPSON DESERT

Simpson Desert Conservation Park
(Desert Parks Pass required prior to entry)

STRZELECKI

DESERT

Innamincka Regional
(Desert Parks Pass required prior to entry)
Reserve

Sturt Stony Desert

STRZELECKI
Strzelecki Regional
Reserve

DESERT

Strzelecki Regional Reserve

Birdsville
Pandie Pandie
New Alton Downs
Andrewilla Waterhole
Geake Hill
Clifton Hills
Warburton Crossing
Mt Gason
Mt Gason Bore
Cowarie
Kalamurina
Mt Hogarth
Uwinya Hill
Mungeranie Gap
Mungeranie
Mungeranie Roadhouse
Mulka
Etadunna
Dulkaninna
Conical Hill
Clayton
Lake Harry
Attraction Hill
Marree
Callanna
Mundowdna
Muloorina
Mt Nor West
Witchelina
Wilpoorinna
Farina
Termination Hill
Lyndhurst
Avondale
Mount Lyndhurst
Myrtle Springs
Telford
Leigh Creek Coalfield
Copley
North Moolooloo
Leigh Creek
Angepena
Maynards Well
Nepabunna
Italowie Gorge
Balcanoona
Wertaloona
Mt McKinlay
Mount Serle
Owieandana
Benbonyathe Hill
Yankaninna
Arkaroola Village
Arkaroola
Wooltana
Umberatana
Mount Freeling
Mt Freeling
Mt Fitton Talc Mine
Mount Fitton
Mt Babbage
Moolawatana
Freeling Heights
Mt Neil
Paralana Hot Springs
North Mulga
Mt Painter
Gammon Ranges National Park
Arkaroola-Mt Painter Sanctuary
Murnpeowie
Mt Hopeless
Mount Hopeless
Blanchewater
Montecollina Bore
Strzelecki Crossing
Yaningurie Waterhole
Bollards Lagoon
Cameron Corner
Fort Grey
Waka
Lake Stewart
Sturt National Park
Merty Merty
Omicron
Moomba
Moomba Gas Field
Big Lake Gas Field
Della Gas Field
Burke-Dullingari Oil and Gas Field
Epsilon
Santos
Toolache Gas Field
Innamincka
Gidgealpa
Gidgealpa Gas Field
Tirrawarra Oil and Gas Field
Burke and Wills Dig Tree
Nappa Merrie
Kudriemitchie Outstation
Coongie
Walkers Crossing
Cordillo Downs
Arrabury
Planet Downs Outstation
Nullah Outstation
Cadelga Outstation
Frew Hill
The Sisters
Haddon Corner
Lake Yamma Yamma
Smithville House
Lake Wallace
Yandama
Lake Muck
Border Downs
Sanpah
Dog Fence Follows border

SOUTH AUSTRALIA
QUEENSLAND

SOUTH AUSTRALIA
NEW SOUTH WALES

Lake Frome Regional Reserve

Lake Blanche
Lake Callabonna
Lake Frome
Lake Hope or Panda
Lake Gregory
Lake Killalpaninna
Lake Killamperpunna
Lake Kopperekoppinna
Lake Florence
Lake Warrakalanna

Cooper Creek
Strzelecki Creek

TASMANIA

The smallest state has an amazing diversity, from gentle farmlands to untracked wilderness, from the wild coastlines of the west and south to the gentle beauty of the east and north coasts.

With over one-quarter of the state reserved as national parks, state reserves, historic sites and similar there is much more to see and do than can be fitted into the couple of weeks' holiday, which is all most people allow.

Tasmania is steeped in history, much of which has been preserved or restored for posterity. Historic sites showcase the Aborigines, the many early explorers who visited the island, the convict era, pioneer settlement, sailors, timber-getters (piners), miners, foresters and farmers.

Wilderness areas include raging rivers amid lush rainforest, gentle streams meandering across buttongrass plains and alpine moorlands, jagged mountain peaks and serene lakes, waterfalls, wildlife and the ever-present sense of vast space. Most noticeable—in most places—are the lack of crowds. and the world's purest air.

Gentler areas encompass magnificent bays offering a multitude of recreational activities, panoramic views, beautiful caves and woodlands.

There are gentle forest drives and walks, open heathlands flowering profusely in summer, rolling green hills and valleys through which meander lazy rivers.

There are activities for all from gentle strolls to week-long bushwalks, from river and lake cruises to scenic flights, wildlife parks and abundant free wildlife. You can ski, fish, canoe, sail, dive, abseil, ride a horse or a four-wheel

Flinders Peak from Strzelecki National Park

motorbike, a jet boat or camel, four-wheel drive along vast ocean beaches and giant sand dunes, or raft down wild rivers.

For downhill skiers there's Ben Lomond, while Mt Field is for cross-country skiing. Whitewater rafters head for the Franklin River in the Franklin–Gordon Wild Rivers National Park while canoeists will enjoy Lake St Clair and Dove Lake in the Cradle Mountain–Lake St Clair National Park, or Bathurst Harbour in the Southwest National Park to name but 2 parks.

Rock climbers have a great choice of national parks, two of the favourites being Strzelecki National Park on Flinders Island and Cradle Mountain. Fishing, for trout and salmon, is rewarding throughout the high country while the east coast offers great surf, rock, ocean and estuarine fishing.

Surfers will enjoy Bruny Island and the west coast (which can be treacherous); swimmers have the entire north and east coasts at their disposal and, for divers, Flinders Island, Governor Island and Rocky Cape National Parks are enticing.

The mechanically minded can find a wealth of historic machinery and museums from Zeehan and Queenstown's extensive West Coast Pioneer Museums to the Working Horse Museum at Triabunna, from barkmills to sawmills to goldmines and the giant Mt Lyell Mine in Queenstown.

Excellent visitor centres at Cradle Mountain, Strahan and Lake St Clair explain the history, geology, flora and fauna of their regions with visually exciting hands-on displays.

In the northwest you can cruise through pristine rainforest on the beautiful Arthur and Pieman Rivers, while from Strahan you can explore the Gordon River to Heritage Landing and learn about the anti-dam blockades which preserved this World Heritage Wilderness.

Convict history abounds, most infamously at Port Arthur but also at Sarah Island, in Macquarie Harbour, Maria Island on the east coast and in the many historic sites such as Richmond Gaol.

The Walls of Jerusalem National Park in winter

The lives of the 'piners' working the south-west wilderness for Huon pine in conditions no better than the convicts experienced stand in contrast to the amazing exploits of Diego Bernacchi's and his 'empire' on Maria Island.

On Bruny Island you will discover that this area was visited by more early explorers than any other part of Australia. You can also gain an appreciation of the immense dangers to shipping of this wild south coast.

You can walk amid extensive heathlands ablaze with wildflowers, or watch penguins, seals, dolphins and whales. There is the amazingly varied and prolific bird life and the abundant—and frequently very tame—wallabies and possums to enjoy. Kangaroos, wombats, echidnas, platypus, quolls, Tasmanian devils and a great many other creatures are often sighted.

The lowering clouds engulf ragged ranges, drawing back occasionally to allow glimpses of their peaks, as you stroll across the high country amidst glacial tarns, ferns and buttongrass.

A walk deep into a rainforest—its trees and branches adorned with mosses, lichens, fungi and epiphytes in a patchwork of verdant hues—is most relaxing. You see a myriad ground ferns dancing under the drip-drip from the forest canopy or stroll through forests of giant treeferns or pandani. There are steep tracks to climb leading to magnificent waterfalls, most of which run all year round.

Visual thrills include watching the sunset burnish the peaks of Cradle Mountain as the shadows on the lake darken, or watching the sun disappear into the ocean off the west coast or rise from the seas along the east coast at such magnificent locations as the Freycinet Peninsula or the Bay of Fires.

The superb white sands of the east coast beaches, between headlands of giant, granite boulders encrusted with orange lichen, offer much: you can swim, surf, dive, fish or just stroll along the water's edge.

The Bass Strait islands have spectacular coastal scenery, plentiful wildlife and a very rich history involving shipwrecks, sealers, whalers and Straitsmen.

There are marine reserves, such as Governor and Ninepin, which offer excellent diving; trout fishing in the highlands, flights into the Southwest Wilderness, and guides who will take you bushwalking, or show you historic sites and Aboriginal cultural sites. The Aboriginal shelters in the sea caves of Rocky Cape National Park with their giant mounds of shells and bones from innumerable feasts are such a site.

Spectacular natural coastal formations highlight the awesome power of the sea while the effects of giant glaciers can be seen in the highlands. Examine the fragile ecology of the Walls of Jerusalem National Park which survives amid stunning scenery of lakes and rocky towers.

Those of us not fit enough for walking for hours or days into the Franklin-Gordon Wild Rivers National Park, the awe-inspiring wilderness panoramas can be taken in from lookouts along the Lyell Highway. A gentle stroll to Nelsons Falls along the Franklin and Collingwood Rivers will also give a taste of the wilderness.

Mt Field has a magnificent walk to Russell Falls which is wheelchair accessible. In fact, many of Tasmania's parks and accommodation cater for the disabled.

For history lovers, Waldheim, at Cradle Valley, is a must. This was the home of Gustav Weindorfer, the man responsible for the creation of Cradle Mountain–Lake St Clair

Tranquil Tarn and Denison Crag in Ben Lomond National Park

National Park. Waldheim Chalet is now a museum in his memory.

By way of a contrast, Callington Mill, in Oatlands, gives us a glimpse into early days as settlers tamed the land. This restored windmill complex is a little piece of the English southwest transplanted to a faraway land.

Tasmania has an extensive network of limestone caves, the most accessible being Marakoopa and King Solomons Caves near Mole Creek. Hastings Caves, in the south, are not limestone but no less fascinating, with wonderful thermal pool for relaxation.

The weather is as varied as the scenery. The north coast enjoys a mild climate; the east coast has been likened to the south of France with its 300 days of sunshine per year. The mountain weather is extremely fickle and unpredictable. Bitterly cold in winter, as you would expect, it can be hot, dry and dusty in midsummer, but a few days later, a sudden snowstorm can blow in! (You must be prepared with a range of clothing.)

The west coast boasts 360 days of rain a year, with rainfalls up to 3600 mm. You can't have rainforest without a lot of rain! The islands of Bass Strait—King and Flinders—enjoy a very temperate climate, neither too hot in summer nor too cold in winter. They are, however, eternally windy.

Winter brings its own special magic to the highlands, particularly to Cradle Mountain–Lake St Clair National Park. Often hot and dusty in summer, under a mantle of snow it becomes gloriously serene and peaceful. Brilliantly crisp, sunny days are not uncommon at that time of year and you can rug up to enjoy the many beautiful walks. Wildlife congregates around the lodges much more so in winter than summer when food is plentiful.

Perhaps the most beautiful time to visit Tasmania is during autumn. The lowlands have a huge number of European trees creating a riot of colour while in the mountains the fagus, or deciduous beech, which is Australia's only deciduous native, is a blaze of golden orange at every turn.

Tasmania is a kaleidoscope of attractions, activities and facilities even if the predominant colours are green, green and green. Lacking only deserts and coral reefs, there really is something here for everyone.

	Ranger/Park Tel.	Ranger/Information	Camping	Caravan	4WD Access	BBQ/Fireplace	Picnic Area	Marked Walking Tracks	Bushwalking	Kiosk/Restaurant	Fishing	Swimming
1 Adventure Bay Coastal Reserve	(03) 6298 3229					*	*		*		*	*
2 Arthur-Pieman Protected Area	(03) 6457 1225	*	*	*		*	*		*		*	*
3 Asbestos Range National Park	(03) 6428 6277	*	*	*	*	*	*	*	*		*	*
4 Bay of Fires Coastal Reserve	(03) 6376 1550	*	*			*	*		*		*	*
5 Ben Lomond National Park	(03) 6390 6279	*	*			*	*		*	*		
6 Boltons Beach Coastal Reserve	(03) 6250 3497						*				*	
7 Bruny Island Neck Game Reserve	(03) 6293 1419	*	*			*	*		*		*	*
8 Burnie Fernglade Conservation Area	(03) 6431 1033					*	*	*	*		*	*
9 Callington Mill Historic Site	(03) 6254 1101						*		*			
10 Cape Raoul State Reserve	(03) 6250 3497							*				
11 Central Plateau Conservation Area	(03) 6259 8148	*	*	*		*	*		*	*	*	*
12 Clifton Beach Coastal Reserve	(03) 6233 8399						*		*		*	*
13 Coal Mines Historic Site & Lime Bay Nature Reserve	(03) 6250 3497	*	*	*		*	*		*		*	*
14 Coles Bay Coastal Reserve	(03) 6257 0107						*	*			*	*
15 Coningham State Recreation Area	(03) 62336560						*	*				*
16 Cradle Mountain–Lake St Clair National Park – Cradle Valley/Pencil Pine	(03) 6492 1133	*	*	*		*	*	*	*	*	*	*
17 – Lake St Clair	(03) 6289 1172	*	*	*		*	*	*	*	*	*	*
18 Cressy Beach Coastal Reserve	(03) 6257 0107						*				*	*
19 Denison Rivulet Coastal Reserve	(03) 6257 0107						*				*	*
20 D'Entrecasteaux Monument Historic Site	(03) 6233 6560						*					
21 Devils Gullet State Reserve	(03) 6363 5182							*	*			
22 Douglas–Apsley National Park	(03) 6257 0107	*	*			*	*	*	*			*
23 Eaglehawk Bay Coastal Reserve	(03) 6250 3497							*				
24 Entally House Historic House	(03) 6393 6201	*					*					
25 Fossil Bluff Coastal Reserve	(03) 6458 1415						*				*	
26 Four Mile Creek & Lagoons Beach Coastal Reserves	(03) 6376 1550		*	*							*	*
27 Franklin-Gordon Wild Rivers National Park	(03) 6471 2511	*	*			*	*	*	*			*
28 Freycinet National Park	(03) 6257 0107	*	*	*		*	*	*	*		*	*
29 Governor Island Marine Nature Reserve	(03) 6233 6191											
30 Granite Point Coastal Reserve	(03) 6357 2108					*	*	*	*		*	*
31 Gunns Plains State Reserve	(03) 6429 1388	*				*	*					
32 Hartz Mountains National Park	(03) 6298 1577					*	*	*	*			
33 Hastings Caves State Reserve	(03) 6298 3209	*				*	*	*		*		*
34 Hellyer Gorge State Reserve	(03) 6428 6277					*	*	*	*			
35 Highfield Historic Site	(03) 6443 4215	*					*					
36 Humbug Point State Recreation Area	(03) 6376 1550		*	*		*	*	*	*		*	*
37 Ida Bay State Reserve	(03) 6298 1241							*	*	*		
38 Interlaken Lakeside Reserve	(03) 6259 8148		*	*		*			*			
39 Kangaroo Bluff Historic Site	(03) 6248 4053						*	*				
40 King Solomon Cave State Reserve	(03) 6363 5182	*					*	*				
41 Labillardiere State Reserve	(03) 6298 3229	*	*	*		*	*	*	*		*	*
42 Lake Barrington State Recreation Area	(03) 6491 1301	*				*	*	*	*		*	*
43 Lavinia Nature Reserve	(03) 6457 1225	*						*	*		*	*
44 Liffey Falls State Reserve	(03) 6336 2678	*					*	*	*			
45 Lillico Beach Coastal Reserve	(03) 6428 6277							*			*	
46 Lime Bay Nature Reserve	(03) 6250 3497	*	*			*	*		*		*	*
47 Low Head Coastal Reserve	(03) 6428 6277						*				*	*
48 Lyons Cottage Historic Site	(03) 6458 1415	*										
49 Maquarie Harbour Historic Site	(03) 6471 7122							*	*		*	*
50 Marakoopa Cave State Reserve	(03) 6363 5182	*					*	*				
51 Maria Island National Park	(03) 6257 1420	*	*			*	*	*	*		*	*
52 Marriotts Falls & Junee Caves State Reserve	(03) 6288 1149							*				
53 Mayfield Bay Coastal Reserve	(03) 6257 0107						*				*	*
54 Mole Creek Karst National Park	(03) 6363 5182	*					*	*	*			
55 Mt Barrow State Reserve	(03) 6336 5397	*					*	*	*			
56 Mt Field National Park	(03) 6288 1149	*	*	*		*	*	*	*	*	*	*
57 Mt Nelson & Truganini Reserve	(03) 6233 6560						*	*				
58 Mt William National Park	(03) 6357 2108	*	*	*		*	*	*	*		*	*
59 Musselroe Bay Coastal Reserve	(03) 6357 2108						*		*		*	*
60 Ninepin Point State Reserve & Marine Reserve	(03) 6233 6191											*
61 Notley Gorge State Reserve	(03) 6336 2678	*					*	*	*			
62 Ocean Beach Coastal Reserve	(03) 6471 7122							*				
63 Peggs Beach Coastal Reserve	(03) 6458 1415	*	*	*		*	*		*		*	*
64 Pieman River State Reserve	(03) 6471 7122	*				*	*	*	*	*	*	*
65 Point Puer–Crescent Bay State Reserve	(03) 6250 3497							*				
66 Policemans Point Coastal Reserve	(03) 6357 2108	*	*				*				*	*
67 Port Arthur Historic Site	(03) 6250 3497	*	*	*		*	*		*	*	*	*
68 Raspins Beach Coastal Reserve	(03) 6257 1420											
69 Recherche Bay Coastal Reserve	(03) 6298 1241	*	*					*			*	*
70 Richmond Gaol Historic Site	(03) 6260 2127	*						*				
71 Risdon Cove Historic Site	(03) 6233 8399	*					*	*				
72 Roaring Beach Coastal Reserve	(03) 6250 3479											*
73 Rocky Cape National Park	(03) 6458 1415	*				*	*	*	*		*	*
74 Sarah Island Historic Site	(03) 6471 7140							*				
75 Scamander Coastal Reserve	(03) 6376 1550		*	*			*				*	*
76 Seal Rock State Reserve	(03) 6457 1225											
77 Seven Mile Beach Protected Area	(03) 6248 4053						*					*
78 Shot Tower Historic Site	(03) 6227 8885	*										
79 Snug Falls State Recreation Area	(03) 6233 6560						*	*				

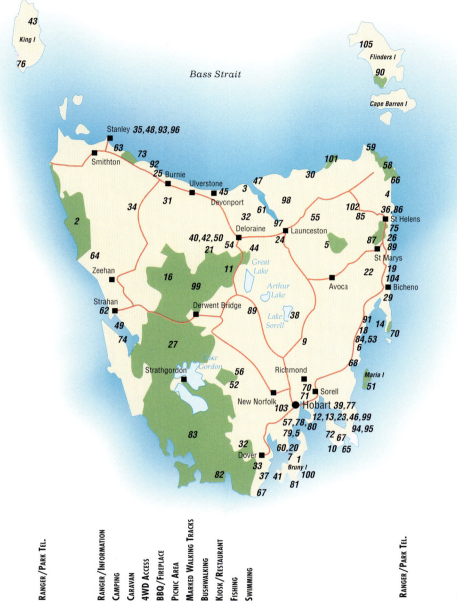

Bass Strait

43 King I
76

105 Flinders I
90

Cape Barren I

Stanley *35,48,93,96*
63
Smithton *73*
92
25 Burnie
Ulverstone
34 *31* *45* *3* *47*
Devonport *98* *30*
61 *101* *59*
32 *97* *58*
2 Deloraine *55* *102* *66*
40,42,50 *54* *24* Launceston *85* *4*
21 *44* *5* St Helens *36,86*
64 *11* *87* *75*
Zeehan *16* Great *26*
99 Lake *89*
Strahan Arthur St Marys *19*
62 Lake Avoca *22* *104*
49 Derwent Bridge *89* Lake *9* Bicheno *29*
74 Sorell *38* *91* *14*
27 *18*
Strathgordon Lake *84,53*
Gordon *56* Richmond *6*
52 *70* *68*
New Norfolk *71* Sorell Maria I
103 Hobart *39,77* *51*
*57,78,*80* *12,13,23,46,99*
83 *79,5* *72* *94,95*
32 *60,20* *67*
Dover *7* *1* *10* *65*
33 Bruny I
37 *41* *100*
82 *81*
67

	RANGER/PARK TEL.	RANGER/INFORMATION	CAMPING	CARAVAN	4WD ACCESS	BBQ/FIREPLACE	PICNIC AREA	MARKED WALKING TRACKS	BUSHWALKING	KIOSK/RESTAURANT	FISHING	SWIMMING
80 SOUTH ARM STATE												
RECREATION AREA	(03) 6233 8399					*			*			*
81 SOUTH BRUNY NATIONAL PARK	(03) 6293 1419	*	*	*	*	*		*	*		*	*
82 SOUTHWEST NATIONAL PARK												
(VIA COCKLE CREEK)	(03) 6298 1577	*	*	*	*	*	*	*	*		*	*
83 SOUTHWEST NATIONAL PARK												
(VIA MAYDENA)	(03) 6288 1283	*	*	*		*		*	*		*	*
84 SPIKY BEACH COASTAL RESERVE	(03) 6257 0107								*		*	
85 ST COLUMBA FALLS STATE RESERVE	(03) 6376 1550					*	*	*	*			
86 ST HELENS POINT STATE												
RECREATION AREA	(03) 6376 1550	*			*	*	*		*		*	*
87 ST MARY'S PASS STATE RESERVE	(03) 6376 1550								*			
88 ST PATRICKS HEAD STATE RESERVE	(03) 6376 1550							*				
89 STEPPES STATE RESERVE	(03) 6259 8148		*			*	*	*				
90 STRZELECKI NATIONAL PARK	(03) 6359 2217	*	*			*		*	*		*	
91 SWANSEA COASTAL RESERVE	(03) 6257 0107								*		*	
92 TABLE CAPE COASTAL RESERVE	(03) 6458 1415											
93 TALLOWS BEACH	(03) 6458 1415				*				*		*	*
94 TASMAN ARCH STATE RESERVE	(03) 6250 3497						*		*			*
95 TESSELLATED PAVEMENT												
STATE RESERVE	(03) 6250 3497						*					
96 THE NUT STATE RESERVE	(03) 6458 1415					*	*		*	*		
97 TREVALLYN STATE												
RECREATION AREA	(03) 6336 2678	*			*	*	*		*			*
98 WAG WALKER RHODODENDRON												
RESERVE	(03) 6336 5397					*	*		*			
99 WALLS OF JERUSALEM												
NATIONAL PARK	(03) 6363 5182	*							*			
100 WATERFALL CREEK STATE RESERVE	(03) 6298 3229							*	*			*
101 WATERHOUSE PROTECTED AREA	(03) 6357 2108	*	*	*	*	*			*		*	*
102 WELDBOROUGH PASS RESERVE	(03) 6376 1550	*							*			
103 WELLINGTON PARK	(03) 6233 6560				*	*	*	*	*			
104 WHALERS LOOKOUT RESERVE	(03) 6257 0107								*			
105 WYBALENNA HISTORIC SITE	(03) 6359 2217										*	*

BEN LOMOND NATIONAL PARK

Ben Lomond National Park is a 1300 metre high plateau, just 60 km from Launceston, and the massive bulk of Ben Lomond Plateau can be seen from all points of the compass.

It was named by Colonel Paterson who founded Tasmania's first settlement, in 1804, at George Town near the mouth of the Tamar River. He called it after the mountain with the same name in Scotland.

THE PARK'S ATTRACTIONS

In winter this 16 527 hectare park becomes the state's major ski resort offering cross-country and downhill skiing from beginners to advanced. There are 8 ski tows, a ski school, ski hire, a kiosk and a day visitors' shelter featuring heating and cooking facilities.

In spring, when the snows have disappeared and the ground dried out, Ben Lomond becomes a popular spot for day visitors. While lacking the dramatic wilderness scenery of Tasmania's west and south, the park is a pleasant, unspoilt spot for walkers. Measuring just 14 km by 6 km, the plateau contains alpine moors, scree slopes and dramatic dolerite cliffs.

Starting from the ski village, you can either take an easy 1 km walk to Hamilton Crags or a steep climb to the 1572 metre Legges Tor. This is Tasmania's second highest peak and will give you panoramic 360 degree views. You should allow 2 hours each way for this walk. You can continue down to Carr Villa, another ½ hour.

The vertical dolerite columns here also attract rock climbers.

WILDLIFE

There is not a lot of wildlife in the park. The main attraction is the bird life: black currawongs, green rosellas, dusky robins, yellow-throated honeyeaters, Tasmanian thornbills and wedge-tail eagles.

ACCESS AND ACCOMMODATION

The road up to Ben Lomond is not for the faint-hearted: the final ascent is steep, winding and narrow. The section known as Jacobs Ladder has 6 hairpin bends, vertical drops and no safety barriers, and it is often closed in winter. A shuttle bus operates from the snowline or you can get a bus from Launceston.

Apart from private clubs, the only accommodation is at Creek Inn which has log-cabin style units sleeping up to 6 people. Creek Inn also has a licensed restaurant with log fires. Creek Inn and the kiosk operate only during the ski season.

There are no formal camp sites but bush camping is allowed.

All walkers and cross-country skiers should register details of their trips at the registration booth in the village. Be prepared for sudden weather changes.

Ben Lomond Plateau in winter

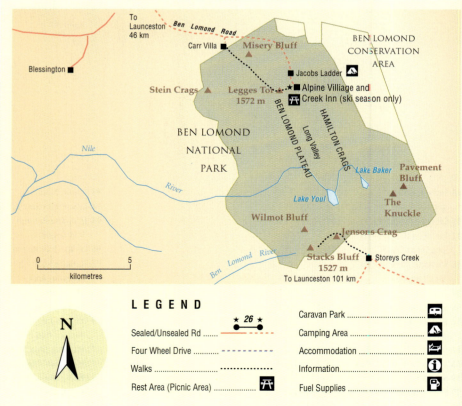

LEGEND

★ 26 ★

Sealed/Unsealed Rd

Four Wheel Drive

Walks

Rest Area (Picnic Area)

Caravan Park

Camping Area

Accommodation

Information

Fuel Supplies

Jacobs Ladder, the access road to Ben Lomond (facing page)

CRADLE MOUNTAIN–LAKE ST CLAIR NATIONAL PARK

IN BRIEF

MAP REFERENCE: PAGE 382 E 9

Location Cradle Valley is 85 km, about 1½ hours' drive from Devonport via Sheffield or Wilmot, or from Burnie airport; Lake St Clair is 175 km from Hobart, via the Lyell Highway and Derwent Bridge. Roads may be closed in winter
Best Time November to Easter
Main Attractions Bushwalking, rock climbing, fishing, canoeing, windsurfing, trail rides, boat cruise, wildlife, 4WD
Ranger Cradle Mountain, phone (03) 6492 1133; Lake St Clair, phone (03) 6289 1115

Accommodation:
Cradle Mountain Resort, phone Toll Free 1800 338 894
Lakeside St Clair Wilderness Holidays, 5 km north of Derwent Bridge has camping, back-packers' accommodation and luxury cabins for 4 to 8 people, phone (03) 6289 1137

Camping: The Ranger's Office, phone (03) 6492 1395

Cradle Huts, Launceston, phone (03) 6331 2006
Craclair Walking Tours, phone (03) 6424 7833

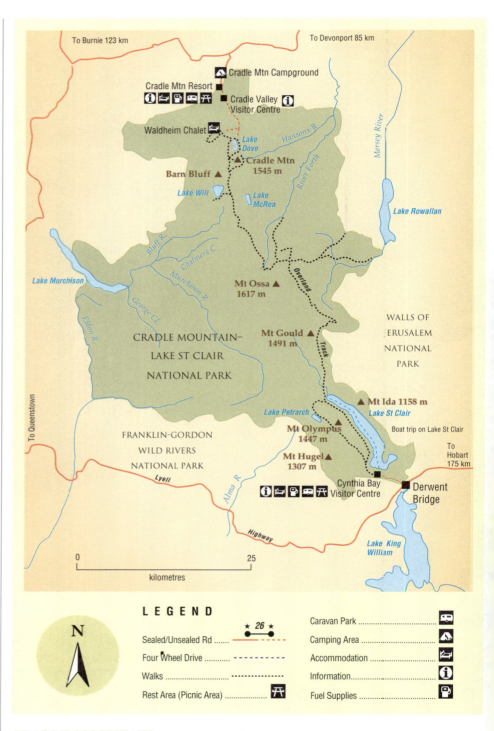

LEGEND

Sealed/Unsealed Rd	★ 26 ★
Four Wheel Drive	
Walks	
Rest Area (Picnic Area)	⛱

Caravan Park	🚐
Camping Area	⛺
Accommodation	🏨
Information	ℹ
Fuel Supplies	⛽

Cradle Mountain–Lake St Clair National Park, part of the Tasmanian Wilderness World Heritage Area, is listed by the World Heritage Commission as one of the most precious places on earth.

This stunningly beautiful area contains rugged mountain peaks, steep forested gorges, moorlands, rainforest and glacial lakes and tarns. Erosion by glaciers and water, some 500 000 years ago, carved the valleys and lakes. Plants reflect their ancient heritage with a closer relationship to plants in New Zealand and South America than to those of mainland Australia. With snow gums and giant grass trees, or moss- and lichen-clad pencil pine forests, the varied terrain contains a wide range of flora including buttongrass sedges, daisies and herbs.

With rain falling on an average of 275 days per year and snowfalls averaging 54 days a year you can expect sunny weather only on some 32 days! But even in winter the park has a splendour and beauty; under a mantle of snow it takes on a fantasy land appearance.

CRADLE MOUNTAIN
Enduring Monument

Gustav Weindorfer, an Austrian naturalist, is considered the 'father' of this 131 915 hectare national park. He built his forest home, Waldheim Chalet, in the wilderness at Cradle Valley in 1911 when everything, including the bathtub, had to be carried in on foot.

After Weindorfer's death in 1932, Waldheim was purchased by his friends and continued to be run as a guesthouse until 1975 when it was closed because of its dilapidated state. Faithfully restored by the Parks and Wildlife Service, with wood work of King Billy pine, it is now a monument to this far-sighted pioneer.

Naturalists' Delight

The national park is a magnet to all nature lovers. Prolific wildlife includes many migratory birds, such as honeyeaters, wrens and robins, which depart the high country in winter for coastal areas, leaving it to the resident bird life,

Deciduous beech (*Nothofagus gunnii*), facing page

including eagles, currawongs and parrots.

A largely nocturnal marsupial population includes wombats, tiger cats, possums, quolls and Tasmanian devils. During the day the many Bennett's wallabies and pademelons will approach looking for handouts.

Luxury in the Wilderness

Nestled in this wonderland is Cradle Mountain Resort, a wonderfully relaxing wilderness retreat offering a wide range of accommodation, from camping—in one of the prettiest and best equipped camp grounds in the country— through dormitories and the self-contained Waldheim Cabins to the upmarket Cradle Mountain huts. The cabins cater mainly for bushwalkers, and sleep 6 to 8 people with shared facilities and generator power. Scattered among the bush are delightful, self-contained family huts, sleeping 4 to 6, plus some luxury double huts where you can soak up the view from your own spa!

The Lodge, which is the hub of Cradle Mountain Resort, has cosy lounges and bars with roaring log fires and a first-class licensed restaurant.

The Lodge's dining facilities include the Tavern Bistro as well as the timber-lined dining room with panoramic views. The latter is open to all for breakfast, Devonshire teas, lunch, afternoon tea and dinner with a well-stocked wine cellar in which you are welcome to browse. These wonderful amenities are most welcome in cold weather when you can warm up with a drink from the bar before tackling a huge, and delicious, dinner. Later, relax with an after-dinner drink enjoying friendly conversation in one of the lounges.

Not to Be Missed

The highlight of an evening at Cradle Mountain Resort is the 9.30 pm animal feeding on the 'Critter Stand' outside the Tavern Bar with fresh fruit and vegetables on offer to the rufous wallabies, quolls, brush-tail possums, tiger cats, Tasmanian devils and wombats. The very fat possums are so tame they climb onto the verandah railing to be hand fed and are not even fazed by the blinding of camera flashes!

Walks for Everyone

There are numerous signposted walks in Cradle Valley starting with a gentle half-hour return stroll along the Enchanted Walk. The King Billy Track (one hour return) takes you through beautiful moss-clad forests of myrtle beech, sassafras, celery-top pine and ancient— 1500–1700 years old—King Billy pines.

Starting behind the visitor centre, an easy, 500 metre Rainforest Walk follows a circular boardwalk going through a rainforest of pencil pines, around roaring Pencil Pines Falls. It will take about 20 minutes.

A very popular 3 hour return walk goes to the Ballroom Forest. It follows the western shore of Lake Dove, which reflects the craggy peaks of Cradle Mountain, to a primeval wonderland of myrtle, sassafras, fagus (also known as deciduous beech) and pandani.

Mountain guides from the Cradle Mountain Resort lead regular daily walks, but if you are trekking independently, it's important to register at the Ranger's Office in the Visitor Centre for any walk over an hour. Weather in these regions is notoriously fickle and you'll need to be well prepared for sudden changes. Japara coats, waterproof pants and even gumboots can be hired from the store if necessary.

Other Things to Do

Tasmania's lakes and streams are renowned as some of the best in the world for chasing the elusive trout. All the major waterways are open to the public for fishing from July until April (an annual Inland Fisheries licence is necessary). Even the pond beside the Lodge is stocked with trout, although all fish caught here must be released.

Drive 8 km down to the shores of beautiful Lake Dove amidst spectacular scenery and a mob of wallabies will converge on you looking for handouts. Other activities at Cradle Valley include canoeing, white-water rafting, panning for gold, 4WD tours, trail rides on mountain ponies, and even abseiling for the more adventurous.

The Cradle Mountain Visitor Centre, at Cradle Valley (open 8–5 daily), has a wealth of information on this World Heritage Area including 'hands-on' exhibitions and a model of the Cradle Mountain region. A good selection of

Richea scoparia which grows on Cradle Mountain

maps and books is also available in the shop.

The store in Cradle Valley has a wide range of souvenirs plus enough provisions so you can handle your own catering if you wish. Petrol (unleaded only) is also available.

Scenic flights are on offer from a small runway a few kilometres away and what a breathtaking panorama they open up!

Driving

Within the national park itself there are no roads, apart from the road to Lake Dove. There are numerous 4WD tracks around Cradle Valley, to places such as Lake Lea and over the Middlesex Plains, but most tracks are on private property and permission must be gained before use. Cradle Mountain Resort runs regular 4WD tours, mostly of 3 hours duration, which will take you into areas otherwise inaccessible.

Grand Adventure

For the dedicated trekker the 60 km Overland Track from Cradle Valley to Lake St Clair offers one of the world's great walks. Evocative names, such as Cathedral Mountain, the Acropolis and

Mt Olympus, indicate the reverence which trekkers, from the earliest times, have accorded this stunning area.

Starting from the historic Waldheim Chalet, the track meanders among rainforests, across swift-flowing creeks and wet, peaty buttongrass moors amid 'kame and kettle' formations: hummocks, or mounds, formed by glacial debris, which may hold pools of water.

The track winds around Lake Dove and ragged Cradle Mountain to Barn Bluff, past many glacial lakes, around Mts Pelion (East and West) and Mt Ossa—Tasmania's highest peak at 1617 metres—and down to Lake St Clair, head-water of the Derwent River.

The Overland Track requires a minimum of 5 days and is not for the unfit or ill-prepared. Lives have been lost on the track, particularly during blizzards. Although there are some public huts along the trail, tents should always be carried.

Guided treks are available from Craclair Tours. Those seeking a little luxury can indulge themselves in a 'walk on the wild side' with Cradle Huts, a Launceston-based company which has 4 well-appointed lodges along the Overland Track, the only private accommodation allowed in this wilderness. These cosy huts, with warming pot belly stoves have been

Cradle Huts run 6 day walks, averaging a daily walking time of 5 hours, including a full day at Pelion (midway) to rest—or you can climb Mt Ossa if you wish. A 17 km boat trip down Lake St Clair completes the trek which begins and ends in Launceston.

LAKE ST CLAIR

This beautiful lake, in the south of the national park, is an easy half-day drive from Hobart. Surrounded by magical mountains, Lake St Clair is Australia's deepest lake (up to 200 metres in places) and very cold. Its beauty and serenity, where its shallow fringes lap large boulders and sandy beaches, backed by gnarled cypress pines and eucalypts, create a very contemplative mood. Lake St Clair is one of the prettiest spots in Tasmania and one of the most popular with day visitors, particularly people passing through to the west coast, but it is not hard to escape the tourist hordes to find peace and quiet.

Trout fishing at Cradle Mountain Resort

A new, and excellent, visitor centre has interpretation displays of the geology of the region, a video on glaciers and a giant hologram of a family of thylacines (the Tasmanian tiger). The visitor centre also houses the offices of the Parks and Wildlife Service, a shop and an 80 seat restaurant. It is a great place for children to learn about animals and places in Tasmania. Information on trout fishing is available here.

Other Activities

A ferry runs regular cruises to the mouth of the Narcissus River at the northern end of the lake and is frequently utilised by walkers finishing the Overland Track.

Lake St Clair is a lovely spot for canoeing, windsurfing, trout fishing and even swimming (if you're feeling brave!).

Easy Walking

A beautiful, 3–4 hour (return) walk following the roaring Hugel River leads to the lovely Shadow and Forgotten Lakes. Two short, new walks at Cynthia Bay are the Platypus Bay Loop (one hour return) and the Woodland Nature Walk (1½ hours return).

Another easy track, suitable for families, (45 minutes return) is the Watersmeet Nature Trail which leads to the start (or end) of the Overland Track passing through eucalypts, rainforest and across buttongrass plains to the Hugel and Cuvier Rivers. Abundant wildlife, particularly birds and wallabies, can be seen along all these tracks.

CAMPING

Phone the ranger's office for details of camp sites. On the Overland Track it is preferable to camp near the huts to prevent degradation of the country. There is no camping in the Cradle Mountain day walk areas.

There are camp sites at Shadow Lake where you can enjoy superb lake and mountain views.

A lone pencil pine on Barn Bluff, Cradle Mountain National Park

designed to the strictest environmental guidelines. After a welcome hot shower to ease aching muscles you can relax in the company of fellow trekkers while the guides prepare a delicious meal.

Visitor Facilities

Cynthia Bay, on the southwest corner of the lake, is a popular picnic area with BBQs, toilets, picnic shelter, kiosk and, frequently, hordes of tourist buses and mobs of wallabies.

DOUGLAS–APSLEY NATIONAL PARK

IN BRIEF

MAP REFERENCE: PAGE 383 N 8

Location 150 km southeast of Launceston via St Marys or Bicheno. There is no road access within the park
Best Time Summer and autumn
Main Attractions Bushwalking, swimming, flora, fauna
Ranger Phone (03) 6257 0107 or (03) 6375 1236

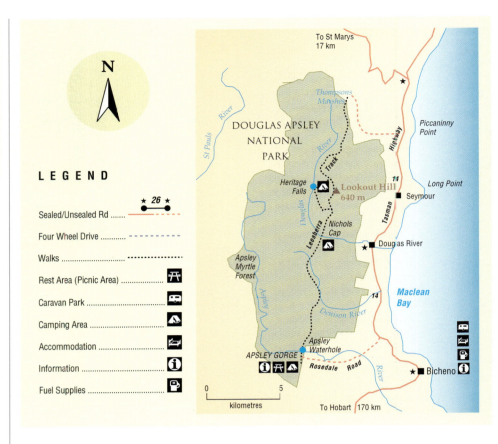

LEGEND

★ 26 ★

Sealed/Unsealed Rd ....

Four Wheel Drive ....

Walks ....

Rest Area (Picnic Area) .... 🏕

Caravan Park .... 🚐

Camping Area .... ⛺

Accommodation .... 🛏

Information .... ℹ

Fuel Supplies .... ⛽

Containing Tasmania's largest remaining area of dry, sclerophyll forest, this 16 080 hectare park is a dolerite-capped plateau on the east coast. Dissected by gorges cut by the 2 rivers for which the park is named, it has a rich diversity of plant life, including many rare or vulnerable species such as Barbers gum. Over half of Tasmania's eucalypt species are represented here.

Forest-clad ridges overlook marshlands, steep river gorges, cascading waterfalls and, in deep gullies, patches of rainforest are dominated by sassafras and myrtle. Wet forests, mainly of stringybark, are also found on moist slopes while the drier areas contain casuarinas and the beautiful Oyster Bay pine (*Callitris rhomboidea*).

HISTORY

The area is not exactly a pristine wilderness; it was mined for coal for over a century as well as being used for farming, trapping and limited logging. It was declared a national park in 1989 to protect one of the few, largely uncleared, dry forests in Tasmania. Its unique diversity of flora and fauna made its protection even more essential. Now, with a total lack of vehicular access beyond the boundary, it is regenerating to its original magnificence.

WILDLIFE

The park contains much wildlife, including vulnerable Tasmanian bettongs and 2 types of pygmy possums.

There are also reptiles which can be found in the park, such as snakes and tiny mountain dragons.

At least 62 different varieties of birds inhabit the region including peregrine falcons, black cockatoos and a great many of the parrot species.

A PARK FOR WALKERS

This park is strictly for walkers and the facilities in the park are basic. There are a number of walks from Thompsons Marshes, in the northern sector, but these are for the very experienced only. One walk takes you to the Heritage and Leeaberra Falls, set deep in a eucalypt-clad ravine of the Douglas River: this is a 5–7 hour

return walk. Passing wildflower-rich marshlands, open forest and wet gullies, it is steep and difficult but the falls are quite spectacular, especially after rain.

If you are prepared for bush camping, an overnight hike continues onto a rainforest circuit via the 640 metre Lookout Hill which

gives stunning views of the east coast. (Water should always be carried in with you as there is none available on the walk.)

The 2½ day Leeaberra Track runs the length of the park from Thompsons Marshes, via Heritage and Leeaberra Falls and Lookout Hill to the Apsley River in the south. This extremely

Nichols Cap, above the Douglas River

challenging, 28 km walk takes in the many habitats of the Douglas–Apsley National Park and its 2 rivers and has some long, steep sections. It can only be walked from north to south to prevent the plant fungus, *Phytophthora cinnamomi*, which is endemic in the south, taking hold in the northern areas of the park.

All the above walks have little signposting and previous bush navigation experience is recommended. Detailed maps from Tasmap or the Parks and Wildlife Service are also recommended. Water must be carried for the stretch between Heritage Falls and Douglas River (one day's walk).

Apsley Waterhole, in the south of the park, is the most convenient visitor location and some of the most magnificent scenery is easily accessible from here. There is even a wheelchair accessible viewing platform which gives stunning vistas up and down Apsley River Gorge. From the car park a 10 minute walk leads to superb pools for an enjoyable swim or a picnic.

The 3–4 hour Apsley Gorge Circuit track meanders along the river between sheer dolerite cliffs and dramatic scenery. Rated as moderate, it involves some steep scrambles up and down sloping banks and should only be attempted in dry weather and when the water level is low.

ACCESS AND CAMPING

The Apsley Waterhole car park is 7 km along Rosedale Road off the Tasman Highway, 4 km north of Bicheno.

Access to Thompsons Marshes is via Forestry Road E off the Tasman Highway between Bicheno and Chain of Lagoons; 20 km in look for the national park sign (it's easy to miss). High clearance vehicles are needed for the last 2 km which are steep and rough.

Bush camping is allowed anywhere in the park except within 50 metres of the river in Apsley Gorge.

Apsley Waterhole has a camp site with toilets, a picnic shelter and an information booth.

Commercial camp sites and accommodation are plentiful along the east coast. Fuel and food supplies are available from Bicheno and St Marys (although diesel may not be available at the weekends).

The Douglas River

FRANKLIN–GORDON WILD RIVERS NATIONAL PARK

IN BRIEF

MAP REFERENCE: PAGE 380 D 2

Location 180 km west of Hobart, along the Lyell Highway via Derwent Bridge. No vehicular access to park apart from 4WD access to Mt McCall
Best Times Late spring and summer
Main Attractions Beautiful rivers, magnificent scenery, rafting, walks, 4WD
Ranger Queenstown, phone (03) 6471 2511; Strahan, phone (03) 6471 7140

Peregrine Adventures, phone (03) 9663 8611
Tourist Visitor Information Centre, Strahan, phone (03) 6471 7488
West Coast Yacht Charters, phone (03) 6471 7422
Wilderness Air, phone (03) 6471 7280

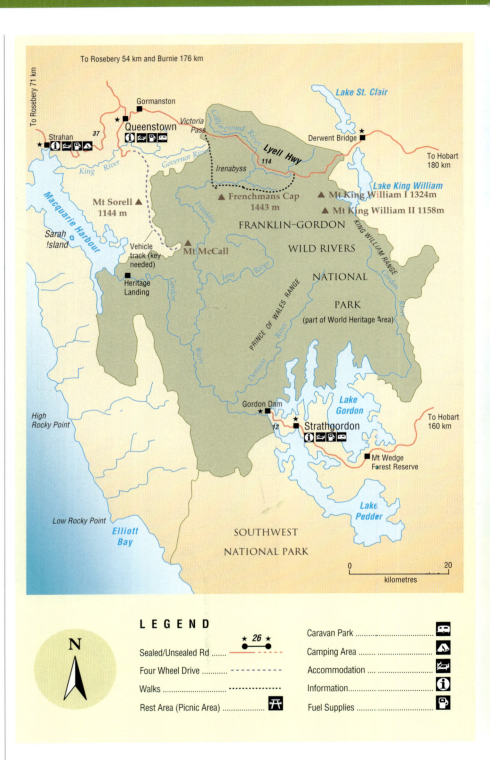

One of the greatest wilderness adventure trips in Australia is to float down the often tranquil, sometimes rapid-churned Franklin River to its junction with the reflective wide waters of the mighty Gordon River in southwest Tasmania. Born out of the greatest environmental battle fought in this country, the Franklin–Gordon Wild Rivers National Park now protects the Franklin River and much of the lower reaches of the Gordon River.

While for many the rivers are a remote, challenging experience, for others who are not so fit or adventurous, there are 'softer' adventures that one can enjoy and gain an experience of this great natural expanse of forested mountains, gnarled peaks and tumultuous rivers. Here you can touch a tree that has lived for over 2000 years, marvel at the thought that this area has been inhabited for over 20 000 years or thrill to the sound of rapids that are known to rafters around the world as 'Thunder Rush' or the 'Churn'.

HISTORY

Carved and shaped by glaciers, the great valleys of the Gordon and Franklin Rivers have played host to one of the oldest records of human habitation in Australia. Between 13 000 and 20 000 years ago Kutikina Cave, on the edge of the Franklin River not far upstream from its confluence with the Gordon, was continually occupied by Ice Age people. As weather patterns changed and the ice retreated, dense temperate rainforest re-invaded the valleys and the evidence of human activity decreased—the

people probably moved closer to the coast. The large numbers of shell middens dotted along the beaches and cliffs testify to their occupation there 6000 years ago.

European exploration began with the voyage of Abel Tasman in 1642 but it was not for another 160 years, when the first English settlement began on what was Van Diemen's Land, that real exploration and exploitation began. In 1815 Macquarie Harbour was discovered along with

the source of the fabled Huon pine.

By 1821 one of the most notorious penal colonies in history had been established on Sarah Island at the head of Macquarie Harbour. This was set up to harvest the rich bounty of timber from the banks of the surrounding rivers. Working in atrocious conditions, the convicts not only harvested the Huon pine but also built a number of ships and smaller craft.

By the time the prison closed in 1834 other

The Gordon River and its pristine river banks

tough individuals were using the rivers to bring down the wealth in logs. In 1842 Governor Franklin journeyed from Hobart to the west coast via Lake St Clair. He passed Frenchmans Cap and crossed the Franklin, which was named after him, just above a major tributary of that river now called the Jane, named in honour of his wife and companion.

For the next 100 years only weatherbeaten loggers plied the region searching for the rich Huon which was floated down the Franklin and Gordon Rivers to be milled at small towns that had sprung up on the wild and wet west coast.

It wasn't until the 1950s that the Franklin River was first canoed over its entire length and in that same decade a young emigrant, Olegas Truchanas, paddled a canoe from Lake Pedder to Strahan via the Gordon River. In the late 1960s the dam that was to flood the pristine natural surrounds of Lake Pedder was begun on the upper reaches of the Gordon. The fight to prevent this was a fight that the fledgling conservation movement lost, but when the Tasmanian Hydro-Electric Commission released plans to flood the lower Gordon and the Franklin Rivers the battle lines were drawn and the conservation movement was determined that this time it would win.

It was during this time that world focus was

FRANKLIN-GORDON WILD RIVERS NATIONAL PARK

Frenchmans Cap towering over the Franklin River

directed onto these 2 great rivers and the first commercial rafting trips began down the Franklin, while pleasure cruises took in the lower, tannin-stained waters of the picturesque Gordon River.

In 1981 the threat of a dam on these rivers was finally defeated in the High Court and soon after the Wild Rivers National Park was formed, amalgamating some smaller, older parks and joining 2 bigger parks, the Southwest National Park and Cradle Mountain–Lake St Clair National Park into one continuous band of green which is now a declared World Heritage Area.

THE LAST WILD RIVER

The Franklin River is the largest river in Tasmania to run wild and free for its entire length from its source in the Cheyne Range, just to the west of Lake St Clair, to its meeting with the Gordon River 45 km from the sea at Macquarie Harbour.

For most, a rafting trip on the Franklin begins on one of the Franklin's tributaries, the Collingwood. It's only a short run to the Franklin but you soon leave the modern world behind.

Soon after, the Franklin begins its great arc around the sheer gigantic bluff of Frenchmans

Shooting Big Fall on the Franklin River

Cap, but unless you leave the river for a hard day's hike you will never see it, for the peak remains hidden behind high walls of rock and veils of green vegetation.

The Irenabyss is one of the delightful glens to be found on the upper Franklin and here, beside the slowly eddying current, a small camp site is located which is a good stepping-off point for the climb to the top of Frenchmans Cap.

As the giant rock buttresses of Frenchmans Cap disappear from view, the river enters a series of gorges separated by rapids of varying intensity. Inception Reach, Serenity Sound and Transcendence Reach are cut by rapids that carry such descriptive names as the Churn, Coruscades, Thunder Rush and the Cauldron, the latter depositing you in Deliverance Reach, the last great stretch of placid water in the Great Ravine. You breathe a little easier once you get here!

From here the river passes through a number of lesser but still spectacular gorges as well as delightful peaceful reaches and over a number of rapids, some quite long while others are just a single drop of white water.

Below Big Fall the river slows and spreads out, waiting to join the Gordon and you need to put a bit of paddling in. It depends on which operator and what sort of craft picks you up, on how much paddling you have to do downstream. No matter what, you will be glad to see the pick-up boat or floatplane or chopper.

THE TRANQUIL GORDON

The Gordon is regarded by many as the monarch of all rivers. Rising in the King William Range south of the Lyell Highway, it too was a wild river until the great dams were built, forming those fabulous stretches of trout-filled water now known as Lake Gordon and Lake Pedder. Below here the river flows through ever narrowing gorges until it passes through the infamous Gordon Splits. Further on, just below its junction with the Franklin River, the river divides and runs around Butler Island, turns north and then west to Heritage Landing and finally to the sea at the eastern end of Macquarie Harbour.

Today, because of water released at unexpected times from the dams, the river is out of bounds. It is too dangerous to raft or paddle, apart from the placid stretches of the lower Gordon which are accessible by boat from Strahan on the northwestern shores of Macquarie Harbour.

That doesn't mean to say the Gordon River has lost any of its beauty—far from it. The lower reaches are magnificent, known for their fantastic reflections that, like the very best mirror, refract the images of the dense forests crowding the pristine river bank.

ACCESS
By vehicle

There is very limited vehicle access to the Franklin and Gordon areas; in fact, there is only one vehicle track which takes you anywhere near the river and it is accessible only by 4WD. This is the Mt McCall Track, constructed by the hydro-electric commission in the days when it was thought the dam was going to be built. It gives access to the Franklin River just below the Great Ravine. There has been an ongoing fight about this track but it remains open—though you will more than likely have difficulty getting a key for the gate from the Queenstown office of the Parks and Wildlife Service

The track takes you through some pretty spectacular country and ends, 22 km later, near Mt McCall above the Franklin River. It is well above the river, and it is a fit person who can

Cruising on the Gordon River

walk down beside the ruins of the steep railway to the river and back and not feel completely exhausted!

Some of the commercial rafting operators start or finish sections of their rafting trip here. The driving time for this track is approximately one hour each way.

By Walking

A number of walks leave the Lyell Highway, including some short ones and others that are really only suitable for the well-equipped, experienced bushwalker.

The Donaghys Hill Wilderness Walk is a short, easy walk of 2 km return that leaves the highway south of the Collingwood River and gives great views of the Franklin River and Frenchmans Cap. You should allow about 40 minutes return.

You can reach the Irenabyss on the Franklin River by leaving the Lyell Highway at Victoria Pass and heading south. This is a much tougher walk and once you have crossed the Franklin you can take the well-worn track to the top of Frenchmans Cap. It's a 3 day return walk of about 54 km and it's hard.

By Raft

For most people wanting to experience the Franklin a rafting trip is the best way, the most exciting and the most rewarding.

You can do it yourself but it takes experience, planning and the right equipment— the Franklin trip is not a trip to be undertaken lightly. It would be much better to join one of the commercial operators—such as Peregrine Adventures— who run a variety of trips down the river during the summer months.

By Boat

There are any number of cruise boats operating daily out of Strahan, taking sightseers to the lower reaches of the Gordon. Powered craft are only allowed up the river as far as Horseshoe Bend. Near here, at Heritage Landing, a loop walkway of about 10 minutes through the rainforest has been constructed to allow you to experience this ancient forest. A large Huon pine, some 2000 years old, is the highlight here.

West Coast Yacht Charters also operate trips out of Strahan on a classic yacht that takes you up the Gordon, generally further than any of the other boat companies.

Contact the Tourist Visitor Information Centre in Strahan, at the wharf, for a detailed list of the choices you have.

By Plane and Helicopter

A number of companies with float planes, such as Wilderness Air, operate out of Strahan taking tourists over the great rivers and around the high peaks. The standard flight takes you up the Gordon as far as a small landing where you can walk to the Sir John Falls—this is much further upstream than most of the boats are allowed to go. It is also a great way to see this region.

CAMPING

There are a few bush camps suitable for bush-walkers scattered through the area. The bridge over the Collingwood is one, Irenabyss Camp on the Franklin is another, along with Warners Landing on the Gordon. Otherwise you pitch a tent where you find room in amongst the dense forest or on a flattish slope on the edge of a cliff!

The township of Strahan has all facilities and is a really delightful place to spend a few days.

FREYCINET NATIONAL PARK

Dramatic red granite peaks reflect in clear blue waters lapping sands of dazzling white. Spectacular coastal scenery is everywhere on the Freycinet Peninsula. The 3 peaks, Amos, Dove and Mayson, known as the Hazards, dominate the skyline from all directions; long before you reach the peninsula they beckon across the expanse of Great Oyster Bay. Such breathtaking panoramas, abundant wildlife and a wealth of outdoor activities make this 10 000 hectare national park a great holiday area.

Freycinet National Park consists mainly of coastal heathland, which is an artist's palette of colour in spring, dominated by awe-inspiring peaks and cliffs. Magnificent white sand beaches, such as Wineglass Bay (mostly accessible only by boat or on foot), alternate with towering cliffs above the rocky coastline.

This east coast of the state enjoys a climate similar to the south of France with over 300 days of sunshine a year.

HISTORY

The Freycinet Peninsula was named in 1802 by the French explorer Nicholas Baudin for his cartographer Henri Freycinet. Schouten Island, located at the peninsula's southern tip and named by Abel Tasman in 1642, once had a whaling station as well as tin and coal mining.

The peninsula became a national park in 1916, and together with Mt Field is Tasmania's oldest. Schouten Island became part of the park in 1967.

GREAT WALKS

The park is largely a wilderness with very little vehicular access. This is a bushwalker's paradise with walks ranging from 1 to 10 hours, and there are several camp sites for overnight hikers on the 27 km circuit track of the park.

There are several walks from the car park. One is quite steep, leading to the saddle between Mts Amos and Mayson and provides superb views of Wineglass Bay and Mts Graham and Freycinet. You should allow about 1½ hours for this 1 km return walk.

Another popular walk—particularly at sunrise—is to the summit of Mt Amos for stunning views south across Wineglass Bay and the peninsula, or north across Coles Bay and beyond (2½ hours return).

Very popular also is the 2 day walk across Mt Graham to Cooks Beach.

HIGHLIGHTS

One of the few areas with vehicular access and one of the most spectacular is Cape Tourville. Here the lighthouse offers splendid vistas of the Tasman Sea and Cape Forestier; the cliffs drop sheer to the ocean hundreds of metres below.

Bluestone Bay (4WD only) is quite fascinating and different: instead of sand it has blue-grey, egg-shaped rocks ranging in size from a few centimetres to a metre or more. They look for all the world like a pile of dinosaur eggs.

The abundant wildlife is rich and varied. Black cockatoos, green rosellas, yellow wattle-birds, butcherbirds and wedge-tail eagles are all seen, while gulls, gannets, fairy penguins and white-breasted sea-eagles are some of the many seabirds. Mammals are represented by walla-bies, possums, echidnas and potoroos among others. Venomous snakes are also found here.

OTHER ACTIVITIES

The Hazards, about 485 metres high, present a challenge to climbers, while the fishing in the park is good: flathead, trumpeter, trevally and salmon are taken regularly. Fishing charters are available from nearby Coles Bay township, as are fuel, supplies, boat and sporting equipment hire. Water sports include swimming, water skiing, diving, sailing and canoeing.

The clear blue waters of Freycinet National Park

Freycinet Lodge nestled below the Hazards

To the north (about 10 km from the highway) are the Friendly Beaches, also part of the national park. This is a great area for anglers and drivers of 4WD vehicles. From here the Freycinet Experience runs 4-day walks in the national park starting with a boat ride to Schouten Island. They have simple cabin accommodation en route with more luxurious accommodation tucked away out of sight at the Friendly Beaches.

ACCESS AND ACCOMMODATION

The park is about a 3 hours' drive from Hobart along the Tasman Highway, or 3½ hours from Devonport on the state's northern coast.

Accommodation ranges from the delightful waterfront camp sites just inside the national park, through youth hostels to B&Bs. The hedonists are well catered for with the Freycinet Lodge situated in between the Hazards and the clear waters of Honeymoon Bay. An environmentally friendly resort, it consists of timber lodges set in bushland with stunning views across Great Oyster Bay. The Lodge offers many nature-based and educational activities.

There is also a variety of accommodation available through the Freycinet Experience, while there are several camp sites for the use of overnight walkers.

LEGEND

Sealed/Unsealed Rd	★ 26 ★
Four Wheel Drive	- - - - - - - -
Walks	....
Rest Area (Picnic Area)	⛺
Caravan Park	🚐
Camping Area	⛺
Accommodation	🛏
Information	ℹ
Fuel Supplies	⛽

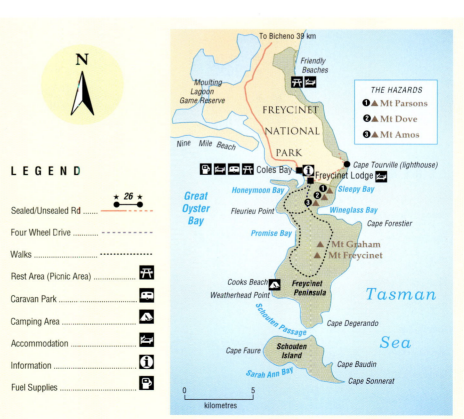

MARIA ISLAND NATIONAL PARK

IN BRIEF

MAP REFERENCE: PAGE 381 N 3

Location Access is by passenger ferry only several times daily, from Triabunna and the Eastcoaster Resort

Main Attractions Walking, wildlife, history, diving, fishing

Best Time Spring to autumn

Ranger Phone
(03) 6257 1420

To book camping/dormitory accommodation at Darlington, phone the ranger, (03) 6257 1420

This tranquil and beautiful island, just 15 km off Tasmania's east coast, boasts magnificent coastal scenery of dazzling white beaches, wonderfully shaped and coloured cliffs, open forests and a mountain range high enough to support a rainforest habitat. Maria is virtually 2 islands joined by a narrow isthmus, and habitats range from coastal heathland and dunes to dry woodlands of blue gums, black and silver wattles, together with rainforest species, such as native laurel and celery-top pine, more usually found in western Tasmania.

UNIQUE HISTORY

Over 20 km long by 13 km at its widest point, Maria was named by Abel Tasman, in 1642. It was explored and charted by Nicholas Baudin in 1802 and saw some whaling and sealing activity in the early 19th century.

In 1825 a penal settlement was established on Maria Island, and, at its peak, Darlington township held up to 900 prisoners. It was abandoned in 1832 for the newly opened Port Arthur but from 1842 to 1850 it again was used as a convict probation station.

Then in 1884 an Italian, Diego Bernacchi, arrived on Maria Island. He had grandiose visions of an empire founded on the production of wine, silk and cement. He rebuilt Darlington township, naming it San Diego; it had a population of over 250 with a post office, bank, store, school, baker, butcher, blacksmith and shoemaker.

Bernacchi died in 1925 although he had long since lost control of his 'empire'. With the Depression businesses folded and Darlington's population dwindled to a few farmers and fishermen. Many buildings were removed, others fell into disrepair.

So Maria Island slumbered, almost forgotten, until it was declared a national park in 1972 and the restoration of many of the buildings began.

EXPLORING THE PAST

Disembarking from the ferry you walk past the silos and the beautiful Commissariat building, now a visitor information centre, and up an avenue of trees to the grassy slopes around Darlington.

The former penitentiary now provides dormitory accommodation for school groups, the chapel contains displays of memorabilia and 3 white-washed terrace houses have been restored externally.

The Coffee Palace still gazes out over the blue waters of Darlington Bay surrounded by the convict-era mess hall, bakehouse and the remains of solitary cells.

Atop a hill is a large convict-built barn housing a great array of old farm machinery and surrounded by rusting relics and concrete bins. On the headland is the cemetery which has only a handful of headstones still standing.

WALKS

Walking tracks vary from half an hour to several days taking in the wilder southern areas. South of Darlington lie the Painted Cliffs, brilliantly coloured and spectacularly eroded by wind and sea. The Fossil Cliffs, full of millions of fossilised shellfish, are found to the east of Darlington. The Fossil Cliffs Nature Walk is an easy 1–1½ hour stroll.

Inland the dolerite peaks of Bishop and Clerk are a half day return walk rated as difficult, potentially dangerous.

The Mt Maria Trail is a 4–6 hour return walk, rated potentially hazardous in places.

Maps and notes on all walks are available from the Visitor Centre.

ABUNDANT WILDLIFE

There are large numbers of very tame Bennett's wallabies, forester kangaroos, pademelons, potoroos, bettongs, possums and emus in the park. The numerous birds include the introduced Cape Barren goose and the endangered forty-spotted pardalote. Some of the animals were introduced to the island in 1965 when a preserve was established to protect fauna that was threatened on the mainland.

The island's waters are rich in marine life with abalone, rock lobsters and giant kelp featuring prominently. Seals and whales are frequent visitors and some of the waters have been declared a marine reserve.

ACCESS AND CAMPING

The ferries run from Tribunna and the Eastcoaster Resort between Orford and Tribunna. The trip takes about ½ hour. Orford is 77 km from Hobart via the Tasman Highway.

There is no transport on Maria Island, no stores, no electricity, and very limited tank

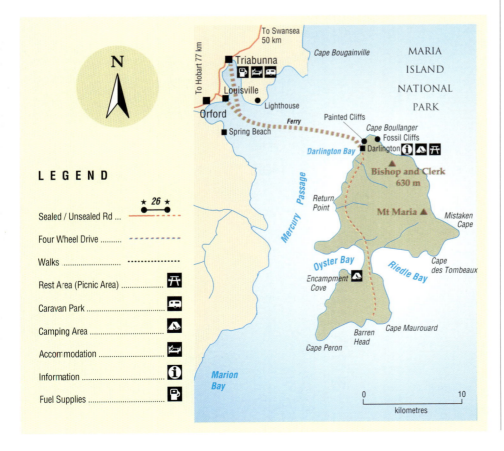

LEGEND

Sealed / Unsealed Rd	⭐ 26 ⭐
Four Wheel Drive	
Walks	
Rest Area (Picnic Area)	🛆
Caravan Park	
Camping Area	
Accommodation	
Information	🅸
Fuel Supplies	

The Painted Cliffs, Maria Island National Park

water so visitors must be totally self-sufficient.

BBQs, picnic facilities and toilets are provided at Darlington Beach; the Commissariat has excellent historic and environmental

displays, brochures and maps for self-guided walks of Darlington township. The rangers also lead regular walking tours.

Camp sites are available at Darlington, as is

basic dormitory accommodation. You can also camp at French's Farm and Encampment Cove.

There is a full range of accommodation available at the mainland ferry terminal.

MT FIELD NATIONAL PARK

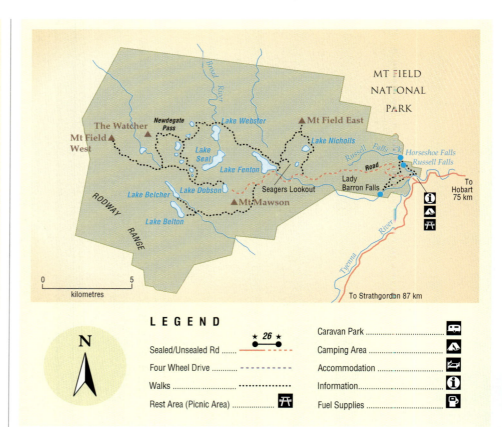

LEGEND

Sealed/Unsealed Rd .... ★ 26 ★
Four Wheel Drive ....
Walks ....
Rest Area (Picnic Area) ....

Caravan Park ....
Camping Area ....
Accommodation ....
Information..................
Fuel Supplies ....

Mt Field is Tasmania's oldest national park and one of the prettiest, with a great variety of scenery from low level rainforest to high altitude moorlands, brooding mountain ranges, waterfalls and many beautiful lakes. Mt Field has something for everyone from gentle walks to strenuous overnight hiking, from wildlife spotting to winter skiing.

The lower levels of this 16 257 hectare park consist of tall swamp gums, sassafras, myrtles, celery-top pines, rainforest and 'manfern' gullies. At higher altitudes the vegetation changes to subalpine conifer woodlands of King Billy and pencil pines, soft tea-trees and snow gums. Alpine moorlands of pineapple grass, cushion plants, pandani, waratahs and sword grass are dotted with many lakes and tarns.

Pandani, Tasmania's tree heath

HISTORY

The 300 acres around Russell Falls were proclaimed a reserve in 1885. This area was enlarged in 1916 and declared a national park. Originally called simply National Park, it was renamed Mt Field National Park in 1947 after Barron Field, a NSW Supreme Court judge and keen amateur naturalist. The first trout were released in the lakes in 1898.

WALKING TRAILS GALORE

The whole of Mt Field National Park is a walkers' paradise with walks ranging from 10 minutes to overnight hikes.

A large picnic area at the park entrance is the starting point for a 1 km Nature Walk which winds through giant tree ferns, swamp gums and a great variety of small ferns to the magnificent Russell Falls. Russell Falls Creek and Nina Creek, which flow from the slopes of Mt Field East, join to cascade in silvery ribbons over these superb falls. Dropping 45 metres in 3 stages, they measure 12 metres across the base. A boardwalk crosses between the 2 lower levels. It is also wheelchair accessible. The walk returns along the Russell Falls Creek, in which you can often see brown and rainbow trout. You can continue onto Horseshoe Falls and the lovely Lady Barron Falls.

On the road to Lake Dobson there are signposted, short walks. One of these, the Tall Trees

Walk, is a 900 metre boarded walk with signs detailing the history of these 45 metre giant swamp gums. Further up the road, along the 15 minute Lyrebird Walk, you see the transition from rainforest to yellow gums and 250–300 year-old gumtop stringybarks adorned with kangaroo ferns and other epiphytes.

Numerous other marked tracks lead to the many lakes and peaks in the park: to Beatties Tarn, Lake Nicholls and across Windy Moor to Mt Field East; around Lakes Webster and Seal, over Newdegate Pass and the Rodway Range to Mt Field West. Some of these are extended, overnight hikes and there are a number of hikers huts in the further regions.

The weather, at these high altitudes, is very changeable and visitors should be prepared for sudden storms; even for snowfalls which can occur at any time of year.

A good map is essential for any one of these longer walks.

BEAUTIFUL LAKE DOBSON

A 16 km drive (unsealed, very corrugated but accessible to conventional vehicles in summer) climbs steeply up to Lake Dobson. The terrain becomes progressively more rugged, with mountain peaks all around, the flora changing noticeably from the rainforest of the lower levels through subalpine conifer woodlands, tea-tree and snow gums which then gives way to the

heath of the alpine moorlands

Lake Dobson is a beautiful mountain lake and the only one accessible by car. It was carved out, about 18 000 years ago, by a 15 km long glacier, which moved down the slopes of Mt Mawson, on its way dumping the giant boulders on the lake shore.

The lake has a circular walk, the 45 minute Pandani Grove Nature Walk, which leads through marvellously mysterious, almost primeval, scenery, much of it along boardwalks. These 'pandani' look like pandanus palms but are actually a tree heath (*Richea pandanifolia*), native to Tasmania. A large, bushy crown of long, narrow leaves—up to 1.5 metres long—wraps around a trunk growing 12 metres high, eventually becoming top heavy and falling over!

This marvellous Pandani Grove is a unique sight but mostly the lake is lined with snow gums—straighter and spindlier than on the mainland—yellow gums and King Billy pines.

Pineapple grass, small *Richea* species and sphagnum moss cover the ground and the air is heady with the perfume of lemon-scented boronia. Dwarf pines and hardy, ancient pencil pines have grown in wondrously warped shapes. Much of the lake is lined with giant granite boulders coated in colourful orange lichen. Extensive views across the lake and the subalpine woodlands are superb. There is a picnic area here with toilets, and fishing (with a licence) for brown trout is allowed at Lake Dobson.

SKIING

Snow-covered in winter, the park offers great scope for ski touring, although the downhill skiing is limited. There are 4 tows, ski hire and instruction but the accommodation is basic. It is more a case of walk in and carry your own gear.

WILDLIFE

Abundant wildlife includes Bennett's and rufous wallabies, wombats, barred bandicoots, Tasmanian devils, native cats while there are platypus in Lake Dobson and the Tyenna River.

Birdlife is also prolific. Lyrebirds were introduced from Victoria in the 1930s and have thrived. Other birds common to the park are black cockatoos, grey thrushes, olive whistlers, green rosellas honeyeaters, currawongs and wedge-tail eagles.

ACCESS AND CAMPING

The park is situated 75 km northwest of Hobart and is off the Gordon River Road. The entrance is 35 km from New Norfolk.

The road to Lake Dobson is open to conventional vehicles in summer; in spring and late autumn it may be suitable only for 4WD while in winter it may be closed due to snow. Anyone travelling up to the higher altitudes in

Marion Falls in Mt Field National Park

winter or spring should carry chains. Visitors should also check the status of the roads before setting out.

At the national park entrance is a large picnic area with BBQs and a kiosk selling basic foodstuffs and souvenirs. A visitor centre provides information about the park, its history, flora and fauna. There's a pretty camping area nearby with full facilities. To book a camp site, contact the ranger.

There is some fairly basic accommodation in the nearby hamlet of National Park but unless you are planning to camp or do really long walks, it's an easy day's trip from Hobart.

The rugged mountain ranges, wild moorlands, rainforests, beautiful waterfalls and lakes make Mt Field a truly magnificent and popular destination.

MT WILLIAM NATIONAL PARK

MAP REFERENCE: PAGE 383 P 4

Location From Devonport it is an easy 2½ hours' drive via Gladstone; from the south it is 50 km from St Helens. There is little vehicular access
Best Time Spring to autumn
Main Attractions Beach and bushwalking, fishing, swimming, surfing, diving, boating, wildlife
Ranger Phone (03) 6357 2108

LEGEND

★ 26 ★	
Sealed/Unsealed Rd	
Four Wheel Drive	
Walks	
Rest Area (Picnic Area)	🏕
Caravan Park	🚐
Camping Area	⛺
Accommodation	🛏
Information	ℹ
Fuel Supplies	⛽

One of Tasmania's lesser known national parks, Mt William National Park combines natural beauty and abundant wildlife in a coastal setting with great appeal for surfers, anglers, bushwalkers and nature lovers. Originally set aside to protect the then-rare forester kangaroo, the 13 812 hectare park covers the northeast tip of Tasmania and encloses coastal heathland, dry sclerophyll forest and some of the most beautiful beaches you'll see anywhere.

For almost a century the north of the park was a grazing property until taken over by the National Parks Service in 1973 for the conservation of the forester kangaroo.

Some of the most spectacular coastal scenery is in the south around Eddystone Point. The Eddystone Light, a circular tower built in 1889 from locally quarried granite, is 35 metres high and sits 45 metres above the ocean on Tasmania's easternmost tip. Eddystone Point offers superb panoramas of the Bay of Fires stretching away to the south. (The lighthouse is open Tuesdays and Thursdays.)

Eddystone Point, like so much of this coast, is fringed with giant granite boulders coated in orange lichen, a colourful contrast to the deep blue-green water. A little natural harbour among the rocks, just north of the lighthouse, offers a great boat launching site.

A rough track of about 4 km follows the coast northward around Picnic Rocks to Deep Creek.

FLORA AND FAUNA

The bush consists of black peppermint, black and white gums, banksias and casuarinas. Grass trees, or kangaroo tails, are very common while behind the coastal dunes are a number of paperbark salt marshes.

The heathlands are a blaze of colour in spring and early summer: pink and white heath, white tea-tree, yellow wattles, banksias and guinea flowers abound.

There are hundreds of forester kangaroos, particularly along the 15 km Forester Kangaroo Drive in the park's north. Large numbers of Bennett's wallabies, pademelons, wombats and echidnas roam the park. Less obvious, since they are nocturnal animals, but still common are brush possums, native cats and Tasmanian devils.

The varied bird life of over 100 recorded species includes many honeyeaters, finches, robins, wrens and pardalotes. The seabirds that are commonly seen are gulls, albatrosses, oystercatchers and white-breasted sea-eagles.

ACTIVITIES

Swimming surfing and diving among the rocks and reefs are popular as is fishing for flathead, pike and salmon. Musselroe Bay, to the north, also has good bream fishing.

Stumpys Bay Beach in Mt William National Park

Long, white beaches and a network of fire trails allow for a variety of bushwalking. An easy 30 minute walk from the car park to the top of Mt William (only 216 metres high) results in sweeping views of the park, from the wide sandy beaches and rocky headlands to the forested inland areas and across to the mountains of Flinders and Cape Barren Islands in Bass Strait.

Cape Naturaliste is the major coastal highlight in the north with superb beaches of white sand stretching south through Stumpys Bay to Boulder Point and Cobbler Rocks.

ACCESS AND CAMPING

Situated about 140 km northeast of Launceston via the Tasman Highway and Gladstone, much of the park is inaccessible with no tracks at all; only the northern and southern tips can be explored by vehicular traffic.

Camp sites are dotted among the dunes near Picnic Rocks and on a grassy area beside Deep Creek. The latter has fireplaces, tables and a toilet; the former a bore fitted with an old-fashioned hand pump. In other words, campers have to be totally self-sufficient.

In the north there are quite a few camp sites around Stumpys Bay and north of Cape Naturaliste. Nestled among casuarinas on the foreshore, they have fireplaces, picnic tables and several have a water bore but there are no other facilities.

IN BRIEF

MAP REFERENCE: PAGE 381 K 8

Location 15 minute ferry ride from Kettering, 37 km south of Hobart on the Channel Highway
Best Time Spring to autumn
Main Attractions Wild coastal scenery, heathland walks, scenic drives, fishing, boating, swimming, surfing, 4WD
Ranger Phone (03) 6293 1408

Towering, fluted cliffs above wild seas alternate with gentle heathlands and lovely swimming bays in Tasmania's newest national park. Encompassing the south coast of Bruny Island, it stretches from Partridge Island and Labillardiere Peninsula across Cape Bruny, Cloudy Bay and Tasman Head, then up the east coast to Adventure Bay.

Adventure Bay was visited by more explorers than any other part of Australia: Abel Tasman Tobias Furneaux, Bruni D'Entrecasteaux, James Cook, William Bligh, Matthew Flinders to name just a few. The French, particular, took a very keen interest in the area which prompted the British to set up the new colony of Hobart Town.

DRAMATIC SCENERY

The convict-built Cape Bruny Lighthouse is Australia's oldest manned lighthouse. Built in 1838 it is 105 metres above sea level and offers breathtaking views of Lighthouse Bay, rugged West Cloudy Head and across to East Cloudy Head, Tasman Head and the Friars Rocks.

Both Jetty Point and Cape Bruny are easily accessible by vehicle although the road gets a bit rough. The drive from Lunawanna provides absolutely breathtaking scenery of a rugged coast. Cloudy Bay, a popular surfing spot, can become wild in winter. A small isthmus at the north divides it from Cloudy Bay Lagoon which is sheltered and popular for water sports.

In places no more than 100 metres wide, the park continues around more giant cliffs at East Cloudy Head Pyramid Bay and Tasman Head. Wild seas here are part of spectacular scenery which can only be reached by 4WD tracks.

North of Mt Bruny and up the east coast past Mangana Bluff and the Bay of Islands, the park is totally wild with no access at this stage.

Partridge Island, at the western tip of the park, can only be visited if you have a boat.

WALKS AND OTHER ACTIVITIES

Fluted Cape, in the northeast of the park, is reached via a 2½ hour walk from the Adventure Bay Caravan Park. From the site of the old

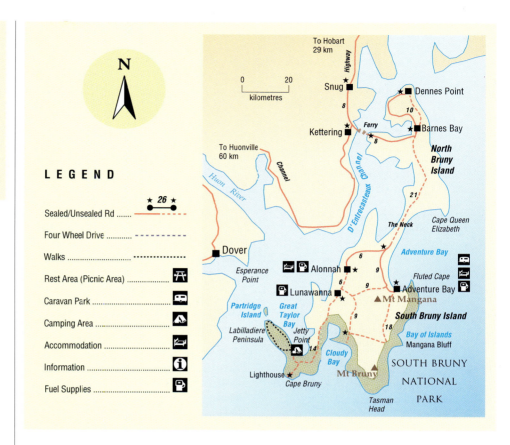

LEGEND

Sealed/Unsealed Rd	★—●—★ 26 ★
Four Wheel Drive	– – – –
Walks	•••••••
Rest Area (Picnic Area)	🏕
Caravan Park	🚐
Camping Area	⛺
Accommodation	🛏
Information	ℹ
Fuel Supplies	⛽

Cookville Whaling Station to Penguin Island, out at the tip, is easy going but then the track becomes steep and difficult. The walk offers spectacular coastal scenery of high, inaccessible cliffs and sweeping panoramas across Adventure Bay toward the Neck which separates North and South Bruny.

The Labillardiere Peninsula, stretching northwest from Cape Bruny, consists of heathlands which are a mass of colour in spring and summer with tea-tree, banksias, orchids, red and white heath. A 7–8 hour walk encircles the peninsula via wild Standaway Bay, Hopwood Point, Great Taylor Bay and lovely Jetty Point.

There is excellent fishing in most areas, with swimming at Great Taylor and Adventure Bays, a range of other bushwalks and 4WD tracks.

ACCESS AND CAMPING

Ferries run 9 times daily (more often in peak times) from Kettering. Alonnah, which is the business centre of the island, is 35 km from the ferry terminal, and Adventure Bay is 37 km away. Cape Bruny is some 20 km south of Alonnah.

Adventure Bay is the 'holiday resort' of Bruny with 2 caravan parks

and other low-key accommodation. It has a long sweep of white sands lapped by clear waters, and is safe for swimming and boating.

Fuel is also available here. There is a range of B&B, homestay and cabin accommodation across the island—none of it upmarket—but nothing south of Adventure Bay.

A basic camp site sits in a sheltered spot above Jetty Beach; a 'wild' camp site at Cloudy Bay is only accessible along the beach by 4WD.

The Neck separating South and North Bruny

SOUTHWEST NATIONAL PARK

IN BRIEF

MAP REFERENCE: PAGE 380 F 7

Location The northern section is 74 km from Hobart via the Lyell Highway. There is little vehicular access. The southern section from Cockle Creek is 2 hours drive from Hobart via the Huon Highway
Best Time Summer and early autumn
Main Attractions Bushwalking, fishing, photography, wildlife, water-skiing, sailing, canoeing
Ranger Phone (03) 6288 1283; Cockle Creek, phone (03) 6298 1577

Accommodation:
Lake Pedder Motor Inn, Strathgordon, phone (03) 6280 1166
National Park Hotel, National Park, phone (03) 6288 1103

Par Avion's Wilderness Experiences cost from $130 per person, phone (03) 6248 5390

The southwest corner of Tasmania is a vast wilderness of soaring mountain peaks, temperate rainforests, unspoilt rivers and a superb coastline forever protected with a World Heritage listing. Unless you're an energetic bushwalker, however, you will see little more than the fringes of this very special place. There are, though, a few corners with vehicular access to give us a taste of the superb scenery and wildlife in this national park while commercial light plane operators will fly you into Bathurst Harbour on the south coast.

HISTORY

This region was inhabited by cave dwellers as long ago as 23 000 BC. For at least the last 3000 years 4 Aboriginal tribes have lived around the coastal area.

In the 19th century the Europeans arrived and they included whalers, sealers, hunters, miners and timber-getters chasing the valuable Huon pine. Lake Pedder National Park was proclaimed in 1955; between 1968 and 1981 this park was extended and renamed Southwest National Park. In 1990 the park was further extended to its present size of 605 000 hectares.

WILDERNESS DRIVE

The Gordon River Road traverses the park's northern boundary, between Lakes Gordon and Pedder, to the Gordon Dam and Power Station. En route is Strathgordon, the former construction village.

From the Maydena Gate entrance to the Southwest National Park to Strathgordon, it is 82 km of steep, winding road through really wild country. The road is fully sealed but subject to ice and snow, so requires a certain degree of caution.

Lakes Pedder and Gordon are vast, covering 500 sq km, and contain 37 times the volume of Sydney Harbour. Mountain peaks, such as Scotts Peak and Mt Solitary, form islands in the lakes.

This is one of the wettest parts of Tasmania—with up to 3 metres of rain annually! The atmosphere is frequently wet with low-level clouds obscuring the superb views. However, these low-flying clouds occasionally clear to give tantalising glimpses of the many mountain peaks.

The Scotts Peak Road, which runs off the Gordon River Road at Frodshams Pass, 28 km from the Maydena Gate, is 36 km of steep, corrugated and deeply pot-holed gravel track. It runs through forests, vast valleys and across wild moorlands, giving stunning views of mist-shrouded mountains in all directions.

The dark dolerite mass of Mt Anne, the highest peak in the southwest, dominates the skyline along with odd-shaped peaks such as the Needles and the Thumbs. This unique, temperate rainforest wilderness suddenly opens up to reveal the vast expanse of Lake Pedder. There are a number of lookouts offering breathtaking panoramas of Lake Pedder, the Arthur Plains, the Arthur, Maydena and Jubilee Ranges, Weld River Valley and much more. The most spectacular 360 degree views can be had from Red Knoll Lookout, 2 gut-busting km past Scotts Peak Dam.

Visitors can buy or hire an audio cassette full of stories, interviews and facts about the area from the Maydena Gate entrance.

Silver wattle, leatherwood and crimson waratah are just a few of the colourful flowers to be seen on the drive. Common birds include robins, wrens, thornbills, rosellas, honeyeaters and currawongs.

THINGS TO DO
Water Sports

Some of the best fishing in Australia is to be found in the park with giant trout being taken—artificial lures only—in Lakes Pedder and Gordon from August to April (a licence is required, available from the Maydena Gate entrance). There are a number of boat ramps, but fishing is not allowed in tributary rivers.

The lakes are perfect for water-skiing, sailing and canoeing but take care—these are almost inland seas!

Walking

A number of picnic areas and walking tracks are found along the Gordon River Road. The Florentine River is reached through rainforest along Timbs Track (4 hours return). Mt Wedge is a 4–5 hour return walk with spectacular views from the summit.

Lake Pedder in Southwest National Park

CREEPY CRAWLY NATURE TRAIL

Two km from Frodshams Pass, along the Scotts Peak Road, is the Creepy Crawly Nature Trail. One of 5 such walks funded by a Commonwealth Rainforest Conservation Project, this excellent 1 km, fully duckboarded walk weaves in and out of rainforest habitats giving visitors the chance to touch, hear and smell this remarkable environment.

It is an easy, ½ hour walk but not recommended for anyone unable to climb a lot of steps or duck under low branches.

OTHER WALKS

Several other walks start from the Scott Peak Road. Lake Judd is an 8 hour return walk while Eliza Plateau is a very difficult 5–6 hour return trek, offering breathtaking views from the summit (for experienced walkers only).

Two tracks—also for experienced walkers only—cross this wilderness. The 54 km Port Davey Track, from Lake Pedder to Melaleuca on Bathurst Harbour, takes 4 to 5 days, one way. As there are no roads to Melaleuca, visitors must sail, walk or take a plane in and out. You can continue walking along the 66 km South Coast Track to Cockle Creek. You should allow between 5 and 9 days for this section, depending on your level of fitness. (Cockle Creek is at the end of the Huon Highway, the southernmost point you can drive to in Australia.)

At Cockle Creek there is a 16 km, 4 hour return walk to South Cape Bay. From here the next landfall across the Southern Ocean is Antarctica! There are also some shorter walks in the area which provide excellent views of the spectacular coastline.

Apart from the Creepy Crawly Nature Trail and the shorter walks at Cockle Creek, the walks in Southwest National Park are for very experienced walkers only. All walks must be registered in log books at the start of each track (and signed out on return).

ACCESS
By Vehicle

The northern section of the park is 75 km from Hobart via the Lyell Highway to New Norfolk and then onto the Maydena Gate entrance.

The southern section is accessed through Cockle Creek which is about 2 hours from Hobart via the Huon Highway to Geeveston.

All roads in the park are subject to snow and ice and visitors should be prepared for sudden weather changes. There is a motel, fuel and food at Strathgordon.

The Easy Way—by Plane

One of the most exciting ways to experience the heart of this magnificent wilderness is on a Par Avion Wilderness Flight to remote Bathurst

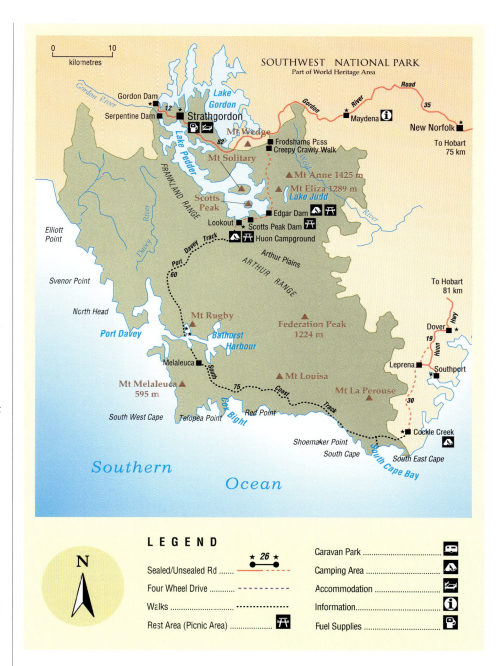

Harbour on the southwest coast. From Cambridge Airport, Hobart, you fly in a 5 passenger, high-wing aircraft, which is perfect for sightseeing, across Hobart and the Derwent River and around Mt Wellington.

Forty minutes after take-off, you are circling the sprawling Bathurst Harbour dotted with islands. As you step out onto Melaleuca airstrip you are greeted by a vista of rolling hills and ragged mountain ranges. A nearby bird hide offers a close-up of rare orange-bellied parrots and firetail finches.

A number of options are available at Melaleuca: you could spend the day in these magical surrounds, camp for a night—or a

week—in Par Avion's Wilderness Camp, or spend a few days cruising Bathurst Harbour, Port Davey and the Davey River aboard the 4 star MV Southern Explorer.

CAMPING

The Huon Campground is 1 km south of Scotts Peak Dam and is the start of the week-long Port Davey Track. This track was put in many years ago to provide an escape route for any shipwreck survivors on the southwest coast.

There is also a picnic and camping ground at Edgar Dam.

At Cockle Creek there is a large camp site near Rocky Bay.

STRZELECKI NATIONAL PARK

IN BRIEF

MAP REFERENCE: PAGE 383 J 3

Location On Flinders Island,
½ hour's drive from Whitemark
Best Time Spring to autumn
Main Attractions Walking,
water sports, wildlife, magnificent scenery, 4WD
Ranger Phone (03) 6359 2148

Largest of the Furneaux Group, Flinders Island is a picture-postcard gem in the middle of Bass Strait. Its many granite peaks, beautiful beaches and plentiful wildlife make it a mecca for all lovers of the outdoors. Strzelecki National Park on the southwestern tip of Flinders Island is 4215 hectares of extremely rugged country with towering granite peaks rising almost sheer from the sea. The highest peak, Mt Strzelecki, is only 756 metres but the range dominates the south of the island behind a narrow coastal band.

About 2.5 million years ago volcanic activity created a land bridge between Victoria and Tasmania. Some 10 000 years ago this bridge was flooded and a chain of granite islands formed which enjoy a mild climate, neither too hot nor too cold but always windy!

The Strzelecki Peaks and Flinders Peaks, along with Mt Belstead, Mt Razorback, Butcher Peak and Lovetts Hill, are mostly barren rock littered with giant boulders.

In 1842 the Polish explorer and scientist Paul Edmond de Strzelecki climbed some of the peaks of Flinders Island, and it is in his honour that the national park is named.

The Strzelecki Peaks seen from Trousers Point

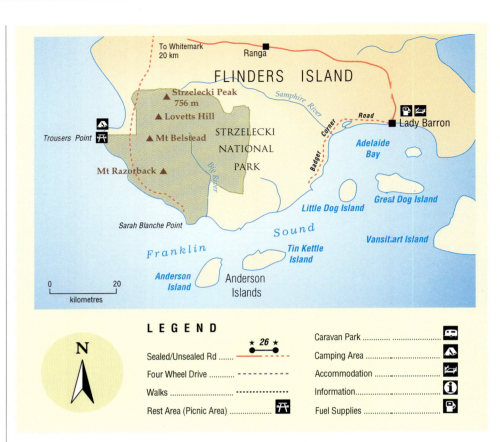

LEGEND

Sealed/Unsealed Rd ....
Four Wheel Drive ....
Walks ....
Rest Area (Picnic Area) ....

Caravan Park ....
Camping Area ....
Accommodation ....
Information...............
Fuel Supplies ....

THE PARK'S ATTRACTIONS

A rough 4WD track runs along the south coast through heathland, melaleucas, casuarinas and Oyster Bay pines to Big River. Along this narrow coastal plain are pretty little coves, tannin-stained rivers and salmon-coloured rocks.

To the east of the park is the Samphire River. Its tea-coloured waters drop down from the Flinders Peaks through rainforest gullies, over falls to flow amid ferns and paperbarks into Adelaide Bay. Close by is Badger Corner with picnic and BBQ facilities and a boat ramp.

Bennett's wallabies, pademelons, wombats, echidnas and brush-tail possums are very common throughout the island and care should be taken on all roads. Some 150 recorded bird species include green rosellas, black curra-wongs, forty-spotted pardalotes and black cockatoos. Also common, unfortunately, are tiger, copperhead and whip snakes—all of which are highly venomous!

In the park's west is the stunningly beautiful Trousers Point, with headlands of jumbled granite boulders encrusted with orange lichen. Dazzling white sand in numerous tiny bays is lapped by aquamarine waters. The name—Trousers Point—is said to derive from a ship-wreck survivor who landed minus his pants.

This is a magnificent spot for rock fishing, swimming, or canoeing or just taking in the view. In one direction are the rocky tors of the Flinders and Strzelecki Peaks while across the Franklin Sound are Cape Barren Island and the Chappell Islands.

ROCK HOPPING

There's just one, steep, walking track to the peaks offering sweeping views from the summit of Mt Strzelecki. Rated at medium difficulty you should allow at least 4–5 hours return.

An overnight walking track runs around the coast from Trousers Point to Badger Corner. Snakes aren't the only hazard; because of the cutting grass, long pants and sleeves—even gloves—are recommended.

The peaks are popular with rock climbers and there are a number of short climbs.

ACCESS AND CAMPING

Flinders Island is an hour's flight from Melbourne, and the park is ½ hour's drive from Whitemark. There is no public transport on the island but hire cars and bikes are available. The roads are mostly unsealed but good, while traffic is almost non-existent.

Camping is allowed right around the island's coast; however, gas bottles cannot be carried on planes. There is a small, sheltered picnic and camping area among the casuarinas at Trousers Point with BBQs, toilets and a water tank. Trousers Point is the only spot on the island with a water supply for camping.

MAP REFERENCE: PAGE 382 G 8

Location Approximately 110 km west of Launceston. Access via the Bass Highway or via Lake Ada

Best Time Summer and autumn

Main Attractions Scenery, hiking, cross-country skiing

Ranger Phone (03) 6363 5182 or (03) 6363 5133

A subalpine wilderness, this 5 800 hectare national park is a stunningly beautiful, but very fragile place. Wedged between Cradle Mountain National Park and the windswept Central Plateau, it is part of the World Heritage Area. This part of Tasmania, particularly the lowlands to the north, was settled by strongly religious groups which would explain the biblical names.

For a long time this isolated, rugged wilderness was the haunt of escaped convicts and wallaby hunters.

A PARK FOR THE FIT

This national park is strictly for the very fit. If you don't slot into this category, you should change your destination!

Bushwalking, plus some rock climbing and cross-country skiing are the activities here; there is no vehicular access.

The main entrance is via Fish Creek in the northwest. From the car park a strenuous 3 hour walk entails a steep climb up to Trappers Hut and onto Solomons Jewels, a chain of beautiful little lakes.

Another steep ridge brings you to Herods Gate between 2 giant rock formations and beyond to sublime Lake Salome. This 900 metre high 'amphitheatre' is surrounded by dramatic cliffs. The West Wall towers 300 metres above the lake, as does the Temple, an impressive mountain. Mt Jerusalem, the highest mountain in the park at 1458 metres, is to the north.

Beyond Lake Salome are the Pools of Bethesda and Siloam. There is no camping at Siloam, but Bethesda has a magnificent wild camp site set among pencil pines.

These, and many other glacial tarns, are surrounded by forests of rare, endangered pencil pines. Although able to survive sub-zero alpine conditions, they cannot survive fires. Most of the specimens around here are a mere 300 years old but could live for several thousands of years, growing into wonderfully convoluted shapes.

Wallabies, pademelons and wombats roam the Walls, as do Tasmanian devils, although you're unlikely to see the latter unless they raid your food supply during the night.

LEGEND

Sealed/Unsealed Rd	★ 26 ★
Four Wheel Drive	- - - - - -
Walks	··············
Rest Area (Picnic Area)	🌐
Caravan Park	🚐
Camping Area	⛺
Accommodation	🛏
Information	ℹ
Fuel Supplies	⛽

TAKE CARE

At this altitude weather can be very unpredictable at any time of year, with sudden and dramatic changes. It's most important to be well prepared and appropriately dressed.

ACCESS AND CAMPING

There is no vehicular access into the park. Fish River Road which leads off Mersey Forest Road ends at a car park. From there a rough walking track heads off into the park.

A somewhat less strenuous route into the Walls is from the southeast via Lake Ada. It's flat walking but is very isolated. This means that a good map and compass are essential.

If access in summer is not easy, it is much more difficult in winter but there are people who enjoy coming here to cross-country ski.

There are no facilities in the park, but bush camping is allowed. Because of the magnificent pencil pine's extreme vulnerability to fire, only fuel stoves are allowed.

For further information, please contact the district ranger.

Pencil pines in the snow in Walls of Jerusalem National Park

CALLINGTON MILL HISTORIC SITE

The third oldest windmill in the country, Callington Mill is being painstakingly restored in Oatlands, a historic town with Australia's largest collection of sandstone buildings.

The Lincolnshire-style tower mill—the entire cap revolved to keep the sails side-on to the wind—was built in 1837 by John Jubilee Vincent. In 1845 he added a steam-driven flour mill; a homestead, a miller's cottage, stables and coach-house were added in 1854.

The mill was closed in 1891, and the sails were removed; fire ravaged the mill in 1913, and the tower was finally used as a water reservoir.

In 1970 the Tasmanian Government started preservation work; the National Trust took over in 1987. The old tower has been largely restored. The other buildings are in good condition; the former steam-driven flour mill now houses a National Trust shop.

Visitors can again climb to the top of the windmill and gaze across a rural 19th century scene with stone walls, farmyards and cottages.

Oatlands is 85 km north of Hobart on the Midland Highway. For further information, ph: (03) 6331 9077.

CENTRAL PLATEAU CONSERVATION AND PROTECTED AREA
89 200 HECTARES

This high, windswept plateau, another part of the World Heritage Area, contains a great many lakes which make the area a world-renowned trout fishing venue. It also abuts the Walls of Jerusalem National Park.

Surrounded by mountain peaks, frequently snow-clad, the plateau is often snowbound and one of the coldest parts of the state; the little hamlet of Liawenee regularly records Tasmania's lowest temperatures. It is covered in sparse, alpine scrub, with occcasional stands of eucalypts and pencil pines.

There are few walks and limited facilities in this park. This is strictly trout fishing country with many little shacks scattered along lake shores and a great many anglers waist deep in freezing waters! Brown trout caught here average 1.5 to 3 kg with occasional catches up to 5 or 6 kg. The season runs from August to April and a licence is necessary.

If fishing is not your thing an interesting 225 km round trip from Launceston will give a taste of the Central Plateau, much of which is inaccessible to vehicles. Drive south through Longford to Poatina on Route B51, then there is a steep climb—with great views—up the 1000 metre Western Tiers. Catch sight of Great Lake and Arthurs Lake before turning right onto Lake Highway (which is largely unsealed and frequently icy or boggy) and around the bottom of Great Lake past Shannon Lagoon and Miena.

Lake Highway passes through Liawenee following the western shore of Great Lake although it is frequently obscured by thick scrub. Through Breona and a descent of the Western Tiers—with spectacular views to the north coast—onto bitumen and Deloraine, then back to Launceston on the Bass Highway. This drive is accessible to conventional vehicles, except, of course, when the road is under snow! The round trip from Launceston takes 3–4 hours.

The Central Plateau is approximately 100 km from Launceston; summer and autumn are the best times to go. Fuel and food are available at Miena; Great Lake Hotel has accommodation and camping. Check the road conditions before setting out and take the appropriate clothing.

For further information, contact the ranger, ph: (03) 6259 8148, or the Great Lake Hotel, ph: (03) 6259 8163.

COAL MINES HISTORIC SITE
214 HECTARES

In a peaceful setting of lawns overlooking pretty Norfolk Bay, on the northwest tip of the Tasman Peninsula, some 25 km from Port Arthur, are the relics of a sad saga. When the first known reserves of Tasmanian coal were discovered at Norfolk Bay in 1833 a party of convicts and overseers was sent to begin mining.

The horrors of convict transportation and the penal settlements in Australia early last century are well documented. Convicts at Port Arthur who committed serious crimes were either flogged or sent to the coal mines.

Up to 560 prisoners toiled night and day in cramped, wet shafts 1.2 metres high, in 8 hour shifts. The main shaft was 46 metres deep: coal

Underground cell at Coal Mines Historic Site

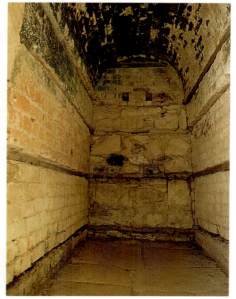

was transported to the jetty via a 1.8 km tramway. Working in the coal mines was bad enough but, if further punishment was considered necessary, they were locked in dark, dank log cells in the mine tunnels!

The mines closed in 1848; today only a few walls and ruins remain, and the main shaft is largely filled with rubble. Down by the jetty on Plunkett Point the ground still has a thick layer of coal.

The Coal Mines Historic Site was declared in 1966 and interpretive signs have been erected around the main settlement and several underground cells have been restored. There is still much work to be done to preserve what is left of the prisoners' barracks, chapel, officers' quarters and solitary cells. Little remains of the bakehouse, guard house and overseer's quarters but explanatory leaflets bring it all to life for those who take the trouble to seek out this fascinating site.

For further information, ph: (03) 6250 3497.

GOVERNOR ISLAND MARINE NATURE RESERVE
50 HECTARES

This reserve is at Bicheno on the east coast and is an important marine breeding ground. It includes the rocky bulk of Governor Island and Alligator Rock where a great many seabirds can be seen.

Divers can view deep-water marine species in a setting of spectacular and unusual granite formations and coves. The Bicheno Dive Centre has equipment for hire and runs diving trips. Boats can be launched in the adjoining Gulch—between Governor Island and the shore—which provides shelter for the fishing fleet. Glass-bottom boat tours to the marine reserve are available, run by Bicheno Penguin and Adventure Tours.

No fishing is allowed within the marine reserve, only swimming, diving and boating.

Bicheno is 176 km from Launceston, or 228 km from Hobart. There is a wide variety of accommodation in and around Bicheno. For further information, ph: (03) 6375 1236.

HARTZ MOUNTAINS NATIONAL PARK
7140 HECTARES

The Hartz Mountains National Park contains superb scenery ranging from rainforest, rugged dolerite ranges, tarns and mountain lakes carved out by glaciers, to high altitude moorlands and alpine heathlands. The wildflowers, particularly the red Tasmanian waratah, attract bushwalkers in spring and summer.

From the main car park just inside the park a 5 minute walk, lined with flowering shrubs, leads to Waratah Lookout with panoramic views across the Huon Valley, and Mt Wellington; nearby Keogh Falls drops down to the valley hundreds of metres below.

A 10 minute walk to the Arve Falls winds between snow gum woodland and alpine herb fields with mountain peaks all around while the little Arve River gathers momentum and tumbles over cascades before dropping over a 500 metre precipice. A wooden walkway and lookout cross these cascades and overlook a wilderness wonderland stretching for miles.

A short distance further along the Hartz Mountain Road is the start of more strenuous walks to Hartz Peak and Hartz Lake (2 hours each way) for spectacular views of the magnificent Tasmanian Wilderness World Heritage Area. Another energetic, 2 hour walk takes you to Lakes Perry and Osborne beneath the rocky ridges of the Devil's Backbone.

In winter the higher slopes of the park are popular with cross-country skiers.

The Hartz Mountains National Park is a little over 75 km from Hobart, on mostly sealed roads, through the Huon Valley to Geeveston. Arve Road (C632) is a steep, winding 13 km of fair, unsealed road; the Hartz Mountain Road, a further 13 km, is accessible in good conditions by conventional vehicles but may be closed by snow in winter. Being so close to Hobart, the park is popular for 4WD vehicles on a day's outing. There are no facilities other than a hikers' shelter and fireplace, BBQs plus toilets.

For further information, ph: (03) 6298 3198.

HUMBUG POINT STATE RECREATION AREA
1620 HECTARES

Just beyond Binalong Bay, this reserve is one of the prettiest in the state, enjoying the east coast's famed warm, sunny weather. Rocky headlands of orange-coated granite boulders enfold many secluded little bays with white sandy beaches and clear, blue water.

The woodlands and heath are a blaze of colour in spring: wattle, clematis, tea-tree, heath, banksias and orchids.

Of the many bird species the yellow-tailed black cockatoo is probably the showiest. Numerous seabirds include majestic, white-breasted sea eagles and an occasional albatross.

This is a wonderful spot for fishing, swimming, sailing, bird watching, bushwalking and horse riding, and a great deal of it is wheelchair accessible.

Two walking tracks—Moulting Bay to Humbug Point and Skeleton Bay to Grants Point—will soon be linked in a 13 km circuit. Fishing for flathead, pike and salmon is popular as is enjoying the stunning beach scenery.

Binalong Bay is just 11 km north of St Helens on a sealed road. The reserve has camp sites,

A mountain brush-tail possum, common in Tasmania

picnic and BBQ areas, toilets and boat ramps; fuel, food and accommodation in St Helens.

For further information, ph: (03) 6376 1550.

IDA BAY STATE RESERVE

An open eucalypt forest stretches down to the sparkling, azure waters of Ida Bay and Deep Hole Bay which are lined with dazzling white sands. The reserve also surrounds Southport Lagoon and gives views of Cape Bruny.

Long-gone Ida Bay was a saw-milling town at the start of the century. The tiny cemetery, overlooking the bay and disused jetty, contains graves of 12 of the 22 members of the Tyler family who operated the mill.

The Ida Bay Steam Railway—Tasmania's oldest surviving railway—runs for 7 km through this reserve from Lune River to Deep Hole Bay. It has run this narrow gauge track continuously, except for the years 1975–7, since 1912. It was built to carry limestone (used in the manufacture of acetylene gas) to the Ida Bay wharf for shipment to Hobart. The line was extended to Deep Hole Bay when Ida Bay silted up.

The railway is fairly basic and unsophisticated but it is a genuine part of Australia's heritage and worth a look. The trip to Deep Hole and back takes about an hour and the train runs every 90 minutes, 7 days a week.

The beach at Deep Hole is a perfect spot for a picnic, a nature walk and a swim. The tourist complex includes a small restaurant, cabin accommodation and camp sites.

Lune River is a hamlet from where access to Ida Bay is available via bush tracks. It is 108 km south of Hobart via the Huon Highway and has Australia's southern-most post office but there is little else.

For further information, ph: (03) 6298 3198.

MOLE CREEK KARST NATIONAL PARK
1345 HECTARES

Two of Tasmania's finest cave systems, Marakoopa and King Solomons, are now combined into one national park, together with over 200 caves and sinkholes in the area.

King Solomons Caves are so-named because of the profusion of light-reflecting calcite crystals which glisten like diamonds. Covering just 164 hectares, King Solomons Caves are small, dry caves with some fascinating formations such as the 'Temple', the 'Crystal Dome' and the vast 'Bridal Chamber'.

A fern-lined pathway leads to the larger Marakoopa Caves—part of the World Heritage Area—which contain 2 underground streams and stretch for 6 km. 'The Gardens' consist of a multitude of stalactites, stalacmites and flowstone. The beautiful rimstone pools of the 'Pink Terraces' reflect the surrounding beauty.

Marakoopa is the only cave system open to the public in Tasmania with glow-worm colonies shimmering on the cave roof above the stream.

There are no bats in Tasmania's caves although they do contain 'cave spiders' (troglodyte huntsmen) which can measure up to 15 cm across and weave a one metre web! However, you are unlikely to see them or the cave crickets unless they are picked out by the ranger's torch. Almost colourless mountain shrimps in the underground streams are likewise hard to find.

The caves are open daily, with regular guided tours. They are well lit and are designed for easy walking.

Nearby are shelter huts with log fires which are most welcome in winter. There are picnic and BBQ facilities, toilets and nature trails to

OTHER PARKS OF INTEREST

enhance your enjoyment of the area.

The park is 85 km west of Launceston via Deloraine and Mole Creek.

For further information, ph: (03) 6363 5182.

NINEPIN POINT STATE RESERVE AND MARINE RESERVE

Dark brown, tannin-rich waters from the Huon River mix with the clear water of the D'Entre-casteaux Channel creating unusual light conditions which have influenced the development of plants and animals inhabiting the marine reserve. Poor sunlight penetration through the dark surface layers means that seaweeds, needing a lot of light, can only grow in water up to 6 metres deep. Thus red seaweeds, often found at much greater depths because of low light tolerance, thrive here in the dark shallows.

At a depth of 8 metres a fascinating rocky reef is crowded with brightly coloured sponges, anemones and other creatures such as sea dragons. Many of these, and associated fish, are usually found in much deeper water. There is no other known, easily accessible, community such as this one at Ninepin Point.

For non-divers, it's a very pretty drive around the southern tip of the Huon Peninsula with beautiful views across the D'Entrecasteaux Channel to Bruny Island. The return drive from Hobart will take 2–3 hours. The only facility is a short, marked walking track. You should allow ½ hour for the walk.

Ninepin Point is 60 km south of Hobart via Huonville and Cygnet, or 80 km via Kingston and Kettering. For further information, phone (03) 6233 6556.

The Pieman River

THE NUT STATE RESERVE
60 HECTARES

The Nut is a giant, 152 metre high, lump of solidified lava looming above the historic town of Stanley. This windy plateau, believed to be millions of years old, and the town are connected to the mainland by a 7 km isthmus and are thus almost surrounded by water.

Sheer on 3 sides, the Nut offers spectacular views up and down the north coast, inland across Stanley and out over Bass Strait. Large muttonbird colonies inhabit this reserve and a short nature walk circumnavigates the summit.

A walking track to the top starts opposite the post office—allow 1–2 hours—or you can take the chairlift from behind the Nut Shop Tea Rooms. Here there is a picnic area and toilets.

Stanley is 130 km west of Devonport via the Bass Highway.

For further information, ph: (03) 6443 4215.

PIEMAN RIVER STATE RESERVE
3314 HECTARES

The Pieman is a mighty river despite being dammed upstream to form Lake Pieman. Its tannin-stained waters meander to the west coast, amid dense rainforest, to Hardwicke Bay where the surf rolls in from 20 000 km away. Forests of sassafras, laurel, celery-top pine, myrtle, beech, Huon pine and giant tree ferns are reflected in its mirror surface.

At Hells Gate cliffs tower 30 metres above equally deep waters. Several rivers flow into the Pieman before it reaches the treacherous Pieman Heads.

Pieman River State Reserve is a pristine, 800 metre wide wilderness corridor of cool temperate rainforest with vehicular access only at Corinna, a fishing hamlet 20 km upstream. To explore the river you will need a boat, or canoe. The 50 year-old Huon pine vessel, MV *Arcadia II* will take you on a 4 hour return cruise to Pieman Heads.

A gold mining town in the late 1800s, Corinna still has an original (non-operative) pub, a boat ramp, camp sites, a few self-contained cabins and a kiosk selling basic supplies.

Corinna is 206 km southwest of Devonport, or 127 km from Rosebery on the Murchison Highway.

For further information, ph: (03) 6471 7122. For cruises, ph: (03) 6446 1170.

ROCKY CAPE NATIONAL PARK
3064 HECTARES

Tasmania's smallest national park contains rocky, north coast headlands, small, sheltered beaches, hills covered in heath and woodlands, plus some of the state's richest Aboriginal sites.

Vehicular access is limited to Sisters Beach in the east and Rocky Cape Road in the west.

Rocky Cape National Park

Beautiful Sisters Beach is wide, clean and shaded by she-oaks. Postmans Track, from the eastern end of the beach, is a 2 hour circuit walk, taking in the beach, wooded hillsides and lookouts with views across Breakneck Point and Bass Strait.

At the western end of Sisters Beach signs lead to cave shelters—Wet Cave and Lee Archer Cave—with interpretive signs detailing some of the history of the Aborigines who lived here up to 10 000 years ago. You should allow one hour for this walk. A 6–7 hour circuit walk leads from Sisters Beach to the western boundary via the Coastal Track and back on the Inland Track.

There is an abundance of bird life, and the hills are a riot of wildflowers in spring: heath, boronia, Christmas bells, grass trees, tea-tree, west coast peppermints and saw banksias.

At the western end of the park the Rocky Cape lighthouse towers above orange-coated rocks, and sea caves dot the cliffs. Two of the most impressive Aboriginal shelters are just a short walk from the car park.

The park has several picnic areas, with BBQs, near safe swimming beaches. There are no toilets or drinking water in the park and camping is not permitted. Accommodation, food and fuel are available at nearby Boat Harbour and on the Bass Highway at the Rocky Cape Road turn-off.

The park is approximately 90 km west of Devonport via the Bass Highway.

For further information, contact the ranger, ph: (03) 6443 4215.

SARAH ISLAND HISTORIC SITE

Australia's most notorious penal settlement was on this very small (4.8 hectares) island at the southern end of Macquarie Harbour on Tasmania's bleak west coast.

Between 1821 and 1833 prisoners here endured conditions so appalling that hanging was considered a merciful release. They worked at timber cutting and ship building; over 100 Huon pine boats were built in the little quay. Few escapees survived the harsh wilderness; among the most notorious survivors (but not for long) were Matthew Brady, who turned to bushranging and Alexander Pearce, who resorted to cannibalism.

Although grassy and well-treed now, it was so barren then that the inmates had to build high timber palisades around the settlement for protection from icy winds.

Of some 30 original buildings only the remains of 13 are now visible but walkways and interpretive signs, using old sketches, show clearly how it once looked. This historic site also includes the nearby speck of rock called Grummet Island, once home to women convicts.

A number of cruises operate from Strahan; just one—Heritage Wilderness Cruises—allows a stopover on Sarah Island and provides informative leaflets for a self-guided tour.

For further information contact the ranger, ph: (03) 6471 7122, or Heritage Wilderness Cruises, ph: (03) 6471 7174.

SEA ELEPHANT—LAVINIA NATURE RESERVE AND WILDLIFE SANCTUARY
6800 HECTARES

This stretch of King Island's east coast is an important autumn stopover for the rare orange-bellied parrots en route from southwest Tasmania to Victoria.

It is a combination of heathlands, swamps, scrub, beaches and lakes and home to a large number of parrots, honeyeaters, seabirds, waterfowl, sea-eagles and many other birds including hundreds of thousands of mutton-birds. Other prolific wildlife includes Bennett's and rufous wallabies, emus and echidnas. The sandy soils produce masses of wildflowers.

Sea Elephant River, the longest on the island, is reached via Sea Elephant Road from Naracoopa. It travels through approximately 20 km of heathlands, saltmarshes and impenetrable melaleuca scrub. The tannin-stained river is dotted with swans but there is not much out here for the visitor. There is no way across the river and the area to the north, along Nine Mile Beach, is wild and virtually inaccessible.

The rest of the park is reached in the far northeast. Lavinia Beach has long, white sands with rolling surf between Lavinia Point and Boulder Point. Named after the *Lavinia* which was wrecked here, this is a dangerous beach for swimmers or surfers.

Inland is Penny's Lagoon, a very pretty, 'suspended' lake, popular with campers, canoeists and swimmers. It is surrounded by most attractive woodlands, crisscrossed by

innumerable very sandy, 4WD and 'wallaby' tracks on which it would be easy to get lost. It has a picnic area and toilets.

Martha Lavinia Lagoon is also popular with campers and anglers if you can find it. Sign-posting on King Island leaves a lot to be desired.

Access to the Lavinia area is from the top end of North Road, via Haines Road; the beach is approximately 50 km from Currie.

For further information, ph: (03) 6457 1225.

SEAL ROCKS STATE RESERVE, KING ISLAND

King Island's most famous natural features are its storm-lashed cliffs which claimed over 70 ships last century. Few places are wilder and more forbidding than Seal Rocks in the southwest, where giant cliffs overlook jagged, rocky outcrops, once home to a great many seals.

Although almost wiped out early last century, the number of seals has increased but you will see more muttonbirds and penguins here than seals. The adventurous visitor can explore caves in these steep, dangerous cliffs.

On the nearby cliff top is the Petrified Forest, a lunar-like landscape of 30 million year old fossilised tree stumps and branches. Now fenced off for protection, there is a walkway and very windblown lookout.

Seal Rocks is approximately 32 km south of Currie via South Road, with another 6.6 km of sandy track leading to a small picnic area.

For further information, ph: (03) 6457 1225.

TESSELLATED PAVEMENT STATE RESERVE
4 HECTARES
TASMAN ARCH STATE RESERVE
138 HECTARES

These are possibly the most visited state reserves in Tasmania, being at the entrance to the Tasman Peninsula and Port Arthur.

The Tessellated Pavement is at Pirates Bay, one of the best fishing and surfing spots in the area. A 5 minute walk from the car park leads to intriguing geological features at the water's edge which have an appearance remarkably like paving stones. At low tide a 1½ hour return beach walk to Clydes Island reveals fascinating sea life in many rock pools.

Eaglehawk Neck, joining the Forestier and Tasman Peninsulas, was the site of a convict-era guard station and the infamous Dog Line where savage dogs were tied in a line to prevent prisoners escaping overland from Port Arthur.

The Tasman Arch Reserve includes the spectacular Blowhole and the Devils Kitchen (a great rock crevice in which the sea boils and churns).

A 2 hour return walk from the Devils Kitchen to Waterfall Bay follows the clifftops,

giving spectacular views of the Tasman Peninsula and the waterfall.

There are no facilities at Eaglehawk Neck or the Tessellated Pavement; Tasman Arch has a picnic area and toilets. These reserves are 70 km from Hobart on the Arthur Highway.

For further information, contact the ranger, ph: (03) 6250 3497.

WYBALENNA HISTORIC SITE

The tranquil setting at Wybalenna Point on Flinders Island, with Cape Barren geese feeding on lush green lawns, belies a sorry history. In the years 1831–47 George Augustus Robinson rounded up the remnants of the Tasmanian Aborigines, some 160, and transported them to Flinders Island. He set up a 'sanctuary' at Wybalenna but it was a disastrous experiment. Over 100 people died; the rest were finally taken to Oyster Bay near Hobart.

Once a small village, most of the buildings have now disappeared but Wybalenna is regarded as one of the most important historical sites in Australia because of its association with last of the Tasmanian tribes.

The little chapel—used as a shearing shed for many years—was purchased in 1973 and restored by the National Trust Furneaux Group. A little cemetery has only a few headstones left, with memorials to both blacks and whites. The chapel, between Pea Jacket Hill and Wireless Hill, overlooks this historic site. Being the only building associated with the original Tasmanians, it is rated the third most important historic building in Tasmania.

Superb coastal views from the settlement extend to the beach and the remains of the old Port Davies wharf. Beautiful little bays of opaline water and pure white sand are bounded by headlands of granite boulders.

In the nearby hamlet of Emita is a museum full of old archives of sealers, whalers and Straitsmen (descendants of white men and Aboriginal women). Wybalenna Historic Site is some 20 km north of Whitemark.

For further information, ph: (03) 6359 2217.

The Tessellated Pavement

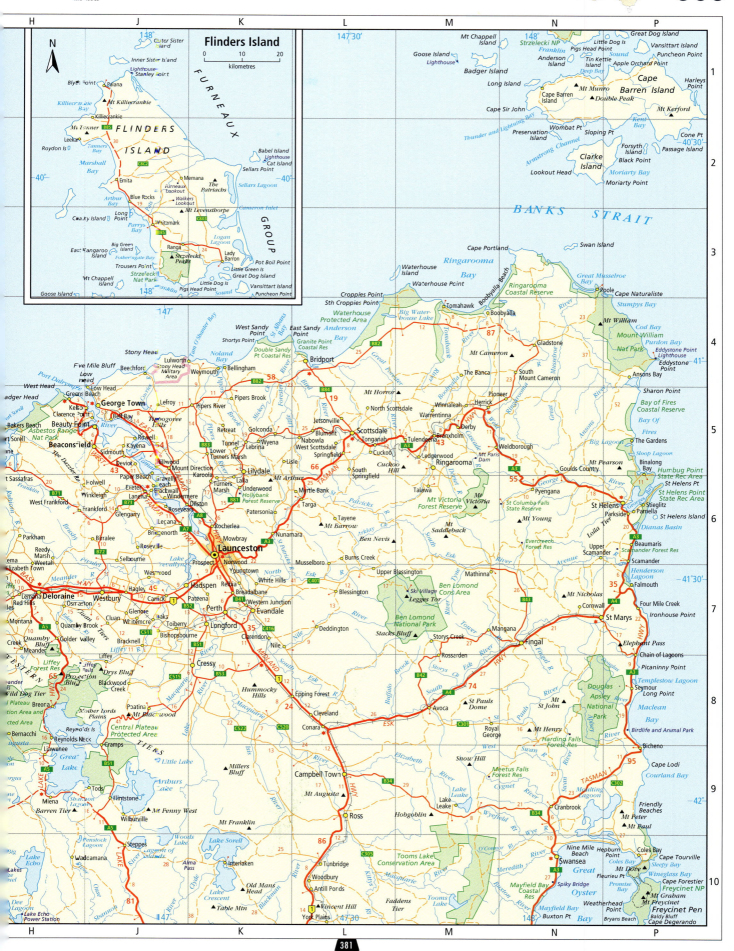

INDEX

Numbers in **bold type**
refer to main text entries

O

PARK NOTES